Learn FileMaker® Pro 10

Jonathan Stars

Wordware Publishing, Inc.

Library of Congress Cataloging-in-Publication Data

Stars, Jonathan.
Learn FileMaker Pro 10 / by Jonathan Stars.
p. cm.
Includes index.
ISBN-13: 978-1-59822-071-1 (pbk.)
ISBN-10: 1-59822-071-3
1. FileMaker pro. 2. Database management. I. Title.
QA76.9.D3S72466 2009
005.75'65--dc22 2007030011

1100 Summit Ave., Suite 102
Plano, Texas 75074

Printed in the United States of America

ISBN-13: 978-1-59822-071-1
ISBN-10: 1-59822-071-3
10 9 8 7 6 5 4 3 2 1
0812

All inquiries for volume purchases of this book should be addressed to Wordware Publishing, Inc., at the above address. Telephone inquiries may be made by calling:

(972) 423-0090

Contents

Part 4
Creating a Real Solution

Part 5
Sharing Your Database

Part 6
Protecting Your Information

Part 7
Beyond FileMaker

Preface

My Intent

This is meant to be a hands-on book. The idea is to have you do various exercises so that you become familiar with FileMaker Pro. The book doesn't have that much to do with theory, although you will learn some along the way. There are other books for theory, if that's something you care about.

The FileMaker Pro PDF manual shows you features. What I want to do is take you through a group of exercises that use those features. That way, when you're done, you've actually created some databases that you can use, and you'll know what it feels like. I want you to learn how to drive by getting behind the wheel. You can read the manual for the rules of the road.

Updating this book has been a combination of excitement and frustration. The excitement comes from discovering a new way of describing some feature of this program in a way that has the potential to really make it understandable. The frustration comes from knowing that someday there will be a better way. Let's face it: Indexes just aren't good enough, especially if

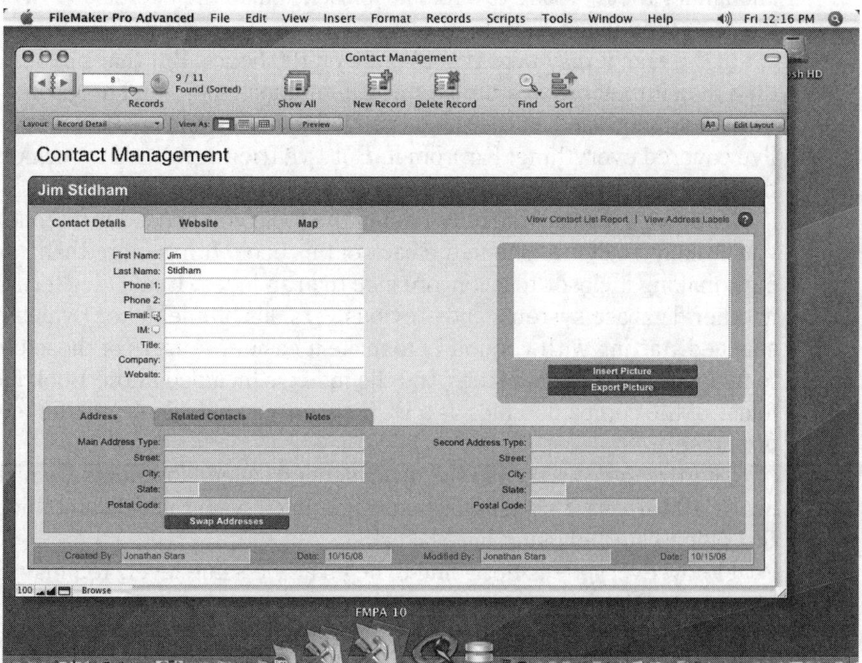

FileMaker Pro as seen in the Macintosh OS X environment.

you don't know the terminology. See if you recognize this: "How do I make the program do that thing I want it to do or that was called by another name in some other database I used to use?" Another frustration is that I'll give you an overview of an area, only to tell you there's more in another chapter. Somehow, I want to inject it into you all at once, like in a vaccination but with less pain! Something like what they did with those knowledge chips in *The Matrix*.

There will come a day when you'll be able to just think about what you want to do, and it will be done. You probably won't even be near an object we now think of as a computer. You won't even have to know that what you want to do is accomplished with a database. That day can't possibly arrive soon enough for me! Until that day arrives…

I recommend that you work at your computer with this book. I don't recommend that you read this lying down. The thing that will keep you awake is getting your hands dirty working with the program.

Try to follow the steps exactly as given in the examples. You may have to do some of them over. There is so much detail that it may be hard to get the big picture the first time. I originally designed the book so that most readers could complete each chapter in about one hour. As features have been added to each new edition of FileMaker, some chapters have gotten a bit longer than that. Regardless, you can't put this book under your pillow for three nights and get it. You may be struggling with the details of a layout or a calculation or a script and miss the overall concept that I'm trying to present to you. If you're anything like me, hearing the definition of a new term once is not enough for the message to sink in. Go back and do the exercises in a chapter a second time if you need to.

In the end, it may take you 40 or 50 or 100 hours. But that's a lot less time than it took me to stumble through multiple books and magazine articles trying to understand all the things you'll find in this one book. Not to say that I've covered everything. Far from it. But I've tried very hard to include all of the little things that you will absolutely need to get started.

If you've ever had difficulty finding the topic you needed in an index, you'll really enjoy the one in the back of this book. It has more than 3,000 listings, making it closer to a concordance than an index. It includes terms used in other database systems and previous versions of FileMaker (which have changed starting with version 7) to make it easier for users of those programs to find what they need faster. (And the index is included in the Book files folder of the companion files as a PDF, so you can quickly search for any word or phrase.)

There is even an area in the index section called "Problems," which lists nearly 100 areas for potential troubleshooting. I wish I'd had something like that when I started using FileMaker!

I know everyone is not going to begin at the same level. You may already have some FileMaker experience. Although I want you to do the exercises, if you're further along, I don't want to force you to do the early exercises just to get the files ready for the chapter in which you want to work. So I've included a set of files in the downloads for this book (www.wordware.com/files/fmpro10) that go along with each of the applicable book chapters starting with Chapter 4. You can take the files in the folder for the chapter where you want to begin doing the exercises and start following along with the text.

If I had written an introductory book on FileMaker about 10 years ago, it would have been much shorter. But, as is the case with most software, the programmers are constantly trying to give us users more powerful tools. That means just listing the tools takes longer. And showing you how to use the tools takes longer still.

I've had some readers complain about my references to the Help files. Some of the Help files are really well done. There is simply no need to make the book longer just paraphrasing what you can get right at your fingertips on screen. I want to give you the basics using real-life scenarios rather than simply list all of the features. And I'll try to include all the details about the little things that might drive you nuts if you don't know about them. You can dig deeper with the Help files if you need to. I use them often myself.

Those few complaints aside, I've had many people write to me saying that they had worked their way through two or more other FileMaker books, only to finally understand the program when they read my book. Flattering, yes, but I'm pretty sure the exposure to those other books got them ready to better understand any book on FileMaker. On the other hand, they tell me that my FileMaker 7 book was the best-selling FileMaker book of all time. Maybe after all of the previous versions, word of mouth is that I write in a style that is easier to understand. That would be rewarding, because doing these books has turned out to be torture. I toss and turn at night trying to think of better ways to make topics understandable. I swore I'd never write another. And yet here I am again. So I hope my pain makes the program I love so much easier for you to understand.

There's a lot of detail in some of the pictures in the book. You may need a magnifying glass to see it. The only way to show more would be to flip the pictures sideways. We simply made the choice not to do that. But really, the idea is for you to bring the same dialogs up on your computer screen. I just want to give you some idea of what you're looking for.

This book assumes you already have access to a copy of the FileMaker manual PDF file. Honestly, you don't need the manual to get most of what you need from this book. It's just that there is not enough space to cover everything in a tutorial like this.

I know some people who find this type of reading exactly what they need to get over a bout of insomnia. I've come to understand that computers, and FileMaker Pro in particular, are just not for everybody. But if it's something you need to learn, I've done my absolute best to make it as easy as possible and keep it interesting. Some people find it easier to learn when they work with videos. They sure have helped me at times. You may find you need to use video sources to augment what you get here. FileMaker is now providing some in a link on their web site, which you can find in the Learn More section of the Quick Start dialog. You might want to give that a try.

And in the end, if you should happen to come to love FileMaker as I have, you'll understand why I say, "Data never knew how beautiful it could be until it was touched by FileMaker Pro."

About the Author

An award-winning Las Vegas singer, songwriter, and comedian with 10 albums, **Jonathan Stars** began using the earliest version of FileMaker in 1986 to keep track of his entertainment business. People who saw his work began asking him to design databases for their businesses.

Among his many projects, Jonathan has developed databases for State of Michigan governmental agencies, CRG Regional Telephone Directories, ICT Cable, various international associations, Farm Bureau Insurance, Harvard Translation Center, Marco Music Publishing in Nashville, Tennessee, and Yale University's NARCOMS database. He is a member of the FileMaker Business Alliance, a FileMaker Certified developer, and a writer for *FileMaker Advisor* magazine.

Acknowledgments

Thanks to Jeff Gagné from FileMaker, Inc. (now at Apple) for giving me the lead that got me started on this book.

To Randi Roger from MacMillan & Company who took it to the next step.

To Jeff Johnson and his business partner, Deborah, from Bake N' Cakes for letting me learn the relational details of FileMaker Pro 3.0 while building a set of files for Bake N' Cakes, their bakery in Lansing, Michigan. They made me a professional.

To writer Thom Cannell for convincing me I could write this book and keeping me going with each update by reminding me how it affects my career.

To Bill Harrison of Custom Photographic in Lansing, Michigan, for letting me try out the web stuff at his Internet Express office.

To Andy Frederick who showed me the basics of FileMaker 1.0 and kept me interested.

To Darren Terry of Pacific Data Management, Inc. (formerly the technical liaison for developer relations at FileMaker, Inc.) for solving a sticky problem I had with networking and another on the FileMaker 7 relational model.

To Ken Black, Dave Folmsby, David Smith, Gene Burd, and the rest of the gang at Eubulus Computer Solutions who sent me out on so many jobs. (The company is now called Capitol Mac.)

To Corey Clemons (formerly of Eubulus) for helping me test out all the finer points of web publishing in Windows 2000.

To Jason Hoss (formerly of Eubulus) who helped me work out the networking issues with Windows XP and FileMaker Pro's Instant Web Publishing.

To Frank Holcomb from ACD.net for showing me detailed changes to the network control panels in Windows 2000.

To Dave Dowling who created the XML examples and helped me to understand what XML is all about.

To Kevin Mallon from FileMaker, Inc. who made sure I got all the latest versions of the software and answers to questions.

To Andy LeCates from FileMaker, Inc. who answered my final set of questions on FileMaker Pro 7.

To Hudson Akridge from FileMaker, Inc. who answered all my in-depth technical questions on FileMaker Pro 6 to keep me on the straight and narrow. He also kept track of my bug reports so they were fixed in the updates.

To Naoki Hirata from FileMaker, Inc. who helped me work through the complexities of ODBC.

To Cathy Switzer from FileMaker, Inc. who always knows who to put me in touch with for answers to my technical questions so I can make sure I'm giving you my best interpretation of the facts.

To Jim Hill (formerly of Wordware Publishing) for agreeing to take the first book to the final printed version, encouraging me throughout the process, and suggesting improvements and other opportunities along the way. I'm a little whiney and he was a good baby-sitter.

To Wes Beckwith (formerly of Wordware) who explained a lot of the details of the publishing business and worked very hard to get the book a better placement in bookstores and online publishing outfits.

To Tim McEvoy, publisher at Wordware, for working with me on the past three versions of the book.

To the rest of the crew at Wordware: editors Kellie Henderson (on the first two editions), Martha McCuller (who really cleaned up the FileMaker 9 book, finding things we had missed in many previous editions — it was a pleasure working with her), and Beth Kohler, production specialist Denise McEvoy, and cover designer Alan McCuller. These people do way more than I ever imagined to make what I wrote sound and look professional and accurate. Many of them have special talents that I never knew existed.

To William Moss for being technical editor for the first four editions. He really makes me look like I know what I'm talking about, and he submitted all his suggestions without making me feel foolish. I used many of his comments verbatim.

To Arthur Evans from AWE Consultancy in London, England, for taking over the technical editor job, keeping me from goofing up too much, and being such fun to work with.

To Jerry Robin from FMPtraining who provided technical edits to some of the early chapters of the 8.5 book and made many suggestions for improving the format. His encyclopedic knowledge of FileMaker is awesome.

To Alan Stirling of Alan Stirling Technology in England who helped me better understand the security issues of Instant Web Publishing.

To FileMaker developer Kevin Frank for his contributions to the better understanding of the anchor-buoy method of working with the relationships graph.

To Marcel De Maria at FileMaker, Inc. for his Hands-On-Training (HOT!) files that helped make the new features in FMP8 so easy for me to understand.

To Janice Child, co-author of the FMP7 book, who came at it with completely fresh eyes. She rewrote much of what you see from the perspective of a beginner — exactly what we needed with a software product that changed so dramatically with that version. She spent months being confused so that you won't have to be.

To Beverly Voth from Tier3 Data & Web in London, Kentucky, who put some files on a remote server for us testers to use so I didn't have to learn a new database platform in order to tell you how the great External Data Sources feature works.

To Jonathan Monroe from Actual Technologies in Libertyville, Illinois, makers of ODBC drivers for Mac OS X, who provided test drivers for developers and authors so we could try before we buy, and spread the word about their easy-to-use interface.

To Rick Kalman from FileMaker, Inc. who provided the best advance information and videos of the new features that we've ever had.

Special thanks to Mom, who actually did the exercises in the first edition of the book. She saved all of you much time and frustration by finding a number of major omissions. She also added immensely to the clarity of my approach in a number of areas. If you find this book reasonably easy to understand, it is largely thanks to her. It was a tough job, but that's what moms do.

And finally, to the unknown guy at Kinko's in Salt Lake City, Utah, who showed me FileMaker for the first time. Read on…

Introduction

How It All Started

It was about 3:00 A.M. in Salt Lake City, Utah. The year was 1986, might have been spring. I had just finished performing a solo music and comedy show at a Fraternal Order of Eagles club. I needed to print out some promotional materials, so I headed over to the all-night Kinko's copy shop.

I was complaining (I do that a lot) to the guy behind the counter about how much trouble I had using a three-ring binder to keep track of all the clubs I was playing. He said, "Oh, you need a database."

I said, "What's that?" And he proceeded to show me FileMaker.

Well, I had just bought a Mac Plus computer so I could make MIDI music. It wasn't too much of a leap to buy the FileMaker software to experiment with.

Here's how running my entertainment business using FileMaker went: I'd sit down to make some calls to line up shows, and I'd think, "It would make more sense to move this field over there. Shouldn't I have a field for mileage? Hey, I'll bet I could print my contracts from here!" I'd look up and an hour had gone by. "Man, I'd better make some calls." It was fun, and I got a lot better at booking shows. I could make twice the number of calls in half the time because I was organized.

When I finished that tour, I joined a Mac user group back in my hometown of Lansing, Michigan. The group's president, Andy Frederick, happened to be pretty good at FileMaker and showed me a lot of things I didn't know existed — because I'd never read the manual. You know, Mac software is so easy, you don't have to read the manual, so I didn't. Good thing Andy was around.

Pretty soon, other members of the user group saw what I was doing and hired me to make databases for their businesses. I thought it was pretty neat to be doing that work, but I didn't think of it as a serious business. I was going to be a famous recording artist.

My first big relational job was for the bakery owned by my wife, Deborah. (We're not married now, but we're friends.) Her partner, Jeff Johnson, challenged me way beyond my knowledge and gave me nothing but encouragement to experiment.

A few years went by. As far as the entertaining business went, I was getting tired of all the driving, living out of a suitcase, setting up and tearing down equipment — and I wasn't getting famous! I mean, I was making a living, and I'd won some awards, but it seemed as if I was always begging for my next gig.

Meanwhile, my phone kept ringing to do FileMaker work. And I really enjoyed it, too. It was like getting paid to do puzzles. Well, after about two years of ignoring the obvious (you only have to hit me over the head with a sledgehammer three or four times), I decided to make it my primary business. Besides, it felt a whole lot better to have my phone ring than to beg.

When I wasn't doing work for clients, I was tinkering. Then I got an e-mail saying that *FileMaker Advisor* magazine was looking for writers. So I submitted a couple of article proposals that came out of my tinkering, and they got accepted. One thing led to another until I was invited to write this book.

Conventions Used in This Book

- File, Open — Any menu title followed by a comma followed by another capitalized word indicates that a selection is being made from one of the menus. A second comma indicates a submenu. For example: View, Toolbars, Standard. To see the submenus, you have to pull down to the menu choice and the submenus will pop out.
- Screen — The whole computer screen. If I say look in the upper-left corner of your screen, on the Macintosh you will see the apple and on Windows computers you'll probably see the name of the program you're in.
- Active window — The frontmost working area on your computer. You can have many programs and files open at one time, but only one is the frontmost active window.
- (Macintosh) — Refers to a command or menu choice for the Macintosh (or Mac) operating system.
- (Windows) — Refers to a command or menu choice for the Windows operating system.
- FileMaker Pro, FileMaker, and occasionally FMP, FMP7, FMP8, FMP8.5, FMP9, and FMP10 are used interchangeably throughout this book.
- Key combinations are shown using a plus sign (+) between the keys. For example, Ctrl+N means hold down the Control (or Ctrl) key and press the letter N. There are a few cases where other symbols are used in the combination. For example, Ctrl+– means hold down the Control key and press the minus key (–). There may also be lengthy combinations such as Ctrl+Option+Shift+F.
- Unless otherwise noted, the Windows and Mac screens are interchangeable. There are slight differences such as the color and shading of the borders, but in general, you should not be confused by seeing one screen or the other. In the few cases where they differ significantly, I include screens for both platforms.

- With the update of the book to version 5.5, I started including a little "5.5" in superscript to indicate new features since version 5.0. I repeated that with 6.0. Starting with version 7, the file structure is so different from earlier versions that you'll need to convert your files before using them. Many, many features and ways of doing things are different this time around. I added a superscript 7 to items that were completely new in FMP7, and I'm continuing that in this book with the superscript 10. That should help users of previous versions know they're looking at something new.
- In the 6 and 7 editions, Jim Hill (the publisher of the first three versions of this book) and I brought in Nonie Bernard to contribute additional text so it better fits an educational format. She also added extra items to the chapter quizzes. I'm not a big fan of such tests, so I asked the current publisher, Tim McEvoy, if we could omit those items starting with the FMP9 book. So far nobody has complained. If you really miss that style of learning and let us know, we will consider put them back in for the next edition.

Updates

FileMaker Pro 7 was arguably the most dramatic upgrade in the history of the program. (I don't know who would do the arguing. I think it was revolutionary.) The most dramatic changes were the relational model and the Accounts & Privileges security system. Since that introduction you can now build multiple tables in a single file (simplifying security design), and tables can be linked via multiple unequal relationships and represented graphically. The old users and groups security was completely replaced by the Accounts & Privileges system, which is much more useful and intuitive. I also find it comforting that the files themselves are much better protected from the harm caused by a computer crash. FileMaker Pro 10 continues to build on that wonderful base, improving and solidifying the previous features, and adding even more. Some say that the new features in version 8 made it the program FMP7 was actually meant to be. Version 8.5 added the amazing Web Viewer tool, which is described in detail in Chapter 25. Even though it's in the section of the book titled "Beyond FileMaker," be sure you don't skip over this wonderful tool.

The 8.5 release provided Universal Application support for Intel-based Macintosh machines, which allows the program to run something like 1.5 to 3 times faster. With this release FileMaker, Inc. also launched its Learning Center. Although it is aimed at new users who are downloading the trial version, it will also be useful to those who are moving into specific areas of the program for the first time — such as Accounts & Privileges and the server version of the application. The center includes videos, a tab for advanced content, and links to other resources such as user groups.

The outstanding feature added in FileMaker 9 was its advanced ability to connect to external SQL data sources. In earlier versions you needed to build SQL queries using ODBC in order to reach out to other database systems. Now you can pull the tables right into FileMaker as if they were from another FileMaker file. This makes the whole process much more intuitive and has resulted in a lot of happy campers in large organizations. FMP10 gives you the ability to connect to a total of eight data sources. FileMaker can finally be the easy-to-use front end to those exclusive behemoths.

FileMaker 10 has completely revamped the Status area so that it's more in keeping with the toolbars in other programs. It's now at the top of the window and it's called the Status toolbar. Another new feature is Saved Finds, which lets you, well… save find requests. And I'm sure Script Triggers will prove to be very popular with developers, along with the ability to send e-mail right from FileMaker.

FileMaker requires that you activate your software to protect you from counterfeit copies and to protect FileMaker, Inc. from losing revenue. (After all, we need them around to get us the next set of great features.)

If your software is not activated, you'll see a dialog inviting you to activate it whenever you start up. You'll have 30 days to respond. If you don't have an Internet connection, you'll need to call FileMaker customer assistance. When you need to uninstall or move your copy to another machine, go to the Help menu and choose Deactivate (or call customer assistance) before uninstalling. You can find out more by going to the Help menu and searching for "Activating." (Don't look for "activate" or "activation." You won't find anything.) That's also where they list the phone numbers for your country. In the U.S., it's (800) 252-3640.

Of course you'll find the changes listed throughout the book, but here are a few that don't seem to fit anywhere else:

If you're creating shared solutions, keep in mind that users who have software previous to version 7 won't be able to open FileMaker 7 or later files.

There have been quite a few keyboard command changes that deal specifically with moving, grouping, and locking objects in Layout mode. To get the lowdown, go to the Help menu, choose Content & Index, and choose the Index tab. Type "keyboard commands" and double-click "Layout mode keyboard commands…" for the OS you're using. Scroll down to "Object arrangement keyboard commands."

FileMaker 6 had changed how dates are handled to provide a more consistent conversion of two-digit years. For all the details, go to http://www.filemaker.com, click the "support" link, and select Knowledge Base. Enter 1138 in the Search Text field, select Answer ID from the Search By drop-down, and click the Search button. I personally enter all dates using four digits for the year. That avoids any confusion. But imported data may need some special attention.

FileMaker has been certified for the Windows 2000 and XP (both Pro and Home editions) logos since version 6, and Windows Vista as of the 9 release. It is accessible for the visually- and hearing-impaired, and includes support for OnNow power management for laptops. It is also easier to provide software updates in large organizations.

Where there will be multiple users of FileMaker on the same Windows computer, each user can have a different user name and network protocol when they launch FileMaker for the first time. You can use Windows XP Fast User Switching between various user accounts without having to quit FileMaker.

FileMaker Pro began supporting Mac OS X starting with version 5.5. FileMaker 7 will not run on OS9, and FMP8 required OS X v10.3.9 or greater. FileMaker 9 went even further, requiring version 10.4.8 or later on the Mac. OS X does not support the Dial Phone script step or AppleTalk (which has been abandoned in favor of faster, more reliable protocols). Any plug-ins you expect to use must be written specifically for OS X. While these limitations may cause some hesitation in adopting the Mac OS X platform, there is one big advantage. Since OS X features protected memory, when one program crashes, others remain untouched. And there's really no way around it — if you want to use FileMaker 10 on a Mac, you have to use OS X. Not only are FileMaker files safer in OS X, but they look great, too! FileMaker, Inc. is making a lot of headway to allow deployment outside the Mac and Windows platforms. For example, FileMaker works with XML and SQL data sources and uses the Web Viewer to plant web pages right onto a FileMaker layout.

FileMaker, Inc. has decided to discontinue support for FileMaker Mobile. Since its introduction I had always felt it wasn't particularly valuable because its feature set was too limited and it wasn't relational. Apparently enough other people agreed with me and it never sold well enough to warrant keeping it in the fold. That said, FileMaker 10 includes the plug-in so that it can communicate with Mobile so users aren't prevented from using the solutions they have already built.

The Help menu has been expanded so you can quickly get to a variety of product documents and FMP's Learning Center. And FileMaker wants to know what you think. Let's say you're having problems with a function that just doesn't make sense. Or maybe there are features you'd like to suggest. If your computer is connected to the Internet, click the Help menu and select Send us your Feedback. That will bring up a web page where you can fill out a form that will help them understand exactly what you'd like to see in FileMaker. Obviously they can't add every feature that everyone comes up with. But who knows. Maybe your suggestion will have a profound effect on what happens next. It sure made a difference to version 7! After all, a million heads are better than one. FileMaker really *is* listening. That's what makes a great company, and I'm proud to be associated with them.

Companion Files

A variety of files are available to be downloaded from www.wordware.com/files/fmpro10. These are divided into the following folders:

- Book files — These files go along with the book, chapter by chapter, for readers to learn to work with FileMaker Pro. This folder also contains a PDF of the index so you can quickly search for any word or phrase and find it in multiple places in the index, regardless of where it is.
- Developer files — Most of these solutions were provided by other FileMaker developers; some of these may require a fee to use beyond a trial period.
- Author files — These include an explanation of what they're for. Simply click the question mark button on the main page of each file.

The download page also includes a link to FileMaker Inc.'s plug-ins page, which lists all registered plug-ins.

See the included Read Me file for more information.

Part 1

Learning the Basics

Chapter 1

Getting Acquainted with FileMaker Pro

Introduction

I'm assuming you've already installed FileMaker Pro and the template files that come with it on your computer. If you haven't, do that now, because when I am done with this first part, I want you to be able to get started right away.

The author of one of the first books I ever read on FileMaker Pro spent the first half of the book on database theory. Great reading if you need to fall asleep! I don't want to waste too much of your time before you get your hands on the program. I guarantee you'll be working with FileMaker in five minutes (unless you're a very slow reader!), but I do want to get you excited about what is coming your way.

FileMaker Pro is the easiest relational database system to use on the face of the earth. I would argue that it is the best desktop database system as well. Pretty strong words, eh? Let's look at the facts.

Developers who create database systems in both FileMaker Pro and Microsoft Access say that when they prototype a system concept for a client in order to get a job, they do the work in FileMaker. Why? Because it takes half the time! That's significant because the developer often isn't being paid for his prototyping time. When the client is paying for the work and wants it in Access, of course the developers will do the work in Access. It takes twice as long and they make twice the money! The fact that you're reading this book means you won't be wasting your time and money either. You made the right choice in database applications.

FileMaker Pro is also the best-selling stand-alone database application in the world. There are more installed copies of Microsoft Access because for many years it was part of the Microsoft Office suite, but many owners don't use it. That means it's very possible that FileMaker is the most-used database system in the world. It is certainly the best-selling cross-platform database application. Access does not work on a Macintosh. Those who are serious about database systems research what's out there and they buy FileMaker Pro.

Its ease of use does not mean FileMaker is wimpy. It is just cleverly built to be easier — "user friendly" in the best sense of the phrase. The creators of FileMaker took a very different approach to their program from systems that came before. They were daring. And we reap the benefits. By the time you finish these 27 chapters, you'll be well on your way to understanding that power.

What Is a Database?

A *database* is simply a collection of information, or data. A *database system* is a set of procedures, devices, and rules for managing the information in a database. A database system can be as simple as a set of Rolodex cards used to keep track of your contact information. Because computer people love to shorten terms to the point of obscurity, they will often refer to computer-based database systems simply as databases. A single file with one or more tables, a group of related files, and the program that created the files (such as FileMaker Pro) are all sometimes referred to interchangeably as a database. Like most people, I'll be using the term loosely throughout the book. But I thought it'd be wise to point out the difference between the two terms while we're just starting out.

Database systems don't have to involve computers at all, but because computers are so good at storing, organizing, and retrieving data, a computer-based database system can be very powerful and flexible.

Sounds kind of boring. Put simply, a computer-based database system is the most glorious Rolodex ever built. Sorting those Rolodex cards by last name never worked very well for me because I can't remember names worth a rip. However, with a computer-based database system you can often find a person based on any piece of information in the file — sometimes even if you can't spell it!

For example, imagine you're trying to get in touch with a salesman about a product. You remember that his first name is George, but you can't recall his last name. In a database, you can do a search for George in the First Name field and just page through the few records that come up. Maybe you've forgotten his name completely, but you remember that he sells key chains and that you'd typed that information in the Notes field. Bingo! Try that with a Rolodex.

FileMaker Pro is a *relational* database system. That means you can create special rules for retrieving more information based on the information that you have already found. These connecting rules are called *relationships*. Going back to the Rolodex contact cards, imagine that on each person's card you wrote his or her favorite hobby. As you thumb through the cards one by one, you decide it would be handy to know who shares the same hobby. I see that Michael Cloud's favorite hobby is playing piano. Who else in my card database has playing piano as their favorite hobby? Doug Deal likes chess. Who else likes chess? To answer these questions, you'd have to compare the hobby on the current card with the hobby on every other card and see which ones match. This would take considerable effort with physical cards, but by using relationships you can have FileMaker provide the information quickly and automatically for each person in your database. Relationships are very powerful, but they can be a complex topic. We'll cover this in more depth in Chapters 2, 6, and 7.

You can use FileMaker Pro for something as simple as a mailing list, inventory system, convention registration, or scheduling, all the way up to purchase orders, billing, and accounting. You can share your files with other users on a network. And with some great tricks provided by the geniuses at FileMaker, Inc., you can share information with many other computer programs and even on the World Wide Web.

I promised you I wouldn't take more than five minutes. Are you fired up yet? Let's go!

Using FileMaker Pro

FileMaker Pro is the *application*, or program, in which you create files and tables and manipulate data. You have to get the program started before you can do anything else.

Opening FileMaker Pro

Start the FileMaker Pro application. If you're using a Macintosh computer, go into the Applications folder, open the FileMaker folder, and double-click on the FileMaker Pro icon. If you're on a Windows machine, find the Start menu, go to Programs, find FileMaker Pro 10 (the list may not be in alphabetical order), and choose FileMaker Pro. If you chose to have an alias put in the Macintosh dock, or a shortcut created on the Windows desktop during the installation process, you can double-click the shortcut to start FileMaker Pro.

When FileMaker opens, you should see a window similar to the one in Figure 1-1a. The drop-down menu in the upper-right corner has been artificially expanded to show you some other choices for converting existing data into a FileMaker file. One of the options that will be of particular interest to Macintosh users is Bento Source. Click the Learn More button in the lower-left corner and you'll see some options new for FileMaker 10. You must be connected to the Internet to take advantage of them. If you or somebody else has been using FileMaker already on this machine, this window may have been turned off in FileMaker's Application Preferences.

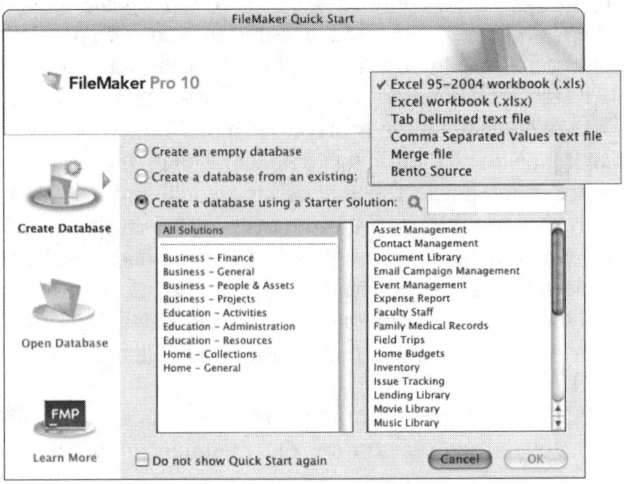

Figure 1-1a
When you first open FileMaker Pro, you should see a window that looks like 1-1a. Clicking the Learn More button reveals 1-1b.

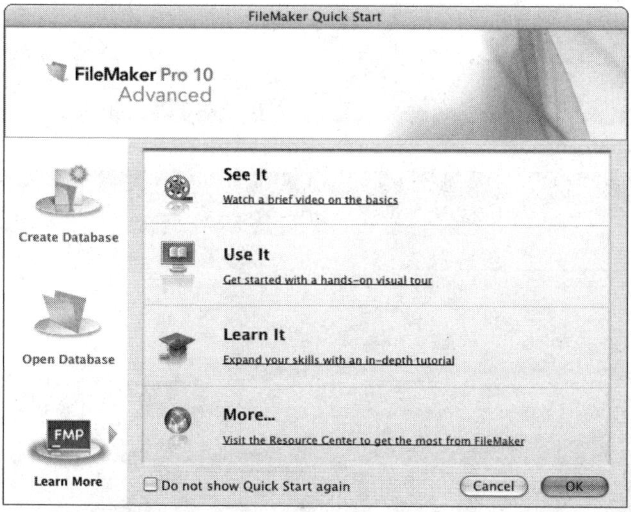

Figure 1-1b
These options are available when you click the Learn More button.

NOTE You can also open the FileMaker Pro application by double-clicking on the icon of any FileMaker Pro file. Of course, that file will open. With some versions of OS X, you may find that it will not bring the FileMaker program to the front.

CAUTION If you open one of the template files by double-clicking its icon, any changes you make to the file will become a permanent part of the template.

Opening a FileMaker Pro File

If you don't see the FileMaker Quick Start window, go to the File menu in the upper-left corner of the screen and choose New Database. (From now on, when I want you to choose an option from a menu I'll write it like this: File, New Database.)

Once you get going, you'll want to work with files that have your data in them. When you want to open a file you've already created, choose File, Open. To find the files you need, you will have to navigate your way through the directories on your computer. You can also open a file by double-clicking on the file's icon. That will also work with an alias of the file (Macintosh) or a shortcut (Windows).

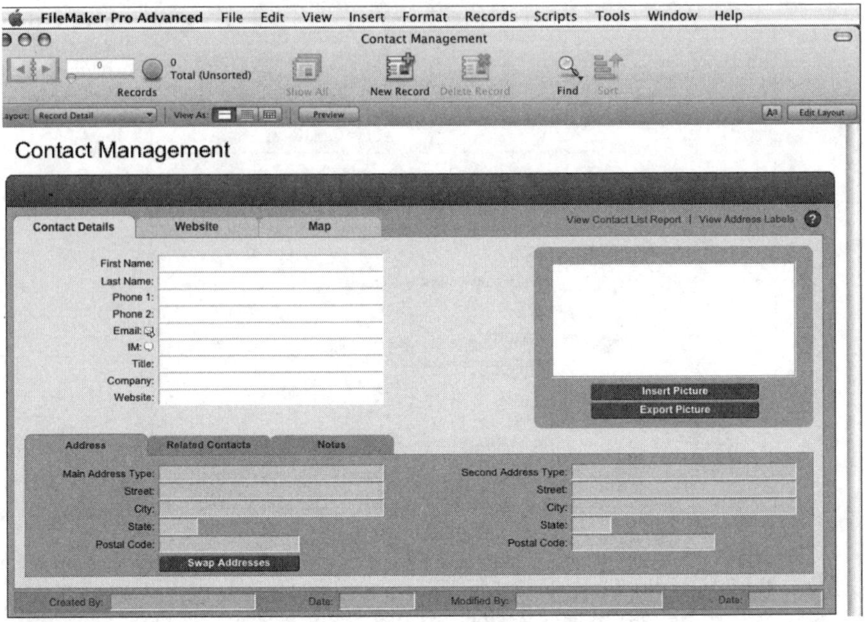

Figure 1-2
The FileMaker Pro screen. Notice the Status toolbar across the top, under the menu bar.

The advantage of using the FileMaker Quick Start window at this stage is that FileMaker knows where to find the templates, so you don't have to go searching through folders on your hard drive. The Create Database icon is automatically selected. Your options are Create an empty database, Create a database from an existing, and Create a database using a Starter Solution (one of the templates). We'll open one of the starter solutions (or templates) in a minute.

By clicking one of the other two icons along the left (Open Database or Learn More), you are presented with other choices that don't really need much explaining. So go ahead and take a look. To take advantage of the items in the Learn More section, you'll need to be connected to the Internet.

Database Concepts

I think it's easier to understand terminology if you're looking at the items I'm talking about as we go. So while we're in the middle of opening this file, I'll explain, continue working, and explain some more.

Files

A FileMaker *file* holds both your information and instructions on how you prefer to keep that information organized. This is similar to the way a word processor or spreadsheet stores its data. All of these applications keep track of the data you create in files on your hard disk.

To create a database system you'll need at least one FileMaker file, but your system can use many files if you prefer. Think back to the Rolodex. Our Rolodex was our database of contact information, but if we have both a business life and a personal life we could keep everyone in the same system or we could keep two separate systems. Similarly, we could keep everyone in the same FileMaker file or split them into two files. Which is the "right" way? It depends on what we think is convenient and appropriate. Sometimes, only our experience will tell us.

Fortunately, FileMaker provides tools to allow separate files to communicate when they need to, as well as tools to partition and order the data into separate areas for clearer organization within a single file. With this in mind, don't get too hung up on how many files your database should have. FileMaker files are organizational tools like a set of drawers in your desk or filing cabinet.

Click the Create Database icon and the radio button labeled "Create a database using a Starter Solution." Click All Solutions in the left column, then find the file called Contact Management in the right column. Click on it so it's highlighted and click the OK button or just double-click the words. FileMaker will display a second window that asks you where you want to save the copy of the file. (See Figures 1-3 and 1-4.) Always pay attention to what folders you put your files in; you'll probably want to find them later. Also notice that FileMaker 10 files have the ".fp7" extension. That is as it should be, because the underlying file format has not changed since FileMaker 7. There is no such thing as an ".fp10" file.

TIP If you develop a system to organize your files now, you'll be much better off later. After all, getting organized is what this is all about, right? If I'm on the Macintosh platform, I often save my new files to the desktop so I can find them later and put them where I want them. I have to override the fact that OS X wants to automatically put my files in the Documents folder. On Windows computers, I save new files in the My Documents folder. But you need to remember to go in there later to put things away. It's easy to forget and create quite a clutter.

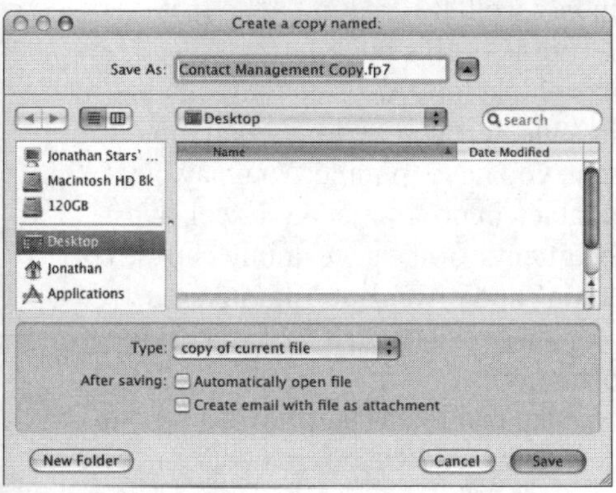

Figure 1-3
The Macintosh window for creating a copy named Contact Management. If the window is abbreviated, click the triangle to the right of the file name to expand it.

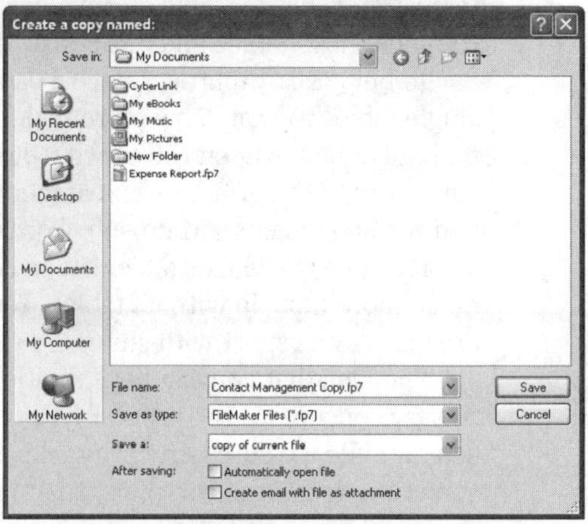

Figure 1-4
The window for creating a copy named Contact Management in Microsoft Windows.

The Contact Management file will probably open to a blank form. Regardless, click on the question mark in the upper-right corner of the screen (see Figure 1-2). This will take you to an informational screen about this page area on the FileMaker starter solution. Take a moment to read this screen. Scroll down if you need to.

Near the upper left of the page is some blue text that says "Return to Previous Layout." (There's an arrow pointing to it in Figure 1-5.) That text is actually a button — sort of like a hyperlink on a web page. Click on it. Notice how the screen appearance changes as you are returned to the blank form. I'll teach you how to create your own buttons later. It's really easy to do and you'll love the power it gives you.

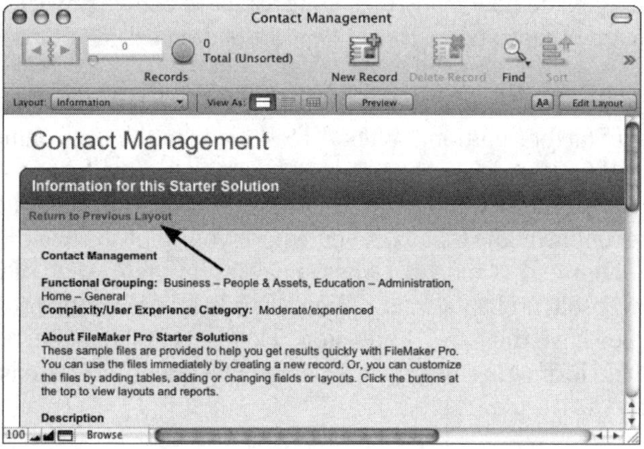

Figure 1-5
The Return to Previous Layout button in the Contact Management information window.

Tables

Tables are collections of data concerning a specific subject, such as a list of customers or invoices. A FileMaker file can hold rules about just one type of table or many different types. For example, a file could have a table for customers and another table for invoices. In fact we'll be creating a file that contains those tables and more over the course of this book.

To help clarify a little, I have a database I use for groceries that only has a single table. You can have more tables in a file, but you certainly don't need to. It all depends upon the specific purpose you have in mind. You may be familiar with the grid-like appearance of tables in programs like Excel, and you can add tables to Microsoft Word documents. You can certainly choose to display your FileMaker table data in columns and rows. But FileMaker is much more flexible with its tables. You can display data so it looks like a form, or labels, or a report with summary information.

The idea that you can have multiple tables in a FileMaker file is a revolutionary concept for the program. Prior to version 7, developers needed a separate file to represent each table. The single-table-per-file arrangement sometimes required complex programming to move between the files to accomplish fairly simple tasks. This newer multiple-tables-per-file system allows people who work with FileMaker to streamline their work considerably. And it allows newcomers to take advantage of some of FileMaker's more powerful features more quickly than ever before.

Records

Look over near the upper-left corner of the window in the Status toolbar. See the icon that looks like an open three-ring binder? There are arrow/triangles on the "pages." That's called the Book. It's a navigation tool that we'll get into later. To the right of the Book is a box with a "0" in it and under it is the word "Records." That means there are 0 records in this table. Oh? "What's a record?" you ask. It's like a card in our Rolodex. *Records* are what you add to a table as you are filling it up with your data. It's the information that you enter about a particular person, place, or thing. What's actually in a record depends on the rules that you've set up in the table.

Take your pointer and click in the white box to the right of the words First Name. Oops! No records, eh? Click the OK button to get rid of the dialog box. Choose Records, New Record. Notice in the menu that you can also make a new record by pressing the Command+N (Macintosh) or Ctrl+N (Windows) key combination. If you look back over at the Book you should now have one record in your file — unless you were trying out the key combinations and now have two or three records. It's okay; try it out. You're not going to hurt anything. The worst that can happen is your computer will blow up, you'll lose a lot of important files, be fired from your job, and end up homeless. So go ahead — give it a shot. (Now isn't this a lot more fun than that sleep-inducing database theory book?)

Fields

You may notice that the cursor is blinking in the white box next to First Name. If you click and hold down your mouse button on the light gray background to the left of the words First Name, you'll see that most of the other white boxes have dotted lines around them. Those boxes are *fields*. That's where you put your information. A field is a little piece of information that's part of a record of your data. By itself it may not describe much, but when grouped with the other fields in the record it should give you a unique and useful description. Go back and click into the First Name field, and type your first name. Press the Tab key and the cursor moves to the Last Name field.

Type your last name. Tab again and enter your phone number. To the right of the field boxes is a gray rectangular panel with a couple of buttons on it that are labeled "Insert Picture" and "Export Picture." You can store a picture (and some other cool things) in the white container field that appears just above the buttons. Go ahead and click in it. Notice that the cursor doesn't blink when it's in a container field. Look at the choices you have under the Insert menu. Yep, you can put a movie or a sound file in there if you want. You could also click the Insert Picture button, but then you can only put a picture into the field, not the other file types.

Look in the center of the Status toolbar. See that New Record button? Click it. You just created a new record without the key combination or the menu command. The flexibility is amazing.

Hey, your name disappeared! Relax; it's still in the file. It's just in a different record — same as if you were on a different page of a book. Go to the Book and click on the left page, the one with the arrow on it. Look at the record. There's your name. Now click on the right page of the Book to return to the blank record. Fill in the fields with information about someone you know.

Each record is like one of those Rolodex cards I told you about. Is the pattern starting to become clearer now? A record is just a collection of one or more fields, a table is just a collection of one or more records, a file is just a collection of one or more tables, and a database is just a collection of the data in one or more integrated files. A database system is FileMaker itself and all of the rules that we put in our files for managing our information. And what is our information? Can you say "database"? I knew you could.

SHORTCUT Another way to navigate between records without using the Book is to hold down the Control key and press the up and down arrows — Control+arrow (Macintosh) or Ctrl+arrow (Windows). It's not particularly intuitive. You click the down arrow to flip the right page of the book onto the next page. In contrast — and more in keeping with clicking the down arrow key — if you are viewing items in a list, you actually move down to the next record.

Layouts

Layouts are just different views of data and tables in your files. In the upper-left corner of the window under the Book is the Layout drop-down list. Click on the arrow or the text that reads Record Detail and choose Record List. This brings you to the Record List layout. You should see a list of the few records you have in the file. Some of them may be empty. Notice that this list does not have all the fields that were on the form. All the rest of the data is still in the file; it's just not visible on this layout. You can even have a layout with no fields on it at all. You could use a layout like that to make notes to yourself using the Text tool (more on that later) or to store some of your favorite icons that you would use on other layouts. Click the column headings (First Name, Email, etc.) to sort the records. There are short "scripts" that run to sort the records and change the little icons you see next to the column heads. Clicking on the little red triangle to the left of the person's name will take you back to the form.

You could even have a layout containing nothing but buttons to act as a menu to other layouts or reports. That can be a great organizational tool and I often do just that for my clients. Think how cluttered the Record Detail layout would be if you had to cram every button for every function on there.

Look at the top of the window for the Magnifying Glass icon with the word Find under it. Click the icon. You're in the same layout, just in Find mode. Every field has a magnifying glass in it to help make it clearer that you are indeed in Find mode. (You can set it up so they don't show if you turn off field frames. See Chapter 15, "Making Sense of Your Information with Layouts.") And the standard set of icons in the Status toolbar all have magnifying glasses incorporated into them. If you click somewhere on the layout background so your cursor is no longer in any of the fields, the magnifying glasses in the fields go away.

Above the container field (the gray rectangular area above the Insert Picture button) is some text that reads "View Contact List Report." Click on it now. The narrow gray bar just below the Status toolbar is called the Layout bar. Notice the blue "Continue" button over on the right. (There's an arrow pointing to it in Figure 1-6.) When you clicked the words "View Contact List Report," FileMaker started running a script. Click on one of the items in the list, then click the Continue button to take you back to the form. Now choose View, Layout mode. Move your mouse pointer up into the Status toolbar and pause it on one of the icons there without clicking. You should see a Tooltip that will tell you what the icon is for.

Click repeatedly on the right page of the Book until the number 6 appears in the box to the right of the Book. If you look at the Layout drop-down list below the Book, you'll see that this layout is called Avery 5160. Before long you'll be able to create your own labels and even custom letters that combine data from your records into the text of your letters.

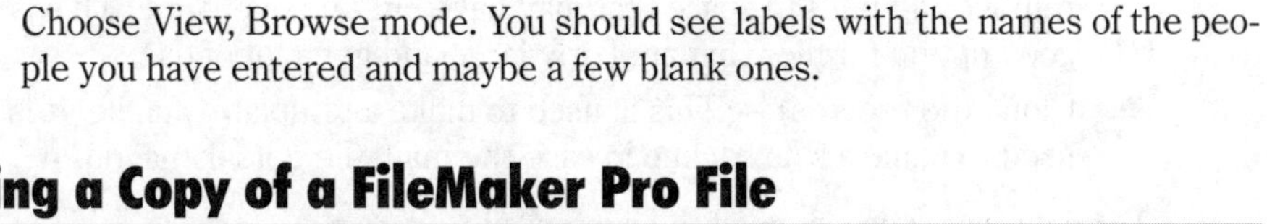

Figure 1-6
The Return to Previous Layout button in the Contact Management window.

Choose View, Browse mode. You should see labels with the names of the people you have entered and maybe a few blank ones.

Saving a Copy of a FileMaker Pro File

As the psychiatrists say, "Our time is almost up," so we need to do a little housekeeping before we finish. FileMaker saves your work as you go. This is a little different from word processors, which often require that you save every few minutes to avoid losing your work. However, you will want to make various backups at the end of a session.

Choose File, Save a Copy As and click on "copy of current file" at the bottom of the window to look at your other choices. The Macintosh and Windows dialogs are somewhat different, so I've included both in Figures 1-7 and 1-8.

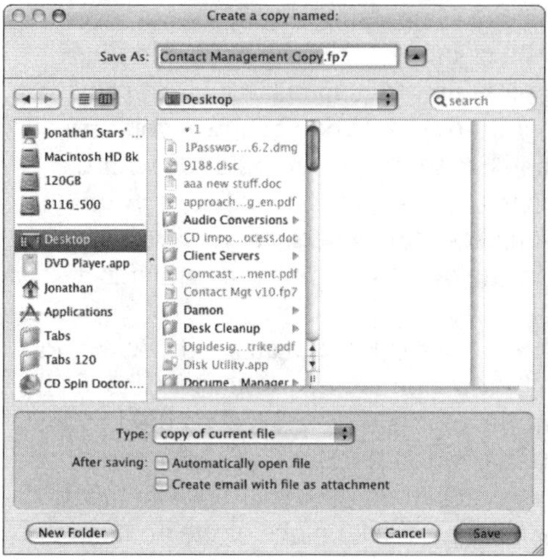

Figure 1-7
The Macintosh window that appears when you choose Save a Copy As from the File menu.

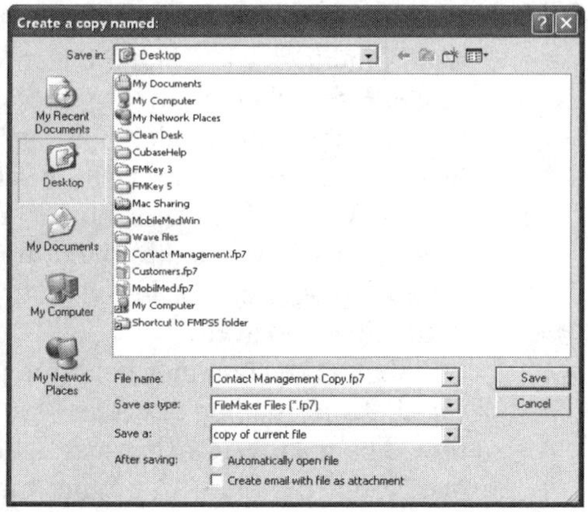

Figure 1-8
The window that appears when you choose Save a Copy As from the File menu in Microsoft Windows.

Notice that next to the file name, FileMaker knows to insert the word "Copy" at the end of the name. You can type over the name and call it anything you like. If you choose "clone (no records)" from the Type pop-up, FileMaker inserts the word "Clone" instead.

NOTE In this book we will use the terms "pop-up" and "drop-down" interchangeably when we talk about a control that lets you choose from a predefined list of options, such as the Type pop-up.

The three Save As file types and their purposes are:

- Copy of current file — Makes a copy of the file with all the data.
- Compacted copy (smaller) — FileMaker goes through the file and removes all unused space that may have built up over time. This is a good option for files that are fairly large and get a lot of use.
- Clone (no records) — This is used to make a template of a file. It is often used to make a safe backup in case the main file gets damaged.

For now, just save a copy of the current file.

CAUTION Save a Copy As in FMP is different from the Save As menu command you may be used to in other programs. In many programs when you choose Save As, the document you are working in immediately takes on the new document name. When you choose Save a Copy As in FileMaker, you remain in the document you were working in before you saved your copy.

Closing a FileMaker Pro File

There are a couple of ways to close your file. You can choose File, Close. On the Macintosh, you can click the red button (the Close button) in the upper-left corner of the file window. On a Windows machine, click the X box in the upper-right corner of the file window. (If you click the X in the upper-right corner of the whole screen, you'll exit the whole FileMaker program.)

SHORTCUT To close a window, use Command+W (Macintosh) or Ctrl+W (Windows).

Quitting FileMaker Pro

Quitting or exiting is done the same way as with any other program I can think of. Choose File, Quit (Macintosh) or File, Exit (Windows). In addition to the following keyboard shortcut, on a Windows machine, you can click the X box in the upper-right corner of the screen. You don't get a similar choice on the Mac.

SHORTCUT To quit FileMaker Pro, use Command+Q (Macintosh). In Windows you can use either Ctrl+Q or Alt+F4.

Summary

This first chapter should have given you a certain comfort level with FileMaker Pro. You now know how to open and quit the FileMaker Pro application as well as how to open and close individual files. We've looked at fields and how any one field may or may not appear on various layouts. We've also seen that there are records in a table, one or more tables make up a file, and one or more files make up a database. Many of the chapters to come still deal with basics. As you're learning these basics, you should start to get some of those "Ah-ha!" moments. That's when you'll recognize that FileMaker Pro can help you accomplish what you need to do in more ways than you'd dreamed. That's when you begin to control your destiny!

Are you having as much fun as I am? Check out the Q&A that follows and try the Workshop exercise. Then go get yourself some coffee, juice, or a soft drink. You deserve it. I'll see you in Chapter 2.

Q & A

Q How do I get my data back if I click the Delete button or choose Records, Delete Record, and then click the Delete button in the dialog box?

A You'd better hope that you have a copy of the record in a backup somewhere. Once a record is gone from the database, it's gone. That's why backing up regularly is so important. See Chapter 23 for more details.

Q What's that slotted gadget underneath the box to the right of the Book for?

A That's the Slider. You can use it to move between records by clicking and dragging it right and left. It can be quite helpful in tables with a large number of records for moving to the first or last record or somewhere between.

Workshop: Try it out on your own

Start FileMaker Pro and open a file from one of the templates folders. Try out some of the buttons. I don't mind if you even take a look at some of the other menus — it'll probably get your mind going with some questions. Create a new record or two and enter some data. In general, just rummage around. The worst you can do is... well, just try it out. Then see if you can save a copy of the file and quit or exit.

Chapter 2

Menus and Modes

Introduction

Welcome to the second chapter. This chapter continues to familiarize you with FileMaker Pro. First of all, I want to get into more detail about the various menus. Menus in FileMaker Pro, as well as most other modern computer programs, are the words that sit across the top of your screen and show you various commands of the program that you're working in. We're going to look at many of the specific FileMaker commands. You will find one of the most important commands under the File menu: Manage. From here you can manage your database by creating tables, fields, and relationships; value lists, which are options that frequently appear in fields (items such as Male and Female, or a drop-down list of employees); external data sources, which we will explore in Chapter 14; and accounts and privileges, which give or limit access to information.

Under the View menu you'll find FileMaker's four modes: Browse, Find, Layout, and Preview. These modes are where you do most of the work with data entry and choose the way information appears. You might do a lot of your initial design with fields and scripts, but you and the people who share your data will work in these different modes.

Manage Database

Even though we'll go further into the details of table, field, and relationship definition in Chapter 3, "Creating Your First Database," I want to show you around the neighborhood so you'll be familiar with it when the time comes.

Open up the copy of the Contact Management file you created in the last chapter. If you deleted it or just can't find it, go back to Chapter 1 and follow the directions there to create a new copy.

Once the file is open, choose File, Manage Database.

SHORTCUT To bring up the Manage Database window, use Command+Shift+D (Macintosh) or Ctrl+Shift+D (Windows). You'll be returned to the tab you were on when you last left Manage Database.

You'll see a window that looks like the one in Figure 2-1. If not, click the Tables tab.

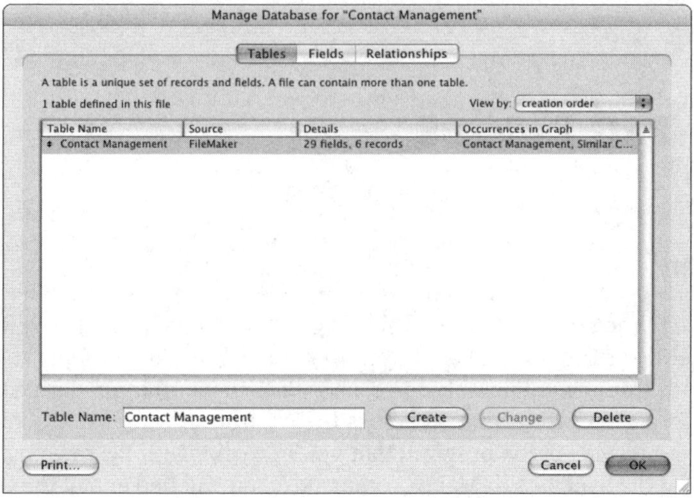

Figure 2-1 The Manage Database Tables tab.

Tables Tab

Since FileMaker now allows multiple tables in a file, you need a place to create and name them. The Tables tab is that place. In the Contact Management file, there's currently only one table. When you first create a file, the first table is automatically given the same name as the file and the Manage Database window's Fields tab is displayed. For every table you want to add to the file, you need to return to the Tables tab. No need for too much detail right now; I just want you to take a look around.

Go to the upper-right corner of the window and click on the pop-up list next to View by. Since there's only one table in this file, you really can't tell what effect making a selection would have. But "creation order" and "table name" are pretty obvious. Look at the little arrows to the left of the words Contact Management in the Table Name column. If there were other tables in this file, you'd be able to reorder them by clicking on the arrows and moving the table names up or down in the list. If you did move one of the table names, the View by pop-up would change to "custom order." You can also sort the list by table name by clicking the words Table Name at the top of the column. Clicking the other column heads has no effect on sorting the table names. The second column (Source) shows whether the data comes from FileMaker or some other data source. We'll learn more about that in Chapter 26. Notice that you can tell how many fields and records are in a table by looking in the third column. The fourth column lists the table occurrences in the relationships graph, which is displayed when you choose the Relationships tab. We'll take a look at that in a minute.

Fields Tab

Click the Fields tab. You should see a window that looks like the one in Figure 2-2. A field is the basic storage area of information in any database. When we were investigating the Contact Management records in the previous chapter, you typed information into some of the fields.

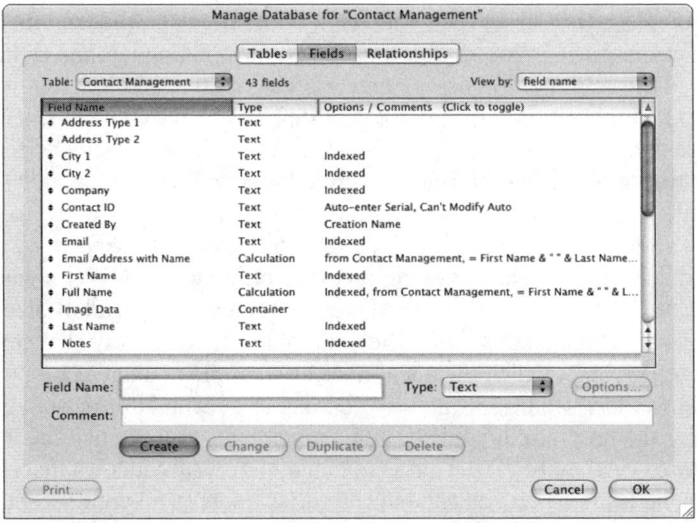

Figure 2-2
The Manage Database Fields tab.

Next to the name of the table, Contact Management, in the Fields tab you'll notice that there are 43 fields in this table. The three column headings are Field Name, Type, and Options/Comments. The Type column matches the categories you'll find in the Type drop-down menu: Text, Number, Date, Time, Timestamp, Container, Calculation, and Summary. If you have a repeating field (which will be discussed in Chapter 4), you will see the number of field repetitions in this column as well. Options are determined in part by the field type and can be edited by selecting the field name and clicking the Options button.

The first field in your list is probably Address Type 1. Go to the upper-right corner of the window and click in the pop-up next to View by. The fields have been sorted by creation date. If you choose "field name" in the View by pop-up, the field names sort alphabetically. Try some of the other choices from the View by pop-up.

Now click on the words Field Name at the top of the first column. The field titles are once again sorted by name. Click it again and they sort in reverse alphabetical order. Notice that your last choice in the View by pop-up has now been replaced with "field name."

Click the Type column header. Click it again. I think you get the idea. Now click the Options/Comments column header. When you click this header, the column alternates between displaying options and comments. If the fields had any comments, they would show up here. Click the column header again to redisplay the options.

> **NOTE** Sometimes field names aren't long enough to be descriptive. You can use the Comment area to make whatever notes you like to indicate the purpose of the field. You enter this information in the Comment field in the lower portion of this screen. The Comment area will hold up to 30,000 characters per field. The only problem is that all your comments are on one line. Someday we may get a scrolling paragraph block. But for now, a sentence or two should be enough.

When you place the cursor over the vertical line between the column headers, the cursor turns into a double-headed arrow pointing left and right. You can resize the columns by clicking and dragging on the line. You might be surprised to find that the columns don't stay that way. After you exit the Manage Database window and then return, they'll be back to their original sizes.

Use the scroll bar on the right to scroll down until you see a field with text in the Options/Comments column that extends off the window to the right. To view a little more of the text, you can expand the window by pulling on the knurled area in the lower-right corner of the window. When you leave the Manage Database window, FileMaker remembers the window size setting. The same applies to all the other resizable windows. Any changes are memorized globally, which means no matter what file you have open, each resizable window will be set the way you like it — even after closing and reopening the program. If you're using a Macintosh, you can use the left-right scroll bar to view more text. That is not an option on a Windows machine, but it's not a big issue when you can expand the window to fill your screen. If you click on the rows, you'll notice that the field name appears in the Field Name box and the Type pop-up changes to match the entry in the Type column. You can also double-click anywhere on one of the rows to see the Options field or to bring up the Specify Calculation window, or you can highlight a row and click the Options button. You might try that now, but be cautious not to permanently change anything in any of these windows. Feel free to make any changes you like and see what they'll do — as long as you make sure you click the Cancel button when leaving the Options area. That way none of your explorations will become permanent. Again, we'll deal more with field definitions in the next chapter.

After you're done exploring the Fields tab, click the Relationships tab.

Relationships Tab

The Relationships tab is where you build connections to other tables either in the same file or in other files. If you're not already in the Relationships tab of the Manage Database window, choose File, Manage Database, and click the Relationships tab to open it. There are six table occurrences defined for this file already and five relationships between them. Your window may not be arranged exactly the same as the one in Figure 2-3, but it should have all the same elements. Take the time to read the yellow text block that explains a little more about what you see in this dialog. I'll show you how to add text to this window later on in the book.

I want to have you create a relationship so you understand a little more about how it all works.

1. Click on the first icon under Tables/Relationships (there's an arrow pointing to it in Figure 2-3) in the lower-left corner of the window. This opens the Specify Table window, from which you can add a table to the relationships graph.

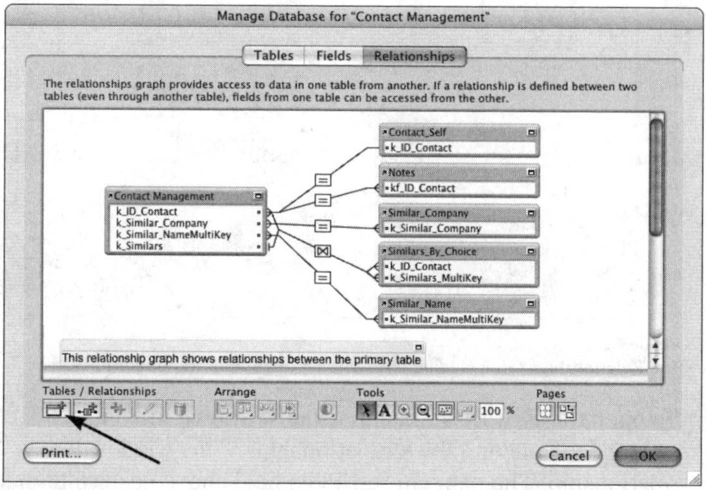

Figure 2-3
The Relationships tab showing the relationships in Contact Management.

2. In the Specify Table window (see Figure 2-4), you can click on the **Data Source** drop-down and choose **Add FileMaker Data Source.**
3. Work your way back through the files on your machine until you find the Templates folder called Business - People & Assets and choose the **Asset Management** file. Highlight it and choose **Open**, or double-click it. You may still have to click **OK** to bring back the Relationships tab, which should now look something like Figure 2-5 with the Asset Management table added.

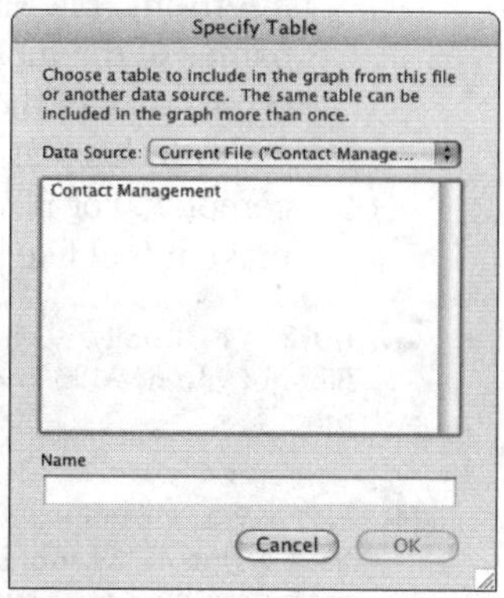

Figure 2-4
The Specify Table window.

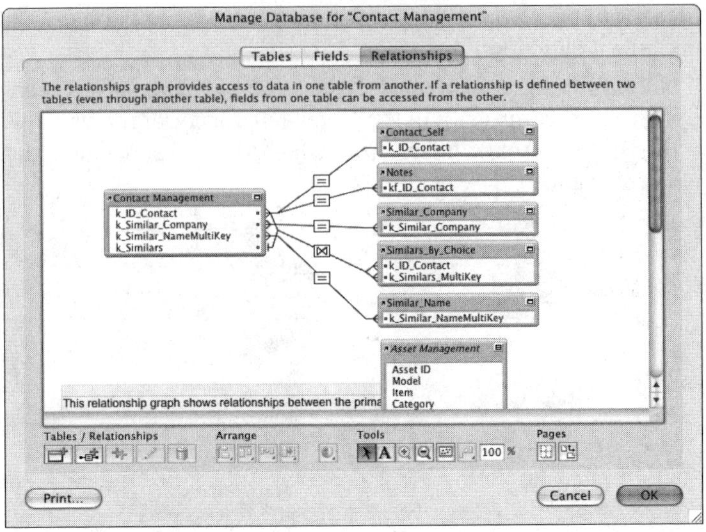

Figure 2-5
The Relationships tab including the Asset Management table reference.

4. To open the Edit Relationship window, shown in Figure 2-6, click on the second icon under Tables/Relationships. This window lets you create a relationship. The name in the Table field above each column should say Table <unknown> at this point. Click in the pop-up for Table on the left and choose **Contact Management**. On the right, choose **Asset Management**. FileMaker automatically uses the names of the tables for the names of the table occurrences used in the relationship. If a second occurrence of the table is needed, you'll see a dialog. But let's not go too far with this just yet. In fact, some of this next part may seem a little complex. For now, just follow along so you get a feel for the tools. Try to make it feel like play. Don't get bogged down in the details.

NOTE Normally, we'll be building relationships to other tables within the same file. But you need to know that you can also build relationships to other tables in other files.

TIP For a faster way to create relationships between tables, simply click on a field in one of the tables and drag to a field in the other table. The fields will move into the upper section of the table icons, and you'll see an equal sign on the line between the icons. You can double-click anywhere on the line between the icons to open the Edit Relationship window and make changes or just see the details.

TIP You can build as many relationships to a table (or tables in other files) as you like and you don't have to use the name of the table. However, you are limited to using a different name for each table occurrence in the graph. Try to use names that will make sense to you in case you have to come back and work on it later. I'll show you a naming standard called anchor-buoy in Chapter 6. Also, some dialogs in FileMaker are not expandable, so it's a good idea to use the shortest names possible while still being descriptive.

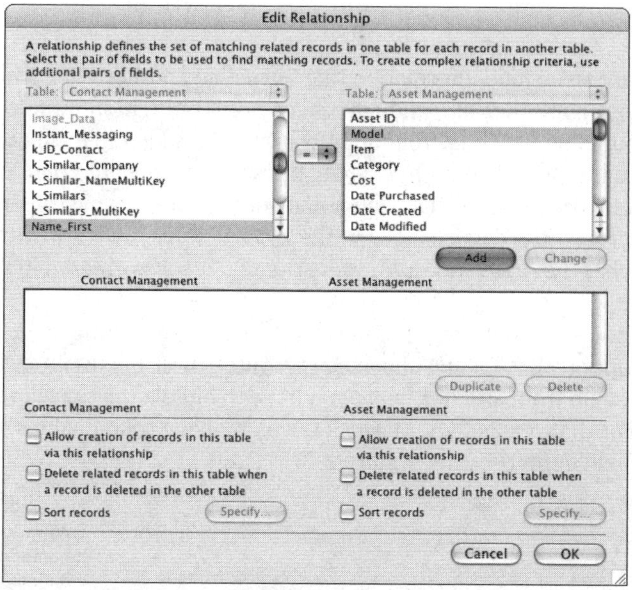

Figure 2-6 The Edit Relationship window showing the two columns of fields from both tables.

The two lists are the names of fields in the two files. Choose Name_First in the left column and try to choose Picture in the right column. You can't. Picture is grayed out because you cannot establish a relationship to it. The Picture field, a container field, holds a different kind of data than most other fields and cannot be indexed. You can only establish relationships between the fields that appear in black.

⌘ **TIP** When you place fields from a related table on a layout, four dots (::) will appear before the field name. The four dots, or double colon, indicate that these are related fields from another table. FileMaker won't allow you to use a double colon in the name of a table reference.

Look at the check boxes near the bottom of the window. Deleting, creating, and sorting related records based on the relationship are all valuable options that are available in this window. We'll get into the reasons for each in Chapter 6, "Working with Related Tables — Part 1."

Click Cancel twice to return to Browse mode in the file. Using relationships, you can display the related data on your layouts or you can create lookup fields that pull the data into your table. That way you can work with the data and even edit it without changing the original data in the source table.

Lookups

When you want to include information that "lives" in another table (this could mean a table from another file) and have a copy of it brought into the current table, you would use a lookup. You might want to use a lookup in an ordering system where the price list might change, but where you want your current orders to reflect the prices at the time you made a quote to a customer. That way, no matter how the data changes in the Prices table, you'll always have a snapshot of what the price was at the time the invoice was created in the Invoices table.

Lookups are created during the process of defining or editing a field by clicking the Options button and choosing the Auto-Enter tab. In order to have the data looked up from another table, you have to build a relationship to the other table. For that reason, FileMaker lets you manage relationships while creating the field definition. See Figure 2-7.

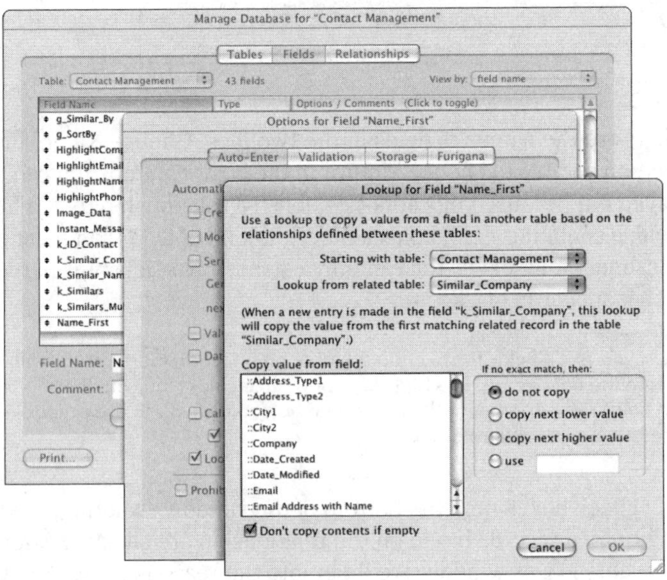

Figure 2-7
One way to automatically enter data into a field is by using a lookup.

Related Data

The other way to use information from another table is to use related data. A field from another table can be placed on the layout of your current table. It can also be used in scripts and calculation fields. Related data that is displayed on a layout can actually be edited from the current table, so you may need to take some precautions depending on what the information is and how it's being used. If the related goodies are line items of an invoice, it may be fine to be able to edit them. But you wouldn't want employees to accidentally change the prices in your products list. We'll discuss lookups and related data (and how to protect it) in Chapter 6.

Modes

Although I've spent this chapter talking about various windows, most of the day-to-day work for the end user is done in the four modes. You can switch modes by choosing them from the View menu. You can also get to them from the Mode drop-down list near the lower-left corner of the window, as shown in Figure 2-8.

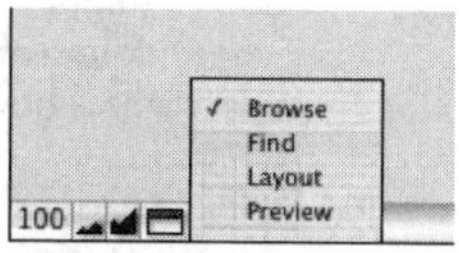

Figure 2-8
The Mode drop-down list in the lower-left corner is available in all four modes.

SHORTCUT Here are the keyboard equivalents for the four modes. I highly recommend that you memorize them. It takes about one second to press the keys and about five seconds to find the menus. Multiply that by the number of times you'll be using them each day and you'll be saving time. Your clicking muscles will thank you, too.

All except Preview are pretty intuitive. (The "P" is already used for the Print command.) I remember it by thinking "vUe."

- Browse mode — Command+B (Macintosh) or Ctrl+B (Windows)
- Find mode — Command+F (Macintosh) or Ctrl+F (Windows)
- Layout mode — Command+L (Macintosh) or Ctrl+L (Windows)
- Preview mode — Command+U (Macintosh) or Ctrl+U (Windows)

Browse Mode

In the last chapter, we learned that Browse mode is where you enter your name and phone number. It's where you view, enter, alter, and sort your data; where you can delete and hide records; and one of the places where you can format and choose which layout you want to use to view the data. Immediately below the Book is a drop-down list of layouts available in Browse mode. Depending on the user's access privileges, the user may or may not see a complete list of all the layouts in the file. Click on it now and take a look.

Layout Mode

Layout mode is where you choose how your data will look on your computer screen or when it prints. Choose View, Layout mode. Now, click on the Layout drop-down list below the Book. Layouts can be excluded from the drop-down that appears in all views except Layout mode — so you have a longer list in this file in Layout mode.

Notice that when you switch to Layout mode, the window looks nearly the same except that there is no data. Using the drop-down list, go to the Record List layout. If you switch back to Browse mode, you'll see that Browse and Layout mode do not look the same for this layout. Also, take a look at the menus that appear under the headings across the top of the screen. Compare how they change when you switch between Layout and Browse modes.

NOTE One of the hardest concepts to grasp has to do with the terminology used with layouts. I will often use the word "layout" to describe a particular view of the data. I might say, "When you're on this layout...." That phrasing gets confusing when I later refer to being in Layout mode where you can move objects around and control how the page looks. When I say, "Go to the List View layout," I mean choose List View from the Layout drop-down list below the Book. You could be in either Layout mode or Browse mode, depending on the context of the discussion. If you get the subtle differences between these concepts straight now, you'll be way ahead of the game.

When you look at the fields in Layout mode, you can see the field names (assuming that View, Show, Sample Data is not turned on). Switch back to the Record Detail layout and make sure you're in Layout mode. If you look at the field next to IM, you'll see that the field name appears to be Instant_Messaging instead of IM. Double-click on that field to bring up the Field/Control Setup window and you'll be able to see the field name there, too. Not only that, but you can actually change what field is in that position in this window. Click Cancel to prevent accidentally changing the field.

Choose View, Show, Sample Data. Take a look at the fields now. When users see something that looks like real data when they're in Layout mode, it's easy to see how they might get confused and think they're in Browse mode. Choose View, Show, Sample Data to turn that option off before *you* get confused!

CAUTION Before we move on, you had better acquaint yourself with the Undo command, which is the first choice under the Edit menu. If you move, change, duplicate, or delete a layout object accidentally, you can change it back with the Undo command, as long as you don't do anything else after making the mistake. Command+Z (Macintosh) or Ctrl+Z (Windows) will accomplish the same thing and is the convention for most other computer programs. If you really mess up a layout and haven't returned to Browse mode, go to the Layouts menu and choose Revert Layout. (An alternative is to click the Revert button on the right side of the Layout bar.) All changes you've made will be discarded. Starting with FMP9, you get multiple levels of Undo and Redo when you're working in a text block. See the section titled "Multiple Level Undo/Redo of Text" in Chapter 5.

For an extra level of protection, you can make a change to FileMaker's Preferences. Windows users choose Edit, Preferences. Macintosh users click FileMaker Pro, Preferences. Now click the Layout tab. Uncheck the box next to "Save layout changes automatically (do not ask)." Now whenever you leave Layout mode you'll be asked if you want to save your changes. Although it can be a pain, the time will come when you thank the day you changed this setting. If you never goof, just go back into Preferences and check the box again. If you get tired of always being asked to save the changes, you have one other safety net. As long as you haven't left Layout mode, you can choose Layouts, Revert Layout or use the Revert button.

Make sure you're still in Layout mode, then click on the First Name field label to the left of the Name_First field. Notice that little squares appear on the corners of the label. These are the selection handles.

Selection handles refer to the small squares that appear at the corners or ends of layout objects. A line object only has two handles, while all other objects (even circles and ovals) have four. The color of the handles changes depending on the color of the background. If the color is solid, the object can be moved or reshaped. If the color is faded or speckled, the object is locked.

If you click and drag one of the handles on this or any other unlocked layout object, you can stretch or shrink the object. Since the handles are so small, positioning the tip of the selection arrow tool in just the right place may take a little getting used to. You can move an object simply by clicking on it and dragging. If the object is currently selected (the selection handles are showing), you can move it by clicking anywhere except the selection handles and dragging. Try to move one of the fields or the field labels now. Use Undo to put it back. Being able to make layouts look exactly the way you want is part of the power of FileMaker. I've seen some pretty amazing layouts from FileMaker users.

You can also copy and paste items, which is a valuable feature when adding a new field or heading to match the formatting of an object already on your layout. Just copy, paste, and change the text or field as needed. All the formatting is maintained.

CAUTION If a layout object is very large, its boundaries may extend off the screen and you may not see the handles. It is also possible to select and move multiple items when you don't intend to. And keep in mind that some objects may be grouped with others. Moving one grouped object will move the other objects in the same group.

Layout Types

You may want to create some layouts from scratch, but this can be a tedious process. Fortunately, FileMaker has a number of preset layout types from which you can choose. FileMaker provides a Layout Assistant that simplifies the process even more. Although we'll get into how to use the Assistant in Chapter 9, "Creating New Layouts with the Layout Assistant," I want to acquaint you with the various layout types.

Choose Layouts, New Layout/Report to see a list of the layout types (see Figure 2-9). If you click on the name of each layout type on the left, over on the right you'll be able to see a thumbnail sketch of what the layout looks like.

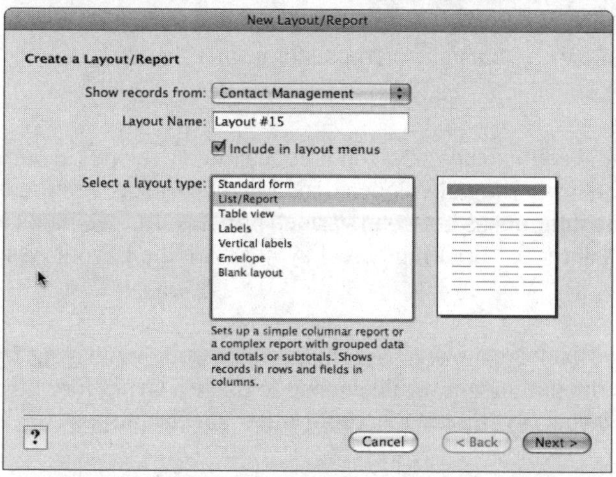

Figure 2-9
Choosing New Layout/Report under the Layouts menu brings up the first window of the Layout Assistant. The seven layout types are listed here.

Click Cancel to exit the Assistant.

Standard Form

In a Standard Form layout, items appear straight down the page — field label on the left and field on the right. It is not a particularly easy or attractive way to enter data, but it's not a bad starting point. Later I'll teach you how to take a Standard Form layout and make it look any way you choose.

List/Report

In this layout, field titles appear as column headings across the page. The data in a single record appears as a row, and all records appear in rows one after the other. A row can be as narrow as one field or as wide as the body in a layout.

You can look at any layout this way by choosing View, View as List. Go to the Form - Main Address layout and choose View as List. You may not be able to see the difference, but if you use the scroll bar on the right, you'll be able to scroll through the records. It's a little confusing, so switch back to View as Form. Then go to the List layout for a more conventional example.

Table View

Table View layout is very similar in appearance and behavior to a spreadsheet. You can turn any layout into a Table view by choosing View, View as Table.

Labels

FileMaker has well over 100 predefined labels, and you can also make your own custom size label layouts. Switch to the Avery 5160 layout to look at an example.

Vertical Labels[7]

Vertical labels were introduced in FileMaker 7. When you click to select them, the window says they're "adjusted to rotate Asian and Full-width characters so the labels can be used vertically." Once you make this choice, the windows that follow are the same as those for regular labels.

Envelope

Envelope layout is self-explanatory. You'll be making envelopes. There can be some issues with formatting envelopes depending on the orientation of the envelope and the differences between various printers. But we'll talk about that briefly in Chapter 9, "Creating New Layouts with the Layout Assistant."

Blank Layout

You would use a Blank layout as a basis for building your own layout from scratch. This is the option you would choose to make a layout for buttons like on the Reports layout, to store icons, or for other special purposes.

Find Mode

This is the mode you use to ask FileMaker to search for records that contain specific data you're interested in. When you choose View, Find mode, you are presented with a blank record of whatever layout you are viewing so you can make your request. The blank form looks similar to a new blank record. FileMaker 10 makes it a little easier than previous versions to know you're in Find mode because there is a magnifying glass in every searchable field except the one that holds the cursor. Pay attention to the Perform Find button in the Status toolbar. That's another strong clue that you're in Find mode. In fact, there are many differences between the Find and Browse mode Status toolbars. Switch back and forth between the modes to familiarize yourself with the differences. And finally, there is also a dashed border around data entry fields in Find mode that is slightly different from the dotted lines in Browse mode.

Preview Mode

Preview mode is a way to see what the page will look like when it's printed. Often your records will look the same in Preview mode as they do in Browse mode. However, variable data using special layout characters (like current date and page number), page margins, and column arrangements (like those used in mailing labels) will only appear on the printed page and in Preview mode. Conversely, some objects that appear in Browse mode can be made not to appear on a printout or in Preview mode. What you see in Preview mode will also depend on the settings in the Page Setup dialog. Previous to FileMaker 10, sub-summaries only appeared in Preview mode. Now they appear in Browse mode as well, which makes them much easier to work with.

Menu Commands

The fact that the menus change depending on what mode you're in certainly expands the possibilities of what you can do with FileMaker; it also makes it a lot more difficult to show you everything in this chapter. But there are a few more commands I'd like you to see now.

Sort Command

Choose Records, Sort Records. The Records menu only appears in Browse and Preview modes.

Notice the two columns in the Sort Records window. On the left is a list of fields on the current layout. You can click on the pop-up at the top of the column to see all the fields in this table or to get a list of relationships to other tables. Choosing one of the relationships gives you a list of the fields in that table, so you can sort by that data, too. Not only that, but at the bottom of the pop-up is Manage Database, which means you can add fields and make a new relationship right from here!

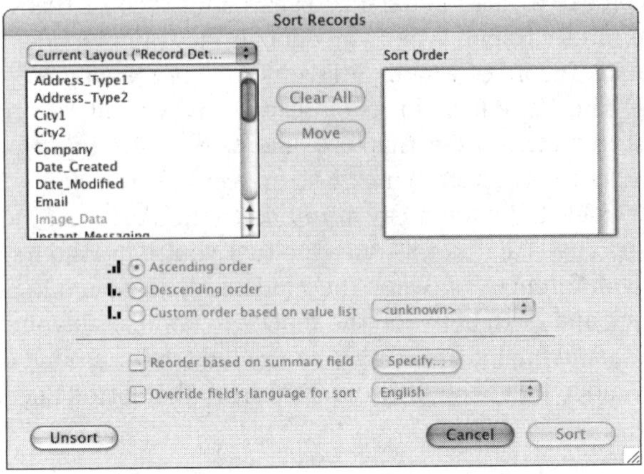

Figure 2-10
FileMaker's Sort Records window showing the field names in the left column. Double-click on an item in the left column to move it to the column on the right.

Double-clicking an item in the left column moves it to the Sort Order column on the right. Move a couple of the fields right now. To the left of the field names is a little double-pointed, vertical arrow. You can change the order of the fields by positioning the cursor over the arrow and using the old click-and-drag technique. Notice the radio buttons and other options at the bottom of this window. We'll spend more time on this in Chapter 8, "Finding and Sorting Your Data." Click the Cancel button to exit the window.

You also have the ability to access the Sort Records window by Control+clicking (Mac) or right-clicking (Windows) when in Browse mode. If you use these same keyboard/mouse shortcuts when clicking in a field, you'll see the context menu shown in Figure 2-11, which will allow you to sort by that specific field. This feature will save developers a lot of time, as they won't have to create sort buttons at the top of columns in various list views. You can turn off this feature for selected users in the Passwords area by selecting Minimum in the Edit Privilege Set window. We will talk more about passwords in Chapter 22, "Keeping Your Data Secure."

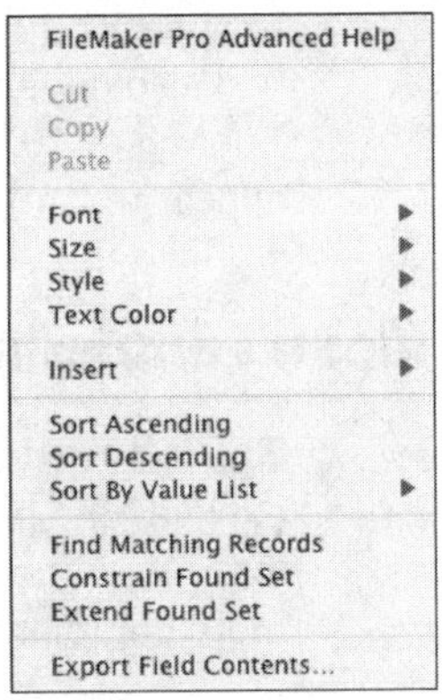

Figure 2-11
FileMaker's Sort context menu.

The Export Field Contents choice at the bottom of the context menu hides a lot of power. FileMaker 8 and later allow you to export the contents of any single field and send it as an attachment to an e-mail automatically.

Manage Scripts

This is my very favorite part of FileMaker. You can make your files jump backward through hoops of fire with scripts! Choose Scripts, Manage Scripts to open the Manage Scripts window. You'll see a list of scripts that were created in the template. You can change the order by dragging the double-pointed arrow. You can also make a script available under the Scripts menu by checking the box to the left of the script name or by highlighting the script name and checking the box labeled "Include in menu" above and to the right of the script name in the lower part of the window.

You can see the contents of a script by highlighting it and clicking the Edit button or by double-clicking on its name. Open the script called Go to Record Detail. (See Figure 2-12.)

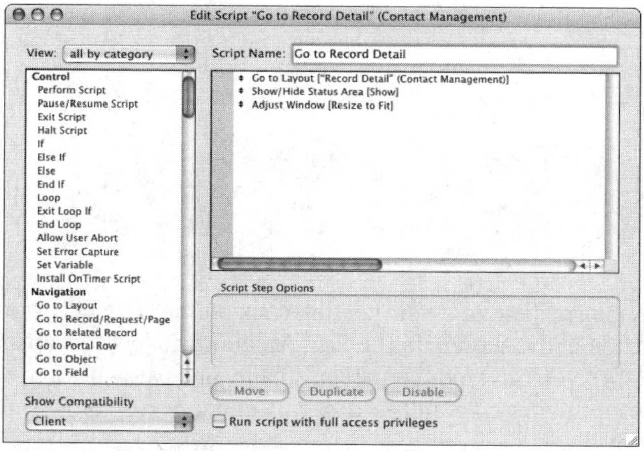

Figure 2-12
The Edit Script window for the Go to Record Detail script in the Contact Management template. Available script steps are in the left column and the actual script appears in the right column.

The right column shows the programmed steps for the script. This script is not too difficult and it even looks like English. Notice the list of available script steps in the left column. Use the scroll bar and take a look at what's available. Click the Close button on the title bar to leave here without changing anything.

Double-click the Swap Main and Second Addresses script. There's a lot going on there! Don't worry; it won't be that bad once I show you around. We'll spend more time with scripts in Chapter 3, "Creating Your First Database," Chapter 8, "Finding and Sorting Your Data," and Chapter 14, "Automating Your Database with Scripts." As far as I'm concerned, scripts are the most powerful tool in FileMaker and they're a blast to work with. But then, I could be biased. Click the Close buttons (choose Don't Save) to exit the script and the Manage Scripts window.

Accounts and Privileges

If nobody ever touches your computer, you're not on a network, and you don't use a broadband connection, you should never have a need to deal with FileMaker's accounts and privileges settings. But as more and more of us sign up for always-on, fast Internet services, security is becoming an issue. You may not know it, but when you're online, depending on your other settings, you may be sharing your computer with the world! This is just a brief introduction; we'll really get into this in depth in Chapter 22, "Keeping Your Data Secure."

Choose File, Manage, Accounts & Privileges. If you're working with the Contact Management file, you should see the window shown in Figure 2-13.

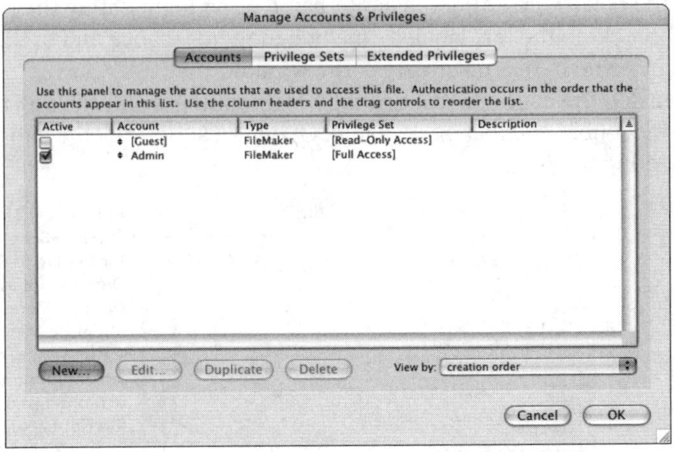

Figure 2-13
The Manage Accounts & Privileges window showing the privilege check boxes.

To add access information for a new person, click on the New button in the lower-left portion of the screen. In the Edit Account window that appears (see Figure 2-14), you can type the person's name and password and select one of the preset privileges — full access, data entry, or read only — that he or she will have.

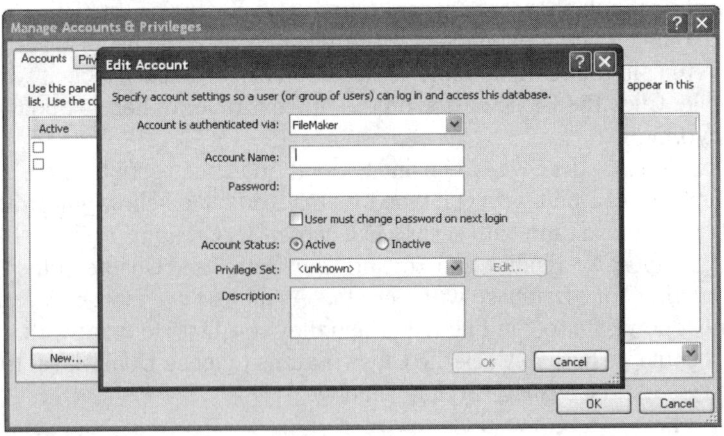

Figure 2-14
The Edit Account window opens when you click the New button on the Manage Accounts & Privileges window.

If instead you select New Privilege Set from the Privilege Set drop-down, you'll be taken to the Edit Privilege Set window. From this window, you can make a variety of decisions about what the user can do in the database. (If you select one of the preset privileges in the Edit Account window, you can click the Edit button to take you to the Edit Privilege Set window.) Feel free to investigate, but for now, delete any passwords you create. It might be disconcerting to lock yourself out of a file at this point. When you're finished, click the Cancel button, then the Discard button in the final window.

You may be asked for your name and password. If you have an account with full access, it will warn you if you haven't assigned a password. For now, just click Allow. If you've made any changes at all, you'll be asked for your account name and password. For now, if you haven't assigned a password for Admin, just enter Admin and click the OK button.

Summary

In this chapter I've continued your guided tour, giving you a chance to become familiar with various windows and menus as well as the four modes. We looked at the Manage Database window's Fields and Relationships tabs, learned how to get around layouts, and found out about the various layout types. I also showed you the Sort Records, Manage Scripts, and Manage Accounts & Privileges windows. In Chapter 3, you'll actually start using what I've been showing you by creating a database from scratch. Don't worry, I'll be with you the whole way.

Q & A

Q When we were in Layout mode, I noticed the Status toolbar had some new items. What are they?

> **A** That is the Tool panel. These are the tools that control what you put on your layouts and how you change the appearance of layout objects. (The Tool panel is covered in Chapter 3.)

Q What are the little icons at the lower-left corner of the window?

> **A** Those are the Zoom and Status toolbar controls. Click on them yourself and see if you can figure out what they do.

Workshop

In the Contact Management file, go to the Record Detail layout. Click the tabs for Related Contacts and Notes and notice the fields that display in those tabs. Go into Layout mode on each of the layouts and see what fields are there. Notice that the field names don't always match the labels that are near them.

Under Layouts, choose Duplicate layout. Below the Book, check to see that the new layout has the word "Copy" added to the end of it. Then, move various layout objects around to see how they're constructed. When you're done, choose Layouts, Delete Layout.

Chapter 3

Creating Your First Database

Introduction

Now that you have some idea of how to get around in FileMaker Pro, we can move to the next step: creating a database file from scratch. You'll find that it really isn't that difficult. And you'll learn some new tools and tricks along the way that will make creating a more complex system of interrelated tables a lot easier than you might imagine.

In this chapter, you'll learn about:

- Planning the database
- Creating and adding fields of various types
- Cleaning up your layouts with FileMaker's layout tools
- Creating scripts
- Attaching a script to a button

When you finish this chapter, you will have a fully functional, single-table database. You'll also have a pretty good idea about how to build a simple database of your own.

Planning the Database

There can be a lot of things to consider when planning a database. It all depends on what you intend to do with it, how many tables might be involved, how they'll interact, and who will be using it. Our planning in this chapter will be basic. We'll get into planning for a more complex system in Chapter 6, "Working with Related Tables — Part 1."

One of the great things about FileMaker Pro is that you can make changes to the structure of your files fairly easily. One of the worst things about FileMaker Pro is that the ease of change also makes it easy for users to skip the planning stage. If you learn to plan ahead now, you'll be ready when you work with more complex systems later on.

You can use the following questions as a checklist to work with every time you start a new database project. Although a more in-depth discussion will follow in Chapter 6, this list is the real deal.

1. What problem are you trying to solve?
2. If there is a current system (maybe even a paper system), what does it do well, and what could it do better?
   a. What things would you add to improve on the way the work has been done?
   b. If other people are involved, be sure to talk with them about the details of their job and why they do it the way they do. Also, ask them what they'd like to add.
3. What fields will you need to hold the necessary information?
4. Can the fields that are needed be divided into smaller sets? That will help determine what different tables you may need.
5. What will the relationships be between the tables? Are there other tables or files already in use from which you can draw information rather than creating new tables and files from scratch?
6. What do you want your screens (layouts) to look like? How many will you need and for what jobs?
7. If you will be sharing your data with other users:
   a. How will you need to adjust your layout for the way they'll be accessing it?
   b. How will you protect the data with FileMaker Pro security?

As you answer these questions, draw out a map of the files, tables, fields, and layouts and the connections between them. As a first-timer, much of this will probably be quite confusing. But as you gain more experience, it will all become more clear to you. So just stay with me a while longer.

Planning This Database

Since I'm going to lead you through the creation of this first database, we need it to be as simple as possible. For that reason, let's duplicate the functions of the old trusty Rolodex in the much easier-to-use form of a table in a FileMaker Pro file. We'll assume that no one else will be using the file. If we ask the seven planning questions listed above, we would answer them like this:

1. What problem are you trying to solve?

   A: I can't remember people's last names, so I can't find their cards when I need them.
2. If there is a current system (maybe even a paper system), what does it do well, and what could it do better?

   A: See answer to question #1.
   a. What things would you add to improve on the way the work has been done?

      A: I want to be able to make more notes about the person than I can get on a card. I might even want to type notes when I talk to people on the phone. And my handwriting is terrible! Typing will be a big improvement.

  b. If other people are involved, be sure to talk with them about the details of their job and why they do it the way they do. Also, ask them what they'd like to add.
     A: Not applicable.

3. What fields will you need to hold the necessary information?
   A: Name, address, four phone numbers, e-mail, web site, and notes.
4. Can the fields that are needed be divided into smaller sets? That will help determine what different tables you may need.
   A: It's really all one set.
5. What will the relationships be between the tables? Are there other tables or files already in use from which you can draw information rather than creating new tables and files from scratch?
   A: Not applicable. It's all on paper and will need to be entered by hand.
6. What do you want your screens (layouts) to look like? How many will you need and for what jobs?
   A: Just one screen. But, wait. I might want to send letters. That means envelopes and labels. And since my computer isn't always on, maybe I should print out a list (in alphabetical order) to keep by the phone. Well, maybe I should keep it simple for now. One screen.
7. If you will be sharing your data with other users:
   a. How will you need to adjust your layout for the way they'll be accessing it?
      A: Not applicable.
   b. How will you protect the data with FileMaker Pro security?
      A: Not applicable.

I made a drawing of what the screen might look like. The screen space might be used a little more efficiently, but everything seems to be there. I think we're ready to give it a try.

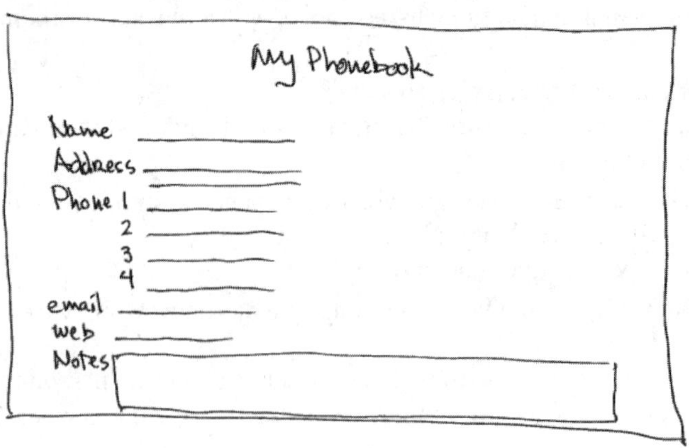

Figure 3-1
Hand drawing of what a phonebook file main layout might look like.

NOTE I want you to understand that I've made some choices in this design that will make data retrieval harder later on. We'll use FileMaker's easy change capabilities later in this chapter to fix them. It's almost as important that you learn how to rework things as it is how to create them in the first place.

Creating the File

1. Open FileMaker Pro. When the Quick Start window appears, select the **Create Database** icon on the left, click the **Create an empty database** radio button, then click **OK.** If the New Database window does not appear, choose File, New Database.
2. The next window will prompt you for a file name and a place to save the file. Call the file **My_Phonebook** and save it in the **My Documents** folder or whatever other place you may decide to use to keep yourself organized.

BEST PRACTICES Notice that I used the underscore character in the file name. Using FileMaker Pro's Instant Web Publishing allows users to share files on intranets or the Internet. FileMaker also allows sharing by way of ODBC and JDBC. Browser and SQL languages don't take kindly to spaces. For the same reason, we will use similar methods for creating field names. Another option is to run words together using a capital letter at the beginning of each word, which is known as "camel case." An example of camel case would be ContactSerNum.

If you are absolutely positive you'll never use your files for these purposes, you don't need to worry about spaces. But once you start using FileMaker, you might be surprised what you'll end up doing with files you create! If you start using underscores or skipping the spaces altogether, you'll be way ahead of the game.

Adding Some Fields

1. When the Manage Database window appears, choose the **Fields** tab if necessary and notice that the cursor is already blinking in the Field Name box and that Text appears in the Type drop-down list.
2. Type **Name** and click the **Create** button. Name is still highlighted in the Field Name box.
3. Now type **Address** and click the **Change** button. Drat! The Name field just became Address. It's better if you make this mistake now rather than later.

TIP If a field name is highlighted in that lower part of the window, it can be overwritten. You don't need to do anything special except make sure you don't click the Change button unless you mean to change the name of the field.

4. Highlight the word "Address" in the Field Name box, type **Name**, and click the **Create** button. It's okay, really. You do want to change it back this time.
5. Now type **Address** and click **Create**.

6. Now type **Phone1** (with no space) and click the Type drop-down list. Select **Number** and press the **Enter** or **Return** key this time instead of the Create button.
7. Type **Phone2** and press **Enter** or **Return**. FileMaker leaves the field type the same until you change it.
8. Go ahead and create the **Phone3** and **Phone4** fields.
9. Switch back to the **Text** field type and create the **Email**, **Web**, and **Notes** fields.

⌘ **TIP** If you should accidentally click the OK button too early, you'll have to choose File, Manage Database and go back to the Fields tab to finish creating your fields. When you're done, if the fields aren't on the layout, you'll have to use the Field tool to drag them there.

10. There are a couple more useful fields we haven't considered: a **CreationDate** field and a **SerialNumber** field. Add them now using **Date** and **Number**, respectively, from the Type drop-down. (Remember, we're not using spaces in field names so that the file will be compliant with other database systems and the web.)
11. Just for the sake of introducing it, add a **CreationTime** field and choose **Time** from the Type drop-down.

Adding Field Options

1. Click on the **CreationDate** field to highlight it, and then click the **Options** button.
2. Make sure the **Auto-Enter** tab is active and click the check box next to **Creation**. Also check that Date appears in the drop-down list next to Creation. That means that whenever you make a new record in this file, FileMaker will put the date in that field for you.
3. Click the **OK** button.
4. Click on the **CreationTime** field and do the same thing to it, except notice that Time already appears in the drop-down next to Creation. You can use that to keep track of changes made to individual records. Notice that there are other choices in the drop-down, even though you can't choose them.
5. Click **OK**.

   (Just under the Creation check box is the Modification check box. If you were to create a field to keep track of when the record was last modified, you would check this box. Take a moment to look at the drop-down list beside Modification. You might find this field useful when you need to backtrack to find out when information was last entered.)

   Another way to look at a field's options is to double-click the field name in the list. Try it. The Options for Field window will open.

6. Select the **SerialNumber** field and click **Options**. Notice that you can use any of the choices from the drop-downs next to Creation and Modification this time, because a number field does not have the specific limits that date and time fields have. But don't make any of those choices. Instead, click the check box next to **Serial Number**. FileMaker tells you that it will start by numbering the first record with a 1 and the serial number will increase by one for each new record. You can actually begin with any number you choose.
7. Click **OK**.
8. When you're done, the window should look something like Figure 3-2. Click **OK** to exit the Manage Database window.

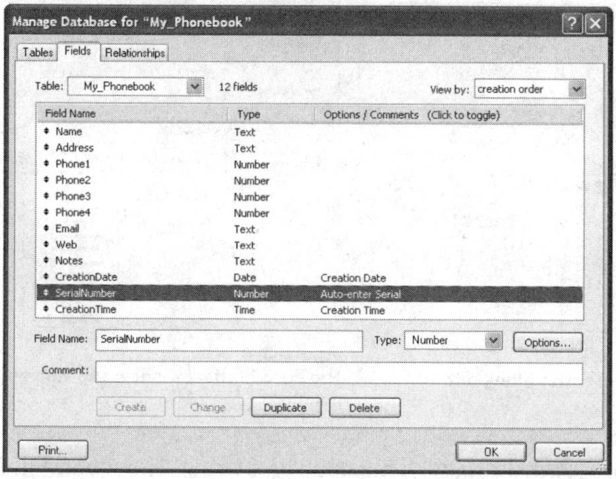

Figure 3-2
The Manage Database window should look like this after you create the basic fields.

After the Manage Database window closes, you will be returned to Browse mode and you'll see the results of your work. It doesn't look much like those colorful layouts in the template. That's one reason FileMaker, Inc. gives you the templates. It also gives you something to shoot for in your own designs. The Layout Assistant can help, too. For now, let's clean up our layout and see what we can make of it.

Cleaning Up the Layout

I like to see borders around fields on my layouts. To place borders around fields, follow these steps:

1. Choose **View, Layout mode.**
2. Click on the **Name** field (look for the selection handles) and choose **Format, Field/Control**[8], **Borders**.
3. When the Field Borders window appears, click the four borders: **Top, Bottom, Left**, and **Right**.
4. In the Format drop-down, make sure **Borders** is selected.

5. To the right of the word "format" are (from left to right) the color, pattern, and line width palettes. Click on the color palette and choose the black square.
6. Click on the pattern palette and choose the solid pattern (top icon of the second column from the left, which shows a solid black square overlapping a transparent square). Choose the **1 pt** line width from the third palette. You can see two of the palettes in Figures 3-3 and 3-4. Look in the Sample area at the right side of the window to see what the borders will look like. While you're at it, notice that the border tools are very similar to the Line and Fill tools in the Status toolbar. Click **OK**. Then choose **View, Browse mode.**

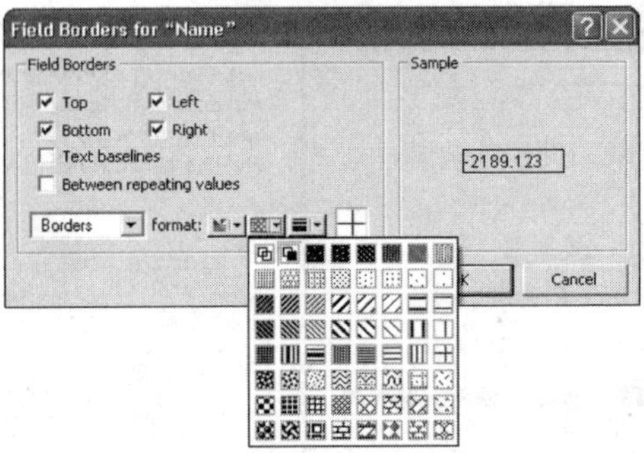

Figure 3-3
The Field Borders window showing the pattern palette.

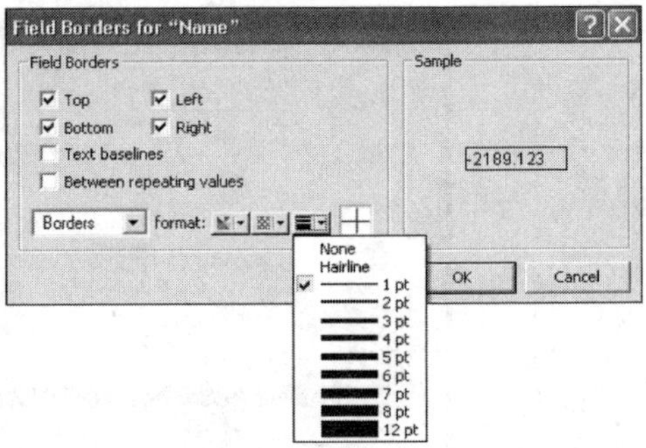

Figure 3-4
The Field Borders window showing the line width palette.

One field down, 11 to go. This could get tiring. However, FileMaker provides you with a few shortcuts that will apply to this and many other layout chores.

7. Choose **View, Layout mode**. You can hold down the Shift key and click on each of the fields one after the other. But there's another, still faster way.
8. Click with your selection pointer outside of the group of fields, and drag diagonally until you have a dotted rectangle that surrounds all of the

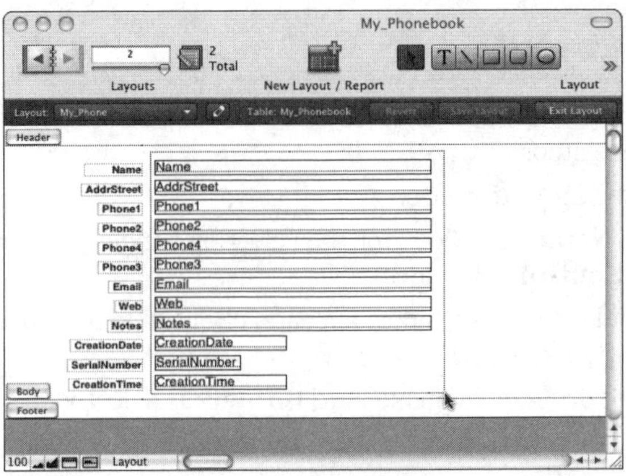

Figure 3-5
Using the Selection tool in Layout mode to surround a group of fields in order to format all of them at one time.

fields but not the field labels. See Figure 3-5. Now choose **Format**, **Field/Control**[8], **Borders** and give all 12 fields the same borders at one time. To see the results, click **OK**, then return to Browse mode.

Format Painter

For an even faster method, try the Format Painter. With it you can copy the formatting of any FileMaker layout object and "paint" the format attributes onto any other layout object. It's a simple three-step process:

1. Go to Layout mode and click on an object that has the formatting you want to copy.
2. Go to the Status toolbar and click the **Format Painter** icon. It looks like a paintbrush and is the rightmost tool in the Tool panel, as shown in Figure 3-7a. You can also access it by choosing Format, Format Painter.
3. Click on the object you want to change. You can also click and drag to form a selection rectangle around one or more objects you want to change.

As soon as you finish your selection, the tool is turned off. If you want to change a number of objects that are spread apart, you can lock the Format Painter by double-clicking the icon in the toolbar. Once you're done, you need to unlock it. Just select one of the other buttons in the Tool panel.

The Format Painter will not work on graphic objects you may have brought in from other applications. But it will work to change buttons, lines, and shaped object attributes, in addition to fields and text. You can even move the background color from a layout part (header, body, footer, etc.) to a layout object, but not vice versa. You can also make it work across files. The only requirement is that both files be in Layout mode when you start. One of the files can even be hidden (minimized).

That all sounds great, but the Format Painter won't pass on such attributes as value lists or number or date formats.

I would also advise exercising some caution against having more than one item selected when first clicking the Format Painter tool. You don't know which attributes from which of the objects the tool will memorize.

Duplicate

Another nice tool is the Duplicate command. Click on any layout object (or group of objects) to select it, then choose Edit, Duplicate to place an exact copy of your selection six pixels down and to the right of the original. This is very valuable when you want to copy a field that is formatted with numerous settings. If your selection was a single field, FileMaker presents you with the Specify Field window so you can even choose a different field if you like, which is usually exactly what you want to do.

Knowing that the new object's position is only off by six pixels means you can reposition it with six quick clicks on one of the arrow keys (see the upcoming "Arrow Keys" section). That puts it exactly vertical or horizontal of the original object, which is often just what you need.

A *layout object* is anything on a layout. That includes pretty much anything — fields, text, portals, lines, rectangles, ellipses, buttons, or images pasted into the layout.

SHORTCUT Using context menus, you can make a number of menu choices without having your mouse make the trip to the menu at the top of the screen. On the Macintosh, hold down the Control key while clicking on a layout object to access the menu. On the Windows platform, right-click on the layout object. See Figure 3-6. What's on the menu depends on the context of the mode and the type of item on which you click.

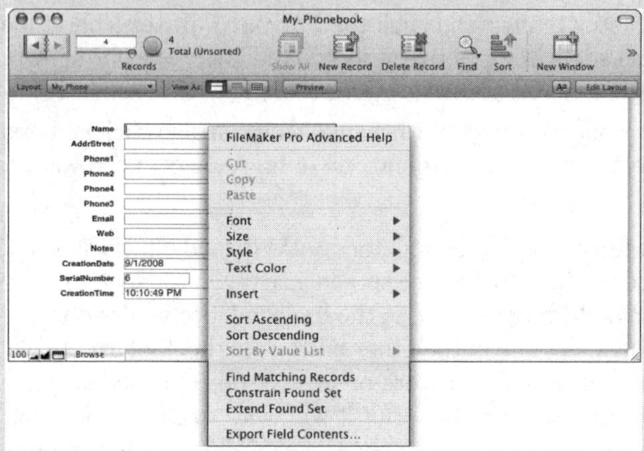

Figure 3-6
The context menu. Use this as a substitute for some menu choices at the top of the screen.

Now go back into Layout mode so I can show you some of the other layout tools.

Tool Panel

The Tool panel is the group of icons that appear in the Status toolbar when you're in Layout mode. See Figures 3-7a through 3-7e for a word or two about all the layout tools.

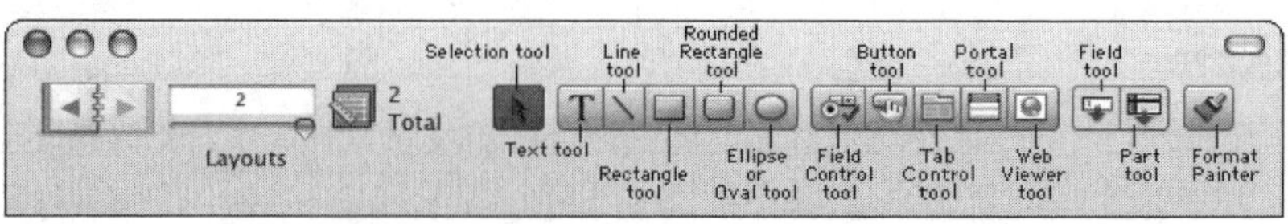

Figure 3-7a
The Tool panel section of the Status toolbar is on the right, as seen in Layout mode.

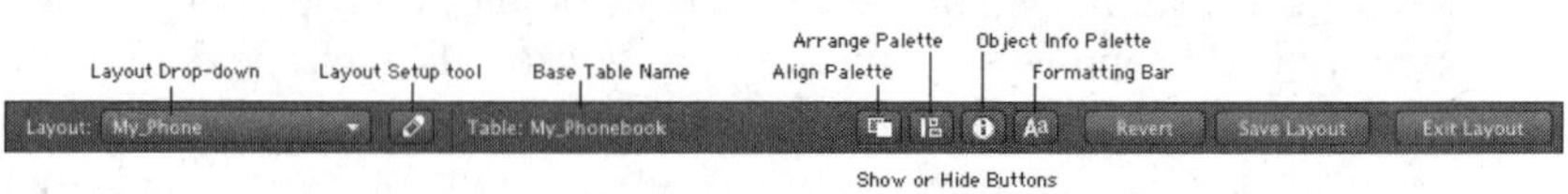

Figure 3-7b
The Layout bar in Layout mode

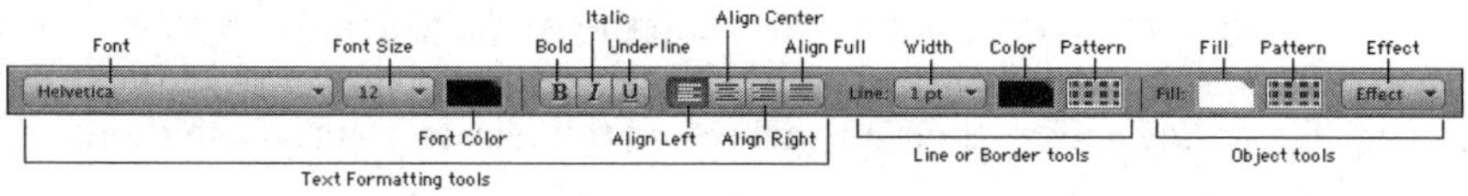

Figure 3-7c
Formatting bar

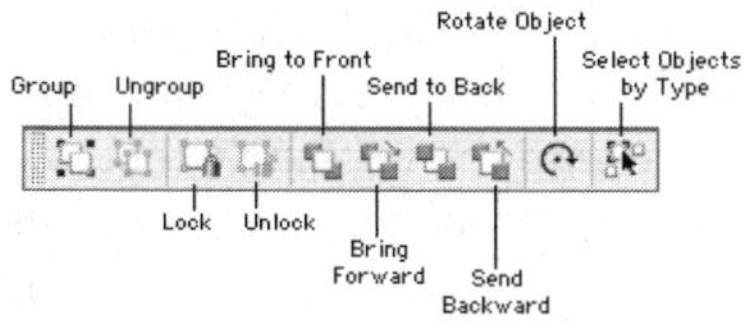

Figure 3-7d
Arrange palette

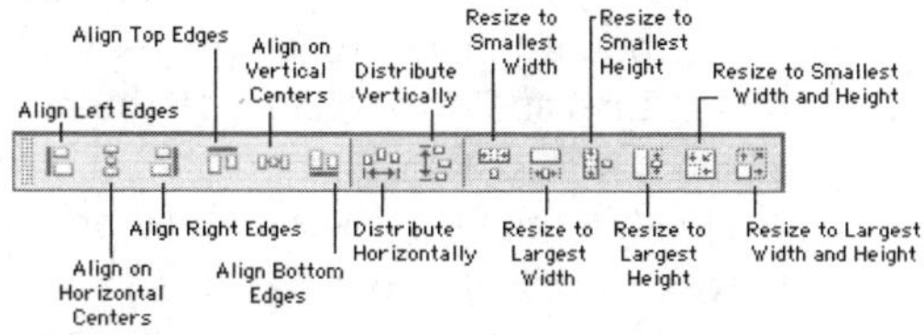

Figure 3-7e
Align palette

Layout Status Toolbar and Palettes

By going to the View menu, you can decide which toolbars and palettes appear onscreen in Layout mode. You can also turn most of them on and off using the buttons in the middle of the Layout bar as shown in Figure 3-7b. In Layout mode the three palettes are Arrange, Align, and Object Info. Switch to the other modes and look at the Layout bar to see how it changes. You'll notice that it's mostly the same on the left, but on the right it changes to provide buttons specific to the mode. The other toolbars are the Status toolbar and the Formatting bar. If you hide the Status toolbar, it stays hidden no matter what mode you're in. The Formatting bar can be on or off separately in Browse, Layout, and Preview modes.

> ⌘ **TIP** The Allow Toolbars script step lets you hide the Formatting bar and disable the View, Formatting Bar menu item. The Show/Hide Status Area script step toggles the Status toolbar. If hidden via a script, it also disables the Status toolbar menu. If you're working with an existing file and you can't get to the Formatting bar and/or Status toolbar, it may be because one or both have been turned off by a script. For more on scripts, see Chapter 14, "Automating Your Database with Scripts."

You can "tear off" the Align and Arrange palettes individually to position them anywhere on the screen that you like. If you move a palette near the side of the screen, it will reposition itself vertically. Once a palette is no longer docked near one of the edges of the screen, you can even resize it by pulling on the lower-right corner of its window. The Object Info palette operates differently. More about that shortly.

FileMaker remembers where you leave the three palettes so they're always in your favorite place onscreen. If you ever use more than one monitor and spread the palettes across both of them and then switch back to a single monitor after restarting the computer, the palettes will reposition themselves so they'll be onscreen.

One other small detail regarding the Arrange and Align palettes is that the buttons remain grayed out until the proper object or objects are selected. Then they appear their normal colors to indicate you can use them.

Drawing Tools

Four of the layout tools are called drawing tools. They are the Line tool, Rectangle tool, Rounded Rectangle tool, and Ellipse or Oval tool. Click on each one in turn and draw shapes in the blank area on your layout. You can constrain how the objects are drawn (i.e., a square with the Rectangle tool or a circle with the Oval tool) by holding down Option (Macintosh) or Ctrl (Windows) while you draw.

With one or more of these objects selected on your layout, experiment with various items from the Object and Line or Border tools to see what effect they have. Switch to Browse mode to see what it really looks like. Return to Layout mode and delete what you've added while leaving the fields and field labels alone.

> ⌘ **TIP** When you finish drawing an object, the Tool panel switches back to the Selection tool (the arrow). To lock a tool on, double-click it. When the tool is locked, the icon looks subtly darker on the toolbar.

Whether a tool is locked or not, to switch between that tool and the Selection tool, press Enter (Macintosh) or Ctrl+Enter (Windows).

Object Grids

The Object Grids option is used to assist with consistent placement of layout objects. When you move objects on a layout with the Object Grids option turned on, they move in a jerky motion as they align to an invisible grid in six-pixel increments relative to where the object was when you started moving it. When you first create a file, the Object Grids option is turned on. You can turn the option on and off by choosing Arrange, Object Grids.

The word *pixel* is short for picture element. It's the smallest picture-forming unit on a computer screen. It's the size of the period at the end of a sentence or the dot on the lowercase letter "i."

> **NOTE** Both Mac OS X and Windows tout sub-pixel rendering, especially in antialiased text. Most of FileMaker deals with pixel-based rendering, except for antialiasing and hairline line widths. Hairline width lines on my screen look gray, but when you zoom to 400% magnification or print the layout, the line appears solid black but very thin.

> **SHORTCUT** You can turn the Object Grids option on and off by pressing Command+Y (Macintosh) or Ctrl+Y (Windows). You can temporarily override the effect of the grid by dragging objects while holding down Command (Macintosh) or Alt (Windows).

T-Squares

Another very handy layout tool is the T-Squares tool found under the View menu. When it's turned on, a pair of intersecting lines appears on the layout, one horizontal and one vertical. This option is meant to imitate a tool used by drafters and architects for drawing perpendicular lines. The lines of the T-Squares have a magnetic quality to them in that objects brought within six pixels of either line are pulled to it. Each line of the T-Squares can be moved independently. This tool can help greatly with positioning, resizing, and aligning layout objects.

Arrow Keys

When you don't want to haul out the T-Squares and the object grids aren't giving you the results you want, you can get pixel-level control of layout object placement with the four arrow keys available on most keyboards. One press on an up, down, left, or right arrow key moves any selected object one pixel. Once I discovered the arrow keys shortcut, I find I use it more than any other object positioning option.

Object Info Palette

Choose View, Object Info to bring up the Info palette. (In earlier versions of FileMaker, the Object Info palette was known as the Object Size palette. I will refer to it as both the Info palette and the Object Info palette.) Depending on your screen resolution, the Info palette is only about an inch and a half wide and four tall, and it's free floating, so it's easy to miss. You may have to look around your screen to find it, but you're looking for what you see in Figure 3-8. Click on any layout object. The first set of four boxes in the Info palette tell you where the object is on the layout:

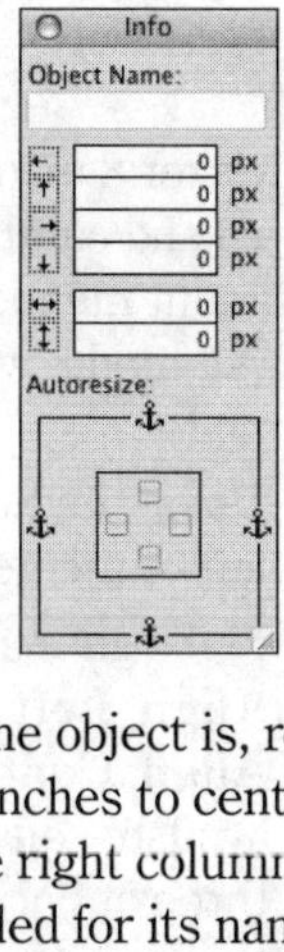

Figure 3-8 The Object Info palette

- How far the left edge of the object is from the left border of the page. (This includes any fixed margins or the default paper size of the current printer.)
- How far the top edge of the object is from the top of the layout (including margins).
- How far the right edge of the object is from the left of the layout (including margins).
- How far the bottom edge of the object is from the top of the layout (including margins).

The last two boxes show you how wide and how tall the object is, respectively. You can change the unit of measurement from inches to centimeters to pixels by clicking on the two-letter abbreviation in the right column.

The new feature in the Object Info palette that called for its name change in FMP8.5 is the Object Name box at the top. You can now name any object on a layout. The power of the Object Name is unleashed when you use scripts to go to specific objects and perform actions on them. When we look at the tab controls in Chapter 17 and the Web Viewer in Chapter 25, you'll see how using Object Name can help you work with layout items.

The Autoresize[9] feature at the bottom lets you specify how layout objects will stretch when you resize the window. We'll look at it in detail in Chapter 17.

Here's how you can use the Info palette to resize fields (not to be confused with Autoresize):

1. Click on the **SerialNumber** field and copy the number in the width box of the Info palette (highlight the number in the box second from the bottom, then choose **Edit**, **Copy**).
2. Now click on the **CreationTime** field and notice the Info palette numbers reflect its size and position. Paste the SerialNumber field's width in the width box. (Highlight the number in the width box again, and choose **Edit**, **Paste** (Mac) or **Paste Formatted Text** (Windows), or just use the keyboard shortcut, which is faster.)
3. Now click in any of the other size boxes, or press **Enter**, **Return**, or **Tab** instead.

Actually, you don't need to perform the copy-paste routine. You can simply type over any number in any box. It might seem a little tedious, but there are things you can accomplish with the Info palette that just can't be done any other way.

Another way to resize objects is with the selection handles. I discussed using them back in Chapter 2, but it's worth mentioning again here.

First, select a layout object, then click and drag one of the little black squares at the corner of the object to resize it. You can choose Edit, Undo Resize to change it back if necessary.

Alignment[8]

FileMaker 8 made some changes in how you align layout objects. Goodbye to the old and cumbersome Set Alignment window. Hello to some very nice alignment menus, tools, and shortcuts. Before you start this exercise, go to Browse mode, which will save the layout the way it is. Now go back to Layout mode.

1. Using the Selection tool, drag a rectangle around all the field labels to the left of the fields like we did for the fields themselves in Figure 3-5.
2. Make sure all of their selection handles are showing and select **Arrange**, **Align**, **Left Edges**. Makes sense, doesn't it? Now choose **Arrange**, **Align**, **Centers**. Figure 3-9 shows a composite of all three pop-up menus available on the Arrange menu (even though you would never see all three at once). Remember that you can perform the same functions as the menu items using icons in the Align palette.

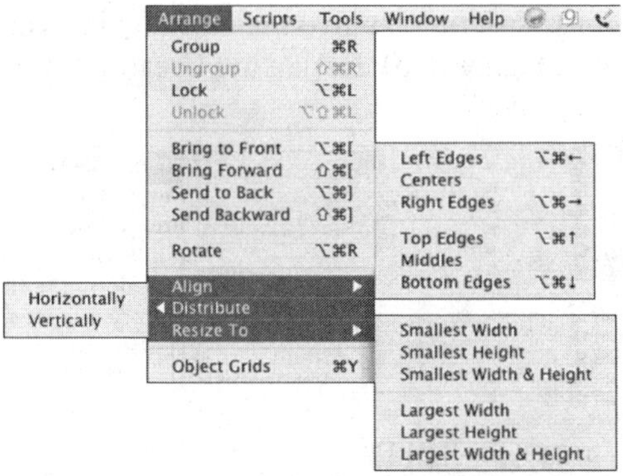

Figure 3-9 The Arrange menu allows you to select alignment options.

Try some of the other combinations. My favorites are the Distribute and Resize To items. Resize To is best used with fields that you want to make the same size. Go ahead and experiment with these options on the fields to see what I mean.

3. Go to the **View** menu, and notice that there is a check mark in front of Arrange Palette. The icons on the right of the Align palette in Figure 3-7e perform some of the same actions. Go ahead and give them a try.
4. When you're done, choose **Layouts**, **Revert Layout**.

These tools can be very helpful when you've been moving a lot of layout objects around and need to clean up quickly. The alignment functionality only works on the selected set of objects and how they align with each other. It has nothing to do with where they will end up on the page.

NOTE When you choose Align Top Edges, Bottom Edges, Left Edges, or Right Edges, the objects will always align with the farthest item in the direction named. For example, if you choose Align Left Edges, the objects will align with the leftmost object. The Centers choice uses a line vertically or horizontally equidistant from the outside edges of the farthest objects. (Whew! That's a mouthful.) Distribute takes the farthest objects and evenly divides the space between them among all objects in the selection.

Locking Objects

You may want to lock various layout objects to keep them in place while you're working with other objects or to prevent other people from changing your layouts. In addition to preventing movement, locking prevents changes to an object's attributes (borders, fill, text style).

You can lock a selected object by choosing Arrange, Lock, or by pressing Ctrl+Alt+L. You can unlock an object by choosing Arrange, Unlock or by pressing Ctrl+Alt+Shift+L. This only locks the object in Layout mode and has no effect over data entry in Browse mode. Also, locking does not require passwords.

Using the tools I've just described, move the layout objects around until they look like the layout in Figure 3-10. Resize the CreationDate field with the arrow keys or the Size palette.

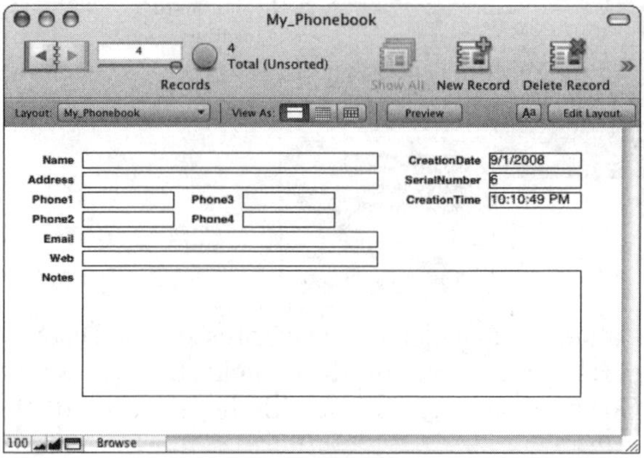

Figure 3-10
My_Phonebook in Browse mode after the layout has been redesigned to take better advantage of screen space.

We'll be looking at efficient layouts in Chapter 17, "Designing Your Screen Layouts." But examine this redesigned layout and start thinking about why this makes better use of the screen space.

Adding Some Data

Go back into Browse mode. Create a new record (Records, New Record) and enter the following information:

Name	*Address*	*Phone1*
Rich Bailey	123 Main St., Wilson, OH	333-4444
Bobby Joe Gentry	1919 Choctaw Ridge, Tallahassee, FL	333-1332
Richard Harris	500 MacArthur Park, Los Angeles, CA	121-9765

We'll do some experiments with this data in just a few minutes.

Adding a Script

In the last chapter, we looked at some scripts in the Contact Management template. You're going to create a couple of fairly easy scripts right now.

Simple New Record Script

To create a script that will make a new record, follow these steps:

1. Choose **Scripts**, **Manage Scripts.**
2. When the Manage Scripts window appears, click on the **New** button.
3. In the Edit Script window, New Script will be highlighted in the Script Name box (see Figure 3-11). Type **New Record.**

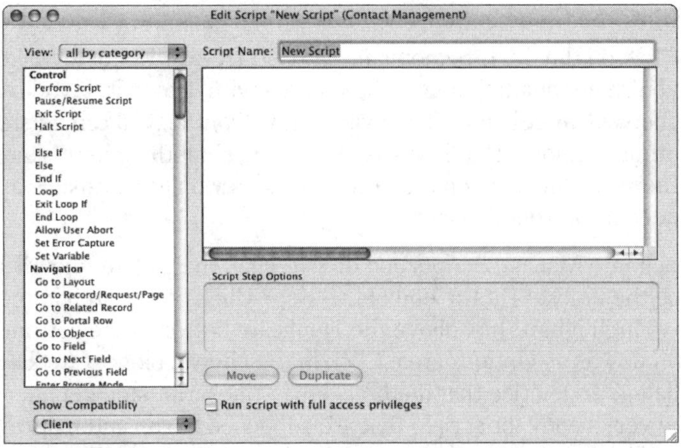

Figure 3-11
The Edit Script window.

4. Scroll down the left column until you see the Records heading and double-click **New Record/Request** (or highlight it and click the Move button).

> **TIP** If you know the heading for the script step you want, choose it in the View pop-up at the top of the script steps column. Then you don't have to scroll up and down the list.
>
> I've gotten to know where most script steps are by heart, so I can just click the right number of times on the gray bar just above the bottom arrow. That moves down the list one full screen at a time.

5. Click the **Close** button to close the Edit Script window, click **Save**, then click the **Close** button on the Manage Scripts window.
6. Click the **Scripts** menu and choose the **New Record** script. Voilà! A new blank record.

Notice that you can also access that script by pressing Command+1 (Macintosh) or Ctrl+1 (Windows). Of course, you can also create a new record by choosing Records, New Records, with the key combination or with the New Record button in the Status toolbar, so at this point, we're not doing anything really amazing. But there are other reasons you might want to do this with a script. For example, there may be times when you'll want to hide the toolbar. Regardless, just wait until you see what else you can do!

Simple Delete Record Script

To create a delete record script, follow these steps:

1. Choose **Scripts, Manage Scripts.** Click on **New.**
2. When the Edit Script window appears, type **Delete Record.**
3. Scroll down the left column until you see the Records heading. Double-click **Delete Record/Request.**

4. Click the **Close** button, click **Save**, then click the **Close** button again.
5. Click on the **Scripts** menu and choose **Delete Record**. Make sure you're not deleting one of the records with data in it. If you're not sure, choose **Cancel** and take a look first. Of course, you can delete a record by other methods. But, hey, we're learning something here. And again, there are times when the other methods won't be available and you'll need a controlled delete.

Go back into Manage Scripts and double-click the Delete Record script. Notice the brackets at the end of the step? Click on the step in the box on the right to highlight it. Just above the Duplicate button in the bottom center of the window is an Options area. Click in the check box next to "Perform without dialog" and notice that the brackets in the script step get filled in. That can be very handy for scripts that are supposed to run automatically for other purposes, but it can be dangerous if you're working with live data. Uncheck the box now, click the Close button, click Save, then Close again. That way, whenever the button is clicked, any user will have the option to cancel before records disappear from the file.

Simple Find Script

To create a Find script, first locate the record for which you want to create the script. Enter Find mode, type Richard in the Name field, and click the Find button in the Status toolbar (or press Enter or Return). Richard's record appears. Notice the new information in the Status toolbar — how many records were found and the pie chart. Do another find for Rich. Now you get two records.

Go to the Records menu and scroll down to Saved Finds[10]. You'll notice that FileMaker remembered what you were looking for under the Recent Finds heading. Since it doesn't remember everything forever, we need a way to save a find permanently. We'll look more at Saved Finds in Chapter 8, "Finding and Sorting Your Data."

We create the script as follows:

1. Choose **Scripts**, **Manage Scripts**. In the Manage Scripts window, select **New**.
2. When the Edit Script window appears, type **Find Rich**.
3. Under Navigation, double-click **Enter Browse Mode** and **Go to Layout**.
4. Under Found Sets, double-click **Perform Find**. Click the **Specify** button (above the OK button in the Script Step Options area) to open the Specify Find Requests window. Just click **OK** to verify the find criteria — My_Phonebook::NameFirst: [Rich] — as seen in Figure 3-12.

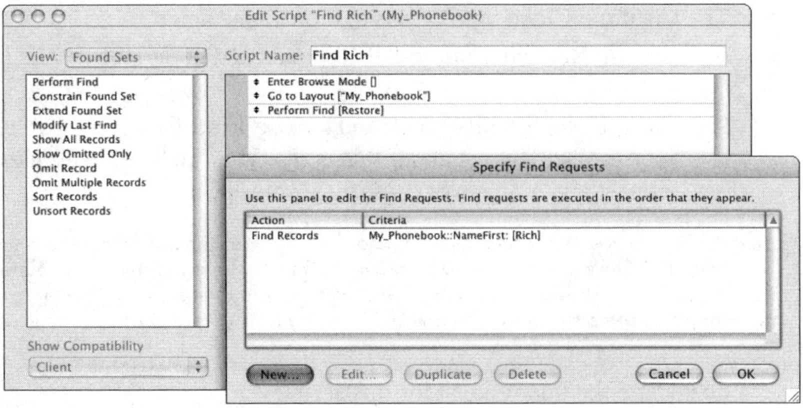

Figure 3-12
The Specify Find Requests window showing the details of the Perform Find script step.

5. When you return to the script you should see that the word Restore has appeared in the brackets after Perform Find and there is a check mark next to Specify find requests. FileMaker remembers any find you perform manually prior to adding the Perform Find script step, even if you don't click the Specify button. Of course, it won't perform that specific find unless the box is checked. But any time you click the Specify button later on, you can see what criteria were found manually and you can change them if you want to so you can include them in your script.
6. In the right column, click once on **Go to Layout**. Above the OK button next to the word Specify is a pop-up list of all the layouts in our file, as well as some other options for selecting layouts. (Currently there is only one layout.) Click on whatever appears there (probably "original layout") and choose **My_Phonebook.** When you're done, your window should look like the one in Figure 3-13.

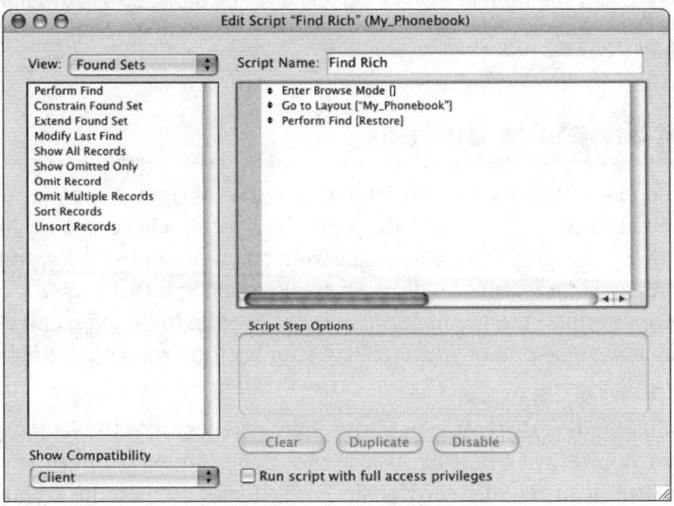

Figure 3-13
The Edit Script window showing the script Find Rich.

7. Click the **Close** button, **Save**, then **Close** again.
8. Choose **Records**, **Show All Records** and notice the details in the Status toolbar.
9. Click on the **Scripts** menu and choose **Find Rich**. The two records appear. What's great about this is that you can build a complex find request and Manage Scripts can memorize it.

NOTE If you ever accidentally delete one or more steps when editing a script, click the Close button, click Don't Save, and immediately click the Edit button again. The previous set of steps will be restored, but any changes you may have made to the script since you opened it will be lost.

To change the find request for this script:

1. Go into Manage Scripts and double-click the **Find Rich** script.
2. In the upper-right box, double-click the **Perform Find [Restore]** step to bring up the Specify Find Requests window.
3. Click the single request to highlight it and click the **Edit** button.
4. Highlight the single find request in the upper part of the window.
5. In the Criteria area, change Rich to **Richard**, click the **Change** button, and click **OK**.
6. Rename the script **Find Richard**. Click the **Close** button, **Save**, then **Close** again to return to Browse mode.
7. Choose **Records**, **Show All Records**, and run the script. Now we're talkin'! Of course you could have separate scripts for Find Rich and Find Richard, not to mention Show All Records.

NOTE For users of versions of FileMaker Pro prior to version 7, the Keep/Replace dialog does not appear anymore. Instead, you'll be working with details in the specific script steps. However, you can simulate the old method by manually performing your find, sort, export, import, and/or print. Then go into the script or scripts you want to change. Double-click the desired step(s) from the list on the right, and click the Specify button to check your request. Delete the old step and move the new one into place.

Assigning Scripts to Buttons

You can place buttons on your layouts that run scripts you create. This puts the power of the scripts right there on the screen where you or your users can see them at a glance. You might want to create buttons for your scripts so that only certain features will be available on specific layouts. As you begin to use more scripts, the list of scripts can get confusingly long, and clarity should always be one of your goals. Using buttons can help with clarity.

1. Enter Layout mode.
2. Click on the **Button** icon in the Status toolbar. It's the icon with the finger pointing at a button. As you move the mouse pointer over to your layout, it turns into a crosshair. Find a blank area on the layout and click

and drag until you've drawn a rectangle about an inch square. The Button Setup window appears with Do Nothing highlighted in the left column.

3. Click on **Perform Script** in the left column. Then click on the **Specify** button in the Options area. When you do, you'll see a new window, "Specify Script" Options, as shown in Figure 3-14.

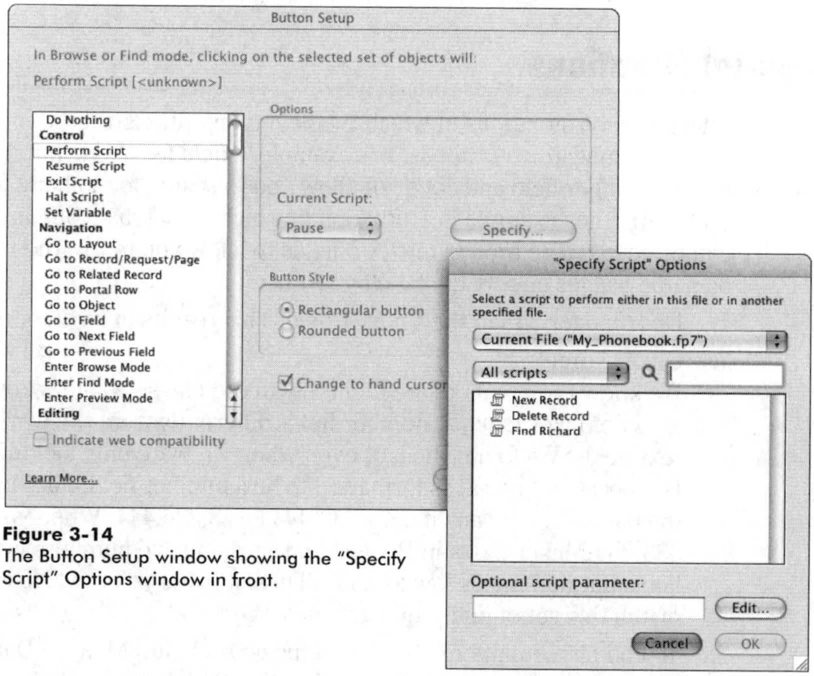

Figure 3-14
The Button Setup window showing the "Specify Script" Options window in front.

Before we move on, I want you to notice the "Optional script parameter" text box near the bottom of the "Specify Script" Options window. If you click the Edit button you'll see FileMaker's Specify Calculation window. This is a powerful tool introduced in FileMaker Pro 7 that allows a single script to work differently depending on choices you make here. We won't talk about it in detail until Chapter 14, but I wanted you to know where to find out more in case you were getting curious.

4. Select **Find Richard** and click **OK**. You are back on the Button Setup window. The box next to "Change to hand cursor over button" has been checked. This will make the cursor turn into a hand whenever it's over the button in Browse mode. Click **OK**.

5. You should now be back in Layout mode with the cursor blinking in the button you just made. Type **Find Richard**. FileMaker expands the button to accommodate the words and the current font size. If you don't like the way the text looks, you can resize the button or the font. Click somewhere off the button and resize it if you need to.

6. Go to Browse mode and try it out. Choose **Records**, **Show All Records** and try the button again.

7. Create another button and attach the New Record script to it. You get the idea.

⌘ **TIP** If you need to edit the text on the button, click on the Text tool (the A icon), then click on the button. The text cursor will begin to flash in the button. Type away.

Special Situations

There may be situations in which the field type or the structure of a field does not accommodate your needs. For example, a field for phone numbers is set up as a number field and does not allow you to search for a phone number prefix. Another example is a situation in which a field that contains customer names needs to be broken into two fields to allow you to use the first name on name badges or sort the field by last name.

1. Do a find for 333 in the Phone1 field. This results in an error message.
2. Click **Cancel.**

   We know the numbers are definitely in the file, so what's wrong here?

   FileMaker looks at number fields differently from the way it looks at text fields. We found Richard even when we were only looking for Rich. But because Phone1 is formatted to be a number field, FileMaker ignores the dash. That means it sees 333-4444 as 3,334,444. When you ask for 333, FileMaker looks in Phone1 and says, "I have numbers in the millions, but nothing as low as 333." Thus, it gives you the "No records match this set of find requests" message.
3. To find phone numbers by the prefix, go back into Manage Database, Fields and change the field type for all of the phone numbers to **Text**. Then try the find again.

Now look at the Name field. It's okay to have one field for the name, but there are some limitations. You might want to create form letters and include the person's first name in the salutation. But you'll be forced to use "Dear Rich Bailey" instead of "Dear Rich." Not very personal. Also, if you ever want to print out a phone list for times when you can't get to your computer, you'll probably want to sort by last name.

1. To create two name fields, go back into Manage Database, Fields and change Name to **NameFirst**, then click the **Change** button.
2. Create a new field called **NameLast**.
3. Go back to Layout mode. The new field may have appeared on the layout. If not, use the Field tool (click and drag on the Field icon) to place the NameLast field on the layout. You may have to change the formatting of the field so that it matches that of the other fields on the layout. Remember, you can use the Format Painter tool.

4. Now go back to Browse mode and go through the records, moving the last names into the NameLast field.

TIP Break the data into the smallest *usable* bits of information that make sense. In addition to NameFirst and NameLast, when it comes to ways of dealing with names, you may see databases with fields for TitleCourtesy (Mr., Mrs., Ms., etc.), TitleProfessional (Dr., Prof., etc.), NameMiddle or NameMI (for Middle Initial), and Nickname, as well as complex considerations for spouses with different last names and people living together.

BEST PRACTICES The reason we're using NameFirst and NameLast is so the field names having to do with name will be grouped together when the field list is sorted by field name. This method is very useful when you use the Sort Order window and when importing and exporting records.

The same goes for address information: AddrStreet, AddrCity, AddrState, etc. Since the field labels on the layouts will be different, users may be a little lost the first time they need to work with the actual field names. But most users understand exactly why you name the fields this way the first time you show them.

Consider companies with multiple contact people in different departments. Do you list the company as the primary contact and create many fields to accommodate all the different people, mailing addresses, and phone numbers? Or do you make each person a separate contact with many records that have the same company name? (Answer: probably the latter.)

Look at the Address field again. There's sure a lot of information there that should be separated. Not to mention, where's the zip code? Once more, go back to the Fields tab of Manage Database and add AddrCompany, AddrCity, AddrState, and AddrZip fields. And after our experience with the phone numbers, make the zip code field a text field. What about the additional four numbers used in zip codes now? We should make a separate field for that as well, and call it AddrPlusFour. When you're done, use your newfound skills with the layout tools to move the fields around until your layout looks like the one in Figure 3-15. Remember to rename the field labels so they make sense. Then go back to Browse mode and break the address data into the right fields. It'll take a little while, but you'll be developing your skills.

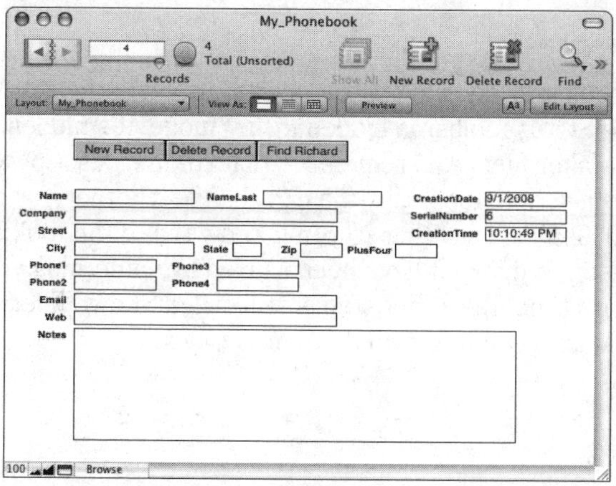

Figure 3-15 The updated layout with changes to accommodate new fields and the buttons.

Customizing the Status Toolbar[10]

Users of versions of FileMaker previous to 10 are in for a surprise. The Status area is now called the Status toolbar and has moved from the left side of the FileMaker window to the top. You can customize the Status toolbar by adding and deleting various functions. And you can customize each of the four modes separately. There are also some limitations and cautions that we'll look at shortly.

The Standard Sets

When you first install FileMaker 10 and open your first file, the default set of toolbar tools will show in each mode. They should look like the ones in Figures 3-16a-d.

Figure 3-16a
The standard tool set in Browse mode.

Figure 3-16b
The standard tool set in Layout mode.

Figure 3-16c
The standard tool set in Find mode.

Figure 3-16d
The standard tool set in Preview mode.

Whether the Status toolbar is showing or not applies to the entire FileMaker application. When the Status toolbar is hidden in any mode, it's hidden in all modes — for *all* FileMaker files. And remember that running a script with the Show/Hide Status Area script step in any file can change whether you see it and interact with it in all files. I say that so you'll know that if the toolbar disappears for some reason, it may not have been caused by something you did. (By the way, as of press time, the script step is still called Show/Hide Status Area even though that area is now called the Status toolbar.)

There is a key combination to show and hide the Status toolbar, assuming you have access to it. It's Command+Option+S (Macintosh) or Ctrl+Alt+S (Windows). If the menu item is grayed out, the account you're logged in under may not allow you to use it, or maybe it's been turned off and locked using a script. The Customize Status Toolbar menu item will be grayed out if it's locked, even if the toolbar is showing. If you have access to Manage Scripts, you can create your own script to give you access to the locked toolbar.

One final way to show or hide the Status toolbar is to use the fourth icon in the lower-left corner of the FileMaker window as shown in Figure 3-17.

Figure 3-17
The Show/Hide Status Toolbar button.

The Customize Palette

When you go to the View menu and choose Customize Status Toolbar, on the Macintosh a palette of possibilities pops open as shown in Figure 3-18a. On Windows, you get a Customize dialog and a list in the Commands tab as shown in Figure 3-18b. On either platform, the items you see will differ depending on which mode you're in at the time. Most of them are self-explanatory, but a few may not be completely clear to you until you get a little farther along in the book.

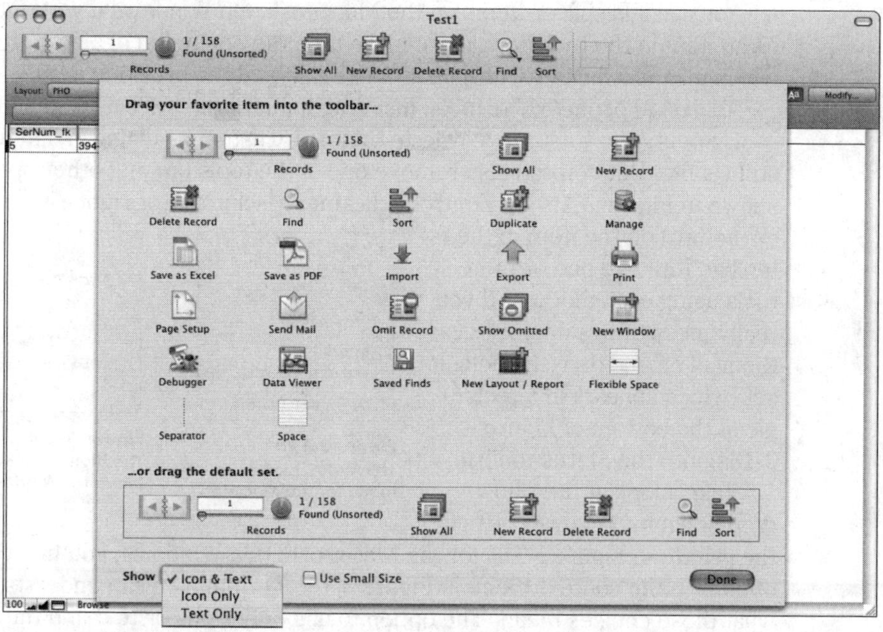

Figure 3-18a
The Customize Status Toolbar palette shown in Browse mode for the Macintosh.

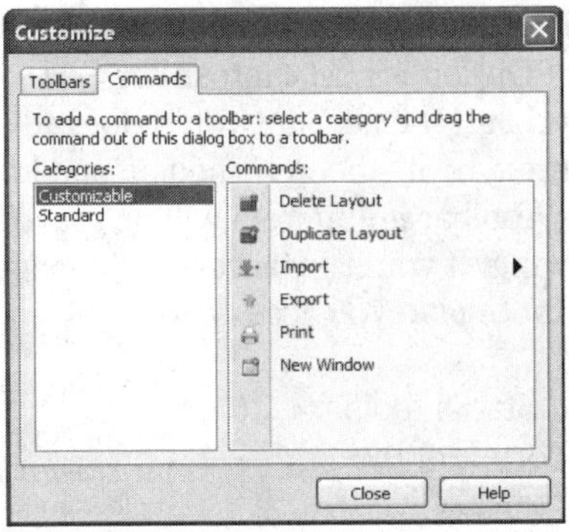

Figure 3-18b
The Customize dialog shown in Layout mode for Windows.

To get a tool into the Status toolbar, you simply drag it where you want it in the horizontal row. Try adding some now. You can reorder the tools by dragging them to a new position. If you add more tools than will show in the current window size, a double arrow ">>" will appear on the right. To see the added items, click the arrow and the other tools will appear in a drop-down list. Oddly, some items seem to be inactive once they move to the drop-down. I think not being able to see the tool in the toolbar sort of defeats the purpose. I mean, it's really not quite so quickly available now, is it? And sorry, you can't stack the tools vertically.

You can add spacer items on the Macintosh. On Windows if you right-click on an item in the toolbar, you can make it be the beginning of a new group, which means a divider will appear between it and the previous item.

To get rid of one of the tools, just drag it out of the toolbar in any direction — assuming the Customize palette (Mac) or Customize dialog (Windows) is still visible. But you can also remove one of the tools (among other options shown in Figure 3-19) by Control+clicking (Macintosh) or right-clicking (Windows) on the item in the toolbar. Remove one or more tools using each method. If you really mess things up, just clear them all off and drag the default set (which appears in a rectangle at the bottom of Figure 3-18a) into the Status toolbar.

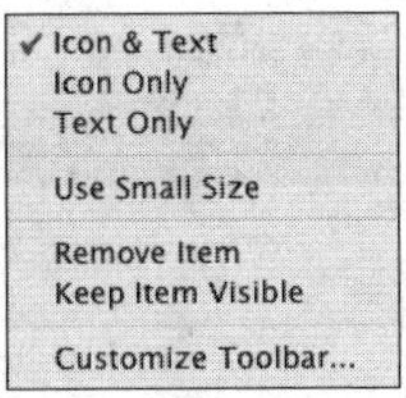

Figure 3-19a
The Status Toolbar context menu for the Macintosh.

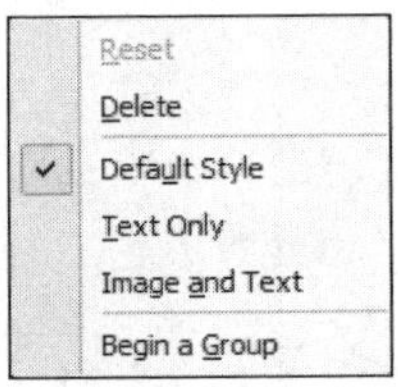

Figure 3-19b
The Status Toolbar context menu for Windows.

Take a look at the Show drop-down in the lower left of the palette in Figure 3-18a for the Macintosh. (On Windows, you find these options in the context menu in Figure 3-19b.) I think you can understand what those choices mean. The option to use only icons or text and the check box for Use Small Size is Mac only. You really can't squeeze more than one or two extra icons on the bar, but that may be enough for you.

Notice the Keep Item Visible choice in the context menu shown in Figure 3-19a (Macintosh only). What that does is keep the tool showing in the toolbar regardless of how narrow you make the window. That means that tool won't move offscreen into the drop-down menu when there are too many tools to display horizontally. Of course if you force all of the tools to stay visible and you narrow the window, they'll pop offscreen as if none of them are checked. Hey, something's gotta give!

Only Windows users can click the arrow on the right of the Status toolbar to get to the set of menus seen in Figure 3-20 where you can uncheck menu items to remove them from the toolbar.

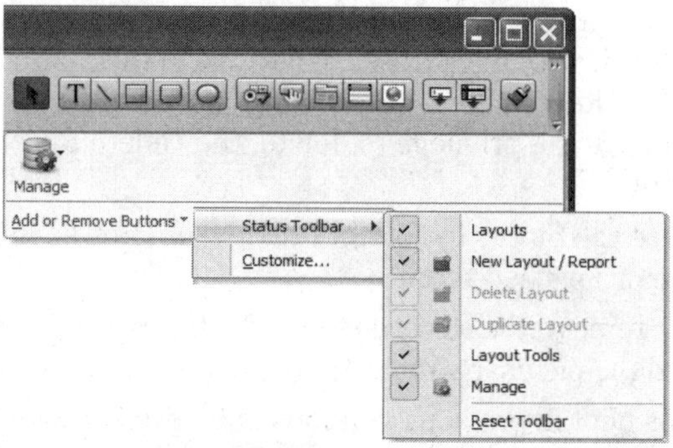

Figure 3-20
The Windows Status Toolbar items checklist.

Limitations and Cautions

The following are some things to keep in mind when using the Status toolbar.

- If you are developing solutions for other people and they remove an essential item from the toolbar on their machine, you'll be fielding frequent support phone calls. For instance, if someone removes the New Record tool, they may not know there is a menu item for that function. You might still need to provide redundant buttons at the top of the layouts for functions you want to be sure everyone will have access to at all times. And it may be a little more clear to have a button that reads "New Customer" or "New Invoice" rather than "New Record."
- You cannot add any of your own buttons to the Status toolbar. Well, that's not exactly true. If you have a copy of FileMaker Pro Advanced, you can create a custom menu in which you can make a script replace a standard menu item. You can even change the text that appears on that menu and the tool that shows in the toolbar. Since customizing menus is an advanced feature, I won't be covering it in this book. But I want you to know it's available, especially with regard to controlling what happens with the toolbar items. Just keep in mind that any given tool may not be there for all users. That's what the "custom" in "customize" means. (Don't worry; you won't need me to train you on custom menus. FMPA comes with a very good PDF document on the topic.)

  "But, ah!" you're thinking. "Why not run a script that includes the Show/Hide Status Area [Lock; Show] step when the file first opens? That will keep them from messing with the tools." Sure, but it will only lock the tools in their current state. If they removed the tool you need them to have before your script runs, you're back where you started —

without the tool. And don't forget, users can create their own scripts in another file with the script step Show/Hide Status Area [Show]. Without that magic word "Lock" in there next to "Show," they can do whatever they want from that moment on.

- If the Status toolbar is hidden, the keyboard commands for Go To Next Record (Control+down arrow) and Go to Previous Record (Control+up arrow) are disabled. Of course you can still get to the next record in a list by clicking on it.
- If you have one file open with full access, all buttons in the Status toolbar work, including Delete Record. If you then bring another file to the front in which you do not have the privilege to delete, the Delete Record button will be grayed out.
- You cannot customize the Status toolbar in Preview or Browse mode if you're in the middle of a paused script.
- On the Mac you can remove the Records tool, which consists of the Book, the slider, and the pie chart. You can't do that on Windows.
- If you have solutions built in previous versions of FileMaker with scripts that adjust window size, you need to be aware that hiding the Status toolbar now happens from the top rather than the side. That will affect the size of the windows. You may have to make some adjustments.

Summary

We did a lot in this chapter. You've learned about planning a database, creating fields, and moving the fields around with the layout tools. You also created a few scripts and attached them to buttons. And you learned some important things about formatting fields and customizing the Status toolbar. I'll bet you can feel the momentum building. Notice that as we got going, I didn't have to tell you every little move to make. I've gone from using the phrase "Go to the View menu and choose Layout mode" in the first chapter to "Go to Layout mode." And you knew what I was talking about and how to do it. You're gettin' good at this!

Q & A

Q What if I decide I want to change what a button does?

A Go to Layout mode and double-click the button. You'll see the Specify Button window again. You can assign the button to a different script or some other function in the list.

Q What if I want to change the text that's on a button?

A Use the Text tool. That's the icon with the letter "A" on it in the toolbar or in the Tool panel. Then click on the button and type away.

Q What if I don't like the font that appears in a field?

A To permanently change the default font for the field in all records, go to Layout mode. Click on the field, choose Format, Font, and select the font you want. That will only affect the way that particular field appears on that layout. All other occurrences of that field can be formatted separately.

If you only want to change how a particular bit of text looks in a particular record in Browse mode, highlight it. Then choose Format, Font and make the change. All other records will be unaffected.

Workshop

Think of at least one field you would want for this file that I haven't given you. Add it using the correct field type and put it on your layout in a logical place with a field label to identify it.

Create a script with the single step Show All Records. Then create a button that uses it. Click Find Richard and look at the information in the Status toolbar. Then click your new button and watch the numbers change in the Status toolbar.

Part 2

Using FileMaker Pro

Chapter 4

Creating a New Database

Introduction

In previous chapters, I showed you how to work with one of the template files and what to do when creating a database from scratch. In this chapter, I'll show you some things to consider when deciding which option to choose.

Then we'll dig deeper into the mysteries of fields — field-naming recommendations, details about the field types, what fields are used for, and how to format them in a layout. And, of course, we'll do all this while working in real files.

Considerations

In the last chapter, I gave you a questionnaire that you'll be able to use from now on to help you decide what elements you'll need in your database. Once you've done that, a good next step is to see if you have any files that already contain the elements you need.

Predefined Databases

Aside from the template files provided with your copy of FileMaker Pro, there are numerous commercial products already developed in FileMaker that may provide some or all of what you need. I've listed a number of resources for ready-made solutions in Appendix B and have also included a few in the downloadable files for this book. Then the problem is how to find what you need, and how to know if it's any good.

Many companies have web sites that offer free downloads of limited versions of their products. You can get a copy, work with it for a while, and decide if it will work for your situation. An important consideration is whether the solution is open or not. An *open* database is one where the developers allow you to have full access to the files so you can add your own fields and scripts. That way you can make your own changes and integrate the commercial files with files you've created.

Freeware and shareware databases are available for download as well. Again, look in Appendix B and in the downloadable files.

Even if there is an existing solution, you may still have solid reasons to build something from the ground up. I had a client ask me recently what it would take to have me create an accounting system for them. Their needs were fairly simple, but it still cost more to build their bare-bones files than it would have to purchase a premade, full-featured system. However, with a custom system they have exactly what they want with the capability to change it anytime they choose. Cost is not the only consideration.

As you work more with FileMaker Pro, you will build up a library of your own files that you will be able to use as templates for new work.

Creating Your Own Database

If you followed along with all the steps in the last chapter, you have a rough idea of what it takes to start a file from scratch. Of course, at this point, it's not exactly second nature. Remember how difficult driving a car was the first time — now you can pretty much do it without thinking. As you develop more skill, building databases in FileMaker will become not only more comfortable but also fun as well. It's like doing a jigsaw puzzle except that when you get all the pieces to fit, you'll have something that will be much more useful.

You can also start your files from the ground up and use layout elements from the templates. All the background layout objects can be cut and pasted for use with your fields. You can even copy the fields, but you'll have to reassign them in your new file. As you learn more about layout tools, you will find that there is a faster way than trying to create all those elements yourself.

And, of course, the Layout Assistant can be a great help. See Chapter 9, "Creating New Layouts with the Layout Assistant," for more on that topic.

A great feature of FileMaker Pro is the ability to import scripts. As much as I like creating scripts, there's no point in creating the same script over and over by hand. You can create a library of commonly used scripts and simply import them into your new files; with a little touch-up, they're ready to use. This can be a big time-saver. We'll examine this in greater detail in Chapter 14, "Automating Your Database with Scripts."

What Are Fields?

A *field* is the area on a layout where the data goes. A field can also contain information that's calculated. In the My_Phonebook file that we created in the previous chapter, we tried to get the fields down to the most basic bits of information we might want to search for and sort on. On the other hand, with a field like a notes field, you can store a lot of useful information that doesn't need to fit in a one- or two-word field. And don't forget that a container field can store pictures, movies, OLE objects (Windows only), and sounds.

NOTE OLE objects allow you to use information from other applications right in FileMaker. OLE stands for Object Linking and Embedding. With it, you can place things like spreadsheets, images, and sounds in container fields. While support for OLE objects is built into the Mac system, it is not supported for the Mac version of FileMaker Pro. In Windows applications, the OLE objects will automatically update from the originating application.

Creating a Field

Open up an existing file such as My_Phonebook, then choose File, Manage Database, and click the Fields tab. To clarify the process I introduced in the last chapter, to create a field you:

1. Type a field name.
2. Choose a field type.
3. Click the Create button, or press Enter or Return.

Remember that after you have a field name and type, you can simply duplicate the field. Highlight the field you want to copy and click the Duplicate button. FileMaker automatically appends the word "Copy" to the end of the name and you can change it in almost any way you like.

About Field Names

There are some considerations to take into account when naming fields.

You cannot define fields with the same field name twice in the same table. That is not the same as having the same field appear on different layouts or even having multiple copies of the same field on the same layout.

When I gave you field names in the last chapter, I left out the spaces between words. I did that for the same reason I used the underscore character in My_Phonebook. If the file might ever be accessed using a browser, the HTML web language doesn't do well with spaces. Also, Open Database Connectivity (ODBC) doesn't work properly with spaces in field names, and SQL keywords would also be a problem. See Chapter 21 for more information about FileMaker and ODBC.

Try to choose field names that will be short, yet descriptive. One of the reasons is that long field names in combination with relationship names can be difficult to read quickly in some of the windows. But keep clarity in mind. Remember that other people may have to fix something in your files when you're not around. You might even have to work on the file sometime in the future. Use names that make sense. Some of my old (and occasionally more recent) files are a little embarrassing to look at in that regard. I had shortened the field names using acronyms that meant something at the time but lost their meaning after a few months had passed. You can use the field comments area to make notes. But remember that you won't be able to see those comments when you're trying to decide which fields to place on a layout or which data you want to export.

When you name fields, tables, or files, you should avoid using any of the characters or items listed in any of the areas above the Formula box in the Specify Calculation window shown in Figure 4-1. Specific characters to avoid include & / " * ¶ - ( ) + = ≠ > < ≥ ≤ ^ . ; (semicolon) :: (two colons in a row) ' (apostrophe) , (comma). It's okay to use the colon symbol, but I try to avoid it since it is a special character and may cause confusion with the double colon. I often create calculation fields that use the names of two other fields. For those, developers often use the "|" (pipe) character between the fields they're combining. For example, if I were to combine NameCompany and ID I might call it NameCompany|ID. That's because you can't use the & symbol or the word "and" in a field name if it might be used somewhere else in a calculation.

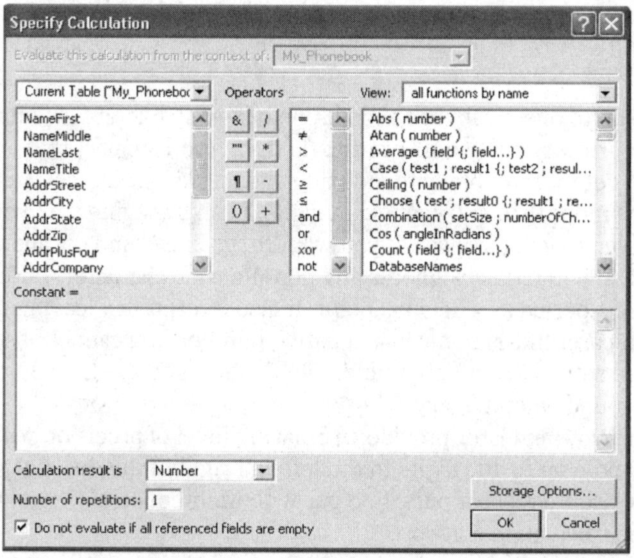

Figure 4-1
The Specify Calculation window showing operators and functions lists, and the mathematical and text operators buttons. Avoid using these symbols and functions when creating field, table, and file names.

It probably sounds like a lot to worry about. But, in general, you won't be using symbols and function names in your field names if you're using good descriptive titles in the first place. FileMaker will warn you if you use illegal characters in a field name.

The Eight Field Types

In the previous chapter, I had you add text, number, date, and time fields to your file. FileMaker also provides timestamp, container, calculation, and summary field types. I want to give you the lowdown on all of them. In Chapter 10, "Keeping Your Data Clean and Neat," I'll discuss the Auto-Enter, Validation, and Storage field data entry options that can be accessed from the Fields tab.

Text Field

As we saw in the previous chapter, sometimes you will use a text field for data you wouldn't expect, like phone numbers. You can also use it to store numbers that begin with one or more zeros. (If you were using a number field, FileMaker would ignore leading zeros.) What I didn't tell you is that a text field can hold one gigabyte of data. That's something like one billion characters. You read that right! That's roughly equivalent to 500,000 pages of text. That's up quite a few pages from FileMaker's old six-page limit. And if you're using a repeating field, the limit applies to each repetition separately. I really can't imagine anyone ever needing even close to one billion characters in one repetition, but if you get too much text in there, you'll get the following warning: "Sorry, this operation could not be completed because you have reached text block limits." I'm betting your brain or your hard drive explodes first, though!

Number Field

You can store up to one gigabyte or about one billion characters in a number field. I'm not sure why you would want to do that. And I suspect that you would start to get into trouble with indexing and display problems when using anything much more than 400 significant digits. I can't imagine why you would want to go that far, anyway. If you want to, go ahead and try and then report back to me. FileMaker ignores any non-numeric characters, although it does recognize a period as a decimal point. It also interprets a leading dash or a leading open parenthesis to mean a negative number. You cannot use a return/carriage return in a number field. FileMaker just plays the operating system beep sound when you try.

FileMaker Pro 7 and later provide an amazing level of precision with numbers. It will handle up to 400 digits to the left and right of the decimal point with complete accuracy. That puts it on par with Mathematica — until now the standard in calculation software.

If you choose to display numbers using the General Format, a number like 8,877,780,000 would appear as 8.8778e+09 once you exit the field. You can also type scientific notation directly into a number field and it will work in calculations with other fields or constants.

Date Field

A date field accommodates dates only. When you enter a date in Browse mode, it all goes on one line (no returns allowed). Although you can format how the date displays, you must enter the date as numbers in a form specified by your regional or international settings. (See the following Note.) For example, in the United States you must enter a date using: month, day, year. Actually, the year portion is optional. But with all the lessons we've learned about Y2K, you should get into the habit of entering the year in four-digit format.

Normally, people use the slash (/) or the dash (-) character to separate each item. But you can actually separate them with any non-numeric characters. You can get pretty wild here, but you must use the same character within a date. If you try two different separators, you'll trigger a warning. Try a few experiments in the CreationDate field.

NOTE At the time each file is created, FileMaker sets up number, date, and time (including timestamp) fields to display using the Regional Options from the Control Panel (Windows) or the International system preference (Macintosh).

Time Field

Time fields hold time data only and it goes on one line, too. You have a lot of freedom in how you enter the time: hours, hours and minutes, or hours, minutes, and seconds. Again, use matching, non-numeric characters to separate the numbers. The standard is a colon (:). If you enter characters or times that are incorrect or too large, you get a warning. You might try putting some correct and incorrect times in the CreationTime field to see what happens. Oddly enough, you can put some numbers in the field that would seem wrong but will still work. For example, try 32766 or 1:32766.

You can use 12- or 24-hour (often called military time) format. If you use the 12-hour format, you only need to add PM for times after noon. FileMaker assumes you mean AM if the number for the hour is 0 to 11.

Timestamp Field[7]

This feature was added in FileMaker Pro 7. It combines the date and time into one field. It keeps track of the date and time in increments of one second starting from the date 1/1/0001. If you plan on performing calculations on the data in this field type, it helps to know that there are 86,400 seconds in a day.

> ⌘ **TIP** When you're working on a network, keep in mind that everyone's computer clocks are not likely to be synchronized. A record may be created on one person's machine at a real time of 1:00 PM and another might be created at a real time of 1:05 PM. Yet the database may show the 1:05 PM record being created at 12:58 because that's the time setting on that computer. To avoid any mix-ups of that kind, when you create a time field, instead of using Auto-Enter Creation Time, check the box next to "Calculated value." When the Specify Calculation window appears, choose Get (CurrentHostTimestamp). When you click OK, check the box next to "Do not replace existing value for field (if any)." For you old-timers, this will work even for FileMaker Server, which now has its own calculation engine and will pass the server time down to the user. (You can use Get (CurrentHostTimestamp) in scripts, too.)

Container Field

Container fields can hold sounds (i.e., music), pictures, movies, PDF files, and just about any other type of file you can think of — including other FileMaker files. This makes FileMaker a terrific document-tracking tool.

With my music background, I've had a lot of fun with container fields. I store songwriting ideas in a container field and then write a description of the idea or the lyrics in a text field for easy searching. I've also stored scanned photographs with a description of where to find the film and negatives. Starting with version 6.0, Mac OS X users could import a batch of photos directly from a digital camera into FMP fields. Although there was no announcement, I found that Windows can import files from a digital camera into FMP8 and later. FileMaker 10 ships with a photo template. Look in English Extras, Templates, Home – Collections, Photo Catalog.fp7. For examples of many of the other uses of container fields, take a look at the companion files to this book, which are posted on the Wordware web site at www.wordware.com/files/fmpro10.

1. Go into Manage Fields and create a container field called **Pic**.
2. Exit Manage Fields and go to Layout mode.
3. If the new Pic field doesn't appear automatically, use the **Field** tool to place a copy somewhere on the layout. Resize it so it's about **1.5** inches wide and **2** inches tall.
4. Now switch to Preview mode and choose **Edit**, **Copy**.
5. Go back to Browse mode, click in the **Pic** field, and choose **Edit**, **Paste**.

The result will depend on how the field is formatted as a graphic, but you can do some pretty impressive tricks by copying and pasting a page in Preview mode. And just wait until you start putting photos of people or QuickTime movies in a container field!

⌘ **TIP** The cursor doesn't flash when you click in a container field, but once you've clicked on it, the field is active. Then you can paste items from the clipboard or go to the Insert menu and choose Picture, QuickTime movie, or Sound.

Calculation Field

A calculation field uses data in each record or from related records to display a result. The calculation can also be or include constants or status functions as well as images. It sounds complicated, but FileMaker offers so many calculation options that it's hard to get a feel for it without a little more experience. You probably normally think of the result of a calculation as a number, but FileMaker goes way beyond that. You can also display the calculation as a text, date, time, or container result. The fact that you're able to display so many types of calculation results can be very powerful.

Follow these steps to test this out:

1. Go into Manage Fields and create a new field called **AddrCombo**, choosing the **calculation** field type. The Specify Calculation window appears.

⌘ **TIP** You can type directly in the Specify Calculation window, or you can build the calculation by double-clicking on items in the field, function, and comparison operator lists and single-clicking on the comparison and logical operator buttons.

2. Enter the calculation exactly this way:

```
NameFirst & " " & NameLast & "¶" &
AddrStreet & "¶" &
AddrCity & " " & AddrState & " " & AddrZip & "-" & AddrPlusFour
```

When you see the quotation marks with a space between them, be sure you actually press the Spacebar once there.

TIP You can put carriage returns (the Return key) between elements of a calculation without affecting the results of the calculation. This can be extremely valuable when trying to visualize what's going on when you work with longer calculations. You can even indent parameters of functions if that will make it easier to understand.

3. In the lower-left corner of the window you'll see the "Calculation result is" drop-down list. It always defaults to Number. Click the drop-down and choose **Text**.

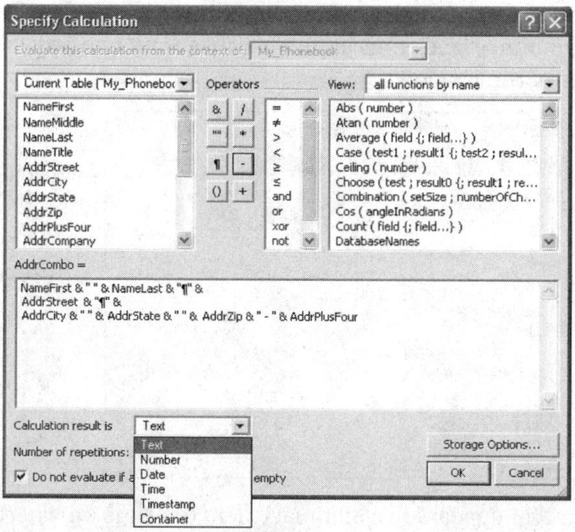

Figure 4-2
The Specify Calculation window for the AddrCombo field. Note the "Calculation result is" drop-down in the lower-left corner.

CAUTION If you build a calculation and forget to choose the correct calculation result from the drop-down, you can get some pretty strange results. The data in the field can look completely foreign. The data might look just fine on the layout, but it might give incorrect summaries. It can also cause a lot of headaches if you use a calculation as part of a relationship to another table. You might have meant to link the tables by the same field type but actually chose two different type results.

4. Click **OK** and **OK** again to exit.
5. Go into Layout mode and place the new AddrCombo field on the layout if it's not already there. You'll want to grab one of the selection handles with the Selection tool and open up the field to accommodate at least three lines of text.
6. Now go into Browse mode and take a look at the results. Notice that a dash appears whether or not there are Zip and PlusFour values. You can further refine the calculation using Case or If functions to prevent that. For now, just make up some zip codes. Notice that you can't type data directly into the calculation field. Click through some of the other records in the file to see what they look like, too. If you want to experiment, go back and choose Date as the calculation result. Just don't forget to change it back.

Summary Field

Summary fields grab data from a single field across one or more records in the same (or related) tables. That might sound a little complicated, but think of a situation where you might want to see the grand total of all invoices written today. That would be a summary field. (In contrast, calculation fields work on one or more fields within a single record, such as Price x Quantity = Amount Due. There are exceptions, but this is a good general definition.) Summaries can calculate total, average, count, minimum, maximum, standard deviation, and fraction of a total, as shown in Figure 4-3. Notice that some fields cannot be summarized. You can tell because they are gray in the field list in the center of the window.

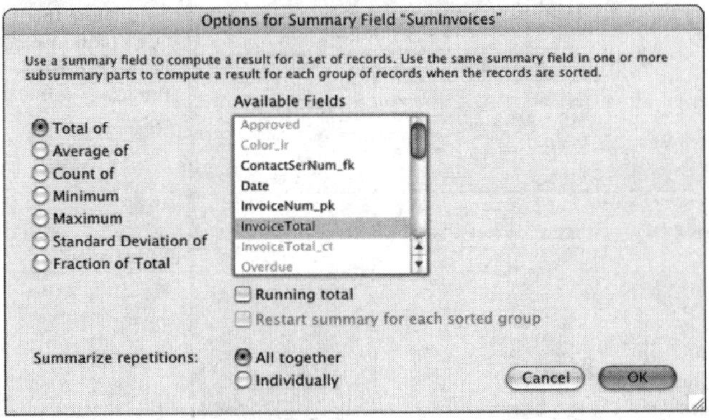

Figure 4-3 Window used to make choices for summary fields.

The information that appears in a summary field depends on where it is on a layout, what records are found, and how they are sorted. You also need to understand layout parts so your reports properly reflect the results you're after. More on that in Chapter 15, "Making Sense of Your Information with Layouts."

When the Options for Summary Field window first appears, the "Total of" radio button is automatically selected. Below the field list is a "Running total" check box. That allows you to view running totals when a copy of the summary field is placed in the body part of the layout. Click down the radio buttons on the left and watch how the options change for the check box.

1. Create a summary field called **CountSerial.**
2. When the Options for Summary Field window appears, choose the **Count of** radio button and the **SerialNumber** field, and check the **Running count** box.
3. Exit and go to Layout mode. Place a copy of CountSerial in the body part of the layout over on the right as shown in Figure 4-4.

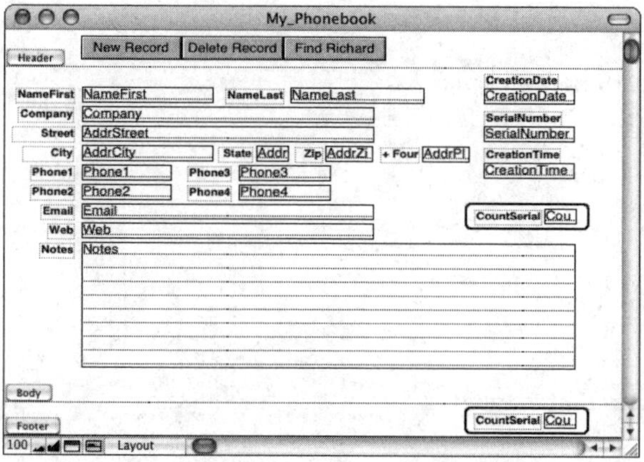

Figure 4-4 Layout mode showing the placement of two copies of the CountSerial summary field enclosed in rounded rectangles.

4. Then place a second copy in the footer part.
5. Go into Browse mode and choose **Records**, **Show All Records**. Click through the records and notice how the numbers change in the body but remain the same in the footer.
6. Now choose **Records**, **Omit Record** and look at what happens to CountSerial in the footer.

Global Storage Option

A field with the global storage option selected contains one value or container type item that is shared across all records in a table and can even be placed in other tables in the same file. You can specify global storage for a field of any type except summary.

Global fields can be used as temporary storage areas to move data between records, tables, or tables in another file. You can use them in conditional parts of scripts. For example, you can tell a script to start at the first record in a table and cycle through the records until it finds a company name that matches one stored in a global field.

A global field cannot be indexed. (I'll discuss indexing in Chapter 10.) When you enter Find mode, you can't get into a global field. It wouldn't do any good anyway, since the search would just find all records. (Remember, it shares the same value across all records.) But values in global fields can still be viewed in Find mode and passed to other fields in the find process using a script. You can also perform a find request in a calculation field that uses a global field as part of its calculation. Basically, what I'm saying is that you can do a lot of neat tricks with global fields.

Part 2

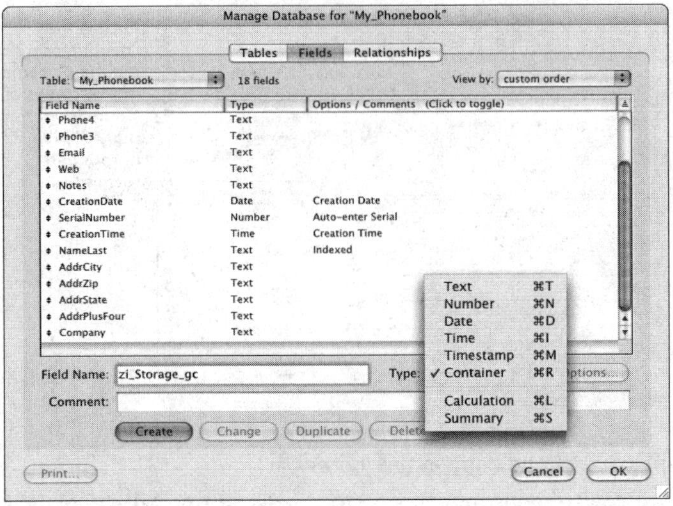

Figure 4-5
A global field begins as any other field.

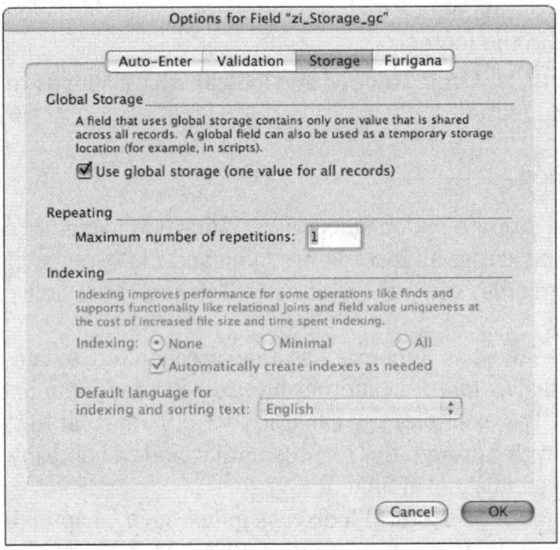

Figure 4-6
Selecting "Use global storage" in the Storage tab of the Options for Field window is what makes a global field.

For example, you could store a logo for a company in a global field formatted as container type and drop the field on various layouts. If the logo changes, you update one field and every occurrence of that logo changes throughout your tables. If you format it as a text type field, you can do the same thing for an address.

When I first read about global fields, I just couldn't figure out what I would use them for. But after a while I found them to be extremely valuable. We'll use them later in the book in some exercises so you'll get a better feel for how you might be able to use them.

> **BEST PRACTICES** Notice the zi at the beginning of zi_Storage_gc and the gc at the end. When I have fields that are really not meant for regular data entry, I put a "z" at the beginning to make them appear at the bottom of the field list when the list is sorted by name. That way, I can find all my utility fields together at the bottom of the list. I use the "i" for interface, which is a general category for something the user sees or might interact with. The "gc" means the field is formatting globally and that it's a container field. For more information on naming conventions, review the information in the downloadable files.

Take a minute to create a global field and pay attention to the windows you'll see. Choose the field name and type, and click the Create button. Then click on Options and, under the Storage tab, check the "Use global storage" box. Scripts and calculations won't work the way you expect if you're using a standard text or number field but think you're getting data from a global field. I tell you this because I've done it more than once. Even more than twice. Okay, I've probably done it as many as 30 or 40 times!

Repeating Field

A repeating field is not a field type. It is a way of formatting any of the other field types except summary. You can format a field with up to 32,000 repetitions.

Repeating fields were originally invented before FileMaker was a relational database. Back then it was especially valuable for invoices. You could use one repeating field, and each repetition would represent another line item on the invoice, as shown in Figure 4-7.

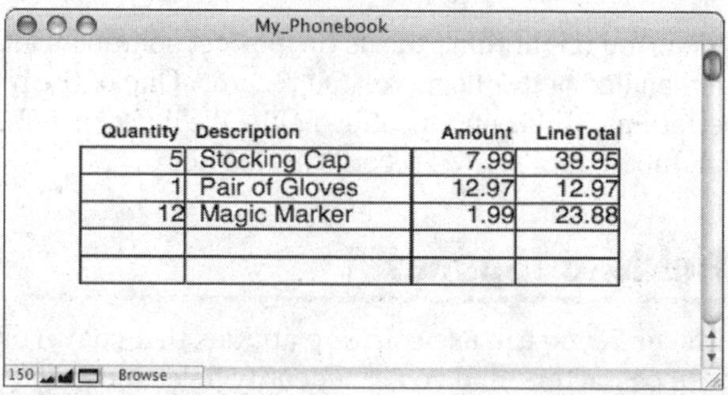

Figure 4-7
Number (Quantity and Amount), text (Description), and calculation (LineTotal) fields formatted as repeating fields.

You choose the number of repetitions in the Storage tab. (In a calculation field, you'll find the number of repetitions in the bottom left of the Specify Calculation window.) Then you choose how many of those repetitions are visible as part of the formatting of the field on the layout (Format, Field Format).

Since FileMaker Pro became a relational database with version 3.0, repeating fields are not used as often. You can do so much more in the way of reporting when line items are created as individual records in a related table. It probably sounds confusing at this point, but I think it will get clearer once we start working with our first relational tables. These days, the repeating field format is most often used for storing multiple values in global fields.

That's interesting because globals were introduced in version 3.0 — the same time FileMaker went relational.

Another common use for repeating fields was for phone numbers. To see how this worked, follow these steps:

1. Go back into Manage Fields and double-click **Phone1**.
2. When you see the Options for Field "Phone1" window, click the **Storage** tab.
3. In the Repeating area, you can select the number of repetitions of this field that will appear on the layout. Type **10** after "Maximum number of repetitions:" and click **OK** and **OK** again.
4. Go into Layout mode and make a copy of the Phone1 field. Paste it in a blank area on your layout.
5. While the field is still selected, choose **Format**, **Field/Control**[8], **Setup**.
6. At the bottom of the Field/Control Setup window is the Repetitions area. As you can see, 10 repetitions are defined. You can show up to 10 repetitions on your layout, and you can start with any repetition[8]. If you want to show only the first six, change the 1 to the right of the word "through" to 6.
7. Now select the orientation of those repetitions — whether they will appear horizontally or vertically — on your layout. Click **OK**.
8. Go to Browse mode. Notice that the number you typed in there earlier is still in the first repetition. Make up a number or two to fill in more repetitions.

Well, you get the idea. You might think this is the perfect solution. But even phone numbers are handled better using related records. One of the reasons is that there are script limitations on repeating fields. We'll take a look at how to turn the phone numbers into related records in Chapter 6.

Formatting Your Fields in Japanese[7]

Starting with FileMaker 7, you can use software utilities that convert keystrokes into Japanese characters, and you can identify fields for which you would like a phonetic translation of that Japanese text.

Beyond that thin explanation, what I have to tell you here is really a cop-out. If you don't want to hear my sad excuses, just go to the Help files and do a find for "Formatting fields in Japanese" and "Furigana." In order to make use of these capabilities, there are some system requirements and extra software utilities I don't have. So my attempts to test these were futile. If you're determined, and you can get your machine set up correctly, I'm sure these are very useful functions.

Field Formats on Layouts

Once you have created your fields, you need to decide how they'll appear on your layouts. FileMaker provides you with many very useful choices. Let's use My_Phonebook to continue our experiments.

Aside from borders and fonts, most fields won't need much formatting at all. But when you need special formatting, you must know where to go to do this. Keep in mind that you can format a number of fields of the same type at the same time, rather than one at a time. Just Shift-click on the fields you want to format and choose the appropriate menu to access the Format window. You can also use the Format Painter to do the formatting.

Date Format

First, let's look at the CreationDate field.

1. Go into Layout mode, select the field, and choose **Format, Date.**
2. Click the **Format as** radio button and click on the **Format as** pop-up list to see the list of common choices. (See Figure 4-8.) Pick any one of them and look in the Sample area near the bottom of the window to see what it will look like. If you switch to the Custom radio button, you can build your own date display including European format, which puts the day before the month. However, when you enter dates in Browse mode, you must still use the format month, day, year.
3. After you exit the field, it will display in the format you've chosen. Notice that by clicking the **Text Format** button in the lower-left corner of the window, you can even access the font, size, color, and style for customizing without going back to the program menus. You can even go one level deeper by clicking the **Paragraph** button in the lower-left corner of the Text Format window.
4. Click **OK** or **Cancel** to exit.

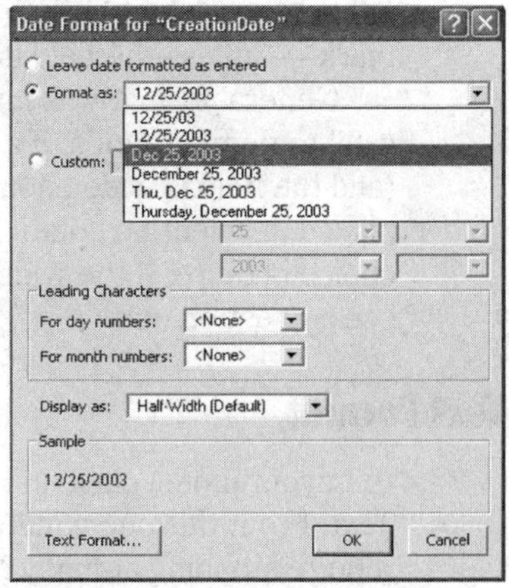

Figure 4-8
The Date Format window showing the choices in the "Format as" pop-up list.

Number Format

The only number field in our file is the SerialNumber field. Right-click on it in Layout mode and choose Format, Number. There just isn't enough space to explain every detail of this window, but as windows go, this one is pretty easy to understand. Notice that you can access the text formatting from here as well. Click **OK** or **Cancel** to exit.

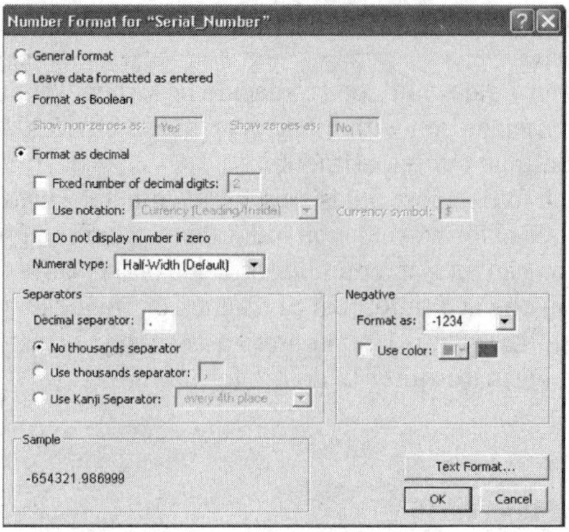

Figure 4-9
The Number Format window where you make choices about how a number field will display on your layout.

If a number is longer than the field width, FileMaker will display a question mark — unless the field is formatted with the "General format" radio button.

General format was introduced in FileMaker Pro 5.0 and applies specifically to number fields. If a number field contains more than nine characters (and the field is wide enough to hold 10 characters), the number will be displayed in scientific notation. This may or may not be what you want, but the choice is there. If the width of the field is smaller than 10 characters, you'll see a question mark.

Text Format

In Layout mode, click on the Notes field to select it. Then choose Format, Text. From this one window, you can access text formatting that would require stopping at many of the program menus at the top of the screen. If you click the Paragraph button in the lower-left corner, you can even format the fields for alignment, indentation, and line spacing. Clicking the Tabs button takes you one layer deeper to build a set of custom tabs. There is plenty of information in the FileMaker manual PDF file and the Help menu on these settings.

Time Format

In Layout mode, click on the CreationTime field and choose Format, Time. Click the radio button next to "Format as" and choose the format that suits you. Most of the time I prefer "hhmm." Then I usually click the button next to "12 hour notation." It's important for you to know that no matter how you format time, date, and number fields on the layout, the data is actually stored the way it was entered.

Here's an interesting little item: If you have a timestamp field, you'll notice there is no layout format for Timestamp. Instead, you choose Format, Date Format and make some choices there. Then you choose Format, Time

Format and make some choices. If you select "Leave date formatted as entered" or "Leave time formatted as entered" in either of the windows, the entire timestamp remains unformatted. You might try creating a timestamp field, creating a new record, and trying the layout format choices to see what happens.

⌘ **TIP** I find it helpful to format my timestamp field with a dash between the date and time so it's easier to read. To do that, use the Custom button to format the date. In the fourth box on the right (after the year) type " - " (space, hyphen, space). After you click OK, choose your time format. When you're done, your timestamp field should display something like 12/7/2008 - 2:11 PM.

Summary

In this chapter, we looked at the options available when creating a new database and what to consider when deciding whether to make one from scratch, from a template, or from a commercial product. Then we looked closely at the various field types and how to make them display on a layout. In the next chapter, we'll talk about what you'll be putting into those fields.

Q & A

Q With all these new fields we're creating, I'm starting to run out of room on the layout. What do I do?

A Go into Layout mode and notice the separators between layout parts. Near the left edge of the layout, you should see some tabs titled Header, Body, and Footer. Each has a dotted line running horizontally across the layout. If you click and drag on the Body tab, you can move it downward to expand your work area. You can also click on the dotted line, but it's a little harder to grab.

Q Some of the database tables I want to create are going to have more fields than will fit on one page. What then?

A Take a look at the Contact Management template again. By making use of the tab control in the middle of the page, you can switch to different layouts and group similar types of data that may not need to be seen on your main screen. For more on tab controls, see Chapter 17.

Workshop

Go back to the Contact Management file. Take a look at the Manage Database window and go to the Fields tab. Scan down the list of fields and see if you can tell what the fields are for without too much trouble. Would some of those fields suit a purpose you might have for a database? Take as much time as you can spare and look at the other template files, keeping in mind how you might be able to use them in your work.

Chapter 5

Entering and Modifying Your Data

Introduction

In this chapter, I want to show you more about creating new records and entering data in those records. Along the way I will give you a number of pointers that should make data entry much easier than having to type all the information into every single field.

We'll look at:

- Tab order
- Getting data from other records with duplicate information
- Deleting records
- Using value lists
- Auto-complete fields and Calendar drop-down fields
- Placing movies, sounds, and pictures into container fields

If you don't already have My_Phonebook open, go ahead and open it back up now. We'll use it sparingly at first, but then we'll pick up some steam.

Creating a New Record

It's not as if you don't know how to create a new record by now. In fact, we even created a button for it. As I mentioned before, I still prefer the key combination — Command+N (Macintosh) or Ctrl+N (Windows) — over the use of a button. I just don't like putting all those miles on my mouse muscles.

One method I didn't discuss is creating a record by choosing Records, Duplicate Record. If you're creating a new record that will have much of the same data as the current record, use the menu command or press Command+D (Macintosh) or Ctrl+D (Windows). Then you only have to change the data that is different for the newly duplicated record. This works very well for companies where you'll be using the same address and phone, but you want to have a different record for each person in the company. However, duplicating a record will not duplicate any items in a portal or a related table. (We'll discuss that in the next chapter.)

Of course, you can create scripts and attach them to buttons for any of these tasks (that is, if I can't talk you into learning the key combination). On the other hand, one advantage of creating a script is that you can have it run a subscript in another table or file. That way, you could perform some specific initialization task or duplicate related items if you needed to.

TIP When you create a new record or duplicate an existing record, the record is added to the end of the table. However, if the records are sorted at the time the record is added and committed, the new record appears after the final item matching the currently selected record.

Since that sounds a little complicated, let me give you an example. Imagine the records are sorted by last name, and among the records you have a number of people with the last name Smith. If the first Smith record is selected and you add a new Smith record, it will appear after the last Smith record in the list. When the records are unsorted again, any new records will appear at the end of the table in creation order.

One further subtlety is that regardless of how records appear because of a found set or a sort, all new records are actually added to the end of the existing records in the table. That means that by unsorting the records, you can always spot any new records because they'll be at the end of the list.

Selecting the Record

I already showed you how to get to a record in the found set by clicking pages of the Book in the Status toolbar. There are a few other ways to move among records.

One such method also has to do with the Book. Notice the number to the right of the Book that is circled in Figure 5-1. In Browse mode, this is called the Current record number. If you click on it, the number will become highlighted, and you can type in a different number. When you press the Enter or Return key, FileMaker will go to that record. A second keep-your-hands-on-the-keyboard way to do the same thing is to press the Esc key to highlight the number, type a new number, and press Enter or Return. (The Esc key only takes you to the record number box if the cursor is out of all fields first. If the cursor is in a field, simply press the Enter key first.) If you type a number larger than the current found set, FileMaker takes you to the last record. I often type a string of ones to go to the last record.

Figure 5-1
Status toolbar showing the current record number with a circle around it.

NOTE In Preview mode, the number next to the Book is called the Current page number. In Find mode, it's the Current request number, and in Layout mode, it's the Current layout number.

The "Current record bar," a narrow vertical black line located at the very left edge of the window, indicates the currently selected record. This is most obvious when you choose View as List or View as Table. To demonstrate how this works, look at our file, and choose View, View as List. Go to the first record using the technique I just described, and click in the NameFirst field.

At the left edge of the page, you can see the Current record bar. It appears in Figure 5-2 surrounded with a rounded rectangle.

If you use the scroll bar on the right to move to the third record, you'll see the Current record bar is gone. If you click in any of the fields in that record, the bar appears on the left to indicate that it is now the current record. This is important because you can be viewing a record that is not the current record. If you then press Tab, thinking you are editing the record you were viewing, the screen will snap to the true current record, and you'll end up editing the wrong record. You can always be sure you're editing the record you're viewing by clicking into it. To return our file to the way it was, choose View, View as Form.

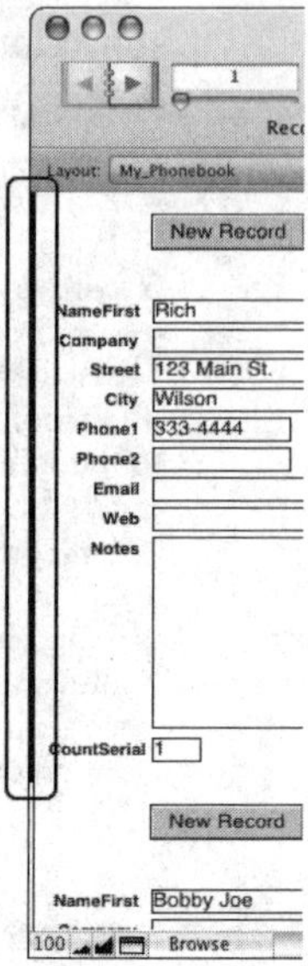

Figure 5-2
The Current record bar outlined with a rounded rectangle.

Let's look at another example. Open up the Contact Management file. Add a few records to the table and switch to the Record List layout from the drop-down. Make sure you have more than one record showing. If not, choose Records, Show All Records. It's a lot easier to see the Current record bar here. If you click on the red triangle, FileMaker will take you back to the Form layout and show you the name you clicked on. Switching to a list like that is a great technique for finding the record that you want to view in detail from a group. You might be working in a table that has thousands of entries and want to do a find for anyone with the name Jim. Scrolling through a list of records in the Form layout could take a long time. By switching to the List layout as shown in Figure 5-3, you can find the person you want much more quickly.

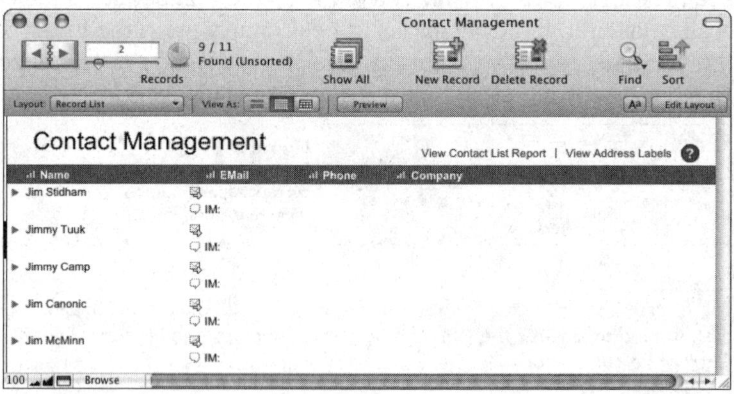

Figure 5-3
List view of a database showing a number of entries with the first name Jim. Clicking on the arrow icon to the left of the entry switches to the Form layout, where the details of Jim's record are available.

A couple other items of interest: When you view the list and someone has an e-mail address (which would show up under the mailing address), clicking on the envelope icon runs a script that begins an e-mail to that person. When you're back at the form, you'll see that envelope next to the e-mail address that performs the same function.

The final method to get to a specific record is to use a script.

1. Choose **Scripts**, **Manage Scripts** and create a script called **Go to Record.**
2. Double-click **Go to Record/Request/Page** from the Navigation heading.
3. Look at the choices available to you in the Specify pop-up in the Options area in Figure 5-4. Choose the **By Calculation** option. When the Specify Calculation window appears, as shown in Figure 5-5, type **0** (zero) in the empty box in the lower portion of the window.

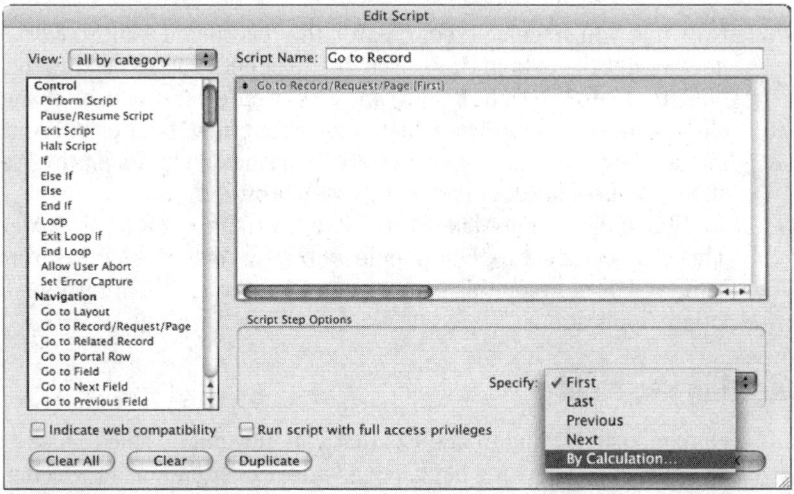

Figure 5-4
The Edit Script window showing the choices from the Specify pop-up for the Go to Record/Request/Page script step.

4. Click **OK**. Now click the **Close** button, **Save**, then **Close** again to take you back to the screen in which you are viewing records as a list.

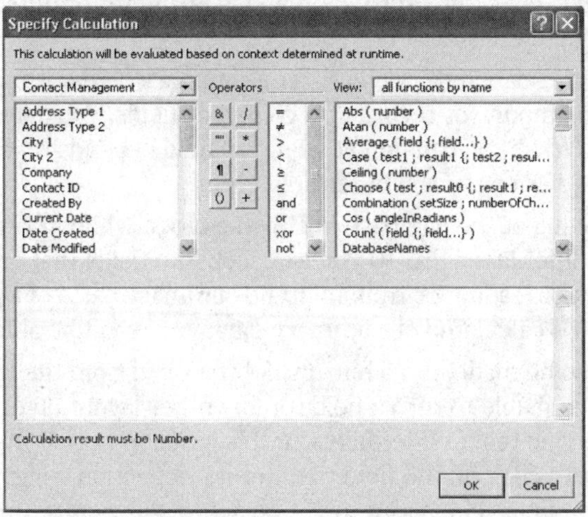

Figure 5-5
The Specify Calculation window.

5. Choose the script from the Scripts menu. Type in the number of the record you want to go to, then click **OK** or press Enter or Return, and you're there. You can make a button for that if you want. It won't be very helpful in your My_Phonebook file because you just created the script in the Contact Management file. We'll be adding a feature like this in our file later.

Adding Data

Now that you've selected or created the record you want to work with, you need to get the data in there. You or the people you're making the file for need to get to the right field(s) and either enter new data or change what's already in there. Here we'll be talking about how to enter information directly into a FileMaker file. In Chapter 20, "Sharing Your Data on the Web," I'll show you how to enter data with a web browser.

Starting with FileMaker Pro 6.0, you can import a whole folder of files. This can be a great tool for people who want to store pictures from a digital camera. For more on this feature, see Chapter 21, "Sharing Your Data with Other Applications."

Selecting the Field

One important thing to know is that you may not be able to make entries into all fields. The following list gives a variety of situations in which a field is not accessible.

- If you didn't set up the database, some fields may be locked through validation at the Manage Database level to prevent change (Manage Database, Fields, Options, Validation tab).
- They can also be locked at the Field Format level by having the "Allow entry into field" check box turned off. (This is different from locking the field in place on the layout.)
- You cannot enter data into calculation or summary fields. And, although you can paste, import, or record into container fields, you cannot type data in them. What you can do with a global field depends on how it's been formatted as one of the other field types.
- If you are looking at the database in Browse mode while in List view, starting with FileMaker Pro 10 you can click into fields that are in the header, footer, or leading or trailing grand summary parts of the layout. Of course, if it's calculated or summary data, you won't be able to alter it.
- A field can also be made into a button and removed from the tab order on the layout. Being able to turn a field (or any other layout object) into a button is a terrific tool in FileMaker. In this case, you could make it so that when users click on the field to enter it, that action triggers a script attached to the field. The script might be set to allow entry only under certain conditions, such as who the user is.

- One final way that fields can be made inaccessible or read-only is through the use of access privileges. Individual fields can be restricted on a per-layout basis.

As you can see, there are plenty of paths to follow in troubleshooting why a field seems to be frustratingly unalterable. On the other hand, each of these limitations can be used as a tool for various purposes, including preventing accidental alteration of your data.

Well, that takes care of why you may not be able to get into a field. Now let's talk about how you *can* get into a field. Yes, you can click on it, but let's look at the more conventional ways.

Using Tab Order

In the early days of computing, the only way to get from field to field was to use the Tab and arrow keys. Then Douglas Engelbart invented the mouse. There are a lot of newcomers who think the only way to get around a screen is with the mouse. But that ends up being a pretty inefficient way to enter data. You don't want to take your hands off the keyboard every time you need to get to another field. That's where the tab order comes in.

Remember when we first looked at the Contact Management file? Tabbing through the record would be a little awkward if you went from First Name to Image to Last Name. It just wouldn't make sense. This is where the Set Tab Order dialog comes in, and there have been significant changes in how this works over older versions. If it's not still open from the last exercise, open Contact Management now.

1. Go to Layout mode, and choose **Layouts, Set Tab Order**. Tab arrows will appear on the layout, as shown in Figure 5-6. You'll also see the Set Tab Order dialog (shown with both pop-up lists open in Figure 5-7) in the foreground, which you can move around if it covers up some of the fields.

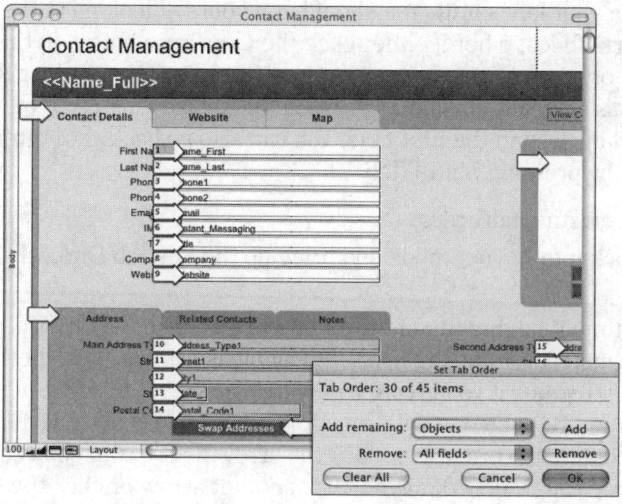

Figure 5-6
The Contact Management file open in Layout view with the tab arrows on the layout in the background.

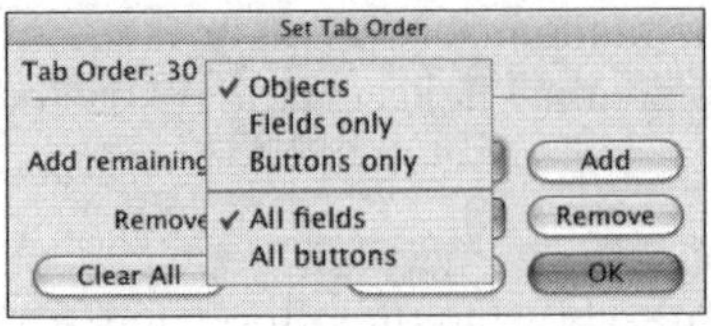

Figure 5-7
The pop-ups next to Add remaining and Remove let you choose the tab order from objects, fields, buttons, all fields, or all buttons. (Both pop-ups are expanded here for illustration only.)

Notice that you can add fields, objects, or buttons and remove all fields or all buttons. Yes, buttons can be included in the tab order. Once you've tabbed to a button, simply press **Enter** or **Return** and the script runs. Since tab controls are essentially non-scriptable buttons, they too can be part of the tab order. You'll see a tab control at the bottom of the Form view layout. The leftmost tab reads "Address." (Tab controls are discussed in detail in Chapter 17.)

Notice that arrows pointing to the right indicate fields and arrows pointing to the left indicate buttons.

2. Click the pop-up list next to **Remove** to see that you can remove the tab order associated with either all fields or all buttons. For this demo, select **All fields** and click the **Remove** button to clear the numbers from the arrows.
3. Then simply click on the blank arrows in the order you choose. You can even leave out some fields. For example, you would probably want to leave out the Image field. Before you leave here, click the **View Contact List Report** text (which is actually a button) near the upper-right corner of the layout. When you're done, click **OK**.
4. Now go to Browse mode and tab through the record. When you get to the last field and press **Tab** again, FileMaker will highlight the **View Contact List Report** button. (It might take a minute since you'll have to tab through all the visible fields before you get to the button.) Press the **Return** key (or Windows users press the Enter key on the main alpha part of your keyboard). You should find yourself looking at the List Report. To leave here, either click the **Continue** button in the upper right, or press Enter or Return. Once the View Contact List Report button was selected, if you had pressed the Tab key instead, you would have ended up back in the first field. You can also go backward through the tab order by pressing Shift+Tab.

To edit an existing tab order:

1. Go back into Layout mode and bring up the Set Tab Order dialog box again.
2. This time type directly in the arrows and change the order of just a few fields instead of starting over with all blank arrows. This method would be a bit tedious if you create a new field and want to add it high up in the tab order. But starting with FileMaker 10, you can add a layout object into the existing tab order. Just click the arrow next to the object and type the number you want. When you click another arrow or click the OK button,

the object that had that number previously will advance along with all other objects with greater numbers. Conversely, if you remove a number from the arrow, all numbers will fall back once you click the OK button. Previously you had to renumber every object manually. This is a welcome improvement.

3. Click in the **View Contact List Report** button arrow near the top of the layout and remove the number there. Click **OK**, go back to Browse mode, and check your work.

If things get really messed up while you're still editing (Oops! Too late now. I already told you to click OK.), you can just click the Cancel button and FileMaker returns the tab order to what it was before you started. And don't forget, you can always choose Layout, Revert Layout to return the tab order to what it was even after you've left the dialog. The default tab order is to start numbering from the upper left and move through the fields from left to right and top to bottom — like reading a book in English.

The other part to address here is the pop-up list next to "Add remaining" in the Set Tab Order dialog. Your choices are Objects, Fields only, and Buttons only. After making your selection, click the Add button. You can play around here all you want and not mess anything up as long as you click Cancel before leaving.

Oddly, if you've removed the tab order for both buttons and fields, any tab controls hold onto their tab order number and have to be emptied manually. I say "oddly" because a tab control seems like a layout object to me. The only reason this matters is that the tab numbers won't start over from 1 until all the tab numbers are cleared.

You can view items hidden behind the tab control area by clicking the tabs themselves (Related Contacts and Notes). When you choose to add all fields or all objects, these hidden fields will be included. The top of the Set Tab Order dialog shows how many items are included. If more show than what you can see, it's possible that they're behind the tabs of the tab control.

NOTE For any of you acquainted with previous versions of FileMaker, there used to be a dialog that came up when you closed the Set Tab Order dialog, bugging you that some fields were omitted from the tab order. You won't see that anymore. Will you miss it? I say good riddance!

TIP If you have fields that are close together, the tab arrows may overlap so you can't get to them. Go to the lower-left corner of the window and click the Zoom In tool. (See Figure 5-8.) It allows you to magnify the layout until you can see enough detail to get to the arrows you need. When you're done, click the Zoom Out tool or click the number in the lower-left corner to revert to 100. The Zoom tools are available in all modes.

Occasionally fields will be too close to each other to work with even at 400% magnification. In that case, I will move a field up or down 10 clicks so I can see the arrows that overlap. After setting the tab order, I move the field back into place.

Part 2

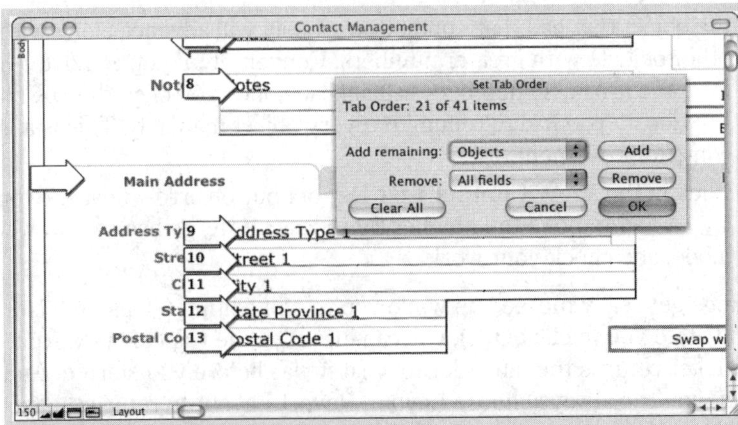

Figure 5-8
Layout mode showing how using the Zoom In tool gives better access to overlapping tab arrows.

Data Entry Shortcuts

You already know how to enter data using your keyboard. But after the thrill wears off (sometime in the first five minutes) you'll need better, more accurate, and faster ways to fill up those fields. One great shortcut is not to have to enter any data at all in some fields. You do this by using predefined information and lookups as part of the field definition. I'll talk more about that in Chapter 10, "Keeping Your Data Clean and Neat."

Insert

Current Date — Go into My_Phonebook, be sure you're in Browse mode, and highlight the date in the CreationDate field. Now choose Insert, Current Date. Notice the key combination in case you might need to place today's date often. Use Command+– (Macintosh — that's Command and the minus sign) or Ctrl+– (Windows). Do the same with the CreationTime field except use the Current Time option from the menu. We'll show you a drop-down calendar in a few minutes.

Current User Name — Since we know that the Web field is empty, click on it and choose Insert, Current User Name. What pops in there will depend on your Preferences settings. If nothing appears, you can investigate further by choosing FileMaker Pro (Macintosh) or Edit (Windows), then Preferences, Application and looking in the General tab under User Name.

NOTE Let's say that several people in a company have access to the database and can enter and change information. The database owners sometimes ask developers to provide ways to identify the person who adds or changes information. It's usually not intended as a way to place blame for incorrect information, but to determine if further training with the program is needed. Developers use the Current User Name field, which goes to the computer of the person making changes and fills in that person's name in the field. However, the Current User Name field cannot be relied on completely, because it collects the name each time the record is touched. If three people made changes to a record within minutes of each other, the name of the person who touched the record last would appear.

TIP Triple-clicking in a field selects the current line. Since one line is all there is in a time, date, or number field, you select the entire contents. You can select the current paragraph of a multi-line text field by clicking four times. Clicking five times selects the entire contents of the field.

From Index — Click in the NameFirst field and choose Insert, From Index. FileMaker brings up a window with a list of all the values that are currently in any of the records in that field. If you click the "Show individual words" check box near the bottom, it does just that. To choose one of the items, double-click it, or highlight it and click OK. You can get to items in the list by typing one or more letters. You can also move among items in the list by using the up and down arrows on your keyboard.

NOTE FileMaker keeps indexes of the field contents of your files. By using Insert, From Index, you can see what the index of a specific field looks like. In some cases, indexing may be turned off for individual fields. The indexing system follows certain rules that may limit how many words or characters of a field are indexed. To find out more about using FileMaker's indexing system, see Chapter 10.

From Last Visited Record — If you're entering a lot of data, chances are you'll have a number of records in a row with information that will be the same from one record to the next. You can create a new record and type any information that is different in field after field. Then when you get to the field where the data was the same in the last record, use Insert, From Last Visited Record. To test this:

1. Go to the first record in the table.
2. Click in the **NameFirst** field.
3. Now go to the next record. If the cursor is not already there, move it into the NameFirst field.
4. Choose **Insert**, **From Last Visited Record**, or you can just press Command+' (Macintosh) or Ctrl+' (Windows). Memorize this key combination because it's another one you may use quite often. If you want to get the original name back, press **Command+z** (Macintosh) or **Ctrl+z** (Windows).

Copy and Paste

If there's a lot of data in one field to transfer from one record to another or even from one application to another, you can use copy and paste. To do this:

1. Highlight the data you need, and choose **Edit**, **Copy** to place it on the clipboard.
2. Go to the field where you want the data to end up, and choose **Edit**, **Paste**. Don't forget these keyboard shortcuts for copy (Command+C for Macintosh and Ctrl+C for Windows) and paste (Command+V for Macintosh and Ctrl+V for Windows).

Remember that you have to work within the limits of the various field types. For instance, you can't paste "Rich" into a date field, but you can copy a date into a text field.

Drag-and-Drop

Another choice for moving data is to use the drag-and-drop feature. To turn that option on and use it:

1. Choose **FileMaker Pro** (Macintosh) or **Edit** (Windows), then **Preferences, General**.
2. Click the check box for **Allow drag and drop text selection** and click **OK**.
3. In Browse mode, highlight some text.
4. Click and drag the text to another field.

I often find that I need to move data out of one field into another. An example might be when I'm looking at a list and I want to move the name of a city into a group of records. Rather than use cut and paste, I highlight the data I'm moving and drag it to the field in the other records. The data stays highlighted in the original record, and I can continue to return to the original and drag as many copies as I need. To clear out the original, since it's still highlighted, all I have to do is press the Delete key.

You can also effectively move data between two files (or two windows of tables in the same file) by positioning them next to each other on the screen so that the source field and the target field are both within view. Try using the drag-and-drop operation with two fields on the same layout.

You can also use the drag-and-drop feature between applications on both Macintosh and Windows. For example, if you have an e-mail from a client open and you can see a FileMaker field, you can just highlight the text in the e-mail window and drag it into the FileMaker field.

On the Macintosh, you can also use clipping files. Clipping files are a big advantage if you need a temporary drop spot as you're moving data between records or applications. Just drag some data off to the desktop, and drag it back on when you find the right field. They also come in handy in Layout mode for moving fields and other layout objects around, either individually or as a group.

Getting items into container fields will be discussed later in this chapter. Another great feature is the ability to import data from other files and applications, which I'll show you in Chapters 21 and 23.

Using Value Lists

Value lists are great tools for reducing the possibility of misspelled words and providing faster data entry. It will become obvious that this works best when you have a field that will use the same group of data over and over. There are five types of value lists provided by FileMaker:

- Drop-down list
- Pop-up menu
- Check box set
- Radio button set
- Drop-down calendar

FileMaker also gives you three ways to create a value list:

- In Layout mode, by selecting a field and choosing Format, Field/Control, Setup.
  a. Select one of the value list options.
  b. Click on the drop-down menu next to "Display values from."
  c. Select Manage Value List.
  d. At the Manage Value List window, click on New.
  e. At the Edit Value List window, give your value list a meaningful name.
  f. Make sure that the radio button next to "Use custom values" is selected, and begin filling in the appropriate information in the box underneath.
  g. Click OK three times to return to your layout.
- In any mode, by choosing File, Manage Value Lists. This takes you to the Manage Value List window. See above for the process.
- In any mode, by choosing Manage Database, selecting the field, and clicking on Options.
  a. At the field Validation tab (Manage Database, Fields, Options, Validation), select the "Member of value list" check box when you're defining a field's options.
  b. Click on Manage Value Lists and continue the process.

CAUTION With check boxes and radio buttons, once you have tabbed into the field (whether it looks like you are actually in the field or not), any items already entered are actually selected as if highlighted. If you then press the Backspace or Delete key, or press Command-x (Macintosh) or Ctrl-x (Windows), you will delete the entire contents of the field. Yikes!

There are many subtleties and possibilities for value lists, and to cover them all would require more than one chapter. However, let me at least expose you to some of the possibilities by saying that value lists include the ability to create a list based on:

- A fixed list you type yourself when you create the value list
- A conditional value list that uses a relationship to generate the values
- A value list from another file
- Data that is already entered in a field
- Values that are not currently in the list but can be added as you go

Of the three ways FileMaker gives you to create a value list, the one I use the most is in Layout mode. Let's create a value list now:

1. Go into the My_Phonebook file and go to Layout mode.
2. Click on the **AddrState** field and choose **Format**, **Field/Control**, **Setup**. You'll see the window in Figure 5-9.

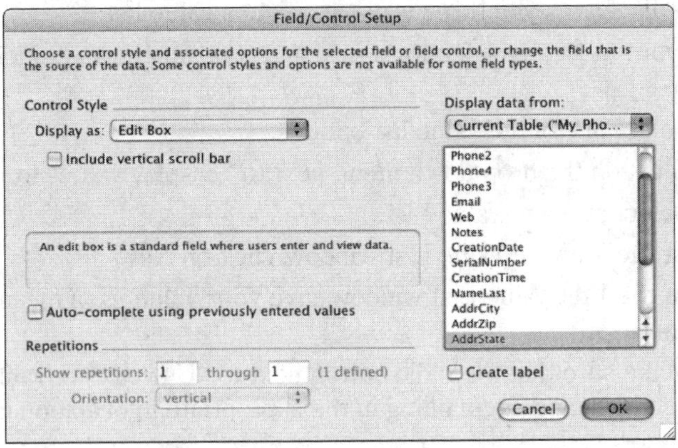

Figure 5-9
The Field/Control Setup window.

3. Click the drop-down next to "Display as" and choose **Drop-down List.** You'll notice the window now has some new choices (which are not shown in Figure 5-9). Click on **<No Lists Defined>** and select **Manage Value Lists** from the drop-down next to "Display values from." (After the first list has been created, when you want to select a list from the drop-down you will either see <unknown> or a list that has already been selected.)
4. When the next window, Manage Value List for "My_Phonebook," appears, click the **New** button.
5. You will see an Edit Value List window that looks something like Figure 5-10. In the area next to Value List Name, type **State**.

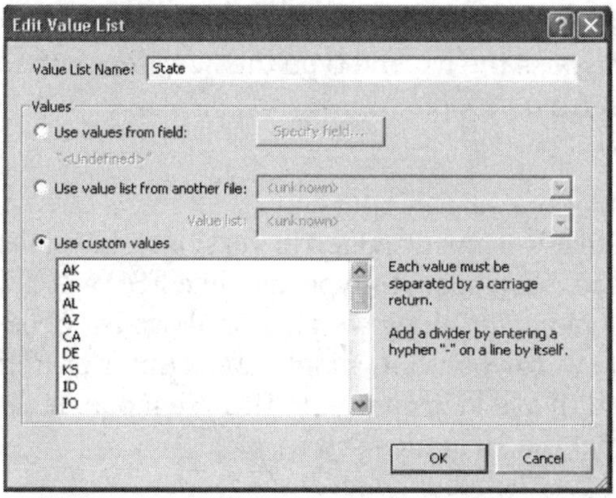

Figure 5-10
The Edit Value List window showing the value list called State.

6. Make sure that **Use custom values** is selected, and begin entering abbreviations for a few states in the box below. (Look at the directions to the right of the custom values box.)
7. Click **OK** three times, and you are back at the layout in My_Phonebook.

Let's say that you forgot to add Vermont and you want to edit your list.

1. Go back into Layout mode, right-click on the **AddrState** field, and choose **Field/Control Setup**. (Yes, this is a different way to bring up the window. Also notice the shortcut key combo.) Once again, you'll see the window in Figure 5-9.
2. This time, check the **Include 'Edit...' to allow editing of value list** box. (This check box is only visible once you have selected a value list.)
3. Go back to Browse mode. Click on **State**, and when the drop-down menu appears with your list of states, you'll see that the final option is Edit. When you click on **Edit**, you'll be taken to a screen called Edit Value List State.
4. Click in the box next to the final state you have listed, press **Enter** or **Return**, and add **VT** to your listing. Click **OK**.

For an easier way to build the list, read on.

1. Choose **File, Manage Value Lists** and double-click on the **State** value list.
2. Click the radio button next to **Use values from field.**
3. In the next window, Specify Fields for Value List, you must select the file from which to select your field. To do that, click **<unknown>** under "Use values from first field." The first item should be My_Phonebook. When you click on **My_Phonebook**, you see a list of all the fields available. Select **AddrState**. Click **OK** three times.
4. Click in the **State** field. FileMaker shows you a list that represents the states that are already in the file. Backspace over the state that's in the field and type **VT**. Click in the field again and you've changed the value list.

This way, the list builds as your file does. If an item isn't in the drop-down list, just press Esc to dismiss the list and type the new item into the field. It will be added to the list from now on.

Auto-Complete[8]

This is a great feature that was finally added in version 8. In some programs this is called "type ahead." You begin to type and, like ESP, words fill in that might be what you're looking for, along with a drop-down list of other alternatives. Once you see the word you want, simply press Enter or Return. It works in Find mode and (if a field is empty) in Browse mode. It also works on global fields despite what the Help files say.

Let's test it in the My_Phonebook file.

1. Enter Layout mode and double-click the **NameFirst** field. Yes, this is yet another way to bring up the Field/Control Setup window.
2. In the lower-left corner of the window, check the box next to **Auto-complete using previously entered values**. Leave the "Display as" drop-down list set to **Edit Box.**
3. Click **OK** and start a find.
4. Type **r** in the field labeled First Name. You should see both Rich and Richard. You could create a few more records with names that start with r and see how the feature works.

There are a number of subtleties to this area. It's not always convenient to have a drop-down list appear when setting up a field for auto-complete.

1. Go back into Layout mode and double-click **NameFirst**.
2. In the Field/Control Setup window, choose **Drop-down List** next to "Display as." Notice the window has changed. Over on the right is a list of fields in the current table. You can change what field is on the layout from here. This Field/Control Setup window actually combines the functions of a couple other windows into one neat place.
3. Next to "Display values from," click on **<unknown>**, and select **Manage Value Lists.**
4. Click the **New** button and call this value list **First Names.**
5. Click the radio button next to **Use values from field**. Click **<unknown>** at the top of the left column and choose **My_Phonebook.** Click **NameFirst** in the list.
6. Click **OK** three times. Make sure there's a check mark next to "Auto-complete using value list." Add a check mark next to **Include arrow to show and hide list**. It's just under the name of the value list.
7. Click **OK** once more and go to Browse mode.
8. Start a find, click in the field labeled **First Name**, and type **r**. Rich should auto-complete without the drop-down list appearing.
9. Now click the arrow at the right edge of the field to reveal the list.

A lot of professional programs use that format. For my money, the value of auto-complete is the ability to reduce all that mouse clicking. I'm not sure how this would be more useful. But if you want it, there it is. If you don't want your file set up this way, go back to Layout mode, change the field back to an edit box, and uncheck the Auto-complete box.

Oh, and one more thing (actually there is a lot more you can find in the Help files), if you use a feature that displays value lists from a second field (as in step 5), auto-complete won't work.

Calendar Drop-down[8]

Nothing could be more intuitive for date entry than clicking on a calendar. Starting in FileMaker 8 we have the choice to attach a calendar to date fields. Third-party companies have been providing add-ons to FileMaker for some time to accomplish this. Looks like they're out of business. Guess you gotta watch it when you come up with a good idea. Somebody might just take it for their own!

1. In the My_Phonebook file, go to Layout mode and double-click the **CreationDate** field.
2. In the Field/Control Setup window, next to "Display as," select **Drop-down Calendar**. Notice that there is a check box next to "Include icon to show and hide calendar." You can try that out on your own if you like; again, that requires an extra click to get the calendar to display. Leave it unchecked for now.
3. Click **OK** and go to Browse mode. Click in the **CreationDate** field and the calendar magically appears!
4. Click on some other date. Try the various arrows on the calendar: up, down, left, right. Now try the arrow keys on your keyboard.

In the case of the CreationDate field, you probably wouldn't want people changing that date. Since it's historical information, the field should probably be protected from modification at the field level. This is just a quick demo, but you can see that it's a pretty nice tool. And it works in Find mode, too. Too bad you can't use it to easily get a date range. Maybe in the next version.

Using Container Fields

Depending on what type of work you intend to do, container fields can be the answer to some of your needs. For example, you can store employee or product photos, and build training files that include multimedia presentations. You can also store QuickTime movies and PDF files. In fact, you can store *any* kind of file in a container field — including other FileMaker files. I think of FileMaker as the ultimate document management application.

Insert QuickTime

The following assumes you have a QuickTime movie, audio file, PDF, or any other type of supported media file on your computer and that you have QuickTime installed. If you have some other file type, just use one of the other Insert choices.

1. In our My_Phonebook file, go to Browse mode and click on the **Pic** field.
2. Choose **Insert, QuickTime.** (If QuickTime is not installed, the QuickTime menu option will be gray.)
3. Find the file you want to place in the field by searching through your files and folders. It's best to keep the items in the same folder as the FileMaker file that will be using them. If it's a movie, once it's in your file, you will see the first frame.
4. Click on the picture to pop out the control bar, and use the controls to play the movie.

You can use the same controls to view a PDF file. The only difference is you don't want to click the Play button since it will flip through the pages too quickly for reading. Instead, use the arrows to go forward and back one page at a time. Of course you will need to change the size of the field so you can read the document. You'll need to have Adobe Reader on your computer to read the PDFs. It's a free download.

Other file types cannot be viewed from within FileMaker and need to be exported first. You could also write a script that will simply open the file. A script like that is a bit complicated, but it can definitely be done. I won't include it here in this book, but if you send me an e-mail, I'll put it on my web site (DataDesignPros.com).

NOTE When any file is stored by reference, the reference refers to the path relative to the machine from which the file was inserted. That means that other users may have some difficulty finding your file unless you plan ahead. If all users are on the same platform (Mac or Windows), you would just make sure the files are on a server that everyone has access to and that the file is inserted pointing to that location. There is more complexity to this issue if you are working with both Mac and Windows users who need to access the file. My solution would be to use two separate fields, one to hold the path for Mac users and a separate one for Windows users.

There are two basic ways to handle FileMaker document storage: 1) Importing a document into a Container field, and 2) Importing a reference to a document into a Container field. Option 1 works best in cross-platform environments, but the FileMaker file that stores the docs can get quite bloated depending on the resolution and quantity of the scans. Option 2 offers faster access to the documents but is much more difficult to implement in a Mac/Windows environment. There doesn't seem to be a perfect solution.

Insert Picture

Insert Picture works similarly to inserting a QuickTime movie, except the picture formats that are available are different on the Macintosh and Windows machines. See Figures 5-11 and 5-12. To keep the size of your FileMaker file down, you can click the check box next to "Store only a reference to the file." This is often the better choice since the size of your file expands when you actually store the images. However, if someone removes the file from the referenced location, it will no longer show in the field.

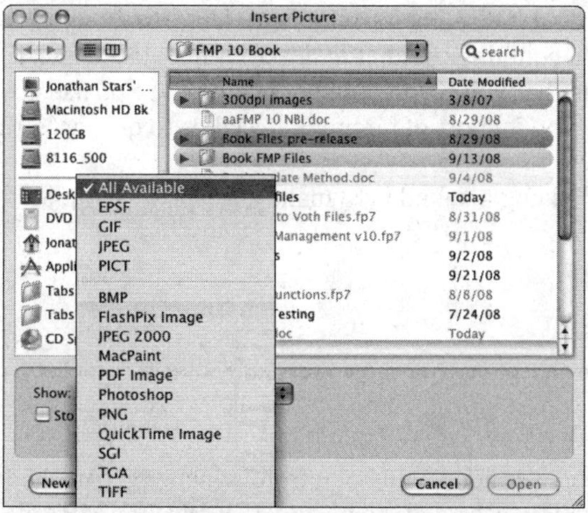

Figure 5-11 The Insert Picture window on the Macintosh showing the pop-up list of acceptable image file formats currently available.

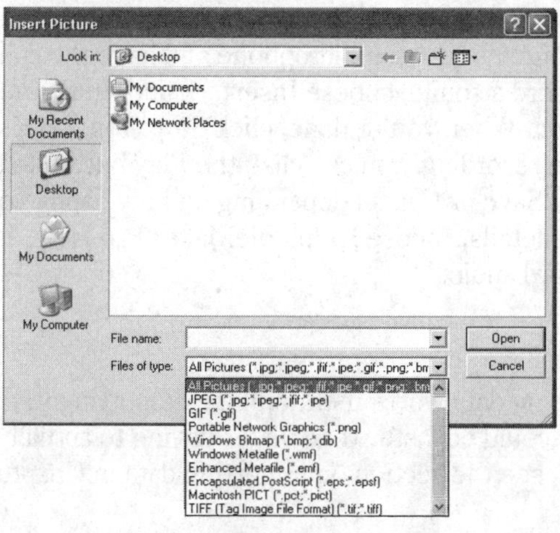

Figure 5-12 The Insert Picture window on a Windows computer showing the pop-up list of acceptable image file formats currently available. The "Store only a reference to the file" check box is not visible because it's under the pop-up list.

1. Go to Browse mode and click on the **Pic** field.
2. Choose **Insert**, **Picture.**
3. Find the file you want to place in the field by searching through your files and folders. As with movies, it's best to keep the items in the same folder as the FileMaker file that will be using them.
4. If your picture doesn't look right, go to Layout mode. Select the **Pic** field, then click **Format**, **Graphic** and either **Reduce** or **Enlarge.** Go back to Browse mode to see if it looks right. The field that holds the graphic must be formatted correctly. One option is the "Maintain original proportions" check box, which will make the image look right regardless of the

size. To learn more about formatting graphics, go to Chapter 17, "Designing Your Screen Layouts."

Insert Sound

There are three ways to get a sound into your files: by copying and pasting it, using a script, or recording it directly into the field. Unfortunately, if you copy and paste a sound into a container field, it is not driven by the QuickTime application. That means that when you double-click on the Speaker icon to make it play, you can't stop it short of forcing FileMaker to quit or letting the sound play to the end.

My favorite way of adding a sound is to make a script with the following steps:

```
Go to Field ["Pic"]
Insert QuickTime []
```

NOTE You need to have QuickTime installed on your computer in order for the previous script to work.

When you run the script, a window will open from which you can choose the file you want to import. The file needs to be an AIFF, WAV, or MP3 file.

Finally, you can record a sound directly into the field. Of course, you must be connected to a sound source such as a microphone and have the computer configured properly. To record a sound, choose Insert, Sound. In the next window, click the Record button. When you're done, click Stop. You can also choose to Pause during the recording. You can click the Play button to listen to the recording, then click Save or Cancel depending on how happy you are with the results. For more details, choose Help, FileMaker Pro Help. In the search field, look for "Record audio."

Importing Data

One other method of entering data worth mentioning is importing it. After all, what method of data entry could be faster than never having to actually type anything at all? For details, see the section on importing data in Chapter 23, "Backup and Recovery."

Changing Data

There are various ways you might want to change your data. Of course, FileMaker provides a number of methods for making those changes.

Highlighting

I often want to call attention to information I have in a text field. To do so, highlight the text, choose Format, Text Color, and make a selection. You can also choose Font, Font size, Style, etc. This process overrides the formatting of the field chosen in Layout mode. The new format stays with every occurrence of that field on any other layout, table, and even in other files that have a relationship to this one. You can also use these characteristics to call attention to digits in a number field. You can even pass that formatting on to a calculation field as long as the result of the calculation is text.

Spellchecking

FileMaker has a very helpful spell checker. I won't go into all its capabilities, but let's take a quick look. Enter some text into a notes field and highlight it. Then choose Edit, Spelling, Check Selection.

You can also have the checker examine the whole record, a set of records, or all text on a layout when you're in Layout mode. On faster machines, you can have your spelling checked as you type. Choose File, File Options and click the Spelling tab.

To select a specific dictionary, go the Edit menu and choose Spelling, Select Dictionaries. The US English Medical dictionary is available in my program. There is also a legal dictionary available, and you can create your own. I tell FileMaker to use the standard English and my own user dictionaries. That way, any words or proper names that I use a lot don't keep popping up. If you have access to a text file with a specialized set of words, you can choose Edit, Spelling, Edit User Dictionary and click the Import button.

Visual Spell Checker[8]

Spelling challenged? Well, maybe not you, but how about someone else in your office? Here's a feature you can turn on and off for each individual machine. I don't know why anyone would want to turn it off. Imagine! Some people find those red underlines irritating.

Type something in the Notes field in My_Phonebook. Include one or more misspelled words. If you see any of the words underlined in red, the Visual Spell Checker is on.

To turn it on and off, go to File, File Options and click the Spelling tab. Notice that you can choose "Beep on questionable spellings." To hear the beep, you'll need your computer's speakers turned up to an appropriate level. Windows users can choose to have the menu bar flash. Personally, I find the underlines enough.

Assuming you have Visual Spell Checker on and can see the red underline, Control+click (Macintosh) or right-click (Windows) on the questionable word and scroll down to Suggested Spellings. You can choose one of the suggestions, tell it to ignore the spelling, learn, or bring up the regular spell checking dialog. The learn option is especially helpful for people in professions that require jargon of one type or another. Let FileMaker know you like that spelling and it won't bother you again.

FileMaker 9 introduced the Field-level Control of Visual Spell checking[9] option. Aside from the global setting for the file, you can decide which specific fields have it turned on. When you're in Layout mode, click on the Email field and choose Format, Field/Control, Behavior. Right in the middle put a check in the box next to "Do not apply visual spell-checking." Click OK, go back to Browse mode, and type something outrageous. You'll see no underline and hear no beep.

The important thing to remember here is that spell checking must be turned on for the file in order for the individual fields to be affected.

Replace Command

The Replace command is a tool I use almost every day. Let's say you decided you would rather have the serial number for all the records start at 1000 instead of 1.

1. First, choose **Records**, **Show All Records.**
2. Click in the **SerialNumber** field and choose **Records, Replace Field Contents.**
3. When the window shown in Figure 5-13 appears, click the radio button next to **Replace with serial numbers** and type **1000** in the "Initial value" box.

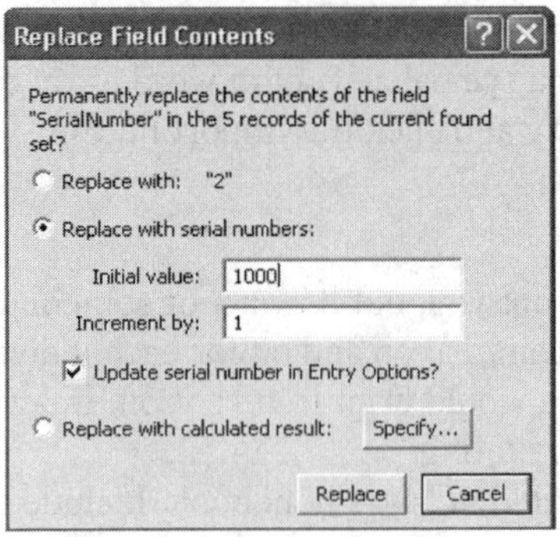

Figure 5-13 The Replace window with the "Replace with serial numbers" radio button selected and the "Update serial number in Entry Options?" box checked.

If you also choose the "Update serial number in Entry Options?" check box, FileMaker will make sure that new records you create will begin with the next available number. This check box will only be active if the field was defined for auto-enter serial numbers, as this one was. Using this option for serial numbers is highly recommended.

> **CAUTION** Be careful with the Replace command when the field you're using it in is a key field. You could easily lose all references to any related data. See Chapter 6 for more on related data.

Another use for Replace would be if you found a number of records with the same word misspelled — let's say in the City field.

1. Perform a find for all occurrences of the misspelled word.
2. Click in the field and spell the word correctly.
3. Bring up the Replace window, leave the "Replace with" radio button selected, and click **Replace.**

It is worth mentioning the last radio button in the Replace window, even though this option won't make sense until we cover calculations later in the book. The "Replace with calculated result:" option allows you to perform extremely sophisticated replacements for data that might be in a field based on calculations. You can read more about it in FileMaker Pro's Help files and in the application manual. I am very enthusiastic about this choice, and it would be worth your time to investigate it further.

You can also call the Replace command with a script.

Find/Replace

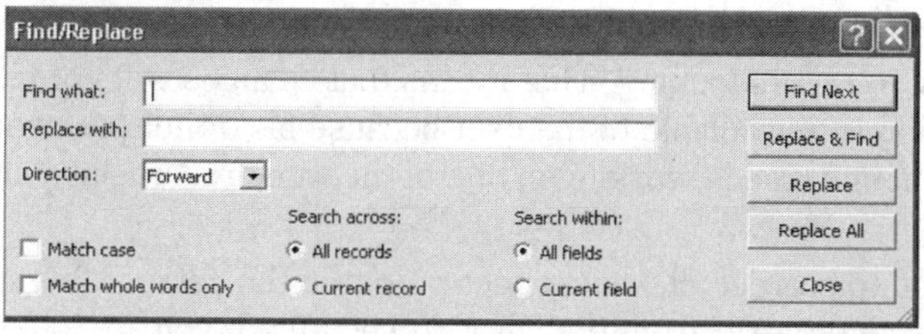

Figure 5-14 FileMaker's Find/Replace window.

Take a look at Edit, Find/Replace, Find/Replace... The window that appears, shown in Figure 5-14, should be very familiar to people who work with word processing programs. FileMaker even provides the summary dialog seen in Figure 5-15 when the replace is finished. You can use the Find/Replace window to look for specific text and make the requested changes. But there are some subtleties you will be interested in:

- You can make it work in all fields on the layout, including portal fields.
- It works on text, number, date, time, and timestamp fields, whether they are regular or formatted for global storage. (You can also have it perform the find in calculation and summary fields, but it can't perform the replace.)
- Replace will not be performed on fields formatted as radio buttons, pop-up menus, or check boxes. That's because those formats are used to restrict data entry. Bypassing that could cause problems.
- It also works in Layout mode. That means you can change text on your layouts without having to go through the tedious process of first selecting the text everywhere it might appear. You will still need to go to each layout, though.
- It can work on one record or a found set of records.
- If it is working on a found set of records, it only works on items in that found set, not on omitted items. Even though the function is called Find/Replace, you should not confuse it with FileMaker's Find mode. You can have Find/Replace perform its magic on whatever found set of records you want without messing up records you want to leave alone.
- It is scriptable. The Open Find/Replace version of it is under the Open Menu Items category. It will open the window even if you have restricted the user's access privileges from reaching that menu.

- The Perform Find/Replace script step is under the Editing category. The script creator will see the Find/Replace window in Figure 5-16 (which is very similar to the one accessible from the menu). With this step you would be able to have users enter text into a global field on a layout and control what happens next. (More on scripting in Chapter 14, "Automating Your Database with Scripts.")
- You should be certain that the user is on a layout and in the table you want him or her on before allowing access to this potentially destructive tool. It might replace text you don't want touched. And it might do that in a bunch of fields! If you do script it, be sure you consider adding the Go to Layout script step before the window appears.
- It is subject to record locking. That means that changes will not take place if a field is unavailable to the user because his or her password limits it or someone else is working in one of the same records in a shared file.
- If you intend to correct all occurrences of text in the current found set, you need to select "All" from the Direction pop-up. If you are looking at any record and the pop-up reads "Forward," the action will not correct the current record. Apparently, Forward implies "not including this record." However, when you perform the Find/Replace using the "Backward" setting, it does include the current record. This behavior does not make sense to me, but you do need to know what to expect.

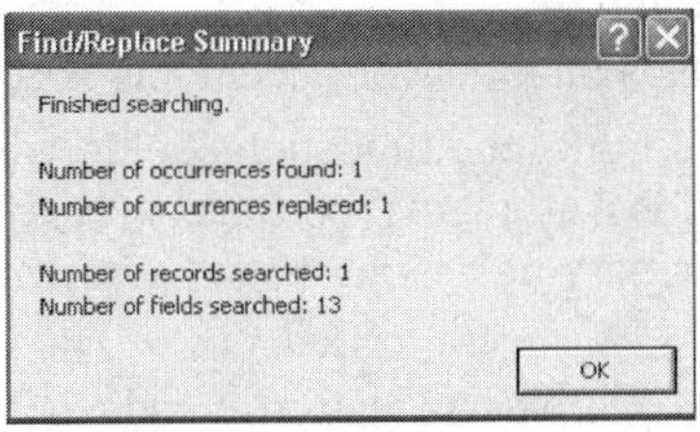

Figure 5-15
The Find/Replace Summary dialog that appears at the end of the process. This dialog will not appear when called by a script if you check the "Perform without dialog" check box.

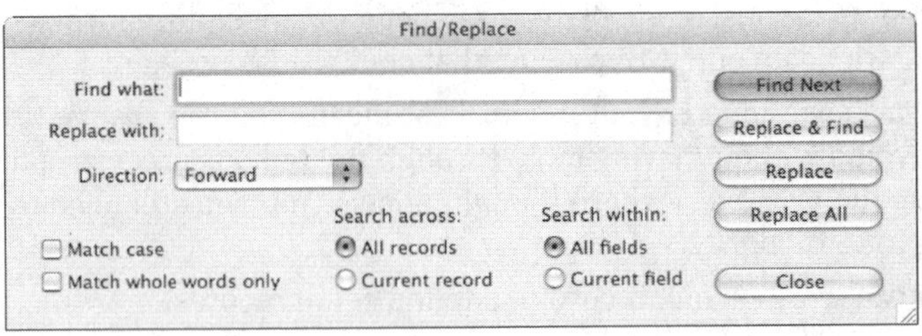

Figure 5-16
The Find/Replace window where you select various options when creating the Perform Find/Replace script step.

CAUTION Don't change data that is used as a key field in a relationship to another table or file without careful consideration. The connection to any attached records will be lost and very difficult to retrieve. You can read more about key fields in Chapter 6.

Revert Command

A tool you should really know about once you start editing your data is the Revert command. If you've gone from field to field making changes here and there without exiting this specific record, you can revert to what it was before you started editing the record. Keep in mind that if you leave Browse mode, click on the layout outside the fields, or press the Enter key, you will exit the record. Give it a try.

1. Go to the **NameFirst** field and make the name bold.
2. Now tab to or click into the **NameLast** field and make that text red.
3. Choose **Records**, **Revert**.

Pretty smooth! Just remember, once you press Enter, change modes, or click outside of the fields, you won't be able to revert.

Another time-saving technique when changing data is to use the Relookup command. You'll find it under the Records menu. I'll talk more about that when we get to the "Looked-up Value" section of Chapter 10.

Multiple Level Undo/Redo of Text[9]

Right after Revert, we need to talk about the Undo and Redo commands that were introduced in FMP9. Prior to FMP9, you could only go back one step when editing text in Browse or Layout mode. (Remember, in Layout mode you can always cancel *all* your changes by choosing Layouts, Revert Layout. But now you can use these new commands to move backward and forward when working with a block of text in Layout mode.) As long as you don't exit the field (or text block) you're in (by clicking out of the field, tabbing into another field, clicking the Enter key, going to another layout, etc.), you can use the Edit, Undo or Edit, Redo commands to move backward and forward through the changes you've made in that field.

The keyboard shortcut for Undo is Command+Z (Macintosh) or Ctrl+Z (Windows). Redo is Command+Shift+Z (Macintosh) or Ctrl+Shift+Z (Windows). The keyboard shortcuts show up in the menu if you forget what they are.

There is also an Undo/Redo script step under the Editing heading. That means you can place buttons on your layout that will do the job for you. Remember, though, that buttons don't work in Layout mode.

Of course, none of this applies to deleting one or more records. That's still the same — once they're gone, they're gone. Unless you have a backup.

Deleting Data

You have a few options open to you when it comes to getting rid of data, depending on what you're trying to do. If you want to get rid of data in an unprotected field, other than a calculation or summary field, simply highlight the data and press the Backspace or Delete key.

To delete a single record (in this example, the target record will be a blank record):

1. Choose **Records, Show All Records.**
2. Click through the records until you find a blank one. If you don't have any blank records, create one using one of the techniques I taught you.
3. When you have a blank record in front of you, look over by the Book and note how many records are in this table.
4. Choose **Records, Delete Record.** (Make sure you *do not* choose Delete Found Records!) FileMaker warns you that it's about to delete this record.
5. Click the **Delete** button. How many records are in the table now?
6. Find one of the records that has some data in it. Choose **Records, Duplicate Record.** Now you have two copies with the same information. You don't need that second record. Press **Command+E** (Macintosh) or **Ctrl+E** (Windows). You get the same delete warning. Go ahead and delete it.

To delete a group of records, choose Records, Delete All Records. A warning dialog box appears that says, "Permanently delete All -- (the dashes represent the number in the currently found set) record(s)?" Now that's a warning to pay attention to! Click the Cancel button for now. But now you know what to do if you really wanted to get rid of a batch of records.

What if you had an invoicing system with 1,000 orders that had been carefully entered over six months and somebody chose that option and clicked the Delete button? You'd better have a recent backup somewhere!

CAUTION Always be very careful when deleting records. You cannot use Undo or Revert after you confirm that you want to delete one or more records. Unless you have a copy of the file somewhere else, you're out of luck.

I have seen someone accidentally choose Delete All Records in a large file. It takes a few minutes to complete the process, so when the person realized what he had done, he pulled the computer's power plug out of the wall. Then the company went through a lengthy process to recover the files afterward and even then, some of the records were already deleted. This is not recommended because recovery may not be successful, and it definitely endangers the integrity of the file(s). But that was the only option at that point. They hadn't backed up in a couple of weeks. To revamp an old carpenter's saying, "Think twice, delete once."

Summary

In this chapter, I showed you more about creating records and ways to select a particular record. Then we looked at ways of getting into the fields, including how to create a tab order, and a number of shortcuts for inserting repetitive data into the fields. I showed you a little about placing movies, pictures, and sounds into container fields. Finally, I covered ways to change data.

Q & A

Q What if I want to allow the user to select more than one of the choices given in a drop-down list?

A You should format the field with check boxes instead of a pop-up.

Q I was working with the tab order and missed a few of the fields. How do I correct it?

A If the Set Tab Order dialog is still on the screen, just click Cancel and the tab order will revert to what it was before you started. If you've already returned to Browse mode, you can go back into the Set Tab Order dialog, and click the Clear All button. Then make a selection from the "Add remaining" drop-down and click the Add button. This won't return you to your previous tab order, but you don't have to start over from scratch either.

Workshop

Go into the Contact Management file to the Record Detail layout and enter Layout mode. Examine the text buttons in the upper-right part of the window to the left of the question mark. Double-click them one at a time. Look at how the buttons are attached to scripts.

Go to Layout mode in My_Phonebook and select the State field. Use the Field Format window and see if you can format the field using the other types of value lists. (Hint: You may have to open up the field a little larger to show all the choices.) Make six copies of the field in a clear area of the layout, one for each value list type plus one formatted without a value list. Open up the unformatted field and make choices in the different value list fields to see how it affects the plain field.

Chapter 6

Working with Related Tables — Part 1

Introduction

Now that you have some of the basics under your belt, let's move on to working with related tables. In this chapter, we'll:

- Create a file with related tables
- Look at the tools for working with relationships
- Look at how the tables are related to each other
- Examine a number of items to be aware of when working with multiple tables
- Create a portal and see how it works

This chapter and the next may be the most difficult for you. Not only will I show you the complicated topic of relationships, but I introduce a naming convention that makes table names sound like gibberish. And all this is on top of a pile of acronyms. You may need to read the chapters and do the exercises two or three times. Please don't move forward until you understand most of what is happening here. Even if it takes you a week, you'll be way ahead of the years it took me to understand all the nuances you'll get here. And try to avoid the temptation to speed up each time you start over. The idea is once you get beyond the steps, you'll begin to get a picture of how the pieces fit together. Hang in there. You can do it.

One or Many Tables?

How do you know if it's time to work with more than one table (or file)? And how do you decide which items go in which tables? As you'll see, the answers are not cut and dried. However, the next two sections should go a long way in helping you know the answers.

One Table — Flat File Design

When there seems to be a logical connection between a group of fields, those fields should probably all be in the same table. For example, in a Customers table there is only one field for customer number, one field for first name, one for last name, one for company name, etc. Your customer doesn't have two first names or three customer numbers. That means all these bits of data probably belong in the same table.

Many Tables — Relational Design

What's the difference between a file and a table? In early versions of FileMaker Pro, a table and a file were the same thing. There was only one table per file; when you created fields, they were created in that single table. You could view the data in Table view, but you also had other options about how your data looked depending on what you decided to do with your layouts.

When you developed a solution that brought together the information in several files, you linked those files with relationships, and when users opened the solution, the files opened as they were needed. The desire for convenience of having a solution open more quickly across a network and the simplification of the administration of accounts and passwords led FileMaker to develop multiple tables per file.

Starting back with FileMaker Pro 7, a file can have more than one table. Since each table is part of the same file, the entire solution opens as quickly as one file opens.

You start any database by creating a table and defining the fields for it. At this point, My_Phonebook is a file with one table in it. In this chapter, we're going to add additional tables to our file.

> **NOTE** We began by creating the file My_Phonebook. At this time the file contains only the one table of records about people with whom you have contact. That will be changing, and we will be referring to the Contact area as only one of the tables within the file.

The first thing we want to do is to change the name of the file to Business, because the tables we'll be creating in this file need a name that more clearly suggests the scope of the tables that we'll be using.

> **NOTE** I don't want you to get confused between a table and a view of a layout that looks like a table. They're not the same thing. A table is a collection of data — or fields — that relate to a subject. In the database file My_Phonebook, you collected information — name, address, and phone numbers — about people you know. If you selected Table view (View, View as Table) you would see the information you collected in a tabular format, like a spreadsheet. Each record takes up one row, and each field will be a column.

As we saw in our My_Phonebook file, customers may have more than one phone number. That situation required us to create four fields for phone numbers, and there could conceivably be more than that! Let's say someone with bad handwriting takes a message for you, and all you can read is the phone number. To find the record in your database you would have to search in four separate fields. Maybe it's time to think about creating another table. I've been to offices where they created a dues payment field for each year their members rejoined. That's another example where a separate table is probably needed.

Another reason you might want to work with a multiple-table system is for reporting. For example, in an invoicing table, you need to have a number of lines on the invoice so your customers can buy more than one item. You certainly don't want to make out a separate invoice for every single item in their shopping cart. You could create a separate field for every line on the invoice, but then it would be pretty difficult to find out how many widgets you sold in the month of May because you'd have to perform a find in each field. By moving the invoice lines to a separate table, you can get that report in short order. Every line will be a separate record that will either be part of your find or not.

You can see a pattern developing when you look at My_Phonebook and an invoicing system. Whenever you find yourself making a list of similar types of items in your database, you probably need another table. Let's create one.

Manage Your Tables

Because our file will now be home to multiple tables, we need a name that will better describe the purpose of the file. It's a good idea to think about these naming issues before you start a project.

1. Save a copy of the My_Phonebook file and name the copy **Business**. Pay attention to where you save it.
2. Close My_Phonebook and open **Business.**
3. Select **Manage Database**, **Fields** and change the name of the SerialNumber field to **ContactSerNum_pk.**

> **NOTE** The "pk" stands for primary key. Shortly we'll use "fk" as a code to represent foreign key. The codes also operate as a reminder that these fields should not be deleted or tampered with for fear that our file structure may fail. The abbreviations aren't required for building our relationships, but they are a common way developers comment the special purpose these fields serve. You can also use field comments in addition to or instead of these conventions. But you can't see the field comments when you're building relationships between tables.

When you rename a field, click on the field in the list, highlight the field name in the Field Name box, and begin typing the new name. Then click the Change button. If you highlight the field name and press Backspace or Delete, FileMaker assumes you want to create a new field. That means that after typing the changed name, the Change button will not be one of your choices.

Now start a new table called Phone in the Business file.

1. First, choose **File**, **Manage Database** and select the **Tables** tab.
2. Click the name of the **My_Phonebook** table to highlight it in the list. Click on the text in the Table Name field, change it to **Contact**, and click the **Change** button.

3. To add another table, highlight the word **Contact** in the Table Name field. Type **Phone** and click on **Create**.
4. Click the **Fields** tab, make sure the Phone table is selected from the Table pop-up, and add the following fields:

Field Name	*Type*	*Options/Comments*
ContactSerNum_fk	Number	Foreign key
Notes	Text	
Phone	Text	
Type	Text	

5. Your screen should look like Figure 6-1. When you're finished, click **OK**.

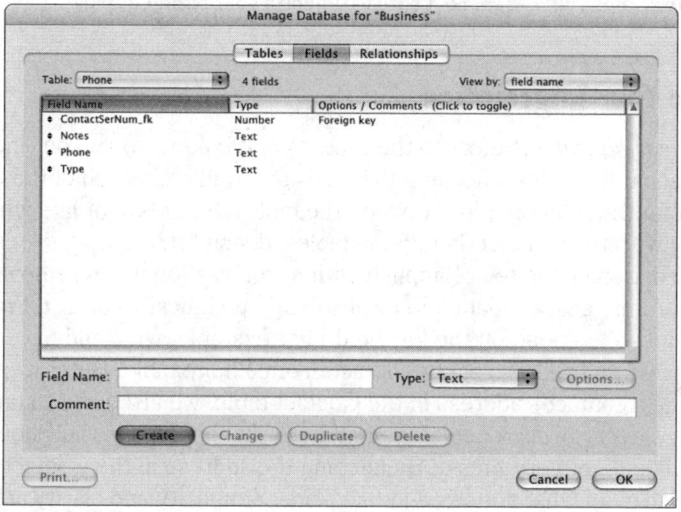

Figure 6-1
The Manage Database window's Fields tab for the Phone table. Notice the "_fk" extension and the comment indicating the foreign key field.

Go to the Layout drop-down below the Book. (See Figure 6-2.) You have two layouts: Phone and Contact. Look at the Phone layout. It doesn't matter what the layout looks like because you'll almost never be viewing the data from the Phone table. Now switch back to the Contact layout.

Figure 6-2
The Layout drop-down list showing the Contact layout selected.

Part 2

TIP Aside from having multiple tables in a file, you can have many files open at one time. You can stack them one on top of the other, or you can have files open but hidden. To hide a file, make it the frontmost window, then choose Window, Hide Window. When you open a file to a layout that displays data from a related file, the related file opens hidden (if it's not already open).

You can also choose Window, Minimize (Windows) or click the Minimize button (minus sign) in the upper-right corner of the window (Windows) or the Minimize button (yellow dot) in the upper-left corner of the window (Macintosh). On Windows computers, that has the effect of stacking a little rectangular representation of the window along the bottom of your screen. On a Mac, it will move the window to the Dock.

One of the major advantages beginning with FMP7 is that you can hide minimized windows that used to pile up at the bottom of the screen on Windows machines. On the other hand, FMP7 and later allow you to open a table in a new window. These options make it easy to organize your screen display.

Normalize Your Information

Data normalization refers to the process of breaking down your information into separate tables, choosing the fields that will be in each of the tables, and creating the relationships between the tables. Sounds a lot like what we're doing with the Contact and Phone tables, doesn't it?

What you hope to accomplish with normalization is the removal of duplicate or unnecessary data. (To be absolutely technically correct, I mean data that doesn't depend on the key field.) For example, we could have included the name and address of our contact in our Phone table. But if we need to change a contact's address in the Contact table, we also have to find and change every occurrence of their address that appears in the Phone table. That could get very messy. By keeping the address in the Contact table, you can find all of what you need in one place. Simplicity and clarity are the goals of normalization.

Determine Your Match, or Key, Fields

When you create a relationship between tables, you choose a field in each table that will compare data. These are the *match*, or *key*, fields. When there is a match in the data in the key field, FileMaker allows you to display information from any of the other fields in any records that also have a match. In Figure 6-3, you can see that more than one record in the Phone table has the same field, ContactSerNum_fk. We'll discuss how to get those records over into the Phone table in just a bit.

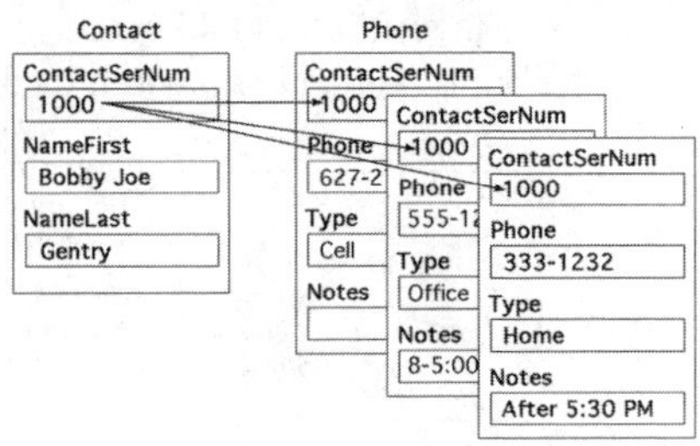

Figure 6-3
The Contact and Phone tables showing match, or key, fields. More than one record can have a match, which is the case with multiple phone numbers.

NOTE I'd like to say a little about "match fields" and "key fields" here. In versions of FileMaker previous to 7, the only kind of relationship possible between tables was when values were an exact match. Starting in FMP7, you can have unequal relationships. Using symbols like <, >, and ≠, you can tell FileMaker to show you items that are less than, greater than, or even completely unlike a value. It would seem then that the term "match field" would apply specifically to equal relationships. I think we'll see the term "key field" coming more to the forefront.

NOTE I've been teaching you to give your key fields identical names (except for the suffix) in both tables. In my quest to show you good database technique, I may be causing some confusion. You can build relationships between tables using any two fields regardless of their names. You can even use fields that have incompatible types of data. The relationships may be invalid and unusable, but you can do it. I encourage you to experiment. There have been some very exciting discoveries made when developers tried things that "couldn't be done." However, you should know good technique so that when you make decisions to go against the standard, you'll know why.

Way back when we created My_Phonebook, we created a SerialNumber field, which we've now changed to ContactSerNum_pk.

TIP Try to use the same basic* name for the key fields in both tables. For example, use InvoiceNum in both the Invoice and Invoice Line Items tables. That way, no matter which table you're in, it'll be easy to trace the relationship back.

(* I say "basic" name because I still want you to use development conventions by starting and ending the field names with other descriptive elements like _pk and _fk for the key type.)

You might think you could use a person's name or a product name as the key, and you can. But let me suggest that you save yourself a lot of the trouble I once had by not making that your primary key. To make critical relationships work, it's best if you use a unique key in one of the two tables. You want to use a field that does not contain active or volatile data. Instead, use a field that is somehow independent from the other information and something you won't be tempted to change.

For example, let's look at the Business table. What if you used a person's name as the key? If you had someone named John Smith in your table, as soon as you entered a second John Smith, the phone number of John number one would instantly appear in John number two's portal! (We'll get to portals in a minute.) And what if you had a woman who changed her name when she got married? As soon as you changed her last name in her contact record, all phone numbers in the portal would disappear!

I'm speaking from the experience of many wasted hours when I tell you that you're much better off using unique numbers right from the start. A number is a good choice because it can be made unique. Use auto-entered serial numbers (without leading zeros), and protect them against modification. In fact, go into Manage Database in the Contact table and double-click the ContactSerNum_pk field. Choose Options, and on the Auto-Enter tab, click the box next to "Prohibit modification of value" to check it. That doesn't mean that you can't create other relationships between tables based on information in other fields. It's just that your primary relationship should use that unique (and unmodifiable) serial number as your key.

Introducing "Anchor-Buoy" Relationship Design

Before we get very far along, I need to bring in elements from a relationship development standard called "anchor-buoy." As explained in some detail in Appendix A, anchor-buoy is a method of organizing the relationships graph so that, as a solution gets more complex, you'll usually know where to go to solve a problem that has to do with relationships. The anchor-buoy standard also makes it much easier to work in various dialogs because table occurrence names group together logically.

The idea is that every layout will be connected to a main anchor table occurrence. We'll stack them down the left side of the graph. Then other table occurrences will string out to the right of the anchors like buoys, depending on their function. I'm sure some of it will be confusing, but I'll fill in more details as we go along. You may need to come back and study it further in the future. For now, I'll just give you instructions.

1. If you're not already in the Manage Database window, choose **File**, **Manage Database**, **Relationships**, then click the **Relationships** tab.
2. Double-click the rectangle that represents the **Contact** table to open the Specify Table window.
3. At the bottom of the window, change Contact to **CON** and click **OK**.
4. Double-click the rectangle that represents the **Phone** table.
5. Rename this **PH** and click **OK**.
6. Now click in the gray area next to PH and move it down and under the CON table as shown in Figure 6-5.
7. In the lower left of the window, just above the Print button, are the Tables/Relationships tools. Click the first button on the left.
8. In the Specify Table window, click on **Phone** in the upper area. The word Phone appears in the Name area. Change it to **con_PH__SerNum**. Use one underscore between con and PH and two underscores before SerNum. Do not include the period. Click **OK**.

The name of this third table occurrence reflects the position in the string of tables it will hold on the graph, going from left to right. The lowercase "con" means that it's connected to the Contact table (abbreviated to CON). The capital "PH" in the second position means that it's the second table in the string as in Figure 6-5, and that its base table is the Phone table. The final item, SerNum, is an arbitrary code that represents the key field.

Making the Relationship

Now let's build the relationship.

1. Click on the second icon from the left under Tables/Relationships in the Manage Database window. This will take you to the Edit Relationship window shown in Figure 6-4.

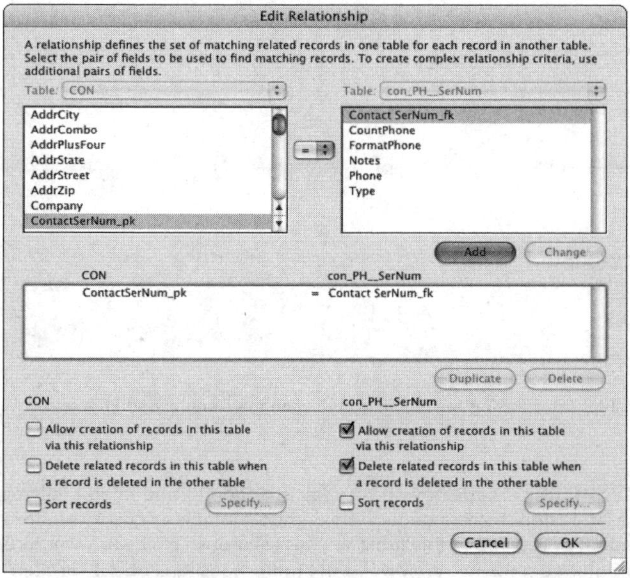

Figure 6-4 The Edit Relationship window showing the key fields.

2. Select **CON** from the Table pop-up list on the left and **con_PH__SerNum** from the Table pop-up list on the right.
3. Select **ContactSerNum_pk** from the list of fields on the left and **ContactSerNum_fk** on the right and click **Add.**
4. Make sure that the equal sign between the tables is selected.
5. Click on the following boxes in the lower-right corner of the box: **Allow creation of records in this table via this relationship** (see the Note below) and **Delete related records in this table when a record is deleted in the other table.**
6. Click **OK**, and **OK**.

These will be the match, or key, fields between the tables. See Figure 6-5. (If you create files and tables regularly, please see "Notes to Developers about Naming Conventions" in Appendix A for information about naming fields and relationships.)

Part 2

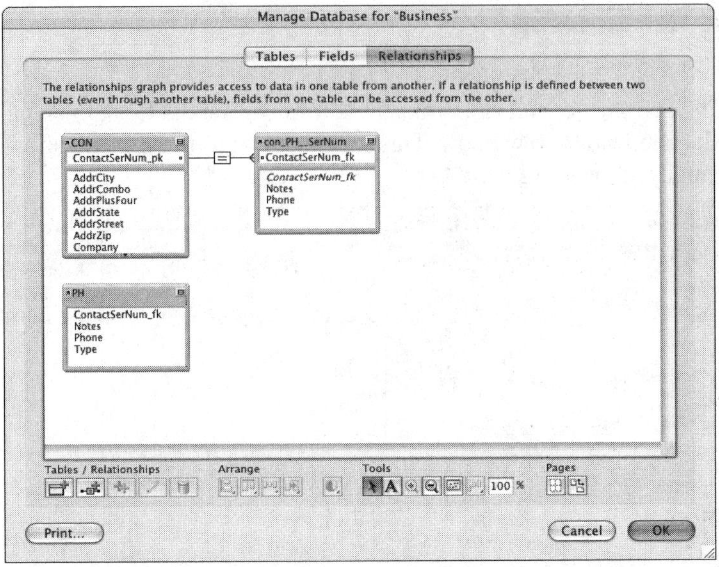

Figure 6-5
The Relationships tab showing the key fields between the Contact and Phone tables.

IMPORTANT NOTE!!! Focus now. If you pay attention to one thing I tell you in this book, this is it. I cannot stress enough how important it is to check the box next to "Allow creation of records in this table via this relationship" if you want to be able to create related records in the portal. I get more questions about "broken" portals because of that check box than all other questions combined. The Edit Relationship window is the only place you can set this up. You might think there should be something in the Portal Setup window itself, but it's not there. And once you've started working with the portal, it's hard to know what's gone wrong and where to fix it. To commit this to memory, when you get to the section titled "Adding Data to a Portal Field" on page 125, turn the check box off and test the portal. Now turn it back on. Do that about 10 times until you know you'll never forget it. There, I just saved you a headache and a panic attack. See what a nice guy I am?

Relationship Tools[7]

Now that we actually have a relationship between tables in our file, I can tell you about the relationship tools in the relationships graph. Take a look at Figures 6-6 and 6-7.

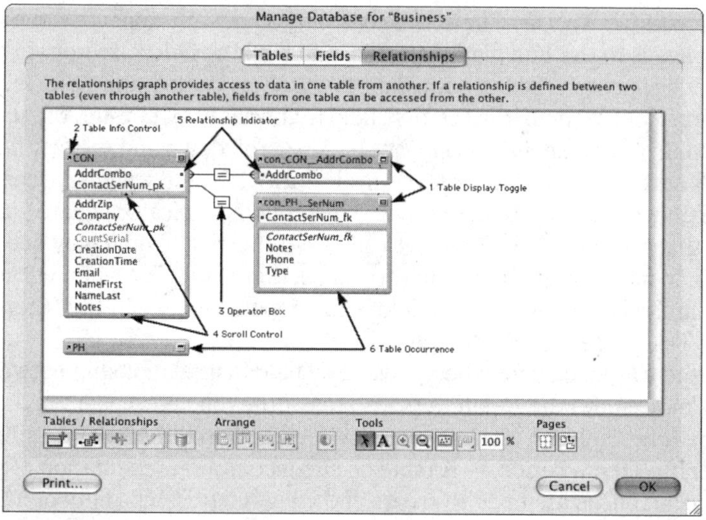

Figure 6-6
The tools in the relationships graph.

Each of these rectangles represents one of the tables in this file. (Figure 6-6 is a different version of the file we've been working with.) When in this window, I will refer to the rectangles as table occurrences or TOs. We'll talk more about the names of the items in this window in just a bit.

There is something that is not apparent from this figure: When you add a table occurrence from another file, the name of the table is italicized. It's just another visual aid to let you know what's going on with the relationships.

The numbered items in Figure 6-6 are explained below.

1 Table Display Toggle — The table display toggle allows you to vary the appearance of the table occurrence between Full, Related Fields only, and Table Name only. The CON and con_PH__SerNum tables are set to Full, con_CON__AddrCombo appears as Related Fields only, and PH shows the Table Name only setting. You may notice there is a slight difference in the appearance of the little toggle icon depending on which appearance variation the TO is in.

2 Table Info Control — When you hover your mouse pointer over the table info control arrow, you can see the source table and the source file. This is helpful because these TOs can be named something other than their actual table name. And you can have tables from other files in this window. Yes, you can double-click the Table Occurrence icon to display that information, but you may find this faster and more to your way of working.

3 Operator Box — The operator box gives you some information about the type of relationship between the TOs. Starting with FileMaker Pro 7, you can build other than equal relationships between tables. That includes <, =, >, ≤, ≥, ≠, and x. If there is more than one criteria between the two TOs, it is considered a complex relationship and the symbol will appear as an "x."

4 Scroll Control — The scroll control triangle only appears if the table occurrence is in the Full display setting and if all the fields are not visible. The fields appear in the list according to the View by pop-up in the Tables tab. If the first field in the list is the first field in the View by pop-up, the upper scroll control triangle will disappear. As you scroll down and the last field appears at the bottom, the bottom scroll control triangle will disappear.

5 Relationship Indicator — The relationship indicator square simply shows that there is a relationship to and from this field. You'll only see a relationship indicator if the field is in the top section of the TO. They will appear either on the left or right of the field name depending on whether there is a related TO on the left and/or right of it.

By the way, once a field becomes a key field in a relationship between TOs, it moves into the Related Fields area at the top and appears in italics with the other fields in the lower area, depending on the display setting.

6 Table Occurrence — A table occurrence is a representation of a table. Table occurrences are used to create and view relationships between tables. Notice that we have two occurrences of the Phone table: PH and con_PH__SerNum. They're really two occurrences of the same table. If you were to look at the data in the table occurrences, you'd see it is identical.

NOTE Much of this window was heavily influenced by the terminology of graph theory. Each little group of rectangles and lines is a "graph." The table occurrence boxes would be called "nodes," while the lines relating the nodes together would be called "paths."

You can resize the table occurrences by clicking and dragging either the sides, corners, top, or bottom. Well, sort of. If the TO is in the Full display setting, you can grab just about anywhere on the frame of the TO to resize it except the scroll control. In the other display settings, you can only grab one of the four sides to resize it.

You can also move and resize table occurrences with the arrow keys. Select one or more table occurrences. Press Control+right arrow to move the TOs. Press Control+Shift+right arrow to make the TOs wider. Try the other Control and Control+Shift+arrow combinations to see what they do. They all give you a little better control over moving and resizing than you can get with click+drag. Also, try using the arrow keys by themselves to move among the objects in the relationships graph.

Now let's look at the tool icons at the bottom of the window.

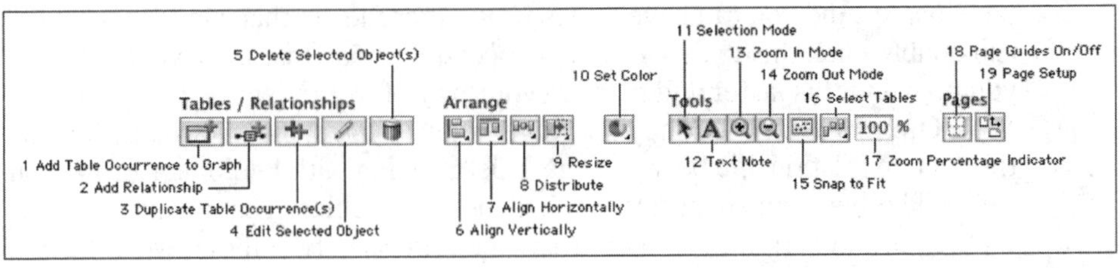

Figure 6-7
The relationships graph tools.

Tool Icons

1 Add Table Occurrence to Graph — This is where you go to add a table occurrence to the window. Clicking the icon brings up a Specify Table window. You can add table occurrences from the current file or from other files. When you click a table in the list, its name appears in the Name of Table Occurrence area. FileMaker keeps track of the names of your TOs. If you already have one called Phone, it will add a number for you, calling it Phone 2. Since I suggest removing spaces, you'll want to rename it Phone2. But when you add the next occurrence of the Phone table, FileMaker will name it Phone 2 (Phone space 2) again. If you remove the space this time (thereby making it Phone2), you'll be warned that the name is already in use. Try Phone3. If you don't know how many occurrences there are, go ahead and let FileMaker name it. Then look around the Relationships window to locate the other occurrences, double-click the new occurrence, and give it the sequential name you want. This is another reason I prefer to leave auto-naming behind and use the anchor-buoy method of organizing the relationships graph.

2 Add Relationship — Click this icon to bring up the Edit Relationship window seen in Figure 6-4. The Table pop-ups will bring up the current list of TOs available. If the table you need isn't there, click the Cancel button and create one with the Add Table button. After you choose the tables and create the relationship between them, if FileMaker needs another table occurrence for one of the tables it will tell you.

3 Duplicate Table Occurrence(s)[8] — This button allows you to duplicate one or more table occurrences and the relationships between them in a single stroke. Previously you had to add each TO one at a time, name them, and recreate the relationships between them. Very tedious! This is a welcome addition for developers of complex solutions.

4 Edit Selected Object — The Edit Selected Object icon will be gray until you select a single TO or a relationship indicator. You cannot select more than one item. If you select a TO and click the pencil, you'll see the Specify Table window. If you select an operator box and click the pencil, you'll see the Edit Relationship window. I personally find it easier to double-click the items to bring up the window. The only time I've used the Edit Selected Object icon is to write this paragraph. Okay, so I didn't really write with the little pencil, but you know what I mean.

Originally I thought you would use the pencil to draw relationships between tables. Nope. But you can accomplish that by simply clicking on the name of the field you want to use as the key field in one TO and dragging to the second key field in the other TO.

5 Delete Selected Object(s) — What else would you use a trash can for? You can select multiple TOs (and the relationships between them) or single relationship indicators, then click the trash can. Yep, you could also just press your Backspace or Delete key — which is how I do it.

6 Align Vertically[8] — For this and the next three icons, you'll notice a little triangle in the lower-right corner. When you select any of them, a list drops down with choices appropriate to the tool. The Align Vertically button choices are Align Left Edges, Align Centers, and Align Right Edges. Any questions?

Many of the choices for these buttons are similar to the tools used to align layout objects. I'm quite fond of them because I obsess over the TOs looking messy. You might want to exercise some caution when using these tools because they can easily pile a bunch of table occurrences on top of one another. Keep your other hand poised over the Undo key combo. And you can always click the Cancel button to undo all changes. But I've often done up to an hour's work in Manage Database before clicking OK. I think it's probably better to exit there more often than that in case you goof something up.

7 Align Horizontally[8] — The choices are Align Top Edges, Align Centers, and Align Bottom Edges.

8 Distribute[8] — Your choices here are Distribute Horizontally and Distribute Vertically. I use it when I have TOs stacked in either rows or columns so that there is even spacing between them.

9 Resize[8] — Choose from Resize to Smallest Width, Resize to Smallest Height, Resize to Smallest Width & Height, Resize to Largest Width, Resize to Largest Height, and Resize to Largest Width & Height. This helps you to make all the TOs in the selection the same width and height.

10 Set Color — You can select one or more TOs and give them a color. This can be helpful especially when you start getting a fairly complicated system. You might choose to make all TOs of the same table the same color. Or you could make specific groupings the same color. Just keep in mind who will be using your color system. About 7 percent of the population has some level of color blindness. And watch out! It is possible to turn the TO white, leaving only the text and a few of the control icons visible.

11 Selection Mode — This makes your mouse the selection tool so you can select TOs or relationship indicators. It's the setting you'll probably be using most.

12 Text Note[8] — This very highly requested feature lets you leave yourself a note about what you're trying to do with a particular TO or group of TOs. Click on the tool and move the cursor into the graph area and it turns into a crosshair symbol. Click and drag and you'll see the Edit Note dialog. Type your note, and choose the font, font size and color, and background color. You can move these notes so they cover one or more TOs and when you let go, the TOs always come to the front and the note block goes to the back. Many developers enlarge the note block so they can drop groups of TOs onto the note color for easy visual identification.

13 Zoom In Mode — Turns the mouse pointer into a magnifying glass, allowing you to increase the magnification. If you're already at full magnification, the tool will be grayed out. If you're zoomed out and using the Zoom In Mode tool, once you get to full magnification the pointer switches to Selection mode and the icon turns gray. If the tool is active, you can use it to zoom out by holding down the Option key (Macintosh) or Alt key (Windows) and clicking with the tool.

14 Zoom Out Mode — Turns the mouse pointer into a magnifying glass, allowing you to decrease the magnification and get a better picture of the overall structure of your tables. You can go all the way out to 1% magnification. That's so small that with the four TOs shown in Figure 6-6 I couldn't even see a gray dot on the screen. I can't imagine that level of magnification would be of much use. If you're using the Zoom Out tool, once you get to 1% magnification the pointer switches to Selection mode and the icon turns gray. If the tool is active, you can use it to zoom in by holding down the Option key (Macintosh) or Alt key (Windows) and clicking with the tool.

15 Snap to Fit — If you can't see all your TOs, just click this button and the entire window will reset to the zoom level that shows them all. The window doesn't change size; just the zoom level does. You can expand or contract the window manually using the knurled area in the lower-right corner. A change in the window size will affect what zoom level is needed to display all your TOs.

16 Select Tables[8] — Click on one or more table occurrences and choose from "Select related tables one away" and "Select tables with same source table." Many developers use the Set Color tool to identify all TOs with the same base table with the same color. If you have a lot of TOs, some with cryptic names, it can be hard to spot them all. This tool makes it easy. The one table away choice makes it easy to spot items in a group. You can also make that choice multiple times to include TOs farther away.

17 Zoom Percentage Indicator — This little box just shows you the zoom percentage. You can type a number directly in the box and then press the Tab or Return key. When I pressed the Enter key on the number pad, it was the same as if I'd clicked the OK button. I was kicked out of the window and back into Browse mode.

18 Page Guides On/Off — You click this icon to see where your pages will begin and end when printing your relationships graph.

19 Page Setup — And this simply brings up the Print window.

Allow Creation of Related Records

Each layout is automatically set up to show records from one table. When you navigate a list of records with the Book in Browse mode, you won't ever jump into a different table. (Although it is possible to end up in a different table if you click a button that takes you there.) However, on your layouts, you can draw a portal to another table and see related records from that other table.

A *portal* is a data window from one table occurrence into another table occurrence (in the same or a different file). Depending on how the relationship is set up, the data in the fields in the portal can be viewed and even altered. But the field definitions and the actual data viewed through the portal can exist in the table that's related to (but *usually* different from) the table that's part of the current layout. (I say *usually* because in a situation called a "self-join," tables can relate back to themselves. There will be a discussion of self-join relationships in the next chapter.)

Checking the box next to "Allow creation of records in this table via this relationship" (which we've already done) allows you to click in a portal that uses an equal relationship and add new data that will end up in the other table. In some cases, you may only want related data displayed in a portal and not created. Of course, you would leave the check box empty in that case. Our situation calls for checking the box, so that's why we checked that box when we created the relationship between CON and con_PH__SerNum.

One important note here: If you create a relationship between table occurrences that is anything other than equal (using something other than the "=" sign), the check box for "Allow creation of records in this table via this relationship" turns gray and inactive. If you've created an equal relationship and check the box, and then go back and change the relationship to unequal, the box will become unchecked without warning.

Parent and Child

In a typical relationship, a single record in one table will relate to several records in another table by way of the key field(s). The table that has the single record is known as the *master*, or *parent*, table. The table with potentially several related records is known as the *related*, or *child*, table.

In our Contact/Phone relationship, the child table is the Phone table, because a single contact record can relate to several phone number records as in Figure 6-3. You can also think of the parent creating the children, which is pretty much what happens when new portal records are created. Not all relationships allow creation of related records. (Okay, in real life it takes two parents to create the children. But let's not get too literal here.)

In FMP7 and later, since relationships to tables within the same file now go both ways, the determining factor of master/related or parent/child is whether a field on one side of the relationship has a unique value. (Having an auto-entered serial number provides implied uniqueness.) In our example, ContactSerNum_pk in the Contact table is unique. ContactSerNum_fk in the Phone table does not have to be unique. In fact, we want to be able to have more than one phone number related back to each contact record. That makes the Contact table the master or parent.

When you check the box next to "Allow creation of records in this table via this relationship" beneath one of the tables, you signal your intent to add records to that table through the portal (usually) and that this is the child table. When you look at the line or path that goes between the table occurrences for a parent/child relationship, you'll see a single line coming from the parent and a triple line or *crow's-foot* attached to the child table as shown in Figure 6-6 between the CON and con_PH__SerNum table occurrences. Every crow's-foot does not imply a parent/child relationship. The crow's-foot means it's a one-to-many relationship. We'll be looking at that more in the next chapter.

Of course, there is nothing that would prevent you from creating a different relationship in the Phone table that named the Contact table as its related table, and there may be instances where you would want to do exactly that.

(Probably not in the Phone table, however.) In this case, the Phone table would be the master table, and the Contact table would be the related table. If the master table is not going to be making records in the related table, it cannot be called the parent, since the parent creates offspring. In that case, it would be confusing (not to mention inaccurate) to call the Phone table the *parent* and the Contact table the *child* because the Phone table will not be creating contacts.

CAUTION It is possible to allow creation of related records in the table that would normally be considered the parent from the child table. I experimented with this by building a portal in the Phone table. I was able to create multiple records in the Contact table that had an identical serial number. I even went back and changed the ContactSerNum_pk in the Contact table so it was unique. I was still able to create Contact records by bypassing a warning dialog.

Creating parent records from the child table can really cause a mess because of identical serial numbers. When new phone numbers (or invoices or whatever) are created in a portal on the Contact layout, they appear in each of the contact records that have that duplicate serial number. Let's just consider this a form of incest — something I'd highly advise against.

Allow Deletion of Related Records

If you lost track of someone in your Contact table and wanted to delete their record, you would probably want to get rid of the phone numbers, too. Checking the box next to "Delete related records in this table when a record is deleted in the other table" takes care of that for you.

If you had old phone numbers lying around in the Phone table, it probably wouldn't hurt anything. On the other hand, if you had an invoicing system where line items were left behind, that could be a different story. Let's say a report created in the InvoiceLineItems table showed that 25 widgets had been purchased in May. But if 20 of those widgets were really orphaned records of a deleted invoice, your books could be off.

Protecting against orphaned records is part of a practice known as *referential integrity*. Good database design will make sure that if a record is deleted, any child records are either deleted or reassigned to another parent record. Another choice is to prevent deletion of the parent record if any child records exist.

Aside from using the "Delete related records in this table when a record is deleted in the other table" check box, complex methods for maintaining referential integrity with scripting and locking of menus exist. The details go beyond the scope of this book. But you need to know that such a concept exists and that FileMaker has provided a way to handle many situations without too much trouble.

Some people find it difficult to keep from deleting inactive records from their files. It's a matter of compulsive housekeeping. But once you learn that there could be an accounting reason to keep them, it's easier to let go of that urge. I think it's even a good idea to keep failed prospect records so you don't keep bothering those contacts when their names appear on new lists of potential clients. All those "leftover" records are your history. Hold onto it.

CAUTION You should be cautious about turning on the option to allow deletion of related records when you're in a child table and creating a relationship back to the parent table. If you're working in an invoice and you delete an invoice line item, you will be unpleasantly surprised to find the whole invoice disappear before your eyes!

Sort Related Records

When you check the box next to "Sort records" in the Edit Relationship window (see Figure 6-4), FileMaker brings up the window shown in Figure 6-8. In this window, you can decide in what order items will appear in the portal. You can choose field values or a custom sort order based on a value list, and you can create the value list from here. You may want a portal to sort items by date, in alphabetical order, or by some other criteria, and you can sort by multiple items.

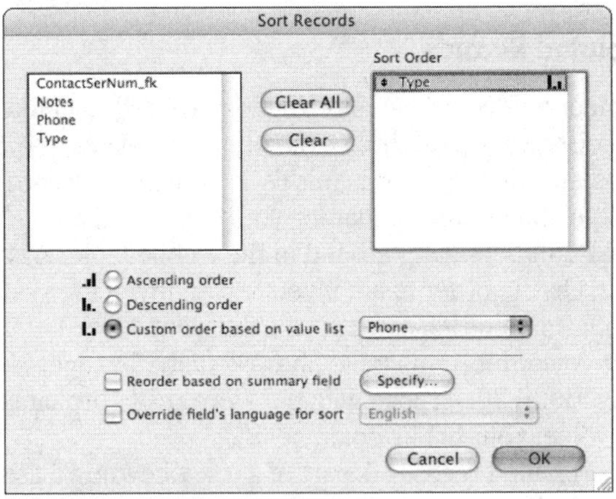

Figure 6-8
The Sort Records window where you choose how items will sort in a portal that uses the relationship.

To demonstrate this option, open the relationship by double-clicking the equal sign between the TOs.

1. Click the check box next to **Sort records** in the lower-right side of the Edit Relationship window.
2. In the Sort Records window, double-click **Type** in the left column to move it to the right column.
3. Highlight **Type** in the right column and click the radio button next to **Custom order based on value list**.
4. Click on the pop-up next to "Custom order based on value list" and choose **Manage Value Lists**.
5. When the next window appears, click the **New** button and name this list **Phone**.

6. Now enter the following values in the box at the bottom of the screen, putting a Return between each item: **Home**, **Office**, **Cell**, **Car**, **Email**, **Web**. Click **OK**, **OK**, **OK**, and **OK**.

Perhaps this is a little detailed for you, but please don't get discouraged. You can do some very sophisticated work and never have to go this far, but I do want you to know it's there if you want it.

> ⌘ **TIP** When you want to edit a value list, you must get to the Manage Value Lists area one way or another. Then you can double-click the list you want to work with. It can be a little confusing because there is no option called Edit Value List menu. (However, there is an Edit button in the Manage Value Lists window.)

> **NOTE** You can specify that any specific portal on a layout sorts independently from the sort you choose in the Manage Relationships area. See the section titled "Sorting a Portal" later in this chapter.

When we get done with the next section, you'll see how this value list affects the order in which items appear in the portal.

Making a Portal

So that nothing goes haywire, make a copy of the CON (or Contact) layout by following these steps:

1. Below the Book, click the Layout drop-down list and select **CON** if it's not already chosen.
2. Go into Layout mode.
3. Choose **Layouts**, **Duplicate Layout**.
4. On this new layout, delete all four phone fields as well as the Email and Web fields and their labels.

Drawing the Portal

To create a portal, follow these steps:

1. Click on the **Portal** tool, which is to the left of the Web Viewer tool (the little globe inside a square). (You can also select Insert, Portal or use the icon on the Tool panel.)
2. Draw a rectangle a little longer than the Company field in the newly cleared area of the layout and slightly taller than a field.
3. When you let go of the mouse button, you'll see the Portal Setup window shown in Figure 6-9.

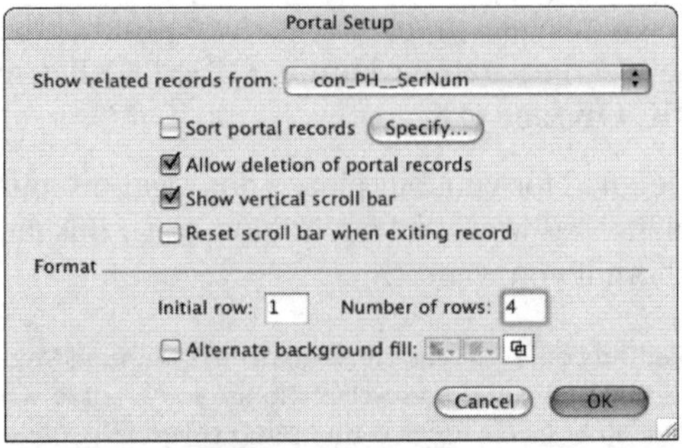

Figure 6-9
The Portal Setup window showing the settings to use for this particular portal.

4. Choose **con_PH__SerNum** from the pop-up.
5. Select **Allow deletion of portal records** and **Show vertical scroll bar**. Then enter **1** in the "Initial row" box and **4** in the "Number of rows" box.
6. Click **OK**.
7. At the next window, Add Fields to Portal, select **Type**, **Phone**, and **Notes**. Click **OK**.
8. If you can't see the scroll bar, it's possible that you have no line width selected for your portal or no solid line color. If this is the case and you can't remember what to do, go back to "Cleaning Up the Layout" in Chapter 3.

You may have to resize the fields and the portal to match the one in Figure 6-10. When you select the portal, notice that the handles only appear in the first portal row. If your screen doesn't look exactly like this one, you may want to move the fields to make them line up. Pay particular attention to the fields within the portal. If a field is even one pixel beyond the border of the portal on the left or the top, the information will not appear properly. Notice in Figure 6-10 that this layout has room to add another row to the portal.

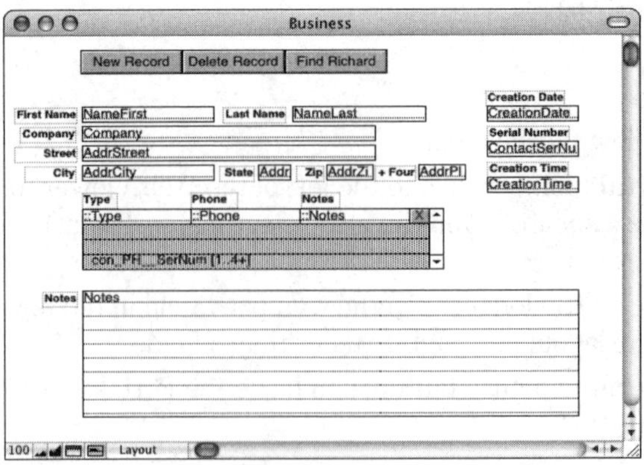

Figure 6-10
The Layout mode in the CON table showing the placement of the Phone portal and the fields from the Phone table.

Depending on the size of the rectangle you draw to represent the portal, you can get some strange results. See the following sidebar titled "Portal Tool Behavior."

Portal Tool Behavior

When you draw the area you want for your portal, there are a number of things that happen depending on how large you draw the rectangle that represents where you want the portal to go.

If you draw a rectangle slightly taller than the currently selected font size, the rectangle will represent the size of the top portal row. The dialog will show the number of rows as 1. You can type over that number. When you click OK, the Add Fields to Portal window opens.

After you select your fields and click OK, the field size expands or contracts vertically to fill the portal row, allowing a buffer of one pixel above and two below in the first portal row. (Keep in mind that depending on your default settings, the portal itself may have one of the effects from the Emboss palette applied to it.) You will probably want to resize the field height. In some cases, the field height will not be tall enough to see the bottoms of the letters in the fields. In other cases, the field height will be too tall and you'll need to change the field height to match the height of the font you've chosen. If you selected more than one field, the width will be squeezed or expanded horizontally to fit the portal row.

If you draw the rectangle slightly taller than the height of two (or more) fields of the currently selected font size (plus the three buffer pixels), the rectangle will represent two (or more) portal rows. The dialog will show the number of rows as 2 (or more). You can type over that number, too.

If you draw the rectangle smaller than the font height, the dialog shows the number of rows as 0. You must type a number larger than 0. Now this is where things get weird. When you type a number (let's say 3) and click OK, depending on the size of your layout, you may get a warning that "This operation will cause objects to extend off the layout." If you click the OK button, the portal rows draw quite tall based on some multiple of the rectangle you drew, and the layout gets expanded to accommodate all the portal rows. Then you move on to the Add Fields window. If you click the No button instead, you are moved to the Add Fields to Portal window. When you finish adding your fields and you're returned to Layout mode, the portal borders are invisible! If you can find the edges of the portal (you'll probably need to move a field or two out of the way), you'll find it has line size and color attributes assigned to it. There is nothing you can do with any of the palettes to bring back the visibility of the portal! However, if you double-click the portal, the number of rows will show as zero. If you change it to 1 or more and click OK, when you go back to Layout mode the portal now has visible borders and can be resized. Of course you'll need to resize the fields and the portal height. If the portal doesn't cause the layout to expand, the portal rows and the field height both draw quite tall based on some multiple of the rectangle you drew.

Placing the Fields in a Portal

When you create a portal with FileMaker Pro 7 and later, the fields appear in the portal in the order in which you selected them. You probably want to add field labels to the layout. To do that, follow these steps:

1. Double-click on the field.
2. At the bottom of the window, check the **Create field label** box.
3. Move the label where it will make the most sense on your layout, using Figure 6-10 as a guide.

   Notice the double colon in front of the field name. That means this field will contain data from another table occurrence; in this case, the Phone table via the con_PH__SerNum table occurrence. (It is also possible to use data from the same table as your layout using a self-join relationship, which is discussed in Chapter 7. Even then, you will still see the double colon in the field name.) If the field font is too large or the wrong style, reformat it now.

> **CAUTION** It is very important that you choose the right fields for your portal. This will usually consist of fields from the same relationship that you used to set up your portal. If you choose fields from the parent table or some other relationship, your portal may behave unpredictably. Using the wrong fields can yield some pretty weird results. Sometimes FileMaker will display the words "<Unrelated Table>" in the field in Browse mode. Other times, your only clue that you have the wrong field is if you see the same values repeated in each portal record instead of separate values. For the specifics, see the "Portable Portals" section in Chapter 14.

> **CAUTION** Placement of the fields in a portal is also important. The top of the field can lay exactly on the outline of the portal, but if it goes one pixel higher, only the first portal row will show and you wouldn't be able to enter new data in the second row. Or if data already existed, you wouldn't be able to see beyond the first row. Pay attention to the left margin, too. If your field is one pixel over the border of the portal, you won't be able to key information into that field. When FileMaker places the fields within the portal, it provides a slight buffer between the fields and the top and bottom of the portal. In our example here, I've removed that buffer, making the layout more attractive. It took a little time to do this, but I think it's important to make your layouts look professional. Practice lining up and resizing your fields. As you become more skilled, you'll be very pleased with the results you achieve.

4. Resize the fields as necessary, then add the field labels as shown in Figure 6-10.

   Notice that I didn't have you place the ContactSerNum_pk field in the portal. The key field only makes the connection between the tables and is not necessary in the layout. I've also left a little space to the right of the Notes field before the scroll bar. Make sure your layout has that little space. We will be adding a button there later. You may have to resize the portal again to make everything fit.

5. Before we try it out, double-click the **Type** field to bring up the Field/Control Setup dialog. In the pop-up menu next to "Display as" select **Drop-down list**. Then choose **Phone** from the value list choices beside "Display values from." Click **OK**. Now go to Browse mode.

Adding Data to a Portal Field

To add data to the portal field, click in the Type field and choose Home from the drop-down list. Don't type the word Home. Use the drop-down list to make sure the data is entered consistently. (To ensure that users do not override your drop-down list choices, format the field as a pop-up menu instead.) Then, make up a phone number and enter it in the Phone field. In the Notes field, you can add an extension number or the best time to reach the person, or just leave it empty. Notice that there is now a new line below the one you're working in because we checked the "Allow creation of related records" box in the Edit Relationship window. But if you try to click on the third line, you can't enter anything there. FileMaker creates a new record in the Phone table when you enter data, and then it gets ready for you to enter new data.

Enter some other phone types. Notice that as you work, the portal is moving the records around — sorting them according to the sort order we defined as part of the relationship. (You need to exit the portal before they'll sort.) If you don't make a choice from the drop-down list, blank items will sort to the bottom of the portal. Of course, you can turn that feature off by going back into Manage Relationships.

NOTE Records created in a portal do not officially exist until you press the Enter key or exit all fields one way or another. I have a client who had spent four hours entering many line items in the details of a quote when his computer lost communication with the server. After restarting FileMaker he discovered all his hard work had been lost. FileMaker saves automatically, but you need to get out of all fields occasionally to help it out.

TIP When the entire portal row is selected, you can choose Records, Duplicate Record, and FileMaker will duplicate the portal record. This can be handy if the data in most of the fields in your portals will be the same. Just to be clear, it is not enough to have the cursor in a field in the portal. The whole portal row must be selected. You can tell if it's selected because the row will be highlighted.

To select a portal row, you must click somewhere on the row outside the fields. Because of the way I set up my portals, that can be a little tricky since I usually close up all available space between the fields. You could leave some space for that purpose. Or you could create a button in the portal with these two script steps:

```
Go to Portal Row [Select; No dialog; Get (PortalRowNumber)]
Duplicate Record/Request
```

See Chapter 14 for more on scripts.

CAUTION When duplicating or deleting portal rows, be sure that you have the row selected or you may inadvertently duplicate or delete a parent record. In the case of a deletion, FileMaker brings up a warning screen that asks "Permanently delete this one related record?" But people tend to ignore warnings after a while.

Continue to make up information until you've filled up four rows. To get to the fifth row, use the vertical scroll bar on the right side of the portal. If you're in a field in the fourth row, you can also use the Tab key on the keyboard to move to the fifth row. Using a portal like this allows you to add as many phone numbers or other information as you want. Notice that using a portal this way can save space on your layout and you get more data. Before we put the portal here, we only listed the phones. Now, we not only have the phones, but we also have a Type and Notes field as well. And we can have unlimited numbers. When you look at your record in Browse mode, you will see the number of rows of data that you chose to display when you created the portal. If all rows are filled and you want to know if there is additional data in the portal, use the scroll bar. You could create a calculation to tell you if there are extra rows, but I'll leave that up to you to experiment with. (Hint: You'll need a self-referencing relationship and a field that counts matching data.)

Sorting a Portal

Before FileMaker 7, you had to make a separate relationship for every portal that required a different sort. It's true that portals will inherit any sort defined in the relationships graph, but you can override that sort and add sorts specific to each portal if you prefer.

To "customize" the sort in a specific portal, go to Layout mode and double-click anywhere below the first row of the portal to bring up the Portal Setup window. Click the Specify button next to "Sort portal records" to open the Sort Records window. You'll notice that the only fields available are the fields from the related table. How the heck do you include fields from other tables? What follows is not particularly intuitive, but it is the proper procedure and gives you all the power you need over the portal.

If you want to use fields from the portal table, double-click them to move them to the Sort Order area on the right, then click the OK button. If you don't want to use any of these fields, just click the Cancel button. Clicking either button will return you to the Portal Setup window. Notice the "show related records from" pop-up at the top of the window and memorize (or write down) the table occurrence that is associated with this portal. By choosing a different table occurrence from the pop-up, you can click the Specify button as many times as necessary to fill the Sort Order area with fields from any table occurrence you want. (In the case of our current Business file, there are no other available TOs to choose from, but this is the process.) The most important thing to do as you finish making your field selections is to reselect the table occurrence you started with from the pop-up in the Portal Setup window before you click the final OK button.

Investigating the Related Table

Now that we have created our portal field, we can examine how related tables work. From this example, you will see that when we enter phone information for a person in the Contact table, the data is actually going into the Phone table.

To begin, switch to another record and make up some phone numbers there. Go to the Layout drop-down at the left of your screen and select PH. Click through the records. To see all the records in a list, you can go into Layout mode, shrink the body part, and remove the header and footer altogether as shown in Figure 6-11 (or you could just choose View, View as Table). We already talked about using NameFirst and NameLast as field names in Chapter 3. We'll change their labels later on.

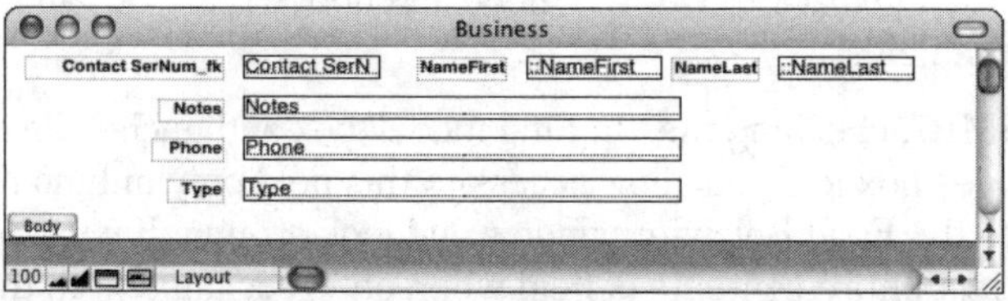

Figure 6-11
Layout mode in the PH table showing header and footer parts removed and placement of related fields from the ph_CON__SerNum table occurrence.

TIP If you are looking for a table in another file, choose Window and select the name of the table. If you don't see it there, try Window, Show Window. Remember that the file must be open, because only open files appear in the Window menu. Hidden windows show in the Window, Show Window menu.

TIP To remove a layout part (header, body, footer, summary, etc.), click on the part's name tab and press Backspace or Delete. If there are layout objects in that part, you'll be warned and will have a chance to change your mind before the part is deleted.

You can also remove a layout part by clicking on the tab and dragging the part upward until it disappears into the window border (if it is the topmost part) or the part above it. If there are layout objects in that part, you won't be able to do that until you've deleted those objects.

Now go to Browse mode and choose View, View as List. Notice that the ContactSerNum_pk field has been entered without any effort from you. That happens because we checked the box for creation of related records when we made the relationship to the Phone table. FileMaker places the number from the key field in the parent table into the key field in the child table.

Notice that you can enter the ContactSerNum_pk field and change the number. That could cause trouble if other users access that field and change the data. You can choose to prohibit modification as part of the field definition, but that might pose a problem if you had to reassign the record to a different parent record to maintain referential integrity.

Here's another solution:

1. Go to Layout mode, select the **ContactSerNum_pk** field, and choose **Format, Field/Control, Behavior.**
2. To protect the information in the ContactSerNum_pk field so that it cannot be changed by mistake, make sure that the "In Browse mode" box is unchecked.

   If it turns out you need to get into the field regularly, you can check the box in the future or create a special layout that allows entry into a copy of the field. You could also create a special script for the purpose of entering the field. If you're beginning to wonder, the answer is: Yes, you can set up the same field with different properties on different layouts — or even on the same layout.
3. Click **OK**, then go back to Browse mode and notice that you can no longer enter the field.

Starting with FMP7, checking the "In Find mode" box and unchecking the "In Browse mode" box lets you allow access to this field only in Find mode.

Go back into the Field Behavior window and look around. If you check the box beside "Select entire contents of field when entered," all text in the field is selected when you click into that field. If you need to delete the text, simply press the Backspace or Delete key. (Of course you won't be able to select the text if you've unchecked "Allow field to be entered in Browse mode.") If the text is selected and you need to edit it, click in the field a second time. The reason you might want all text selected is so you can easily replace the text without having to manually select it first.

If you use a software utility that converts keystrokes to Japanese characters, check the box next to "Set input method to" and choose the appropriate method from the drop-down list, as shown in Figure 6-12. (See Chapter 4 for a brief explanation of the Furigana options you have when you define fields (File, Manage Database, Fields tab, Options, Furigana).)

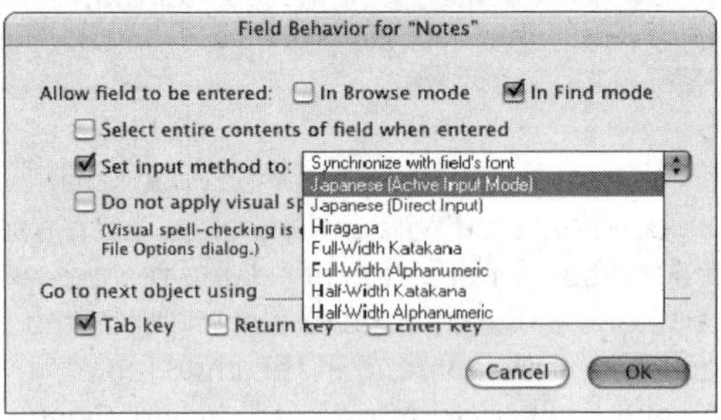

Figure 6-12
Field Behavior window showing Japanese character options.

NOTE Even though I had some Japanese fonts installed, I couldn't get any field to hold onto those font formats. Maybe it's because I don't have the appropriate software utility. I suspect that's why the drop-down did not display the input methods shown in Figure 6-12. If this is something that is important to you, the Help files might give you more to work with, although I found them a little skimpy on the subject. Look under the topic "Setting the text input method for fields." One other note: The list in the pop-up on the Mac is much more limited than in Windows.

You can decide which key or keys are used to navigate to the next field. This is a very handy feature that can prevent extra returns at the end of data fields. It's also useful for people who will use the number keypad for data entry.[7]

Relating a Table Back to the Parent Table

(If you are not trying to create a relationship between files, you may want to skip this section.)

In older versions of FileMaker, if you wanted to display parent data you needed to create a relationship in the child file back to the parent file.

In version 7 and later, with multiple tables within a single file, a relationship travels in both directions. So once we created the relationship from Contact to Phone, we automatically have the data from Contact available to the Phone table. However, if you find it necessary to use multiple files instead of multiple tables within one file, you will still need to create a relationship back to the parent file.

NOTE You may need to use a multiple file system in cases like the following:

- If you converted a set of files from previous versions of FileMaker and there isn't time or budget to change all the files into multiple tables within one file.
- If there is so much data in a single file that it would cause the file to approach FileMaker's 8 terabyte file-size limit, or the limits of the hard drive the file is on.

Here are some examples:

- If you store images, rather than references to images
- If you import large amounts of text into single fields
- If you want to store data on separate servers
- If there is a security problem raised by having a two-way relationship

A table of secret agents would need to set up a relationship into a table of world leaders to keep track of who is spying on whom. But if these tables were in the same file, someone could follow the relationship from the other direction and get a list of which secret agents are spying on particular world leaders. By keeping the tables in separate files, it's possible to make the relationship flow in only one direction. Secret agents may be a silly example, but there are all sorts of laws dealing with student grades, medical records, credit reporting, and even telemarketing phone numbers where privacy is legally required.

The instructions that follow assume that you have created a separate file called Phone and that you've made a relationship to it from the Contact table in the Business file. Since a file for phone numbers is not likely to become large enough to need this, we'll pretend it's a security feature to prevent someone from using a telephone number to look up a contact name. To create a relationship back to the parent file and table, in this case the Business file and the Contact table, follow these steps:

1. Open the Phone file.
2. Choose **File**, **Manage Database**, **Relationships**.
3. The table for the Phone file appears. Click the **Add Table** tool, the first icon on the left under Tables/Relationships.
4. In the File pop-up in the Specify Table window, select the **Business** file.
5. You should see the Business file tables. Select **Contact** and click **OK**.
6. You should see table reference icons for both Phone and Contact. Click the **Add/Edit Relationship** tool, the second icon under Tables/Relationships.
7. In the Edit Relationship window, select **Phone** in the Table pop-up on the left and **Contact** in the Table pop-up on the right side of the window. Select **ContactSerNum_pk** under both tables. Click **Add**. Do not check any other boxes. Click **OK**.
8. In the Relationships window, you can see that the relationship exists. Click **OK**.
9. Now go back to the Contact table. Go to **File**, **Manage Database**, **Relationships**. You won't see a relationship between your table named Phone and the Contact table unless you already created that relationship in the Business file.

When you are working with external files, you may need to create a relationship from the parent to the child and from the child to the parent to make data appear in both tables. (Don't get confused between the Phone table in the Business file and the Phone file outside the Business file.)

Performing a Find in a Portal

The reason we started this portal was to be able to perform a search in one place for multiple phone numbers. Click in one of the Phone fields with a number in it, select the whole number (Edit, Select All), and copy it.

> **SHORTCUT** To select the entire contents of a field, place the cursor in the field and choose Command+A (Macintosh) or Ctrl+A (Windows).

Enter Find mode and paste the number in the Phone field in the first row of the portal. Click the Find button or press Enter or Return. The Status toolbar should show one record found.

Performance Considerations

Finding data in a portal works just fine in a table with only a few records. But you need to know that the more records in the current table, the slower the portal search. You had a glimpse of the concordance FileMaker keeps for certain fields when you selected Insert, From Index while entering data in Chapter 5. This index is what makes FileMaker's searching so speedy when you perform a find in the active table on a layout. But these indexes aren't much use to FileMaker when you're searching through a relationship in a portal or in a related field. Searching indexed fields becomes just as lethargic as searching unindexed fields when you access the same data through a relationship. I have a Contact table with over 3,000 records, and a find is instantaneous — even across multiple fields. A find in a calculated field in a portal that has 100,000 child records is something else. In a case like that, it may be better to use scripts that structure the find in the child table and bring you back to the related records in the parent table. If you'll be running a report like that once a month with an unshared file, speed may not be a big issue. But if this report will be a daily process with files shared on a network, you may want to reconsider.

CAUTION Running complex finds and reports on a network with very actively shared files can cause severe slowdowns and sometimes even crashes. When such reports are going to be run, it may be best to ask other users to quit the program. Another option is to run FileMaker Server, a separate, specialized program from FileMaker, Inc. to be used for just such a busy network.

NOTE When I say that records in a portal are treated as unindexed, I don't want to give you the impression that they are unindexed anywhere other than through relationships. If you go to the related table and perform a find in those very same fields, as long as the fields have been indexed, the find will run more quickly.

NOTE Finding in fields displayed from an External SQL Source (ESS) will not operate the same as local FileMaker fields. Those records will always act as though they are not indexed. And if there are hundreds of thousands of records in the ESS, a find can be very slow. However, that is a small trade-off for getting such convenient access to these other data sets. For more on ESS, see Chapter 26, "Working with External Data Sources."

Another choice may be to create redundant lookup fields in the parent table for the purpose of such reporting. See Chapter 7 for more on lookup fields. Just remember, when you do that you reduce the level of normalization, which may create pockets of out-of-date data in your database. If you decide to use lookups to duplicate data, try to use fields that contain information that won't change or that need to stay static for archival purposes. An example would be an invoice system where you want prices to reflect what they were at the time the invoice was created. (Starting with FMP10, you can use Script Triggers to more easily synchronize related lookup data, which we will discuss in Chapter 16, "Working with Script Triggers.")

Deleting a Record from a Portal

What if you find you no longer need one of the lines in the portal? Sure, you could just clear the fields, but then you have an empty line in the middle of the portal. This could be a big deal in an invoicing system where reports may turn up these empty records.

Remember that little space I had you leave in the portal just to the right of the Notes field? Go back to the CON Copy layout and click in it now. One line of the portal should become highlighted. If that's not what happens, go back into Layout mode, click the portal, and pull the selection handle to create the space as shown in Figure 6-10.

Go back to Browse mode and click in the space. While that portal row is highlighted, choose Records, Delete Record. A warning dialog box will appear as shown in Figure 6-13. Note that this dialog is different from the one that appears when you try to delete a parent record, because it mentions the "related record." If this is for one of those made-up phone numbers and you don't care about it, go ahead and click the Delete button. Just remember, there's no undo or revert for this.

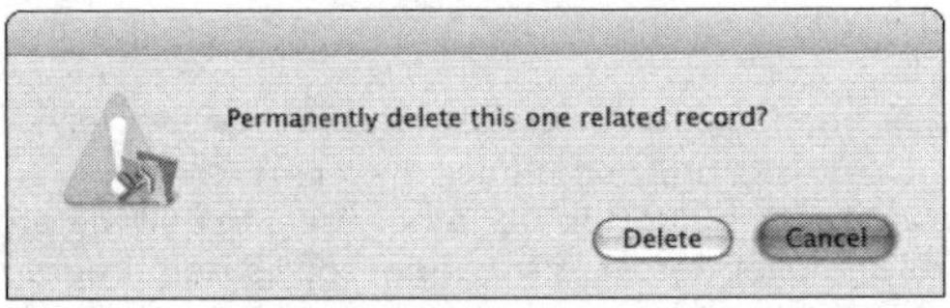

Figure 6-13
A warning dialog box that appears when you try to delete a related record.

Another alternative is to create a script that will delete a portal row and attach the script to a button. Make the button small enough to fit on one line of the portal and drop it in the first portal row. The button will automatically be repeated for every row of information plus the one empty row that's always waiting for new data.

Dealing with "Portal Pop"

If you have more items in a portal than the number of rows can show, you can scroll down to take a look. But there has been a little annoyance since portals were introduced way back in FileMaker 3. As soon as you entered any other fields on the layout, the portal would "pop" back to the top, and the lower records would once again be hidden from view. If your portals are doing that, and you want them to stay put, here's what you do:

1. Go to Layout mode and choose **Layouts**, **Layout Setup** or click the little pencil icon to the right of the Layout drop-down.
2. On the **General** tab, uncheck the box next to **Show field frames when record is active.**
3. Click **OK**, go back to Browse mode, and notice that your portals will stay put as long as you are on that record.

Ah, but there is a price to pay. By unchecking the "Show field frames" box, you no longer see the field frames — those little dotted lines that appear around all fields in which you can enter data — while you enter data. And the magnifying glasses you see in the fields when you're in Find mode also disappear. If you really need your portals to stay in place, you may want to provide your data entry fields with borders so they're easier to spot. One subtle effect of having field frames turned off is that you can never tell when your cursor is in a container field. There is simply no change in appearance to the field. The Insert menu items are active, so you know you're in the field, but that's it.

An added detail introduced in FMP8.5 is that you can override the field frames setting.

1. Go to Layout mode and double-click the portal.
2. Check the box next to **Reset scroll bar when exiting record.**
3. Click **OK** and go back to Browse mode.

Now, even though field frames are turned off, the portal scroll bar will zip back to the top unless you clicked in a field somewhere. Regardless of how you have it set, when you leave a layout or switch to another record and then return, the scroll bar will always be reset to the top.

Before We Go

Prior to creating the portal for phone numbers, we created a duplicate layout for Contact so that we could move fields around and add new features. Since this layout works so well, you'll probably want to delete the first Contact layout we developed.

1. Go to Layout mode. From the Layout drop-down list, select the **CON** (or Contact) layout.
2. Go to **Layouts, Delete Layout.**
3. At the "Permanently delete this layout?" prompt, select **Delete.**
4. Now go to the **CON Copy** layout. Select **Layouts, Layout Setup.** Under Layout Name, rename this layout **CON_Contact** and click **OK.** Notice that we're using the same three-letter code to show us this layout is associated with the CON table occurrence.
5. For naming consistency, switch to the PH layout and rename it **PH_Phone.**

I also need to let you know that you can create relationships to tables in other files the same way we just created the relationship to the Phone table. But there are a couple of immediate advantages to working under the umbrella of a single file structure:

- Managing security in a single place
- Managing your schema in a single place

That's not to say there aren't reasons to work with multiple files. But you get immediate benefits with consolidation and it should be well considered when making plans for your database system.

In earlier versions of FileMaker, whenever you went to what was called the Define Relationships window from various other windows, you would see the currently selected relationship highlighted in a list of relationships. That is no longer the case now that we have the relationships graph. Now you need to know what you're looking for. And as your solution gets more complicated, that will get more difficult. Sounds like another good reason for taking some time with color coding the table occurrences and organizing the window as you build relationships in it — and for working with the anchor-buoy standard of development.

Summary

In this chapter, we learned when and why to use more than one table in our database. We built a two-table system complete with relationships, a portal, and related fields. We also looked at a number of potential problems in a multiple-table system and discussed ways of protecting against them.

Now we're gettin' into the good stuff! Are you starting to get the hang of it? You should probably find yourself being able to switch between the tables and modes, and moving fields around on the layouts pretty easily by now. If not, take the time to do the exercises in this chapter again. I learned everything the hard way over a period of years. You can learn it in a matter of days by working on this until you get it. In Chapter 7, we'll use our Contact table to build a real invoicing system using a total of five tables!

Q & A

Q All this, and it still doesn't look like the templates. How do I get that great, finished look?

A You can use the Layout tools to pull apart the templates, copy and paste any elements from there, and create whatever your heart desires. The more you practice, the better you'll get at it. We will deal more with layouts in Chapter 9, "Creating New Layouts with the Layout Assistant."

Q When we were in the Phone table and made a relationship back to Contact, who was the parent and who was the child?

A I believe that the names "parent" and "child" should be reserved specifically for relationships where creation of portal records takes place from the master side. "Master" and "related table" would probably be the more all-encompassing terminology to cover all relationships regardless of parenting capabilities. Whatever table is handing out its keys is the master table for that relationship. And whatever table is holding copies of those keys is the related table. That means that a table can be both a master and a related table to another table. It can also be master and related table to many other tables. So the Phone table is still the child, although it would be more accurate to call it the related table, and the Contact table is the master.

Workshop

Create a temporary relationship to one of the tables in the template files using anything that resembles a serial number. If there is no field like that, choose anything. In this case, check the box to allow creation of related records in the relationship. Put a portal on your layout and add some fields. Be sure to choose fields that are from the right relationship. Add a few records.

Now try changing the relationship by choosing a different key field from the template file. What happens to the records in the portal? What happens when you change the relationship back? When you are done, remove the new portal and fields from the layout, then delete the temporary relationship and the file reference.

Chapter 7

Working with Related Tables — Part 2

Introduction

In the last chapter, we created a fairly simple, two-table relational database. In this chapter, we'll build on what we learned there when we make a working invoicing system. As part of the project, we'll:

- Look at different types of relationships
- Learn how to diagram a multiple-table database
- Learn when to use related fields and when to use lookup fields
- Create the tables we diagram and enter some data

Along the way, I'll show you a number of potential stumbling blocks and ways to keep your footing among them. As in the last chapter, understanding these concepts is crucial to making FileMaker work really well for you. Don't hesitate to reread this chapter in order to let it all soak in. Many of the items I include may not be relevant to the solution we're creating, but they are important to more complex solutions. Grab what you need now and know that you can always come back here later and fill in those little details that didn't make sense the first time through.

Planning Your Database

Planning — I hate it! Some developers swear that 80 percent of your work should be gathering information, and that you shouldn't even turn on your computer until the last 20 percent of the job. This can be pretty hard to take if you're the type of person who likes to get your hands into the computer part of a project. The other side is that without good planning, you will probably end up wasting a lot of your time. If you intend to build FileMaker databases for other people as a profession, that can mean you'll end up working for free whenever you have to fix errors caused by bad planning. I've done it, and I've learned my lesson (although maybe not to the 80 percent planning level). Let me pass the lesson along to you.

The great thing about spreading out the data between more tables in a multi-table solution is that you have better possibilities for accurate reporting. At the same time, you increase the complexity and number of things to be careful about. All the more reason for good planning. You may have noticed that once we went from our single table, My_Phonebook, to the relational tables, Contact and Phone, there were quite a few extra steps and cautions to take into account.

Part of this planning can take place using the questionnaire I gave you in Chapter 3. Then you have to sit down and lay it all out on paper. Understanding the types of relationships and how to sketch them out will go a long way in the planning of your database.

Tricky Terms and Catchy Phrases

To get things started, you need to know that there is more than one type of relationship.

ER Diagram

An ER diagram is a way to represent how relationships work between files and tables. ER stands for entity-relationship. In database terminology, an *entity* generally refers to a file or a table. I don't know why they just don't call it a file- or table-relationship diagram — probably because the term came before FileMaker was invented. Figure 7-1 shows the basic ER diagram for our Business file. A more complete ER diagram would include fields, and the lines between the table occurrences would point to the key fields. Hmmm... Didn't we see something like that back in Chapter 6 when we looked at the Relationships tab in the Manage Database window in the Contact Management file? That's right! Starting with FileMaker Pro 7, one form of an ER diagram is created automatically. Complete ER diagrams can show more detail about the types of relationships using little one-letter codes and icons. I won't go into that here. You might also want to know that you usually only want to show the main relationships between TOs at this stage of planning. Often, a number of utility relationships don't need to be indicated. If you get too many lines going, you won't be able to read the diagram.

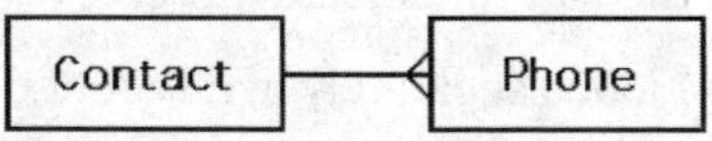

Figure 7-1
Basic ER diagram for the Business file.

One-to-Many Relationship

When you created the Phone (con_PH__SerNum) table and built the relationship to it from the Contact (CON) table, you made a one-to-many relationship. One contact can have many phone numbers.

> **NOTE** Technically, this specific diagram could indicate a many-to-many relationship since one phone number could belong to many people, since we haven't determined a unique key. Take, for example, the case of a small company where many people share a common phone number. But for now, let's keep it simple.

In Figure 7-1, you can see one line on the Contact side and three lines (a crow's-foot) on the Phone side. That means it's a one-to-many relationship.

In an invoicing system, for example, you can put many products on one invoice.

The inverse of this is the many-to-one relationship. When we created a relationship from the Contact table to the Phone table, a relationship was automatically created from the Phone table back to the Contact table. Using that, we can display the person's name in the Phone table. That is a many-to-one relationship. I've used it a lot. This inverse relationship is shown by a set of crow's-feet attached to one of the tables in the diagram and a single line attached to the other table.

NOTE Even though there is an automatic relationship back to CON from con_PH__SerNum, since we'll be using the anchor-buoy method, we won't likely use it. With anchor-buoy there will not be a layout associated with the con_PH__SerNum table occurrence. For more on anchor-buoy, see Appendix A.

One-to-One Relationship

Putting everyone's last name in a child table instead of the parent table would be an example of a one-to-one relationship. It can be done, but why would you want to? (This assumes the use of a serial number as the primary key.) This relationship is sometimes used to keep confidential information (such as an employee's evaluation) away from prying eyes. But you could probably accomplish the same thing in a single file by using password protection to make the data in specific fields inaccessible (or grayed out).

There are some legitimate reasons to implement two files with a one-to-one relationship, so I don't want to leave you with the impression that it should never be done. For example:

- If a file were reaching FileMaker's 8-terabyte limit, the developers might store some of the data in a separate file. You're more likely to run out of hard drive space first, which brings us to…
- If a file were reaching the limits of the size of the hard drive.

And what if two complex files were developed separately in different departments and then brought together? It might be simpler to create a one-to-one relationship than to rebuild. I'm sure you can picture what a one-to-one ER diagram would look like — two boxes joined by one line.

In FileMaker's relationships graph, a relationship will only appear to be one-to-one when both fields in a pair are defined as unique (validation) or expected to be unique (auto-enter serial number).

Oh, a terabyte? That's equal to 1024 gigabytes. And you can now have a file up to eight times that! That's a whole lot bigger than the old file size limit of 2 gigabytes. Now that's power! To give you some perspective, the largest FMP file I have is 1.5 gigabytes. It contains the full text of every e-mail I've sent or received in the past 10 years. (That doesn't include any files that were attached.) Assuming my e-mail activity stays about the same, it would take more than 50,000 years before I hit the file size limit!

Many-to-Many Relationship

In an invoicing system, one invoice could have many products on it, and one product from the Product table could appear on many invoices. This would be considered a many-to-many relationship. It's sort of a double-sided one-to-many.

There are uses for a many-to-many relationship, but it's simply not allowed when it comes to making a relationship that allows creation of records in a portal.

Although rarely used in this context, one other option is to use a multi-valued field. You could have a number of product IDs in a single text field on one invoice. FileMaker is one of the few databases that supports multi-valued keys. This is a method that is difficult to support, so I won't go into detail about that here.

You also can't have a "many" side to the invoice relationship if the invoice has a unique serial number. Unique denotes one, not many. So you would have to remove the unique feature. But what's the use of a bunch of invoices with the same number? Sound confusing? Just don't do it. Instead, use another table.

I do often use a many-to-many relationship to root out duplicate names and addresses in my files. Back in Chapter 4 in the section titled "Calculation Field" we created a field called AddrCombo. Using two table occurrences of the Contact table joined on both sides with AddrCombo, we can see when there are multiple copies of that specific name and address. You can see what this looks like in Figure 7-6 with the double crow's-foot symbols between the AddrCombo fields in the CON and con_CON__AddrCombo TOs. A portal displaying this relationship would always show at least one item — the record itself. To really make this effective, you'd want to create a multi-criteria relationship (see the section coming up shortly) so that the portal only displayed other records with a matching name and address. Of course it wouldn't help you spot records where the data entry people used Bob one time and Robert the next, but it certainly will help you spot absolute duplicates.

In FileMaker's relationships graph, a relationship will only appear to be many-to-many:

- When both fields in a pair are neither unique (validation) nor expected to be unique (auto-enter serial number)
- When the relationship uses the Cartesian "x" symbol between two fields

> **NOTE** Selecting the so-called Cartesian "x" symbol from the pop-up in the Edit Relationship window means that all records in one table are connected to all other records in the other table. It is especially useful for passing data into special-purpose fields formatted as global storage. It helps to eliminate the need for special constant calculation fields and relationships between those constant fields used by developers in earlier versions of FileMaker. It can also be useful for displaying all records from a special table that stores choices you might want to display in a portal.

The Join, or Link, Table

The way to handle a many-to-many relationship is to create an in-between table called a *join*, or *link*, table. Each record in the join table would contain key fields (probably serial numbers) for both the invoice and the product. These are often called *foreign* keys because they refer to a specific record in another table. The fields in the join table don't need any auto-enter options turned on because they will be created from the other tables. For an invoicing system, this table would contain the invoice line items. We'll call it InvoiceLineItems and code it ILI to stand for invoice line items. Then you have a one-to-many relationship from Invoice to ILI (one invoice shows many items purchased) and a one-to-many relationship from the Product table to the ILI table (one product can show up in many lines in the portal of the invoice).

Does this sound complicated? Don't worry. You'll understand it much better when you work through the example later in the chapter.

> **BEST PRACTICES** LI is an abbreviation often used to refer to line items. Accepted abbreviations like this make field names shorter, yet understandable.

If you find yourself drawing a many-to-many ER diagram when planning your files, just put another table between them as in Figure 7-2.

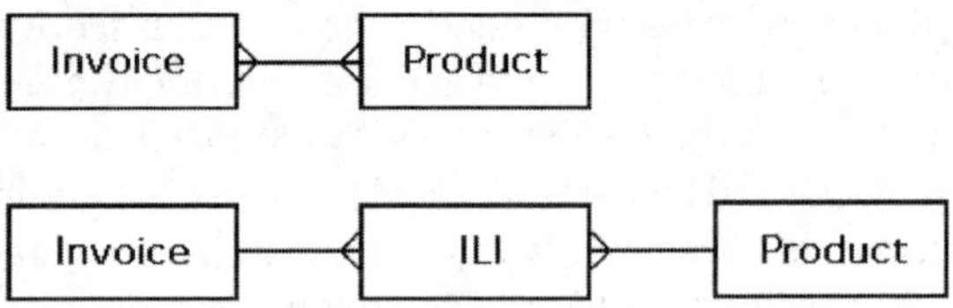

Figure 7-2
ER diagram showing a many-to-many relationship for an invoicing system and how it should be restructured using a third table. ILI becomes the join table between Invoice and Product.

Whenever you see a table with two (or more) of the three-pronged crow's-foot symbols attached to it, that table is a good candidate for *reporting*. The reason you do a report here is that it's more flexible than either of the other tables.

For example, let's say you have an invoice all nicely laid out in the Invoice table with a portal that shows 10 lines. A customer comes in and orders 12 items. Even though you can use the scroll bar and enter the data, only 10 lines will print out. You can expand the portal, but eventually some customer may order so many items that your portal extends down to another page. When you print invoices from now on, you'll have to print all those empty lines and a second page with your total at the bottom, even if other customers only order one item. This looks tacky and is unnecessary. Instead, print your invoice from the layout associated with the ILI table occurrence and the "report" (invoice) can show just as many or as few items as your customer orders.

I've been involved in situations like this a couple of times. My client swears, "We'll *never* need more than X repetitions." So I build a report, or a contract, or an invoice in the "one" side of the relationship. Eventually the system improves their business, and the "never" day comes. The temptation to build the report in only one table comes because, when you use data in a related table, you have to create one layout for day-to-day work and another for printing. And the amount of time you thought you'd have to spend on the work didn't include extra layouts and scripts. But experience dictates the need for both layouts.

Self-join Relationship

A self-join relationship is also called a self-referencing relationship. When you call up the relationships graph or Edit Relationship window, you can create a relationship to the table you're in. You can create a self-join for any of the other types of relationships, although I use it most often with the one-to-many relationship. In our Contact table, we might have a number of people who work for the same company. You could create a self-join relationship by choosing Company in both of the field lists. Then you make a portal on the layout that would show the names of anyone else who works at that company. To make this work, you will need to make sure the company name is spelled exactly the same in each record, which is not always an easy thing to accomplish.

If you need to create a self-join relationship, you can choose the same table on both sides of the Edit Relationship window. But as soon as you select the fields and click OK, you'll find that FileMaker requires that you add another table occurrence to the graph. In our example, FileMaker would create a table occurrence called Contact 2 with all the same fields as Contact. If need be, you can create other self-joining relationships for the same table using multiple table occurrences. There are a couple of self-join relationships in Figure 7-6 between the various Contact table occurrences. The relationship between CON and con_CON__x is a multiple-criteria relationship, which we'll be discussing next.

NOTE FileMaker will add a space and a number to each subsequent table reference. The next references would be Contact 3, Contact 4, and so on. We will change those names using the anchor-buoy naming convention. (See Chapter 6.) Since it also removes spaces from TO names, it is in keeping with the requirements for web sharing and ODBC.

Multiple-Criteria Relationships[7]

FileMaker Pro 7 and later allow you to create multiple pairs of relationship criteria between the same pair of table occurrences. What advantage is there to this arrangement? Let's say you built a relationship between two TOs of the Contact table to show all the people in your file who work at the same company (Company = Company). A portal on the CON_Contact layout using that relationship would also display the name of the contact person whose record you're looking at. There's not much value in that. Using the multiple-criteria relationship tool, you can edit the relationship and add a second criterion where ContactSerNum_pk ≠ ContactSerNum_pk. Now no matter whose record you look at in that company, the only names to appear in the portal are the names of other employees.

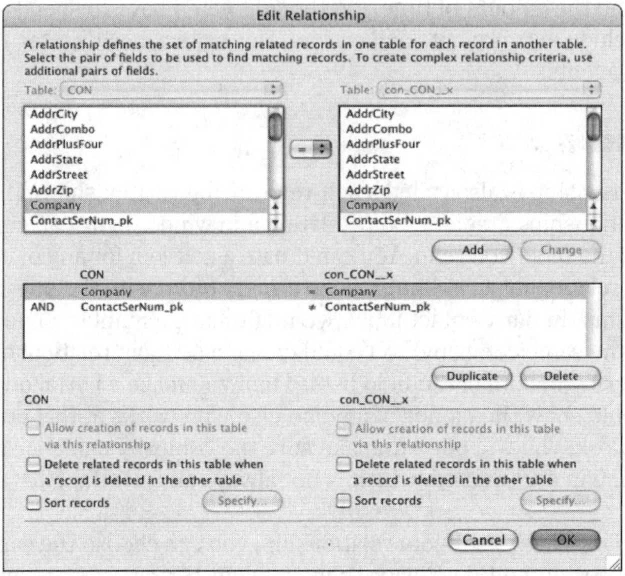

Figure 7-3
The Edit Relationship window showing a multiple-criteria relationship that includes an unequal relationship.

There are a couple of multiple-criteria relationships in Figure 7-6 between CON and con_CON__x and between INV and inv_INV__DateRange. These also happen to be unequal relationships, which we'll be discussing next.

There are some limitations to this arrangement depending on the scheme with which you intend to work. Sometimes the field pairs you choose will prevent creation of records via the relationship. But that's not too hard to figure out since that choice is grayed out once you create your second pair of fields. But here's something that might not be so obvious: If you add a second pair of relationship criteria to a relationship that allows creation of related records, the check mark disappears without warning. Even if you immediately delete the second criteria set, if you click the OK button when leaving the Edit Relationship window, you may be surprised to find you can no longer create records in the portal.

Unequal Relationships[7]

Previous versions of FileMaker only allowed equal relationships between fields. FMP7 and later versions let you create various unequal relationships. This includes relationships based on field values being less than, greater than, and not equal to each other. For example, using the relationship symbols, you can build a portal to show all invoices created between two dates. A simplified version of the relationship would look something like this:

```
Date ≥ zi_DateStart_gd and
Date ≤ zi_DateEnd_gd
```

zi_DateStart_gd and zi_DateEnd_gd would be formatted as global storage. You could put the fields on your layout and put any dates in them you want. Quick, easy, and flexible reporting! If your invoices included the name of the salesperson, you could add a global field to filter for that, too. There's a lot of power here.

The most important part of this kind of report would be putting the right portal on the right layout. In this case, the inv_INV__DateRange portal goes on the INV_Invoice layout. You also need to make sure the two date fields come from the INV table occurrence (TO).

There are a couple of unequal relationships in Figure 7-6 between CON and con_CON__x and INV and inv_INV__DateRange. You'll see the quick report I just talked about using the date fields at the bottom of the middle column in Figure 7-6 in the inv_INV__DateRange TO. Also notice how the relationship lines (paths) next to zi_DateStart_gd and zi_DateEnd_gd have a little vertical line attached to them and don't quite touch the side of the INV table occurrence. That indicates that the fields next to them cannot be indexed. In this case it's because the fields are global. A second interesting aspect of this particular relationship is that both of the global date fields in INV terminate at a single date field in inv_INV__DateRange.

NOTE When you use one or more global (or any other unindexed) fields on one side of a relationship, you can only find or display related records properly that "live" on the other side of the relationship. Even then, it only works if the key related field(s) are indexed and the portal (or related fields) are displayed on a layout that uses the appropriate table occurrence. Indexed records cannot find or display unindexed records. The only way to identify "related" records is if they're indexed. Relationships with one or more unindexed fields on each side of the relationship will simply not work properly and should be considered invalid.

The Relationships Graph

FileMaker's relationships graph can be very helpful in understanding your table relationships at a glance.

You may also be able to see if you have an invalid relationship. For example, if any relationship shows even one unindexed field on each end of the relationship, whatever function you intend to perform will fail.

I said you can learn a lot at a glance. But as your solutions become more complex, the graph can get so cluttered you may not be able to tell what's going on. Right now we only have a few connections (or paths) to ContactSerNum in our Business file. But it is conceivable that there could be dozens. When more than one path connects to a field on the same side of the table occurrence, you may not be able to tell which is a one, many, or unindexed connection. You may need to move the table occurrences around the graph and double-click the path symbol to view the details in the Edit Relationship window.

After I've spent some time organizing my graph, I really don't want to move TOs around too much. So I discovered another method of opening the Edit Relationship window. You already know which two TOs and relationships you want to examine. Of the two, one of them has many other TOs connected to it. Don't click on that one. Instead, click on the TO with the fewest TOs attached. Then press the arrow key on your keyboard in the direction of the busier TO of the two. It will highlight the operator box and you can press Command+O (Mac) or Ctrl+O (Windows) to open the Edit Relationship window.

By the way, double-clicking anywhere on the line that connects two table occurrences opens the Edit Relationship window. The problem is that where the TOs are tightly packed, you can't even get to the lines easily. But the TOs are always fairly easy to click on.

Other Notes

You don't need to tell FileMaker what type of relationship you're using, but knowing the relationship types is extremely helpful for good planning. That's how you recognize where data storage problems with a proposed system lie, and where you should do your user interface and reporting development.

Notice that the one-to-many (and its reverse, the many-to-one) relationships are the only ones that are regularly used. Your ER diagrams will probably also reflect that.

> **NOTE** If you put enough thought into it, it's possible to complicate everything into a many-to-many relationship. This is especially true if you look at your data independent of time. For example, a person may only have one spouse at any given time, but looked at over a long time, a person could have had many spouses. The goal isn't to make your database cover every situation; it's to make it descriptive of the information you need to gather and use. Make the entities and relationships in your database system as simple as possible, and no simpler.

Occasionally, you may see a dialog with the following warning: "This name is already in use. Please provide a unique name." The solution is simple: Just give the table occurrence a different name. You can make as many relationships to a table as you need. The only requirement is that each table occurrence has a different name. One other advantage of the anchor-buoy standard is that there is never a question regarding the name of a TO.

Invoice System ER Diagram

Now that you know how to create and use an ER diagram, let me show you the ER diagram for the invoicing files we'll be building in this chapter. Figure 7-4 gives you some idea of how the Contact and Phone tables we've already made will be connected to the invoicing system.

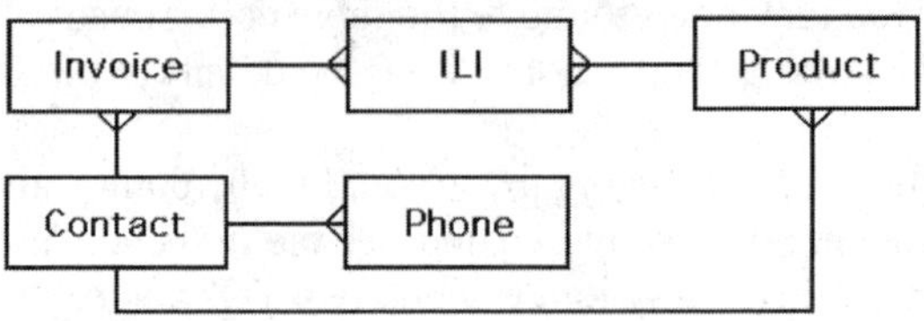

Figure 7-4
ER diagram for a basic invoicing system integrating the Contact table created earlier.

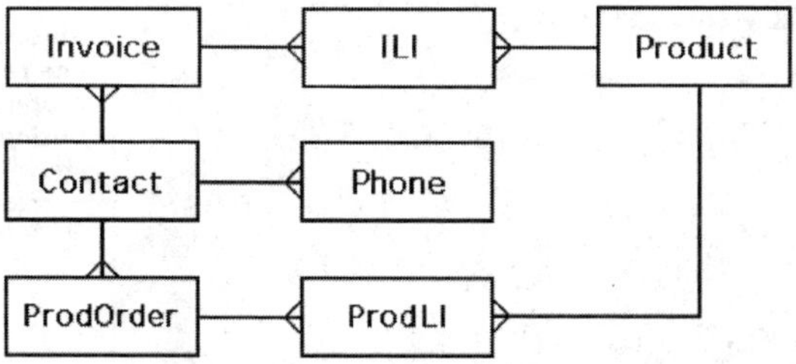

Figure 7-5
ER diagram for an invoicing system integrating two files for product orders.

NOTE The ER diagrams shown here are valid; however, FileMaker's relationships graph won't let you create a "circular" relationship like the one shown in Figure 7-4. That circle is created when Product connects back to Contact. In FileMaker you would create a second occurrence of the Product table. Don't worry, FileMaker will tell you when you've got it wrong!

Some of the people in the Contact table will be customers. One customer will (hopefully) have many invoices with your store. The reason Contact and Product are tied together is that your suppliers — as well as your customers — can be in your Contact table. One contact (manufacturer or distributor) will supply you with many products. Tying these together may not be practical in some cases where it would require too many specialized fields, but let's assume this for now.

Connecting one contact to many products sounds good, but there is a potential problem. You may not order a given product from the same manufacturer every time. Prices change, and you'll want to take advantage of the best deal. Figure 7-5 shows how the ER diagram would change to accommodate that arrangement.

Notice that ProdLI (code PLI) now has the double "many" symbol attached to it. That means the reporting will be done there. You might fill out the orders in ProdOrder (PRO), but you should print from PLI. Also notice that the "many" symbol that was attached to Product in Figure 7-4 has now turned around. Product is now "one" attached to many PLI records.

One more thing: Remember that every time you create a relationship, you have to identify key, or match, fields. So, take this planning time as an opportunity to think through the fields that you'll need to create in each table, how each table will relate, and the kinds of reports you'll need.

If this is your first time working with a database, you're in for a real treat. The more you work on your database solution, the more things you'll discover that you want your database solution to do. You'll discover just how powerful a tool FileMaker Pro is, and you'll wonder how you ever got along without it.

So, it's important to gather as much information as possible about the system you'll be building. It's also important to realize that every solution is not cut and dried.

I won't be demonstrating the modification that connects products to contacts in our basic invoicing system, but by the time you finish this book, you should have the knowledge you need to fill it out yourself.

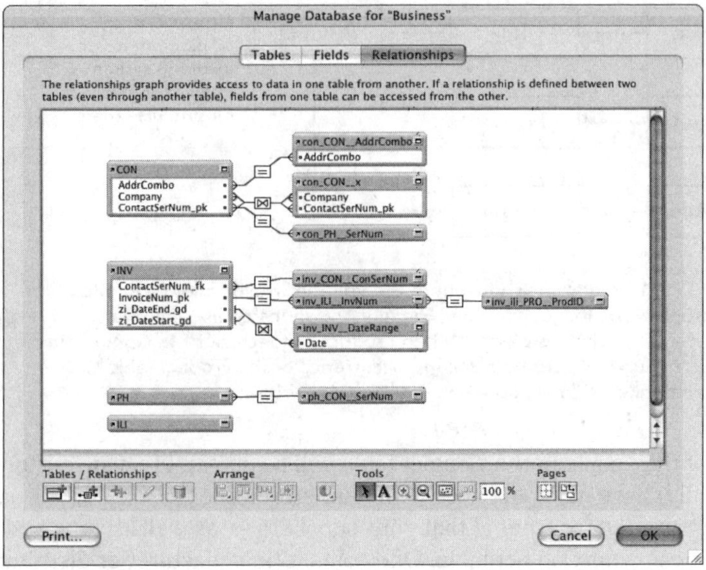

Figure 7-6 The relationships graph in the Business table showing a variety of relationships.

Create the Tables

Looking back to Figure 7-4, you can see that we need to create three more tables: Invoice, InvoiceLineItems, and Product. You already know how to create files, fields, and layouts. So rather than tell you every little step, I want you to go ahead and do what you already know how to do. Even though the graph in Figure 7-6 has more elements than you'll have when you complete this exercise, it may give you some clues as to what the relationships will consist of. (You may need a magnifying glass.)

Invoice Table

Start a new empty table called Invoice and add the following fields:

Field Name	*Type*	*Options*
InvoiceNum_pk	Number	Auto-enter Serial, Prohibit Modification
ContactSerNum_fk	Number	
Date	Date	Creation
InvoiceTotal	Number	

NOTE This table needs to be easy to work in on a day-to-day basis. It needs to be clear so the order taker knows what he or she is supposed to do to take the order. It doesn't need to be as pretty as the printouts from the InvoiceLineItems layout we'll use.

InvoiceLineItems Table

Start a table called InvoiceLineItems and add the following fields:

Field Name	*Type*	*Options*
InvoiceNum_fk	Number	
ProdID_fk	Text	
Description	Text	
Price	Number	
Quantity	Number	
LineTotal	Calculation	= Price * Quantity (result is Number)

> **TIP** You do not need to add the equal sign (=) in the Formula window for this calculation. In fact, if you try to place it there, you'll get a warning when you click the OK button. This is just the way it shows up in the field list when you're done.

This table has to look good for printing reports. You'll probably want your company logo to appear here. One report could actually be the invoice itself, and customers will surely see that.

Importing a Table[8]

If you have downloaded this book's companion files you can use a feature introduced in FileMaker 8 that allows you to import a table and the data in it all in one quick step. Look in the Chapter 7 folder for Products.fp7. (If you don't have that file, you can download the files from the publisher's web site at http://www.wordware.com/files/fmpro10 and click on the link for "Book files." Otherwise, skip to the next section and create the table manually.)

> **Note** FileMaker Pro 10 files still have the .fp7 extension and are compatible, but FMP8, 8.5, 9, and 10 features won't be available to users of the FMP7 program.

FileMaker 8 introduced the ability to import a table from another file. Many buyers of FMP7 complained that this function should have been available with version 7. You, dear reader, get the benefits of their outcries. Now that the howling has subsided, here's what you do:

1. Choose **File**, **Import Records**, **File** and locate the file that has the table you want. In our case, it's called **Product** in the Chapter 7 folder.
2. In the upper-left corner of the Import Field Mapping dialog, click the drop-down next to **Source**. In the case of the Product file, there is only one table.
3. In the upper-right corner, click the drop-down next to **Target**. Pull down and select **New Table ("Product")**. Import arrows automatically fill in. If you switch any of the arrows off, the data for that field will not import. Notice that only the "Add new records" radio button is active in the Import Action area.

4. Click the **Import** button and you've got a fresh new table with data ready to work with.

Here are some of the finer points:

- If you already have a table with that name in your file, FileMaker will add a number to the end of the name.
- Only the current found set of records will be imported from the file.
- If some of the imported fields include calculations that refer to fields in other tables, the calculation will be "commented out." You'll be able to see what the calculation should be so you can fix it.
- Fields that include lookups may need to be repointed once you build the relationships.

Product Table

If you didn't create this table by importing it in the section above, create the table called Product and add the following fields:

Field Name	*Type*	*Options*
ProdID_pk	Text	Unique Value
Description	Text	
Price	Number	

Notice that ProdID_pk is a text field. Many companies have their own product IDs that may incorporate numbers and letters. The ID is very ingrained in the way the entire company refers to the product line. A text field will allow for such an arrangement, as long as the ID is unique. You can find the Unique Value option under the Validation tab.

NOTE The ProdID refers specifically to product numbers internal to the company. If the company is dealing with parts that come from other manufacturers, you will probably want a separate field for MfgProdID. In that case, you will want to allow duplicate values in that field, because different external manufacturers may have matching product ID numbers.

This is a utility table, so you don't have to worry about making it beautiful. But you should design it to be easy to work in for taking and printing inventory.

Other Possibilities

If you're really serious about this system, you'll probably also want to include the following fields in the Product table. I'll leave them out for the purpose of this demo. But I'm sure you can see their importance, and you may want to add them to your system.

Field Name	*Type*	*Options*
Cost	Number	
Quantity	Number	

Field Name	*Type*	*Options*
MfgNumber	Text	
Picture	Container	
Taxable	Text	Yes/No
TaxRate	Number	Lookup from Global
zi_TaxRate_gn	Number	Global

Notice the Quantity field. In the process of taking orders, it would be possible to have items removed from inventory. You could easily generate a report to be run whenever you choose that will list the products whose quantities had fallen below the warning level.

Example Data

Add the following example data to the Product table:

ProdID_pk	*Description*	*Price*
1001	Small Widget	9.99
1002	Medium Widget	14.99
1003	Large Widget	19.99

Create the Relationships

Now let's build the relationships between the tables.

Invoice and InvLI

1. Go to **File, Manage Database, Relationships** (see Figure 7-7).

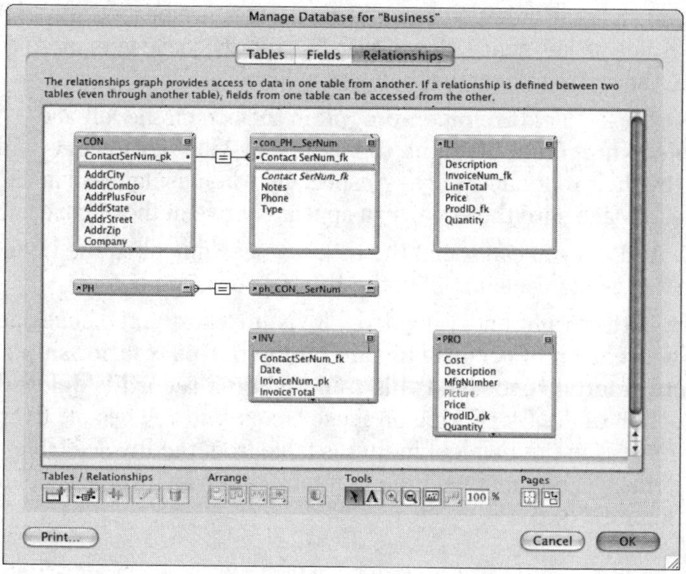

Figure 7-7
The Manage Database window's Relationships tab showing various table occurrences.

2. Because we're using the anchor-buoy system, we need to give these new TOs abbreviated names and stack them down the left side. They will be associated with their own layouts. Double-click the new TOs in turn. Change InvoiceLineItems to **ILI**, Invoice to **INV**, and Products to **PRO**.

   We'll add utility TOs as we need them for various purposes. Our first goal is to build an invoice. It seems as if an invoice should appear on a layout of its own. The INV table occurrence looks like the logical place to start, so we'll add TOs to the right of it to provide functionality to the invoices we'll be creating. We'll need a copy of the InvoiceLineItems, but we don't want to use the ILI occurrence because the A-B method insists we reserve that strictly for a layout of its own.
3. Click the lower-left button just under the word Tables to add a new TO. Select the **InvoiceLineItems** table in the upper area of the Specify Table window.
4. Now, take a look at how we connected the second Phone table occurrence (con_PH__SerNum) to the CON table occurrence. Can you guess what we should name this new TO? (See if you can get it without peeking.)
5. Name this TO **inv_ILI__InvNum** and click **OK.**
6. Move this new TO to the right of INV.
7. Click on the **Edit Relationships** icon, the second from the left under Tables/Relationships. You can use this icon not only to edit relationships but also to create them, as we demonstrated in Chapter 6.
8. From the Table drop-down on the left, select **INV**. In the drop-down on the right, select **inv_ILI__InvNum**. Yes, there are a lot of TOs in the drop-down list. But notice how this new TO falls alphabetically right after INV. Kinda makes sense, doesn't it? As your database gets more complicated, this arrangement will be more valuable.
9. Select the key field **InvoiceNum_pk** in the box on the left and **InvoiceNum_fk** on the right. (Sometimes I will refer to fields with suffixes by their root name only — especially when using them in TO names.) Make sure the equal sign appears between those boxes.
10. Click **Add**. As you can see in the box, InvoiceNum_pk in the Invoice table equals InvoiceNum_fk in the ILI table occurrence.
11. At the bottom right under inv_ILI__InvNum, click on the boxes next to **Allow creation of records in this table via this relationship** and **Delete related records in this table when a record is deleted in the other table**. By clicking on these boxes, you will be able to create new records in the InvoiceLineItems table from the Invoice table and all line items will be removed from that table when an invoice is deleted (see Figure 7-8).

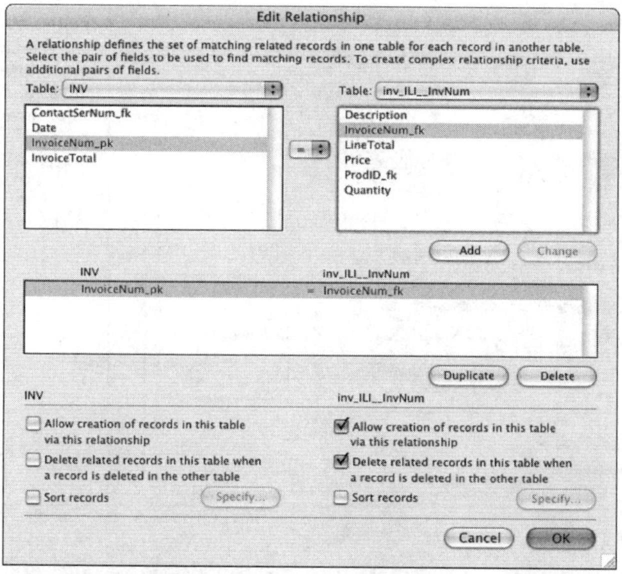

Figure 7-8
The Edit Relationship window showing the relationship between INV (Invoice) and inv_ILI__InvNum as well as the check box selections.

> **CAUTION** Do not check the boxes in the lower left. Why? With the Delete option checked, any time you delete a line item from the invoice (customers do change their minds), the entire invoice will disappear! There is no point to having invoices created from the InvoiceLineItems table. In some cases, you may choose to sort the portal. You don't need that here.

> **CAUTION** If you start moving your table reference icons around the relationships graph, the appearance of the Edit Relationship window may change. For instance, if you drag the inv_ILI__InvNum TO to the left of the INV TO (and it was initially on the right), the line between the tables will snap over to the left of INV. Double-clicking the equal sign will now show the columns in the Edit Relationship window have reversed with inv_ILI__InvNum on the left and INV on the right. You don't need to be alarmed — only the appearance has changed. But if you're moving tables around and always expect to be clicking the Delete box on the right, you could be in for a rude awakening. Pay attention to *everything* in the Edit Relationship window whenever you make changes there. If you stick with the anchor-buoy system, this probably won't be a problem — another advantage of the system!

12. Click **OK**. As you can see in the relationships graph, you've created a one-to-many relationship between INV and inv_ILI__InvNum. An equal sign is part of the link, and the field InvoiceNum shows in italics in the lower part of each TO. Not only that, the upper block in each table in a relationship includes the key field name with the link from that key field to the corresponding key field in the other table in that relationship. If the equal sign is blue, it is currently selected. Look at Figure 7-9 to see what your graph should look like. Notice that I've closed up some of the TOs to make it easier to read. You can always pop them back open by clicking that little Table Display toggle box in the upper-right corner of the TO.

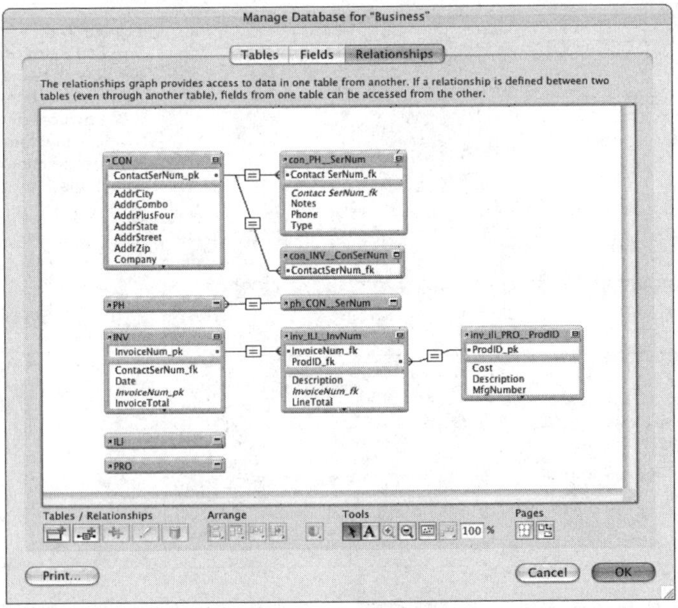

Figure 7-9
The relationships graph once the tables and relationships have been added.

- As I mentioned earlier, if you want to edit that relationship, double-click on the equal sign or anywhere on the line itself, and you will be taken to the Edit Relationship window.
- If you want to cancel the relationship, select the equal sign and press the Delete key. However, any table occurrences created will remain unless you delete them.

Invoice and Contact

Now we need to create a relationship with Contact (CON) as the parent and Invoice as the child using ContactSerNum as the key field. Call the Invoice TO **con_INV__ConSerNum**. In this case, you don't need to click any of the boxes under Contact or Invoice in the lower part of the Edit Relationship window. Refer to Figure 7-9. We'll eventually use this in order to be able to view invoices that belong to a contact and to be able to create invoices directly from the contact.

InvLI and Product

Create a relationship between inv_ILI__InvNum and the Product table using ProdID as the key field. Again, create a new TO for Product. Since this will go to the right of the new line items table, its name will be a little longer and reflect its position in the string: **inv_ili_PRO__ProdID**. Kind of cryptic, but the name does tell the story about where it belongs in the relationship. You needn't click any of the boxes in the lower part of the window. Notice that in this case the relationship is a many-to-one (inv_ILI__InvNum to inv_ili_PRO__ProdID).

The first table we created in this Business file was Contact. From there, we created the Phone table. In the Contact table, you want to be able to have multiple phone numbers. When we created the relationship between these two tables, we selected "Allow creation of records in this table via this relationship" in the Phone table.

Whenever your intent is to create new data in the child table from a portal on the parent table, you check the "Allow creation of records" box under the child table.

You might ask if the parent table — or the "one" table of the one-to-many relationship — must appear as the left table reference in the Edit Relationship window. The answer is no. As mentioned in the previous Caution, the columns may change whenever you move the table reference icons in the relationships graph.

BEST PRACTICES When you name a table (and the table occurrences), even if you don't follow the A-B method, make sure that you don't separate words in the name. It could be a problem if your data is used for the web or ODBC. You can have multiple table references because of the equal and unequal relationships between tables. To rename a table, double-click on it. You'll see the Specify Table window. You can change the name near the bottom under Name of Table Occurrence.

CAUTION Once you begin building lists of external data sources and relationships between files and adding scripts, don't change the names of the files. (You don't have to worry about that when dealing with tables within a single file.) It's usually best to keep related files in the same folder. Versions of FileMaker previous to 7 would search the entire network in an attempt to find a file, sometimes finding the wrong file! With the Manage External Data Sources window, once it has searched the places listed it will stop and present you with the File Not Found dialog. Even if you identify the file at that point, you really need to update the data source in order to avoid seeing the File Not Found dialog in the future. Even then you may have problems with scripts and value lists that depend on external files. The FileMaker Advanced product has a feature that helps you easily rename related files and takes care of all the internal renaming automatically.

However, it's still a good idea to rename backup copies to prevent them from accidentally being opened. You might try putting an "X" or the date in front of the name of your backups. If you ever have to use the files again, just undo the changed name (and rename the ones you're taking out of service). If FileMaker finds an older version of a file or a file with the same name in some other database system, you may get some unpleasant surprises. FileMaker can now keep track of the network address of the machine of the data source. That's just fine unless the server bites the dust and you put the files on a new server with a different machine number. Unless you assign the old machine number to the replacement server, all your external data sources will need to be reset. Better to reset the machine number!

Add the Lookups

When you enter information in an invoice, you'll want to do it as quickly as possible. After all, the customer is waiting. It would be great if we could just choose the ProdID and have the description and price appear automatically. We can do that by using FileMaker's lookup capabilities.

The reason we want to use lookup fields is that products and prices may change. We want any invoice, even the old ones, to reflect the products and prices as they were at the time the order was placed.

The fields we want to make into lookup fields are in the InvLI table.

1. Go to the ILI layout.
2. Go into **Manage Database**, **Fields**. You should be viewing the fields for the InvoiceLineItems table.
3. Select the **Description** field and click on **Options**.
4. At the **Auto-Enter** tab, check the box beside **Look-up value.**
5. At the drop-down beside "Starting with table," select **inv_ILI__InvNum.**
6. At the drop-down beside "Lookup from related table," select **inv_ili_PRO__ProdID** as the related table (see Figure 7-10). Again, notice that using the A-B system, it is very clear which tables are related to this version of the line items table. You'll also notice that if you left ILI in the "Starting with table" drop-down, there are no related tables at all!
7. Select **Description** under "Copy value from field."
8. Click **OK** and **OK** again.
9. Now do the same for the **Price** field, except you want to copy the data from the Price field into the InvLI table's Price field (not the Description field). Click **OK, OK.**

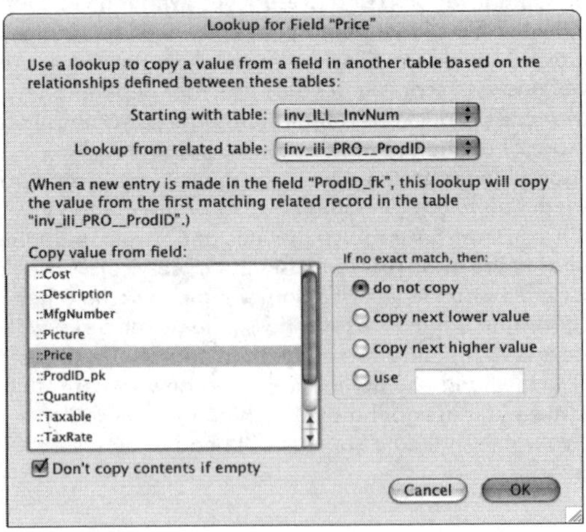

Figure 7-10
The Lookup window for the Price field in the inv_ILI__InvNum table occurrence.

The Invoice Layout

Go to the INV layout in Layout mode. Rename this layout **INV_Invoice**, and move the fields around until they resemble Figure 7-11. I'll explain about the Customer field when we get to the section about adding drop-downs, so skip it for now. Add the inv_ILI portal and place the fields in the upper row of the portal, being very careful that they stay within the boundaries of the portal.

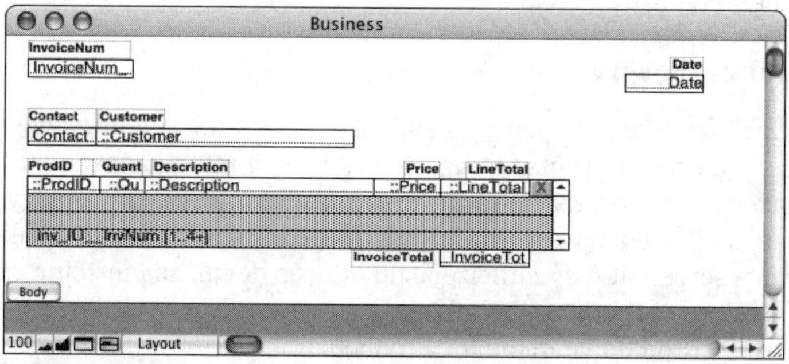

Figure 7-11
The INV_Invoice layout showing example positions of the fields and the portal.

If your fields don't have borders in Browse mode, go back to Layout mode, select them, and right-click on one of them (Control+click (Macintosh)). Select Field Borders. Make sure that you've specified borders at the top and bottom, left and right. Then go to the format section at the bottom of the window. Now make sure that you've selected black and a one-point line.

The X on the right of the portal is a button that will delete portal records. Notice that I shortened the field labels for ContactSerNum and Quantity. Whenever possible, I like to have the full name of the field on the label, but sometimes it's better to abbreviate to keep the layout from being too crowded. Unless your customers are ordering hundreds of thousands of items, you won't need a large space for the Quantity field, for example. Abbreviate the field labels to match the size you need for the field. As an alternative, you can rotate the field label. (Select the field label, then go to Arrange, Rotate. It may take more than one rotation to get the appearance you like.) If the field names are long, though, the rotated version will take up a lot of real estate on your layout, too. The best alternative is to abbreviate the labels. I also removed the header and the footer layout parts.

The Product ID, Quantity, Price, LineTotal, and InvoiceTotal fields have their text aligned to the right so the number columns will line up. LineTotal and InvoiceTotal are formatted as numbers with two decimal places to represent price.

1. To do this, click on both fields. Select **Format, Number.**
2. At the Number Format window, select **Format as decimal.** Select **Fixed number of decimal digits** and type in the numeral **2.**
3. Click **OK.**

Adding Drop-downs to the Invoices

Some of the drop-downs we need to add to fields that appear on invoices will actually come from other tables. (If you intend to include value lists from other files, it's best to build them in the other files first.) When we click on the ProdID field, it would be very helpful to see both the ProdID and the description because most people don't memorize the ID numbers of the products for their company.

Products Drop-down

What's the difference between a pop-up and a drop-down menu? There's no difference. We use the terms *pop-up* and *drop-down* interchangeably. Starting in FileMaker 8 it seems that they have standardized their terminology to drop-down, so I've tried to switch to that. Depending on where the field appears on a screen, it may either pop up or drop down, and in some cases it might pop out to one side or the other.

To create a drop-down menu for Products:

1. Choose **File**, **Manage Value Lists**.
2. At the Manage Value Lists window (see Figure 7-12), click on **New**.

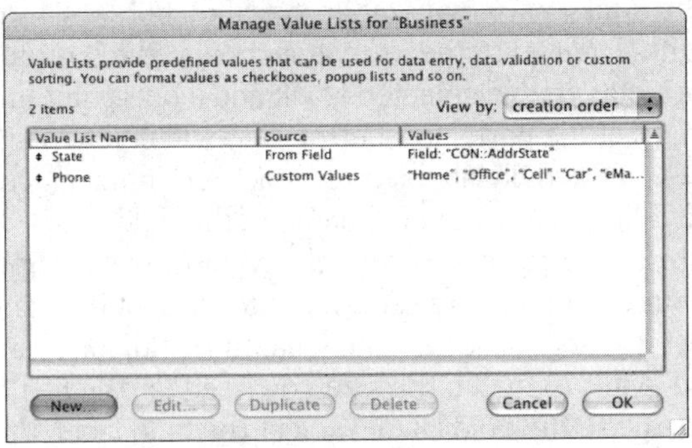

Figure 7-12
The Manage Value Lists window.

3. The next window will be the Edit Value List window, but it is also the window from which you can create value lists. Name the value list **Products**, and select **Use values from field**.
4. At the next window, Specify Fields for Value List "Products," use the drop-down menu under "Use values from first field" to select **PRO**. When you do, the three fields in the Product table will appear in the box below (unless you added the extra fields mentioned earlier).
5. Select **ProdID_pk**. When you do, other options that were previously grayed out will become available.
6. Select **Include all values.** Include all values gives you access to all information in that field in the drop-down. If you selected "Include only related values," you would see only information for which you had previously set up a relationship. (For example, let's say you were creating a drop-down for customers so you create a relationship back to the Contact table. There's no point in having family, friends, and other non-customer

names appear in the pop-up. It would be better to create a check box field in Contact that identifies customers. Then you could have a global field in Invoice that holds the word "customer" matching the word "customer" in the check box in Contact.)

7. If you want to display values from a second table or select a second field from the table you've already selected, click in the check box beside **Also display values from second field.** If you wanted to include information from a different table, you would choose the table from the drop-down menu. This was introduced in FileMaker 7. I'm not sure how you would use values from a different table, and to this day I still haven't seen any developers make use of it.
8. Make sure that **PRO** is the table selected and, when the fields appear, select **Description.** (Notice that we don't need to select a TO that's related to the invoice. We can go back to the base table for the value list.)
9. Next to "Sort values using," select **Second field.** (The radio buttons for first field and second field do not refer to the first and second fields in either list. Rather, they refer to the field selected in the first column — the one on the left — and the field selected in the second column — the one on the right.) In our case, the first field is ProdID, and the second is Description. When the items appear in the drop-down list, they'll be sorted alphabetically by the product name instead of the ID. In some companies, people will know the ID better than the product name. If you need to change it, this is the place to do it.
10. Click **OK**, **OK**, and **OK**.

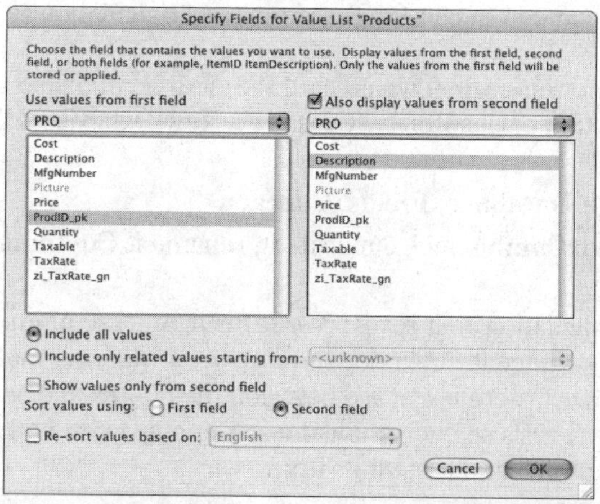

Figure 7-13
The window to specify fields for the value list.

(If you were planning to use a value list from an external file, you might want to create a value list in that file first. Then you would come back to this file and create an external data source and create a value list that refers to that file and the value list in that external file.)

To try out your new drop-down, go to Layout mode, select the ProdID field in the portal, and format it with the Products drop-down list. Now go into

Browse mode and try it out by adding a few items to the invoice, but you'll need to create a new invoice first.

Getting the Invoice Total

You may have noticed that InvoiceTotal is empty. We couldn't make the correct calculation until the relationships were in place. Go back into Manage Database, Fields, and change InvoiceTotal into a calculation field that reads: **Sum(inv_ILI__InvNum::LineTotal)**. Be sure that you choose **Calculation result as Number**. Click **OK** and **OK**. Like magic, you'll see the total. Look again at the calculation. It's actually adding numbers based on the relationship. (If you have not followed along exactly, naming your relationships and fields as I have, you will not get the total. In fact, FileMaker won't let you leave the area where you create the calculation unless it's formatted correctly.)

Customers Drop-down

Wouldn't it be great to have a list of customers drop down like the products did? But what would you want to appear in the second field — First Name, Last Name, or Company? You'd probably want a combination of fields. We can make a new field that concatenates (kon-KAT-e-nayts) all three of the other fields into one.

Concatenation is the process of combining character strings in a calculation. You can combine text from fields with other fields or any alphanumeric data you put in the calculation. The ampersand (&) is the concatenation symbol. In this case, you need to choose Text from the "Calculation result is" pop-up.

We did the same thing when we created the AddrCombo field in the "Calculation Field" section of Chapter 4, "Creating a New Database." We can build on that.

1. Go to **Manage Database, Fields, Contact**.
2. Select the **AddrCombo** field, duplicate it, rename it **Customer**, and click **Change**.
3. Change the calculation so it reads: **NameFirst &** " " **& NameLast &** " - " **& Company**. (Since it might not show up very well in print here, you need to know that there is a space between the quotes and before and after the dash. That's so everything doesn't end up crammed together.) Make sure the calculation result is **Text**.
4. Click **OK** and **OK** again.
5. Now choose **Manage Value Lists**. Create a value list called **Contacts**, and set it up like Figure 7-13 except choose **ContactSerNum** from the list on the left and the new **Customer** field on the right.
6. Click **OK**, **OK**, and **OK**.
7. Back in Layout mode, select the **ContactSerNum** field and format it with the Contacts drop-down list. Now go into Browse mode and try it

out. You'll probably want to make up a few company names to go in the records in the Contact table.

CAUTION Here's a little glitch. There's a problem with having the Customer drop-down sort by full name. If there are two people with the same name, FileMaker will only show you one! That's because FileMaker uses its indexing feature and only shows you unique values. If you have two John Smiths with no company name, you'll only see the first one. You can fix that by indexing on the unique ContactSerNum. Of course, then the list won't sort alphabetically. There are other solutions that require calculations, but that's beyond our purpose today.

NOTE When using concatenated fields as a key, you need to be aware that FileMaker has a 100-character limit with regard to evaluating the uniqueness of any single word. (A "word" can consist of any combination of letters and numbers as long as there are no spaces in the string; however, I advise against using special characters such as #, %, *, etc. Stick with upper- and lowercase letters and numbers.) That means any field used as a key needs to determine uniqueness in fewer than 100 characters. I have sometimes found it necessary to insert spaces between the parts of a concatenation to make a calculated field work reliably as a key. If a single string concatenation without spaces doesn't seem to work for you, try inserting spaces before and after the dash character using the method described above. This has nothing to do with FileMaker's ability to find records; FileMaker indexes every word in an indexed field regardless of the field length.

Placing the Customer Field on the Layout

Now you'll want to put the Customer field on the layout.

1. Go into Layout mode and use the **Field** tool.
2. When the Specify Field window appears, click **Current Table ("INV")** to activate the drop-down. Uh, oh! In the upper area under "Related Tables" there are no TOs that can give us the customer information. We'll just have to create one.
3. Click **Cancel** and go to **Manage Database, Relationships.**
4. Click the **Add Table** button, choose **Contact** and call it (can you guess?) **inv_CON__ConSerNum.**
5. Place this table somewhere to the right of INV and create a relationship between the TOs based on ContactSerNum.
6. Click **OK** to exit Manage Database.
7. Go back to the layout and add a field.
8. When the Specify Field window appears, choose **inv_CON__ConSerNum** from the drop-down and double-click the **Customer** field. Place it on the layout as shown in Figure 7-11.
9. Go back into Browse mode and try it out by choosing a ContactSerNum. Notice that when you choose a different ContactSerNum from the drop-down, a different customer appears in the Customer box.

Since Customer is a calculated field, you can do a find request in it, but the data cannot be altered accidentally.

⌘ **TIP** Sometimes you'll need to protect data in a field, but that data will have to change in the future. That means selecting "Prohibit modification of value" is out of the question. And if you turn off "Allow entry into field," your users can't perform a find request in that field.

Before FMP7, you had to create a new calculation field equal to the first field and place that on the common layout. Then you had to make a separate, password-protected layout where the original field could be modified. Starting in FMP7 you can go to Layout mode and choose Format, Field Behavior and uncheck the box next to "Allow field to be entered In Browse mode." As long as the box is checked next to "In Find mode," your users can find in the field, but not enter it in Browse mode. You could also protect specific fields from alteration by various users with accounts and privileges. For more on that, see Chapter 22, "Keeping Your Data Secure."

Other Considerations

For ease in data entry, you'll probably want to remove most of the fields from the tab order. The only fields you really need to tab into are ContactSerNum, ProdID, and Quantity.

When I was telling you about ER diagrams, I said that reporting would be done in the ILI table. The question now is: How do you make the contact information appear and print in that table? One way to do this is to create new fields in the Invoice table that would look up the company name and full address from the Contact table using the Contact relationship. (Hint: In the Lookup dialog, the starting table will be INV and the related table will be inv_CON__ConSerNum.) Each record created after the addition of those fields would have a copy of that information. Why not just show the related data from the Contact table? Well, what if the company changes its address? With invoices, it's important to have a copy of that information just the way it was when the invoice was created. If the IRS ever did an audit, you wouldn't want to try to explain why the addresses from an old invoice don't match their old location!

If you decide to add those fields on your own, you'll have to update all records created before you added those fields. To do that, go to the Invoice layout, and choose Records, Show All Records. Click in the ContactSerNum field (click a second time to dismiss the drop-down), and choose Records, Relookup Field Content. When you click the OK button, all records will now have the current company and address information filled in. You can go back into the InvLI layout and make that same data show by dragging fields onto the layout and using the Invoice relationship from the drop-down list at the top of the Specify Field window.

⌘ **TIP** Whenever you leave a window (Manage Database, Specify Button, Manage Scripts) where you've just been looking around, unless you intended to make one or more changes, get in the habit of choosing the Cancel button. Many times I've watched users go to a window or dialog and make a change accidentally, only to have it become the new setting when they clicked OK. Of course, once it becomes a habit, you can just as easily forget to click OK when you really mean to make a change.

External Data Source[9]

FileMaker can now connect with a number of ODBC databases by pulling a table occurrence right into the relationships graph. Even though we'll discuss this in more detail in Chapter 26, "Working with External Data Sources," I want to tease you a little bit here.

When you are in Manage Database on the Relationships tab and click the button to add a table, if you click the Data Source drop-down you'll see the list shown in Figure 7-14. It's the "Add ODBC Data Source" item that holds the power here. You first need to define a data source elsewhere in your system, as outlined briefly in Chapter 21, "Sharing Your Data with Other Applications." Once that's set up, when you make the Add ODBC Data Source selection, the tables will be listed in this dialog. There are some complexities to this feature because you'll need to be acquainted with one of these other database systems to some extent. Refer to Chapter 26 for the details.

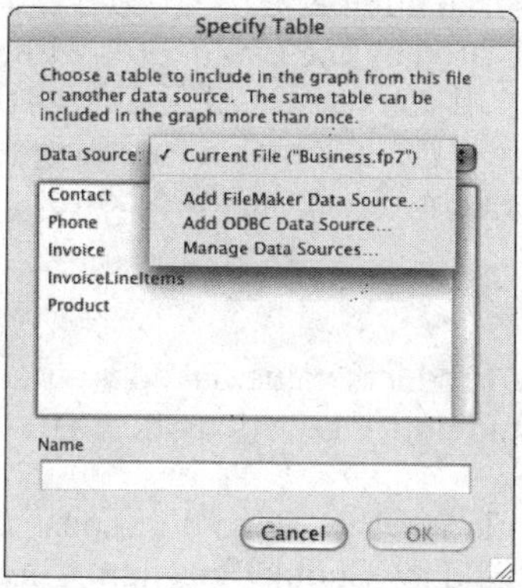

Figure 7-14
The Specify Table window showing FileMaker 9's new Data Source[9] drop-down.

Summary

This chapter has covered some of the serious stuff. If you're following along with what we've been doing, you're well on your way to understanding the whole thing. Granted, there has been a lot of jumping around between tables and some strange table occurrence names. But if you're starting to catch on to why, that's what counts. If you find it's all getting a little confusing, take a break and then go back and review some of the earlier chapters. There's more on relationships in Chapter 14, "Automating Your Database with Scripts," in the section called "Portable Portals."

In this chapter, I showed you the three types of relationships and how and when to use a join table. That led directly to learning how to draw a diagram of the relationships between tables. Then you built the tables from the diagram, added lookups and pop-ups, and entered some data. Good job!

Q & A

Q It seems that there can be quite a bit of variation with how the same files can be put together. Isn't there one right way?

> **A** No, because each situation will be different. That's why it's so important to gather as much information as you can before starting. Keep asking, "What if I (or some other users) do such and such?" and "How will I be able to show that report?" Then draw the ER diagram until it's clear.

Q After a while, I may have quite a few people in my Contact table. I won't want all of them showing up in the drop-down list. How do I limit it to real customers?

> **A** You can add two more fields to Contact. One would be a text field called CustList that you format with a radio button with values of "Yes" and "No." The second would be a calculation field (call it CustListCalc) that would read as follows: If (CustList = "Yes", ContactSerNum, ""). This If statement says to show the serial number if the record is marked "Yes"; otherwise, show nothing (indicated by the two quotes with nothing between them, not even a space). If you use CustListCalc as the first field in your drop-down, any contact with "No" or where nothing is selected in the CustList field will not show up in the drop-down.

Workshop

Go into the Product table and change the Products value list so it sorts by the first field. Now go back into the invoice and notice how that affects the sort order of the ProdID drop-down.

Follow the directions in the section titled "Other Considerations" near the end of this chapter to place a lookup field for ContactSerNum. Then go back into Invoice and create a few line items. See if you can make the contact show up in the ILI table.

Take a look at the Relationships tab. Does your handwritten ER diagram resemble the one created there by FileMaker?

Chapter 8

Finding and Sorting Your Data

Introduction

Having all this data isn't much good unless you can find it when you need it. You need to organize it in a way that will make sense so you can make decisions — what products to order, what customers to give a price break to, what zip codes to send a mailing to, what payments you deducted from employees' paychecks, and what old records to delete from the file or send off to the archives.

In this chapter, I'll show you how to:

- Find the records you need
- Omit any leftover records
- Use Saved Finds[10]
- Sort the remaining records
- Do any repetitive versions of these jobs with the help of scripts

Finding Records

Remember when we were finding Rich and Richard back in Chapter 3? Then you have a pretty good idea of where we're going. When you choose View, Find mode, FileMaker presents you with a blank record. You then type the data you're looking for in any of the fields or related fields. When you click the Perform Find button in the Status toolbar and press Enter or Return on your keyboard, FileMaker shows you the records you requested. If no records are found, FileMaker displays a dialog box telling you "No records match this set of find requests."

If one or more records were found, the Status toolbar shows how many. A green pie chart indicates how many of the total records are in your found set. Then you can click through the found set of records, or do whatever else it is you need to do.

Any records that are not found are still in the file; they're just hidden or omitted from the current found set. To bring all records back, choose Records, Show All Records, or press Command+J (Macintosh) or Ctrl+J (Windows). You can also click the pie chart to show just the omitted records and hide the found records. That's the same as if you went to the Records menu and selected Show Omitted Only. One thing that can be a little confusing: After you choose Show Omitted Only and then choose it again to bring back your found set, you lose any sort you may have had going. That means any sub-summaries that showed up won't appear until you sort the records again. For more on that, see the "Dynamic Sub-Summaries" section later in this chapter.

Methods

1. Go into the **CON_Contact** layout and run the **Find Richard** script or click the button.
2. Now choose **Records**, **Modify Last Find**. FileMaker remembers the find you just performed and allows you to make a change. This can be a great time-saver if you've just run a complex find and need to rework it. (A find performed with a script will not show up in the Saved Finds menu, which is described later in this chapter.)
3. While you're still in Find mode and your cursor is in the First Name field, backspace until all you have left is **Rich**.
4. Finish the find. You should have a different group of records. (I know, the First Name field is really NameFirst. But as far as the user is concerned — and that's you right now — the field is called First Name because that's what the field label says. When we're in Browse or Find mode that's what we'll call it. When we're defining the fields, working with scripts, importing, exporting, or sorting, we'll call it NameFirst.)

⌘ **TIP** Modify Last Find is also referred to as Refind. The keyboard shortcut is Command+R (Macintosh) or Ctrl+R (Windows).

5. Run Modify Last Find again. This time FileMaker remembers Rich.
6. Now put = (equal sign) in front of Rich so it looks like **=Rich** and run the find. This time, Richard is not in the found set. The equal sign is one of FileMaker's find symbols. It stands for an exact match and means that you only want to find records that have that exact combination of letters in the field. Your search may result in records that contain other words or characters in the field, but they must be separated from the search string by spaces, returns, or certain Unicode characters. This may sound confusing the first time you hear it. Test it out using single words, as well as multiple words and spaces strung together, to get a better handle on it.
7. Duplicate the record so that you have two records with Rich.
8. In the second record, add the middle initial **A.** (include the period) in the First Name field.
9. Modify the last find. (Modify Last Find allows you to make changes to a find, although in this case, we are not going to make changes; we are just going to repeat it. Choose **Modify Last Find** to re-examine your last request, so that you can check the spelling or other criteria you may have

entered. This is particularly useful for complex finds, in which you don't want to retype everything.)

10. Complete the find. You should show both records. The equal sign will also allow records with other information in the field to be found, as long as one of the words is an exact match.
11. Do a Refind (**Modify Last Find** or use the keyboard shortcut), add a second equal sign in front of Rich so it looks like **==Rich**, and perform the find. You should only find the one record now. The double equal sign finds only records that have exactly the data that follows them and nothing else in the field. (That means that FileMaker will not find any records that contain any additional words or characters — including spaces or returns that you can't see — in that field. This contrasts with the single equal sign in that records *will* be found that contain other characters as long as they are separated by spaces or return characters. Results may vary if the field is indexed with Unicode.)
12. Do a Refind and add an **A** (without the period) in the First Name field. No records are found. That's because you don't have a "Rich A" — you have a "Rich A." instead.
13. Try it again and include the period. Now try Refind and add an extra space between Rich and A. This find symbol won't let you get away with anything! FileMaker Pro also has a set of features a bit different from Modify Last Find that allow you to extend or constrain your find. For details on those features, look further in this chapter.

The Find Symbols

All the find symbols are available in Find mode from a drop-down list in the Status toolbar as shown in Figure 8-1. Click the triangle next to the word Operators to make the list appear.

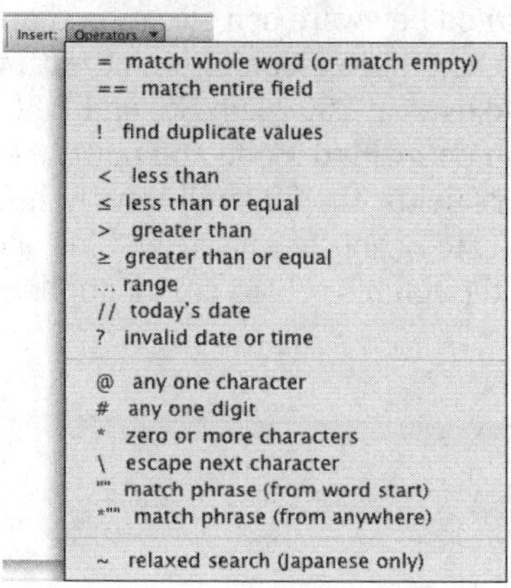

Figure 8-1
The Find Symbols pop-up list.

You may remember some of these other symbols from math class. Let's look at what the symbols mean.

Match Whole Word (Or Match Empty) (=)

We've already looked at this, but there's a twist. You can use this symbol to find fields that are empty or have unindexed values. Since many of the Notes fields are empty, do a find in the Notes field and only put the equal sign in there. In essence, you're asking FileMaker to find all records that are equal to nothing in that field. Remember, though, that many keyboard characters are unindexed. For instance, if you only had a dash or an underscore character in the field, those records will turn up in your find as well. This can cause you some headaches when it comes to finding e-mail addresses, since all e-mail addresses include the @ symbol. Well, you can actually find e-mail addresses if you add the backslash character (\) just before the @ symbol. So if you were performing a find for my e-mail address, you would type JStars\@DataDesignPros.com. Another option would be to index the field as Unicode, although there are drawbacks to that. To learn how to index a field for Unicode, see the "Find Strategies" section later in this chapter.

Match Entire Field (==)

We talked about this before. The double equal sign only finds records where the entire field contents match the data that follow the equal signs exactly. If there is an extra space in the field in a record, that record will not be among the found set. You can use the field content match when searching in date, time, and number fields, but I can't think of a reason you would want to.

Find Duplicate Values (!)

The find duplicate values symbol can be handy for finding people with different names who live at the same address. Choose the field for which you want to find duplicates, and type the exclamation symbol. Of course, you might find people who live at the same address in different cities.

To take this to the extreme, you should be aware of a situation that could yield unexpected results. Let's say you had three records: John Smith who lives at 100 Elm Circle, John Smith who lives at 200 Main St., and Jalil Petroch who lives at 200 Main St. If you enter Find mode and put the exclamation symbol in the Name and Address fields, the find will return the second John Smith. His name is a duplicate of another name and his address is a duplicate of another address, even though his record isn't a duplicate as a whole.

⌘ **TIP** A trick to finding duplicate entries in a database is to build a calculation field that concatenates people's names and their street addresses. For example, DupCheck = NameFirst & NameLast & AddrStreet. Notice there are no spaces or dashes between the elements. That's because all we need is the data. Perform a find in this field, and you'll see all entries that are almost certainly duplicate records (barring data entry differences like William vs. Bill, or St. vs. Street). Then you can decide which ones you want to keep and which ones to delete. (If you have nothing but numbers in your field, make sure that the field calculation result is text.)

Using the multiple-criteria relationship discussed in Chapter 7, you can accomplish much the same thing without building this field. The relationship would be:

CON::NameFirst = con_CON__x::NameFirst
AND CON::NameLast = con_CON__x::NameLast
AND CON::AddrStreet = con_CON__x::AddrStreet

If any records are visible in the portal, there's a duplicate! (This assumes there is only one pre-existing Contact table and you create the con_CON__x table occurrence for the purpose of this relationship. I only mention that because I had already displayed some other Contact table occurrences in Figure 7-6 in the last chapter.)

Less Than (<)

The less than symbol is used to narrow your searches by eliminating values that are higher than or equal to your selected limit. As an example:

1. Select **Show All Records** and note the number in the ContactSerNum field in the last record.
2. Start a find, and click in the **ContactSerNum** field.
3. Choose the less than sign (<), follow it with the serial number you just memorized, and finish the find. You should have all records except the last one. You can also use the less than symbol to find dates, times, and even text.
4. Start a find, type **<G** in the Last Name field, and finish the find. You should find the Bailey records and any others you might have that begin with letters lower in the alphabet than G. It also works for partial or whole words. Do a find for "<Gump." This time FileMaker includes Gentry (at least in my file) because it's less than Gump.

⌘ **TIP** You don't need to choose the find symbols from the pop-up list; you can simply type the symbols right from your keyboard.

Less Than or Equal (≤ or <= on Macintosh, <= on Windows)

This is much the same as less than, except it will also include the item typed in the results found. In the find for ContactSerNum we tried above, you would have found all records.

Greater Than (>)

Just the opposite of less than. If you tried to find records greater than the last ContactSerNum, you wouldn't have found any.

Greater Than or Equal (≥ or >= on Macintosh, >= on Windows)

This finds all records with a value greater than and including the item typed. In our example, you would have found the last record.

Range (...)

This is used mostly for date fields, but it works for numbers, times, and even text. To try it out, start by finding all records. Then go into the CreationDate field and put in a variety of dates. Perform a find using one of the earlier dates and one of the later dates. Structure your find like this: "5/22/2007...7/7/2008." The earlier date (meaning year, month, and day) should always go first. One little caution: If you try to use a date range in a text field, you won't get the results you expect.

> **NOTE** When you perform a find using a date range in a date field, FileMaker will reject invalid dates. For example, if your date range includes February 30, you will get a warning that the date is invalid.

Today's Date (//)

This only works in a date or timestamp field. FileMaker knows that when you put these two slash symbols in a date field, you want to find items with today's date according to your computer's clock.

Invalid Date or Time (?)

FileMaker won't let you put an incorrect date or time in a date, time, or timestamp field. For example, 7/44/2008 is an unacceptable date. However, incorrect data can be imported, entered by a script, or caused by converting some other type of file to FileMaker format. When data is incorrect in a date or time field, a question mark appears in that field. (You'll also see a question mark in a number field if the number is too long to fit in the space allotted for it.) If you need to check date or time fields for improper data, do a find using the question mark. Again, this won't work for a number field.

Starting with version 6, FileMaker handles two-digit years in date fields in a single, consistent manner. Look near the end of the FileMaker Pro 10 manual for the details. But once again, use four-digit years in a date field to be safe. And be aware of potential problems when importing data from other sources.

Any One Character (@)

You can use the at symbol (@) as a substitute for one character of which you're unsure. For instance, if you're looking for someone named Smith in your file, but you're not sure if it's spelled Smyth, type Sm@th and perform the find. However, you have to be sure of the rest of the letters. In our file, if you type Bail@, you won't find any records. The Any One Character find only works in a text field. To find text that includes the @ character, see the "Escape Next Character" section coming up.

> **NOTE** If a field is formatted using Unicode and you want to find just the @ symbol and nothing else, put it in quotes. See the "Match Phrase (From Word Start)" section later in this chapter.

Any One Digit (#)

The number or pound symbol (#) can be used when performing a find in a number field to represent a number character you're not sure of. For instance, all the MiniDiscs in my audio database are numbered from 7000 to 7999. To find them all, instead of typing 7000...7999, I can simply type 7### and they'll all show up. From this example, you can see that you're not limited to using it only once in the field.

Zero or More Characters (*)

This find symbol is more flexible than the @ symbol. In our previous example, if you instead type Bail*, you'd find Bailey and Bailor if we had them in the file. You can also use the symbol more than once in the text. For example, *i*y will work just fine and be helpful for people playing Wheel of Fortune. This symbol only works in text fields.

Escape Next Character (\)[10]

Sometimes you want to find text that includes one of the find operators. Finding an e-mail address is a good example. Until FileMaker 10, looking for JStars@DataDesignPros.com was impossible unless you formatted your field as Unicode or put quotes around the entire email address (making it a Match Phrase From Word Start find). But then the problem was you had to make sure you were absolutely positive about which other letters were uppercase or lowercase. Very inconvenient! By adding the \ character before the special operator, you are telling FileMaker, "Hey, I know you usually use this next character to mean something special when performing a find, but for now, ignore that and include the character in the find." So in my e-mail example, you would enter Find mode and type JStars\@DataDesignPros.com. It works great! You would also include the \ in front of any of the other characters that appear in the operator drop-down. For double and triple characters like <= or *== you would add multiple backslashes, one before each character, like this: \<\= or *\=\=.

Match Phrase (From Word Start) ("")

The literal text quotes are used to locate a word or phrase exactly as it appears between the quotes, starting at the beginning of a word, including symbols, spaces, and punctuation. For example, use the quotes to find "meet @ 2:00". If the elements of the text appear in the field in any other order, for example "@ 2:00 meet", the record will not be found. This can be very handy for finding odd symbols in text fields, too. The literal text search will also work with a number field, but non-numeric characters cannot be found in a number field.

Match Phrase (From Anywhere) (*"")

Use this to find a phrase where you need to leave out one or more characters at the beginning of the first word. The phrase goes between the quotes. So if you were looking for Smith Barney and weren't sure of the spelling of Smith, you could type *"th Barney" as your find request.

Relaxed Search (Japanese only) (~)

This one isn't as much fun as it sounds. It's only used for phonetic matches in Asian alphabets. Honestly, a lot of developers were hoping for some kind of best-guess mechanism like we see in Google.

AND Finds

When you're in Find mode, you can put find data in more than one field. That effectively performs an AND find. For example, if you want to find all people named Smith who live in California, you'd type "Smith" (not including quotes) in the Last Name field and "CA" (not including quotes) in the State field. You are requesting "Smith AND CA".

OR Finds

I used FileMaker for three years before someone showed me that you could make more than one find request at the same time. (I probably just didn't read the manual.) This is very handy. Here's how you do it:

- While you're in Find mode and you've entered some data for which to search, choose Requests, Add New Request. You get another blank record to enter new find criteria. If you're on a layout in List view or Table view, you'll be able to see your multiple requests. Otherwise, look in the Status toolbar just to the left of the Book and you'll see the current number of requests.
- Clicking the pages of the Book allows you to fine-tune the requests as you go. You can enter data in the same or different field(s) as the first find request. Your find could be for "Bailey OR Harris".

- You can also combine the AND and the OR requests by putting data in more than one field in more than one request. This gives you tremendous flexibility.

Constrain and Extend Found Set

Both Constrain Found Set and Extend Found Set were introduced in FileMaker Pro 6. They perform variations of a function that I like to think of as a find within a find. They act in ways similar to Modify Last Find but with more flexibility and sometimes more simplicity.

Instead of starting your find with the whole database of records, the Constrain Found Set and Extend Found Set commands start with just the currently found (or visible) records. If you've just run a Find command, you could simply use the Modify Last Find command to enter more options to get a smaller or bigger group of records. So why would you want to use the Constrain Found Set and Extend Found Set commands? Speed of searching is the biggest reason. If you have a large database, it's often much faster to constrain or extend the current found set than it is to redo the last find on the whole database. This is especially true if your find uses unindexed fields (like in a portal) and if your constrain or extend does not involve the unindexed fields. If you do the first find with only the indexed fields, and then constrain (or extend) the found set with the criteria in the unindexed fields, you'll get a faster result since FileMaker doesn't have to compute all the unindexed field values for every field in the database.

Additionally, there are situations where your found set wasn't created with the Find command, such as when you're using the Omit Record commands or a Go to Related Record script step. The Constrain Found Set and Extend Found Set commands give you much more flexibility than any of the other finds. Let's take a look.

Constrain Found Set

1. Go to our **CON_Contact** layout and add someone named **Rick Cooper**.
2. Perform a find using **Ri** in the First Name field. You should see four records: Rich, Rich A., Richard, and Rick.
3. Enter Find mode again, type **Rich** in the First Name field, and choose **Requests**, **Constrain Found Set**. You're telling FileMaker, "Limit my last find by showing me only people with Rich in the First Name field." Yes, you could have selected Modify Last Find and added the "ch." But Constrain/Extend Found Set become more valuable when your finds are more complex and across multiple requests. Say you had just performed a complex find, looked at the results, and needed to clean it up a little. Just enter Find mode again, make the change, and choose the extend or constrain function that suits the situation.

Extend Found Set

This works the same as Constrain Found Set except you use it to widen your find. Although the specifics of the Constrain Found Set and Extend Found Set functions turn out to be a bit complex, here are some points that may give you some ideas as to how they can be useful to you:

- You can perform an endless series of extend and constrain functions in any order on a set of records.
- You can perform a Modify Last Find and constrain or extend from there.
- You can manually omit records from a found set and continue to constrain or extend from there. The omitted records will not be included in your next move unless they are part of your new request.
- You can combine omitting records using the "Omit" check box (Find mode) with a request to Constrain Found Set or Extend Found Set.
- In effect, you can say things like, "Oops! I didn't mean to remove those people from the found set. Let me put them back in and try again."
- If you have been moving through a series of steps, extending and constraining a set of records, and you accidentally perform a regular find (rather than selecting Requests, Extend/Constrain Found Set), your found set will be replaced with your last find request. This point leads to one of the limitations of these functions, which is…
- You cannot go backward through the steps of your find.
- The functions are scriptable. (Use the Perform Find script step and make your choice from the Options Specify pop-up.) What happens in the script depends on whether the "Restore find requests" option is checked. If it is not checked, the script step will use the last manual or scripted find performed before this step runs.
- The functions allow you to perform an inclusive OR, an exclusive AND, or any combination of either. (This terminology may only be pertinent to mathematicians and statisticians.)

A couple of years ago I worked with a client to create a file that printed labels based on a complex find in fields for counties, school grades, and buildings, each allowing multiple choices. It required some pretty tricky scripting, a set of special fields to mark records, using the Replace functions on a special layout, and an extra script to clear the marked records. Using Constrain Found Set, we were able to shorten the scripts, the process became easier to understand, and we were able to get rid of the extra layout and the special marking fields.

For many finds, I still prefer to see the full construction of the requests by creating a series of simultaneous requests or performing a Modify Last Find. Modify Last Find is especially handy when you've messed up your Find command and you want to make changes. With constrain and extend, you end up keeping much of your find in your head, something that is easier for some people than others. But you can look at the found set and fine-tune your find without having to build a complex series of find requests. To put it simply, you can operate more intuitively. And after all, that is one of the hallmarks of FileMaker Pro.

CAUTION Manage Scripts can only memorize one Find command with the Restore option checked. However, if you uncheck the Restore option, you can add any number of find steps with constrain and extend options to a script.

Quick Find8

At user request, the wizards at FileMaker, Inc. have created a great tool for finding data quickly. This feature assumes you're looking at a field in a record that contains the data you want to find. Let's try it.

In our Business file you're probably still on the CON_Contact layout.

1. Choose **Records**, **Show All Records** and click through until you find someone whose first name starts with "Ri." Highlight **Ri.**
2. **Control+click** (Macintosh) or **right-click** (Windows) to open the context menu and choose **Find Matching Records**. You should find Rich, Richard, and Rick.
3. Click through the found records and duplicate Rick Cooper's record. Change the first name to Bob.
4. Highlight **Cooper** and use the context menu to select **Extend Found Set**. This time you should find the people with "Ri" in their first name plus all the "Coopers." It just happens that Rick Cooper is in both groups.
5. Click on the Last Name field while invoking the menu and select **Constrain Found Set**, but don't highlight any text this time. If you don't highlight anything, Quick Find assumes you want to match the entire field contents.

You can go on all day extending and constraining and switching from field to field as you wish. You can even combine the Quick Find from the context menu with the extend and constrain choices from the Requests menu. The only difference between the quick find and regular find is that you're limited to one field at a time. Of course you can't use this tool if you don't have access privileges to the field or it's not a searchable field (summary, global, or container). Also, if a script is running but paused, the context menu won't be available.

Auto-Complete8

We discussed auto-complete in Chapter 5. I just want to remind you that it's a tool you can make available to your users for various fields in Find mode as well as for entering data. Maybe you want to control data entry separately from how your people will perform a find. You can have separate layouts with fields formatted differently on each layout.

Other Find Tricks

While you're in Find mode, you can switch to another layout with the same base table if one of the fields you want to search for isn't on the layout you're currently viewing. To do this:

- Open the Contact Management file, go to the Record Detail layout, and enter Find mode.
- Click the Layout drop-down below the Book and switch to the Record Table layout. FileMaker stays in Find mode the whole time.

Of course, you can search in related fields just like we did in our Contact file when looking for phone numbers in the portal. That means you can do a find that combines data from fields in the parent record and the child records in the portal.

> **NOTE** This doesn't work when you're switching to layouts that use different tables. If you do switch tables, the find will only be performed in the last table you were in. If you switch back to the first table, the found set will be the same records you found previously in that table. To keep everything straight, just be sure you stay with various layouts of the same table and you'll be fine.

Within Scripts

Back in Chapter 3, when we created the Find Richard script, you learned that scripts can memorize a set of find criteria. FileMaker can remember more complex, multiple-request finds as well.

Using scripts, you can have control over the way the requests are made. Go back to the CON_Contact layout in our Business file and create a new script called Find Rich. Double-click script steps until you have the following:

```
Enter Browse Mode []
Go to Layout ["CON_Contact" (CON)]
Enter Find Mode [Pause]
Insert Text [Select]
Perform Find []
```

Be sure you select the Perform Find under the Found Sets heading. (Do not use the Perform Find/Replace step under the Editing heading.)

To clean up the script:

1. Click the **Enter Find Mode** step and uncheck the **Pause** box in the Options area.
2. Double-click the **Insert Text** step, and double-click the **NameFirst** field.
3. Click the lower **Specify** button and type **Rich**. Click **OK**.

When you're done, your script should look like this:

```
Enter Browse Mode []
Go to Layout ["CON_Contact" (CON)]
Enter Find Mode []
Insert Text [Select; CON::NameFirst; "Rich"]
Perform Find []
```

It might not look as if much has changed, but here's what we did: In the third step, one of the Enter Find Mode options is to specify a find request. We certainly don't want that. It could really mess up what we're trying to do if any of the fields are already filled in. We also don't need the script to pause because we want it to move ahead and do the find for us. In the fourth step, we tell the script to put Rich in the NameFirst field. Then in the fifth step, it's possible to specify a request. That's why we can use just the brackets; in effect, we're saying, "Just find what we already told you to find." The reason I had you leave the Go to Layout script step is because Insert Text can only be done on a layout that has a copy of the target field. Click the Close button, Save, then Close again. Now try it out. Yes, it still finds Richard as well as Rich.

Go back into the script, select the Insert Text step, click the lower Specify button, and change it to include the equal sign (=) in front of Rich. Click OK, click the Close icon, Save, then Close again. Try that out.

Although we will be spending more time with scripts in Chapter 14, "Automating Your Database with Scripts," this chapter is about finding, so let's dig a little deeper. To tell you the truth, the original Find Richard script could just as easily have been two steps:

```
Go to Layout ["CON_Contact" (CON)]
Perform Find [Restore]
```

> ⌘ **TIP** When you use the Perform Find [Restore] step, you must be on a layout based on a table occurrence that includes the criteria you're finding. But the field doesn't actually need to be on the layout. It's not the same as Insert Text, which requires the field to be on the layout.

So why build the long script instead of the simple find? First of all, you can see what the longer script does so it's easier to fix if you have problems with it. On the other hand, you can show what the find was in the short script by adding a Comment step, which can be found at the bottom of the steps list. Type whatever comment you want to remind yourself why you did something. Using comments is very, very helpful. There is nothing more confusing than coming back to one of your files a year later and trying to figure out what the heck you were thinking. Start developing this habit now.

I must admit, to my thinking, shorter scripting is better, but it's also helpful to know that there's more than one way to do things. Another instance in which you might want to use a longer set of steps is when you run the script under certain conditions. For instance, on a network, if the current user is a specific employee, insert =Rich into the find, and if it's any other employee, insert =Richard. (I would more likely have a script determine what layout a specific user would be switching to. But let's stay with our example for now.) To build on our previous example, it would look like this:

```
If [Get (UserName) = "Jonathan Stars"]
     Insert Text [Select, CON::NameFirst; "=Rich"]
Else
     Insert Text [Select, CON::NameFirst; "=Richard"]
End If
Perform Find []
```

Notice that when you double-click the If step, you automatically get the End If step as well. You can move it up or down in the list as you please. Anything between the If and End If is indented except an Else or Else If step.

> **TIP** You will often see extra quote marks between the brackets in script steps. That's just the way they appear when you are in the Script Definition window. But it can be a little disconcerting trying to figure out exactly what you're supposed to enter in the Formula box. The best advice I can give you is to use quotes to enclose text constants. When you click OK, you'll be warned if there are too many quotes.

One other item I want to cover here is what happens if no matching records are found. The standard dialog box that pops up, as seen in Figure 8-2, can be a little confusing, especially if it arrives when a user clicks a button and doesn't know anything about scripts or what the find might have been.

Figure 8-2 The dialog box that appears when a find results in no records found.

FileMaker generates hidden error messages when it runs scripts (and other processes), and you can use these messages to alter your scripts. Then you can substitute your own message dialog, complete with buttons that let you control what happens next. Here's an example that continues the previous script:

```
Else
     Insert Text [Select, CON::NameFirst; "=Richard"]
End If
Set Error Capture [On]
Perform Find []
If [Get (FoundCount) = 0]
     Beep
     Show Custom Dialog ["Sorry, none found. Want to try again?"]
     Comment [Button 1 = OK / Button 2 = Forget It]
     If [Get (LastMessageChoice) = 1]
          Modify Last Find
```

```
          Go to Field [CON::NameFirst]
     Else
          Halt Script
     End If
End If
```

Notice that you can have the script recall the previous find attempt, and even go to the field where the problem is. Okay, this is way beyond our original three- or even five-step script. But it covers most of the elements you could want in a find script. If you study this one and get it, you're well on your way to advanced scripting. And guess what else — now you're programming!

Find Strategies

For a long time I thought you needed to find a person's whole name. Not so. For example, in our Contact table, you can enter Find mode, type R in the First Name field and B in the Last Name field, and you'll find our dear Mr. Bailey. It's not that the special find symbols wouldn't work; it's just a different technique.

Excluding data from a find is also important — so important that there's a section on it called "Omitting Records" coming up.

You can change the way a find works in a field by indexing it based on ASCII or a language other than English. Go to Manage Database, Fields, choose a field, and click the Options button. On the Storage tab there is an Indexing section with the pop-up list seen in Figure 8-3.

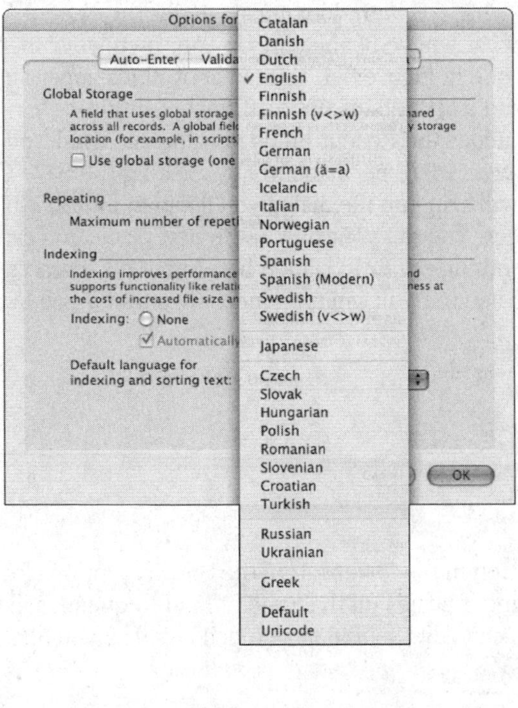

Figure 8-3
The Storage tab of the Options for Field window showing the many language indexing choices.

Limitations

FileMaker can memorize many Find [Restore] steps per script, but if it performs them one after the other, you'll only see the final found set. However, you can run actions on each of the various found sets during the course of the script. Of course, you can construct the script step by step as we did previously, which would avoid the need for a restore.

> **CAUTION** More than once I've started entering data in what I thought was a new record, while I was actually in Find mode. When you go back to Browse mode, all that data is lost. FileMaker warns you after you've created 10 find requests, but that could be a lot of data. If you're still in Find mode when you realize your error, you may want to scribble down what you've entered. Otherwise, when you return to Browse mode, it's gone.

Saved Finds[10]

Previous to FileMaker 10, in order to have quick access to any finds you created, you would need to make a script for each find. For many users, scripting is a scary place to work. FMP10 introduces a very helpful feature called Saved Finds, which puts finds at the fingertips of even absolute beginners. More advanced users can always recall one of the finds and turn it into a script. It does come with some limitations, but let's look at the good stuff first.

Go to the Records menu and come down to Saved Finds. You'll notice that FileMaker remembered what you were looking for under the Recent Finds heading. Depending on what you've been doing on your own, your menu may or may not look like the one in Figure 8-4. Your Recent Finds appear in the lower half of the dialog and FMP retains up to 10 Recent Finds.

The first item listed under the Recent Finds heading is considered the Current Find. You can save it more permanently by clicking the Save Current Find menu item, which will bring up the dialog you'll see in Figure 8-5. The default name relates to how you ran your find in the first place. You can change the name to something easier to remember. About 65 characters will show in the Saved Finds list, but you can type more than that if you like.

Figure 8-4
The Saved Finds menu.

Notice the Advanced button in the lower left of the Specify Options for the Saved Find dialog. Clicking it brings up the Specify Find Requests dialog seen in Figure 8-6, where you can edit the find in as much detail as you like.

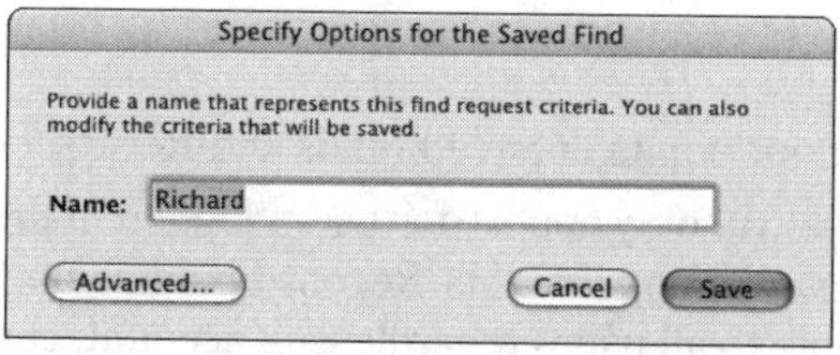

Figure 8-5
The Specify Options for the Saved Find dialog.

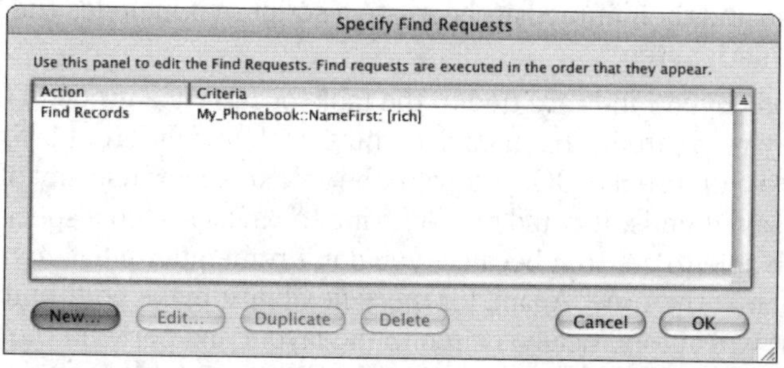

Figure 8-6
The Specify Find Requests dialog.

The final part of the Saved Finds process is the Edit Saved Finds menu item. Clicking it brings up the dialog in Figure 8-7. It lists all saved finds for the account under which you're logged in and allows you to edit them by calling up the dialog in Figure 8-6. The finds listed are regardless of the table occurrence with which they're associated. Once the find is saved, it will show up at the bottom of the Saved Finds list (rather than at the top as happens with Recent Finds). You can reorganize the Saved Finds using the double arrows in the Name column as in Figure 8-7. You don't get that kind of control over Recent Finds. Once you've turned a Recent Find into a Saved Find, it goes to the bottom of the list of Saved Finds, just above the Recent Finds heading.

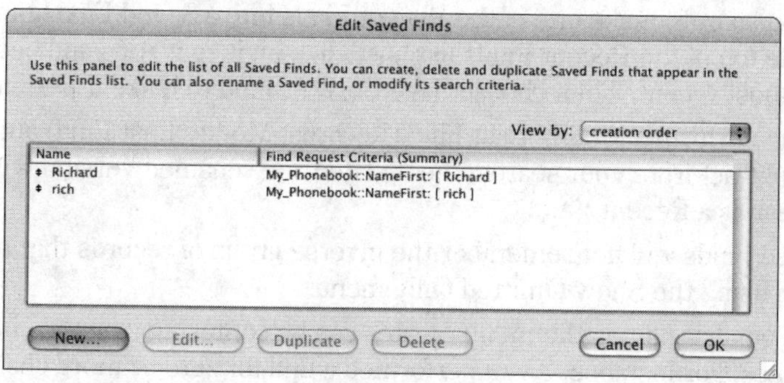

Figure 8-7
The Edit Saved Finds dialog.

Saved Finds will appear for all other users of the file who are logged in with the same account name, and they will come back even after users close and reopen the file. If you are the host of the file, you retain your Recent Finds even after you close and reopen the file. However, guests of your file do not see your Recent Finds. A guest of your file will have his own set of Recent Finds, which will disappear when he closes the file. If FileMaker Server is hosting the file, Recent Finds will disappear when users close the file.

Saved Finds Details

Now let's look at some of the finer points of Saved Finds and Recent Finds.

- All Recent and Saved Finds will only appear for users logged in under the same account (although again, it appears that Recent Finds do not). If you want to make a find available to all users regardless of account, run the Saved Find and then immediately create a script that includes the Perform Find script step.
- Recent and Saved Finds are tied to the table occurrence group (TOG) in which they're created. That means if you switch to a different layout attached to a different TOG, you won't be able to see or use any of the previous saved finds. It could be confusing to have created a special find and not be able to get to it because you don't remember what layout/table you were in at the time. Again, for more flexibility, make your find into a script that will automatically switch to the layout and perform the find. For more on table occurrence groups, see Chapter 14, "Automating Your Database with Scripts."
- The Recent Finds menu remembers attempted finds that turned up zero records; these can be turned into Saved Finds.
- There is a menu choice to Clear All Recent Finds, but you cannot delete them one at a time. Clearing your Recent Finds has no effect on other users' Recent Finds list. Regardless, if you really intend to keep a Recent Find, make it into a Saved Find.
- When a script performs a find, the find does not appear in the Recent Finds list.
- If you want to make one of the Recent Finds into a Saved Find but it's not at the top of the Recent Finds list, just click on it so it runs and becomes the most recent. Then choose Save Current Find to make it permanent.
- If you perform a Modify Last Find (Records, Modify Last Find) and add or subtract from your search, the updated and renamed version will appear as a Recent Find.
- Saved Finds will not remember the inverse group of records that result from using the Show Omitted Only menu.
- The generic names the menu creates can be confusing in some circumstances. For instance, if you performed a find for zero or more characters (*) in the Last Name field and then performed a similar find in the Company field, you would have two Recent Finds named "*", which is not very helpful. There are two ways you can discover what any Recent Find was: Perform it and then choose Records, Modify Last Find to see what criteria were used, or perform the questionable find, choose Save Current Find, and click the Advanced button to look at the details. To avoid actually saving the find, click Cancel and Cancel again.
- After you edit a Saved Find, the name will change to reflect the change, but only if it still has the automatically assigned name. However, if you

have already given your Saved Find a specific name, that name will not be overwritten.

- If you click and hold the Find icon in the Status toolbar in Browse mode (assuming that button hasn't been removed through customization), you can see the Saved Finds menu. You can also add a Saved Finds button to the Status toolbar. When you're already in Find mode, one of the default icons is Saved Finds.
- There is a script step called Open Edit Saved Finds. You can use it to allow users whose privileges wouldn't normally allow them to open that dialog to edit the finds.
- Saved Finds are tied to the table occurrence groups rather than a specific base table. Since I use the anchor-buoy development standard (discussed in Chapter 6 and Appendix A), every layout is tied only to a base table. That should help keep Saved Finds from being a confusing issue. For more about table occurrence groups, see Chapter 14, "Automating Your Database with Scripts."
- Saved Finds for users who log in using external authentication are stored in the file. When an account is no longer active, you might want to delete those saved finds. You would choose File, Manage, Accounts & Privileges and edit the account. Click the User Data button in the lower-left corner. You can then selectively clear data based on user name.
- Running a script that begins with Set Error Capture [On] (and isn't followed by Set Error Capture [Off] later) disables the Saved Finds menu items. This can be important since you may not want the user to override what you want to have happen during the scripting process. Once the script has run its course, the error capture state is automatically restored to "on," which reactivates the Saved Finds menu.

Omitting Records

What to leave out is as important as what to find. When you find one or more records, the other records are omitted, and you can continue to omit records from the found set if they don't apply to your needs.

Methods

1. To give it a try, go to our **CON_Contact** layout and do a manual find (don't use the script) for **Rich.** That should turn up our records for Rich, Rich A., and Richard.
2. Click through the records until you find Richard.
3. Then choose **Records, Omit Record.**

SHORTCUT Omit Record is Command+T (Macintosh) or Ctrl+T (Windows); Omit Multiple is Command+Shift+T (Macintosh) or Ctrl+Shift+T (Windows).

Omit Multiple

1. Choose **Records**, **Show All Records**, and click until you're about half-way through the records.
2. Choose **Records**, **Omit Multiple**. You'll be presented with a window asking how many records you want to omit starting with the current record. You can type in whatever number you want. If you enter a number that is larger than the number of records left in the file and click the Omit button, you'll get a warning.
3. Click **OK** and the original window fills in the correct number.

This is a much easier method than trying to calculate how many records remain in your found set. I usually just type something like 1111, hit Enter and Enter again. It's very fast once you understand the process.

Omit as Part of a Find

You can omit records as part of a find request.

1. Enter Find mode, and type **Rich** in the First Name field.
2. Now look up in the Layout bar and click the **Omit** button next to the words "Matching Records."
3. Finish the find and you'll have everybody except Rich and Richard.

You can even combine a regular find with an omit request.

1. Enter Find mode, and type **Rich** in the First Name field.
2. Choose **Requests**, **Add New Request**.
3. Type **Richard** in the First Name field.
4. Click the **Omit** button, and finish the find.

Using that trick in a larger database, you can, for example, find everyone who lives in California except the people in Los Angeles.

Show Omitted

Sometimes it's easier to find what you don't want, and then find the opposite. Expanding on the last example, let's say you wanted to find everyone in all states in the U.S. except California, but you did want to include the people of Los Angeles. Perform the original find, and then choose Records, Show Omitted. It's a bit deep, but with a little thought you can get just about anything you need.

Within Scripts

The same types of omits are available as script steps. You can find them under the Found Sets heading. Use the same omit methods mentioned previously, and combine them with what you learned in the previous "Within Scripts" section. With the Omit Multiple script step, you have the option to show the window asking for how many records to omit. You can also choose a preset number to be omitted, whether the window appears or not.

Strategies

Just as you can have multiple find requests, you can have multiple omit requests. You need to know how omits are constructed to get the most out of your find requests. When performing a find, FileMaker starts with your first request and moves forward.

For example, if you construct a find in the Contact table that places Richard in the first request and omits Rich in the second, FileMaker won't find any records. If you reverse the requests to omit Richard in the first request but find Rich in the second, all records will be found. For that reason, it's usually more logical to place your omit requests after any finds you want. You have to think it out, give it a try, and then fine-tune.

Limitations

You can also omit records from a portal as part of a find. However, the individual portal record is not omitted from the portal. Instead, the parent record is omitted from the find.

Sorting Records

I already introduced you to the Sort window under the Records menu back in Chapter 2. Sorting isn't really that complicated. We looked at how to sort portals in Chapter 6. Portals are sorted as part of the relationship definition. The windows are nearly the same, except when sorting records, you have the option to unsort and to include summary fields as a part of the sort.

Methods

1. Choose **Records, Show All Records.**
2. Create a new record and put the name **John Smith** in the appropriate fields.
3. Now create a record for **Sam Smith**.
4. Choose **Records, Sort Records.**
5. Now move **NameLast**, then **NameFirst** to the list on the right, and click the **Sort** button.

As I said in Chapter 2, you can also sort by related fields. The related fields can go anywhere in the sort order list. But if the field to be sorted is in a portal, and the portal itself is sorted as part of the relationship definition, the records will end up sorted by the data in the first portal row. Sorting by related fields works more reliably in a report constructed in a child table or file where the relationship is many-to-one.

You can sort by a custom order by creating a value list as we did when we sorted the portal in Chapter 6. The results are the same.

Starting with FileMaker 10, sorted records can resort on the fly as data changes. Let's say you have a group of sorted records. Now you change some data in one of the sort fields in such a way that it belongs in a different group. When you commit the record, the records will resort. It can be a little disconcerting to be looking at part of a list of records and suddenly have the records jump around. But as long as you understand what's going on, you can get used to it. We'll look at how that happens shortly. The reason for this new behavior is that FMP10 now has the ability to view dynamic sub-summaries in Browse mode without going into Preview mode. For more experienced developers, it's important to know that this live resorting is suspended when importing, during Replace Field Contents, or when a script is running. That's primarily so scripts can work through a group of records without losing their place.

And finally, you can include a sort by a summary field. Because of the complexity of this option, I'll cover this in a minute under the section titled "Strategies."

Within Scripts

Of course, FileMaker can memorize any of the most complex sorts you can dream up. While the sort is still in memory, create a script and add the Sort step by double-clicking it in the left column. When you choose the Sort script step, you have two choices in the Options area: "Perform without dialog" and "Specify sort order" — which allows you to create or modify a sort order from right here in Manage Scripts.

- If you just want the sort to be recreated as is and you don't want to be bothered with the window, leave both of these boxes checked.
- If you'd rather give yourself or your users the option to override the sort, uncheck "Perform without dialog." That way, you'll see what the default sort would be and have a chance to make a change. You may also want the window to appear temporarily as a method of debugging a script.

The only other sort related script step is Unsort. It simply returns the found set to the order in which the records were entered into the file. There are no options available for Unsort.

Strategies

Sorting by a summary field can get confusing because there are so many different areas of FileMaker that have to be in place to make it work — some of which we haven't covered yet. The idea is to get groups of records that already have sub-summaries to sort by a summary field of your choice.

Sort By a Summary Field

To show this feature, I'm going to create a very simple file — one layout — and run the sorts, all without describing every little step. You may not have enough knowledge to make this work at this point. If you should need this capability at a later time, you should be able to come back here and put all the pieces together. There is more about layout parts in Chapter 18, "Designing Your Printed Report Layouts."

Create a database named Sub-sum_Test with the following fields:

Field Name	*Type*	*Options*
SalesPerson	Text	
Amount	Number	
SumAmount	Summary	=Total of Amount

The layout needs to be set up as shown in Figure 8-8. Use the Part tool in the Status toolbar to drag the necessary layout parts onto the layout. Notice that the SumAmount field in the sub-summary part is the same field as the Grand - Sum Amount in the trailing grand summary. It just has a different label.

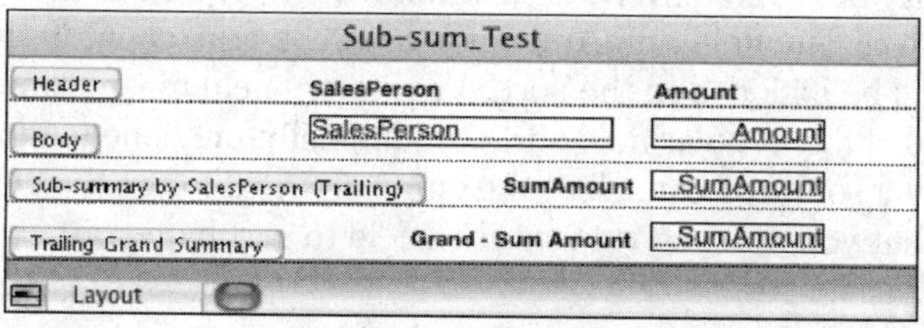

Figure 8-8
Layout showing position of fields and layout parts to demonstrate sorting by a summary field.

⌘ **TIP** Sometimes you may need to move a layout part up or down, but get stopped by objects on the layout. You can make the part border move through layout objects by holding down the Shift key (Macintosh) or Alt key (Windows) while you drag the layout tab or dotted line.

Now, create the records shown in Figure 8-9. As you enter the data, the Grand - Sum Amount amount increases, but none of the sub-summary amounts show. That's because you have to sort by SalesPerson to see those amounts. (Previous to FileMaker 10, sub-summaries only appeared in Preview mode. Now they appear in Browse mode as well.)

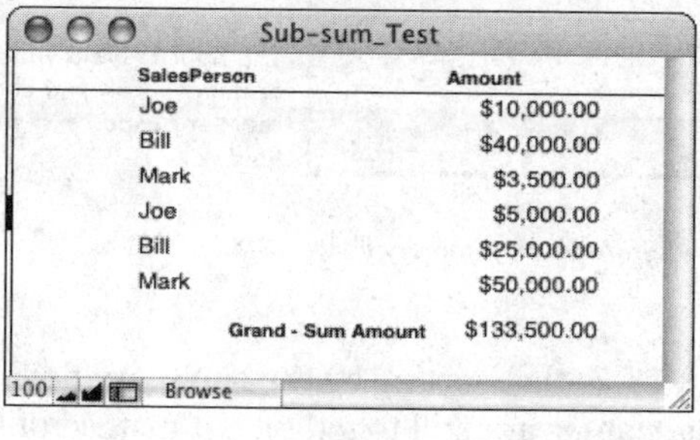

Figure 8-9
Enter this data in the Sub-sum_Test file.

Part 2

Now run a sort by SalesPerson. You should get the results shown in Figure 8-10.

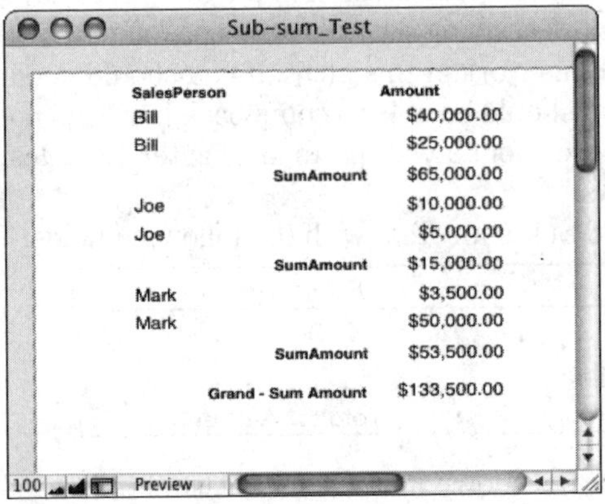

Figure 8-10
What the report looks like when sorted by SalesPerson.

Now run the sort shown in Figure 8-11. To make the summary field, SumAmount, part of the sort, select SalesPerson and check the "Reorder based on summary field" box. In the next window, highlight SumAmount and click the OK button. The field SumAmount will still be grayed out in the left column, but it will be included in the sort. A summary field must always appear at the end of any regular field sorts. Additionally, only one summary field is allowed in a sort. You can move the summary field to the Sort Order list at any time, but you must choose another field to sort by before you are allowed to perform the sort.

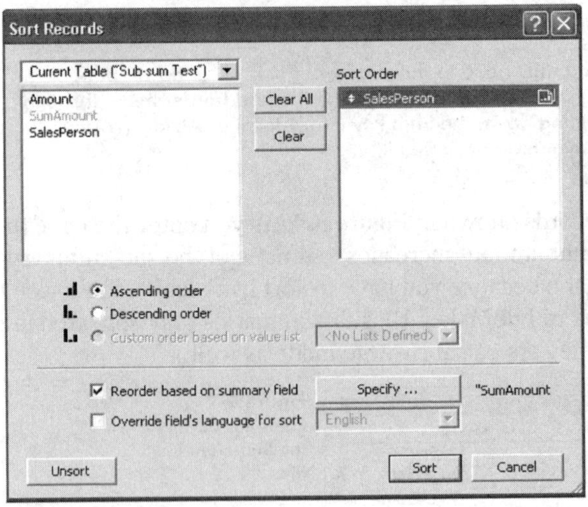

Figure 8-11
The Sort Records window showing the SumAmount summary field being added to the Sort Order list.

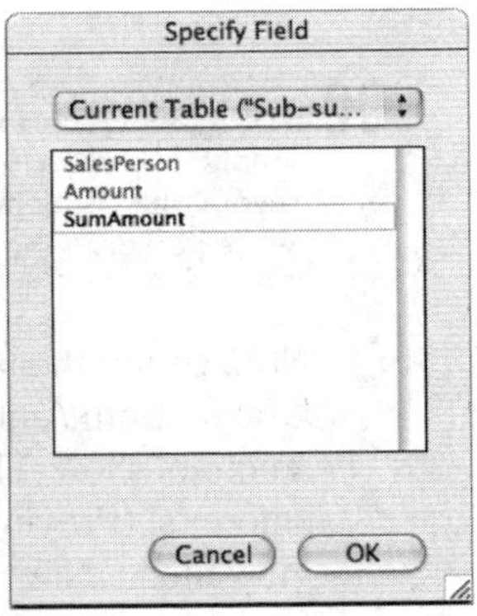

Figure 8-12
The Specify Field window that appears when you choose to reorder based on a summary field.

The result, shown in Figure 8-13, is that sorting by the summary field overrides the sort by name. All the names are still together, but instead of Bill being listed first, based on an alphabetical sort, he's now last because he took in the most money.

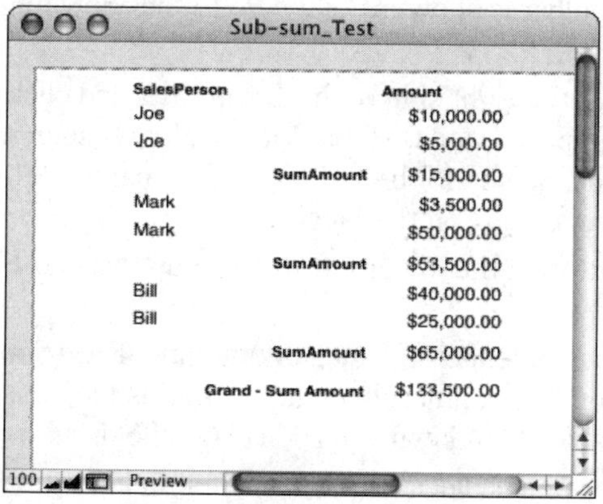

Figure 8-13
The final order using a sort that includes a summary field.

Dynamic Sub-Summaries[10]

Now what would happen if you found you made a mistake and it was Bill who made the $10,000 in the first row? First, highlight $10,000 and format the text color so it's some shade of blue. Change Joe to Bill in the first record and click out of the field. Whoa! Did you see it jump? Now change Bill's $10,000 item back to Joe and exit the field. What if you change the $10,000 to $100,000? Right, Joe goes to the bottom of the list. This is all part of FileMaker 10's new dynamic sub-summaries. It's so much more convenient and intuitive than in the previous versions, which required that you enter Preview mode to see what your report would look like. And when you're in Preview mode, any buttons you have on the layout are inactive. Developers created all kinds of convoluted scripting tricks to work around this limitation. No more! Of course you still won't be able to see page breaks, page numbers, and other features specific to printing. For that, you'll still want to use Preview mode. But I've been using FileMaker for 24 years now, and I can say that the addition of dynamic sub-summaries is a very welcome improvement.

> **NOTE** Sub-summaries in Table view may not display as they do in List view. As we go to press, some developers are reporting that a sub-summary field will not calculate properly in Table view unless the field it evaluates is in the body part. My tests showed sub-summaries don't work at all in Table view.

Modify Table View[10]

And that's not all. You can also add and subtract fields when you're in Table view. These fields only appear in Table view and don't show up in Layout mode. Let me show you what I mean.

1. Create a new text field called **Test** and exit Manage Database.

2. Go to Layout mode. If the new field has been added to the layout, remove it and tighten up the body part again. Now go to Browse mode.
3. Make sure the Status toolbar is showing. Then go to the View menu and choose **View As Table.**
4. Look all the way over on the right side of the Layout bar and click the **Modify** button to bring up the Modify Table View dialog as seen in Figure 8-14. Notice the padlock icon to the left of the field names. That indicates these fields are already on the layout.
5. Click the green plus button in the lower left to bring up the Add Fields dialog.
6. Click the **Test** field (since SalesPerson and Amount are already on the layout). Although we don't have any related tables in this file, just know that you can click the table drop-down and add related fields as well.
7. Click **OK**. Notice there is no padlock next to the Test field in the Modify Table View dialog. Also notice the double arrows to the left of the field names, indicating you can reorganize them. What you do here affects the order in which they appear in Table view.
8. Click **OK** again. The Test field is now added to the layout. Adding this particular field isn't very helpful to us, but you get the idea. If you go to Layout mode, you'll see that the Test field has not been added to the layout at all.
9. Go back to Browse mode and click the **Modify** button again.
10. Click the **Test** field in the list and click the trash can in the lower left of the dialog to get the field off the layout.
11. Click **OK** and it's gone. Click one of the remaining fields in the list. Notice that the trash can is grayed out. You cannot throw away any fields that are in the body part of the layout.

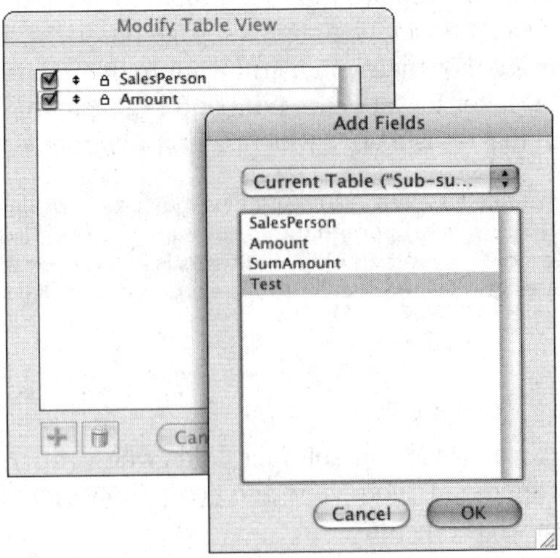

Figure 8-14
The Modify Table View and Add Fields dialogs.

You can also modify the fields you see in Table view even when the Status toolbar is hidden. To do that, Control+click (Macintosh) or right-click (Windows) on any column heading to bring up the context menu. Modify Table View is at the bottom of the list. The only trouble with this technique is it's easy to accidentally resort the fields, and your sub-summaries will disappear until you resort again. Don't ask me how I know.

OK, before I forget, switch back to View As List.

Limitations

FileMaker allows multiple Sort [Restore] steps per script. But unless you pause or print after each one, only the last sort will be in effect when the script is finished running. Use the same conditional concepts I showed you in the "Limitations" section for finding records.

In versions of FileMaker previous to 7, when you called for a sort (either by choosing Records, Sort, or by using the Sort Records script step), the currently selected record would be the first record in the found set. Starting with FMP7, the currently selected record will be the same record that was selected prior to the sort. If you have converted solutions with processes that depend on the first record being selected as part of a script, you'll need to add the Go to Record/Request/Page [First] script step to make everything work properly. On the other hand, this allows us developers to stop creating complex workarounds to get back to the record we began with in case we don't want the first record.

Summary

In this chapter, we looked at finding and sorting records. You learned the ins and outs of finds, including the find symbols and Saved Finds. You also saw how to omit records you don't need, how to sort what you have left, and how to attach even the most complex finds and sorts to a script. And finally you looked at FMP10's new dynamic sub-summaries and how to add fields to Table view without affecting the layout.

This is the area where you make sense of sales figures and get lists ready for mailing labels. This is what keeps you organized. For me, being able to find a customer's record when I needed it is what got me started with FileMaker in the first place. Without finds and sorts, you might as well go back to the Rolodex.

Q & A

Q This AND/OR find terminology is a little confusing. If I wanted to find everyone who lives in Ohio and Florida, that seems like an AND find to me.

A It does, doesn't it? However, you would need to use two requests to accomplish this. That's because you can't type two states in one field. You're not asking for individuals who live in both the state of Ohio AND the state of Florida at the same time. So for clarity, the way to phrase the find is: "show me all the people in my file who live in either Ohio OR (new request) Florida."

Q Do I have to know all this complicated script stuff to be able to get through this?

A No. I used FileMaker for about five years before I discovered how to make scripts do more than change to a different layout. Learning scripting is really not that hard, though. The trick is to do something simple, then build on it. Scripting can't be beat for automating repetitive tasks.

Workshop

Build a complicated find based on multiple fields in more than one record. Include an omit as part of it. Then create a script for it. Now do a Refind (Modify Last Find), change the find criteria, and make a new script for that. Run one script after the other. Now sort the records and add the sort to one of the scripts. Perform a different sort and add that to the second script.

Chapter 9

Creating New Layouts with the Layout Assistant

Introduction

Layout mode operates like a simplified version of most computer drawing programs (like Adobe Illustrator or CorelDRAW). But what sets FileMaker apart is that it's designed to also show data from the fields in the records of your database tables. You can create all sorts of layouts for use on screen or in printed reports. Remember though, no matter what beautiful or ugly way your layouts present your data, you aren't actually changing what's in the tables themselves (you can only do that in Browse mode).

The Layout Assistant gives users a terrific way to create layouts. Almost every window explains what it does in clear language. Because the Layout Assistant offers a number of choices at each point, resulting in millions of possibilities, I won't be able to show you every available combination. I'll only be able to get you started, but you'll do just fine.

We could use some other layouts in our invoicing system. So I'll have you build one of each of the layout types and show you the sights along the way.

Create a New Layout

First, let's create a new layout.

1. Go to the Business file.
2. To make a new layout, you first have to switch to Layout mode.
3. Choose **Layouts, New Layout/Report** or use the keyboard shortcut Command+N (Macintosh) or Ctrl+N (Windows). Notice it's the same shortcut as New Record in Browse mode. You should see the window shown in Figure 9-1.

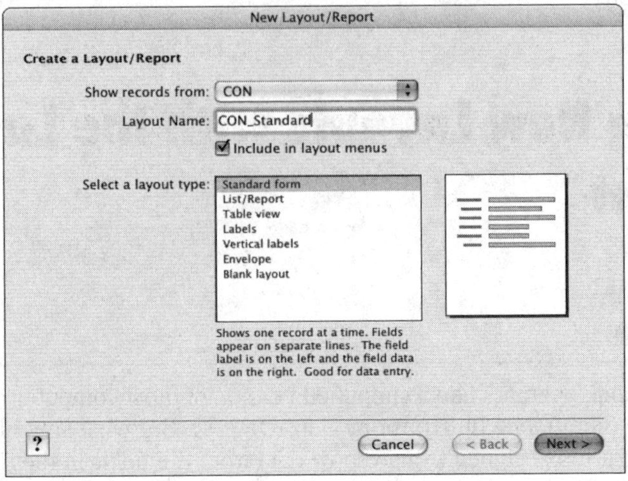

Figure 9-1 Choosing New Layout/Report under the Layouts menu brings up the first screen of the Layout Assistant.

Standard Form

4. Choose the **CON** table occurrence from the "Show records from" drop-down list. We chose Contact because it's the table where the records we're interested in are stored. As you get more comfortable with making relationships, you may find that you'll choose the table that holds the primary keys for the relationship you're interested in. But when you're just starting out and things like keys and relationships don't mean much to you, picking the table that has most of the fields you want to show is a good rule of thumb.
5. Next, enter a name to identify your layout. You can give your layouts any name you like, even if it duplicates the name of another layout. FileMaker has other ways to keep track of the layouts, so the name here is strictly for us humans. For the sake of simplicity, call this layout **CON_Standard**, and select **Standard form** in the layout type list. We're also using the TO code letters (CON) so that when we look at the layout, we can tell immediately which base table it's attached to.
6. Notice the check box for "Include in layout menus." Leave it checked for now, but note that unchecking this box will hide the name from the Layout drop-down below the Book. All layout names will still show up in the drop-down when you're in Layout mode and the layout is still accessible by way of your scripts and buttons. For a final level of protection, you can prevent users from getting to Layout mode by using passwords. We'll talk more about that later.
7. To move on, click the **Next** button.

Specify Fields

If there are any options concerning the layout dimensions you chose (such as when you choose labels or columnar lists), FileMaker will ask you some additional questions. In our case though, you'll see the Specify Fields screen shown in Figure 9-2. This would also be the second window if you had picked Table view from the layout type list. However, it would be the third window if you had chosen List/Report; Choose Report Layout would have been second. In essence, whatever fields you name in the right-hand list will be created on the layout for you (which can be a real time-saver).

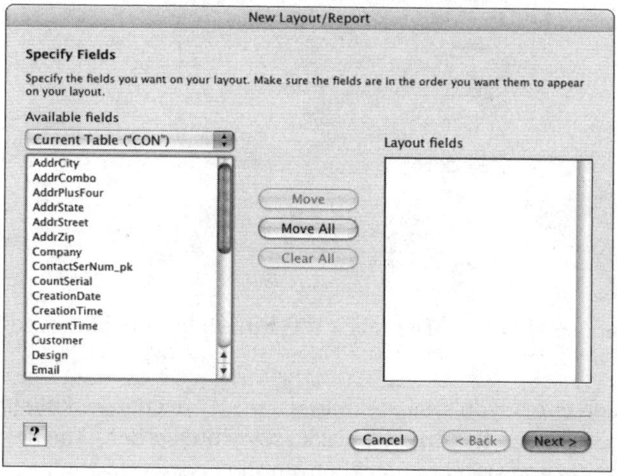

Figure 9-2
The Specify Fields screen of the New Layout/Report window in the Layout Assistant.

8. If you don't have too many fields, click the **Move All** button, then double-click any fields in the Layout fields list that you want to remove from this layout.
9. You can also remove fields from the list by clicking once on the field name to highlight it and clicking the **Clear** button. (Note that the Clear button won't show up until you have at least one field in the Layout fields list on the right.) I think click-click is faster than click-move-the-mouse-click, but it's up to you. Remember, we're not using any of the phone number, Email, or Web fields anymore.
10. Notice the "Available fields" drop-down on the left. You can choose fields from related files and tables, and you can even create relationships from here.
11. Now drag the fields up or down in the list until they're in the order you think you'll find most logical, then click the **Next** button.

Select a Theme

You'll also see the Select a Theme screen shown in Figure 9-3 when you choose the List/Report and Table view layout types. FileMaker 10 has added 10 more themes, all based on the themes in Bento. The themes are also available on the Windows platform even though Bento is a Macintosh-only product.

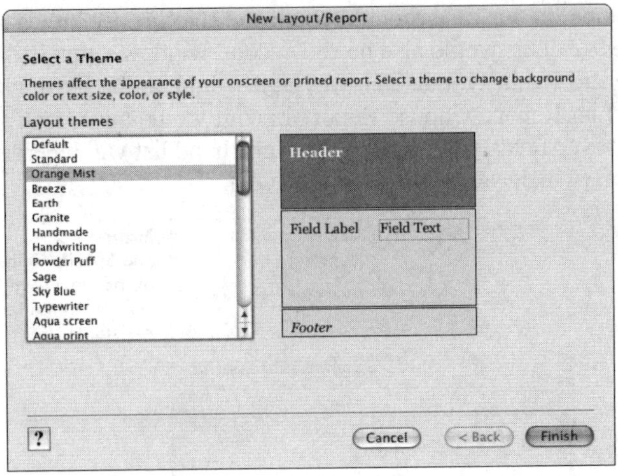

Figure 9-3
The Select a Theme screen is where you choose how the new layout will look.

12. For now, choose **Orange Mist**, click the **Finish** button, and go to Browse mode.

Without too much effort, you've just created a pretty decent-looking layout. It's quite a bit better than the original black and white screen. The fields have some depth to them and stand out nicely from the background.

If you go into Layout mode, you can click on the layout part tabs and change the color of the background using the Fill tools. You can also make any other changes and move fields and labels wherever you like. If you click on one of the fields and then click on the Object Effects palette (to the right of the Fill Pattern palette), you'll see that the fields have an engraved effect applied to them. The effect of this change might be quite subtle. The appearance depends on the theme you select and the field border width; be sure that field borders are turned on. If you left out any fields, just place them where you need them.

⌘ **TIP** Want to place a field on a layout and match the style of another field that's already on the layout? Hold down the Command (Macintosh) or Ctrl (Windows) key and click on the field with the style you want to copy. All the attributes are instantly selected as the default. That includes the color of the field, the borders, and the font size, style, and color.

The defaults can also be set if you change an attribute with no object selected. For example, changing the fill color with nothing selected applies that fill color to any new objects you create. These defaults are also relevant here because the list of themes in the layout wizard includes Standard and Default, and in most cases they look quite similar. Standard is a black and white layout theme. Default uses whatever you have selected as a default attribute (field fill color, line widths, fonts, etc.). Of course you would want to set your defaults before working with the Layout Assistant.

TIP You can create your own themes! On Windows, look in FileMaker Pro 10\English Extras\Extensions\Themes. On Macintosh, look in the FileMaker Pro 10 folder and Control+click on the FileMaker Pro application icon. Choose Show Package Contents, then choose Contents\Resources\English.lproj\Themes. Open the folder, make a copy of one of the themes, rename it, and open it with a text editor. (I would recommend against editing these files with Microsoft Word. Word tends to add headers to the file that will make it unreadable by FileMaker.) The text file is written in XML (Extensible Markup Language), which is similar to the web language HTML. XML is actually fairly easy to read. If you or someone you know is comfortable with HTML, you're on your way to creating quick, custom layouts. In fact, you may be able to figure it out on your own.

List/Report

There are quite a few steps and options to creating this layout type. Since inv_ILI__InvNum has two one-to-many relationships terminating on it, we should be doing some of our reporting there. But following the anchor-buoy standard, we should actually do the reporting using the ILI TO because it's attached to a layout already and it uses the same base table, InvoiceLineItems.

1. Go into Layout mode and create a new layout/report.
2. Choose **ILI** from the drop-down list at the top.
3. Call this layout **ILI_InvoicePrint**, select **List/Report** as the layout type, and click the **Next** button.

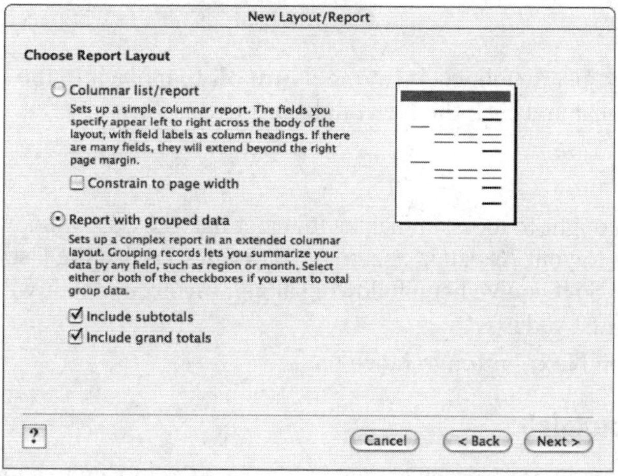

Figure 9-4
In the Choose Report Layout screen, you decide whether to display simple columns of data or a more complex report.

Choose Report Layout

4. Choose the **Report with grouped data** radio button, and check both the **Include subtotals** and **Include grand totals** boxes.
5. Click the **Next** button.
6. In the Specify Fields screen, click the **Move All** button, then click **Next.**

Organize Records by Category

As you can see in Figure 9-5, from the next screen you can choose more than one field to summarize, which you may want to do sometime in the future.

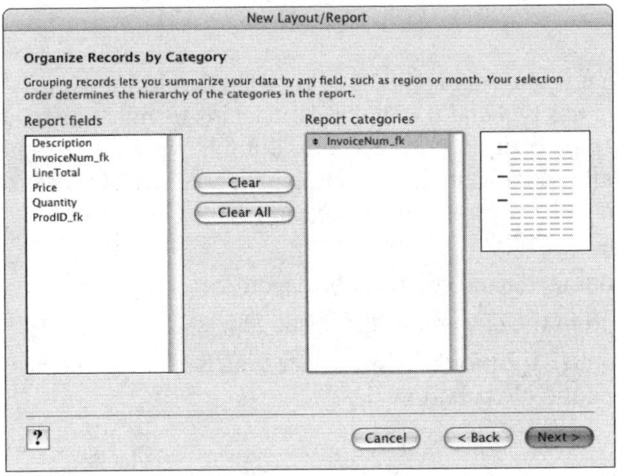

Figure 9-5
The Organize Records by Category screen lets you summarize data by field.

7. For now, just double-click **InvoiceNum_fk** to move it to the Report categories list and click the **Next** button.

Sort Records

This screen ought to look familiar, as it is just like the Sort window. FileMaker's Layout Assistant assumes you want to reuse the last criteria you sorted with. So if you've been following along, Invoice number will be here. Otherwise, just add it.

8. Click the **Next** button to move on.

Specify Subtotals

The Specify Subtotals screen shown in Figure 9-6 offers quite a few choices. When we created our invoice layout in the Invoice table, we created a field to give us the invoice total, but we don't have that here.

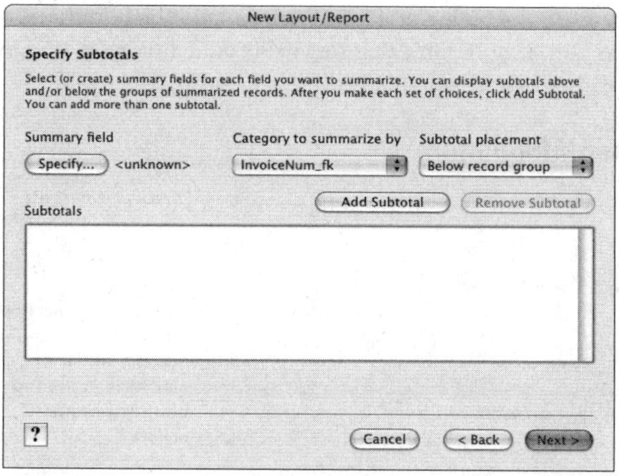

Figure 9-6
The Specify Subtotals screen is where you select or create summary fields for the report.

9. Click on the **Specify** button under the Summary field header to bring up the Specify Field screen.
10. Click on **Current Table ("ILI")** in the drop-down, scroll all the way to the bottom, and select **Manage Database.**
11. Click the **Tables** tab and double-click **InvoiceLineItems**. You'll actually be creating a new field here.
12. Call it **InvoiceTotal**, choose **Summary Type**, and click **Create**.
13. Highlight **LineTotal** in the field list. Be sure the **Total of** radio button is selected.
14. Click **OK**, **OK** again, highlight **InvoiceTotal** in the list, and click **OK** one more time. InvoiceTotal will now appear next to the Specify button.
15. To make InvoiceTotal show up in the Subtotals list, you have to click the **Add Subtotal** button near the center of the window. It should appear as ILI::InvoiceTotal in the Subtotals box. Look at the other drop-downs just so you'll know what's there, but leave them as is. You can choose more than one subtotal in this window. If we had more subtotals, you'd first have to select the one you want from the Summary field drop-down, then click the Add Subtotal button. Since we don't want any others right now, just click **Next**.

Specify Grand Totals

The term "grand totals" may not be familiar to you if you're not a statistics or accounting wizard. It's just a total of all the totals. Look around this screen to get familiar with it. It's not much different from the Specify Subtotals screen. Notice that you can decide where you want the total to appear on the report.

16. Specify the **InvoiceTotal** field.
17. Click the **Add Grand Total** button to move InvoiceTotal to the list, then click **Next**.

18. You've already seen the Select a Theme screen, so these options will look familiar to you. If you don't want to print your invoices in color, select the **Standard** style, and click the **Next** button.

Header and Footer Information

The Header and Footer Information screen, shown in Figure 9-7, tells you what it's for.

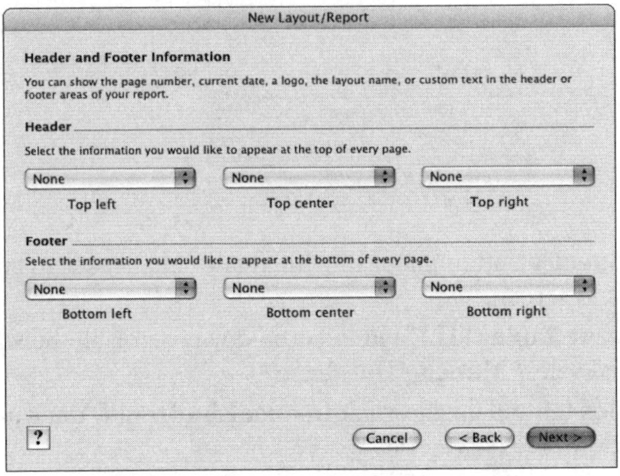

Figure 9-7
The Header and Footer Information screen lets you add a number of clarifying elements in the top and bottom margins of your report.

19. Under the Header section, click the "Top center" drop-down, choose **Large Custom Text**, and type what you like (I typed **My Company, Inc.**). Click **OK**.
20. In the "Top right" drop-down, choose **Current Date**.
21. Under the Footer section, click the "Bottom right" drop-down and choose **Page Number**. You get the idea.
22. Click **Next**.

Create a Script for This Report

Using this screen can save some time in the Manage Scripts department. If you don't like the default script, you can always delete it or edit it.

23. Go ahead and click the radio button next to **Create a script**, name it **Invoice Print**, and click the **Next** button.

> **NOTE** You don't need to be as fussy about script names as you do field names. You can leave spaces between words. Since we're using so many other odd-sounding standards, it's nice to have something that looks like real English!

24. Whatever choice you make in the New Layout/Report window doesn't change much of anything. However, after I create a report, I like to go to Layout mode to do some cleanup. So, check the radio button that will take you to Layout mode and click **Finish**.

Cleaning Up

To make the report look nice, the first thing I'd do is shrink the InvoiceNum, ProdID, and Quantity fields. Then, I'd expand the Description field. Align the text in Price, Quantity, LineTotal, and both copies of InvoiceTotal to the right, and format all values but Quantity to contain dollar signs and two decimal places.

Switch back to Browse mode to make sure that you've left enough space for the numbers in Price, Quantity, LineTotal, and InvoiceTotal and that your layout stays within the page margins.

> ⌘ **TIP** The layout part tabs are tipped sideways. At the bottom of the window, to the left of the Mode drop-down (which should now read Layout), is a little icon called the Part label control, which will flip the tabs back to horizontal. But then, of course, they're in the way. To temporarily turn any one of them horizontal, simply click on the tab and hold for a second. When you let go of the mouse button, it will flip back out of the way.
>
> If you don't want to make the trip to the icon at the bottom of the screen, try this shortcut: Click on one of the part tabs while holding down Command (Macintosh) or Ctrl (Windows). You can toggle the tabs horizontally and vertically.

Well, it's still not exactly an invoice you'd send out, but it's sure a heck of a start. You can see how I changed my final layout in Figure 9-8. I expanded the leading sub-summary (below the header) and added related information about the customer. If you did the Other Considerations exercise at the end of Chapter 7, the customer data should be available in the Invoice table. But there are no occurrences of the Invoice table connected to ILI. To get access to that data, add a TO called ili_INV__InvNum. Place it to the right of ILI and connect it by, what else, InvoiceNum. (Notice that sometimes I'm not using the exact field name when it's included in the TO name. Keeping it short is just fine.) The left- and right-pointing double arrowheads (called chevrons — less than and greater than keys on your keyboard) in the figure mean these are merge fields. I'll show you how to create some merge fields when we get to mailing labels later in this chapter.

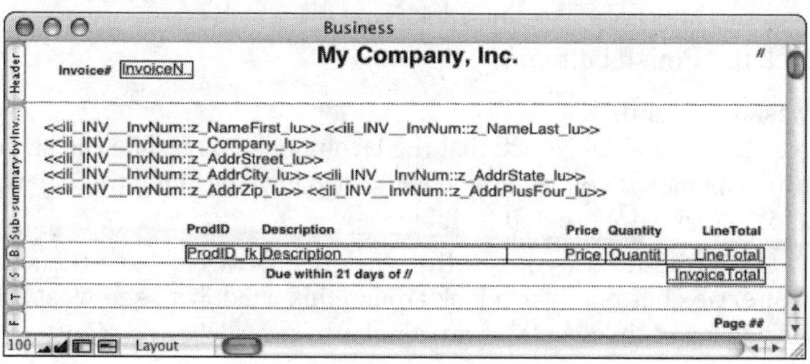

Figure 9-8 The Invoice report in the ILI table as created by the Layout Assistant with a few useful additions.

Sub-summary Part Definition

1. Double-click the **Trailing Sub-summary** tab (just below the Body tab) to access the Part Definition window.
2. Check the boxes next to **Page break after every 1 occurrence** and **Restart page numbers after each occurrence** to make each invoice appear on a separate page. There are other ways to get to the Part Definition window, but I find this the most useful. Click **OK**.

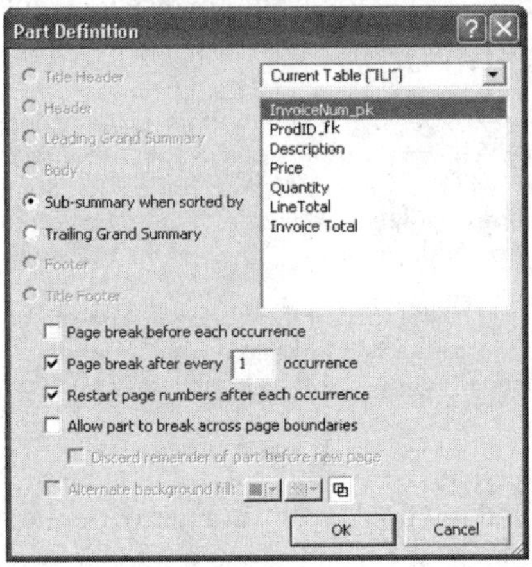

Figure 9-9
The sub-summary Part Definition window showing page break options.

Table View

Let's use the Table view as a way to get a quick overview of our invoices.

1. Go to Layout mode, and start a new layout.
2. Choose **INV** from the "Show records from" drop-down list, and choose **Table view** from the type list. Call this layout **INV_Table**, and click **Next**.
3. Click the **Move All** button, then click **Next**.
4. Choose a style you like, and click **Next**.
5. Click the **Finish** button.

That wasn't too hard.

Go to Layout mode. Notice that the layout looks more like the standard layout than a table. If you want, you could also have changed the view of the first layouts that were created to Table view.

6. Choose **Layouts**, **Layout Setup**, click the **Views** tab, and then click the **Properties** button. Take a look around this window to see what it has to offer. Many of these options are similar to spreadsheet options.
7. Now check the boxes next to **Sort data when selecting column** and **Include header part**. Click **OK**, and **OK** again.

8. While you're still in Layout mode, make a little button that goes to the INV_Invoice layout and put it in the header part.
9. Go to Browse mode, and click the column title bars to see the invoices sort. Then click on one of the invoices in the list, and click the button in the header. It should take you to the invoice detail. This is no big deal with only a couple of invoices, but when the list gets long, you'll appreciate a quick way to move between the Table view and the invoice itself.

> ⌘ **TIP** You can resize column widths in groups rather than one at a time in Table view. To select a contiguous group of columns, Shift+click on the column heads. To select discontinuous columns, use Command+click (Macintosh) or Ctrl+click (Windows). Move your cursor to the divider on the right side of any one of the selected columns until you see the double-headed arrows. Click and drag to change the column size for all the columns.
>
> If you can't see the double-headed arrows, go to Layout mode, choose Layouts, Layout Setup, and click the Views tab. Click the Properties button to bring up the Table View Properties window and check the box next to Resizable columns.
>
> If you have a large number of fields on a layout and they don't all seem to show, it's probably because you've reached the 110-inch layout limit. By resizing the columns you can display more fields.

Labels

1. Go back into the Business file, switch to Layout mode, and start a new layout.
2. Choose **CON** from the "Show records from" drop-down. Name the layout **CON_Labels**, choose **Labels** from the type list, and click **Next**.
3. Take a look around the Labels window. The drop-down has a huge list of Avery labels to choose from that was updated in FMP9. (Check with your office supplier to see which labels you can buy off the shelf. You can work with other label suppliers if you know the Avery number.) If nothing suits you, you can create your own custom labels. What more could you ask for? Use the default setting, and click the **Next** button.
4. Double-click on the field names to create your label until it looks like Figure 9-10. You can choose related fields as well, but what we need is right in this table. Notice the merge characters (« », called chevrons) that set off these special fields. Feel free to type any text you want to appear on the label (commas, returns, even words), but don't add text between the chevrons since FileMaker needs that text to exactly match the name of a field.

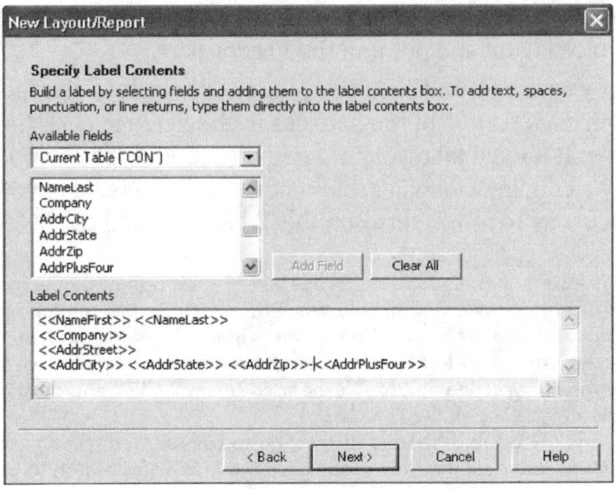

Figure 9-10
The Specify Label Contents window where you choose the merge fields by clicking on items in the list.

5. Click **Next**, then click **Finish**. You'll be in Preview mode, and you should see the current found set as labels. If you only see one, go to Browse mode, choose Show All Records, and return to Preview mode. To get rid of the dashes when there is no plus four zip code, see the Q & A section at the end of this chapter.

⌘ **TIP** If one or more of the labels seem to have incorrect information, you have to switch to one of the data entry layouts to make the corrections. The data in merge fields cannot be edited. (Well, that's not quite true. See the Caution below.) However, you can change which merge fields appear on the layout. If you see labels with blank lines in them, you'll most likely find extra, invisible return characters in one of the fields. Sometimes people entering data press the Return key instead of the Tab key when trying to leave a field. Maybe you did it! To prevent that, see the "Validated By Calculation" section in Chapter 10.

⌘ **TIP** To change a merge field, you must be in Layout mode. Using the Text tool, double-click in the merge text area so the cursor enters the text box. Delete the unwanted merge field using normal text editing methods (backspace over it or highlight and delete). To add a different field, choose Insert, Merge field. Then choose the field from the field list. You can also enter the chevrons and the field names directly.

⌘ **TIP** One nifty thing to note about merge fields is that the only part of the text that FileMaker looks at to get the style information is the first open angle bracket (<) for each of the merge fields. If you format that bracket with the style you want (16-point Arial, for example), then you can highlight the rest of the text and make it a small size (like 6 or 8 point). That way it will take up less space on the screen. Sometimes in places where space is very constrained (like portals or buttons) this trick can help you fit "long" field names in the tight space. The downside is that it's harder to revise later on. And there's no guarantee that FileMaker will continue to support that behavior in the future since it's an undocumented "feature."

CAUTION If you intend to use merge fields to keep people from editing the data, you need to know this: If someone chooses View, View as Table, merge fields suddenly become active, editable fields! This was not the case in versions of FileMaker previous to 7. You can keep users from having access to Table view on a layout-by-layout basis. Go to Layout mode and choose Layouts, Layout Setup, click the Views tab, and uncheck the box next to Table View. Problem solved.

Formatting dates, numbers, and times in merge fields is a different story. For example, let's say you have two numbers that you want to format separately in a single block of text. If you want to format one with a dollar sign and the other with a percent sign, you're out of luck. You'd have to break them into separate blocks of text. Otherwise, you could create some complex calculation that included your own custom formatting and place that concatenated field on the layout.

NOTE Vertical labels are primarily used for Asian languages. They allow users to print labels using characters that go from the top to the bottom of the label rather than from left to right. For more on that, go to the Help menu, select FileMaker Pro Help and search for "Formatting fields and text for vertical writing."

Envelope

This works exactly like the labels. Give it a try and see if you can do it without my help. When it comes to printing, that's another matter. Everything depends on the type of printer you're using and how you intend to feed the envelopes. With my printer, I finally gave up and just selected letter as the paper size instead of envelope. Maybe I gave up too soon, but it works just fine.

Blank Layout

Do you really need to ask? The only thing you need to do is decide on a name for it and decide if it should appear in the Layout drop-down. Then click Finish. If I'm going to use a blank layout for something like a letter, I immediately delete the header and footer parts. They only cause problems trying to get the letter to print where you want it to.

Summary

In this chapter, I showed you FileMaker Pro's Layout Assistant. We added one of each of the layout styles to the invoicing system to move it a little further along the way of making it a usable set of files. We also looked at quite a few of the Assistant's options along the way.

Q & A

Q When I looked at the labels, everyone who didn't have a plus four zip had a dash. What should I do about that?

A Create a calculation field called AddrPlusFourCalc that is figured as follows:

```
If(IsEmpty(AddrPlusFour); ""; "-" & AddrPlusFour)
```

For you real techies, a shorter version would be:

```
If(AddrPlusFour; "-"; "") & AddrPlusFour
```

You can do that because the If function simply tests whether there is data in the field, so you don't need the IsEmpty function. But I think it's more clear the other way.

Make sure you choose Text for the result. Then change the last line of the label so it reads:

```
<AddrCity> <AddrState> <AddrZip><AddrPlusFourCalc>
```

Notice there is no space between AddrZip and AddrPlusFourCalc.

CAUTION I got the short version of AddrPlusFourCalc to work reliably, but I could not repeat it for other calculations. Always test your work — and the testing should be on a copy of the field.

Workshop

In the Business file, I had you create a Table view of Invoice. Using the Invoice table, go back and make a List/Report without the summary information. When you're done, compare it with the Table view and see which you like better. Think about how you might use one or the other for various purposes.

Part 3

Turning Your Data into Information

Chapter 10

Keeping Your Data Clean and Neat

Introduction

Incorrect data can cause problems. Zip codes with too many digits, the wrong price for a product on an invoice, or a check made out to the wrong person — all can cause problems that can bring a business to a screeching halt. We looked at some of the tools FileMaker offers when we used drop-down lists and lookups in our invoicing system. In this chapter, we'll explore data entry in depth, by looking at the details behind the:

- Auto-Enter tab
- Validation tab
- Storage tab
- Furigana tab (briefly)

Not only do the options on these tabs keep your data correct, they often speed up your work. That spells savings.

Field Data Entry Options

The field type determines what lies behind the Options button of the Manage Fields window. All field types except summary have a Storage option. When you click the Options button for text, number, date, time, timestamp, and container fields, you are presented with the Options for Field window shown in Figure 10-1. In the case of a container field, many of the options are not applicable, so they're grayed out. Aside from the calculations themselves, the only options calculation fields have are storage options. You can see them in Figure 10-5.

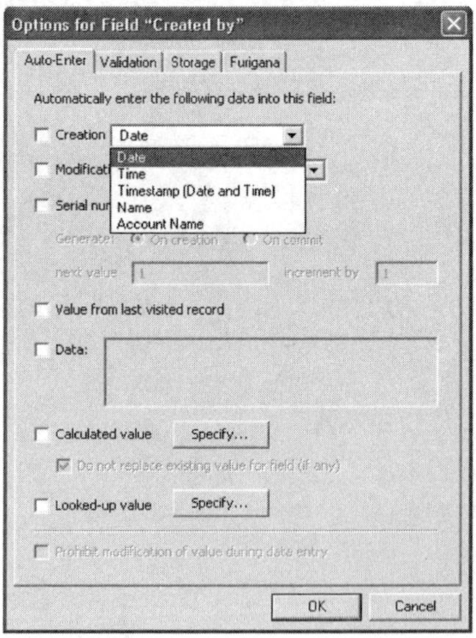

Figure 10-1
The Options for Field window showing the Creation/Modification drop-down list.

Auto-Enter Tab (Automatically Entering Values)

The choices behind the Auto-Enter tab allow you to set up a field so that data entry can be taken care of automatically. We've looked at a few of these choices already, so you should feel somewhat comfortable with them.

Creation

When you select the Creation check box, you can select the automatic entry of the date, time, timestamp (which is date *and* time), name, or account name for a field. If you're storing the data in a text or a number field, you can choose any of the items from the drop-down. Of course, a number field can't index anything other than numbers. But surprisingly you can search for dates and times in a number field. Text data (Name or Account Name) does show up in a number field, but you can't perform a find for it. If you're working with a date or time field, the drop-down displays inappropriate choices in gray.

Modification

The second check box, Modification, gives you the same five auto-entry options — date, time, timestamp, name, and account name. In a business with shared files, having a special field that keeps track of when a record was last modified and another for who did the modification can be very helpful. You can always check back with that person to get more details or use that information to track down problems or to see employee productivity.

Serial Number

We used the Auto-Enter Serial Number option in a number of our tables. One thing I didn't mention is that you can include text as part of what gets entered. For example, having "MC-1" or "5-CR" in the "next value" field would create serial numbers like MC-1, MC-2, or 5-CR, 6-CR, and so on. That could work well for a products file that needs such modifiers. Be careful whenever you put text in a number field, though. Since you can't perform a find for the letters, you should change the field type to text. This may also be a concern if your auto-entered value is being used for a database key. Better alternatives may be to use a calculation to combine two fields (a serial number and a code) or to use a relationship with a compound key.

Notice also that the numbers don't have to increase by a single digit. You can use almost any number you want in the "increment by" box. To be more specific, you may use a range of integers from 1 to 32,767. That rules out using a number like 0.5 or a negative number, in case you were trying to have the value decrement rather than increment.

> **NOTE** Since we're talking about text in the auto-entered serial number, here's something else to consider: If you enter a decimal number in the "next value" field, FileMaker interprets everything to the left of the decimal as text rather than an integer. So if you started with the next value of 6.9, the next number that would appear would be 6.10 rather than 7.0 as you probably intended.

Notice the radio buttons to the right of Generate. Starting with FMP7, you can decide whether the serial number gets created when the record is created or once the user exits or commits the record. Sometimes users create records accidentally or get partway through and decide to stop. In cases like that, the serial numbers are no longer sequential, which bothers some people. The choices here can help prevent that. But it can also create a problem if the serial number will be a key field for records that will be created in a portal immediately after the master record is created. The key field must receive a value before records can be created in the portal.

Value from Last Visited Record

If you're doing data entry for a large number of records, one after the other, that have the same data in one or more of the fields (for example, Company, Address, City, State), turn this feature on for the fields that need it. When you get to the next batch of records that are different, make the changes to the values in the affected fields. All records from then on will copy the new changes.

> **TIP** If you'll be turning a feature like this on temporarily for a number of fields, move the affected fields to the top of the Manage field list. When you want to turn the feature off, they'll all be right there at the top of the list. The View by drop-down will display the words "Custom order." So don't set it back to "field name" or one of the other choices until you're done.

Data

If you check the box next to Data, you can type anything you like, up to 255 characters. You can have text or number data go into a date or time field, too, if you can find some reason for doing that. Should most of the people you enter in your contact file live in the same city and state, you may want those fields set up to fill that in for you and just change them to accommodate the rare cases. Some of my clients have multiple contacts that belong to the same company at the same address. They like to duplicate the first record and have the name and e-mail address fields blank. In that case, we check the box next to Data and don't enter anything in the Data box for the name and e-mail fields. That automatically leaves the field blank.

Calculated Value

This option is interesting! You can have a regular text, number, date, time, or timestamp field that gets filled with a calculated value. But since it's a field that is otherwise modifiable, you can change it manually or with a script. Otherwise, it's protected from the kind of changes that happen to fields that use looked-up values. (See the next section on looked-up values.)

Here's why this is different: In a normal calculation field, if you change the value in any of the fields to which it refers, the calculation result changes. Take our ILI table for example, which contains LineTotal = Price * Quantity. If you change Price or Quantity, LineTotal changes. With a field that enters data using a calculated value, that wouldn't happen.

Also, in a regular field that's defined with the Lookup option, let's say you change the value over in the field that gets looked up. If you trigger a relookup, it overwrites the data in the lookup field. That doesn't happen with the Calculated value option turned on. The only time relookup will do anything with a field like this is if it's empty to start with (or if you uncheck the box next to "Do not replace existing value for field (if any)"). You can empty it first if you do want to trigger a relookup. If you empty the field and change one of the values that the calculation refers to, you'll get the calculation result.

The way I use this most often is if the value I need might come from more than one lookup table. For example, you might have a calculation refer to a regular price table and a sales price table (or a different field in the same table) if purchases are made during a specific date range. That is something you can't do with a regular lookup since a regular lookup must point to a single field.

If you intend to use this function, be sure to turn off the upper five check boxes in the Auto-Enter tab (Creation, Modification, Serial number, Value from last visited record, and Data). Otherwise, the value selected by the upper check box will take precedence, and the calculation won't be triggered. By the way, you can make it act like a looked-up value by unchecking the box next to "Do not replace existing value for field (if any)." That gives the calculated value more power than you can achieve with a regular looked-up value because the looked-up value is limited to grabbing data from a single table with a single relationship. But note that the values will only update if the fields that are being changed are in the current record in a layout that references the table the fields belong to. In other words, your calculation will not change reliably if a related field is part of the calculation and that related field gets changed. To control something like that, you might use script triggers, which are discussed in Chapter 16, "Working with Script Triggers."

CAUTION Don't think of this technique as the same as a lookup. If you change any of the values on which the calculated value is dependent, any value already calculated for this field will not change the way a lookup would. However, with the addition of the "Do not replace existing value for field (if any)" check box introduced in FMP7, you can make it act exactly like a lookup — except with more power! Also be sure you choose the correct table occurrence from the drop-down next to "Evaluate this calculation from the context of" at the top of the Specify Calculation window. It is absolutely critical that you make the right choice when it comes to the context of the calculation. This context drop-down is quite important and will be covered in various references to the Specify Calculation window as we move forward in the book. Test to see if you're getting the results you expect. If not, look to the context drop-down first.

Looked-up Value

We used this feature in our ILI table. Choose the ProductID from a drop-down, and the Description and Price come in automatically since they have been defined as lookup fields.

Zip code databases that include fields for city, state, and phone area code are available at very low cost or free. You can set up a file to look up the other fields based on the zip code as the match field. If you've ever purchased something over the phone, and the order-taker asked for your zip code and then verified your city and state, that's how they did it. Set up your databases to take advantage of this great time-saving feature. Those extra few seconds times how many data entry people taking how many orders every day can cost a lot of money to the company that doesn't take advantage of lookups like this.

You should know that you can relookup the values for fields that use a lookup. Once you've found one or a batch of records, click in the key field for the relationship and choose Records, Relookup Field Contents. You need to be somewhat cautious, though, since you cannot undo a relookup. Also, any other fields that use lookups based on the same key field will be affected.

Prohibit Modification

The last check box in this tab is "Prohibit modification of value during data entry." We used it to protect our InvoiceNum_pk field. I've seen this used in offices to protect a field that keeps track of the modifier name. That way no one can change a record and blame it on someone else — at least not while they're on their own machine! However, you'll also want to use passwords to protect user access to the Manage Database window.

Validation Tab (Checking Data for Accuracy)

The check boxes on the Validation tab help you make sure data gets entered properly. You can check more than one box here to provide multiple validations and you can even send your own message to the user if the data isn't entered properly. Take a look at Figure 10-2.

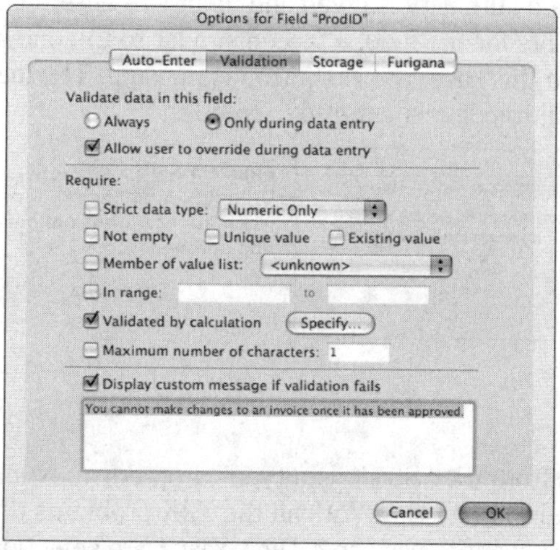

Figure 10-2
The selections under the Validation tab in the Options for Field window.

Validate Data in This Field[7]

The upper section of the Validation tab is titled "Validate data in this field." Here you can select whether the data is validated only at data entry or if it is constantly monitored (including when importing data). This feature was introduced in FileMaker Pro 7. It is most helpful when importing data. I can't tell you the number of times I've imported data that had incorrect date, time, and number formats. With the "Always" radio button selected for the fields targeted for import, you'll be notified that there were errors in the dialog that appears at the end of the import procedure (see Figure 10-3). Of course you'll have to go find the problem records, but that's a lot better than having useless data floating around inside your files.

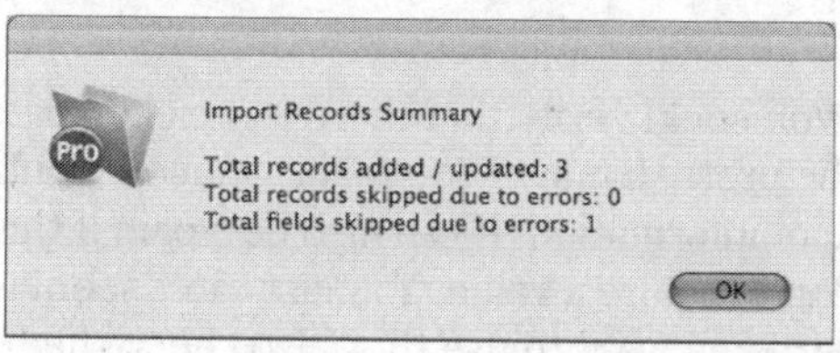

Figure 10-3
Import Records Summary dialog showing fields skipped due to errors in the data.

You can also choose if the person doing the data entry can override the validation warnings. If the person doing the data entry is given authority to override the validation warning and enters information not within the requirements established for the field, he or she will see a message similar to the one in Figure 10-4a. Notice the No button.

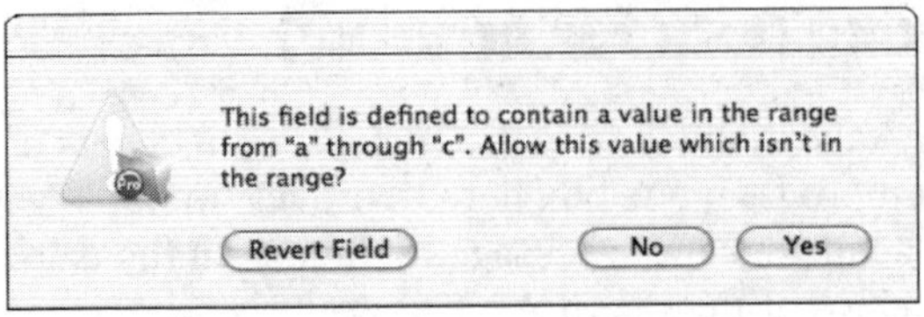

Figure 10-4a
Data validation dialog displayed when the user has override permission.

On the other hand, if no such authority is given and he or she enters information outside the requirements for the field, a screen similar to the one in Figure 10-4b will pop up. In this case, the No button is missing. The dialog will continue to pop up until the data is entered correctly.

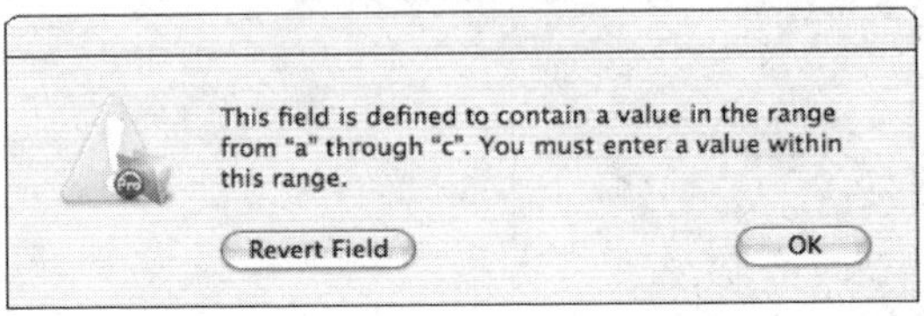

Figure 10-4b
Data validation dialog displayed when the user does not have override permission.

Strict Data Type

You only get three choices from the "Strict data type" drop-down: Numeric Only, 4-Digit Year Date, and Time of Day. With all the Y2K problems the computer industry had, you may want to use the 4-Digit Year Date selection to protect date fields from future troubles. In fact, let me discourage you from allowing entry of dates with only two digits in the year, because FileMaker is going to fill in the first two digits for you and may guess wrong. Let's say that the field is Birthdate, and the person entering the data types in 03/14/32. FileMaker is going to guess that the intended year is 2032. FileMaker is always going to guess that the intended year is either within the next 30 years or the last 70.

CAUTION Whenever you click in the "Strict data type" drop-down, FileMaker automatically selects the check box next to Strict data type. You may unwittingly end up with requests to validate a field that doesn't require it. If that's not what you intend, be sure to uncheck that box.

Not Empty

For a retail ordering system, you could verify that there is a pickup date in every order. This option can be pretty handy if you find that users continually forget to fill in a specific piece of information. It can also be a pain if this option is used on fields that don't require a value. You just can't seem to escape the record. If you're sure you want to use this, also check the box next to "Strict data type."

Unique Value

Remember when we talked about using a unique ProdID in the Products file? This is where you make that selection. Be sure to also check the "Strict data type" check box. Otherwise, users will be able to override the warning box, and you'll have duplicate IDs. You can choose either the "Unique value" or the "Existing value" check box.

Existing Value

Using the "Existing value" check box makes sure that users only select values that have already been entered in the file. (In a case like that, you might consider selecting "Member of value list" instead.) If a new value needs to be entered in the file, turn this option off, make the addition to the record, then turn it back on. Since this is the opposite of "Unique value," you cannot choose "Unique value" at the same time.

Member of Value List

Checking this box urges the user to enter a value from the value list you choose before leaving the record. You can create a value list right from here if you want. You'll probably want to attach the specific drop-down list to any fields with this option turned on. Otherwise, users will have a heck of a time guessing what they're supposed to enter.

Currently on a Macintosh computer, you can't tab into a field that uses a pop-up menu even if you have full keyboard access turned on. However, if you format a field to use a drop-down list that allows tabbing, users can click in the field and type something that's not in the list. To prevent that, you could use this validation. Even at that, since this validation is based on FileMaker's indexing, it is not case sensitive. So you may still want to have users select from a pop-up menu.

In Range

Using this option, you can restrict data entry to a range of values. For instance, you could use a time range to make sure workers punch in and out within certain hours. You can even enter a range of first initials or full words in the range boxes.

CAUTION Avoid getting carried away with using a text range, because it can be tricky. For example, if you used a range from "a" to "bbb," entering something like "c" in the field would set off the warning, but an entry like "abcde" would not.

Validated By Calculation

This is the option with the most power. You can check for such errors as:

- A field that begins or ends with an extra space or contains or ends with a carriage return
- A State field that has more or less than two letters
- A Zip Code field that has anything other than five digits
- A Social Security Number field that is structured with anything other than three digits followed by a dash, two digits, a dash, and four digits.
- A carriage return at the end of various parts of an address field. This usually happens when users hit the Return or Enter key instead of tabbing to the next field.

We'll be looking at calculations in Chapter 11, "Putting Your Data to Work for You."

Maximum Number of Characters

Checking this box lets you limit the number of characters users can enter in a text, number, date, or time field. You can do something similar with the "Validated by calculation" option, but it's a lot simpler here. Just type in a number and you're good to go.

> **CAUTION** Be careful about what other options you choose when deselecting the override option. When you uncheck the box next to "Allow user to override during data entry," and then check the box next to "Existing value" but the value has never been entered before, the only way to escape the looping dialog is to either revert the field or delete the record. You can't even quit or exit FileMaker. Since your users may not know that, they may panic and pull the plug on the machine. Test your work by using as many possible values as you can think of — and even some you can't think of — before inflicting it on other users.

Display Custom Message if Validation Fails

You can have a custom message displayed with or without the override option being selected. Use this to clarify what the user should do to correct his or her data entry if the FileMaker window isn't clear enough.

Try to be concise. You can type up to 255 characters in this box. That's 15 to 55 more characters than will actually fit in the dialog that appears if the validation fails. If you're not sure the text will fit, test it by returning to Browse mode and entering some incorrect data. In some cases you may find the standard error message can actually be more descriptive, especially for range errors. If you're developing for both Mac and Windows, be sure your message will fit in the dialog box on both platforms.

Storage Tab (Global Storage, Repeating Fields, and Indexing)

The Storage tab, as seen in Figure 10-5, contains the choices for global storage, repeating fields, and indexing.

Global Storage

This is the area where you make the choice that turns a regular field into a global field. (The global storage option was discussed in detail in Chapter 4.) Let me remind you again though, that for the sake of best practices, global field names should start with *zx_*, where the *x* will be replaced with some other letter that represents the developer's purpose (control, interface, keys, etc.) and end with *_gx*, where the *x* will represent the field type (text, number, date, etc.). If you're not sure which letter to use in the suffix, you can always find the code in the Field Type drop-down. The keyboard shortcuts and their letters are located there.

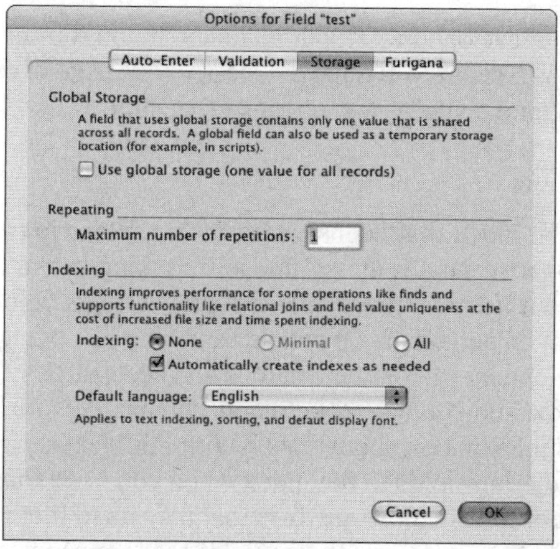

Figure 10-5
Storage tab of the Options for Field window showing global storage, repeating fields, and indexing options.

Repeating Field Options

I covered the repeating field option in Chapter 4. A repeating field is just a way of formatting field types (except summary) with multiple boxes for data entry. It was used quite a bit back in the days before FileMaker became a relational database. It's been maintained primarily so users who had developed databases back then can keep their files as is. However, many developers format global fields as repeating to store multiple values and images for use throughout their files.

You can have up to 32,000 repetitions of a field. When you place a repeating field on a layout using the Field tool or by copying a single repetition version of the field from some other layout, there is no clue that the field repeats. You must choose Format, Field/Control, Setup in Layout mode to access the area where you choose how it will appear on the layout. You can choose to display fewer repetitions (all the way down to 1) than appear in the Storage tab.

> **NOTE** You can perform a find for a value, and if it appears in any of the repetitions, the record will appear in the found set. For example, let's say you had a record with Dog in the first repetition and Cat in the second. A find for Cat in the first repetition or Dog in the second will find the record. If you have the field formatted with a single repetition, you won't be able to see the specified data even if you click in the single repetition. That would be a clue that it is defined as a repeating field.

> **NOTE** When you go beyond simple storage of values and images in repeating fields, my advice is to look to relationships and portals for the answer to that job. There is just so much more you can do with them.

FileMaker's Indexing System

Imagine that you have an encyclopedia without an index. If you wanted to find every reference to Thomas Edison, you'd have to scan every page of every volume to find it. With an index, you're way ahead of the game.

Storage Options

FileMaker Pro has a similar index that keeps track of what data is in each field and what records contain those data. It does a fine job of taking care of everything behind the scenes, but because these indexes can get large, you have the option of turning them on and off on a per-field basis. It's like being able to decide that your encyclopedia will only list names and occupations. That makes for a nice slim index, and you'd be able to find Thomas Edison, but how are you going to find information about Cuba? With FileMaker, you can change your mind and add other fields to the index when you need them.

Remember that number fields ignore any text that may be in them except for periods and dashes. That includes calculation fields that are concatenated from number and text fields, but have a number result. If you look at the field, you'll see the text. But when you search for the text, you may feel as if you're dealing with a ghost. Knowing that is particularly important if you're using a special combination field as a key in a relationship. The relationship and the portal will act squirrelly. Of course the need for most of these calculated "combination" keys goes away for most people now that relationships allow compound keys.

> **TIP** If you have a relationship that is acting up and it's based on concatenated fields, check that the key fields on both sides of the relationship are the same field type. If they're both calculations, see if you have a match in the "Calculation result is" drop-down in the Specify Calculation window.

In indexed text fields, all numbers and letters are indexed; most other characters are not. However, you can search for them by putting quotes around the symbol you want. FileMaker can find it, but it takes a while in a large file. Remember, it has to look on every page.

NOTE You can actually get FileMaker to index the special characters if you really need to. Go into Manage Fields, choose the Storage tab, and select Unicode from the default language drop-down. Then why not just index every text field as Unicode? Because it may give you headaches in other areas. For instance, when you perform a find for Bob, it won't find bob. Upper- and lowercase Unicode characters are not considered the same character. Bummer!

Field Indexing Pros and Cons

Choosing whether to index fields is a balancing act. If every field is indexed in a big file, it takes longer to import records (they'll be indexing as they come in) and perform lookups. The file also gets larger, since the index is stored as part of the file. That's not such a big issue with the 8 terabyte file size limit and since larger hard drives keep getting cheaper almost daily.

On the other hand, if you turn indexing off for all fields, FileMaker will still perform a find for you — it will just take longer. Turning indexing off also makes a field unusable as a key in a relationship from the foreign side (either table or file). Never uncheck "Automatically create indexes as needed" if the field will be used as a foreign key. (Using field naming conventions, you will, of course, note foreign keys by putting an _fk at the end, won't you? Now you're beginning to see why these naming conventions are so important.) Notice the indexing options in Figure 10-5. If you select the "None" radio button and uncheck the box next to "Automatically create indexes as needed," FileMaker will build a temporary index when needed. Unless you know that a field will be searched somewhere down the road, the simplest solution is to just ignore the whole thing and let FileMaker take care of it for you. If you need a more comprehensive explanation of these options, see the Help files.

Limitations

The result of a calculation cannot be stored if it uses data in a field:

- Where the indexing is turned off
- That uses the GetSummary function
- That is global
- That comes from a relationship

That's because the data can change across a set of records too easily. In older versions of FileMaker, if you tried to create a relationship using an unstored key field in a child file or table, FileMaker would show you a warning. That is not the case with FMP7 and later; you have to know the rules. You can go ahead and create the relationship, but nothing connected with it will work correctly.

> **CAUTION** If you create a relationship and later change the key in the child table so it becomes unstored, you will not be notified that the relationship is now invalid. But be assured, if it works at all, it will not work properly. Pay attention to your key fields and treat them with care. This would be another good reason to identify your key fields with pk or fk suffixes. (See "Notes to Developers about Naming Conventions" in Appendix A.)

Furigana Tab[7]

The Furigana tab was introduced in FileMaker Pro 7. It will only be of interest if you are working with Japanese text and looking for phonetic translation of that text. You'll create two fields. The first field will hold the Japanese text, and the second field will hold the phonetic translation. Choose the Furigana tab, check the box next to "Use Furigana Field," and select the first field you created. Then go to the "Translate into" drop-down menu and choose the character set you want to use.

Summary

In this chapter, we looked at what you can do when defining fields to simplify data entry and avoid errors. These options appear behind the Auto-Enter, Validation, and Storage tabs. Good use of these tools makes for faster work and a more reliable database.

Q & A

Q If I choose to prohibit modification of a field, what's the point of allowing users into the field at all?

A If you intend to perform a find on the field, you need to have a way to get into it. However, you can still construct a find in a script that doesn't require entry into the field. Not only that, but you can also copy data from such a field. In order to isolate a record, I sometimes like to copy the text, enter Find mode, paste it back in, and complete the find. (The keyboard commands are right next to each other and the cursor stays in the field.) You need access to the field in order to do that.

Q Why shouldn't every validation message be set up as Strict? Why would I want users to override what I've set up?

A Until you know for sure that you have it set up correctly, you might want to leave yourself an out. You have to balance how serious the results will be: incorrect data entry compared with improperly closed files. You may also want the validation to be a very strong suggestion to the user, but not a requirement. For example, if an international order came into your database, you may want to complain to the user that the zip code doesn't look right or is omitted. If there really were a strange or nonexistent zip code, then you'd probably want to allow the odd data but offer the validation as a "reminder" only.

Workshop

Go to the Contact table and experiment with items under the Validation tab on different types of fields. Try selecting "Numeric Only" on a text field. If you get really daring, try selecting "Validated by calculation" on the AddrState field. See if you can make it check whether you have more or less than two letters in the field. Hint: Click Specify, and look at the text functions in the View drop-down list at the upper right.

Chapter 11

Putting Your Data to Work for You

Introduction

Buttons can do a lot of tricks for you by finding and sorting records, and moving between files and layouts. Lookups and other auto-enter fields do some of the data entry for you. Now let's put down those pocket calculators and let FMP calculation fields do that work for you, too. You got your first taste of what can be done with calculation fields in our ILI table back in Chapter 7. We used them to provide line totals in the portal on the invoice, and the InvoiceTotal that gave us a grand total of all the line totals. We also used calculations to make a field that combined a customer's first and last names as well as company name.

In this chapter, we'll look at the four categories of operators you use in calculation fields that:

- Perform the math
- Make comparisons
- Create complex comparisons
- Build calculations using text

Defining a Calculation Field

The Specify Calculation window should be familiar by now. Using it, you build a formula with FileMaker's functions and operators that combine data from various local fields, related fields, and constants.

A *constant* is a value right in the formula. The value of the constant doesn't change unless you change the formula. The constant can consist of text, date, number, or time information.

You can type the formula directly in the Formula box. But the more common method for entering a formula when you're getting started with FileMaker is to build it by double-clicking on items from the lists or clicking on buttons in the upper third of the window.

There are so many functions that we won't be able to cover all of them; however, Chapters 12 and 13 show some of the more useful functions in detail. It's also valuable to note that you can use scripts to place the results of these same calculations in appropriate field types in one or more records. Don't forget that the Replace window has a "Replace with Calculated Result" radio button that brings up the same Specify Calculation window. FileMaker

Pro 7 and later allow you to specify a calculation when you define a button. It should be clear that developing some level of competency here would yield great dividends.

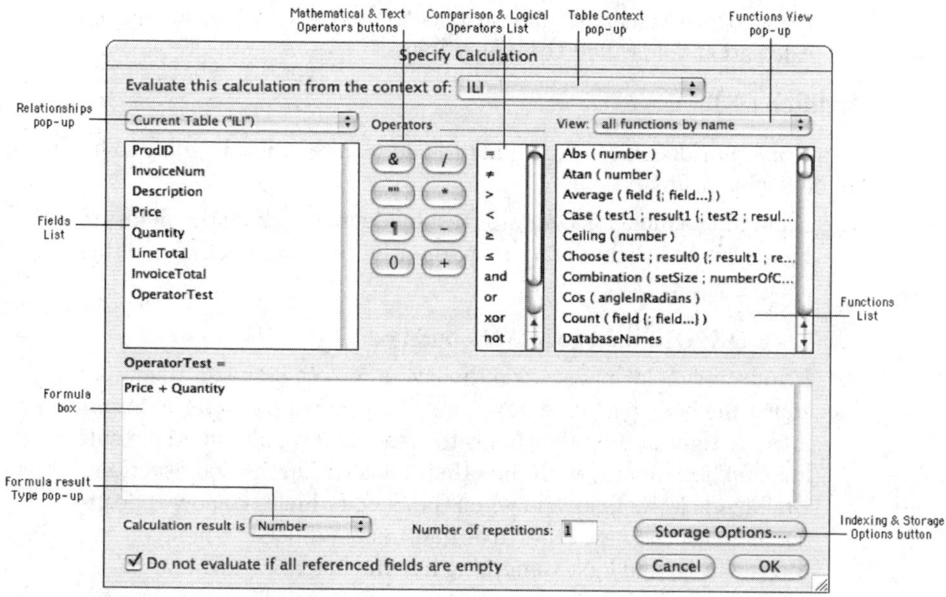

Figure 11-1
The Specify Calculation window.

Operators

Operators are the symbols used to change the behavior of or provide different results from your data. Think of it this way: You have two number fields. Each field has the number 2 in it. They just sit there. Then you create a calculation field using the plus (+) operator between them. You get the idea.

Mathematical Operators

These are the operators you remember from math class. Even though I'm sure you know what to expect here, I want to set up a layout with a few fields where we can try out some examples. Maybe there will be a few surprises.

1. Go into our Business file, start a new layout/report using the ILI table occurrence, and call it **ILI_Calcs**.
2. Choose the **List/Report** type, click **Next**, and at the next window, **List/Report** should already be selected, so click **Next** again.
3. At the Specify Fields screen, double-click **Price**, **Quantity**, and **LineTotal** to move them to the Layout fields list.
4. Then just keep clicking **Next** (and **Finish**) until you're in Preview mode.

5. Enter Browse mode and choose **Show All Records**. Hopefully, you created a few records when we were experimenting with the Invoice table. If you didn't, create a few records now, and make up some numbers for the Price and Quantity fields.
6. Now go into Manage Database, choose the **InvLI** table, and make a new calculation field called **OperatorTest**.

Addition (+)

If this operator doesn't look familiar to you, you're probably going to have a lot of trouble from here on.

1. Build the formula for OperatorTest by double-clicking the fields from the Fields list and clicking the + operator button until it looks like this:

   ```
   Price + Quantity
   ```

2. Click **OK**, **OK**, then go into Layout mode.
3. If your new field appeared on the layout, delete it and its label, then adjust the body part (see next Tip). Copy one of the other fields and paste it to the right of the other fields to create a new column. Make sure it lines up horizontally with the other fields within the body section. Double-click the field, and when the Specify Field window appears, double-click the new **OperatorTest** field in the list. When you're done, the layout should look something like the one in Figure 11-2.

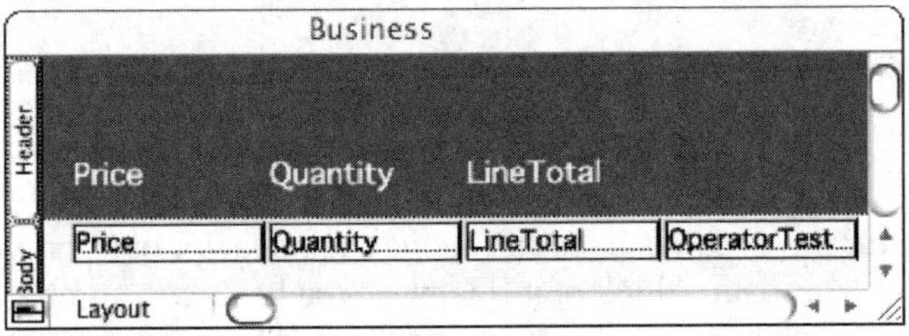

Figure 11-2
The ILI_Calcs layout, which uses the ILI table occurrence showing the position of the fields.

4. Now go back to Browse mode and look at the results. When you add the first two columns, they should equal the new field in the fourth column.
5. Go back into Manage Fields for the InvLI table and change the OperatorTest field so it reads like this:

   ```
   Price + Quantity + 15
   ```

   The number 15 is just an arbitrary figure to demonstrate how the constants work.
6. Click **OK** and **OK**, and go back to Browse mode. As you can see, you can string together any number of fields and constants.

⌘ **TIP** I've mentioned this before, but... You can set FileMaker so it doesn't add new fields to your layouts. Go to the FileMaker Pro menu and choose Preferences. Click on the Layout tab and uncheck the box next to "Add newly defined fields to current layout." I know developers who love to have the new fields dropped onto the layout, so it's up to you which way you prefer. That's why they call it a "preference." I turn it off because some of the complex reports I create get really messed up when the body part moves.

⌘ **TIP** You can use either a number field or a calculation field (with a number result) defined with global storage as a constant in another calculation. In FMP7 and later, you can change a field even while other users are sharing the file. But keep in mind that the value in the global field on everyone else's machine will not change unless you are the host of the file. Even then, other users will receive the change only after they close and reopen the file.

An interesting characteristic in formulas that only use addition is that you can put the values in any order, and the calculation will still work.

Subtraction (–)

The minus symbol is used to subtract the second value from the first one. Here, the values have to be in a specific order. Reverse them and the results are not the same. That's not a FileMaker convention — it's a mathematical convention. In the following example, I want you to change the field by yourself. You should know how to get in and out of the Manage Fields window by now, so do that, and then go look at the results.

1. Go back and redefine OperatorTest so it reads:

   ```
   Price – Quantity – 15
   ```

2. Then change it to this:

   ```
   Quantity – Quantity – 15
   ```

What's the point, you might ask? Sometimes in your search for a solution, you can end up building very complex calculations with unnecessary elements. The last equation could be shortened to just –15.

Multiplication (*)

For an example of the multiplication function, look at the LineTotal field definition. Here again, you can reverse the order and you'll get the same results. Try this:

```
Price * Quantity * .25
```

It gives you a reasonable markup, even though it doesn't round out evenly.

Division (/)

Using the divide symbol indicates that the result will divide the first value by the second value. Change OperatorTest so it reads:

```
Price / Quantity
```

I do this at the grocery store all the time to figure out how much I'm paying per ounce for a product. When you divide, you turn the integers in the operation into decimal numbers, and any number divided by 100 is its percent equivalent.

Power of (^)

The power symbol is used to multiply a number by itself the number of times indicated by the value that appears after the sign.

Let's look at some large numbers:

```
Price ^ Quantity
```

Hey! What are all those symbols in the result? When a number field is first placed on a layout, FileMaker uses the General format that I mentioned in Chapter 4.

1. To change it, go to Layout mode, select the field, and choose **Format, Number**.
2. Click the radio button next to **Leave data formatted as entered** and click **OK**. Now you'll have to make the field quite a bit longer — try 3 or 4 inches. When you go back to Browse mode, you'll see a question mark if the number is still too large. You can click in the field to see what it really is.

Granted, invoices are not the kind of situation where you'll use the power operator. In my 15 years of working with FileMaker, I don't think I've ever used the power operator. It is pretty handy in statistics, probability, and calculating things like compound interest for an arbitrary number of months or the volume of an object.

Precedence ()

You use the precedence parentheses symbols to surround elements of the calculation that are supposed to occur first. Otherwise, the formula is figured from left to right, with multiplication and division results calculated before addition and subtraction.

1. Let's try a few:

   ```
   Price + (Price * .25) * Quantity
   ```

   Wait a minute. That number seems pretty low. I'm trying to mark up the price by 25%, and then multiply by the Quantity. However, FileMaker did the multiplication within the parentheses first. Doing the multiplication before the addition, it multiplied the result by the quantity. Then it added the first Price field last.
2. Rewrite it adding another precedence:

   ```
   (Price + (Price * .25)) * Quantity
   ```
3. Now, to make all the numbers round out nicely, finish it off like this:

   ```
   Round ((Price + (Price * .25)) * Quantity, 2)
   ```

I know I'm supposed to be saving functions for the next chapter, but the fields do look nice in Browse mode, don't they? Don't let the complexity of this calculation frighten you. In the next chapter I'll show you an easy way to add functions to a calculation without getting confused about all the precedence parentheses.

Why, you might ask, would you do it this way instead of just formatting the field on the layout? Because your financial books will be off. The way numbers appear on a layout is independent of the way they are actually figured in calculations. How it appears is for your convenience. How it's figured is for your accountant, but you have to supply the correct figures.

NOTE A common use of parentheses in mathematics is as a shortcut for multiplication. For example: 3 (2 + 4) = 18. You cannot use this shorthand in FileMaker. You must specify 3 * (2 + 4).

Comparison Operators

When you want to find out how similar two values are, you use comparison operators. The values can be fields, constants, or formulas. The calculation returns either True or False. The mathematical equivalent is a 1 or a 0. This type of True or False result is referred to as a Boolean value. Yes and No are also considered valid Boolean results. This concept also applies to the logical operators.

NOTE The term Boolean is named after George Boole and honors his idea that a statement can only be true or false. It's a simple but powerful idea. Formatting a number to display in a Boolean format simply asks FileMaker to narrow down the contents of the field to one of two cases: no or false (0 or empty) or yes or true (1).

NOTE (This note is a little technical, but I had to put it somewhere. If it helps you, great.)

Some computing environments offer a Boolean field type where you can only store a yes or no answer. FileMaker doesn't. You have to be careful because FileMaker can be a bit inconsistent about evaluating a null value. You would think that a field with a null value would be evaluated as false. But if the calculation has a check mark in the "Do not evaluate if all referenced fields are empty" box, the field may not result in either 0 or 1.

A couple of other details to be aware of: FileMaker will no longer evaluate number fields beginning with T or Y as true. Also, if you enter both text and numbers in a number field and you begin with either a T or an F, these fields will not evaluate as Boolean. Instead, they will evaluate as the numeric value in the field. "T111" is a legitimate entry and 111, not 1. "Fall333" evaluates as 333, not 0.

Equal to (=)

If the values on both sides of the equal symbol are the same, the value is 1.

1. Try the following:

   ```
   Price = Quantity
   ```

   You probably won't get any 1s in that batch.
2. Now try:

   ```
   Quantity = 2 * 5
   ```

   If you don't have a match, replace one of the numbers in the Quantity field with a 10.
3. Go into Layout mode, select the **OperatorTest** field, and choose **Format, Number.**
4. Click the radio button next to **Format as Boolean.** Leave Yes and No in the boxes just beneath the radio button.
5. Go back to Browse mode and check out the results.
6. Go back and reformat the field as a number and type **Dah!** over the Yes and **Nyet** over the No.
7. Now try to perform a find for Dah! — it doesn't work. Now try to find for Nyet — failure! What's going on here? FileMaker simply displays what you tell it to when it evaluates a number as Boolean. But you can't perform a find on what it displays. You can only perform your find on that actual value in the field — the Boolean 0 or 1. But it's looking for a word to start with Y, and Dah! just doesn't cut it.
8. Before we move on, change the Dah! back to **Yes**, and Nyet back to **No.**
9. Try this as the calculation:

   ```
   2 * 5 = 10
   ```

   Each record shows a Yes, because you're not referring to any fields, just the constants — all of which have a value.
10. Now select **Show All Records.**

> **NOTE** The equal sign can be a point of confusion for many novice FileMaker users, especially if they've used another programming language or even some spreadsheets. In many other languages, the equal sign assigns a value to the item on the left side of the equal sign. X = 5 + 7 would result in X having a value of 12. In FileMaker, the equal sign is an operator that will result in only one of two values: 0 or 1. So if you had "FieldX = 5 + 7" in a function, you would not be assigning 12 to FieldX. The function would simply return 1 if FieldX held a value of 12. Otherwise, it would return 0.

Not Equal to (<> or ≠)

If the values are different, this will yield a 1.

1. Try it for:

   ```
   Price <> Quantity
   ```

2. Change one of the prices to match the quantity in the same record so you have at least one dissenting value in OperatorTest.

⌘ **TIP** On the Macintosh platform, you can use ≠ (Option+=) in place of <>. If the files are ever moved to a Windows machine, the <> will be automatically substituted in any calculations.

3. Try it with a constant:

```
Quantity <> 10
```

If all the results are the same, change one of the Quantity values to 10.

Greater Than (>)

If the value on the left is greater than the value on the right, this will show a 1.

1. Try this:

```
Price > Quantity
```

2. Now try this:

```
Quantity > Price
```

Depending on the numbers you have in your fields, you may not get the exact opposite results. That's because the opposite of Price > Quantity is Price <= Quantity. Read on.

Less Than (<)

If the value on the left is less than the value on the right, you'll get a 1. Run your own test.

Greater Than or Equal to (>= or ≥)

If the value on the left is greater than or equal to the value on the right, you'll get a 1.

Try the following, but make sure you have at least one Quantity field with 12 in it as well as larger and smaller amounts in other records:

```
Quantity >= 12
```

Less Than or Equal to (<= or ≤)

Be sure to have one record where Price and Quantity are the same. Watch that record change as you switch from the first to the second of the following calculations:

```
Price > Quantity
Price <= Quantity
```

These are the opposite of each other as are Price < Quantity and Price >= Quantity. Notice that if you flip either of them you'll get the same result:

Quantity > Price is the same as Price < Quantity. Price >= Quantity is the same as Quantity <= Price.

Logical Operators

Logical operators also return Boolean results (1 or 0). Understanding what they do is not that hard, but grasping an entire formula can be a little more difficult than simple comparison operators. That's because you're using these symbols to join two or more of the comparisons.

AND

The AND operator will produce a value of 1 or True if all comparisons in its string are true.

1. Change the OperatorTest field so it reads as follows:

   ```
   Description = "Large Widget" AND Price = 19.99
   ```

2. Go into Layout mode, shorten the field up to about 1 inch, and add the Description field to the list. If there are no Large Widgets with a price of 19.99 in the same record, make a couple.

> ⌘ **TIP** FileMaker will recognize both "AND" and "and" as valid in the calculations. If you type AND, FileMaker converts it to lowercase anyway when you click OK. Nothing to be alarmed about.

3. Now try this:

   ```
   Description = "Large Widget" AND Price = 19.99 AND Quantity = 10
   ```

You can go as deep as you want with this. While this might seem like a pointless exercise, you might find yourself in a situation in which someone asks you for specific information about two or more fields. You could scan through all the records, which would take a lot or time, or you could create a calculation that will help you find that information in seconds. Notice that you have to put quotes around the text constant (Large Widget), but you don't have to worry about adding quotes around numbers unless they will be part of a text constant.

4. Now do one more test:

   ```
   Description = "Large Widget" AND Price = Quantity AND Quantity = 10
   ```

If you are confused about these calculations, consider typing it with extra returns and indents, so it reads like this:

```
Description = "Large Widget"
   and
Price = Quantity
   and
Quantity = 10
```

In this one, the middle test compares the values in two fields as well as the two other constants. Of course, to test it in Browse mode, you'll need to make sure that all three conditions are met in at least one record.

OR

The OR operator will produce a value of 1 or True if any of the comparisons in its string are true. Just replace the ANDs from our last formula with ORs:

```
Description = "Large Widget" OR Price = Quantity OR Quantity = 10
```

AND and OR

Now look at combining AND and OR in the same formula by changing either of the ORs back to an AND. For example:

```
Description = "Large Widget" AND Price = Quantity OR Quantity = 10
```

Change the numbers in some of the Quantity and Price fields to see how they affect the calculation. Is it what you expected?

XOR

Aside from wondering what XOR is, you might wonder where the spelling of XOR comes from. It's just short for X or Y, with the Y part left off. (It is also referred to as "Exclusive OR.") It's pronounced like the first part of "Zorro." You get a True result if either X or Y is true, but not both. If neither is true, you get a Boolean False, No, or 0.

1. First try:

   ```
   Description = "Large Widget" XOR Price = Quantity
   ```

2. You can combine this with AND and OR as well. So try:

   ```
   Description = "Large Widget" XOR Price = Quantity AND Quantity = 10
   ```

This can be particularly confusing, because we are asking that the two parts of the Y portion match. In this case, the X part of the equation is Description = "Large Widget," and the Y is Price = Quantity AND Quantity = 10.

- If the Description is "Large Widget" and the Price and the Quantity are both 10, you will get a False result.
- If the Description is "Medium Widget" and the Price and Quantity are both 10, you will get a True result.
- If the Description is "Large Widget" and the Price and Quantity are not both 10, you will get a True result.

It took me a long time to understand this concept. Let me give you a more concrete example of why somebody might want to use XOR.

Let's say I'm adding people to my database. I have two fields describing the person: BoughtMyBook and VisitedMyWebsite. The result of a BoughtMyBook XOR VisitedMyWebsite expression would give me a list of people who did at least one of the two but not both. This would be very handy for marketing to people who have shown interest in my work and getting them to look at other work of mine. That way I can leave out those people who haven't done either, as well as those people who've already done both and might not be receptive to more requests to view my work.

BoughtMyBook XOR VisitedMyWebsite is equivalent to:

```
(BoughtMyBook OR VisitedMyWebsite) AND (NOT (BoughtMyBook AND
VisitedMyWebsite))
```

You can see that the XOR calculation is a handy shortcut, not to mention easier to understand — once you get the hang of it. Don't worry if you don't get it. I don't have to use this one very often, so I have to think it through carefully every time I work with it.

NOT

NOT is not used to combine other elements, although you can certainly use it in formulas that have two or more comparison elements. You have to combine NOT with parentheses that surround the value you're testing. Whatever is true in the parentheses returns a False result. Conversely, whatever is false in the parentheses returns a True (or a 1) result.

For example, if we use the calculation NOT (Quantity) = 10, and there is a 10 in the Quantity field, you'll get a 0. Why would you want to do that? Remember when we were working with Omit? Sometimes it's easier to find what is not true than what is true. For example, using the calculation NOT Left(Description, 5) = "Small", returns a 1 for any kind of widget other than Small. Notice that you can combine NOT with other functions, operators, and constants.

One situation I often run into has to do with whether a field has a value in it. Let's say you need to make sure that every item in the invoice that has a number in the Price field also has text in the Description field. In that case, you have to use something like NOT IsEmpty(Description). It sounds a little weird, but that's how you have to phrase it, because there is no function called IsFull(FieldName).

To see what it does, try NOT IsEmpty(Description). Then go into Browse mode and clear out whatever is in one of the Description fields. We'll look more closely at calculations in the next chapter.

> **NOTE** Length(FieldName) also works. It returns 0 for an empty field and 1 for a field with text.

Text Operators

You use text operators to build calculations with a text result. In a calculation field built with text operators, you can't edit the field directly. But keep in mind that you can use a calculation as part of a script, auto-enter calculation field option, or Replace function to fill a normal text field that *can* be edited.

Concatenate (&)

We looked at concatenation in Chapter 7, when we combined the contact information as follows:

```
NameFirst & " " & NameLast & " - " & Company.
```

You're not limited to concatenating fields. You can combine various constants and fields in any combination you like. Be sure to choose a text result, and try this on for size:

```
"The product is " & Description & " and it costs $" & Price & "."
```

All those quotation marks bring us to...

Text Constant ("")

Anytime you want to have specific text as a constant (appearing the same in every record), you have to place it between a set of quotation marks. Look at our preceding examples. If you forget to put quotes around text you intend to display as a constant, FileMaker will check to see if you are naming a function or if there is a field with the name as the text string. If not, you'll get the warning dialog shown in Figure 11-3.

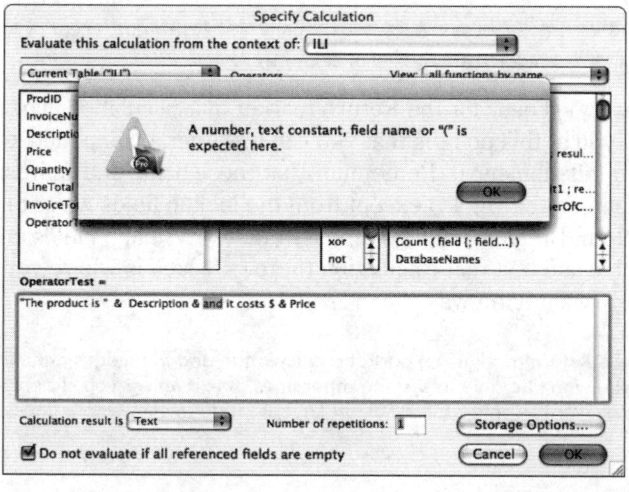

Figure 11-3
A warning dialog box that may appear when leaving a calculation; the warning tells you that one or more of the elements is missing.

FileMaker does a pretty good job of alerting you if a calculation is invalid. It's up to you to test the specific results. If you leave a required element out of a calculation, you won't be able to leave the Specify Calculation window until you correct it.

TIP Let's say you've built a complex calculation but can't seem to get all the elements right. You'll lose all your work if you just click the Cancel button.

Instead, try this: Type /* at the start of the calculation and the reverse */ at the end of it. This is called "commenting out" the text. FileMaker's calculation engine ignores anything between these symbols. You can also use this method to leave behind notes to yourself in the calculation. Anything outside those characters will work like a normal calculation. And you can have more than one area commented out in the dialog. Sometimes I duplicate the calculation that's not working and comment out a second copy so I can come back to it if I really mess up the second copy.

NOTE The Specify Calculation window can hold over 60,000 characters. There is no practical limit to text constants starting with FileMaker 7. Text constants used to be limited to 235 characters. While you could create longer constants, you needed to break them into 235-character chunks and concatenate them. Those days are gone.

Return Marker (¶)

Enclose the Return marker operator in quotes to use carriage returns between items in the text calculation. Before FileMaker provided us with merge fields, people often built address labels like this:

```
NameFirst & " " & NameLast & "¶" & Company & "¶" & AddrStreet & "¶" &
AddrCity & " " & AddrState & " " & AddrZip
```

There are other good uses for the Return marker in a calculation. The only hint I can give you at this point is that you can use it for a compound key in certain types of relationships. (Remember that these name and address fields won't be available in the ILI TO except from the lookup fields we put into ili_INV__InvNum. But you could go directly into the Manage Fields area of the Contact table and test that calculation there — which is where you'd more than likely want it anyway.)

TIP If you have Return markers as part of a calculation and the field is only one character tall, you won't be able to see the other lines of text unless you click in the field. You may want to enlarge the field in Layout mode to show more lines of text.

NOTE Regular returns in calculations don't do what you'd expect. FileMaker treats a regular return the same as it would treat a space character. So if you typed:

```
NameFirst & NameLast &
Company &
City
```

you would get:

```
JonathanStarsData Design Pros, LLCLansing
```

Notice that leaving out the " " causes the words from the next field to run right into the last word of the previous field. And leaving out "¶" causes the fields to appear on the same line.

Other Options

There are other choices to be made in the Specify Calculation window. I mentioned a few of them in the previous chapter. The others we discuss here.

Storage Option

The Storage Options button (in the Specify Calculation window) brings up the window shown in Figure 11-4, which is a slightly shorter version of the one we looked at in Chapter 10. It provides all the same choices minus the Repeating fields option (which you'll find in the lower portion of the Specify Calculation window). Otherwise, everything else applies. Notice, however, that if the calculation result is number, the default language drop-down is grayed out, since numbers don't have much to do with any language.

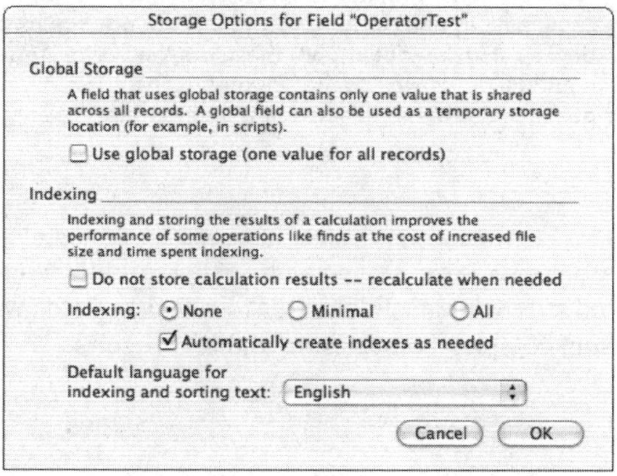

Figure 11-4
The abbreviated Storage Options window accessible from the Specify Calculation window.

Repeating Field

The "Number of repetitions" check box is in the Specify Calculation window (see Figure 11-3) instead of behind the Storage Options button. The meaning is exactly the same as described in the last chapter.

Do Not Evaluate

The "Do not evaluate if all referenced fields are empty" check box allows you to prevent FileMaker from placing a zero in the calculated field until at least one of the fields involved in the calculation has data in it. That can also be a check against incomplete entries. A zero could be a valid result, whereas empty would not be.

Limitations

If the fields you're referencing are not of the type you think they are, your results will probably be off. For example, if you build a calculation field with a number result that gets data from another calculated field that has a text result, the calculation will be wrong. It can happen, 'cause I've done it! If the data in a calculation field looks wrong, this is one place to check. However, it's okay to have data from any other "Calculation result is" type appear in a text result field.

To clarify this a bit further — the result type does not have to match the input types. For example, you could create a field that is the result of a date field plus a number field and choose to display the result as either a date or a number, or even use the GetAsText(date) function and display the result as text. There are a lot of things you can do with the "Calculation result is" drop-down choices. You just need to make sure you choose the right one to get the results you're looking for.

NOTE Speaking specifically about calculations and summaries that have number results, a calculation field is not the same as a summary field. Generally speaking, calculation fields perform calculations on one or more number fields (or other calculation fields with number results) in the same record. Summary fields perform calculations on a single field in one or more records. There are a number of tricks you can use to go beyond this description, but these are the basics. You can use relationships and global fields, as well as the aggregate and GetSummary functions, to push the limits, but I'll leave it at that for now.

Summary

In this chapter, we looked at how to get FileMaker to calculate fields with mathematical, comparison, complex comparison, and text results.

Q & A

Q How many logical operators can I use in a formula?

A The Formula box has a 30,000-character limit. Otherwise, you're only limited to being able to figure out what the darn thing means.

Q Can I use a Boolean result in another formula?

A Yes, but in FileMaker, the result is always seen as a 0 or a 1 regardless of how the calculation is formatted in the field definition or on the layout.

Workshop

Go to our Contact table and create a new calculation field where the calculation result is text. Experiment with some calculations combining various other text, number, and date fields as well as some constant values for each type. Try using some of the Return markers (¶). Don't forget to open up the field so you can see all the lines.

Chapter 12

Real-World Calculations — Part 1

Introduction

FileMaker Pro leaves a Rolodex in the dust once you get started using the operators and functions. This is where you turn your data into useful information. This is also where you check and correct data. You can take large amounts of data from other sources and whip it into shape, making all of it fit the proper format.

Rather than describing each of the functions, I'll show you some basic concrete examples and tell you about several hidden specifics. Then I'll show you tricks for combining functions into more complex calculations. That way you'll have a far better idea of how to make your own. The functions are listed in the FileMaker Pro manual and in the Help files. I don't see the point in repeating something that is right at your fingertips. What I want to give you is the stuff you can't find there.

FileMaker's Help Files

Starting with this chapter, knowing how to use the FileMaker Pro Help files will be extremely valuable. The Help files cover each function in detail and give you comprehensive alternative examples. But I have to say that not all of them are completely lucid. It may not be FileMaker's fault. I can't say I understand astrophysics either.

To use the Help files, you need to have installed them previously. If you did a full install of the FileMaker Pro application, the Help files should already be available. Choose Help, Contents or just type a question or phrase in the Search box. (If you don't see any of those choices, you'll need to get out your CD and follow the instructions for a custom install. Then install only the Help files.) Otherwise, you can go to the Contents tab and click on the list. Each click takes you deeper, outline-style, until you find the topic for which you're searching. Another approach is to click items in the Help Topics area and work your way through those topics

The Help files have become increasingly useful in the past few years, providing better examples and some extremely useful solutions. FileMaker 9 added a number of features that extend the Help even further. When you're in the Specify Calculation window, there is a "Learn More" link in the lower-left corner, which takes you immediately to the Help files.

If you click the Help menu at the top of the screen you can, of course, select FileMaker Pro Help. But a little further down is the Product Documentation drop-down shown in Figure 12-1. The people at FileMaker, Inc. discovered that many users didn't know there were PDF user's guides or tutorials, so they decided to make them available to us here. I'll leave it up to you to rummage around.

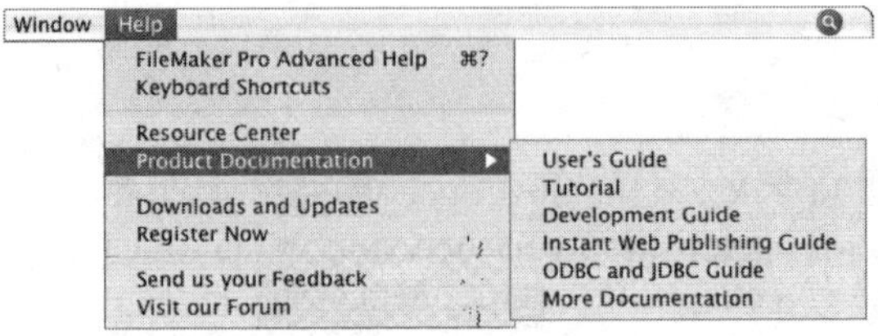

Figure 12-1
The enhanced Help menu showing the Product Documentation drop-down submenu.

Selecting the Resource Center option will take you to FileMaker's web site where there are more tutorials, search tools, and Frequently Asked Questions areas. Of course, a fast Internet connection will help you get the most out of this site.

What Are Functions?

Put simply, a *function* is a formula that crunches data. You choose the function, give it the data to operate on, and it gives you the result. The functions are available from the list in the upper-right area of the Specify Calculation window, next to View or wherever you may find it. That includes:

- When you're defining a calculation field
- When using the Replace menu choice
- When the "Validated by Calculation" check box is selected in Field Definitions
- From within the Set Field, Insert Calculated Result, and Replace script steps
- In the Conditional Formatting dialog[9]

Some of the functions are fairly easy to understand, and some are quite deep. Additionally, you can combine even the easiest functions into complex expressions. You don't need to know them all in order to do well with FileMaker. But you should know which functions are available and where to find out how to make them work for you when the time comes.

The group of functions we'll discuss in this chapter operate on specific types of data: text, number, date, and time.

NOTE An expression in FileMaker is different from a phrase your grandmother used when she was annoyed with the paperboy. An *expression* is a value or a calculation that gives you a value. It can contain field values, functions, and constants.

TIP When you're working out the specifics of a calculation in a table that has a lot of records, it's often better to test it in a script rather than creating a field definition. When you exit Manage Database, Fields, it can take quite a while to recalculate every single record only to find that it's not quite right. Using the same calculation in a script can tell you whether it's working in much less time. You can have it drop the result into an empty field (maybe in one or more temporary test records) to test it out. Once you have it fine-tuned, copy and paste it into the field definition formula box.

TIP Because FileMaker 7 and later allow you to work with multiple tables in a file, it is very important that you pay attention to the table in which you want to perform your work. At the top of the Specify Calculation window is the "Evaluate this calculation from the context of" drop-down menu. Make your table choice there.

Text Functions

Text functions operate on — you guessed it — text. You can use them to pull apart data and to build new groups of text. The calculations can include constants, data from other fields, the expressions we worked with in the last chapter, and even other functions. When we created the AddrCombo field in our Contact table, we were using text functions.

1. Go into the Contact table now, start a new calculation field called **FunctionTest**, and click **Create**.
2. Click on the View drop-down in the upper-right corner, and pull down to Text functions.
3. Double-click on the first function, **Exact**.

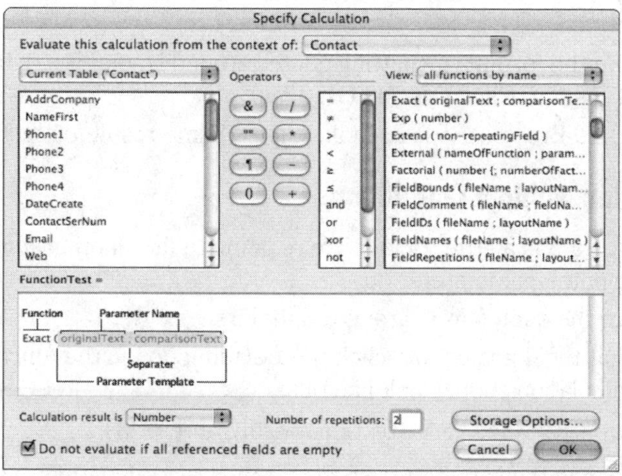

Figure 12-2
The Specify Calculation window showing a diagram of the Exact function.

When a function moves into the Formula box, the parameters or arguments you need to fill in are highlighted between the parentheses. This is called the parameter template. In the U.S. English version of FileMaker, semicolons separate the parameters that you need to replace. In other localized versions,

Part 3

other symbols may be used. Regardless, double-clicking the functions in the list will transfer them to the Formula box with the right types of separators in them.

⌘ **TIP** Unless you know specifically what you want to replace the parameters with, it's usually best to click further down in the Formula box to deselect them. That gives you some time to find their replacements and work on them one by one.

Left

1. Highlight and delete the **Exact** function, then scroll down and double-click the **Left** function. The Left function looks like this:

   ```
   Left (text; numberOfCharacters)
   ```

   Starting from the left, it plucks the number of characters indicated in the numberOfCharacters parameter from the "text" parameter. You can put the number in directly, or have it come from a number field, or it can even come from other functions.
2. Choose **Text** from the "Calculation result is" drop-down (lower-left corner of the Specify Calculation window) and try substituting the following parameters in the formula:

   ```
   Left (NameFirst; 4)
   ```

3. Click **OK** and **OK** again.
4. Go to Layout mode and place a copy of the field on the layout if one isn't already there.
5. Go to Browse mode and look at the results of the calculation in a few of the records.
6. Redefine the formula by putting quotes around NameFirst, which turns it into a constant. Click **OK** and **OK** again.
7. Go back to Browse mode and take a look. Same result for each record!

A Calculation within a Calculation

This next section is a little trickier. We're going to use another function to replace one of the parameters.

1. Remove the quotes from around NameFirst.
2. Highlight the **4** and double-click the **Left** function in the function list. Your calculation should look like this:

   ```
   Left (NameFirst; Left (text; numberOfCharacters))
   ```

3. Now change the parameters so the formula reads like this:

   ```
   Left (NameFirst; Left (AddrStreet; 1))
   ```

I'm asking FileMaker to grab letters from the NameFirst field based on the first character in the Address field (assuming it's a numeral). Granted, it's not a very practical example, but let's fly with it for now.

4. Go to Browse mode and try playing with the data in the Address field, then clicking out of the field to see how FunctionTest recalculates.

This is an example of a nested function. Nested functions are the hallmark of complex calculations. They are complex, but you can keep them manageable by using the techniques described in the section titled "Building Complex Calculations" in this chapter.

The term *nested function* refers to replacing a parameter in a function with another function. Other than the 30,000-character limit of the Formula box, there is no limit to the number of nested functions you can use in a calculation. (In previous versions of FileMaker, you could only nest 125 If functions. I tested it this time and gave up after 250 levels. It would appear that limit is no longer in effect.)

LeftWords

The LeftWords function looks like this:

```
LeftWords (text; numberOfWords)
```

It works just like the Left function, except this does the counting based on spaces and other non-text characters (such as the underscore) between words. Choose Text in the "Calculation result is" drop-down.

Remember back when we had our contact's full name in a Name field? You would have been able to extract the first name from the field this way. It works great for entries with just a first and last name. But you would still have had to figure out what to do with entries that included middle names, initials, and various other combinations. (One way to handle this situation might be to use the Position function described below.)

Length

Length counts the number of characters in a field. It includes spaces, numbers, and special characters as well as text. The function looks like this:

```
Length (text)
```

Choose Number in the "Calculation result is" drop-down and substitute NameFirst for the "text" parameter:

```
Length (NameFirst)
```

By combining it with one of the logical functions, you can use Length to check that phone numbers, Social Security numbers, and credit card numbers are the correct length. This isn't exactly that test, but you might try it for fun:

```
If (Length (NameFirst) = 5; "Five"; "Not Five")
```

The If function can be found in the logical functions. Sometimes I use a field like this that I've formatted to show large red letters on the layout when the validation fails; for example, if a needed field were left empty. (This type of "validation" is not to be confused with Validate by Calculation.) To use it that way, remove the word Five from the second parameter and let the quotes sit next to each other. Then nothing shows if the validation is okay. You could also use a calculation like this in the Validate by Calculation section of a field definition. You wouldn't get any large red letters that way, but once again it shows you how you can solve problems in FileMaker from different directions. Since Validate by Calculation uses Boolean logic, you could use this simpler calculation:

```
Length (NameFirst) = 5
```

> **NOTE** In older versions of FileMaker Pro, sometimes there's no space between the name of the function and the left parenthesis for the parameter. In version 7 and later, FileMaker automatically adds this space. Calculations in files converted from previous versions will work just the same; it's strictly a cosmetic issue.

Position

To use the Position function, choose Number from the "Calculation result is" drop-down. It looks like this:

```
Position (text; searchString; start; occurrence)
```

This returns a number representing the number of characters from the start point (the third parameter) where the first character of the specified string begins. If the calculation returns a zero (0), it means that that particular occurrence of the substring wasn't found in the searched segment of text.

The Position function has the following parameters:

- "text" is usually the data in a field, but it can be an expression.
- "searchString" is a text field or expression. It is the specific text for which you're searching.
- "start" is a number field or expression and it is determined by counting from the left.
- "occurrence" is a number field or expression that specifies the repetition for which you're looking.

Position is often used with other functions to extract data starting with the character found by the Position function.

Let's say you inherited a database with only one field for people's full name. You want to split the first name from the last name and create two fields: NameFirst and NameLast. You can use the position function Position (FullName; " "; 1; 1) to find out how many characters are before the first space. With this calculation, FileMaker starts at the first character (start) in the FullName field and goes to the first space (occurrence), essentially splitting the field in two.

That's great, you say. Well, almost. What happens if some of the names in this field include a middle name or initial or a Junior, a designation, or a degree at the end? You'll need to keep using the Position function to keep splitting the information into fields that make more sense.

It sounds like work, but just think how much more work it would be to manually break out names in thousands of records without this function! And once you've created it, you can use it over and over in different projects.

FileMaker 8.5 introduced the GetAsURLEncoded text function. It will take a string of characters and convert it to the format that the URL box in a browser can use. Of course, it's of most value when you're actually trying to build a URL string. I talk about it a little more in Chapter 25.

Building Complex Calculations

Trying to create complicated calculations to get the result you want can require so many nested functions that your eyes bug out. I've met a few people who can see these things in their heads, but I'm not one of them. So here's a technique I've developed that might work for you.

I've included the answers to the questions that apply to our example calculation. Then I describe the process, including techniques for making it go more smoothly. If you work along on your computer, you may be able to remember some of the methods when it comes time for you to figure out your own calculations.

This example is one I was asked to do for a client who had a number of phone directories stored in a word processing program. The street name needed to be extracted from the whole address string.

The Steps

1. Ask yourself what you want, and describe it in plain English.
   A: I want the street name without the number.
2. What will be the main function?
   A: The Right function
3. How can you single out what you want? What sets it apart (delimits it) from the rest of the data in the field in most records?
   A: There is a space in front of it. Not only that, but it's the first space in the field.
4. How do I define that delimiter? Should I use a constant or a function?
   A: Try the Position function.
5. Test the separate parts of the subfunction(s), and save each part that works.
6. Repeat steps 3 through 5 for each subfunction that will replace a parameter in the main function. Add other functions as you need them.
   A: I might need the Length function.

7. Then use the main function and drop the subfunction formulas into the parameter slots in the parameter template. Start over at step 2 if you find you picked the wrong main function.

Using the Process

1. Go to our FunctionTest field, highlight the existing formula, and delete it.
2. Because we'll be using the Position function as a subfunction, we need to solve that first. Choose the Text functions from the View drop-down, then find and double-click the **Position** function from the list. It will appear with the four parameters highlighted, as shown in Figure 12-3.

```
Position ( text ; searchString ; start ; occurrence )
```

Figure 12-3
Immediately after you move any function into the Formula box, the parameter template is highlighted.

> **TIP** In the function parameter template, starting after the first parenthesis and then after each semicolon, add a Return (carriage return) until it looks like Figure 12-4. That way, each parameter is on a separate line. Even though semicolons separate each parameter, once you start replacing parameters with other functions (each with their own set of semicolons), you'll still be able to figure out where you are.

```
Position (
text ;
searchString ;
start ;
occurrence )

/* Position ( text ; searchString ; start ; occurrence ) */
```

Figure 12-4
The Position function with Returns inserted after the first parenthesis and after every semicolon.

> **TIP** Once you've added a function, click to the right end of it in the Formula box, press Return (carriage return) twice, then double-click the same function again. Once you start replacing the parameters, it's easy to forget which one you're working on. This way, you have the template sitting right in front of you. Don't forget that you can leave these functions in the calculation by commenting them out with /* and */ as discussed in Chapter 11.

Replacing the Parameter Template

3. Highlight the word "text" and replace it with **AddrStreet**, since that's the field we're searching in.
4. Highlight "searchString" and replace it with two quotes with a space between them (" "), because a space is the character that appears before the text for which we're looking.
5. Highlight "start" and replace it with a **1**, since you want to start counting from the first character from the left. Highlight "occurrence" and replace it with a **1**, since you want it to look for the first appearance of the space. When you're done, it should look like Figure 12-5.

```
Position (
AddrStreet ;
" " ;
1 ;
1 )

/* Position ( text ; searchString ; start ; occurrence ) */
```

Figure 12-5
The Position function once the parameters have been replaced with specific data.

Testing the Results

6. Count the number of characters after the space, and compare it with the number in FunctionTest. Uh, oh. That's not right. It's showing the position of the space, not the number of characters we need.
7. Go back into the field definition and look at it again.

What went wrong? What we really want is the number of characters after that space. We still need the position of the space, but if we subtract it from the total number of characters in the field, we'll get the right number of characters.

⌘ **TIP** If you have a calculation that almost works, but you're going to try something dramatic, make a duplicate of the field and add the word "Safety" to the end of it. Then, once everything works, delete the safety copy to prevent cluttering up your files. Also, in FileMaker Pro 7 and later, you can add a comment to the field definition (that's not the same as "commenting" a calculation) to help you spot fields that are temporary. Click the Options/Comments header to view the comments for all the fields.

Making Adjustments

8. Put your cursor just to the left of the "*/" at the end of the dialog and add a **Return** (carriage return) at the end of the Position function, then find and add the **Length** function. Now add a second copy of Length at the top followed by a minus sign. When you get done, it should look like Figure 12-6.

```
Length ( text ) - Position (
AddrStreet ;
" " ;
1 ;
1 )

/* Position ( text ; searchString ; start ; occurrence )
Length ( text ) */
```

Figure 12-6
The calculation after adding the Length function template.

9. Replace "text" with **AddrStreet**. Click **OK** and **Done** and go look at it. Aha! That's the number of characters we need. Now go back to the field definition, and get rid of the extra carriage returns until it looks like Figure 12-7. You can just leave the part that's commented out at the bottom.

```
Length ( AddrStreet ) - Position ( AddrStreet ; " " ; 1 ; 1 )
```

Figure 12-7
The calculation with all extra carriage returns removed.

Inserting Subfunctions

Finally, we need to combine that number formula with the Right function.

10. Add two carriage returns after our calculation, and double-click the **Right** function. Copy the Length minus Position calculation, and paste it into the "numberOfCharacters" parameter. Replace the "text" parameter with the AddrStreet field. And finally, delete the original calculation. The formula should look like this:

```
Right (AddrStreet; Length (AddrStreet) - Position (AddrStreet; ""; 1; 1))
```

11. Change the calculation result to **Text**, and go check it out. It works pretty well. This is exactly how I got the data my client needed.

Different Function, Same Result

Now here's a calculation that will scare you with its simplicity:

```
MiddleWords (AddrStreet; 2; 10)
```

Guess what? It gives you the same information as the longer calculation. (Well, when I did this it dropped the period from "Main St.") The MiddleWords function parameter template looks like this:

```
MiddleWords (text; startingWord; numberOfWords)
```

You can use "10" or some other suitably large number as the "numberOfWords" parameter even when there are not ten words in the field. The function simply stops when it runs out of words to check. There are at least two other calculations that will give you the text we've requested. I didn't figure out this shorter version until later. How I got the answer didn't matter to my client. The main point is that understanding this process will put you on the road to finding solutions with your own complex calculations when you need them.

Make It Permanent

Here's how to turn a calculation field into a permanent, editable, non-calculation field. After you've seen that the calculation works, go back into Manage Fields. Highlight the calculation field, and use the Type drop-down to choose the format you want (usually text or number). Click OK and then Save, and it will be permanently converted.

There are a few situations you need to be aware of to make this work:

- After first creating the calculation or making any subsequent changes to the calculation, you must return to Browse mode. Then return to Manage Fields and convert the calculation to a text or number field.
- You cannot include global or related fields anywhere in the formula. That's because they cannot be indexed. You can, however, use a related field by creating a temporary field and copying the data into the temporary field using a script or a Replace by calculation. Then use the data in

the temporary field in the calculation, convert the calculated field, and delete the temporary field afterward.

- This one is probably obvious, but here goes anyway: Now that the field is no longer based on a calculation, it will no longer update when data changes in the fields that were originally referenced. It's just a plain old static field. As long as it's not locked down by one method or another, you can still change data in it; it just won't happen automatically.

Number Functions

Number functions will probably feel a little more familiar than the text functions. That's because they're more like math.

One of my clients wanted me to set up a table so phone numbers could be entered as straight numerals without dashes, and the dashes would appear automatically in the right places. What seemed to start out as a number function problem ended up using a lot of the text functions. But the trial and error and adjustment cycle in this real-life example is just too good to scrap simply because it's not all numbers.

The following example demonstrates one method that worked in FileMaker previous to version 7, and the lesson is still valid. For a method that works well in FMP7 and later, read the section called "A Calculation for FMP7 and Later."

The Process

To tackle the assignment, I answered the questions in the complex calculation questionnaire and then ran some experiments.

1. I want to put dashes between digits so it looks like a phone number.
2. Try the Left, Right, and Middle text functions.
3. There will be 10 digits. That should be pretty easy to break into smaller pieces.
4. Use a constant as a delimiter.
5. Test...
6. I don't think I'll need any other functions.

This shouldn't be too hard. Let's try it.

1. Go to the Phone table, create a new calculation field called **FormatPhone**, and add it to the layout. So you can follow along, create four new records and add this information in the Phone field in the four records:

```
(613) 477-1234
343-1235
http://www.react.net/utopial
utopia@react.net
```

2. Use the Left, Middle, and Right functions, which start out like this:

```
Left (text; numberOfCharacters)
Middle (text; start; numberOfCharacters)
Right (text; numberOfCharacters)
```

3. Put them together like this:

```
Left (Phone; 3) & "-" & Middle (Phone; 4; 3) & "-" & Right (Phone; 4)
```

4. And here are the results! To get the same results I did, you'll need to go to Layout mode, select the **FormatPhone** field, choose **Format, Number**, and click the radio button next to **Leave data formatted as entered.**

```
(61-3)-1234
343–12-1235
htt-p:/-pial
uto-pia-.net
```

Yikes! Maybe this isn't going to be so easy.

Make an Adjustment

Maybe I need to have the calculation ignore all the symbols in the Phone field. The GetAsNumber (text) function might work. Here's what I tried next:

```
Left (GetAsNumber (Phone); 3) & "-" & Middle (GetAsNumber (Phone); 4; 3)
& "-" & Right (GetAsNumber (Phone); 4)
```

And here's the result:

```
-61-347-1234
343-123-1235
.1--.1
```

It looks as if the conversion of Phone to a number is using the parentheses to indicate that the first phone number is a negative number. Now we're also confronting something I missed before. The second number doesn't include an area code because it's local. And, in the end, we do want the e-mail and web addresses to show up unaltered.

Modify Further

To make negative numbers appear as positive, let's try the Abs function:

```
Left (Abs (GetAsNumber (Phone)); 3) & "-" & Middle (Abs (GetAsNumber
(Phone)); 4, 3) & "-" & Right (Abs (GetAsNumber (Phone)); 4)

613-477-1234
343-123-1235
.1--.1
```

Well, that takes care of the first number, but what about the phone number with only seven digits? We have numbers with 10 digits, some with seven, and anything that's left over should stay as text. This calls for either the If or the Case logical function. Either will allow for different results based on variations in input. If and Case work very similarly. I prefer the Case function because with longer nested functions, it uses fewer characters, so I just use it for everything.

Try, Try Again

Starting over with our first question, here's how we might make the statement in plain English: If the phone number has 10 digits, format it as we already did. If it has seven digits, we only want the left three digits, then a dash, then the last four digits. Anything else should be left as entered in the Phone field to show as text.

Case Function

Since the Phone field can have any number of characters in it, how do we get the calculation to recognize 10 characters? If it's converted to a number, the smallest 10-digit number is one billion. So we can say, "For any number over one billion, format it like a 10-digit phone number." The smallest seven-digit number is one million. So we can say, "For every number over one million, format it like a seven-digit phone number." For everything that's left over, leave it as is.

The Case function looks like this:

```
Case (test1; result1 {;test2; result2; ...; defaultResult})
```

To break it up for easier visualization:

```
Case (
test1;
   result1;
test2;
   result2;
defaultResult)
```

Notice I added three spaces before each result so it would be easy to spot the differences between the test and the result. I also removed the brackets and the ellipsis near the end.

Plug It In

You can run as many tests as you like using the Case function. The only limit is 30,000 characters in the Formula box. (Warning to power users of earlier versions of FileMaker: The Formula box used to allow up to 64,000 characters.) Now, let's plug in the calculations. Be sure to choose Text for the calculation result.

```
Case(
Abs (GetAsNumber (Phone)) > 1000000000;
   Left (Abs (GetAsNumber (Phone)); 3) & "-" & Middle (Abs (GetAsNumber
   (Phone)); 4; 3) & "-" & Right (Abs (GetAsNumber (Phone)); 4);
```

Part 3

```
Abs (GetAsNumber (Phone)) > 1000000;
   Left (Abs (GetAsNumber (Phone)); 3) & "-" & Right (Abs (GetAsNumber
   (Phone)); 4);

Phone)
```

I also added extra carriage returns between each test and result set. It doesn't affect the formula, but it does make it easier to read, though it's still not very easy at that! Notice I've removed the Middle function from the second argument.

In the end, I found that I didn't need to use GetAsNumber. The Abs function converts the parameter within its parentheses into a number. (Abs will convert dates and times in ways you might not expect. It will even attempt to convert text.) In this case, it doesn't matter. It works both ways. The compulsive part of me believes that simpler is better, but where the client is concerned, faster and cheaper is better.

The Real Trick

We're not done yet! Even though users will enter a string of numbers when they're done, you want the delimited calculation to show. So here's how you pull that off. You have to stack the calculated field on top of the original Phone field. By that I mean both fields have to be exactly the same size (use the Size tool under the View menu), and you need to place them so that only one is visible. The Phone field is directly underneath the calculated field and completely obscured from view (use the Arrange menu). The upper field needs to be the calculated field with a solid fill color — white is a good choice. It also has to be formatted on the layout to prevent entry into the field. The Phone field must allow entry and can be included in the tab order. When you click on the upper field, since it's unenterable, FileMaker immediately transports you to the field below. You enter the data, and as soon as you exit the field, you see the properly formatted data in the calculated field.

A Calculation for FMP7 and Later

And now for an even easier method. FileMaker now has a check box for "Do not replace existing value of field (if any)" that can be unchecked, thereby allowing you to replace the value in a field with a calculated value. You can use the "Calculated value" part of the Auto-Enter tab in the field definition and replace the phone number with a fully formatted version of itself. Assuming that the only data in the Phone field will either be a 10-digit phone number or a web or e-mail address, you can use the following calculated value to format only items entered as phone numbers. The Phone field needs to be a text field.

```
If (Length (Phone) = 10 and
PatternCount (Phone; "w") = 0 and
PatternCount (Phone; "@") = 0;
Left (Phone; 3) & "-" &
```

```
Middle (Phone; 4; 3) & "-" &
Middle (Phone; 7; 4);
Phone)
```

As long as the Phone field has 10 digits in it and no "w" (which you would find in a web address — www) and no "@" symbol (which you would find in an e-mail address), it will automatically be replaced with the dashed format. Of course, this assumes the data entry people never make the mistake of missing a digit or entering extra digits. But they'll be able to see that there's a problem in an instant because the phone number won't pick up the dashed format.

Date and Time Functions

When you see a date in FileMaker, you're really seeing a formatting trick. Behind the scenes, FileMaker is keeping track of dates with a numbering system. Starting with 1/1/0001 as day 1, all dates get a serial number. It makes calculations for the program quite easy — all it has to do is use simple math.

The same simple math doesn't necessarily work so well for certain script steps that use dates. Since you can use functions in scripts, you need to know how to handle dates.

In the Set Field and Insert Calculated Result steps, if you're taking a date from a date field or time from a time field and placing it in a text field, FileMaker will now format it so it is recognizable as a date or time (9/7/2004 or 5:55:25 PM). If you want it unformatted strictly as the numbers FileMaker uses "behind the curtain," you need to use the GetAsNumber(text) function, which can be found under the Text functions.

Conversely, if you're taking a date from a text field and placing it in a date field, you need to use the GetAsDate(text) function.

Interestingly, if you click in a text field and choose Records, Replace and select "Replace with Calculated result," you can use a date field and get what looks like a date in the text field. This won't work if you go the other way. You would have to use the GetAsDate(text) function.

Time Clock

Those things being said, let's look at an example that combines both date and time information into a simple time clock for keeping track of employee hours.

1. Start a new table called **TimeClock**, and create the following fields. For the Hours field, be sure to choose **Time** for the calculation result.

Field Name	*Type*	*Options*
Date	Date	Creation Date
TimeIn	Time	Creation Time
TimeOut	Time	
Hours	Calculation (Time result)	TimeOut – TimeIn

2. Use the **Auto-Enter Creation Date** option for the date field, and **Creation Time** for TimeIn.
3. Switch to the **Relationships** tab, move the TimeClock TO over to the left column and rename it **TC.**
4. Click **OK.** Go to the TC layout in Browse mode, and choose **View, View as Table.**
5. Enter some appropriate times in the TimeOut field to see how the calculation does the math for you.

Third Shift

Now, what happens if the company goes to a second or third shift? Workers may arrive for work in the evening and leave after midnight.

1. Create a new record, and overwrite TimeIn with **9:00 P.M.**
2. Fill in TimeOut with **5:00 A.M.** Minus 16 hours?! This employee owes the company some money!

What we need in a situation like this is a field that combines both the time and the date. It's time to use FileMaker's timestamp field type.

3. Go back into Manage Fields, change the name of the TimeIn field to **TimeStampIn**, and change the field type to **Timestamp.**
4. Now click the **Options** button. In the **Auto-Enter** tab, change the Creation drop-down to **Timestamp.**
5. Change TimeOut to **TimeStampOut** and change the field type to **Timestamp.** You won't even need the date field any more.

Rebuild the Calculation

Before FileMaker Pro 7, you would have needed to create a second date field called something like DateOut and add TimeOut to it. Since this chapter is about calculations, I've decided to leave this section in because it will help you think about how hours are figured. There are situations where you may need the information about the number of seconds in a day. By the way, the old method still works. It's just that the new method is simpler. First, I'll describe the old way.

We need to rethink the Hours calculation. We need a combination of date and time data. Here's the trick: Time fields really keep track of the number of seconds since the beginning of a day. You can figure out the number of seconds in a day. There are 24 hours in a day, 60 minutes in each hour, and 60 seconds in each minute. That's 24 x 60 x 60 = 86,400 seconds in a day. The Hours calculation would be:

```
((DateOut * 86400) + TimeStampOut) - ((DateIn * 86400) + TimeStampIn)
```

After you exit Manage Fields, you'll have to go to Layout mode and place the DateOut field on the layout (unless your preferences are set up to add new fields). When you return to Browse mode, the Hours field will be a mess because you don't have any of the DateOut fields filled in. Try a few combinations to check it out.

Another slightly shorter way to write the calculation would be:

```
((DateOut - DateIn) * 86400) + (TimeStampOut - TimeStampIn)
```

A Conditional Alert

Now let's look at the new FileMaker way.

What if you want to be alerted when the employee has too many hours? Create a calculation field (choose Text in the "Calculation result is" drop-down) called OTProblem (OT for overtime) with the following calculation:

```
Case (Hours > 3600 * 12; "Check this out!"; "")
```

The value 3600 is the number of seconds in an hour. The reason I did it this way is that it isolates the number of hours so it's easy to change. You could substitute a field for the 12. That way, by creating a global field formatted as a number, you'd be able to change the results of the calculation without redefining the field.

After you exit Manage Fields, you'll have to go to Layout mode and place the OTProblem field on the layout. I recommend formatting this field with bold, red text. Return to Browse mode, and change the TimeOut field until you trigger the warning.

Commenting Calculations[7]

Some of the calculations we've looked at can be frightfully complex to build. As we've already discussed, starting with FileMaker 7 and later you can leave comments in your calculations. There is more than one way to do this, but I'm just going to show you one method. It's good enough for everything I want to do. If you want other options, look in the Help files for "Adding comments to a formula." This is the same one I showed you before with just a little more detail — mainly that the comments can be anywhere in the calculation, not just at the end.

To add a comment to your calculation, simply start with the characters "/*" (without the quotes), type your comments, and end with "*/" (without the quotes).

If we were to add comments to our last calculation, it might look like this:

```
Case (Hours > 3600 * 12; /* If the employee punched in for more than 12
hours (there are 3600 seconds in an hour)...  */
"Check this out!";  /* ...show me this text... */
"") /* ...otherwise, don't display anything. */
```

This works anyplace in FileMaker where you see the Calculation window — including scripts. Don't forget that in the Fields tab of the Manage Database window you have a Comment box where you can remind yourself what the field is for. It's just much more convenient having it right there in the calculation, line by line.

Summary

In this chapter, we looked at some text, number, date, and time functions, and you learned how to put them together in complex calculations using some logical functions with comments to help you keep it all straight. You also learned that you can get most of the details that you need about specific functions from FileMaker Pro's Help files.

Q & A

Q When I start looking at all those functions with semicolons and parentheses, I just lose my place.

A Join the club! It helps if you try to see separate parts of a formula as groups or modules that can be plugged into one another. Many of the formulas in this chapter have sections that repeat. When I modified them, I could change whole sections by highlighting and replacing.

Using the returns between parameters can also help. Sometimes I'll copy a calculation and paste it into a word processing document so I can print it out. Then I'll draw lines around areas that represent the modules. You really don't have to understand the entire calculation at a glance. You can learn to grasp it in pieces. Think of it as a meal. You don't swallow everything on your plate in one gulp. But taking it one mouthful at a time, the meal gets eaten.

Workshop

Go back into the TimeClock table and create the global field mentioned in that section. Change the number in the field and see if you can make it work with different trigger points. Now create two scripts: one that punches in and one that punches out. I'll leave it to you to see if you can figure that out. But I will give you one hint: Don't forget to add the timestamp to the script. Then add punch in and punch out buttons to the layout. The buttons won't show unless you choose View as Form or View as List. One other detail about a global field: If you're sharing the file using FileMaker Pro Server, the data in a global field does not get saved back to the server. That means you'll need to enter that number every time you want to see the calculation. A better way would be to use a one-record table, which is described in Chapter 23, "Backup and Recovery."

Chapter 13

Real-World Calculations — Part 2

Introduction

This chapter continues our discussion about basic and complex calculations you might really use. Since I introduced you to a number of techniques for building complex calculations in the last chapter, I'll spend more time on specific uses in this chapter.

Aggregate Functions

Aggregate functions are meant to get information from a number of records, related records, or repeating fields. That really makes sense when you look at the names in this group of functions:

Average
Count
List[8.5]
Max (maximum)
Min (minimum)
StDev (standard deviation)
StDevP (standard deviation of population)
Sum
Variance (spread)
VarianceP (population spread)

Aggregate Examples

We already used one of the aggregate functions when we pulled the invoice total from the InvoiceLineItems fields.

1. Go back to the Invoice table, go to Manage Fields, and double-click on **InvoiceTotal** to review the field formula:

   ```
   Sum (inv_ILI__InvNum::LineTotal)
   ```

2. While you're looking at the Specify Calculation window, choose **Aggregate functions** from the View drop-down.
3. Highlight the word "Sum" in the formula and type **Max**.
4. Now click **OK** and **Done**, then look at the amount in the InvoiceTotal field.

5. Click through a few records until you get the idea. Regardless of how many entries there are, the Max function finds the largest number.
6. Now go back into the definition, and replace Max with **Min**.
7. Exit the field definition and look at these new numbers.
8. Now try it with **Count**. Of course, the field is formatted with two decimal places, but the number in each record is correct. Now be sure you change InvoiceTotal back so it reads:

```
Sum (inv_ILI__InvNum::LineTotal)
```

I used the following calculation for a phone number portal that shows five rows. I wanted to know how many rows were beyond the fifth row without scrolling. So I created a field called CountPhone with this calculation:

```
Case (Count (Phone::Phone) > 5; Count (Phone::Phone) - 5; "")
```

The number only shows up next to the portal if there are hidden phone numbers that I need to scroll to see.

You may try the StDev, StDevP, Variance, and VarianceP functions if you like. They test for the amount of variation of values in a field. That can give you some idea of what would be considered a "normal" range.

> **NOTE** The above function was pre-FMP7. Using the anchor-buoy standard, it would be longer, but easier to follow throughout the file, this way:
>
> ```
> Case (Count(ph_PH__ConSerNum::Phone) > 5;
> Count(ph_PH__ConSerNum::Phone) - 5; "")
> ```
>
> As you can see, you would need to add a second Phone TO. Since the calculation is in the Phone table itself, you can use it anywhere you place any other data from the Phone table, not just on the PH layout.

I want to say a few quick words about the List[8.5] function. With it, you can display a list of related items. It will even display related items a number of table occurrences away from the table you're in. That's something you can easily do in a portal, but maybe not as conveniently. Some developers are quite excited about it. They say it makes going to distant related sets of records a quick single jump where it previously required multiple steps. I find it just as easy to go to related records using one of the anchor-buoy TOs with the "Show only related records" and either of the Match radio buttons selected. For example, I'm able to quickly go to all products from the CON_Contact layout through the con_inv_ili_PRO__ProdID table occurrence. But since there has been so much talk about this function, I thought I should mention it. One developer suggested building a calculation in a product table that only displays the product name if there are still items in inventory. We'll have to see how other developers make use of the List function.

Summary Functions

There's really only one Summary function right now — GetSummary. This function was created because there were some limitations with regular summary fields. Previous to FMP10 you could only display summary data in Preview mode. Now that we have dynamic sub-summaries (discussed in Chapter 8, "Finding and Sorting Your Data"), this function is likely to lose most of its power. But even now you still cannot perform calculations on summary data. The GetSummary function bypasses that limitation. Let's take a look.

GetSummary Example

To test various operators back in Chapter 11, we made a new layout called ILI_Calcs based on the ILI TO. Go to the ILI_Calcs layout now.

1. Go into the Manage Database window, create a new field called **SumLineTotal**, and choose **Summary** from the Type drop-down. (You should be in the InvoiceLineItems table.)
2. In the Options for Summary Field window, choose the **Total of** radio button and select **LineTotal** from the field list as shown in Figure 13-1.

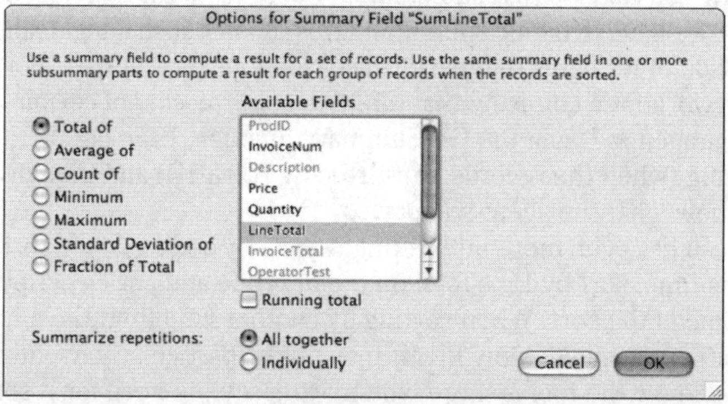

Figure 13-1 The Options for Summary Field window with selections for the SumLineTotal field in the InvLI table.

> **TIP** Even though the GetSummary parameter template should make it obvious that you need a summary field, I've tried constructing a calculation using the GetSummary function many times without one. It just doesn't work. Create your summary field first. After all, you can't "get" a summary if there is no summary to get.

3. Now create a new field called **TotalByItem**, select **Calculation** from the Type drop-down, and press **Create.**
4. When the Specify Calculation window appears, choose **Summary functions** from the View drop-down list, then double-click the **GetSummary** function to move it into the Formula box. It should look like this:

```
GetSummary (summaryField; breakField)
```

5. Replace the summaryField and breakField parameters with **SumLineTotal** and **Description**. Your final formula should look like this:

```
GetSummary (SumLineTotal; Description)
```

6. Click **OK** and **OK**.
7. Go to Layout mode, double-click the **OperatorTest** field, and choose the new **TotalByItem** field from the field list.
8. Go to Browse mode, and choose **Records, Show All Records**. (If that choice is not available, all records are already showing.) The new field is empty! And it should be. When we select a break field parameter, that means we're required to sort the records first. (If all you see is a 1, go back to Layout mode and reformat the TotalByItem field so that it is not Boolean.)

> **NOTE** What is a break field parameter? According to the FMP10 glossary, "In a subsummary part, records are grouped (sorted) by values in another field, called the break field. Whenever the value of the break field changes, the report 'breaks' and FileMaker Pro inserts the subsummary part."

9. Choose **Records, Sort Records** and sort by **Description**.

Aha! Now you can see that sub-summary data. So what's the big deal? Well, now that we have dynamic sub-summaries, it isn't such a big deal. But you can still add other fields that perform calculations on that data. For example, I do some work for a company that offers to split the cost of certain advertising with their agents. Using the GetSummary function, I can get totals for the advertising (when the records are sorted by AgentID) and then divide it by two to show what the agent will pay.

You can get even more interesting results by adding other sorts to the mix. This time, sort by LineTotal on the first line and put Description in the second line of the sort. When sorting by another field first, the amount in OperatorTest changed in my file. It may not be particularly useful in this case, but if you know the tool is there, you may discover a need for it some day. This is a result you simply cannot get even when using the new version of regular summary fields and subsummary parts.

Repeating Functions

Back in Chapter 4, I showed you repeating fields. I also mentioned that there are some uses for them beyond the old method of invoicing and a short list of phone numbers. I'll show you one here. But first, look at Figure 13-2 to see the parameter templates of FileMaker's three repeating functions.

```
Extend (non-repeatingField)
GetRepetition (repeatingField); number)
Last (repeatingField)
```

Figure 13-2
FileMaker Pro's repeating functions.

GetRepetition Example

What I want you to see in this demonstration is how to highlight a field with a color based on a calculation — like the amount of the invoice total. Sound interesting? Well, FileMaker's conditional formatting[9] feature makes this trick kind of old school. (We'll look at conditional formatting near the end of Chapter 17.) But I suggest you do the exercise. It will help you better understand how you can make the repeating functions work in other ways. And it will show you how you sometimes have to invent solutions when the tools you want don't exist yet.

BEST PRACTICES I used the "r" at the end of the upcoming global field because it's a container field. Since FileMaker reserves the "c" for calculation fields, they use "r" in the Type drop-down as the shortcut key combination to call container fields. We'll follow their lead.

1. Go into the Invoice table and create a new field called **zi_Colors_gr**. Select **Container** from the Type drop-down and click the **Create** button.
2. Click the **Options** button, select the **Storage** tab, and check the box to **Use global storage**. Click the check box next to **Maximum number of repetitions**, enter **2** in the box, and click **OK**.
3. Now make a new field called **Color**, click the **Calculation** type radio button, and click **Create**.
4. Click the View drop-down and choose **Repeating functions** from the list.
5. Double-click the **GetRepetition** function, then highlight the repeatingField parameter and replace it by double-clicking the **zi_Colors_gr** field from the field list in the upper left. Highlight the number parameter and type **1**. Your calculation should look like this:

```
GetRepetition (zi_Colors_gr; 1)
```

6. Finally, choose **Container** from the calculation result drop-down, and click **OK** and **OK**.
7. Go to the INV_Invoice in Layout mode, and place a copy of the zi_Colors_gr and Color fields side by side in an empty area of the layout near the InvoiceTotal field.
8. Double-click **zi_Colors_gr** to bring up the Field/Control Setup dialog. Near the lower left of the dialog you'll find the message, "Show repetitions 1 through 1." (Both numbers can be altered, limited to the number of repetitions.) Enter **2** in the through Repetitions box, so it reads "Show repetitions 1 through 2," and click **OK**.
9. Using the Rectangle tool, draw a rectangle on the layout about 1 inch by 3 inches. Format it so it has no borders, and fill it with red. While it's still selected, choose **Edit**, **Copy**, and go to Browse mode.

10. Click in the first repetition of the zi_Colors_gr field, and choose **Edit, Paste**. The red color should not only fill the zi_Colors_gr field, but the Color field as well.

> **NOTE** The color may not completely fill the fields depending on how the field is formatted as a graphic. You can change that in Layout mode by selecting the field and choosing Format, Graphic and working with the choices there. When the patch of color is larger than the field, I usually choose Crop. More on formatting graphics in Chapter 17, "Designing Your Screen Layouts."

11. Go back to Layout mode and select the red rectangle and change it to some shade of blue. Choose **Edit**, **Cut**, and return to Browse mode.
12. Click the second repetition of the zi_Colors_gr field and choose **Edit, Paste**.
13. Now go back to Manage Fields and redefine the Colors calculation, replacing the 1 with a **2**.
14. Return to Browse mode to see that the Color field has turned blue. Now here comes the fun part. We can tie the color change to something other than a constant number.
15. Go back into the Color field definition and put a couple of carriage returns after the formula. Choose **Logical functions** from the View drop-down, and double-click the **If** function.
16. Click outside of the parameter template, add a couple more returns, and double-click the **If** function again so we have a copy to compare to the original.
17. Go back to the first If function, and put a carriage return following the first parenthesis and after each of the semicolons so that the formula looks like this:

```
GetRepetition(zi_Colors_gr; 2)

If (
test;
result one;
result two)

If (test; result one; result two)
```

18. Highlight "test" and replace it with **InvoiceTotal < 0**.
19. Copy the GetRepetition calculation and highlight and replace both "result one" and "result two" by pasting from the clipboard. Change the 2 in the first GetRepetition to **1**. Then delete all the other functions so the formula looks like this:

```
If (
InvoiceTotal < 0;
GetRepetition (zi_Colors_gr; 1);
GetRepetition (zi_Colors_gr; 2))
```

What we are saying here is that if our invoice is less than 0, please Mr. ColorField, grab the color — red — from the first repetition in the zi_Colors_gr field. However, if the invoice is greater than 0, grab the second color — blue.

NOTE I tend to write short calculations using If functions, because that's the way I express the question in my mind. But my technical editor, William Moss, sent me the following clever (and short) formula.

```
GetRepetition (zi_Colors_gr; 1 + (InvoiceTotal >= 0))
```

Here, FileMaker is evaluating whether InvoiceTotal is greater than or equal to 0. The answer is a Boolean 1 or 0. So the result of 1 + 0 or 1 + 2 determines the color that will be displayed.

TIP Be sure you set each test and its result apart with a semicolon. FileMaker will warn you if the function doesn't make sense. However, you might accidentally create a correct formula and still not get the data you're seeking. It is easy to miss a semicolon, especially if you've worked with earlier versions of the program where you needed to use commas.

20. Click **OK** and **Done**, and go back to Browse mode.
21. Since none of your invoices are likely to have a negative InvoiceTotal, enter **1** into the next empty Quantity field, and enter a negative number larger than the current InvoiceTotal in the Price field. You could also enter **Refund** in the Description field. When you're done, you should not only have a negative number in the InvoiceTotal field, but the Color field should have turned red.
22. Remove the negative number and the Color field should turn blue.

You might want to use the trick I showed you in the last chapter (in the section titled "The Real Trick"): Send the Color field to the back and stack the InvoiceTotal field on top of it, then make InvoiceTotal transparent so the color shows through. If you don't want any color to show when InvoiceTotal is a positive number, click in the second repetition of the zi_Colors_gr field and press Backspace or Delete. You might also want to choose a lighter shade of red so the black text is easier to read. You can delete the zi_Colors_gr field from the layout and let the calculation take care of the rest.

It took us 22 steps to get this little trick working. Using conditional formatting in Chapter 17 we do the same thing in 14 steps. Once you get used to that method it won't seem like much work at all. But there are still some other clever uses for this type of calculation. You can store icons in a repeating field, and use the same GetRepetition function so that the icons on buttons change based on data in some other field. The repeating field doesn't always have to be formatted as a container. The GetRepetition function will work just fine on text, number, date, and time fields as well. I used it recently to put different text field labels at the top of a portal based on selections made from a drop-down list. That choice determined how the portal was to be used, so the labels needed to change accordingly. Something like that can make one file useful for multiple purposes. I also know of a few developers who make the text on their buttons change for the various countries in which they sell their software.

Financial Functions

Figure 13-3 shows the four financial functions. The most common of these is PMT because it can be used to figure payments on a mortgage, boat, or auto loan.

```
FV ( payment ; interestRate ; periods )
NPV ( payment ; interestRate )
PMT ( principal ; interestRate ; term )
PV ( payment ; interestRate ; periods )
```

Figure 13-3
FileMaker's four financial functions.

PMT Example

1. Rather than add more fields to our tables, let's just create a new empty database for this one. Call it **Mortgage** and create the following fields:

Field Name	*Type*	*Options*
Principal	Number	
InterestRate	Number	
Months	Number	
Payment	Calculation	PMT (Principal, InterestRate/12, Months)

   You divide InterestRate by 12; otherwise, the interest is figured annually. Most of us make monthly payments, so that's what most people are interested in.

2. Click **OK** and **Done**, and put in a few figures. For a home, try 90,000, .0725, and 360 (30 years times 12 months). I get:

```
613.958652050573
```

   Whew! Maybe we'd better add some rounding to the formula.

3. Find the number functions and double-click the **Round** function:

```
Round (number; precision)
```

4. Now copy and paste our first calculation over the "number" parameter, and replace "precision" with **2**:

```
Round (PMT (Principal; (InterestRate/12); Months); 2)
```

   During data entry, you'll have to put the InterestRate in as a decimal number so that .0725 represents 7.25%. If you want to simplify the data entry process, just change the formula to this:

```
Round (PMT (Principal; (InterestRate/12)/100; Months); 2)
```

On the other hand, you can enter the longer numbers and format the field to display the percent sign (%).

5. To do that, go to Layout mode, and choose **Format, Number**.
6. Click the **Format as decimal** radio button, check the box next to **Use notation**, and choose **Percent** from the drop-down list. You should understand that you can do one or the other but not both. Numbers entered as 7.25 with a field formatted as a percent will show up as 725%!

Another choice would be to build a calculated text field that includes the percent sign, format it as unenterable on the layout, and stack it on top of the regular InterestRate field. I'll leave it up to your level of curiosity to handle that one.

Now before you get carried away and make plans to buy that new Ferrari, wait a second. Don't forget the down payment, taxes, insurance, and various and sundry upkeep costs. Oh, don't worry, the lender will turn you down if you can't afford it. Just don't sign away your house as collateral.

Trigonometric Functions

What is great about using trig functions is that you won't have to get out the old calculator; just plug the numbers into the fields.

See Figure 13-4 for the nine trigonometric functions.

```
Acos ( number )
Asin ( number )
Atan ( number )
Cos ( angleInRadians )
Degrees ( angleInRadians )
Pi
Radians ( angleInDegrees )
Sin ( angleInRadians )
Tan ( angleInRadians )
```

Figure 13-4
The nine trigonometric functions. (Ln and Log are grouped with the Number functions.)

Pi Example

For a quick example, let's use the Pi function to figure the area of a circle in a flash. Go back into the Mortgage file, and add two new fields:

Field Name	*Type*	*Options*
Radius	Number	
Area	Calculation	Pi * (Radius ^ 2)

Now drag the fields onto the layout, and put a number or two into the Radius field. This is another situation where you may want to round the results. After all, Pi goes on to infinity.

```
Round (Pi * (Radius^2); 2)
```

Logical Functions

I showed you an example of the Case logical function in the last chapter when we worked on automatically formatting a field to display a phone number complete with dashes. I want to spend a little more time with this group of functions, because I've found them so helpful. There are now 17 logical functions, as shown in Figure 13-5.

```
Case ( test1 ; result1 {; test2 ; result2 ; ... ; defaultResult} )
Choose ( test ; result0 {; result1 ; result2...} )
Evaluate ( expression {; [field1 ; field2 ;...]} )
EvaluationError ( expression )
GetAsBoolean ( data )
GetField ( fieldName )
GetLayoutObjectAttribute ( objectName ; attributeName
                           {; repetitionNumber ; portalRowNumber} )
GetNthRecord ( fieldName ; recordNumber )
If ( test ; resultOne ; resultTwo )
IsEmpty ( field )
IsValid ( field )
IsValidExpression ( expression )
Let ( {[} var1 = expression1 {; var2 = expression2...]} ; calculation )
Lookup ( sourceField {; failExpression} )
LookupNext ( sourceField ; lower/higherFlag )
Self
```

Figure 13-5
The 17 logical functions.

The If and Case functions are very similar in that you can perform multiple tests and get multiple results. Choose is different because you run a single test that can have multiple results. Whereas the Case function is designed for multiple tests, the If function is really meant to perform a single test yielding one of two results. You can get the If function to perform like Case, but you have to nest successive If statements to get the same results.

Prior to the addition of the Case function, FileMaker Pro users became very adept at building nested If statements. Not to belittle the If function, but many developers use it exclusively, even when the Case function will do a much better job. One thing is clear: When you start nesting If statements, it can be difficult to see where you're going.

If and Case

Look at the following two examples. The Case function requires 63 characters, while the If requires 73. Not only that, but some users find the group of parentheses at the end of the If a little confusing.

```
Case (Grade = 100; "A+"; Grade > 94; "A"; Grade > 87; "B"; Grade > 80;
"C"; "D")

If (Grade = 100; "A+"; If (Grade > 94; "A"; If (Grade > 87; "B";
If (Grade > 80; "C"; "D"))))
```

Of course, adding returns between groups of tests and results makes either formula much easier to read.

```
Case (
Grade = 100, "A+";
Grade > 94, "A";
```

```
Grade > 87, "B";
Grade > 80, "C";
"D")
```

NOTE There is a limit of 125 nested Ifs in the Formula box. The Case function has no such limit, but when you get beyond a dozen or so choices, it may be time to reconsider the arrangement. Whenever you need to update the values, you'll have to refigure the calculation. It may just be better to make the field into a lookup and create a special table listing the values. Such an arrangement is much easier to manage and update than a calculation.

The order in which the tests appear is important. You should use either mutually exclusive cases or continually greater than or less than subsets. Starting from the left, the calculation will display the result for the first test that fits.

NOTE In reference to the previous grades example, I used to think you had to use an AND operator so that it read ">94 AND <100." But it turns out that once the function has determined the value is not 100, it moves to the next test. So ">94" is all you need. The other test works; it's just unnecessarily long.

IsEmpty

I frequently work with the IsEmpty function. You use it to find out whether a field has any data in it. I use it most often in a script, but I want to show it to you here. The IsEmpty function is another one that gives the Boolean results of 1 (true, the field is empty) or 0 (false, the field is not empty). Then you can combine it with If or Case functions to give you all kinds of results.

1. Go into the InvoiceLineItems table and open the Formula box of OperatorTest. Redefine it so that it reads:

   ```
   IsEmpty (Quantity)
   ```

2. Exit Manage Database and go to Layout mode to make sure there's a copy of the OperatorTest field still on the layout.
3. Go to Browse mode. Most of the values should appear as a 0, meaning that the Quantity fields are not empty.
4. Delete the number in one of the Quantity fields.
5. Check for the reverse of IsEmpty by putting **NOT** in front of it. (I wish instead there were a function called IsFull or GotSomethingInIt. That would just be more intuitive to me.)

Evaluate[7]

A lot of developers are fond of the Evaluate function because it allows for more flexible calculation options. The description of this function is that it evaluates an expression as a calculation. I'm going to give you an example by having you create a table that uses Evaluate. In it, we'll create some fields that would logically be multiplied together to yield a line total, but it will actually be a straight number field.

1. Create a table called **NoCalcCalc** and add these fields:

Field Name	*Type*	*Options*
Price	Number	
Quantity	Number	
Calc1_gt	Text	Global
LineTotal	Number	

2. Double-click the **LineTotal** field, go to the **Auto-Enter** tab, and click the **Specify** button next to "Calculated value." Before you do anything else, be sure you choose **NoCalcCalc** from the drop-down next to "Evaluate this calculation from the context of" at the top of the window. I can't stress how important making the right choice is when it comes to choosing the context of the calculation. Enter this calculation:

```
Evaluate (Calc1_gt; [Price; Quantity])
```

3. Click **OK** and uncheck the box next to **Do not replace existing value of field (if any).**
4. Click **OK** and **OK** again to bring you to Browse mode.
5. If you're not already there, go to the NoCalcCalc layout. Choose **View, View as Table.** You'll probably want to make the Calc1_gt field a bit bigger.
6. Create a new record and type this into the Calc1_gt field:

```
Price * Quantity
```

7. Enter a Price and a Quantity. You get a LineTotal that is calculated without being a calculation field! Change one of the numbers. The line total changes. That's because we unchecked that box back in the Fields tab and because we included the field name in brackets in the Evaluate function. If we had only put Quantity in the brackets, the LineTotal would only be recalculated when Quantity changed, not when Price changed. Every time you change one of the numbers, the LineTotal will be recalculated.
8. Create a new record and enter some different numbers for Price and Quantity.
9. Now change the Calc1_gt field so it reads like this:

```
Case (Price * Quantity > 100; (Price * Quantity) – (.05 * (Price *
   Quantity)); Price * Quantity)
```

   Notice that none of the LineTotals have changed. They will only change when one Price or Quantity changes, not when Calc1_gt changes.

10. Create a new record and enter a Price and a Quantity so your LineTotal will be less than 100.

11. Create a new record and enter amounts that will equal more than 100. The calculation now says, in effect, "If the LineTotal will be more than $100, give them 5% off; otherwise, just calculate the LineTotal."

You could use something like this to calculate special prices during a sale and then return them to normal after the sale. The calculation could even be based on specific start and end dates.

Now, what if your Calc1_gt global field used a value list formatted as radio buttons that switched between different sets of formulas? You could add a script that recalculates LineTotal using the same Evaluate calculation and put a button on the layout so you don't have to change Price or Quantity to trigger the auto-enter evaluation. I tried both the radio buttons and a Reevaluate button. Works great!

One thing to be aware of when using Evaluate is that it won't update properly if any of the fields are being drawn from relationships. Normally Price and Quantity would be in the InvoiceLineItems table (rather than this test table), so that wouldn't be a problem. But let's say you wanted to include a tax percent that is kept in a Setup table. Won't work. Instead, you could make the tax percent a field in the InvoiceLineItems table, perhaps as a lookup from the Setup table.

The Evaluate function is really quite powerful. I know someone who has built an industry-standard FileMaker solution for the printing industry. He used the Evaluate function to replace nearly 1,000 calculations he needed in his old FMP6 files. One of the advantages for him is that complex calculations become static numbers. They're faster to draw onscreen because they don't have to refer to other fields, sometimes many calculations deep, to display the current value.

Let[7]

Another logical function that got a lot of attention when it was first introduced in FMP7 is the Let function. There are two parts to the Let function: the area where you define variables and the actual calculation itself that uses the variables you defined.

The main advantage of Let is that it can make a calculation easier to read and, quite often, shorter. You choose some characters to replace an expression with something shorter or more meaningful. For example, you could use the word "Age" to replace this expression:

```
Get (CurrentDate) – BirthDate
```

Written as a Let function, it would look like this:

```
Let (
[Age = Get (CurrentDate) – BirthDate];
Age)
```

Wow! Not much to the calculation part, eh? Yes, the calculation part is that last word — Age. Notice that I'm putting the parts on separate lines. I do that for clarity. It could all go as one continuous string on one line.

If a calculation was quite long and used multiple copies of an expression, it would sure be easier for me to debug if I just saw the word Age in place of the longer expression. The variables can even come from fields on a layout. That means you could put mini-calculations in text fields and use them to change parts (or all) of the calculation without returning to Manage Database.

As we move through this section, we'll use the Let function to change the color of a selection in a text field. Start by looking at the parameter template for the Let function shown in Figure 13-6.

```
Let ( {[} var1 = expression1 {; var2 = expression2...]} ; calculation )
```

Figure 13-6
The Let function parameter template with the optional items highlighted in gray.

Kinda messy! And what the heck does it mean?

First of all, the Help files say that the curly braces {} indicate that the items within them are optional. To my thinking that means you could exclude any characters between the curlies. Not quite true. The square brackets [] absolutely must remain in there, or you can't exit the field definition area. What is true is the curly bracket area is where you define your variables. Within that area, you can have zero, one, or more variables. That includes the entire gray area in Figure 13-6 — which is most of it. If you didn't have any variables to declare, you could just leave the brackets empty and it would look like this:

```
Let ([ ]; calculation)
```

When it's written that way, it would just be a calculation with no variables. You could write pretty much any calculation like that.

```
Let ( {[} var1 = expression1 {; var2 = expression2...]} ; calculation )
```

Figure 13-7
The Let function parameter template with the additional variables section highlighted in gray.

Look at the part in gray in Figure 13-7, showing var2 followed by the three dots (ellipsis). It means you can have as many variables as you want. We could write the Let function in plain English something like this:

```
Let ([Choose something short here to equal (=) something long and
complicated here;
Repeat as many times as necessary for the number of variables you need];
Then use the short thing(s) in place of the long things in this
calculation here.)
```

You might think of the first part of the Let function as a glossary. Any time you need to know what a part of the calculation means, just look in the glossary. (My thanks to Jerry Robin.)

Now, on to our example. I often want to highlight specific text in a field to call attention to it. I want to be able to select some text in any field I choose.

Then I want to run a script that turns it red. (More on scripting in Chapter 14.) First I created a script without the Let function. It uses the Set Field script step and no target field is specified. This is the part that goes in the Specify Calculation window:

```
Replace (Get (ActiveFieldContents); Get (ActiveSelectionStart); Get
(ActiveSelectionSize);
TextColor (Middle (Get (ActiveFieldContents); Get
(ActiveSelectionStart); Get (ActiveSelectionSize)); RGB (255; 51; 51)))
```

I'd say that's pretty much incomprehensible. A debugging nightmare. So I changed it to take advantage of the Let function. I copied out smaller calculations from within the big calculation and gave them simple names.

```
Let (
[Input = Get (ActiveFieldContents);
Start = Get (ActiveSelectionStart);
Size = Get (ActiveSelectionSize);
Output = Middle (Input; Start; Size)];

Replace (Input; Start; Size; Red (Output)))
```

(The Red part is a custom function I created that is explained later in this chapter.) Notice that I used the first three variables — Input, Start, and Size — in the fourth variable, Output. If you count the total number of characters, the Let function version is only about 15 characters shorter than the first version. That's because it takes space to define the variables. But when you read the calculation part, which consists of the last line, it almost makes sense. Also, by reusing the first three variables in the fourth variable, they didn't have to appear twice each in the final calculation as they did in the first version. The Let function is really most valuable when calculations get a lot longer than this example — especially when some functions are repeated a number of times. But it's better to start with an easier example so you have a chance to understand it.

Take a look at the Help files if you'd like to investigate further.

GetLayoutObjectAttribute[8.5]

This function, introduced in 8.5, uses the information you put into the Object Name field in the Object Info palette. Developers are suggesting that FileMaker should automatically name every object on the layout. For now, it's up to you to name the ones that are important to you. This function has some pretty valuable uses. It's especially effective when used with the Web Viewer, which I'll talk about in detail in Chapter 25. (As you near the end of the book, you may be tempted to skip over some of the final chapters. But do read the one on the Web Viewer. It's a very cool tool.) Oh, yeah, and you'll be excused if you find yourself looking for this one among the Get functions more than once or twice. Maybe you can remember where to find it by thinking that it's "illogically in with the logical functions." Actually, it doesn't belong with the other Get functions because they don't have user-defined parameters.

The full function looks like this when it first goes into the Calculation box:

```
GetLayoutObjectAttribute (objectName; attributeName {; repetitionNumber;
portalRowNumber})
```

The first argument is always the object name. In order to use it on any specific object, you have to use the Object Info palette and — guess what — name the object.

Next you choose an attribute. There are a ton of them. Well, 19 to be exact. I hate to direct you to the Help files again, but the description there is quite helpful and complete. And you'll get a good introduction in Chapter 25.

The main thing to know is that the arguments need to be in quotes. An example of a calculation I use in Chapter 25 looks like this:

```
GetLayoutObjectAttribute ("Picker"; "source")
```

Also, in the Help files, the examples near the bottom of the explanation use commas between the parameters. Don't do that. Use semicolons, just the way the calculation template does.

Notice the options for repetition and portal row. You might think this means you need to name each repetition and portal row, but that's not the case. It really just means you can target a specific repetition of the specific named object or portal row on which you want to perform an operation. You can see by my example above that you don't need to include the repetition or row parameters unless you need them for some reason.

You should know that you can choose either a repetition number, a portal row number, or both. But there are some subtleties to using any of the choices.

- If the object is a repeating field, you only need to include a single number as the third parameter. So your function might look like this:

  ```
  GetLayoutObjectAttribute ("Picker"; "source"; 3)
  ```

- If the object is a repeating field and there is no third parameter, the first repetition is assumed. So if your intent is to target the first repetition, you can either enter the 1 or leave it empty.
- If the object is in a portal, you need to include both of the optional parameters, even if the third parameter (repetition number) is just a placeholder. The placeholder can be either the double quotes ("") or a 0 (zero). So your function might look like this:

  ```
  GetLayoutObjectAttribute ("Picker"; "source"; ""; 3)
  ```

- If the object is in a portal and there is no fourth parameter, the first row is assumed.

- If the object is a repeating field that has (or might ever have) a portal in it, you should include both of the optional parameters, even if the portal row number is just a placeholder. (I haven't actually been able to effectively place a portal in a repeating field, so you're on your own with this one.) Such a function might look like this:

```
GetLayoutObjectAttribute ("Picker"; "source"; 3; "")
```

- If you were targeting a specific repetition of a repeating field inside a specific portal row, of course you would fill in both numbers.
- If you specify a number for either parameter and the number isn't available, you'll end up with an empty (null) result.

My advice is to use both of the optional parameters (including the double quotes with no space between them) whenever you intend to target either of them. There's no telling what results you might get if you later added something like a repeating field to a portal, and FileMaker started making up its mind how you wanted the script or calculation to operate. If you always include both parameters, you'll never have to spend days looking for that bug!

Self[9]

Introduced in FMP9, the Self function is an interesting feature that allows some calculations to be more portable because you don't need to name a specific field or object. Let me give you an example and then I'll explain the specifics.

1. Go to the INV_Invoice layout and go to Layout mode.
2. Click on the Line Total field in the portal and choose **Format**, **Set Tooltip.**
3. Type the following calculation into the Tooltip calculation box, being very careful to include every space and quote:

```
"The value in this field is " & "\"" & Self & ".\""
```

4. Before leaving here, highlight the calculation and copy it to the clipboard.
5. Click **OK**, go to Browse mode, and hover the mouse pointer on the field without clicking.
6. Go back to Layout mode and add tooltips to the Price and Description fields by pasting the calculation from Line Total into the Tooltip calculation boxes.
7. Go to Browse mode and look at what the tooltip says. Try it on more than one line of the portal.

NOTE There are an awful lot of quotes in that calculation above. Because we want that first bit of text to appear just as it is, we need quotes around it. The quote mark is programming language for "display everything between the quotes as text." You have to do that because one of the words might be a field name, and that could certainly give you strange results. (For example, if you had a field named "value" the sentence might read, "The 29.99 in this field is..." That's not what we're looking for!)

Next we have "\"". The outside quotes again mean "display everything between the quotes as text." That takes us down to \" as our final mystery characters. In this case, I'm trying to actually display the " character as if it had no programming meaning. By putting the slash before it, we tell the program, "the next character you see (in this case, the quote mark) is a programming language character, but I want you to use it as text." That way we can put quotes around whatever value the Self function provides for us in order to draw attention to it.

You can also apply the exact same calculation to a tooltip attached to the buttons on the page and the labels over the fields.

Now granted, this isn't a very sophisticated use of the feature. You already know what's in the fields and what the labels and buttons say. But I expect developers to come up with a lot of interesting uses for this over time.

One example is where you might want to have a script move from field to field and perform tasks without having to name the field the user or the script is in. In that case it would do away with a whole bunch of If/Then statements.

Here are the specifics:

The Self function provides the text, number, date, time, or timestamp content of an object without requiring you to name the object. That way you can apply the calculation to other objects. It works on calculations for tooltips, auto-enter calculations, conditional formatting, and field definitions. For anything else, it returns an empty string. It isn't really meant to be used in a calculation field formula or in scripts that use the calculation dialog. It's really more for conditional formatting and tooltips. Its real value comes into play when you can use the same formula on different objects. You just copy and paste the same formula. And if you change the field name at a later date, you don't have to go back and change all those layout calculations.

GetFieldName[10]

This is another one of those functions that sounds as if it belongs with the Get functions but doesn't because it has no user-defined parameters. You can tell because the "real" Get functions have parentheses in their names, like Get (RecordNumber). This function will give you the table and field name with a double colon between them. (By comparison, Get (ActiveFieldName) returns just the field name without the table name.)

Beta testing developers are giving this function high marks because it will make scripting more flexible since they won't have to name a specific table and field. That way, a single script can be used with multiple tables and even in different files.

Up until now scripts had no way of knowing what field the cursor is in. I remember a project I worked on some years ago where a script had to tab through the fields on a layout and perform operations depending on which field it was in. I could tell the script to go to a specific field as it started, but if the tab order ever got changed, the whole thing could come crashing down. My favorite use of GetFieldName requires it being combined with a few other functions:

```
GetFieldName(Evaluate(Get (ActiveFieldName)))
```

If I had a script run at the moment the cursor was in the NameFirst field on the CON_Contact layout, the result would be "CON::NameFirst." Once you know the field name, you can push data into it, grab the data from the field and store it in another field or a variable, and use the data when you need it.

NOTE If you were in a different table and the cursor were in the NameFirst field, the GetFieldName function might return something like inv_CON__ConSerNum::NameFirst. This could be valuable information and affect what you intend to have happen next.

One of the examples given in the Help files is GetFieldName(Self). But when you try to put that into one of the calculation dialogs you get the message, "This function cannot be used in this expression." But remember, that's not how the Self function is meant to work.

Get Functions[7]

The status functions from versions of FileMaker previous to 7 are now the Get functions. There are 94 Get functions that gather information about FileMaker Pro or the computer system you're using. I won't list them here, but there are quite a few very useful ones. I find them especially valuable in scripts. Take a look at the following functions.

Get (RecordNumber) Example

1. Go back to the InvoiceLineItems table, and redefine OperatorTest so the formula reads like this:

   ```
   Get (RecordNumber)
   ```

2. Make sure Calculation result is **Number**.
3. Before you close the Specify Calculation window, click the **Storage Options** button and check the box next to **Do not store calculated results**.
4. Click **OK**, **OK**, and **OK** again.
5. Sort the records.
6. Now unsort them.
7. Choose one in the middle of the list and omit it. See what's happening?

> **TIP** Using Get (RecordNumber) in a calculation that uses data from related records can really slow a machine down, especially when scrolling through a long list. Instead, go to the layout, choose the Text tool, and click in the body section with the text insertion I-beam. Now choose Insert, Record Number Symbol. You can also just type "@@." Then return to Browse mode. These numbers will perform the same function as the calculation, but they'll operate more quickly.

Another of the Get functions I use quite a bit is Get (ActiveModifierKeys). I use it to determine how a script acts depending on what modifier key or keys (Shift, Control, Command, Option) the user is holding down. We'll look at this in greater detail in the next chapter.

For those of you who are familiar with previous versions and are reading this to get up to date, four Get functions were introduced in FMP8.5:

- Get (ActiveLayoutObjectName)
- Get (SystemNICAddress)
- Get (WindowDesktopHeight)
- Get (WindowDesktopWidth)

The following Get functions were introduced after 8.5. They tend to be a little more advanced in terms of their uses, and I won't be discussing them any further here or in any of the exercises.

Get (TemporaryPath)[9]

Starting with FileMaker 9, you can use Get (TemporaryPath) to find out where FileMaker wants to put files. Once you know the path, you can use it to store PDF, Excel, text, and other types of files in a place that you can count on to be there. That bit of information can be really valuable if you want to attach one or more of those files to an e-mail. We'll do exactly that in Chapter 14. Other folders may be renamed or moved. If you always use the temporary path, you can pass the path and the file name to plug-ins and other applications for immediate retrieval.

Get (DocumentsPathListing)[10]

This function provides you with a list of folders and files in the Documents folder and any folder within. (You can find the location of the Documents folder by using the Get (DocumentsPath) function introduced in FileMaker 8.) You can use this function to find out if a file with a particular name already lives in the Documents folder before overwriting it or attempting to open it. But there could be quite a few items in that folder. In my test, it returned thousands of items.

A typical list might include items like the following:

```
Library/FileMaker Server/Data/Documents/Personal/contacts.fp7
Library/FileMaker Server/Data/Documents/cakes.fp7
```

Notice that cakes.fp7 is immediately inside the Documents folder, whereas contacts.fp7 is one level deeper, inside the Personal folder.

Get (HostApplicationVersion)[9]

This function simply tells you about the application that is in charge of the database. If you're logged into a file being shared by FMP Server, it will tell you the version number of the server software. If you're the host of the file, it will tell you the version of the software on your machine. If the host machine has an older version than the version that the current user has, the newer features most likely won't operate properly. That could be important!

Design Functions

You may never use FileMaker's design functions (or the external functions discussed in the next section), but you should know they're there if you need them. A few developers have used the design functions to create some excellent tools that analyze whole groups of files, listing everything from layouts and the fields on them to the details of relationships. FileMaker 7 introduced 19 design functions. FMP8 added the WindowNames function. LayoutObjectNames, introduced in 8.5, gives you a list of all named objects on a specific layout in a file. Since there is no easy visual way to tell which objects have names (as there is for Tooltip objects), this may be a necessary calculation for developers.

FieldNames and FieldStyle Examples

1. Go to the Contact table in the Business file and create a calculation field called **Design** with a calculation result of **Text**.
2. When the Specify Calculation window appears, choose **Design functions** from the View drop-down in the upper-right corner.
3. Double-click the **FieldNames** function to move it to the Formula box. It should look like this:

   ```
   FieldNames (fileName; layoutName)
   ```

4. Substitute "**Business**" (include the quotes) for fileName and "**CON_Contact**" (include the quotes) for layoutName so that it looks like this:

   ```
   FieldNames ("Business"; "CON_Contact")
   ```

   Of course, you need to use the name of your file. If you're working in Windows, you may find you need to enter Business.fp7 to make it work properly. (Don't get confused here. Contact is a table in the Business file. But CON_Contact is the layout name — as long as you have followed along with our instructions.)

⌘ **TIP** All parameters need to be put inside quotes when you use the design functions.

5. Click **OK**, **OK**, and go into Layout mode.
6. Make sure you're on the CON_Contact layout, place a copy of the new Design field on your layout, and open it up so that it shows more than one line.
7. Now go to Browse mode, click in the new field, and use your up and down arrows to look at the names of the fields on the layout.
8. Now try changing the Design calculation to this:

```
FieldStyle ("Business"; "INV_Invoice"; "InvoiceTotal")
```

9. Before you close the Specify Calculation window, click the **Storage Options** button and check the box next to **Do not store calculated results — recalculate when needed.**
10. Click **OK**, **OK**, and **OK**.

    My calculation shows "Standard." The part I find most interesting about this is that even though the field is on the CON_Contact layout, it reaches through to one of the other layouts and grabs the information without a relationship.

⌘ **TIP** When using both the Get and design functions in a calculation, they work differently (and probably more the way you would expect) when the results are not stored. When indexing is turned on, FileMaker remembers the results from the last time it stored a change in the record. By turning indexing off, it continues to recalculate, and your results reflect the current status of the database.

11. Go into Layout mode, go to the INV_Invoice layout, and format InvoiceTotal as a drop-down list using the Contacts value list. Click **OK**.
12. Go back to Browse mode on the CON_Contact layout and see what the Design field says.
13. Before you move on, go back to Layout mode on the INV_Invoice layout and format the InvoiceTotal field to **Exit Box**.

External Functions

The external functions deal specifically with getting information from FileMaker's plug-ins. *Plug-ins* are little programs that give specific extra functionality to FileMaker. Not all plug-ins make use of the external functions, but FileMaker's Auto Update plug-in does, and it should have been included when you installed FileMaker Pro.

If you're interested in plug-ins, you can go to FileMaker's web site for more information and for a list of developers who have written them. There are more than 150 registered plug-ins available and probably as many unregistered ones as well. Plug-ins add features not available from within

FileMaker. If there is something you want FileMaker to do that is not among its current feature set, there is probably a plug-in that does it.

This demo simply reaches out to the Auto Update plug-in and tells you which version is installed on your machine. It lacks excitement, but it will familiarize you with the procedure.

1. Windows users should choose **Edit, Preferences, Application.** Macintosh users should choose **FileMaker Pro, Preferences.** Now choose the **Plug-Ins** tab. You should see Auto Update in the list. If there is no check mark next to it, click the box next to it so it gets one, then click **OK.**
2. Go to the Contact table. Choose **Scripts, Manage Scripts,** and start a new script called **Auto Update Plug-in Script.**
3. Under the Fields heading, double-click **Set field** to move it to your script window on the right.
4. Click the **Specify** button next to "Specify target field," and double-click **Notes** from the list.
5. Now click the **Specify** button next to "Calculated result," and choose **External Functions** from the View drop-down. If everything's okay, you should see the list shown in Figure 13-8.

```
FMSAUC_FindPlugIn ( parameter )
FMSAUC_UpdatePlugIn ( parameter )
FMSAUC_Version ( 0 )
```

Figure 13-8
The external functions available to FileMaker's Auto Update plug-in.

6. Double-click the third one: **FMSAUC_Version (0).**
7. Click the **Close** button, **Save,** then **Close** again.
8. Make sure you're on a layout with the Notes field on it, and choose **Script, Auto Update Plug-in Script.** The Notes field on the active record in my file reads, "FileMaker Auto Update PlugIn Version 10."

That's all there is to it. The other items listed for the Auto Update plug-in work with FileMaker Server to update plug-ins on client machines.

Text Formatting Functions[7]

There are currently 10 text formatting functions. Using them, you can target specific text for a font, color, size, or style change. You can use the Position function and various other text functions to make a format change to a specific phrase, word, or character in a field as a calculation or part of a script.

1. Go to the Contact table and create a field called **PrettyType.** Make it a calculation field with a text result.
2. Select **TextColor** from the functions. It should read:

```
TextColor (text: RGB (red; green; blue))
```

3. Now make changes to the formula so that it reads:

```
TextColor (Left (NameFirst; 3); RGB (100; 10; 10)) &
TextColor (Middle (NameFirst; 4; 10); RGB (10; 100; 150))
```

Put the field on the Contact layout and see what you think. Isn't that cool? (Okay, but maybe *not* pretty.) The first names will be in Technicolor. Since this is a calculated field, you can't make changes to it unless you redefine the calculation or use global fields to determine the position of the colors. But if you use a script to make changes to the text color in a normal text field, you can go back and change the colors of the text manually. You can do this with the font, size, and style, too.

Now what if we just used calculations to change the color of InvoiceTotal instead of stacking the highlight field like we did in the GetRepetition example earlier in this chapter? You could use a calculation (with a number result) like this to color your text:

```
Case (
Sum (inv_ILI__InvNum::LineTotal) < 0;
TextColor (Sum (inv_ILI__InvNum::LineTotal); RGB(255; 0; 0));
TextColor (Sum (inv_ILI__InvNum::LineTotal); RGB(0; 0; 255)))
```

Way cool! Well, almost. Unfortunately, formatting the text color like that only works in Browse mode if the cursor is in the field. But it works great when used on text fields. All of this is pretty pointless anyway since you can go to Layout mode and use the Number Format options to make a negative number appear red. Ah, but we now have conditional formatting. I'll show you how to use that in Chapter 17.

Timestamp Functions

It's a little misleading to call this category "functions" plural, since there's only one function here. It looks like this:

```
Timestamp ( date; time )
```

It combines both Date and Time into a single field value. In older versions of FileMaker, developers needed to jump through all kinds of hoops to combine the two in order to accurately express a specific moment and the difference between moments. Thank goodness those days are gone! Just go ahead and use it happily without the old hassle.

Custom Functions[7]

One other item in the View drop-down is called Custom Functions. That heading will probably leave you with an empty list because these functions can only be created in FileMaker Pro Advanced. Once built there, they can be included in any solution for users of the regular version of FileMaker. The custom functions follow the specific file they were created in. There is no way to import custom functions from other files without the use of special third-party tools.

That said, these functions offer a lot of power in that the developer can create special formulas that need to be written only once and can be used over and over in fields and scripts throughout the file. If a change is needed, it can be made in one place.

As I said in the Let function section earlier in this chapter, I often want to highlight specific text in a field to call attention to it, so I created a custom function I call Red. The users see Red (text). All they need to do is drop the text item in place of the word "text" and it will be colored my favorite highlight shade of red. If you were to look at the custom function itself, it's written as TextColor (text; RGB (221; 0; 0)), with the single parameter "text."

Using the example in the section called "Text Formatting Functions," we could shorten that using a custom function for both Red and Black so it looks like this:

```
Case (
Sum (inv_ILI__InvNum::LineTotal) < 0;
Red (Sum (inv_ILI__InvNum::LineTotal));
Black (Sum (inv_ILI__InvNum::LineTotal)))
```

The RGB numbers for black are 0, 0, 0. That way, whenever I want to use it in a script for a field calculation in any file, I don't have to memorize the RGB numbers (assuming I've created the necessary custom function). I just type Red. But once again, it just makes more sense to use the Number formatting option to make it red on the layout (unless we use conditional formatting[9]).

Using some of what we've learned in this chapter, take one final look at this:

```
Let (
[Total = Sum (inv_ILI__InvNum::LineTotal)];
Case (Total < 0; Red (Total); Black (Total))
```

Summary

In this chapter, we looked at a few more of FileMaker Pro's growing number of functions. I demonstrated some of their uses and a few tricks to help make your work better.

Q & A

Q There are so many of these functions. How can I ever learn which is the one I'll need?

A Let the categories be your first clue as to which one you might need. You'll gradually learn new ones when you try to solve specific problems. Even when you search the list for the ones you need, you'll reject ones

Part 3

that don't sound right, which means you're becoming more familiar with them. Don't forget to use the Help files if you're not sure whether a particular function might work for you. That's where I go.

Q When I'm in the Specify Calculation window and I scan down the list of all functions, I don't see many of the Get functions. Where are they?

A Because there are so many of them, the people at FileMaker decided to show them all only when you select "Get functions" or "all by type" from the View drop-down. You'll also notice that only one generic external function, External (nameOfFunction, parameter), appears in the list. That's because the external functions will change depending on which plug-ins you have installed and active. And don't forget that the Get (LayoutObjectAttribute) function is illogically in with the logical functions.

Workshop

Go to the ILI table and rebuild the formula for OperatorTest using either the Case or If function to test this scenario: Price less than 19.99 and Quantity greater than 20. Make the results appear as some kind of text.

Part 4

Creating a Real Solution

Chapter 14

Automating Your Database with Scripts

Introduction

This chapter is all about scripts. If you don't remember my saying this earlier in the book, I love scripts! I could do a whole book on 'em. Now that that's out of the way....

We've built this group of tables, but nothing is set up to work very smoothly for you. We'll use scripting as the cure. In this chapter, we'll look at:

- What scripts are
- How to plan them
- How to debug them
- A quick overview of categories of script steps
- How to import scripts from other files
- The script management features introduced in FileMaker 9 and 10

We'll also create some scripts that will work in our tables using steps from many of the categories.

What Are Scripts?

We spent a little time with scripts in some of the earlier chapters, so this won't be foreign territory. In fact, you already have some buttons that perform simple finds and sorts. Scripts are similar to macros, which you may be familiar with from other applications. They're little program commands within FileMaker that perform one or more tasks. FileMaker's Manage Scripts[10] dialog (formerly known as ScriptMaker) uses what is called a high-level programming language. That means it's written in what looks like English instead of the strange-looking code you may have seen sometime in the past. That other weird code is actually going on behind the scenes, but you won't have to deal with it.

Most of the time you'll create permanent scripts that will be used again and again to perform repetitive tasks. There will also be times when you'll make a temporary script that you'll only use once to perform a specific job on a large group of records rather than do the job manually.

One Step at a Time

1. Open your Business file to the INV_Invoice layout in Layout mode.
2. Draw a button to bring up the Button Setup window. Scripts are often (but not always) attached to buttons. One thing that I mentioned before is that buttons can be attached to many of the individual script steps. That way, a button can perform a simple, one-step task when needed. When you want the button to perform a more complex task, you have to attach it to a script.
3. Click **Cancel** to exit here.

   While I prefer to attach scripts to buttons, the other choice is to have them appear under the Scripts menu. If that's what you want and you're in the Manage Scripts dialog, simply check the box to the left of any script. The next time you click the Scripts menu, your script will be there, ready to use. One other cool thing is that the first 10 scripts will have a keyboard shortcut. If you want to have scripts to help users with data entry or with other tasks that are performed frequently, just make sure that the script is one of the first 10 "visible" in the Scripts menu. Be sure to pick carefully which scripts show up there, though. Some scripts are better left hidden, and once your users get used to the keyboard shortcut, don't change them!

> **NOTE** On Mac OS X, the first 10 scripts are mapped to the Command+numerals 0-9 keys. Don't get these mixed up with the function keys.

4. Now choose **Scripts, Manage Scripts.**
5. At the Manage Scripts window, click the **New** button.
6. At the Edit Script window, name this script **Test**. See Figure 14-1. Notice the asterisk after the words at the top of the dialog. It indicates that this script has not been saved.

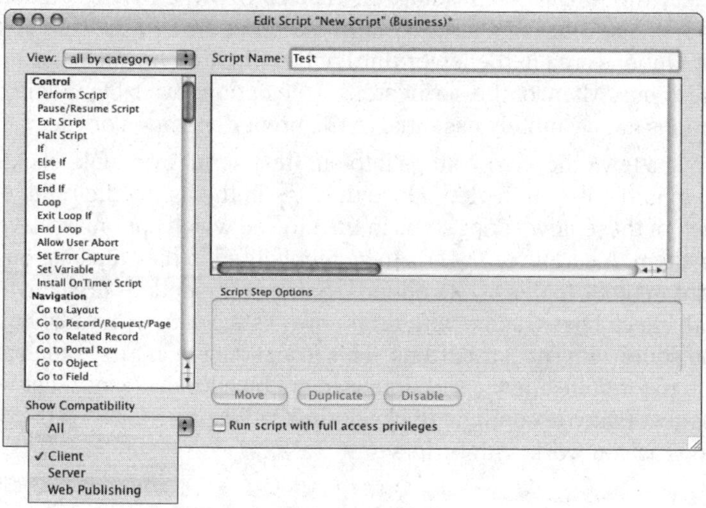

Figure 14-1
The Manage Scripts Edit Script window for the Test script.

NOTE What used to be called Page Setup on the Macintosh pre-FMP7 is now called Print Setup — same as on the Windows platform. You'll find that step under the Files heading.

When you first look at all the script steps available from the list on the left, it can be a little overwhelming. Fortunately, you build scripts one step at a time. You just have to know what you want, and run a set of trial-and-error experiments until you get it. That doesn't sound so bad, but keep in mind, scripts can be destructive. For example, you can construct a script that will show all records and delete all records without even showing the user a warning message!

CAUTION If you're experimenting with a script in a file with some valuable data, it's probably a good idea to save a backup copy of the file in a safe place first. Then run your experiments on the backup file and make the changes to the original file once you've determined it's not destructive.

I'm not too worried about the current set of tables. Even if all the data is gone, the layouts and existing scripts will still be there. But if you've already entered real data for 100 customers or friends and relatives, you might want to make a backup first. I don't intend to show you any destructive scripts, but what if you goof up?! And let me just say, it's not only beginners who make that type of mistake (blush).

While we're here, notice the Show Compatibility drop-down list in the lower-left corner of Figure 14-1. Select any of the three options and you will see that steps that won't run in that situation will turn gray. In the past, this has been most important concerning web publishing since only about half of the script steps can be run from FileMaker's web interface.

Script Options

7. Under the Navigation heading, find **Enter Browse Mode** and double-click it. You'll see that it moves into the script area on the right. Notice the Options area in the lower third of the window now includes a Pause check box. Many of the script steps have options available. Some of the options are absolutely essential to the proper operation of your scripts.
8. Move a few other script steps into our Test script by double-clicking them in the list on the left. Once they are in the list on the right, click each of these new script steps in turn to see which options are available for them. A script step needs to be highlighted in the steps list on the right in order to display its options. Some of the options are activated with check boxes, some with drop-down lists, some with radio buttons, and some with regular buttons. This is an area I didn't pay much attention to for quite a few years. I missed out on a lot that way. I just want to suggest that you continue to check the Options area for each of your steps as you work with scripts.

Planning Your Script

Once you get beyond simple scripts, such as those that find and sort Rich and Richard, you'll have to do a little more planning. The easiest way to begin is to write on a sheet of paper in plain English what it is you want the script to do for you.

Of course, it helps if you understand what scripts can do in the first place. From the work we've already done, you've probably already figured out that you can make a script go to a different layout, perform a find or sort, and even print. But did you know you can have a script find a group of records, go through them one by one correcting specific errors, and then beep and show the message "All Done" after it hits the last record? Yep, and a whole bunch more!

First you have to imagine what you want. Usually that will consist of some chore you have to do over and over manually. Then you have to find a way to get a script to do it for you. The better you know the set of steps from the list on the left, the more power you'll have.

When you double-click the Perform Script step under the Control category, this is what you get:

```
Perform Script [<unknown>]
```

Using this step, you can have this script perform other scripts. That includes scripts in other files. Perform Script offers tremendous power, but the flip side is that debugging (or figuring out why a script isn't working) gets more difficult.

Even if the script you're creating does all its work in the current file, there are some advantages to using subscripts rather than just writing one long script.

- It's easier to debug shorter scripts.
- With good planning, scripts can become modules you can use again in other scripts. One good example is various page and print setups you might use.

Some FileMaker professionals swear that a script should never be longer than the number of steps that can fit in the steps window (not including subscript steps). I wouldn't go that far, but it is easy to get confused when a script gets overly long.

The FileMaker Pro manual contains a marvelous list of considerations to take into account when planning your scripts. By all means read them, but you can start very simply by asking the following questions: Where am I now? What do I want to do? Where do I want to be when I finish? It's also a good idea to add one more question: What can go wrong along the way?

Where Am I Now?

To begin any journey, you have to know where to start. Part of the next suggestion could also apply to the "What can go wrong" category. Users may have the file in some condition you didn't anticipate. For example, if the user is in Preview mode and chooses a script that goes to another layout without returning to Browse mode, none of the buttons on that layout will work. That's why Enter Browse Mode is often the first step in many scripts.

If the script will be attached to a button that only appears on specific layouts, you'll have a much better idea of where the users are when they start. On the other hand, if you allow the script to be run from the Scripts menu, you may need to do a little more planning.

When a script is called up, consider what mode, layout, file, and found set of records may be involved as the script starts. It is possible to have a script run tests to determine any of these various states. But most of the time it's just easier to force the setting to be what you need. For example, if you want the user to go to a summary layout in Browse mode, it would probably be easiest to change the layout and mode. If you're an old-time user, keep in mind that since FileMaker Pro 7 and later allow multiple tables per files, some scripts will work correctly only if the right table is activated by selecting an associated layout from the Layout drop-down.

What Do I Want to Do?

This is usually where the thinking for most scripts begins. Finding the answer to this question actually requires several steps.

- Where do I need to go to accomplish what I want to do? If you have to enter data in certain fields, you may have to switch to a layout that has a copy of the field on it. In FileMaker 7 and later, you need to be sure you're in the table on which you want the script to perform.
- What modes will I have to go through? Will I enter Find mode, run a sort, display the results in Preview mode, and then return to Browse mode at the end?
- What other tables or files will be involved? You'll have to work out a way to get to any external files. Fortunately, the Perform Script step can run a script from another file.

Where Do I Want to Be When I Finish?

After the job has been run, the user should be back where he or she started or in some other familiar area in order to continue working.

In what file, in what table, on what layout, and in what mode do you want the user at the end?

What Can Go Wrong?

When you first start working with scripts, there are all sorts of goofy things that can trip up your plans. But in the end, you'll be inventing your own scripts, some of which may have never been imagined before. Keep in mind that you'll need to learn to think ahead! That's something you'll get with experience. I'll try to give you some tips as we go along.

I already mentioned that being in the wrong mode at the beginning of a script can cause problems. Another common situation is that after performing a find, occasionally no records may be found. You need to plan what you want your script to do when that happens. What if the script has a loop in it, and the Exit Loop If condition is never met?

Script Steps Overview

Look at the category list from the View drop-down in Figure 14-2.

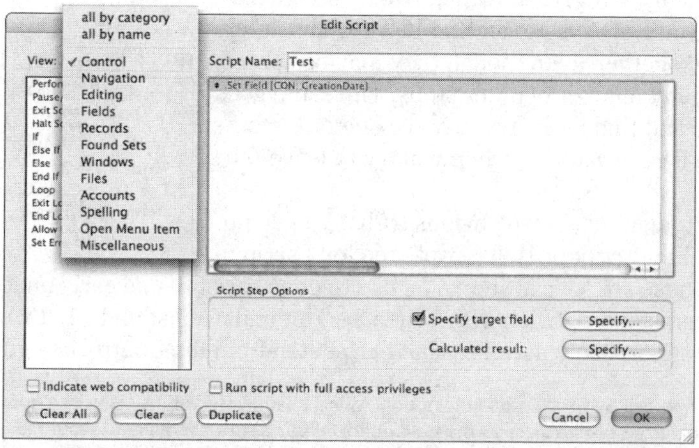

Figure 14-2
The View drop-down list of script categories.

One thing I can tell you is that in a few cases, the steps you're looking for may not be in the category where you expect to find them. Over time, you'll begin to get familiar with where they are. Don't forget FileMaker's Help files. They not only tell what the steps do, but they often give helpful examples.

Script Steps

What I want to do now is build some scripts that you will find useful in our Business file. These scripts will contain steps from various categories. Whenever I introduce a new step, I will put the category after it in parentheses, like this:

```
Enter Browse Mode [] (Navigation)
```

Items in the brackets are choices you make in the Options area. Empty brackets indicate that none of the options are in use. To keep things clear in your mind, I'll include the script names before every script, like this:

```
Script Name: Main Menu
Enter Browse Mode []
```

Control Category

You should still be in the INV_Invoice layout looking at your Test script. When you choose the Control category from the View drop-down, you should see the list in Figure 14-3.

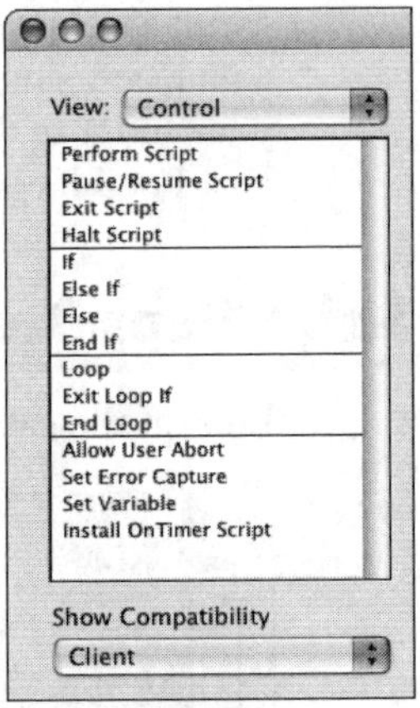

Figure 14-3
The list of Control script steps from the View drop-down.

I've added some dividing lines to the figure that you won't find in your Edit Script window. I've done this for clarity because each of the upper three groups hold steps that are related to one another and tend to be used together. In fact, when you double-click If, you'll always get an End If. They absolutely must be together, even though they may be spread apart by any number of other steps. The same goes for Loop and End Loop. If you leave one or the other out, you'll get a warning when you try to leave the window.

What might not be so obvious is that you do not need an Exit Script or Halt Script step for a script to finish. These are special steps you use to get a script to end early under certain circumstances. Otherwise, when a script ends, it just ends. Let's make a script that purposely uses the Halt Script step from the Control category.

> **NOTE** The Exit Script step has an option called Result[8]. It's a bit subtle, but here goes. It gives you full access to the calculation engine, but usually you would just put some value in there, such as a letter or a number. The Result option has no value to the script itself. It's only useful when the script is called from another script. Then you can use the result to tell the calling script what to do.
>
> For example, you want to prevent deleting too many records. If more than 10 records were found, exit the script and place the value ">10" in the result. When you get back to the calling script, include an If step that displays a custom dialog saying, "Sorry, you're not allowed to delete more than 10 records."

Main Menu Script Example

We'll start by creating a Main Menu layout in the Business file. No matter where you are in your database, you'll always be able to get back here and you'll be able to perform various tasks from here.

1. Use the skills you've already developed to create a new table called **Null** (abbreviation NUL) with no fields in it.

2. Rename the table occurrence **NUL** and move it to the left column of the Relationships tab.
3. Use the Layout Assistant to make a new blank layout using the NUL TO, and call it **NUL_MainMenu**. Delete the header and footer parts.
4. Now create a script called **1 - Main Menu (Halt)** with the following steps:

```
Script Name: 1 - Main Menu (Halt)
Enter Browse Mode [] (Navigation)
Go to Layout ["NUL_MainMenu" (NUL)] (Navigation)
Adjust Window [Restore] (Windows)
Halt Script (Control)
```

The reason for the Halt Script step is that scripts from other files may come here. This way, no matter what other steps there might be in the other script, it will stop here at the Main Menu layout. Putting the word Halt in parentheses in the name of the script signals anyone calling it from any other scripts that everything will stop after that script has run. You also need the Adjust Window step in case the file happens to be minimized at the time the script is called.

⌘ **TIP** The Halt Script step stops everything. If the Halt Script step is in a script called by another script, that's the end of the line.

The Exit Script step only discontinues the current script that's running. If the script with the Exit Script step in it is being called by another script, the original script will continue any remaining steps and subscripts. If the exiting script wasn't originally called by another script, then it will end just like the Halt Script.

⌘ **TIP** If you put a sequential number before each script name as you create it, you will greatly simplify your ability to locate scripts in the scripts list. I use the numeral followed by space, dash, space. The details of this and other methods are in Appendix A under the heading "Notes to Developers about Naming Conventions."

5. Exit Manage Scripts, and draw a button on the new Main Menu layout.
6. In the Button Setup window, choose **Go to Layout** from the list on the left.
7. From the Specify drop-down in the Options area of the screen, choose **INV_Invoice**.
8. Click **OK**, and type **Invoice** on the face of the button.
9. Now go to the Invoice layout and make a new button.
10. Choose **Perform Script** from the Control category, and choose **1 - Main Menu (Halt)** from the Specify drop-down in the Options area.
11. Click **OK** and **OK** again, and call this button **Main Menu**.
12. Copy the Main Menu button, go to the **CON_Contact** layout, and paste the button there.

13. The standard place for this button would be in the upper-left corner of the layout. You may have to move some of your other buttons around to give you enough space up there.
14. Make it non-printing (see the following Note), and put a copy of it on all other layouts in your file. Don't worry for now that it may overlap layout parts or other text.

> **NOTE** To make anything on a layout non-printing, choose Format, Sliding Printing. In the lower-left corner of the Set Sliding/Printing window, check the box next to "Do not print the selected objects." We will discuss this more in the next chapter.

Going to Contact

We're also going to want to get to the Contact table from the Main Menu layout and other places in our database. So let's make one more script in our Business file that will tell any external files what they should do once they get here.

1. Create a new script and call it **2 - Land Here**.
2. Give it the following steps:

```
Script Name: 2 - Land Here
Enter Browse Mode [] (Navigation)
Adjust Window [Restore] (Windows)
Go to Layout ["CON_Contact" (CON)] (Navigation)
```

> **TIP** If you rename your layout, FileMaker will automatically update any scripts using the Go to Layout step with the new name. Other database systems aren't so forgiving. This comes with a warning; not all layout references are updated. For instance, if you use something like If [Get (LayoutName) = "CON_Contact"] and you change the layout name, that reference will not be updated. It's one of the little side effects of the file structure starting with FMP7 that allows a little more flexibility. You'll be able to spot the items that won't be updated because you have to type quotes around the text when you create it. (Even though there are quotes around the layout name in the Go to Layout script step, you don't type them the way you do in the calculation box in the If example I just gave you.)

You might ask why I include the Enter Browse Mode step. In some cases, various functions you intend to have happen may fail if FileMaker is in some other mode. By adding this step to scripts that might be called from external files, you'll avoid that problem. That step is unnecessary when a script is simply going to another table within the same file. However, you can have similar problems if you choose to have multiple windows open in the same file — each window possibly open in a different mode.

3. Click **OK**.

4. This next script will be run from a button on the INV_Invoice layout. Create a new script called **3 - Go to Contact**:

```
Script Name: 3 - Go to Contact
Go to Related Record [Show only related records; From table:
"inv_CON__ConSerNum"; Using layout: "CON_Contact" (CON)] (Navigation)
```

   Well, it's only one script step, but there seems to be a lot to it. I'll actually suggest that we add some extra steps to this script in just a minute.

5. Click **OK**, and **OK** again.

Performing the Go to Related Record step may seem a little fancy when you could simply choose the Go to Layout step. But Go to Related Record (GTRR) is a quick and easy way to go right to the contact listed in the current invoice record. It has no meaning at all when you try to use GTRR from the Main Menu layout (since there is no relationship), but it's really valuable when you want to look at more information about the specific contact while you're looking at their invoice.

A very important detail about this script is the table occurrence we start from, inv_CON__ConSerNum. Keep in mind that when this script starts, we'll be on the INV_Invoice layout, which is connected to the INV TO. When you're in the "Go to Related Record" Options dialog and you click the drop-down next to "Get related record from," you can see only one TO that both begins with "inv" and is followed by CON. This is where the anchor-buoy system begins to show its usefulness.

Fail-safe

Earlier, I mentioned the importance of considering what can go wrong. This script is an example. If for some reason there are no records in the current found set in the Invoice table, or a contact has not been chosen yet, there will not be a matching contact record in the Contact table. You'll end up right where you started. I have to admit, I've only seen this happen a few times in many years, but lightning does strike. So here's the script rewritten to protect against those two possibilities:

```
Script Name: 3 - Go to Contact
Enter Browse Mode [] (Navigation)
If [Get (FoundCount) = 0] (Control)
   Show All Records (Found Sets)
End If (Control)
If [IsEmpty (inv_CON__ConSerNum::ContactSerNum_pk)]
   Beep (Miscellaneous)
   Show Custom Dialog ["Sorry, there is no Contact chosen for this
                      record."] (Miscellaneous)
   #Button 1 = OK (Comment - Miscellaneous)
   Halt Script (Control)
End If
```

Part 4

```
Go to Related Record [Show only related records; From table:
"inv_CON__ConSerNum"; Using layout: "CON_Contact" (CON)] (Navigation)
```

NOTE The Comment step will actually appear in bold in your list of steps on the right. When you print scripts, comments will be italicized. All comments begin with the pound sign (#). You have no control over that.

TIP Adding comments to your scripts can save you time as your scripting gets more complex. Whenever you have a find, sort, import, or export, you can use a comment to remind yourself what you did. You can also use it during the development stage to remind yourself what you still need to do. (Starting with FileMaker 7, the name and file of external scripts show in the Perform Script step. That allows you to reduce some of the script comments that used to be required in previous versions of the program.)

You can also easily view (and modify) sorts, finds, imports, and exports by double-clicking the script step and clicking the Specify button. But you may find that you work faster having a Comment step with that information right in front of you without going into the specific Find or Sort step. I often add comments to show me what the buttons on my windows are. For example, Button 1 = OK / Button 2 = Cancel.

TIP The only way to get to the Get functions is by choosing View, Get Functions. As I mentioned earlier, there are so many Get functions, it would make the "view by name" list prohibitively long.

Let's look at some of the parts of this script, starting with the first If step: If [Get (FoundCount) = 0]).

1. When you click on the If script step in the Control category, the step will appear in the script block. Click on it twice, and you will be at the Specify Calculation window.
2. In the View drop-down menu, look for the Get functions, and select **Get (FoundCount)**. (This particular Get function does not appear in the list of functions when listed alphabetically.)
3. Now look at the second If step: If [IsEmpty(inv_CON__ConSerNum::ContactSerNum_pk)]. This is the one that checks to see if there is a matching contact record before moving on.
4. Finally, take a close look at the final step in this script: Go to Related Record [Show only related records; From table: "inv_CON__ConSerNum"; Using layout: "CON_Contact" (CON)].
5. You select **Go to Related Record** from the Navigation category, and when you double-click, you'll see the "Go to Related Record" Options window. Select the table and the layout, and check the **Show only related records** box (see Figure 14-4). FMP8 added the options "Match current record only" and "Match all records in current found set." Previously, you only found records that matched the current record. This option would allow you to find a group of contacts and find all invoices that belong to all those customers. That was a complex task previously

— and I know because I've had to do it! Nice move, FileMaker! Notice that you can even check a box to show the related records in a new window.

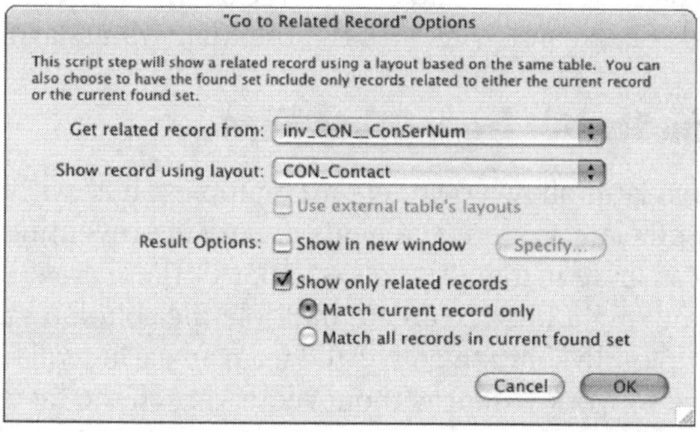

Figure 14-4
The "Go to Related Record" Options window where you make selections for the records and layout.

When you are in the "Show Custom Dialog" Options window for the Show Custom Dialog step, be sure to remove the word Cancel from the Button 2 caption box.

That's a lot of extra steps for a little protection, and you could probably get by without them. However, I've had some late-night phone calls that could have been avoided if I'd known to protect against these two problems.

The first few scripts you try may seem complicated, but don't worry. Pretty soon it will become second nature and you'll love this part of working with FileMaker as much as I do.

6. Now add a little button on the actual invoice layout.
7. Put it to the right of the contact's name, and attach the script to it. I usually type **<--Go** on these buttons. Users only need to see how to use this button once. They never forget it.

Getting Back

After you get to the CON_Contact layout, you'll want to get right back to the invoice you came from. In the Contact table, create a button that goes to the INV_Invoice layout and call it Back to Invoice. Keep in mind that the button could be a little confusing since your users might click it when viewing the contact under other circumstances. It will take you to the INV_Invoice layout, but not necessarily to an invoice pertaining to the contact.

It's a little beyond the scope of these exercises, but let me at least explain how I handle this: I create a tab on the CON_Contact layout with a portal that lists all of the contact's invoices. The user can click a button in the portal to go to a specific invoice. Then the button on the INV_Invoice layout takes the user to the layout with the invoice portal. A tab on the invoice portal layout takes the user back to the main CON_Contact layout. You might try that if you think you've got the idea of portals and the buttons I've mentioned.

Testing

It's time to test the script. Go to Browse mode, and see if it takes you to the invoices. Go to a different invoice and see if the Go button will take you to that contact record. Then come back. Try out the Main Menu layout buttons.

Access the Main Menu Layout from Other Files

FileMaker Pro 7 and later allow you to create multiple tables within a single file. This is a very efficient system and helps greatly in preventing a number of "gotchas" that can arise in a multi-file system. But there are still many situations in which you might need to create multiple-file solution scripts. (You may inherit a multiple-file solution converted from an earlier version of FileMaker and have to work with it without recreating all the tables and scripts in one main file.) Scripting in multiple-file solutions is a little more complicated, but I want to teach you about it for when that need arises.

Let's imagine an example where we have a different department in a warehouse that handles inventory. They want to be in control of their file — changing layouts and adding fields when they need to — but the two departments need to be able to get back and forth between your files on your network.

1. Let's create a new file called **Inventory** with the following fields:

Field Name	*Type*
ProdID_pk	Text
Description	Text
Quantity	Number

2. Add the following example data to the Inventory table:

ProdID	*Description*	*Quantity*
1001	Small Widget	10
1002	Medium Widget	15
1003	Large Widget	20
1004	Terminal Pin	25

3. Now create a script to take you back to the Main Menu layout in the Business file:

```
File: Inventory
Script Name: 1 - Main Menu (Halt)
Adjust Window [Hide] (Window)
Perform Script [<unknown>] (Control)
```

The reason I use the Adjust Window step is that opening a bunch of files can make the screen a mess.

Now you have to fix that Perform Script unknown step.

1. Click on the **Perform Script** step. Go to the Options area and click the **Specify** button.

2. Near the top of the "Specify Script" Options window, click on the words **Current File.** If the Business file were already in the list, you would choose it. Since it's not, scroll to the bottom and choose **Add FileMaker Data Source** to create a connection to the Business file. This will take you to the Specify External Script window.
3. Now all you need to do is choose the **1 - Main Menu (Halt)** script from the list. When you're done, your script should look like Figure 14-5.

```
‡ Adjust Window [Hide]
‡ Perform Script ["1 - Main Menu (Halt)" from file: "Business"]
```

Figure 14-5
Script steps for the Main Menu script in the Inventory file.

Add a button somewhere on the layout in the Inventory file, attach the Main Menu script to it, and call it Main Menu. But remember, if it's really someone else's file, get permission first.

Starting with FileMaker 7, you are able to create buttons that call scripts in other files without creating a script in the current file. That means that to get to the Main Menu layout from the Inventory file you could more easily have created a button right there in the Inventory file and attached it to the Main Menu (Halt) script that lives in the Business file. But since we want to hide the Inventory window, we need the Adjust Window [Hide] step.

Now create a button on the Main Menu to take you to the Inventory file. I think you can figure out how to do that, but be sure to give the script the number 4. (Hint: You'll need to add a FileMaker data source.)

Go back to the Inventory file, and create a script called "2 - Go to Product" with the following steps:

```
Script Name: 2 - Go to Product
Adjust Window [Hide]
Go to Related Record [From table: <unknown>; Using layout: <Current
Layout>]
```

1. Double-click the **Go to Related Record** step to bring up the Options window.
2. Click on **<unknown>** or **Inventory** and scroll down to **Manage Database.** That's right, you can get to the Manage Database window from right here.
3. Click the **Relationships** tab and click the **Add Table Reference** button in the lower-left corner.
4. When the Specify Table window appears, click on **Current File** and select **Add FileMaker Data Source.**
5. Find and double-click the **Business** file.
6. When you get back to the Specify Table window, choose **Product** from the list. Call this TO **inv_PRO__ProdID** and click **OK.**

7. Click on **ProdID_pk** in the Inventory table reference and drag it over to the ProdID_pk field in the inv_PRO__ProdID table occurrence to quickly create an equal relationship between the tables. Before you leave here, rename the Inventory table occurrence **IVT**.
8. Click **OK** again to return to the "Go to Related Record" Options window.
9. Choose **inv_PRO__ProdID** from the "Get related record from" drop-down.
10. Check the boxes next to **Use external table's layouts** and **Show only related records.**
11. Click on **<unknown>** or **<Current Layout>** and choose **PRO** from the drop-down.
12. When you're done, your script should look like this:

```
Adjust Window [Hide]
Go to Related Record [Show only related records; From table:
"inv_PRO__ProdID"; Using layout: "PRO" (PRO)]
```

The great thing about this script in FMP7 and later is that it does away with a number of issues in previous versions of FileMaker. First of all, you were required to create a script in the external file. (In our case, that would have been the Business file.) Secondly, you can tell the script what layout to display in the external file. And finally, regardless of what mode the external file is in, it will return to Browse mode to display the related records — that is, as long as there is a related record. If not, the script just stops.

Unfortunately, we're not done yet. What would happen if there are no related records in the Product table? How could that happen? Data entry errors from either department would be one possible reason. Another might be that one department knows about a new product that the other department hasn't been informed of. The answer to what would happen is — nothing. The user has no idea why he wasn't transported to the Product table. To protect against any confusion, you should probably polish off the script as follows:

```
If [not IsEmpty (inv_PRO__ProdID::ProdID_pk)]
   Adjust Window [Hide]
   Go to Related Record [Show only related records; From table:
   "Product"; Using layout: "Product"  (Product)]
   Open File ["Business"]
Else
   Beep
   Show Custom Dialog ["Sorry, there are no related records to this
   Product. I'll take you to the Product table anyway."]
   #Button 1 = OK
   Adjust Window [Hide]
   Perform Script ["5 - Go to Product" from file: "Business"]
End If
```

What happened? When you got to the Perform Script step, did you discover that you needed a 5 - Go to Product script in the Business file? Did you create one? Whenever you are developing a solution, you may discover that in order to complete one script, you need to create another. Back in Chapter 7, I talked about planning your database. Most of what you need can be pre-planned, but don't be hard on yourself if you discover that you need to take a step backward before you can move ahead.

You may decide that you don't want users to go to the Product file at this point. Maybe you want them to clear up the discrepancy. In that case you wouldn't include the Perform Script step.

Also notice the Open File step. The file is already open, but it's hidden. Unless you run a script in the Business file that brings the window back to the front, it will stay hidden. The second part of the 2 - Go to Product script does run a script that you just created. But that script won't unhide the window unless you include one of the steps that will bring it back to the front. I often use the Select Window [Current Window] step.

Now add a button to the layout and attach this script to it.

To test it out, go to the Inventory file, look at the Small Widget, and click the button. My layout called PRO in the Business file is set up as a table. I can't see the Main Menu button. To change that:

1. Go to Layout mode and choose **Layouts**, **Layout Setup**.
2. Click the **Views** tab and click the **Properties** button.
3. Check the box next to **Include header part**.
4. Click **OK**, **OK** and go to Browse mode. There it is.
5. Click the **Main Menu** button and then the **Inventory** button.
6. Now click the **Go** button next to Terminal Pin. Aha! The Terminal Pin is not listed on the PRO layout.

> **NOTE** I want to mention again that in FileMaker 8 and later, the Go to Related Record script step has the option "Match all records in current found set." This option allows you to do things like find all line items for all invoices belonging to a given customer. Your only choice previously was to go to records that matched the current record.

Using Layouts from Other Files[7]

This next exercise uses a very exciting feature introduced in FileMaker Pro 7. It allows you to build layouts and use data from other files as if they were in the current file!

1. Start a new layout in your Business file and call it **IVT_Inventory**.
2. Click on whatever appears next to "Show records from" and select **Manage Database.**
3. Click on the **Relationships** tab and click the **Add Table Reference** button in the lower-left corner of the window.

4. Click on the drop-down menu next to File and choose **Add FileMaker Data Source.**
5. In the Open File window, select the **Inventory** file. That will take you back to the Specify Table window.
6. If there were more than one table in the file, you would select it here. Name the TO **IVT** and click **OK.**
7. Back at the **Relationships** tab you should see the TO in the graph. Move it over to the left column since it will be associated with a layout of its own. Click **OK** to take you back to the New Layout/Report window.

> **NOTE** If you hover your mouse pointer over the Table Info Control icon in the upper left of the TO, it will show you information about the source file, source table, and file path. If FileMaker can't find the file, it will show the list of unresolved paths.

8. Name the layout **IVT_Inventory**. Choose **Blank layout** as the layout type and click the **Finish** button.
9. Delete the header and footer from this layout, and open up the body a little. Now comes the amazing part.
10. Under the Window menu, go to the Inventory file (**Window, Show Window, Inventory**). Go to Layout mode, select the fields and their labels, and copy them.
11. Go back to the Business file in your new layout and paste the fields. Move them around until you're happy with their position on the layout.
12. Go back to Browse mode.

Amazing! Not only does the data show up immediately, but the table automatically displays all four records. In versions previous to FileMaker Pro 7, you would have had to reconnect every field using the relationship just to display one record. Even at that, you would have only been able to see one record unless you were using a portal. This way, you are actually viewing and able to work with the data as if it were right here in this file — and indeed, it is!

You should be aware of a number of potential problems here:

- The other file needs to be available through the network in order for the data to be available.
- You can overwrite data here.
- You can delete records on this layout.

That's right — if you delete a record in this table, those records will also disappear from the Inventory file! If the other department wants to be in charge of their own file and you have this much power over it right here in your file, you really need to take some precautions.

The Separation Model

The ability to place TOs from other files in the "current" file brings me to a development method known as "the separation model" (TSM). It's a topic dear to the hearts of a number of FMP developers. TSM refers to a style of developing where you attempt to separate the data (or "back-end") tables from the "interface." The interface would be a file that contains the layouts the users see when they're working, the relationship structure of the tables in the graph, and the scripts, but no data. This setup is not unlike a number of other database systems.

One of the big advantages is that you can provide users with updated features by replacing the old interface file with a new one in a matter of minutes. Ask workers to exit the files, stop the FileMaker Server service, remove the old interface file to a safe location, drop the new one into the folder with the data file(s), and start the service back up again. There's no need to import the data into the interface file because it lives in the data file. And if there are problems with the new update, simply "roll back" to the previous interface without worrying about the data — again, in a matter of minutes.

It only gets a bit stickier when you need a new field, because that requires making changes to the data file. (And who hasn't needed to add a field from time to time?) But proponents would argue it's not that difficult to add a field or two along with the new interface file. You can even add fields while workers are still working in the database (see the following Caution). To reduce the need for that, some developers include a number of extra fields of each field type (and even some extra tables with spare fields) using generic field names so they can be brought into service without needing to add anything to the data file.

CAUTION Developing remotely on a "live" database can have disastrous consequences. Developers have reported losing connection with the host, and later finding the entire relationships graph empty and irretrievable! Man, you had better have a recent backup close at hand when that happens. I do not develop using FileMaker's Open Remote option across the Internet without making a backup first. The same caution applies to developing across a local network. If the network can go down, you can lose it all. (Keep in mind that working wirelessly increases your chances of losing your connection. All it takes is a second.)

A much better option is to use a program like Timbuktu, Remote Desktop Connection, Apple Remote Desktop, or PC Anywhere to take control of the remote computer where the files live. That way, once you've reestablished your lost connection, you can take up from where you left off. And if you can't get reconnected, you can have someone at that remote location finish up your work. You would just need to make sure someone is onsite and has some basic knowledge about how they would finish your work using your phone instructions. Of course if you have a commercial solution installed with a large number of different customers, that wouldn't likely be feasible.

FMP9 expanded on TSM now that we can add data from tables that live in SQL data sources into our FileMaker files. For more on that, see Chapter 26, "Working with External Data Sources."

There are arguments both for and against TSM by top developers on both sides of the fence. I only want to let you know about it so you know there is another alternative out there. I've used it in a couple of my solutions when I expected to have multiple clients, each with their own set of files. For example, I worked with a group of insurance agents who each had their own data files. When I added features, I sent each of them the new interface file but didn't need to provide for any complicated method of importing their data since there is no data in the interface file.

Portable Portals[7]

Here's another item introduced in FileMaker Pro 7. (Some of this is pretty deep, but many of us developers are quite excited about the possibilities.) You can copy a portal from a layout within a file and move it to another layout within the same table occurrence group (TOG). The data that displays in the copied portal will change based on the context of the new table. Now I should tell you that this is not possible when you use the anchor-buoy standard for organizing your graph, because there is only one layout associated with any table occurrence group. But if you are not sticking with the A-B method, this is something that might be considered a feature. (Even if you do use A-B, you can still copy and paste a portal in order to take advantage of its esthetics. It's just that you need to redirect all the elements, from the portal itself to the fields and buttons in the portal, to the proper TOs.)

Here's an example of how this might work. Let's say you have a Company file with three tables: Company, Employee, and Appointment. All three TOs are connected on the graph and there is a layout for each TO. (Again, not following A-B.) On the Employee layout you have a portal into the Appointment table listing their appointments. If you copy the Appointment portal from the Employee table and drop it on the Company table, that portal will show all the appointments for all employees with that CompanyID.

You can even do this from multiple tables (or even files) away, as long as they're connected on the graph. In previous versions of FileMaker, you often had to create special "pipeline" calculations in each of the tables between where the information came from and where you wanted to display it. You can also add fields to the portal from any of the tables along the table occurrence (TO) path — with mixed results. This is possible because in the relationships graph, every table in a table occurrence group is related to every other table in that group — not just the ones directly connected to it. In the case of our Business file, take a look at the INV table occurrence. Even though you see three sets of lines between the TOs in that group, there are actually six relationships there. Keep in mind that every relationship acts as a filter of the data.

Even though we can't take advantage of this portal drop when using the anchor-buoy system, we can still take advantage of the ability to display data from table occurrences that are not directly connected to the base table layout. For this example, we'll display every item ever ordered by a contact, regardless of which invoice it's on.

1. Go to **Manage Database** and choose the Relationships tab.
2. Add a new TO using the InvoiceLineItems table and name it **con_inv_ILI__InvNum.** You should have a pretty good idea where it goes in the graph by its name. In case you don't, connect it to con_INV__ConSerNum using InvoiceNum as the key field and place it in what might be considered the third column from the left.
3. Go to Layout mode on CON_Contact and draw a portal about 4 inches wide and 2 inches tall in an empty space.
4. In the Portal Setup window, choose **con_inv_ILI__InvNum** from the drop-down, check the box next to **Show vertical scroll bar**, and click **OK**.
5. In the Add Fields to Portal window, click the Available fields drop-down and select **con_inv_ILI__InvNum.** Then double-click **InvoiceNum_pk**, **Description**, **Quantity**, and **LineTotal** and click **OK**.
6. Go to Browse mode. You should see all the items ever ordered by that contact in the portal.
7. You'll probably need more data to get the full impact, so go over to the Invoice layout and create some more invoices. Be sure you create more than one invoice for your contacts and give them different creation dates.
8. Add another TO to the graph, call it **con_inv_ili_PRO__ProdID**, and add it to the chain.
9. Go back to Layout mode on the Contact layout and make the portal about 3 inches wider.
10. Add three more fields to the portal: **con_INV__ConSerNum::Date**, **con_inv_ili_PRO__ProdID::Price**, and **con_inv_ili_PRO__ProdID::Description**. Go to Browse mode.

All of the fields we added come from tables other than the con_inv_ILI__InvNum portal. Okay, the Description field from the Product table is redundant information. However, it's really coming from a different table, and the data is accurate. That was impossible before FileMaker 7. Additionally, you can edit any of these extra fields as long as they're editable under normal circumstances (meaning they're not calculation fields and you have edit privileges). Could this be the end of pipeline calculations?

Not exactly. Notice that the same Invoice Date is repeated all the way down the portal regardless of the dates on the invoices for this contact. What's going on? Here's the rule for adding a field to a portal from other tables along the path: Look at the graph. If the field you want to add comes from a TO between the layout TO and the portal TO, it probably won't work. Conversely, if the field you want to add comes from a TO farther away from the layout TO than the portal TO, you're likely to get useful data. In short, context is king, and it may still be necessary to create "pipeline" calculations to display the data you want. Regardless of the limitations, this ability to display data from distant table occurrences can be useful and a big time-saver! (To pipeline the invoice date into the portal, you'd need to add a calculated field to the InvLI table equal to Invoice::Date.)

⌘ **TIP** When you transport a portal to a layout represented by a different table, any sort order associated with the portal may act strangely because of the new context. However, you can change the sort order associated with any portal by simply redefining it in the Portal Setup window.

Print Invoices Example

For this next exercise, let's start by assuming that these are invoices you send out through the mail. This is a very common use for a database like this. We'll also assume that when payments come in, they'll be recorded by finding the original invoice and adding a Payment entry in the portal. Our goal is to find all invoices with an outstanding balance, charge 1.5% interest (or reprocessing fee) if they're more than 30 days old, and print them. Sketching that out as a rough pseudo-script, it might look like this:

```
Find invoices with outstanding positive balance.
Sort by Customer
Go to the first record in the found set.
Loop
   If the invoice is over 30 days old, add interest.
   Go to Next Record [exit after last]
End Loop
Go back to the first record in the set
Loop
   Go to the ILI_InvoicePrint layout and Print it out.
   Come back to the Invoice layout
   Go to Next Record [exit after last]
End Loop
```

This demo will not combine multiple invoices for one customer into a single statement. All invoices for the same customer will print one after the other.

Else If[7]

This section is almost a sidebar, taking us away from our current work. It's about the Else If step, which was introduced in FileMaker 7. Nothing that we're building will require it, but I think it is valuable enough to spend a little time explaining it. Previously, when you wanted to have a script evaluate a number of conditions, each would need to be accompanied by another If step followed by a final End If for each If. Not only that, but the steps would be indented another level. Depending on the complexity of the script, it was possible to have steps indent so far to the right that they disappear out of the script box. Here's a fairly mild example of how using multiple Ifs can get a bit complicated. Notice the string of End Ifs at the end.

```
If [Communication Choice = "USPS"]
   Go to Layout ["Letter"]
   If [Communication Choice = "Fax"
      Go to Layout ["Fax"]
      If [Communication Choice = "Email"]
         Go to Layout ["Email"]
      Else
         Perform Script [Dial Phone]
      End If
   End If
End If
```

I have a client who actually uses something very similar to this when contacting club members. It loops through the member records and either prints a letter, sends a fax, or sends an e-mail. In FileMaker Pro 7 and later, the script can be constructed as follows, making it much easier to read, as well as shorter.

```
If [Communication Choice = "USPS"]
   Go to Layout ["Letter"]
Else If [Communication Choice = "Fax"
   Go to Layout ["Fax"]
Else If [Communication Choice = "Email"]
   Go to Layout ["Email"]
Else
   Perform Script [Dial Phone]
End If
```

The Else If step operates the same as an If step, except there must be an If step above it to start the sequence. Whenever an If or Else If step is evaluated as true, all other steps down to the next End If are ignored. That is not as complicated as it sounds. Look at the example script. If the Communication Choice were USPS, you really would want the script to go to the Letter layout and do its work there. You wouldn't want it to continue on and switch to the other layouts. By the way, scripts set up the old way will work just fine. If you find that easier, stay with it.

The Print Script

Let's set up the script that does the printing using the ILI_InvoicePrint layout. But keep in mind that it will be run from the Invoice layout. Now make a script called "6 - Print One Invoice" using the following steps:

```
Script Name: 6 - Print One Invoice
Go to Related Record [Show only related records; From table:
"inv_ILI__InvNum"; Using layout: "ILI_InvoicePrint" (ILI)] (Navigation)
Sort Records [Restore; No dialog]
```

```
#Sort by ILI::InvoiceNum_fk (Comment - Miscellaneous)
Print Setup [Restore; No dialog] (File)
Print [Restore; No dialog]
Go to Layout ["INV_Invoice" (INV)]
```

Double-click the Print Setup step in the column on the right and make your settings there. If you had recently printed something, the settings will be just as they were when you last printed. Whether you like them as they are or make changes, as soon as you click OK, they'll be memorized in the script. Do the same with the Print step. You should be all set — unless somebody changes printers on you. Ah, but this next paragraph might help you with that.

Starting in FileMaker 10, you can select the target printer in the Print script step and the script will remember it. Maybe you use one printer for labels only and another is loaded with a specific preprinted form. In cases like that, this is a very welcome, timesaving feature. If FileMaker can't find the specific printer, it will use the default printer instead. If a specific printer is not really that important, the Any Printer option is probably a better choice. If you replace the printer with another of the same brand and model, you may have to go back into the script(s) and target the replacement. It should be easy enough to run a test or two. Running a script with a Print step that has a saved targeted printer resets FileMaker's default printer. So you'll have to reset the printer manually when you run your next print job — unless that job is run from FileMaker with a script using a different targeted printer.

> **TIP** FileMaker's default printer is completely separate from the system default printer. Go to the File menu and choose Page Setup (Mac) or Print Setup (Windows). The printer and the settings you choose in that dialog become the default. You need to know that the paper and orientation options are saved on a per-file basis, which is something you might not expect. So now you'll know where to look when one file defaults to landscape all the time and a different file defaults to portrait.

> **CAUTION** Different printers have different border requirements. Try to allow a little extra space around all four edges of your printing layouts to accommodate a wider range of printers.

The Invoices Scripts

Now go back to the Invoice layout, find all records with an InvoiceTotal greater than zero, and sort them by ContactSerNum. (It's not strictly necessary to perform the find and sort manually. You can make those choices within the script itself.) Create a script called "7 - Find Invoices with Balance Due" that has the following steps:

```
Script Name: 7 - Find Invoices with Balance Due
Go to Layout ["INV_Invoice" (Invoice)] (Navigation)
Set Error Capture [On]
```

```
Perform Find [Restore] (Found Sets)
#InvoiceTotal > 0 (Comment - Miscellaneous)
If [Get (FoundCount) = 0]
   Beep
   Show Custom Dialog ["Sorry, there are no outstanding invoices at this
      time. Better luck next month!"]
   #Button 1 = OK (Comment - Miscellaneous)
   Halt Script
End If

Sort Records [Restore; No dialog] (Found Sets)
#Sort by ContactSerNum_pk (Comment - Miscellaneous)
```

Make sure you double-click the Perform Find step and click the OK button in the Specify Find Requests window to retain the find you just performed manually. Do the same with the Sort step and check the "Perform without dialog" box in the Script Step Options area.

Back in the Edit Script window, click OK, and start a script called "   8 - Add Interest Item." Notice that I've indented the script name by three spaces. That way it's easier to notice it in the scripts list and see that this is a script that's really meant to be called as a subscript.

```
Script Name:    8 - Add Interest Item
Go to Layout ["INV_Invoice" (Invoice)]
Go to Field [inv_ILI__InvNum::Description]
Go to Portal Row [Last] (Navigation)
Set Field [inv_ILI__InvNum::Description, TextColor ("Interest";
           RGB (255; 0; 0))] (Fields)
Set Field [inv_ILI__InvNum::Quantity; 1]
Set Field [inv_ILI__InvNum::Price, Round (INV::InvoiceTotal * .015; 2)]
```

TIP You will need a set of quotes in the Formula box around the word Interest. Quotes always indicate text constants. If you try to leave the Calculation window without them, you'll be warned that FileMaker can't find the Interest field.

NOTE Here's how to get an RGB color you want: Go to Layout mode, click the paint bucket icon, and choose a color from the Fill color palette. Click the palette again and choose Other Color. Click the sliders icon and pick RGB Sliders from the drop-down list. Now you have the RGB color you want, or you can make your own color by moving the sliders.

NOTE When you call up either the Specify Find Requests or Edit Find Requests window, you can create multiple criteria in each. Once a group of requests are in the window, you cannot move them up and down in the window. However, you can add, change, and remove items from the Edit Find Requests window. You can simulate being able to move items in the Specify Find Requests window by using the Duplicate and Delete buttons.

Notice the Set Field step. You'll find it in the Fields category. It's similar to Insert Text or Insert Calculated Result, except Set Field doesn't require the field to be on the currently chosen layout. It can even reach through a portal to a field that's in the table but not in the portal and add or change data in the remote record.

I'm afraid the use of the word "set" isn't really very descriptive of the power of this step. But I highly recommend you become familiar with it. I rely very heavily on Set Field. To help me visualize what it does, I used to imagine "setting" the TV on channel 10. Substitute the word "values" for channel 10 and "field" for TV, and you've got it. Maybe it would be easier for you to think of someone setting the time on a clock. Whatever works for you is fine. Just don't miss out on the power of this step because the terminology is unfamiliar.

Notice that we're also using the RGB argument of the TextColor[7] function. This will cause the word "Interest" to appear in red on the invoice — as long as you're printing invoices in color. It can alert the clients that if they pay their invoices within 30 days, they can avoid this charge. If you want to keep the text black, your step would look like this:

```
Set Field [inv_ILI__InvNum::Description, "Interest"]
```

CAUTION If you have more than one portal on a layout, you need to name one of the fields in the portal, such as inv_ILI__InvNum::Description, before using the Go to Portal Row script step. Otherwise, the step will attempt to work on the portal that was placed on the layout first, which may produce unexpected results. The order in which a field or a portal is placed on the layout is independent from whether you send a field to the back or bring it to the front of a layout. It is best to get into the habit of adding a field from the portal to the script as we have done here. Nothing will surprise you more than a script that doesn't work after you or someone else has made a change to a layout. Of course, you need to make sure your target field stays on the layout.

Along those same lines, because you can now build portals to display an initial row other than 1, you can place portals next to each other to more conveniently fit your layout purposes. However, this can present problems when scripting various functions, since a script can only identify the first copy of a portal displaying the same related data. If you have rows 1-8 on the left side of a window, and rows 9-16 on the right side, a script can only operate on rows 1-8. But now you can name layout objects using the Object Info palette. Every version of a portal can have its own unique name (as can every field in the portal if you choose). Name the portal and the script can easily navigate to the one you want. For more information, see the section titled "Object Names" in Chapter 17.

Figuring Interest

The Add Interest Item script will create an interest item in the portal. So now we need a script that will determine which invoices to add the interest to. Call this script "9 - Figure Interest on Found Set":

```
Script Name: 9 - Figure Interest on Found Set
Allow User Abort [Off] (Control)
Enter Browse Mode (Navigation)
```

```
Go to Layout ["INV_Invoice" (INV)] (Navigation)
Perform Script ["7 - Find Invoices with Balance Due"] (Control)
Go to Record/Request/Page [First] (Navigation)
Loop (Control)
   If [INV::Date < Get (CurrentDate) - 30] (Control)
      Perform Script ["   8 - Add Interest Item"] (Control)
   End If (Control)
   Go to Record/Request/Page [Next; Exit after last] (Navigation)
   Exit Loop If [Get (ActiveModifierKeys) = 4] (Control)
   #Modifier Key 4 is the Control Key (Comment - Miscellaneous)
End Loop
```

The first step is Allow User Abort [Off]. You don't want anybody stopping this script partway through. If it were started over at a later time, some customers might be charged interest twice. Then you would have to make excuses to irate customers.

Next you see Enter Browse Mode. The reason we add that step is you may choose to have the script run from the Scripts menu or in some cases from another file. In those cases, you could run into problems if the user were in some other mode. If the script will only run from a button on a specific layout in the same file, there is no need for that step. But it doesn't take much extra work to add the step.

You can see there is a set of If steps inside the Loop steps. You can "nest" as many of these as your brain can handle. Just remember, the more complicated it gets, the harder it will be to debug later. When you're tempted to make it complicated, it's usually better to find an easier answer, even if it takes more time.

Notice that the nested Go to Record step includes "Exit after last." Be sure you check this box in the Options area for this step. If you don't, the script will go into an endless loop. That's why I've included the Exit Loop If step.

⌘ **TIP** When you're testing a script with a loop in it and Allow User Abort is Off, include the step Exit Loop If [Get (ActiveModifierKeys) = 4] just before the End Loop or just after the Loop step. Modifier key 4 is the Control or Ctrl key. If the script goes crazy, just hold down the Control key to regain "control." After the script has been tested under all circumstances, you can delete that step.

Printing One Invoice

Sometimes we'll need to print a single invoice from the Invoice table without running the whole billing process. We can use the 6 - Print One Invoice script we already created. Simply add a button to the Invoice layout and attach the 6 - Print One Invoice script to it. Keep in mind that this button will not create an interest item.

I didn't add any protection back in 6 - Print One Invoice, but it's possible for someone to try to print an invoice for a record that has no line items. You can use the If [IsEmpty] steps, mentioned earlier in the "Fail-safe" section, as a template to safeguard against that if you like.

Monthly Billing Script

Finally, we string all of these pieces together with a script called "10 - Find & Print This Month's Invoices":

```
Script Name: 10 - Find & Print This Month's Invoices
Perform Script ["7 - Find Invoices with Balance Due"] (Control)
Perform Script ["9 - Figure Interest on Found Set"]
Go to Record/Request/Page [First]
Loop
   Perform Script ["6 - Print One Invoice"]
   Go to Record/Request/Page [Next; Exit after last]
   Exit Loop If [Get (ActiveModifierKeys) = 4]
End Loop
```

The nice thing about this modular script approach is you can also remove the second step if you prefer not to charge interest.

Testing Monthly Billing

1. To test this properly, you should have about five invoices in your file. If you don't, create some now, choosing a Product ID and Quantity so you have InvoiceTotals with which to work.
2. Set it up so that at least one of your invoices has an InvoiceTotal of 0 by clicking in the last empty line of the portal. Don't choose a ProductID. Make a Quantity of **1**, type **Payment** in the Description field, and make a negative Price equal to the InvoiceTotal.
3. Finally, click through the records to find at least one invoice that has an InvoiceTotal more than 0, and change the date so that it's older than 30 days.
4. Now add a button to your new Main Menu layout, and attach the "10 - Find & Print This Month's Invoices" script to it.
5. Go to Browse mode and see if it works.

Thoughtful Additions

Since the script changes some of the records, you may want to add some extra steps that again take into account what can go wrong.

The very first steps could be to beep and show a message to check that the correct printer is selected and loaded with paper in the correct tray. Then allow users to cancel the script if everything isn't set properly.

You might also add a DateBilled field that could be filled in with the current date as each of the invoices is printed. That way, if there were a computer crash partway through the billing process, you'd be able to figure out where you left off. You could change the Find Invoices with Balance Due script so it only finds invoices that have not already been printed — invoices that have nothing in the DateBilled field.

Printing to PDF[8]

A wonderful alternative to printing to paper is the capability for FileMaker 8 and later to print to PDF. You can choose File, Save/Send Records As, PDF, or use a script — which is what we'll be doing. Among other things, you can e-mail the invoices for quicker response time and no postage — except for your monthly Internet fees. But you're paying for them anyway, right?

1. Duplicate the script 6 - Print One Invoice. (The Duplicate Script button is the fourth icon from the right at the bottom of the Manage Scripts window.)
2. Double-click the script to open the Edit Script window, then rename it **6.5 - Print One PDF.**
3. Remove the Print Setup and Print steps.
4. Insert both a Set Variable (Control) and a Save Records as PDF (Records) script step after the Sort step.
5. Double-click the Set Variable step to open the "Set Variable" Options dialog, and name it **$pdf.** The Set Variable step was introduced in FileMaker 8.
6. Click the **Specify** button across from Value and enter the following line in the Specify Calculation window, being sure to leave a space after Inv:

```
"Inv " & ili_INV__InvNum::InvoiceNum_pk & ".pdf"
```

7. Click **OK** and **OK.**

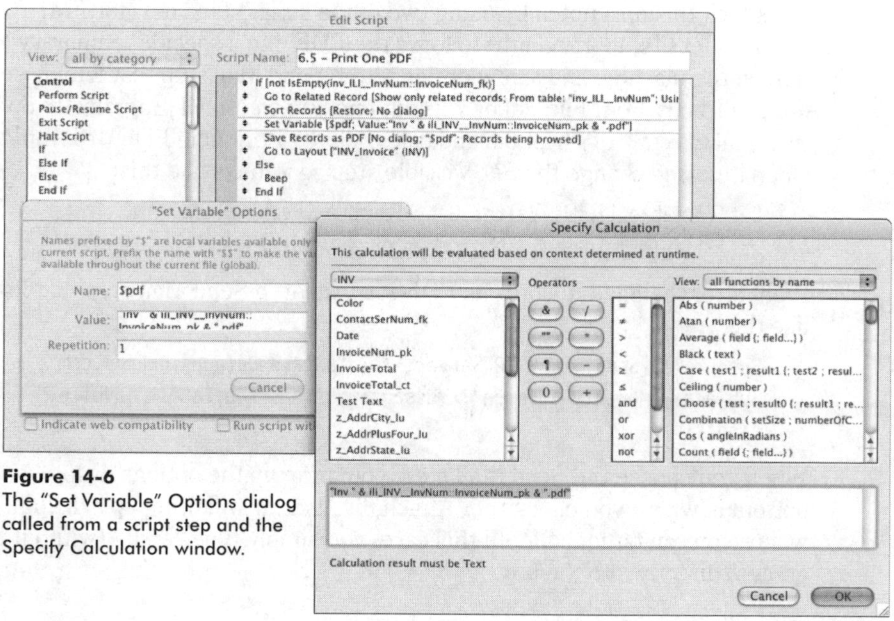

Figure 14-6
The "Set Variable" Options dialog called from a script step and the Specify Calculation window.

8. Double-click the Save Records as PDF step and type **$pdf** in the Specify Output File dialog. Take a look at the options at the bottom of this dialog. You can set it up to create an e-mail automatically with the PDF document attached. All as part of that one script. Very nice!
9. Click **OK**. When you get done, the script should look like this:

```
If (not IsEmpty (inv_ILI__InvNum::InvoiceNum_fk)]
   Go to Related Record [Show only related records; From table:
         "inv_ILI__InvNum"; Using layout: "ILI_InvoicePrint" (ILI)]
         (Navigation)
   Sort Records [Restore; No dialog]
   Set Variable [$pdf; Value: "Inv " & ili_INV__InvNum::InvoiceNum_pk
         & ".pdf"]
   Save Records as PDF [No dialog; "$pdf"; Records being browsed]
   Go to Layout ["INV_Invoice" (INV)]
Else
   Beep
End If
```

We've done quite a few interesting things here. Normally when you specify an output file, you type exactly what you want the file name to be. But we want every PDF to have its own name. If they had the same name, they would overwrite each other. Unfortunately, you can't put a calculation in the Specify Output File dialog — at least not directly. That's why we needed the variable.

Get (TemporaryPath)[10] and Send Mail[10]

Let's kick this up a notch by using two of the script steps new for FMP10. We can use Get (TemporaryPath) to force the PDF into a specific temporary location on the machine and a new option in the Send Mail step that lets us send e-mail directly from FileMaker without opening an e-mail program. To do that, make a copy of script 6.5 and call it "6.51 - Print One PDF to TempPath." Open it up and change the Set Variable step so it looks like this:

```
Set Variable [$pdf; Value: Get (TemporaryPath) & "Inv " &
     ili_INV__InvNum::InvoiceNum_pk & ".pdf"]
```

Right after the Save Records as PDF step, insert a Send Mail step that looks like this:

```
Send Mail [Send via SMTP Server; To: "JStars@DataDesignPros.com";
Subject: "Monthly Invoice"; Message: "Here's the latest invoice.";
"$pdf"]
```

When you choose the Send Mail step, you bring up the options dialog. At the bottom is where you check the "Attach file" box. It will bring up a dialog where you can target a file. In this case, you simply type "$pdf" (without the quotes) directly into the box.

The feature that's new for FMP10 is the "Send via" drop-down near the top of the Send Mail Options dialog, which now allows you to target a specific SMTP e-mail server. Previously the e-mail went out of FileMaker and into an e-mail program like Entourage on your computer. There's a "Specify" button to the right of the drop-down that brings up the SMTP Options dialog. That's where you fill in the specifics for the e-mail server you'll be using.

You can probably get the e-mail server information from your e-mail program. You need to know what you're doing when you get to this dialog. As for me, I gave up after an hour. Either my pre-release version of FMP didn't have that feature completed yet, or at least one of my settings was incorrect (most likely). I have to admit that I panic whenever I see e-mail server dialogs since it always signals to me that I'll be in for a prolonged testing period. There's a little more about all this in Appendix A along with screenshots of the dialogs.

One thing you should know about Get (TemporaryPath) is that anything in that folder is really temporary. When you turn off your machine, that folder gets emptied. If you intend to keep copies of the PDF (or anything else you intend to use the function for), you should send it somewhere else more permanent. On Mac OS X, you can't even open the folder for the temporary path. It's in an invisible directory. There are some utilities you can get to make invisible items visible, but for most of us users, be aware that the function is just meant to provide a transitory holding place.

Even though I never did connect, I think it's fantastic that you can send e-mail directly from FileMaker without an e-mail client or a plug-in.

> **NOTE** If you have your preferences set to low resolution in your PDF driver, the PDFs you generate could look pretty ragged to the person you send them to, especially if the receiver has their PDF reader set to low resolution too. That means even if you send a high-rez PDF, it could still look bad. Nevertheless, it still beats the pants off a fax, and it gets there before the post office thinks about driving down the street to pick up your paper invoice.

Append to PDF[9]

As soon as FileMaker added the Print to PDF feature, users started asking that they be able to add to an existing PDF. In some cases they wanted to build one report and follow it with another on a different layout in the same PDF. Well, now you can!

Let's say that once a year you wanted to add your client's contact information to the bottom of their invoices so they can verify it for accuracy. Here's how:

1. Duplicate the **6.5 - Print One PDF** script and rename it **6.6 - Append to Invoice PDF**.
2. Change the middle of the script so it looks like this:

```
Set Variable [$pdf; Value: "Inv " & INV::InvoiceNum_pk & ".pdf"]
Go to Related Record [Show only related records; From table:
"inv_CON__ConSerNum"; Using layout: "CON_Contact" (CON)]
```

```
Save Records as PDF [Restore: Append: No dialog; "$pdf"; Current record]
Go to Layout ["INV_Invoice" (INV)]
```

3. Save the script and give it a try, assuming you already have a PDF named for the invoice you're looking at.

In a situation like this, you would more than likely use a different layout that has some text explaining why you're including this information with their invoice and remove the buttons — whatever you need to get the job done. You might also find it a little awkward to click a button for each invoice that needs to be appended this way. You might want to put a button on the INV_Invoice layout rather than leave it in the Scripts menu where it could be triggered from any layout. But really, this example is just supposed to get you thinking about how you would use such a feature.

Here are some things you need to know about Append to PDF:

- If the PDF has been moved or renamed, all you'll get is a PDF with the new material.
- If you set up the original PDF to open with a password, you need to include that information when you append to it.
- The options set up for the original file cannot be modified when you append.
- If you want to perform multiple appends to the file in one script, you must not have the Auto Open check box set until the very last append. Otherwise, the file opens before the last append, and ends up "locked" and unable to accept the new material.

Script Variable[8]

A script variable begins with a dollar sign. It's only good during the time the script runs. It's a lot like a global field, and many developers use them instead of global fields. I still like global fields because you can put them on a layout and see what their values are when the script is running. Variables are invisible and they're not easily passed from one script to another. FileMaker Pro Advanced has a data view window you can use when debugging scripts, which really can help do away with those global fields. It's just that if you're working on somebody's machine and you don't have a copy of FMPA with you, you may be stuck unless you use globals.

Anyway, what we've done in script 6.5 is tell the variable to start with "Inv," then use the invoice number and put ".pdf" at the end. Then all that stuff becomes the file name as it hits your desktop. You could even include the customer name in the file name. You might have to limit the number of letters allowed if the customer name makes the file name longer than your computer allows. Having a file name that is too long can cause errors in your script.

To make this whole thing run strictly with PDFs, go back into script 10 and substitute script 6.5 for script 6. You could have a preferences area where you checked a box to choose between printing to paper or PDFs. Then the script would have an If statement that would switch between the two subscripts based on what was in the check box. One step further would be to set it to print one or the other based on specific customer preferences. Pretty flexible!

Match Found Set (Related Records)[8]

If you were strictly printing to paper, you could print all the invoices at once. By using the "Match found set" option in FMP8 and later in the Go to Related Record dialog, you can easily jump right from the invoices with a balance due to the line items for all those invoices. You would be able to do away with the looping script completely. The final script would look like this:

```
Script Name: 10.5 - Find & Print ALL This Month's Invoices
Perform Script ["7 - Find Invoices with Balance Due"] (Control)
Perform Script ["9 - Figure Interest on Found Set"]
Go to Related Record [Show only related records; Match found set; From
    table: "inv_ILI__InvNum"; Using layout: "ILI_InvoicePrint" (ILI)]
    (Navigation)
Sort Records [Restore; No dialog]
#Sort by InvoiceNum_fk (from current base table ILI)
Print Setup [Restore; No dialog] (File)
Print [Restore; No dialog]
Go to Layout ["INV_Invoice" (INV)]
```

Keep in mind that printing all invoices at once won't work when printing to PDF. You would end up with one long document showing every invoice for all clients. You probably wouldn't want to send that out to everybody. You'll still have to loop through each invoice to print PDFs.

Debugging Scripts

Now that you know how to make the scripts, you'll need to know how to fix them when they don't work properly. The very best tool for debugging is the one included in FileMaker Pro Advanced. Along with other features, you can watch your scripts run one step at a time, stop them when you need to, and skip parts manually. If you don't have FMPA, continue reading this section for other methods you can use.

I already gave you a very important debugging tool when I showed you how to exit the loop using the Control key.

Try your scripts under different conditions with different data. Notice the "special situations" data I gave you in the "Testing Monthly Billing" section earlier in this chapter. We have an invoice that's overdue and another with a zero balance, as well as normal invoices with a balance due. That way you have at least one of every combination of data to test for. Keep asking yourself, "What if the user does this..." and then try out those "what ifs" until the script works under all the conditions you can dream up. We never mentioned that an invoice might have a negative balance!

If those tests show there is a problem and you can't spot it, you need to break down the script to find out where it's failing. The way to do that is to run short sections of the script until you find the problem. Simply put a Halt Script step below the section you want to test. Once that section checks out, move the Halt Script step farther down until you've worked out all the kinks.

In some cases, you'll need to preview some data that the script is entering, and then let it continue the rest of the steps. For those times, the Pause Script step is more appropriate.

And finally, there are times when you'll want to debug by temporarily bypassing a section of script entirely. For that, I use an If statement that can't be met, and place it around the steps I want to deactivate. For example:

```
If [1=2]
   [Steps I want to temporarily deactivate go between the If and End If]
   Find (temporarily disabled)
   Print (temporarily disabled)
End If
```

Just don't forget to remove the extra Pause and Halt steps or deactivate the special If steps when you're done testing. That sounds like a given, but you'd be surprised. When you have a bunch of scripts linked together, it's easy to miss one.

⌘ **TIP** If you want to view the details of your script without clicking every Find, Sort, and Print step, here's a great tip: When you print a script, FileMaker prints all the Find and Sort criteria. Choose Scripts, Manage Scripts, and select the script or scripts you want to print. Then click the Print icon in the Manage Scripts window. To select all the scripts for printing, press Ctrl+A (Windows) or Command+A (Macintosh).

Important Hints

- The Commit Records/Requests step from the Records category should often be the last step in a script so that the cursor is out of all fields and any calculations can update. It just depends on what the script does. (This step used to be called Exit Record/Request.) This step has two options: "Skip data entry validation" and "Perform without dialog." Since you can now have FileMaker ask users if they want to save the changes they've made to a record as they exit it, you would probably want to use the "Perform without dialog" option.
- There is a step called Open Record/Request under the Records category. You might think of it as making the record open for business. It actually locks the record from data entry by anybody else who might be sharing the file without requiring the user to put the cursor into a field. But you need to be careful with this step because it's possible to leave a record without releasing the lock by using the Window, New Window command

or New Window script step. You would be well advised to follow it somewhere in the script with the Commit Records/Requests step. Now, is this something horrible? Not terribly so. Whenever someone is editing a record in a table, other users can't change that record (although they can view it and even enter the fields). It's just that starting with FMP7, any user can lock more than one record at a time. If someone locks one or more records and then goes to lunch… Well, I guess it depends on the situation, doesn't it? Users are notified if a record is locked and the dialog allows them to send a message to the person who has it locked. But again, if they're at lunch (or worse yet, gone home for the day), it doesn't do much good. It really could cause problems if you run a process that alters a group of records that includes the locked record(s). You might end up with data that has not been properly updated.

- You can also lock all the child records in a portal by being in the parent record. Interestingly, if you go to the table where the child records live, you can make changes to any of the related records there except any that are being edited back in the parent record — either by yourself or another user. (A record can also be locked with the Open Record/Request script step.)
- Starting with FMP7, you can have multiple windows open. If you've made changes to a record and have a script that calls for a new window without using the Commit Records/Requests step, you could run into problems. If the new window uses the same table as the previous window, the data will not be updated. (The same would apply to a different table that might have a portal that uses records from the original table.) Not only that, but if you try to make changes to the same record as in the previous window, you'll find the record is locked. That could certainly be confusing for users. The answer is to use the Commit Records/Requests script step as part of your script.

NOTE For users of versions of FileMaker previous to 7, the Set Field step also requires a Commit Records/Requests step — even though your cursor has not officially been active in any fields. Some developers also used the Go to Field step without declaring a field as a method of exiting or committing the record. That will no longer work either.

- When using the steps from the Editing and Fields categories that have to do with entering data (which is nearly all of them), pay attention to the Options area. Choosing the Select option causes the new data to replace the existing data. Unchecking the box simply adds to the data that's already in the field.
- A very common mistake is to have a script enter Find mode, enter some data into one or more request forms, and then forget to follow it up with the Perform Find step. I've done this myself in front of a client who was able to spot the problem immediately. Ouch! Even then, to make it work correctly, be sure you uncheck the box next to Restore.

- And finally, sometimes unstored values such as calculations that use related data don't update properly on the screen to reflect the actual values. You may get the correct results by using Go to Layout mode, followed by Go to Browse mode as the last two steps in your script.

Import Scripts

Once you get going with FileMaker, you'll begin to realize that you use many of the same scripts over and over in many different files. Until version 5.0, when the Import Script feature was added, you had to recreate each new script by starting all over from scratch. This feature can be a real time-saver.

1. Open the Contact Management file, choose **Manage Scripts**, and click the **Import** button. (It's the button second from the right at the bottom of the window.)
2. Find and double-click the **Business** file from the Files window.
3. In the Import Scripts window, click the check boxes to the left of the **6 - Print One Invoice** and **1 - Main Menu (Halt)** scripts, then click **OK**.
4. You will get a warning that errors were detected, but just click **OK**.

   Even when scripts import successfully, you need to check all steps that include variables such as subscripts, finds, and sorts. (For users pre-FMP7, the word "imported" is no longer appended to imported scripts.)
5. Double-click the **1 - Main Menu (Halt)** imported script. Because the script doesn't recognize the layouts in this file, this would be considered an error, but it's certainly something that's easy to fix. Imagine importing a long, complicated script, and only having to fix one or two steps! Heavenly!
6. Click **Cancel**, and double-click the **6 - Print One Invoice** imported script. Before you'd make this a permanent addition to your file, you'd want to check all the variables like Sort and Page Setup (Macintosh) or Print Setup (Windows), but it sure beats creating all these steps manually.
7. Before you leave here, delete both of these scripts.

Version 5.0 of FileMaker was quite fussy about imported scripts. Starting with version 5.5, FileMaker no longer requires that the capitalization match in field or relationship names. Also regarding relationships, the key fields are not compared as long as the field names and types are the same. The main point is to make sure you have table occurrences, the relationships between them, and fields with matching names in both files. As always, there is more information in the Help files. Search the Index tab for "importing scripts."

Another related feature is that starting in FMP9 you can highlight a script in the script list and copy and paste it to another location — either into the same file or a different file, effectively eliminating the need to import. More on that near the end of this chapter under the heading "Copy and Paste Scripts."

Button Options (Pause, Halt, Exit, Resume)

Back in your Business file, go to the INV_Invoice layout in Layout mode, and double-click the Main Menu button.

In the Options area, click on the drop-down (see Figure 14-7) under the words Current Script (which are hidden by the drop-down in the figure). Your choices here determine what will happen to any other scripts that may be running when you click the button in Browse mode. Most of the time the Pause default will be just fine, but in certain circumstances, that may not be enough. For example, if some other script just brought a user to a special layout that puts him or her in Find mode and pauses, you'll probably want to use the Halt or Exit option for your Cancel button. If the Cancel button just takes users back to the data entry layout, they'll still be in Find mode. You may not need these button options often, but when you do, this is the only place to find them. You can also check the box next to "Change to hand cursor over button" to make the pointer turn into a hand whenever it's over the button in Browse and Find modes.

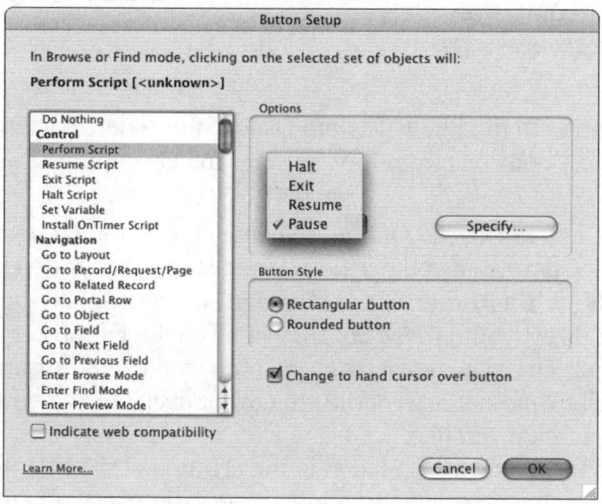

Figure 14-7
The Button Setup window showing the pop-up that determines what happens to the current script when clicking this button.

Startup/Shutdown Scripts

In Browse mode, choose File, File Options. There's just not enough space in this book to go into detail, but notice the two sections titled "When opening this file" and "When closing this file." You can have FileMaker perform a script (including any internal or external subscripts) during either of those operations. This just offers you another level of control over what happens with your files. I use it to warn myself if I don't have enough money in my checkbook (which, of course, I keep in FileMaker). I'll leave it up to you to figure out other situations in which you might use it.

A script set to run with document preferences will not run when a file opens hidden or minimized. To make sure that scripts do run in all related files of a solution, you'll have to add a script that runs when you open the main file. That script will run the external scripts you intended to run from the Preferences window when those files opened.

Show Custom Dialog Script Step

You can create your own dialog boxes and windows. Like the Comment step, Show Custom Dialog is also found under the Miscellaneous heading at the bottom of the steps list.

To show you one way to use this feature, I created a simple script called "11 - Custom Dialog - New Customer."

```
Script Name: 11 - Custom Dialog - New Customer
Go to Layout ["CON_Contact" (CON)] (Navigation)
New Record/Request (Records)
Show Custom Dialog ["New Customer"; "Please provide the name of the New
   Customer"; CON::NameFirst; CON::NameLast]
If [Get (LastMessageChoice) = 2 ]
   Delete Record/Request [No dialog]
End If
```

Pay particular attention to the Show Custom Dialog step. There's a lot going on at this step that isn't obvious from the wording. You have to make several choices here.

1. At the "Show Custom Dialog" Options window, choose the **General** tab, then type **New Customer** in the Title box and **Please provide the name of the New Customer** in the Message box. Since this is just text, you can type it directly into these boxes; when you do, FileMaker will add quotation marks around your message. (You won't see the quotes until you switch to another area of the window or click OK. Or you can put them in yourself if you like.)

   If you need to include a calculation in the creation of the title or message or a field name, you could click on the Specify button to open the Specify Calculation window. A clever technique you could apply here would be to set up a special one-record table and a layout with fields that contain the text you want to use in these dialogs. Then they could actually be edited in Browse mode without needing to edit the script. If you select a field name from a table or a calculation, FileMaker will not add the quotation marks.
2. In the lower portion of this window are the boxes for the text that will appear on the buttons that show beneath your message in the message window. OK and Cancel are good choices for most uses.

NOTE The text entry boxes for the buttons are bigger than the text that will fit on the buttons. The boxes look like they can fit about 20 characters, but you can really fit only about 12 characters on any button. The results will be different on the Mac than on Windows. So if you're creating a solution that will be used on both platforms, you should try it out before giving it to your users.

3. Now, click on the **Input Fields** tab at the top of the screen.
4. Put a check in the **Show input field #1** box.
5. Click on **Specify** to the right of #1. This takes you to the Specify Field window. Select the **CON** table occurrence in the drop-down menu at the top and then select **NameFirst**.
6. Type **First name** in the box beside Label.
7. Put a check in the **Show input field #2** box, and open the Specify Field window. Select **CON TO**, choose **NameLast**, and type **Last Name** in the Label box.
8. Notice the check box for "Use password character (•)." Don't check it now, but keep it in mind if you want to add a degree of security to this window — if you were to use it for some login system, for example.
9. Click **OK** to finish up the script step. But be sure to put a check mark next to **Run script with full access privileges** in the Script Step Options area. That will allow users who don't have privileges to delete the newly created blank record if they back out of the process.

You can probably see pretty quickly how the choices I made in Figures 14-8 and 14-9 combine to create the custom dialog shown in Figure 14-10.

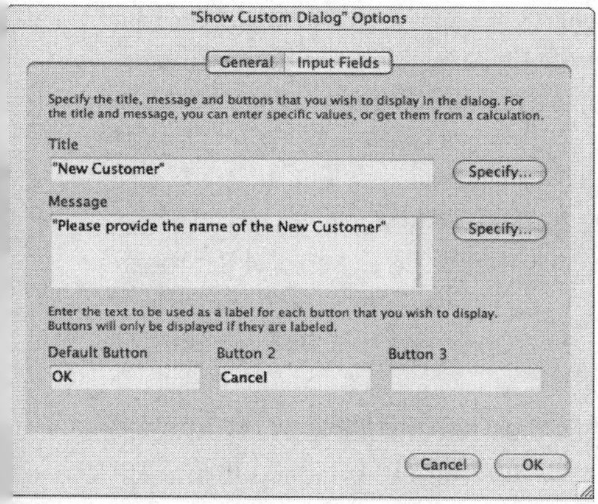

igure 14-8
he "Show Custom Dialog" Options window's General ıb.

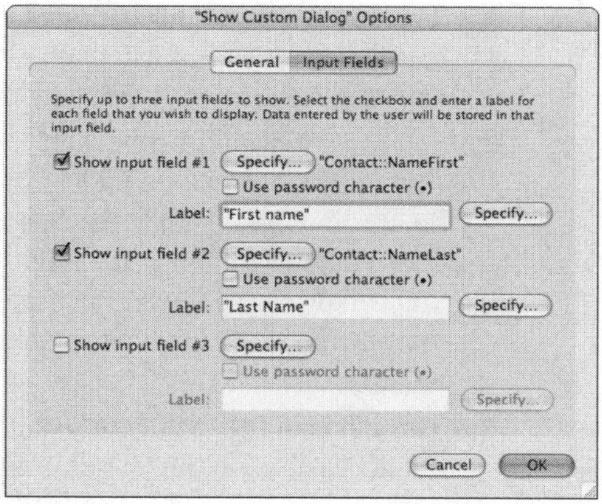

Figure 14-9
The "Show Custom Dialog" Options window's Input Fields tab.

Part 4

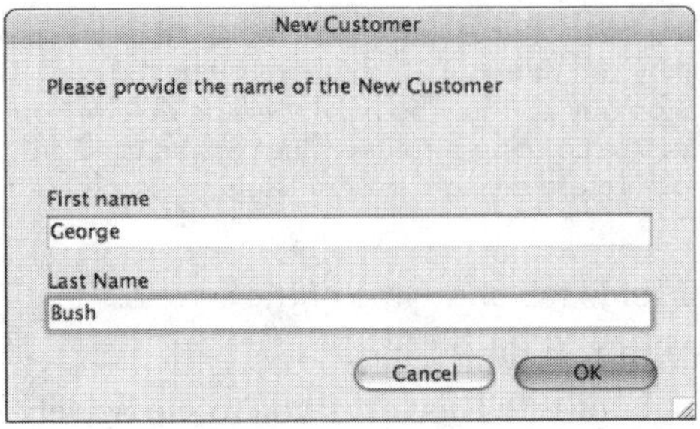

Figure 14-10
The custom dialog box the user sees.

There are a few things that might not be readily apparent about this script step:

- If the dialog appears when viewing an existing record, the data in the fields named in the Input Fields tab will only be displayed and changeable within the limits of the user's access privileges. That's why it's so important that you check the box next to "Run script with full access privileges" if you intend to have all users make the changes.
- If you intend to use fields in the dialog for data entry or change, data will only be affected when the user clicks the default button (the first button on the right). I often make the second button as the affirmative (OK or Do It) button so that users have to click it rather than simply hitting the Enter key. You will not get the results you expect if you do that with the custom dialog.
- If you intend to enter data from the dialog into a new record, you must create the record before displaying the custom dialog.
- The space allowed for the label name in the script step's dialog is a bit more generous than what will actually display when the dialog box appears to the user. It will only display about 50 characters.
- You can choose to display text that comes from a field for the window's title and message (see Figure 14-8) and label names (see Figure 14-9). To do so, you need to click the Specify button and use the Specify Calculation window to choose the fields that will provide the text. That means you can display different messages to different users based on text in various fields. Think how valuable that might be for a multi-language solution.
- The fields in the dialog bypass field validation and allow entry into fields not accessible on the layout in a manner similar to the Set Field script step.
- Because the Input Fields tab has the option to use the "•" password character, Show Custom Dialog can be used to create a custom login system. This will allow for a much simpler system than the various complex systems developers have had to create over the years. Yippee!

Set Field By Name[10]

Set Field By Name is a script step that developers have been wanting for a long time. The reason is, when you use its cousin, Set Field, you have to select the field where you want the data to go from the list of fields in a given table. That means you point to one field and one field only. When you want to point to other possible fields, you need to set up a script using as many If, Else, and Set Field steps as necessary. Using Set Field By Name, you get to determine the target field using the Calculation dialog, which leaves the specific field selection wide open. You'll find this step just under the Set Field step in the Fields category.

As an example, you might create a script or an auto-enter calculation that corrects data that is entered all in caps in the field with the cursor in it. Using Set Field, you would need something like the following script just to cover two fields:

```
If [Get (ActiveFieldName) = "Address"]
   Set Field [Proper (CON::Address)]
Else If [Get (ActiveFieldName) = "City"]
   Set Field [Proper (CON::City)]
End If
```

The script has to be very specific since you need to determine what field the cursor is in and then prepare every possible field in which you might want the change. (Notice that since the cursor is already in the field, the Set Field step doesn't need to name the target field — just the data that will go there.) However, if you were to substitute Set Field By Name, you could use the following single step:

```
Set Field By Name [Get (ActiveFieldTableName) & "::" & Get
(ActiveFieldName) ; Proper (Get (ActiveFieldContents))]
```

Since you don't name the field where the data is going or what data will go there, this script can be used over and over for any field in any table in any file. You could use the example I've given you in a looping script that goes from field to field in a record, as long as you give the script a way to stop itself. So, Set Field By Name is ultimately flexible. This is only an example of how it might be used. Don't get the idea that it can only be used if the cursor is in the field. That was just for illustration. By the way, Set Field By Name could be used to replace the Set Field step altogether. To name a specific target field as you would in Set Field, you have to put quotes around it in the first parameter like this:

```
Set Field By Name ["CON::City" ; "Chicago"]
```

NOTE You might be tempted (as I was) to use the GetFieldName (Self) combination, but it won't work in a script. As soon as you click OK in the Calculation dialog you'll see a dialog that says, "This function cannot be used in this expression." As mentioned in Chapter 13 (and you did memorize that, didn't you?), it works on calculations for tooltips, auto-enter calculations, conditional formatting, and field definitions. It isn't really meant to be used in a Calculation field formula or in scripts that use the calculation dialog. It seems kind of inconsistent because you see the Calculation dialog and think that means it's okay. But you need to know what context you're in when trying to use it.

Other Features

Even though we didn't use any of these next steps in any of our scripts, they are all very clever and powerful additions to the FileMaker arsenal.

New Window[7]

The New Window script step allows you to open a new window on a file. Look at the window shown in Figure 14-11. The options for New Window are very similar to those of Move/Resize Window in terms of input. When you tell it to open a new window without selecting a window name, the script automatically just duplicates the current window. (There is also a New Window menu item below the Window menu that provides a new window without the naming and size options.) The new window is given the name of the file and a number to represent the new window. For example: Business becomes Business - 2. It locates that window slightly offset from the position of the original and overlapping it. If you specify a name for the new window as part of your script, that name will appear at the top of the window regardless of the file name. If you also want to tell it to change to a specific layout or table, you would add the Go to Layout script step before the New Window step. That's important if the rest of your script will only operate on that specific table based on the fields, data, and relationships there.

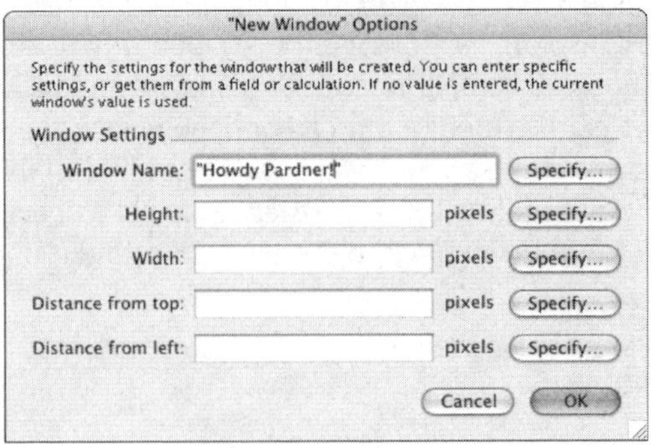

Figure 14-11
The "New Window" Options window.

Why would you want to use either the script step or the Window, New Window menu choice? How about these ideas:

- Perform a complicated find for a set of records and check a different set of records without losing the first group.
- You can have different sorts of the same group of records.
- You can work in Layout mode in one window, Browse mode in another, and Preview mode in yet another.
- Have a List view of a found set of customers, click on a customer name, and have a new window open on the right side of the monitor where you can see the detail view of the customer and either edit the record or make a call. When you're done, dismiss the detail window and go on to your next call in the list.
- Bring up a report in Preview mode where you cannot have any active buttons, and have a small, new window appear at the top or off to the side with active navigation buttons.
- Be working in the file and open a new window in order to answer a question from a customer without losing what you were working on.
- Have a group of records in one window and a subset of that group in another without ever losing the first group.

You can create as many windows as you like, and you're not limited to sticking with the same table in the file either. For instance, you could call the Go to Related Record script step and follow it with New Window. One limitation I spotted was that if you try to view the records using the View As menu choices, each occurrence of the layout will change to your selection.

Let's look at some of the settings in the "New Window" Options window.

You can type the name for the new window directly in the Window Name field, or you can click the Specify button and use a calculation, which could include any number of If, Else, or Then statements or values from various fields.

Then there are the four location fields, each with a Specify button of its own for precise positioning of the window on the monitor. The choices you have in New Window and Move/Resize Window can include field values as well as calculations. By the way, you can use any of the various Get (Window…) functions to set the current window size in a field for later reference from within the New Window script. It is now possible to position a window just about anywhere and any size you want. That includes an unusual option: By using negative values, you can make the window "appear" off the computer screen. I'm not sure why you might want to do that, but it can be done.

NOTE This "feature" that allows a window to be placed off the screen was apparently "broken" in FMP8.5 but returned in FMP9.

To test it out, I created a script that positioned the window off screen and added the script step Adjust Window [Hide]. That baby was gone and untouchable. So then I added a script with these steps:

```
Select Window [Name: "off screen"] (cause that's what I named it)
Adjust Window [Resize to Fit]
```

On a related note, using these script steps may make it difficult to place windows reliably across a computer that uses multiple monitors.

Here's an interesting oddity: If your script calls for a new window with a specific name and you run it multiple times, all the new windows will have the same name. It will not append the window with any numbers. That can make it a bit difficult to select the right one from the Window list. Use some caution in that you can have more than one window open with the same name. When you use the Select Window script step and choose a specific window name, FileMaker will operate on the frontmost window with that name. Or if no name is selected, it will operate on the frontmost window regardless of its name.

The Select Window step brings the named window (or the file in which the script is running if the option is set to Current Window) to the front. Users of previous versions of FileMaker need to know that Select Window now replaces the Refresh Window [Bring to Front] step. It is critical in many applications if a script depends on a specific table and window being frontmost.

All of the New Window functions are subject to the limitations of record locking. If you have not committed the record in a previous window that has a relationship to the new window, you will not be able to enter data in the new window. For the details, see the section titled "Important Hints" under "Debugging Scripts" earlier in this chapter.

Under the Window menu is an item called Show Window. Even if a window is hidden, it appears in this list unless the user's account prevents it.

CAUTION

- You can call a window to the front and not have it show in the Window list.
- You can have many hidden windows, and if one is the active window, watch out! Scripting actions can be performed on the hidden, active window.
- You can have multiple windows with the same name. It's up to you to make sure you have the one you want to operate on.
- It appears that in 8.5 on the Mac some part of the top and/or side of a hidden window may still show. If you have a solution that depends on the window being completely invisible, you need to be aware of this inconsistency. Again, this was "fixed" in FMP9.

Along with New Window, Manage Scripts now offers five other steps in the Window category: Select Window, Adjust Window, Move/Resize Window, Close Window, and Arrange All Windows. Most of them are pretty intuitive. But it's the Move/Resize Window step that offers the same depth that New Window has.

Script Parameters[7]

Script parameters were introduced in FileMaker Pro 7. Scripts now have a sort of temporary storage place. But I'd better back up just a little. What are parameters? One of the $2 definitions according to the *American Heritage Dictionary* is that a parameter is "A constant in an equation that varies in other equations of the same general form." We looked at parameters back in Chapter 12, "Real-World Calculations — Part 1." You'll find parameters whenever you use the various functions in the upper right of the Specify Calculation window wherever you see it. Think of the function Length (text). Remember the word(s) you have to replace inside the parentheses? In this case it would be the word "text." The stuff you replace the words with are the parameters. In our example, Length (text), you would normally replace the word "text" with the name of some field, like Length (NameFirst). In this case, the parameter is NameFirst. I usually think of it as a value because parameters are often numbers. But as you can see, somebody's name isn't really a number. So in the end, parameters can be text, numbers, or calculations.

Now that you know a little more about parameters, what are *script parameters* good for? As I said before, a script parameter is a temporary storage place. You can assign data or calculations to a script without the need to store it in a field. That's right, the entire Specify Calculation window is available to script parameters.

The big advantage is that you can develop generic scripts and have them perform different tasks based on the parameters assigned to them. Let me give you an example that might make sense. (The Help files could fill out your knowledge a little bit beyond what I can do here, although the examples given don't really demonstrate the modularity I think this tool is capable of.)

There are only two places you can assign a parameter to a script: 1) in the window you see when you create a button and assign a script to it, and 2) in the "Specify Script" Options window you see when you add any subscripts to a script. That means the "parent" script can't have any parameters assigned to it — unless it was triggered by a button that has been assigned a parameter. And that makes sense since the purpose is to give scripts the ability to be more multi-purpose. Otherwise, if you intend to assign a permanent value to a script, just dump the value in a global field and get the value from the field each time you need it. On the other hand, you can put global fields on a layout and watch what happens as the script executes. Script parameters are hidden from view — unless you push them into a field somewhere. In that case, why not stick with a global field to start with?

NOTE Remember that data entered into a global field only stays in place for each individual user. If you are the only user and the file is not being served by FMP Server, that is not a problem. If the file is being served by someone else or FMPS and you want to store a global value that every user will have access to, you need to have all users close the file and/or stop FMPS and open the file with the client version of FMP as the only user. Then any changes you make to any global fields will be available to all users. That awkward limitation is why you often see me recommend using a one-record table. Any changes you make there are instantly available to all users without interrupting everyone's workflow, not to mention that it's a lot less confusing.

The best example of this modular approach I've heard so far was discussed at the 2003 FileMaker Developer Conference in Phoenix. This is based on a filtered portal trick some of us developers have been using for quite a while now. By putting a letter into a global field and keying to the first letter of people's last names, you can filter the portal to only display last names that begin with a specific letter of the alphabet. Here's how:

1. In the Contact table create two fields:

Field Name	*Type*	*Options*
FirstLetter	Calculation	= Left(NameLast; 1) [Be sure the calc result is Text!]
zi_Filter_gt	Text	Global

2. Add a new TO based on the Contact table and call it **con_CON__Filter**. Create a relationship between two occurrences of the Contact table where zi_Filter_gt (in CON) = FirstLetter (in con_CON__Filter).
3. Create a portal on the CON_Contact layout using the relationship and just put the NameFirst and NameLast fields in it.
4. Put the zi_Filter_gt field on the layout and type a letter in it. If you have anyone with a last name that starts with that letter in your file, you'll see their name in the list. Now try a different letter.
5. Then you put 26 buttons on the layout, one for every letter of the alphabet. Each button is attached to one script whose single step is Set Field [zi_Filter_gt; "A"] — or whatever letter you'll be using.

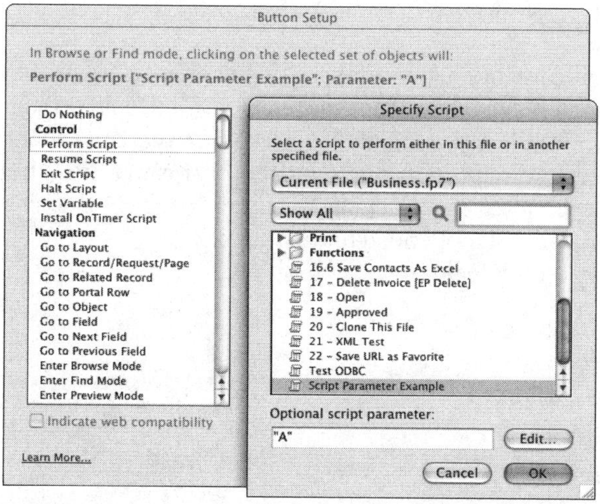

Figure 14-12
The "Specify Script" Options window seen from Button Setup showing the parameter defined as the letter A.

That, of course, requires 26 scripts, which is a lot of overhead. But now that we have script parameters, all 26 buttons can call one script. Each button has the script parameter that represents the letter on the button. So the A button's parameter would be "A," as in Figure 14-12, and the script would read:

```
Script Name: 11.5 - Filter Portal
Set Field [zi_Filter_gt; Get (ScriptParameter)]
```

You still need to make 26 buttons, but you only need one script. Not bad!

Although this method is a good example of how to use script parameters, starting with FMP10 you can accomplish something similar without all the buttons using script triggers, which we'll discuss in Chapter 16, "Working with Script Triggers." On the other hand, a button interface can be very intuitive for users.

The other half of this whole script parameter feature is the Get (ScriptParameter) script step. It really goes hand in hand with specifying a script parameter. If you just specify the parameter without doing anything with it, there really isn't much point, is there?

You can also specify a bunch of data as a parameter and parse it out as needed. I don't want to go into a full-fledged example with regard to a script parameter. But it's sitting out there if you're up to the task.

NOTE *Parsing*, as far as developers use the term, means using a calculation to separate the specific data you need. A simple example would be if you inherited data where people's first and last names were in one field. Using a calculation, you would look for the space between the names as the delimiter to parse the data into two separate fields.

Accounts Script Category[7]

The Accounts script category allows for scripting user accounts without the need to use the Manage Accounts & Privileges area. You could arrange it so that some users who normally wouldn't have access to that area could still set up, enable, and delete accounts. Of course most of that won't mean much to you until you get to Chapter 22, "Keeping Your Data Secure." But since we're talking about scripts here, I feel I need to mention it.

The Accounts category includes:

- Add Account
- Delete Account
- Reset Account Password
- Change Password
- Enable Account
- Re-Login

You can have your users place text in the dialogs these scripts generate or grab data from fields. That also means you can combine it with the Show Custom Dialog script step, which will populate database fields with text from the custom dialog, and then have a script perform the work of any of the other steps in this category. Very powerful! A developer's dream.

External Data Sources[9]

When you added the Inventory file to make this a multi-file database solution, FileMaker did some work for you in the background. Choose File, Manage, External Data Sources. (For readers familiar with versions of FMP7 up until FMP9, that used to be called Define, File References.) You'll see a list of files needed to run your solution. Right now it probably only shows the Inventory file. Every version of FileMaker has always kept track of files for a solution, but they have been hidden from view in versions previous to 7. Having it all available now can be somewhat confusing. In previous versions, the closest we came to this was in the Manage Relationships window, which listed files in the right column. When converting solutions, you may see references that appear to have no use. It's probably best to just leave them alone. Otherwise, you would need to go through your entire solution and double-check every script to make sure it uses the table you intend it to before deleting the reference. When you delete a data source, you do not get a warning that it may be used in a script. My attitude is "If it ain't broke, don't fix it."

There is a lot more detail to external data sources. We'll look at this more in depth when we get to Chapter 26, "Working with External Data Sources."

Script Organization Features[9]

FileMaker 9 introduced a set of script organization features that developers had been asking for since as far back as I can remember. This is the logical place to show them off — and for you to start using them!

First of all, starting in FileMaker 9, Manage Scripts is "non-modal." That means that Manage Scripts is just another window that you can work in and push to the side, allowing you to go back and work in your file. Previously you couldn't work in Browse mode while you worked in Manage Scripts. This change allows for a lot of flexibility, but it can also cause some problems and confusion.

For instance, if you're working on a script and minimize the Edit Script and Manage Scripts windows, you might forget you're partway through the job. If you try to close the file, you'll get a warning that you have one or more unsaved scripts open, as shown in Figure 14-13. Decide if you want to Save All (keep all changes you made — *if* you can remember what you were doing), Revert All (delete all changes you made), or Cancel (don't do anything). If you choose Cancel (my favorite), you can find your scripts by going to the Window menu. (The other two choices close the file, any open scripts, and the Manage Scripts window.) Yes, old-timers, Manage Scripts and any open scripts now appear as windows just as if they were files. A little different, but not at all inconvenient.

If you're happy with the changes you've made to a script, you can simply press Command+S (Macintosh) or Ctrl+S (Windows) to save your changes. If you've made changes (and haven't already saved them), you can click the Close icon in the Edit Script window and you'll be asked if you want to Save, Cancel, or Don't Save the changes. Cancel puts you right back in the script. Don't Save allows you to discard the changes — you know, in case you really goofed up.

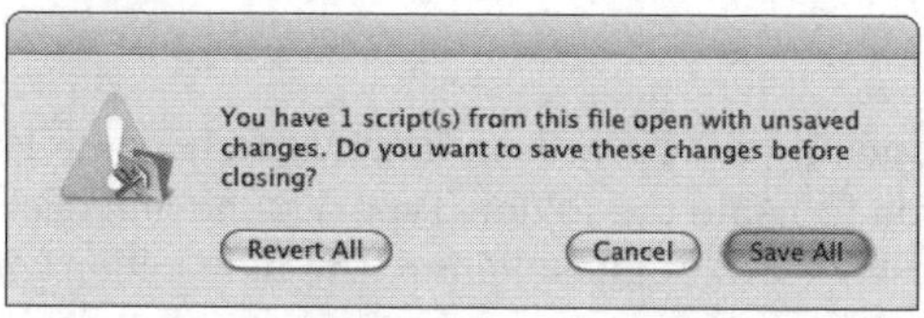

Figure 14-13
The dialog you see when closing a file that has unsaved scripts.

Go into Manage Scripts and let's take a look at some of the features. Figure 14-14 shows the meaning of the unlabeled icons. It's easy enough to find out what the icons mean because hovering your pointer over any of them reveals a tooltip. You can press Command+N (Macintosh) or Ctrl+N (Windows) to start a new script, or click the New button of course. If you click the reveal triangle to the right of the New button, you'll get the drop-down shown in Figure 14-14, giving you access to Folder and Separator as well as Empty Script and Default Script. The Default Script option provides you with a basic four-step script that puts you in Browse mode and remembers your current layout, find (which is the same as the most Recent Find), and sort status. It's a nice starter for beginners. In days of old, every new script in FileMaker had a basic set of steps, but many developers complained and said they just deleted them and started from scratch. Later, others complained that they missed the starter steps. Now everybody can be happy having it whichever way they want. I guess you can please everybody.

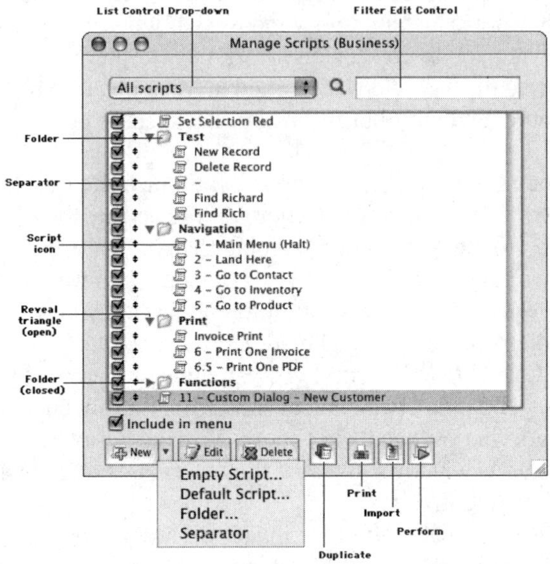

Figure 14-14
The Manage Scripts window showing the meaning of the icons and the New drop-down.

To edit a script you can click the Edit button or you can simply double-click the script name. Notice the little scroll icon to the left of the script name indicating that it's a script (as opposed to a group, which looks like a folder with its name displayed in bold text).

Script Folders[9]

You can create a folder by opening the New drop-down and choosing Folder. You'll see a dialog asking you to name the folder. Type a name and click OK. If you have any scripts and/or folders already selected, the new folder will appear after the last selected item. If nothing is selected, it will appear at the end of the scripts list.

On the Macintosh, when a new folder appears, its reveal triangle is pointing down, as you can see in Figure 14-14 next to the Test, Navigation, and Print folders. On Windows, you'll see a minus inside a square. This indicates that the folder is "open" and ready for you to put scripts or other folders inside it. You can click the triangle (or minus) to toggle it closed. The only time you can put items into a folder is when the folder is open.

It's very easy to move items into and out of a folder. Just click and drag the double arrow to the left of the script name until you reach the folder. If you drag the item down toward the folder from above and nudge the folder, the item will pop below the folder and to the right, indicating that it's now in the folder. If you drag up from below, nudging the folder causes the item to move over to the right. If there are already other items in the folder, the item (script or folder) will slide to the right as it approaches the last item in the folder. If your goal is to move past the folder, just keep going until you drag above the folder icon. There is a subtlety to dragging to get a script to be all the way to the left between two folders, but you'll find you can get the hang of it in just a couple of minutes. Once you've started dragging an item, you can control its horizontal indentation by moving your mouse left or right. Just how this works depends on where you are in the list.

If you only want to move an item a few places, you can select it and press Command+up arrow or down arrow (Macintosh) or Ctrl+up arrow or down arrow (Windows). You can also use these key combinations to precisely move a script (or folder) out of a folder and all the way to the left so it becomes a primary item. If it's the first item in a folder and you move it up one click, it will become a "primary" without moving into the folder above it. If it's the last item in a folder and you move it down one click, it will become a "primary" without moving into the folder below it.

Speaking of key combinations, you can open and close folders on the Macintosh by selecting the folder and then pressing the left and right arrow keys on the keyboard. On Windows, use the plus and minus keys. (In case you didn't know it, those same key presses work to expand and collapse folders on the Mac Finder and Windows Explorer.)

Another very nice feature is that you can move multiple items (either scripts or folders) at the same time whether they're adjacent in the list or not. Just make your selections and drag on the double arrow next to any of the selected items. If the items were discontinuous, they will now be grouped one after the other.

I've already hinted that you can have folders within folders. I don't know the limit to how many levels you can go. But when you're working in Browse mode it gets awkward clicking in the Scripts menu when sub-folders keep jumping out on opposite sides. The idea is to be organized, so keep your folders only one or two levels deep if they'll be available in the Scripts menu.

You may have noticed the Separator option from the New drop-down. A separator is simply a script with no steps defined. After you've added a separator, you can double-click it and see that it's named with a dash, just as it appears in the list.

If you look at Figure 14-14, you'll see how I've organized our scripts into folders. Look at the separator (fifth from the top of the list). Now look at Figure 14-15 to see how this organization affects the Scripts menu back in Browse mode. Rather than one long list of scripts, you see the folder names with triangles indicating there's more inside. In the Test folder, you can see the result of the separator where it sits between Delete Record and Find Richard as a light gray line.

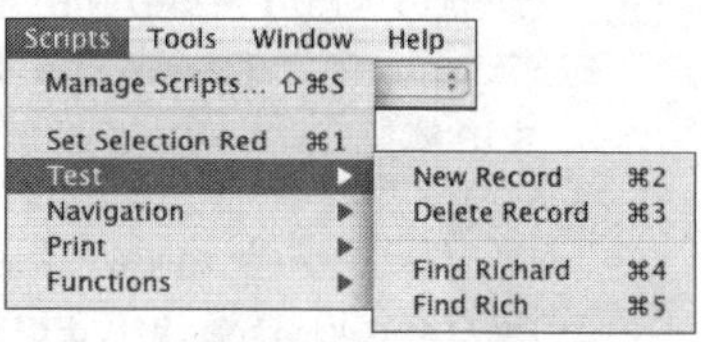

Figure 14-15
What the Scripts menu looks like once scripts have been organized in folders.

Part 4

Also notice that the scripts can be triggered by the function key combinations even though they're inside the folder.

Back in the Manage Scripts window, if you uncheck the box to the left of a folder so it doesn't show in the Scripts menu, all scripts inside it that are checked will now show in the scripts list as if they weren't even in a folder. You have to uncheck any script individually if you don't want it in the list. Regardless of how the folders are collapsed, they appear as folders in the scripts list.

Clicking the reveal triangle (or the minus on Windows) next to an unselected folder can cause the script list to jump in an unexpected way. For example, let's say you selected a script or folder near the top of the list. You scroll down the list and click one of the triangles (or minuses) next to a folder to close it. The dialog will close the folder and jump back in such a way as to display the upper script or folder and keep it selected. No harm done. But if you find that disconcerting you can first click on the folder name you want to toggle.

You're not allowed to delete a folder unless all of the contained scripts can be deleted without errors. An error would be caused if one of the scripts were being called from another script in the same file. That seems like a good, safe warning.

Filter Scripts[9]

You can easily find specific scripts using a couple of techniques. You can select a folder name using the drop-down at the top of the Manage Scripts window (which shows "All scripts" in Figure 14-14). Or you can type any word or character that appears in the script name into the Filter Edit Control box in the upper right. (By the way, the character or characters you type can be anywhere in any of the words in the script, not just at the beginning.) If you have selected one of the folder names from the drop-down, you'll only see items with matching text from that specific folder. To see all scripts filtered, you need to choose the "All scripts" option. Just think how quickly that will work with the script numbering system I've been teaching you.

One developer I know puts a greater than (>) character in the name of scripts he's working on. Then he uses the Filter Edit Control to get a list of all of them very quickly. When he's happy with one of them, he removes the character.

To see all scripts again (either within the folder or from the All Scripts folder), you need to clear the View List Control box. Also, in order to use the technique of typing the first few characters of the name of a script to jump to it in the scripts list, you must be clicked somewhere on a script name in the script list. Your cursor must not be in the View List Control box.

Here's a strange side effect to the View List Control: Let's say you have all the folders neatly closed. Now you use the View List Control to search for something. As soon as you clear out the box, all the folders are left open! How the heck do you close them all back up? Here are some undocumented keyboard commands to help you out. First, select all scripts by pressing Command+A (Macintosh) or Ctrl+A (Windows). (The A is for "All.") Now, on the Mac simply press the left arrow key. On a Windows machine, press the minus (-) key on the numeric keypad. To open the folders up again, select all and press the right arrow (Macintosh) or + key on the numeric keypad (Windows). These key commands actually work on any selected folders. So if you only want to open or close a few folders at a time, simply select them and use the commands.

Copy and Paste Scripts[9]

We've already covered the Import Scripts dialog. But there is another technique that you might find even more handy. Go to the file that contains the script or scripts that you want. Select the scripts you need, go to the Edit menu, and choose Copy (or use the keyboard shortcut). Go back to Manage Scripts in the file you're working in. Select a script in the list near where you want the copied scripts to go and choose Edit, Paste. Easy as that! You do need to be aware that the script(s) you paste may need some touch-up work. Things such as fields and table occurrences won't likely be in the file you brought them into. You won't get the same warning dialog about errors that you get when you import scripts. But other than that it does work very easily — especially now that you can have multiple script windows open at the same time (see below).

Copy and Paste Script Steps[9]

You can also copy and paste script steps between scripts or within the same script, either in the same file or between different files. Again, just highlight the step or steps you need and choose Edit, Copy. Highlight the location where you want them to go and choose Edit, Paste. If the steps you selected were not contiguous in the source script, they will be when they're pasted. But that only makes sense, doesn't it?

Multiple Script Windows[9]

Starting in FMP9, you can have multiple script windows open simultaneously. That means you can set two or more scripts right next to each other and see how they're different. You can also use the Edit menu to copy and paste steps between the windows. How about duplicating a script and making changes to it while looking at the old script or some other script entirely? And each window can be minimized while you go back and work in the file. That includes the Manage Scripts window itself. But it could be easy to forget that you have them open and minimized. To my way of thinking, I'd rather save that minimize feature for some extraordinary situation. (If you activate a script via a button or the Scripts menu, you'll be prompted to save or reject any changes.)

With all these windows open, you might want some keyboard shortcuts to help manage them. When you close a window after making changes, you're asked if you want to save the changes. If you want to bypass that dialog and save your changes, just press Command+S (Macintosh) or Ctrl+S (Windows). Instead of clicking the close window button, you can close any window by pressing Command+W (Macintosh) or Ctrl+W (Windows).

To save all changes and close all open scripts and Manage Scripts, press Command+Option+W (Macintosh) or Ctrl+Alt+W (Windows). You'll still see a dialog asking if you want to Save All, Revert All, or Cancel, but it can be a time-saver if you know what you want to do. (If you'd rather click the close window button, you can hold down the Option or Alt key and achieve the same closing of all scripts and the Manage Scripts window.)

FMP Advanced Features[9]

There is one other change to Manage Scripts starting with FMP9 that's only available to users of FileMaker Pro Advanced. Now multiple users can be in Manage Scripts at the same time editing different scripts. Developers who work in teams have been asking for this feature for years. The only limitations are that each user must be working with a copy of FileMaker Pro Advanced, and they cannot be editing the same script.

And Finally...

As a little last-minute cleanup, you might want to remove the portal from the Contact layout that displays all products a contact has ever ordered. You might also remove the portal that filters by last name, unless you really like it.

Summary

In this chapter, we looked at what scripts are, and how to plan and debug them. We looked at the various categories of script steps and created some scripts using steps from many of the categories. We also looked at how to import scripts from other files, how to use the Show Custom Dialog script step, and how to use some script steps introduced since FMP7. And finally, we looked at an array of features introduced in FMP9 and 10 — from external data sources to script organizing features.

There are so many wonderful things you can do with scripts. It's discouraging that I can't show you more, but the fact is, you'll learn the most by getting in there and trying to make it do what you need to have done. Then you'll be ready for more advanced books on the subject.

Q & A

Q I'm getting lost going back and forth between the files. How can I make it clearer?

A You might draw some boxes on the paper where you do your planning to represent the files. Put numbers in the boxes to indicate the order in which you want the subscripts to perform. Then put the same numbers next to the plain language descriptions of what you want to have happen. You could even draw arrows between the boxes showing the direction of the scripts. Refer to the drawing as you work on your scripts.

Q Let's say I made a script that runs a script in another file. What if I want to change the remote script to a different remote script?

A Good question! When you're in the Edit Script window, select the perform script with the external script in it. Down by the OK button, you'll see the Specify button. When the "Specify Script" Options window appears, you can choose a different script. You can also choose a script from an entirely different file by clicking on the File drop-down.

Workshop

Go to all the other files in this solution and add the Main Menu script. Then add Main Menu buttons to every layout. To keep them consistent, copy the first one you made so they'll all look the same. Just remember to attach it to the proper script once you take it to the new file.

In the "Printing One Invoice" section, I talked about some extra protective steps that could be added to that script. Figure out what the script should be, create it, and add the suggested steps.

Try organizing your scripts into folders. Use Figure 14-14 as a guide.

Chapter 15

Making Sense of Your Information with Layouts

Introduction

How your information is organized on the screen is an extremely important element of how useful it is to you. Remember back in Chapter 5 when you saw how awkward it was to enter data when the tab order was not set up logically? Imagine what data entry would be like if the NameFirst field were in the upper left of the screen and the NameLast field were in the lower right. This is certainly an extreme example, but sometimes in our haste to get all the fields onto a page, it's easy to forget how it will look to the end user. I had one client who hired me specifically to redesign their invoices and it took more than a couple hours to do it right.

In Chapter 17, "Designing Your Screen Layouts," we'll spend some time learning how to make layouts look good and flow logically for the user. In this chapter, I'll take you on an overview of layouts. We'll look at:

- Layout types, both for data entry and printing
- The various layout parts and their uses
- How to work with layout parts

What Is a Layout?

Having already placed fields and objects on a few layouts, you probably have a pretty good idea of what a layout is. The term *layout* is a carryover from the printing industry. Before a newspaper, magazine, or book went to press, the designers and editors would lay out all the picture and text elements on a flat surface, and move them around until they were satisfied with the appearance. Those tasks and the jargon have now moved over to the computer. When you think about it, it really makes sense to use the same term in FileMaker. We get to move all the elements of our file around until it looks just right, and in the end, we're often going to print the results.

The data in your file is actually separate from the field layout objects that display the data. For instance, in a price field, the number $9.99 is the same whether you choose to format the field in 48-point red type without the dollar sign, or 9-point black type with a dollar sign. Of course, if you don't place a field on the layout, you won't be able to see the data in it.

Layout Types

Thus far when dealing with layout appearance, we've spent most of the time looking at data entry. Data entry layouts will often look quite different from the layouts you create for printing purposes. When you run long reports and print invoices for customers, you don't want all those colored backgrounds. You can use up ink very quickly trying to make it look pretty. If you're using black and white laser printers, all the colors just come out as shades of gray — sometimes unpredictably. On color laser printers, printing out a lot of colorful layouts can get very expensive. On the other hand, you need to provide adequate lines and shading to separate sections and make the report readable. And maybe you do want to provide a logo in color.

On-screen Layouts (Data Entry)

For data entry purposes, you want to use colors or shades of gray as well as graphic objects to help group similar items together. When users go to the layout to enter or find data, they shouldn't have to search too far. If you do your job well, you can help direct their eyes to the right data.

It's also important not to get too carried away with colors. Backgrounds and fields with extremely bright colors can make your eyes tired after a short time. You also need to be careful that there is reasonable contrast between the color of the font and the background color of the field. Black text on white or light-colored paper is considered the easiest to read, but some human interface studies compare reading black text on a white computer monitor to reading the words from the surface of a 75-watt bulb while it's turned on. You may want to temper your layouts away from black and white somewhat, but unless you're creating a database for a circus, take it easy with mixing in too many colors.

Look at the templates and the layouts created by the Layout Assistant for some hints. As time goes on, you'll notice other people's work and get ideas from that. A while ago I saw an amazing set of layouts designed for a database that's used by a number of companies in the fashion industry. It was strongly influenced by a science fiction TV series. The futuristic look made sense for trying to appeal to people in that forward-looking industry. Even at that, it was tastefully done, intuitive to negotiate, and easy to work in for hours on end.

Standard Form

We had a quick brush with the Standard form layout in Chapter 9. Before the introduction of the Layout Assistant in 5.0, when you chose the Standard form you got a copy of every field in the file. (There was only one table per file back then.) In a file with 100 or more fields, that was awkward, to say the least. Now you can choose the fields you want from the field list, and even include fields from related tables or files. If you do want all the fields in a particular table, you can get them with the click of a button — and that includes multiple copies of the same field. This is a much better arrangement. Let's take a look.

1. Go to Layout mode.
2. Choose **Layouts, New Layout/Report**.
3. Choose **INV** from the "Show records from" drop-down and **Standard form** from the Layout type, then click the **Next** button.
4. Notice the order of the fields in the list on the left. In my file, they appeared in the order given in Figure 15-1a.

```
InvoiceNum_pk
ContactSerNum_fk
Date
InvoiceTotal
z_NameFirst_lu
z_NameLast_lu
z_AddrCompany_lu
z_AddrStreet_lu
Z_AddrState_lu
z_AddrZip_lu
z_AddrPlusFour_lu
zi_Colors_gr
Color_l
```

```
Color
ContactSerNum_fk
Date
InvoiceNum_pk
InvoiceTotal
z_NameFirst_lu
z_NameLast_lu
z_AddrCompany_lu
z_AddrStreet_lu
Z_AddrState_lu
z_AddrZip_lu
z_AddrPlusFour_lu
zi_Colors_gr
```

Figures 15-1a and b
The list of fields in the Invoice table. The order in which they appear in the Layout Assistant is affected by the choices you make for field order in the Manage Fields window.

5. Click the **Cancel** button and choose **Manage Database, Fields.** In the upper-right corner, choose **View by Field Name** from the drop-down.
6. Click **OK**, and start a new layout, **INV_Standard**, until you get to the Specify Fields window again. The order of the fields has changed so it matches Figure 15-1b. In our file, that's really no big deal, but when you have a file with lots of fields, trying to move the ones you want into the Layout fields list on the right can be a mind bender. Depending on your situation, you may prefer to have them in creation order so the newer fields are at the bottom of the list. At other times, having them appear alphabetically is the best choice.
7. Of course, you can selectively move fields in and out of the Layout fields list, and even reorder them any way you like. While you're here, move the following fields into the list, and include the fields from the INV and inv_CON__ConSerNum tables. Maneuver them up and down in the order until your list looks like this:

    Date
    InvoiceNum_pk
    InvoiceTotal
    ContactSerNum_fk
    inv_CON__ConSerNum::Company
    inv_CON__ConSerNum::NameFirst
    inv_CON__ConSerNum::NameLast

    Before you leave here, notice that this dialog doesn't open up wide enough to see the full field names. That's one of the reasons we use abbreviations as much as possible.
8. Click the **Next** and **Finish** buttons. When you're done, your layout should look similar to the one in Figure 15-2.

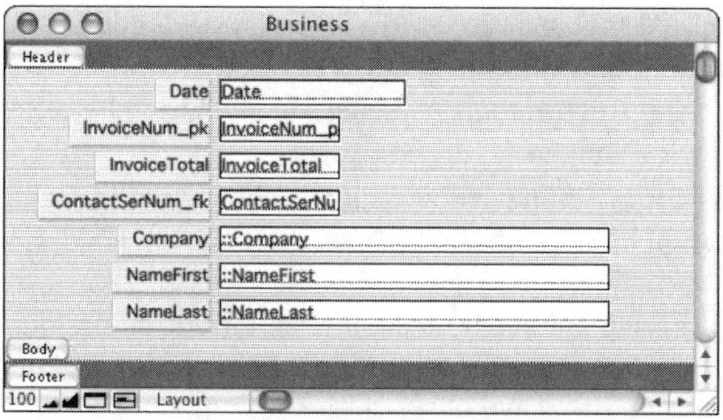

Figure 15-2
Layout mode showing the placement of specific fields when using the Standard layout from the Layout Assistant.

Notice the different widths of the fields. That's because FileMaker uses default sizes for different types of fields.

> **TIP** When the fields are all crowded together in the area you want to work in, it can get a little claustrophobic. You may find it easier to grab the Body tab and expand it downward a few inches. Then choose Edit, Select All, and move the fields and their labels down the layout a few inches. Now you've got room to work.

Since we already have an Invoice layout, let's just delete this layout and move on.

List/Report vs. Table View

In Chapter 9, we created a List/Report using the ILI table occurrence that will be the printed invoice. There are other reasons you might want to make a list. For example, View as Table can be handy for many uses, but it has its limits, too.

1. Go to the Invoice table.
2. Get to Layout mode, and start a new layout. Name it **INV_InvoiceList**.
3. Select **List/Report**, and click **Next**. Click **Next** again.
4. In the Specify Fields window, choose the following fields:
   Date
   InvoiceNum_pk
   InvoiceTotal
   ContactSerNum_fk
   inv_CON__ConSerNum::Company
   inv_CON__ConSerNum::NameFirst
   inv_CON__ConSerNum::NameLast
5. Click **Next** as many times as you need to until you see the Finish button, then go ahead and click **Finish**. When you get back to Browse mode, the layout should look a lot like the Table view. The big difference is what you can do with the body section of the layout.
6. Go to Layout mode, choose **Edit**, **Select All**, and move all the layout objects to the right so you have about an inch on the left.

7. Select the **Text** tool and type @@ close to the left edge of the layout. (@@ displays the record number.)
8. Now select the **Button** tool and make a small button between the @@ and the InvoiceNum field.
9. When the Button Setup window appears, choose **Go to Layout** under the Navigation heading. In the Options area, specify **INV_Invoice** from the drop-down, then click **OK.**
10. When you're back in Layout mode, the cursor will be flashing on the new button. Type **-->** to make an arrow. If the font size is too large, choose a smaller one. You may have to resize the button, too.
11. Go to Browse mode. Now you can see the record numbers, and clicking on the arrow button will take you to the invoice detail. I think it's much more intuitive than the button we placed at the top of our Table layout in Invoice. Jump ahead to Figure 15-6 to see what it looks like.

TIP You may have already run into the warning in Figure 15-3. You'll see it most often when changing the size of text and placing a portal on a layout. The main reason for choosing the No button in this dialog box is that you may have spent hours carefully tweaking a layout only to have it explode from an accident with a layout object. If that won't be a problem, just click Yes.

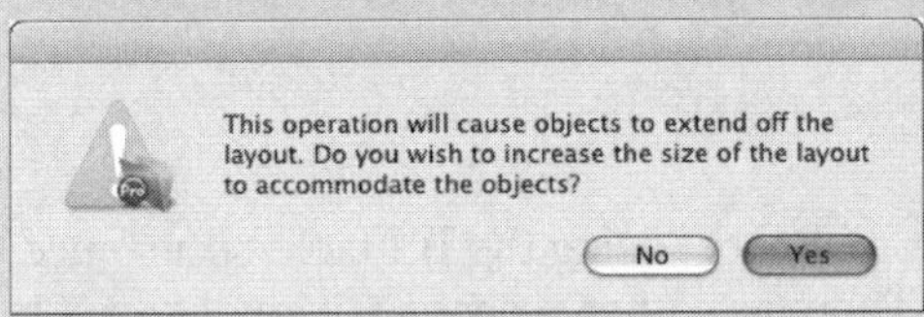

Figure 15-3
The warning dialog box that appears when the position of a layout object might cause the layout to change size.

12. If you're not on one of the INV_Invoice or CON_Contact layouts, go there now. Make a new button near the top of the layout that will take you to the INV_InvoiceList layout, and type **List** on it. Now you can switch back and forth. You might add another button at the top of the List layout that will show all records. You could sort the records by the inv_CON__ConSerNum::Company field, create a script that contains the sort, and make a button for that, too. Now you can see one of the advantages of Table view — you can sort the records just by clicking the column titles, as long as that feature is turned on. But then any buttons you placed in the body area won't show up. Before you leave here, format the numbers and the fields that represent money so they align to the right. Then change the text on the field labels. At this point, the changes you make are up to your taste. You will probably want to protect the fields from accidental entry. When you're done, your layout should look something like Figure 15-4.

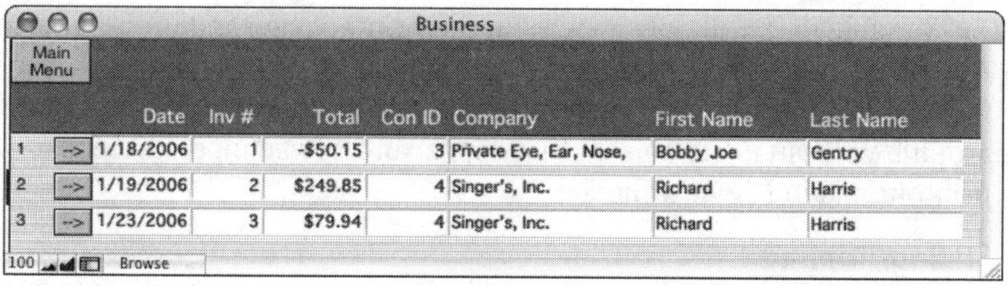

Figure 15-4
Browse mode showing the placement of the fields once they've been moved into more useful positions.

If you really want to take advantage of the capabilities of both Table and List views, try the following:

1. Make sure List view is set up to include a header part (Layouts, Layout Setup, Views, Properties tab).
2. Then place a button in the header section.
3. When the Button Setup window appears, choose **View As** under the Windows heading.
4. In the Options section, choose **Cycle** from the Specify drop-down, click **OK**, and name the button **View**. By clicking the button back in Browse mode, you should be able to switch to Table view to take advantage of sorting field labels, then go to List view to use the buttons in the body.

You can set FMP to show a dialog when leaving a record where data was added or changed. (Leaving or "committing" a record consists of clicking out of all fields, hitting the Enter key, or changing layouts or modes. You do not leave a record when you change windows.) You can turn this feature on or off on a layout-by-layout basis. When you're in Layout mode, choose Layout Setup, click the General tab, and you'll see a check box next to "Save record changes automatically." If that is unchecked, it will bug you each time you change any data and commit the record.

There is also a feature in Layout Setup called "Show field frames when record is active." Field frames are the little dotted lines that appear around the fields that will accept data when the cursor is in one of the fields in a record. FMP has always done that. But now you can choose whether or not to display field frames. The frames are helpful if you have fields without borders, but I can imagine special layouts that might benefit from this feature. This is controllable on a layout-by-layout basis, too.

Printed Layouts

The other thing that sets data entry layouts apart from printed reports is the way data is displayed. As I mentioned in Chapter 2, some elements do not appear when you're in Browse mode. You can see what the printed page will look like by choosing View, Preview mode.

Variable data will only appear on the printed page and in Preview mode. And even though sub-summaries now appear in Browse mode, they will not show at all in either mode unless the layout is sorted correctly. To turn that around, you can make objects that appear in Browse mode disappear on a printout and in Preview mode.

Sliding/Printing

Let's assume you want a quick printout of your invoices. Go to the INV_Table layout. Make sure you're viewing it as a Table, then go to Preview mode. This looks like a pretty straightforward way to print the list, but if you have extra field labels in the header or too much color, or if you made that View button, you won't want to print it as is.

Non-Printing Objects

Try this technique to keep items from printing:

1. Go into Layout mode, click the **Header** tab, and choose transparent (the two interlocking white squares) from the Fill pattern palette.
2. Do the same in the body and footer areas.
3. Now select all the field labels (**Shift+click**) and choose **Format, Set Sliding/Printing.**
4. In the lower-left corner of the Set Sliding/Printing window, check the box next to **Do not print the selected objects**, and click **OK**.

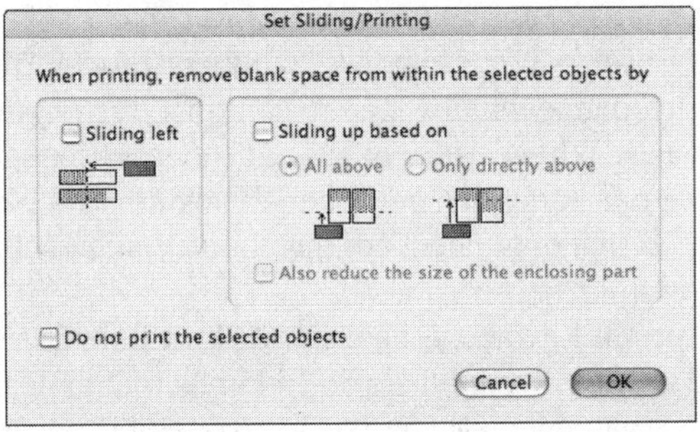

Figure 15-5
The Set Sliding/Printing window.

5. Go to Preview mode and notice that anything that was in the header is gone! If you created that View button but didn't select it during this process, it's still on the page, but nothing happens when you click it in Preview mode.
6. Go to Browse mode, choose **View as List** (or use your View button), and go to Preview mode. The field labels are gone. At this point you have to decide which view you'll be printing. But now you have a technique to avoid printing selected items on layouts.

CAUTION If you're designing layouts for other users, remember that buttons don't work in Preview mode. Since everyone who uses your file might not understand that, it's usually a good idea to take them to the preview by way of a script that includes a Pause step. That way the users can click the Continue or Cancel button in the Status toolbar, which will take them back to Browse mode where you can include Print and Cancel buttons. You want to make sure those buttons are non-printing so they won't show in Preview mode. There's nothing more frustrating for a user than to have buttons in front of them that don't work. An alternative would be to script a new window with buttons on it to control what happens next. Just remember that users may move your windows to other places than the position you script them to be in.

When you use the Layout Assistant, FileMaker colors the layout parts based on the theme. If you go to any of the template files and look at the form in Preview mode, some of the background colors will disappear. That's because the layout part colors have been left transparent, and the colors are provided by colored, non-printing rectangles. Layout part colors cannot be made non-printing. The only thing you can do is change the pattern to transparent.

Sliding Objects

While we're at it, let's look at another feature of Sliding/Printing. One of the contacts in one of my invoices has a long company name. You can rearrange the layout to show the information, and use the Set Sliding/Printing window to make the printout look more professional. (If the names in that field are too short to make sense in this demo, go to the contact record represented on one of these invoices and give it a long company name. Then come back and finish this exercise.)

1. Go to the INV_InvoiceList layout (see Figure 15-6). Drag the dotted line or the tab for the body part down, and expand the inv_CON__ ConSerNum::Company field to show two lines.

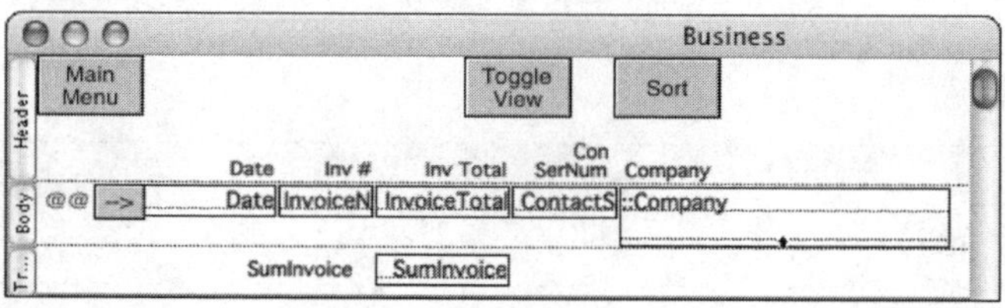

Figure 15-6
The INV_InvoiceList layout in Layout mode showing the Company field opened up to accommodate a long name.

2. Choose **Format**, **Set Sliding/Printing**, and check **Sliding up based on.** Leave the "All above" radio button selected, then check the box next to **Also reduce the size of the enclosing part**, and click **OK**. When you go to Preview mode, any long company names will show on two lines, but all the shorter names will close up tight to each other.

You may have more control over field size when you use the Autoresize[9] feature. You can apply Autoresize to any selected layout object in Layout mode using the Object Info dialog (View, Object Info). For more details, see the section titled “Autoresize Layout Objects” near the end of Chapter 17.

CAUTION Make sure that any expanded fields in the body don't extend into the trailing grand summary, sub-summary, or footer parts. If they do, the fields won't slide properly.

Using Sliding/Printing this way is something you may need to do on the ILI_InvoicePrint layout where a product name or description may be too long to fit on one line. There is a very good discussion of the finer points of Sliding/Printing in the FileMaker Pro manual PDF file and the Help files.

In Table view, you can simply expand the column to the right until it shows the whole company name. If you have a lot of fields, however, you may not be able to make all of them print on a page. In that case, the advantage goes to List view where you can use Sliding/Printing. You can also place fields one after the other in horizontal rows in List view. Remember, you'll never get sub-summaries in a printout of Table view. (You can get grand totals to show in the footer if you set it to show in the Table View Properties area of Layout Setup.) Table view is handy for viewing and printing quick and simple lists regardless of how complex the database, but it's just not meant for reports.

Layout Parts

FileMaker Pro has eight layout parts to choose from. So far, we've created all of our layouts using the Layout Assistant, where FileMaker took care of creating the layout parts for us. Now it's time to learn what they're all about.

Go to ILI_InvoicePrint layout, switch to Layout mode, and look at the Invoice layout we created in Chapter 9, shown here in Figure 15-7. Choose Layouts, Duplicate Layout so you can experiment without ruining the original.

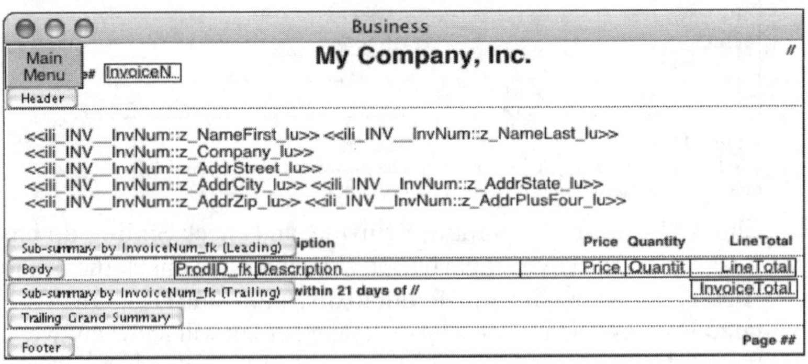

Figure 15-7
The InvLI_Invoice layout showing six of the eight layout parts.

> **CAUTION** Whenever you get ready to experiment with a layout you've worked hard to create, make a copy first.

The Part label control is the icon near the lower-left corner of the window to the left of the Mode drop-down (see Figure 15-8). Clicking on this icon toggles the layout part label tabs between displaying horizontally on the layout and flipping up vertically out of the way. When you use the Layout Assistant to create labels, envelopes, and reports, the tabs are turned sideways.

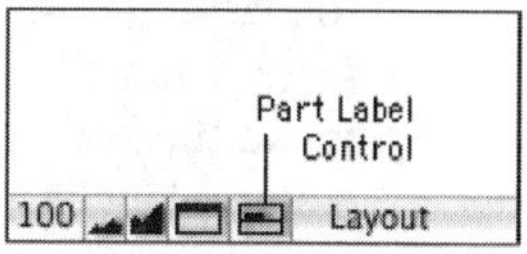

Figure 15-8
Clicking on the Part label control icon toggles the layout part label tabs between horizontal and vertical display.

Double-clicking one of the tabs will bring up the Part Definition window shown in Figure 15-9. You can also call up this window by choosing Insert, Part from the menu bar. From here, you can change the current layout part to a different one. The radio buttons are only active for the specific parts that can go in that position on the layout. All others are dimmed. If you close the window and click on the other parts, you'll see that the available radio buttons will change. Let's look at the various parts and their uses.

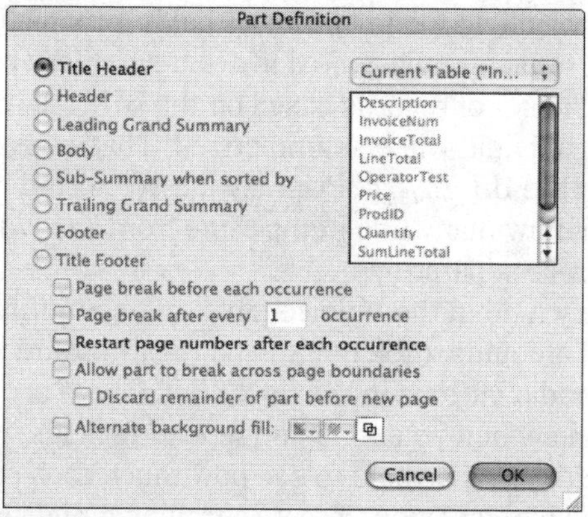

Figure 15-9
FileMaker's Part Definition window.

Title Header

The title header only appears on the first page of a report no matter how many pages the report has. I will often duplicate elements from the header section and put them in the title header when they're needed on the first page.

Header

You'll find the header at the top of every page unless the report has a title header. In that case, the title header replaces the header on the first page.

Body

Even though the body part only appears once in Layout mode, when it comes to printing (and Preview mode) it will repeat as many times as it will fit on a page when allowing for any other layout parts that also have to print. You can make the body print in columns. That's how you're able to print multiple-column labels.

Sub-summaries (Leading and Trailing)

Sub-summaries print before or after a group of records, but only if the records are sorted by the field selected when creating the sub-summary. You can have as many of these on a layout as you can dream up, but the order in which they appear may seem somewhat unpredictable depending on how the records are sorted. When you look at all other layout parts, they print in the same order in which they appear on the page. But a sub-summary part that is lower on the layout may actually appear above a different sub-summary part if they are sorted in reverse order. In some cases, that may be exactly what you want. If the sub-summary parts always appear in the same order as your sort, you'll have no surprises.

You have to create a summary field for any numeric fields for which you want summaries. Placing that same summary field in a sub-summary part will display summary data for the subset of records based on the sort. All records with the same value in the sorted field will be summarized. That's what the InvoiceTotal field did for us on the ILI_InvoicePrint layout. We sorted by InvoiceNum, and regardless of how many line items came from an invoice, we could see the total of each invoice separately.

Now let's create a summary field in the Invoice table called SumInvoices that will total the InvoiceTotal amounts. (You don't need to pay attention to the "Summarize repetitions" radio buttons in the lower left. Those are choices you'll only need to make when you are using repeating fields, which we're not using.) With this field, you'll be able to see how much each contact spent. Now, go to the INV_InvoiceList layout, create a trailing grand summary layout part, and place your SumInvoices field in that part. See Figure 15-10.

Don't get the idea that you need a summary field to take advantage of a sub-summary part. A common use of sub-summary parts is to break a category by a "text" label. For example, in an Employee database, you could have a field for supervisor. If you wanted to print all of the employees grouped by supervisor, then you'd make a sub-summary part, put the Supervisor field in that section, and sort by supervisor. No summary field is needed to accomplish that.

Sub-summary objects and the data in the fields in these parts will show up in Browse and Preview modes or when printed, but only when the records are properly sorted. If a part doesn't show in your report, be sure to check the sort first.

> **CAUTION** If you have a sub-summary that shows up in Browse and Preview modes but won't print, check your print window. Choosing the Current Record option from the FileMaker settings area in your print window will cause the sub-summaries not to print as you expect. If you're trying to get a look at one page of the report, choose "Print pages 1 to 1" in the print window instead.

My experience has been that simply reading about reports and doing a few exercises won't make you a master. You'll have to create some reports of your own based on what you've learned here and what you can get from the manual and the Help files. Then you need to experiment until you get them just the way you want. You know, practice makes perfect.

Leading and Trailing Grand Summaries

These parts only appear once on a report, but you can have one each of the leading and trailing grand summaries. Summary fields that are placed in these layout parts provide totals for all records in the found set.

We've removed the SumLineTotal summary field from the trailing grand summary part on the ILI_InvoicePrint layout. That's because when you print a group of invoices, you don't want that total going to the customer whose invoice prints last. You can avoid that by double-clicking the Trailing Grand Summary part tab, and checking the box next to "Page break before each occurrence." Of course, you'll also have to put the InvoiceTotal field back into that part. If getting the grand total isn't important, you could even delete that part from the layout.

Footer

The footer appears at the bottom of every page unless there is a title footer part. In that case, the title footer takes the place of the footer on the first page of the report.

Title Footer

The title footer only appears once in the report at the bottom of the first page. As with the title header, I will sometimes duplicate elements from the footer section and put them in the title footer when they're needed on the first page.

Working with Layout Parts

Be sure you're in Layout mode, and choose Layouts, Part Setup. You should see the window shown in Figure 15-10. This is a great way to get an overview of the part structure of a layout. As you can see on your screen, some layout parts can be moved, while others are locked in place, as indicated by the padlock icon.

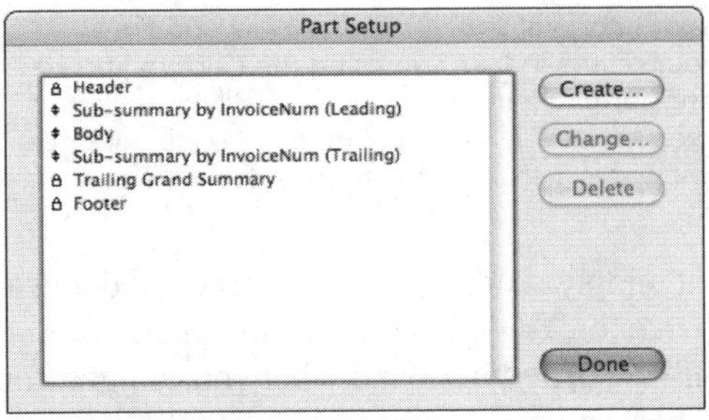

Figure 15-10
The Part Setup window showing the parts on the Invoice layout in the InvLI table.

Double-clicking on the listed part or single-clicking the Create button brings up the Part Definition window, which we've already seen.

Adding and Deleting Parts

If you want to add a part to the layout, you can use the Part tool and just drag parts onto the layout. You can also use Insert, Part from the menu bar. Or you can use the Create button in the Part Setup window. Some parts can only be placed in specific locations or between other layout parts. You can also use the Part Setup window to delete a layout part. Alternatively, you can simply click on the part label, and press Backspace or Delete. FileMaker will warn you if there are any layout objects within the boundaries of the part you're attempting to delete.

Modifying Parts

You can double-click the label of an existing part and designate it to be something else, but you're limited to the parts that can go in that location on the layout.

> ⌘ **TIP** Getting vertical lines for columns to show up across multiple parts was a nightmare until I learned this trick. A line will not print across three layout parts, but you can make a line appear to be continuous across multiple parts by placing one vertical line across the upper and middle parts and overlapping it with another line that crosses the middle and lower parts. Choosing the exact position and length is up to you. Unfortunately, it doesn't work so well when you have sliding elements.

If you followed along and created the duplicate Invoice layout, you may want to delete it now. Or you could give it another name, indicating that it's temporary, so you can experiment with it later.

Summary

In this chapter, we looked at how data entry layouts differ from layouts that will be used in printed reports. I showed you how to keep layout objects from printing but still appear on the screen.

Then we looked at the various layout parts, the differences between them, and how to add and delete them from the layouts.

Q & A

Q It looks as if you're saying we have to make two of every layout — one for viewing and one for printing.

A Not exactly. You probably won't want to print some layouts, and some you'll print so rarely that it won't matter how they look. Reports for internal use and those that customers will be seeing need different consideration. Sometimes a user may just need to see a bit of information from a group of records in order to answer a question. If that's the case, there's no need to print it. But it should still be easy to find the data requested.

Q The details of these layout parts are confusing. How can I figure them out?

A Fortunately, the Layout Assistant takes a lot of the load off. Using it, you can create a complicated report, and then use the Part Definition and Part Setup windows to analyze it. Also read the FileMaker Pro manual PDF file and take a look at the Help files. Sometimes just seeing the same topic from another angle will make it click for you.

Workshop

Experiment with one of the layouts created with the Layout Assistant, and turn off the background colors. Then, substitute colored rectangles and make them non-printing. Once you create one on the layout, you'll have to choose Arrange, Send to Back so it doesn't cover up your other layout objects. Check it out in Preview mode. Using this technique, you can make data entry layouts that can still be printed without wasting ink.

Go back to Chapter 8 and find the section titled "Sort By a Summary Field." If you weren't able to do that exercise then, you should be able to now with what you've learned in this chapter.

Chapter 16

Working with Script Triggers[10]

Introduction

Perhaps the most long-requested feature for FileMaker is script triggers. Well, we've already seen that you can trigger scripts by clicking a button, using the Scripts menu, or running one when you open or close a file. FileMaker 10 introduces 12 ways to trigger scripts. These are broken down into five object-based and seven layout-based triggers. Because the events that trigger them are relatively passive compared to clicking a button, they may seem to happen as if by magic.

A related feature new for FMP10 is the Install OnTimer script step, which can make scripts operate in the background as invisibly as the script triggers. Both of these features will do away with some of the plug-ins that have been required to accomplish similar tasks, and they're done quite elegantly right here inside FileMaker.

Make a Script

Before we can trigger a script, we need to create one that will be appropriate for the demonstration. Remember our little experiments to format a phone number back in Chapter 12? This script is nowhere near as complicated as that example. All this does is format a phone number in a specific way.

Go into our Business file and create the following script:

```
Script Name: 12 - Check Phone Format
If [Length (con_PH__SerNum::Phone) = 10 and PatternCount
(con_PH__SerNum::Phone ; "-") < 2]
   Beep
   Show Custom Dialog ["It looks as if this phone number isn't formatted the
way we want it. Would you like me to do that for you?"] (Buttons: "OK",
"No!")
   If [Get (LastMessageChoice) = 1]
      Set Field [con_PH__SerNum::Phone; Substitute (con_PH__SerNum::Phone ;
           " " ; "")]
      Set Field [con_PH__SerNum::Phone; Substitute (con_PH__SerNum::Phone ;
           "(" ; "")]
      Set Field [con_PH__SerNum::Phone; Substitute (con_PH__SerNum::Phone ;
           ")" ; "-")]
```

```
    End If
End If
```

I used three Set Field steps where a single step with three nested Substitute functions would work, but I wanted it to be easier for you (and me) to see what's happening. The first one clears any spaces. The second removes the leading "(." And the third replaces the ")" with the dash.

Now this script isn't going to perform any miracles. It will only change phone numbers entered as (517) 694-8372 into 517-694-8372. There are many other ways phone numbers could be entered, not to mention international phone numbers, but this example will certainly give you the idea. You could also handle this formatting at the field level, but using a script allows you to perform other actions besides fixing the data and flashing a dialog.

Now let's take a look at script triggers to see what we might do with this script.

Object-Based Script Triggers

Go to Layout mode on the CON_Contact layout. Click on the Phone field in the portal, go to the Format menu, and select Set Script Triggers. You should now see the dialog in Figure 16-1.

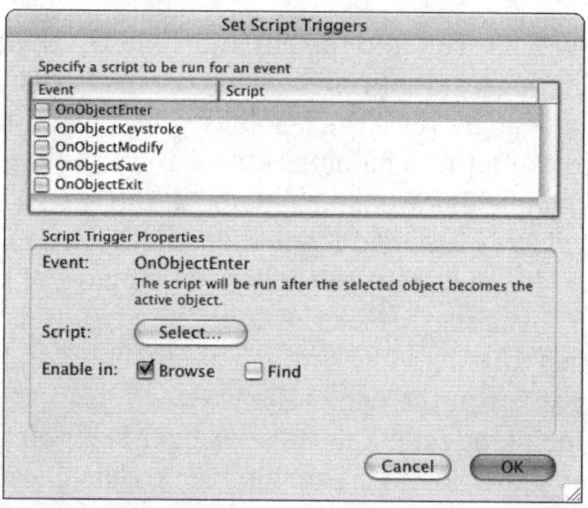

Figure 16-1
The Set Script Triggers dialog.

OnObjectEnter is highlighted in the Event column, and there is a short description of what this script trigger does in the Event area in the middle of the dialog. Go ahead and click on the text (not the check box) for each of the other triggers to see if their description makes sense to you from their name.

You may have noticed that some of the triggers also have a Result section at the bottom of the dialog (not shown in Figure 16-1). That just means that whatever you did to trigger the script will continue from there, such as whether you tabbed to the next field or clicked to go to another record.

Clicking the Select button brings up the Specify Script dialog where you can choose the script that will run — in this or any other file. You can also apply script parameters if you like. Did you notice that the Browse box is checked? With the two "Enable in" check boxes you can specify whether the script will run in Browse or Find mode or both. When both are unchecked, the trigger is deactivated. That's in case you want to keep the trigger in place but just not have it operate for a while. One option that may not be clear is you can have multiple events checked for a layout object. So, for instance, you could perform one script as you enter a field and another script as you exit the field.

OnObjectExit[10]

Okay, now let's attach our little script to the Phone field. You should still have the Set Script Trigger dialog in front of you.

1. Check the box next to **OnObjectExit** and attach the Check Phone Format script. Make sure to enable it in Browse mode.
2. Click **OK**. Notice there is a little red asterisk in the lower-right corner of the field to help you identify objects that have script triggers attached to them. You can turn those on and off by going to the View menu and choosing Show, Script Triggers.
3. Go to Browse mode, enter a phone number formatted like (517) 694-8372, and exit the field by pressing the Enter or Tab key. You should see the dialog. Click **OK** and watch the number reformat like magic. If you click Cancel, the number will remain formatted as is.

Almost every client I work with has run into the situation where they accidentally press the Return key when exiting a field. That means labels will end up with empty lines that aren't caught until the labels are already printed. Wouldn't it be nice to trap for the return character (or pilcrow) and run a script that takes it out of certain fields? Well, maybe not all the time. I often type two lines of text in the address field and I wouldn't want a script trigger to keep me from doing that. (That only goes to show that you have to keep asking, "What can go wrong?") But maybe a script could be triggered on exiting the zip code field (AddrZip) that would go through all the fields and trim out any improper return characters at the end of the text.

This next script uses some of the functions new for FileMaker 10 that refer to the ActiveField. They allow you to create shorter scripts because you don't have to name the field that is being operated on. It also makes it easier to use similar scripts in other tables and files, thereby reducing development time. Build it once and use it many times. Here's the script:

```
Script Name: 13 - Check Fields for Extra Returns
Go to Field [CON::NameFirst]
Loop
   Set Field By Name [Get (ActiveFieldTableName) & "::" & Get
(ActiveFieldName);
   Let ([GAFC = Get (ActiveFieldContents)] ; If (Right (GAFC ; 1) = "¶";
   Left (GAFC ; Length (GAFC)-1) ; GAFC))]
   Go to Next Field
   Exit Loop If [Get (ActiveFieldName) = "AddrState"]
```

```
End Loop
Go to Field [CON::AddrPlusFour]
```

Notice that I've used the Let function so I can shorten Get (ActiveFieldContents) to GAFC. Otherwise, that Set Field step would have taken more than three lines. That's what Let is for. Might as well start using it.

Now attach this as a script trigger to the AddrZip field using OnObjectExit as the event. Back in Browse mode add an extra return to the NameFirst and NameLast fields, which would definitely mess up a mailing label. Continue tabbing until the cursor is in the AddrZip field and tab once more. Go back and see if it took out the returns. This works fine as long as you don't change the Tab order on the layout. (Just one more thing that can go wrong.)

The nice thing about how this trigger operates is that after the script runs it will go to the AddrPlusFour field if you pressed the Tab key, but it will exit the record if you clicked on the background or pressed the Enter key. Yet if you go to another record, the script will run, but the cursor will still be in the Zip field when you get to the next record. It will also run if you close the file since that would certainly be exiting the record. Every one of those actions is perfectly logical and makes operation very smooth.

⌘ **TIP** One little thing I ran into that will likely catch you too is that I had the script loop through the fields until it came back to the AddrZip field rather than the version you see where it stops at AddrState. When I clicked out of the AddrZip field, it triggered the script. But when it got back to the AddrZip field, it triggered the script again and again, and would have continued looping forever until I typed Command+period (Macintosh) or Esc (Windows). This kind of perpetual loop happened to me in at least three different cases, so it's likely to be something you'll want to know. You need to look at the logic of what your scripts are doing and test them thoroughly if other people will be using your file.

By the way, you can remove the return characters at the field level using validation. Can you figure out how? (The answer is elsewhere in this chapter, but you'll have to find it.)

Part 4

Layout-Based Script Triggers

Now let's look at how scripts can be triggered with events that are associated with layouts. There are many interesting uses for this feature, but we'll focus on one that will affect our invoice report. Something that has bothered me about reports for a long time is that the records on those layouts need to be sorted in order to be able to view the sub-summary sections. That's somewhat easier to deal with now that we have dynamic sub-summaries as discussed on Chapter 8. But the sub-summaries can quickly disappear when the records are no longer sorted as expected. Let's work on a script that we can have run whenever we go to the ILI_InvoicePrint layout.

1. Go to the Scripts menu and choose **Manage Scripts**.

2. Duplicate script "**7 - Find Invoices with Balance Due**" and rename it "**14 - Find Invoices with Balance Due & View In Print Layout**."
3. Now change it so it reads like this:

```
Script Name: 14 - Find Invoices with Balance Due & View In Print Layout
Set Error Capture [On]
#ili_INV__InvNum::InvoiceTotal > 0
Perform Find [Restore]
If [Get (FoundCount) = 0]
   Beep
   Show Custom Dialog ["Sorry, there are no outstanding invoices at this
time. I'll show you all invoices"]
   #Button 1 = OK
   Show All Records
End If
#InvoiceNum_fk (ascending)
Sort Records [Restore; No dialog]
```

You'll need to go into the Perform Find step and change the find criteria to match the comment in the line above it. I'm pretty sure you can do that by now. Notice the change in the dialog in case zero records are found, and also notice that the script doesn't halt any more. The sort stays the same, but I added the comment above it so it's easier to see what it is without having to go into the dialog.

4. Duplicate the script once more and call it "**15 - Sort Invoices.**"
5. Get rid of everything except the sort. Then add an If and End If so it looks like this:

```
Script Name: 15 - Sort Invoices
If [Get (SortState) = 0]
    Sort Records [Restore; No dialog]
End If
```

I had to add the Get (SortState) step because when I switched records and tried to type in the Description field (which we'll be doing in a few minutes), it ran the sort script trigger and popped me right back out of the field. By clicking a second time in the field on the same record, I could start typing. The If step looks to see if the records are sorted. If they are, it doesn't sort them again. Just goes to show you how little things can mess you up. Test, test, test! And by the way, it's not sorting by the AddrState field. What it's doing is checking whether the records are sorted or not. 0 means they're not sorted, and 1 means they are.

Now let's attach the script to the layout.

6. Go to Layout mode and switch to the ILI_InvoicePrint layout.
7. Go to the Layouts menu and select **Layout Setup**. Another method to bring up the Layout Setup dialog is to go to Layout mode and click the stubby pencil on the left side of the Layout bar near the Layout drop-

down. You can also Control+click (Macintosh) or right-click (Windows) on any layout part (not including the toolbars) to bring up the context menu. Layout Setup is one of the choices.

8. Click the **Script Triggers** tab and you should see the dialog in Figure 16-2.

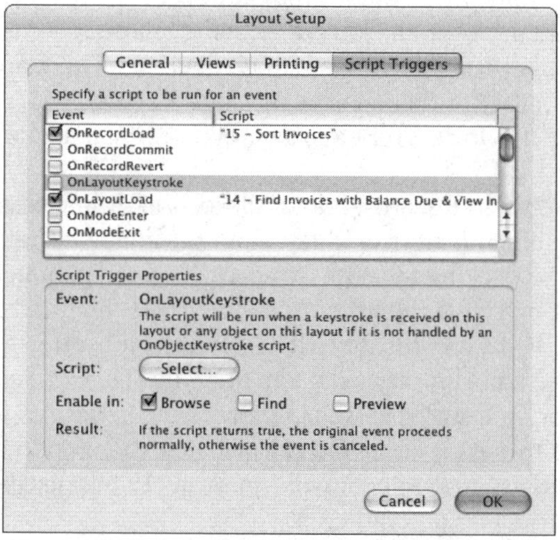

Figure 16-2
The Script Triggers tab of the Layout Setup dialog.

When I took this picture of the screen I deliberately highlighted the OnLayoutKeystroke event because doing so allows you to see the Enable in Preview check box. Not all the other events have that option; to see which ones do, click on each of the events one at a time.

You need to keep in mind that script 14 will also run when you click the button that runs 6 - Print One Invoice. You can see how it might be confusing to end up printing batches of invoices when the script clearly calls for only one. So even though we have these great new script triggers, they can get in the way of our other work as easily as they can solve problems. With that in mind, you may decide to deactivate this one later.

OnRecordLoad10 and OnLayoutLoad10

Here again, you can check two or more events in this dialog. For example, in the case of our invoices, you might want to run one script that shows all records and sorts when you switch to the layout (OnLayoutLoad), and another script that sorts by contact and invoice date when you change any of the data (OnRecordLoad). That way, the sub-summaries will always show. (Well, not quite. But we'll discuss that shortly.)

9. Check the boxes shown in Figure 16-2 and attach our new scripts.
10. Now start in Browse mode from any layout except ILI_InvoicePrint and choose that layout from the drop-down. You should get a report showing the invoices with a balance due.

Of course in order to see anything at all, you'll need some invoices with a balance due. If you don't have any in your file, go back to the Contacts area and create a few now. And also create at least one invoice that is paid off with a balance of zero.

One thing I was hoping to accomplish with this example was to have records sort automatically if you choose the Show All Records menu option or use the key combination. After all, you are "loading" more records, aren't you? But unfortunately that doesn't seem to be the case. There are a lot of ways to load records, just not that specific method. For what I imagined to occur we would need an OnRecordSetChange event, which doesn't exist just yet.

So go ahead and choose Records, Show All Records. You just get a list of line items with no sub-summaries or clues about the contacts. You can activate our Sort script by clicking to another record. To do that, notice which record is selected (it will have the little black bar on the left), and just click on a different line item. Voilà, records sorted! There are a few other ways to sort the records to see the sub-summaries. If you bring up the Sort dialog, FileMaker remembers the sort that was in there when you came to the layout, so just clicking OK gets it back. You can also quickly jump to Layout mode and back to Browse mode and it will run script 15 because you're "loading" the records.

If you have only the unpaid invoices on your screen, and you just want to see the invoices that have been paid off, go to Records, Show Omitted Only or click the pie chart in the upper left of the Status toolbar. That triggers a record load because whatever your current record is it will be replaced with one of the omitted records, and all your paid invoices will be properly sorted.

And finally, you can add a button in the header layout part that will sort the records when you click it. As far as I'm concerned, all these solutions seem to take away a little of the magic. Well, go ahead and add a button, and put the word "Sort" on it. <sigh>

Now look at the report in Preview mode. Notice that every invoice will print on a separate page. So what we see in Browse mode, regardless of how the records are sorted, isn't a completely accurate representation of how the report will print. But in Browse mode you do get the ability to change the data in this report before printing it out. Again, that is something that hasn't been possible until FMP10, regardless of script triggers.

OnObjectKeystroke[10] Example

The OnObjectKeystroke event can cause a script to run when someone is typing in a field and clicks a particular key. Because I think it has so much potential, I want to run you through a simple exercise that uses it. So create the following script:

```
Script Name: 16 - OnObjectKeystroke Example
If [Get (TriggerKeystroke) = "-"]
```

```
   Show Custom Dialog [Title: "Hey..."; Message: "You typed the dash
key!"] (OK button)
Else If [Get (TriggerKeystroke) = "¶"]
   Show Custom Dialog ["Oops!"; "Returns are not allowed here. I'll
remove it for you."] (OK button)
   Halt Script
End If
```

Now attach the script as a script trigger to the Description field using the OnObjectKeystroke event.

Go to Browse mode and add a little text to the Description field and eventually enter the dash character (-). You should get the dialog described above. Try pressing the Return key. Now press the Enter key. Uh, oh!

The Return and Enter key seem to be recognized as the same key. It turns out you need to use one of FileMaker's new functions called Code in order to capture the more specific keystroke. You'll see the solution to that after the next two paragraphs.

I originally thought I could just have the Else If followed by Show Custom Dialog and a Set Field to remove the pilcrow (¶), but when I did, it got stuck in a loop. The first problem is that FileMaker captures the keystroke and runs the script before letting the text go into the field. That meant that after the script runs, the pilcrow character is inserted into the field, and the script runs again and again. So that's why you need the Halt Script step. And once the script halts, the pilcrow doesn't get entered, so you don't need Set Field to take it out. In other words, your keystroke action is never completed.

Now see if you think this next little bit is interesting. There is also an OnLayoutKeystroke script trigger. It can watch for specific keys being typed in *any* field on the layout. So a script like our number 16 above could be made to run when typing in any field. Wouldn't that come in handy on the CON_Contact layout to act as a watchdog during data entry? Since you might want to add returns in the Notes or Street fields, you could exclude them by changing the Else If step to read:

```
Else If [Code (Get (TriggerKeystroke)) = 13 and Get (ActiveFieldName) ≠
"Notes" and Get (ActiveFieldName) ≠ "AddrStreet"]
```

I tried it and it works great!

When to Use Auto-Enter Calculated Value

Now, what can go wrong with script triggers? Well, they're not a good way to validate data all the time. If you think about it for a second you'll realize that we've tied it to either a field on a layout or the layout itself. That means if the same field were on another layout, the data wouldn't get corrected. And there would be no vigilance over data changed using Relookup Field Contents, Replace Field Contents, or any imported data. For really solid control, you need to work that out with field validation or Auto-Enter Calculated value, which is my favorite method. For example, you could set up the NameFirst field to quietly reject Return characters like this:

```
Case (PatternCount (NameFirst ; "¶") =1; Substitute (NameFirst ; "¶" ;
""); NameFirst)
```

Then uncheck the box next to "Do not replace existing value of field (if any)." That way, any time anything is changed in that field on any layout or portal or when data is replaced or imported, it will remove the pilcrow. You would repeat that for any fields that need it.

Now that doesn't make this script we created a completely useless tool. Just don't expect it to take care of every situation the way we've been using it. Besides, you get a lot more control over exactly what happens when you use a script vs. field validation. Uh, but now that we've found a reasonable, if not perfect, use for this script trigger, maybe you'll want to take out the silly stuff about the dash. That could get old after a while.

All this talk about removing the pilcrow brings up something that almost wipes out the other work we've done. There's a feature that was added way back in FileMaker 7 that you can use to prevent someone even entering the Return character in specific fields. To take a look, click a field in Layout mode and choose Format, Field Control, Behavior. At the bottom of the Field Behavior dialog is a section for "Go to next object using" where you can check "Return key." When a field is set up this way, anytime the user presses Return, he or she simply jumps to the next field in the tab order. Try it out. That also means you can't press the Return key to complete a search when you're in Find mode. I prefer to use the Enter key for that, but I am certainly aware that other people don't. After all, isn't that how we ended up with those extra returns in the first place? It all goes to show that FileMaker really does supply you with a lot of great tools, many of which can be used to accomplish similar functions in different ways. Depending on what field you just formatted, you may want to change it back at this time.

OnObjectModify[10] Example

I've shown you some triggers that may be less than useful to you. That's because I'm trying to keep this simple. (Okay, it's also because this is new territory and I don't really know all the cool things that it might be used for.) However, this one might be something you can actually use. I often want to perform a find in more than one field at a time. By making a combination field, you can look in multiple fields while typing in a single field. Using this particular script trigger, the list of found records will change as you type more.

1. Create the following calculation field in the CON table using a Text result:

   ```
   NameCombo = NameFirst & " " & NameLast & " " & Company & " " & Notes
   ```

2. Also add a Global Text field called zi_Search_gt.
3. Make a new list layout based on the CON table and call it **CON_Search**.

4. Add these fields:

   NameFirst
   NameLast
   Company
   Notes
   zi_Search_gt

5. Choose whatever other settings you like and finish up the layout creation process.
6. When you get done, go to Layout mode and put the zi_Search_gt field in the header section.
7. Now, create this script:

   Script Name: 16.5 - Search Name, Company and Notes Using a Script Trigger

```
Set Variable [$$Cursor; Value:Get (ActiveSelectionStart)]
If [$$Cursor = 1]
   Show All Records
   Halt Script
End If
Enter Find Mode []
Set Field [CON::NameCombo; MiddleWords (CON::zi_Search_gt ; 1 ; 1)]
New Record/Request
Set Field [CON::NameCombo; MiddleWords (CON::zi_Search_gt ; 2 ; 1)]
New Record/Request
Set Field [CON::NameCombo; MiddleWords (CON::zi_Search_gt ; 3 ; 1)]
Set Error Capture [On]
Perform Find []
If [Get (FoundCount) = 0]
   Show All Records
Else
   #Sort by NameLast, NameFirst
   Sort Records [Restore; No dialog]
End If
Set Selection [CON::zi_Search_gt; Start Position: $$Cursor]
```

8. Attach the script to the zi_Search_gt field using OnObjectModify.
9. Go to Browse mode and type a few letters in the search field. Just make sure they're letters that represent some of your records. You should be able to watch the list of records get shorter as you type.

In the final step, you only need to specify the starting position of the cursor even though the dialog lets you specify both start and end position. This version of the script lets you find up to three words. You can repeat the Set Field step as many times as you want if you need to find more words. There's a way to shorten the repeating Set Field steps using a loop, but that's for you to work out. Sounds like a good candidate for the Workshop section at the end of the chapter.

One thing I noticed is that if you type multiple words, it will find them as an "OR" find. In other words, if you type Richard Bail, it will find both Rich Bailey and Richard Bailey. What caught me was when I typed Richard, I got a fairly short list. Then I pressed the Spacebar and typed the letter b, and the list got longer.

As your database gets filled up, searching in the Notes field can make it less effective because you'll turn up so many matches. Also, depending on the size of the database, it can be slow when looking in related records. If you type fast, response may seem a bit sluggish because the find has to be performed between each letter.

Script Trigger Notes

There are a lot of subtleties to using script triggers. I'm only listing a few here. If you want more, you should look at a document titled FMP10_Users_Guide.pdf in the Electronic Documentation folder.

- Fields aren't the only objects that can run script triggers. If you set up your tab order to go to various objects on the layout, you can also get triggers to run when typing while in a tab control, button, portal, or web viewer, although I find those options counterintuitive. The part about the portal just applies to the portal object itself. Script triggers attached to portal fields operate just like they do on any other field.
- Making a choice from a drop-down list, radio button, or check box will not fire a Get (TriggerKeystroke) script trigger.
- Operating system and FileMaker Pro keyboard shortcuts will not be processed for script triggers. That's why I couldn't get Command+J (Macintosh) or Ctrl+J (Windows) for Show All Records to trigger the Sort Invoices script. However, if you have a copy of FileMaker Pro Advanced (FMPA), you could use custom menus to substitute a script for the Show All Records menu that will only operate that way on that specific layout. See the section titled "A Case for FileMaker Pro Advanced" later in this chapter for more about FMPA.
- As I already mentioned, in the case of OnObjectKeystroke, the trigger runs the script before the text is actually entered into the field. If the script returns a negative result, the data never gets entered.
- You can trigger scripts when entering and exiting summary and calculated fields. But since you can't alter the data in either of those fields, you can't trigger off of them with OnObjectModify, and the data itself won't be changed.
- You can trigger scripts that run events outside of FMP, like AppleScripts or Window VB scripts.
- You may be disappointed to find that you can't trigger a script using each of the individual tabs in a tab control. Maybe in another version or two.
- Script triggers are not functional in Instant Web Publishing.

Script Trigger Ideas

Here are some uses for script triggers that are being discussed by beta testing developers at the time we go to press:

- Messages that explain exactly what is incorrect about the data entry
- Coding of credit card numbers
- Switching to the proper layout based on a selection from a drop-down list
- Sending automatic e-mail messages if specific data changes, such as when an insurance agent changes something in your policy
- Date checking
- Audit trail (This is a biggie!)
- Changing layouts after data has been entered correctly without clicking a button
- Auto-advancing to the next field when a specific number of characters has been entered
- Switching to a specific tab in a tab control depending on a field value, such as switching to the Credit Card tab when Credit Card is selected as the payment type
- Updating lookup information in related tables to preserve integrity of data normalization
- Creating a group of standard records in a portal, such as a group of meetings that might be attended at a conference. That way the data entry person only needs to click check boxes in the portal instead of selecting session names from a drop-down.
- Running calculations on number data to automatically fill a standard number field rather than using a calculation field. This is especially beneficial when there are many calculation fields that can slow down screen redraws.
- Renaming, resizing, and positioning a layout onscreen as you switch to it. (I notice some of the template layouts have to be resized manually whenever you go to them.)
- Testing whether or not users should go to a layout and leave them where they are if not (rather than showing them a blank layout with no buttons to get back)

Install OnTimer Script10

This is a very cool script step indeed. Basically what this step does is run another script at a time interval measured in seconds. When you first select it, the script step looks like this:

```
Install OnTimer Script []
```

There are two Specify buttons where you choose the script and the number of seconds of the loop. Let's go ahead and create an OnTimer, and then we'll discuss some of the finer points about how to use it.

Because of security reasons, many programs pop the user out of the data entry area if there has been inactivity for a specific length of time. Just to let you know, you can use the Edit Privilege Set dialog to choose "Disconnect user from FileMaker Pro Server when idle." But the way that works is preset, and you have to be using FMPS. Using this OnTimer version, you have complete control over what happens.

1. Create the following three scripts:

```
Script Name: 17 - Start OnTimer - Commit Record and Re-Login
Set Variable [$$Layout; Value:Get (LayoutName)]
Set Variable [$$RecordNumber; Value:Get (RecordNumber)]
Set Variable [$$Field; Value:Get (ActiveFieldName)]
Set Variable [$$CursorPosition; Value:Get (ActiveSelectionStart)]
Install OnTimer Script ["18 - Check for Data Entry"; Interval: 10]

Script Name: 18 - Check for Data Entry
If [Get (LayoutName) = $$Layout and Get (RecordNumber) = $$RecordNumber
and Get (ActiveFieldName) = $$Field and Get (ActiveSelectionStart) =
$$CursorPosition]
   Enter Browse Mode []
   Commit Records/Requests [Skip data entry validation; No dialog]
   Beep
   Show Custom Dialog ["The file has been idle for too long. You must
        Re-Login."]
   Re-Login []
   Perform Script ["17 - Start OnTimer - Commit Record and Re-Login"]
Else
   Set Variable [$$Layout; Value:Get (LayoutName)]
   Set Variable [$$RecordNumber; Value:Get (RecordNumber)]
   Set Variable [$$Field; Value:Get (ActiveFieldName)]
   Set Variable [$$CursorPosition; Value:Get (ActiveSelectionStart)]
End If

Script Name: 19 - Stop OnTimer
Install OnTimer Script []
```

As you finish up script 19, make sure you check the box next to it so you can run it from the Scripts menu. Once an OnTimer gets going, it can be frustrating to shut it off unless you can get to the Stop script quickly. (Don't ask how I know.)

Let's look at what these three scripts will accomplish:

- Script 17 finds out where the user is and even the position of the cursor in a field. It still works if the user isn't in any field at all. I set the interval at 10 seconds so you can see it work. There is no point in setting it to 15 minutes and having you sit around waiting to see if and how it works. You can change the interval later.

- Script 18 checks to see if the user is on the same layout, record, and field with the cursor in the same position before the interval started. If nothing has changed, it beeps and displays the explanation dialog. After that's dismissed, the user will see the Re-Login dialog. Relogging in starts the OnTimer all over again. However, if the user has been working all along, it records the layout, field, and position and starts again.
- Script 19 stops the original OnTimer. You stop an OnTimer by calling another OnTimer with no script and/or no interval or an interval set to zero. In this case, I've selected neither. That's why you see empty brackets.

2. Now go to the CON_Contact layout in Layout mode, bring up the Layout Setup dialog, and click the **Script Triggers** button. You should see script 16 already attached to the OnLayoutKeystroke event.
3. Check the box next to **OnLayoutLoad** and choose **Script 17**.
4. Go to Browse mode and wait 10 seconds. Remember, you can get into the file using Admin for the account name and leaving the password blank.

Did you see the two dialogs? After re-logging in, did you get kicked out again? Remember, you can run script 19 to make it stop.

FileMaker's Install OnTimer Script step only runs during idle time. I was surprised to learn that FileMaker considers typing to be idle time. That's certainly not my definition! That's why I had to create this convoluted solution. The programmers at FileMaker, Inc. mean you are idle if there is no other script running (or paused), no dialog boxes sitting in front of you, and no menus popped open. Once any other scripts are finished or dialogs are dismissed, the OnTimer continues from where it left off.

Now, if a user runs a script that pauses them in Browse mode with their cursor in a field, this OnTimer example will not run until the script finishes. In that case, you may want to be very specific about how long the user is allowed to pause the script rather than leaving it paused indefinitely.

If you really want to use this function, you'll probably want to change the length of time to something longer than 10 seconds. Measured in seconds, to get a 15-minute interval you would enter 900. A user could go "idle" in Find or Preview mode, so you would want to check those boxes in the Script Triggers dialog. Just remember that having those boxes checked will also affect how script 16 works. You'll also want to consider which layouts it should be attached to. We only used it on the one, but in reality, people will be working on multiple layouts and possibly in multiple files. Setting it up like that can limit what else the OnTimer can do because, if you'll remember, you're only allowed one of each type of script trigger per layout. Use up the OnLayoutLoad trigger for this purpose and it's not available for any other.

⌘ **TIP** I find multiplying out all those seconds a little tedious since I'm not among the lucky few who does that kind of calculating in my head. I found that you can just type 60 * 15 and FileMaker will do the math for you.

By the way, the point of this particular OnTimer example is not to catch people loafing. Phone calls, e-mail, and other workers dropping by can easily interrupt data entry. On the other hand, you could use the OnTimer to catch people loafing, but I'll leave that up to you to figure out. Anyway, this is just an example. There are many ways you can use the OnTimer.

Install OnTimer Script Details

Here are some subtleties to the inner workings of the Install OnTimer Script step:

- Only one OnTimer can be running per window. But don't forget that you can have multiple windows open in the same file.
- Any dialogs will come to the front of the current window but not in front of other applications. You can call another OnTimer script to take the place of one that's already running. That's what we did with script 19 to halt the first OnTimer.
- You can use an interval that comes from a value in a field. If you change the number in the field, the OnTimer won't change until you start it over again.
- You can have multiple files all running their own OnTimer scripts, although one must run completely before the next one can begin.
- If you add other steps to the script with the OnTimer in it, the steps before the OnTimer will run, then the Timer will start, and the steps after the timer will execute. But the timer keeps running and repeating the selected script. The other steps in the script containing the OnTimer step will only run one time. If you have multiple OnTimer steps in the same script, only the final one will actually run since it will replace any others.
- Adding a Halt script step after the OnTimer step will not affect the OnTimer. It will keep plugging along.
- You cannot use Install OnTimer Script with web publishing.
- You cannot run an OnTimer as if it were a FileMaker Server scheduled script. That's not to say that it won't run if you're sharing your files with FileMaker Server — just that you would use Server's own timer scripts separately.

OnTimer Script Ideas

Here are some ideas for using the OnTimer:

- Flash reminders on the screen that time is running out for task completion
- Refreshing Web Viewer data
- Combine with an OnLayoutKeystroke trigger to start the OnTimer with every keypress. That way the OnTimer starts as soon as the typing ends.

There will be a lot more to come as developers come up with new ideas.

Functions Related to Script Triggers

Many of the things you'll want to use script triggers for require knowing what's being done on the keyboard. We already looked at Get (TriggerKeystroke) in script 16. Since you'll want to be able to capture the various key codes, it would be helpful to have a translator. We'll use the Code (text) and Char (number) functions for this tool. Code takes text and converts it to a Unicode number. Char does the opposite, converting a number into the text character. Let's take a look. Go to your CON table and add these fields:

Field Name	*Type*	*Options*
zi_Text_gt	Text	Global
zi_Num_gn	Number	Global
GetCode	Calculation	Code (zi_Text_gt)
GetChar	Calculation	Char (zi_Num_gn)

Put them on the CON_Contact layout somewhere out of the way and organize them something like this:

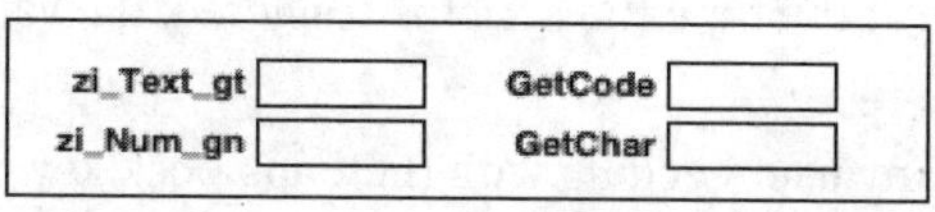

Figure 16-3
Example of GetCode and GetChar.

Now enter any letter into the zi_Text_gt field and press the Enter key; you should get the numeric equivalent. You can now use that number as we did in the altered version of script 16 to trigger a script when pressing a specific key. Try pressing the Return key when your cursor is in zi_Text_gt. Was script 16 looking over your shoulder? Do you know how to fix it? You can even type multiple letters to get a long string of numbers. GetCode will probably display a question mark, so just click in the field to see what the whole number is. Oddly, if you enter multiple letters, the numbers appear in reverse order from the way the letters are entered. What number represents your name?

Now use zi_Num_gn to enter numbers to see the keyboard character. Nothing below 33 seems to show anything. They really do represent keys; it's just that you can't see them. For example, the carriage return equals 13 as we've already seen. Tab equals 9 and space equals 32. Some developers will be happy to know that the invisible line feed character is equal to 10. Now you can watch for that character and either convert it or strip it out of text fields. You should be aware that some key character codes may be different between Macintosh and Windows.

Get (TriggerModifierKeys)

This function grabs the same value as the Get (ActiveModifierKeys) function but only at the time of the trigger event. I would expect it to be used mostly in conjunction with Get (TriggerKeystroke) to determine if a letter is upper- or lowercase or one of the optional characters (like ©, which is entered by pressing Option+g). On the other hand, the definition doesn't appear to prevent it from being used with other script triggers.

You can use the information it captures in a branching script to perform different actions depending on which modifier key or keys are down at the time. If your solution will run on both Mac and Windows, you might need to use the Get (SystemPlatform) function first since some of the keys have different values. When more than one of the modifier keys is down at the same time, the number captured is the sum of the values of those keys. Here are the modifier key values:

Shift = 1
Caps Lock = 2
Ctrl (Windows) and Control (Mac OS) = 4
Alt (Windows) and Option (Mac OS) = 8
Command (Mac OS) = 16
If no keys are held down at the time the script is triggered, the value is 0 (zero).

Here's an example. Since many users end up with the Caps Lock key down, you can make a script to watch for that. Again, keep in mind that it's possible to use up your script triggers on a layout.

```
Script: Caps Lock On
If [Get (ActiveModifierKeys) = 2]
   Show Custom Dialog ["Caps Lock is on."]
End If
```

A Case for FileMaker Pro Advanced

As I mentioned earlier, script triggers can run almost magically and invisibly. That's great until you find one running improperly and you can't figure out what's causing it or what's wrong with it. One of FileMaker Pro Advanced's main features is the debugger. You can start the debugger running and any time one of the events gets triggered, you can watch the script run step by step and figure out what's going on.

A second feature for FMPA is the ability to make custom menus. With this tool, you can set up separate menus for different users. You can also substitute a script for a specific menu item. One popular example would be the Delete Record menu item. Using custom menus in FMPA, you could substitute a script that tracks what was in the record (maybe sending it into a special archive table) and who deleted it before it actually removes the record from the file. I can't tell you how many of my clients find that an attractive feature!

Advanced looks nearly identical to the regular client version of FMP, except that it has a few added menus. But the tools they hold are powerful. You can read about the rest of them on the FileMaker web site. I also recommend the use of a second monitor or at least an 18-inch monitor. Script Debugger sits in front of any active window and you'll need to be able to push it out of the way but still keep it in view.

Summary

In this chapter, we looked at script triggers and several script steps. We created some example scripts and used script triggers to fire them off. We also looked at some of those old demon "gotchas" that can pop up and bite you.

Q & A

Q I'd like to run an OnTimer script step to trigger a script that updates a clock in my application every second. What is the best way to make that work?

A It's not a good idea to run an OnTimer script trigger with a very short interval, because you can effectively lock yourself out of the application. However, there is a very cool JavaScript Data URL clock that I've included in the downloadable files in the Chapter 15 folder. Look for it on the NUL_DataURL layout.

Q I like the idea of checking for data entry errors in some fields, but I don't want to do it in every field or tie up the Layout Setup script triggers.

> **A** You can apply the same script trigger to multiple objects on a layout at the same time by selecting them all at once and going to the Script Triggers menu item. If the script will process different fields in the grouping differently, you can use a series of If and Else If steps to make it behave exactly the way you want.

Workshop

Apply the alternative keystroke trigger suggested for script 16 and apply it to the CON_Contact layout. Here again is the substitute step:

```
Else If [Get (TriggerKeystroke) = "13" and Get (ActiveFieldName) ≠
"Notes" and Get (ActiveFieldName) ≠ "AddrStreet"]
```

Another problem some of my clients have is data entry personnel who like to type with the Caps Lock key on. Create a script that will loop through the fields and correct that. (Hint: Use the Proper (Text) text formatting function. But keep in mind it will also turn names like McCarthy into Mccarthy. How would you implement something like that at the field level?)

Chapter 17

Designing Your Screen Layouts

Introduction

You already know how to create layouts, and you know about layout parts and building reports. This chapter is about design and the specifics of the various FileMaker tools used to accomplish good design. In a way, it's a continuation of the last chapter where you put the right fields on the right layouts. Now you need to organize the fields with graphic elements, make it flow, and make it sing.

Computers are everywhere today. People see a lot of software and know what commercial products look like. With the proliferation of the Internet, we see web pages of all types. If you've done a little web surfing, you know that some web sites are easy to navigate, while others are total confusion. The reason for that is the design of the interface. You need to ask yourself what type of database you want to design — hopefully one that's clear, crisp, and easy to understand. How do you want users to feel while doing their work with what you've designed? I'll bet you thought you were just trying to keep track of data.

Because there are so many good interface designs out there, user expectations are high. You have to do a good job just to make it acceptable. I love it when my clients call to tell me that a report that used to take them two days to produce now only takes 15 minutes. They're using it, and it's saving them time. If you find that some areas aren't being used anymore or they're being neglected, it may be because of bad design.

Basic Design

One of the best ways to get started with design is to look at the FileMaker Pro templates. Use File, New Database, click the Create Database icon, and then choose the "Create database using Starter Solution" radio button. That way you can study these examples, tear them apart, and then delete the files from your computer afterward. You should also give the files names that will let you know they may be deleted later.

Each of the templates follows a modified Aqua or Ocean Blue screen theme of white and various shades of blue. Some text items along the top (which are really buttons) represent layouts that differ in the way information is presented, such as View Contact List Report and View Address Labels.

Some templates (Contact Management under the Business - People & Assets heading, for example) have tabs partway down the screen that take advantage of the Tab Control feature introduced in FileMaker 8. The tabs and icons provide a fairly clear indication of what type of data can be found on those screens. This style of interface will be familiar to anyone who uses computers, and is quickly grasped by first-time users as well. I must admit, I was thrown by the text buttons in the upper right. I'm just not sure it's clear that clicking on the text in the light gray bar near the top will do anything, although the text itself invites you to "View" something. I would probably have used elements that look more like buttons.

A big design consideration should be finding out what the end users already work with. Try to make your design similar to something with which they will be familiar. I often scan paper forms used in the offices, duplicate the forms in FileMaker layouts, and then try to improve on the design. This is really a good time to ask the staff what they would change about their forms. If your screen fields are in the same approximate position as the paper forms, the transition to your system will be that much easier.

Navigating through the database with buttons should mimic or be better than the current workflow. Remember, it doesn't have to be clear to you, it has to be clear to the user. There should always be a Home or Main Menu screen. Users should rarely have to go more than three clicks from the Main Menu to get to a specific area. Warning messages should make it clear what choices are expected from the user. That is why learning to work with FileMaker's custom messages in field validation and scripts can be so valuable to you as a developer.

After you've built a beta version, watch the end users work. See where they get lost, and rethink your work. The big software companies test their applications with video cameras focused both over the shoulders and on the faces of their testers, and even with all that, you've seen how badly designed some of the software is! You can do better than they can if you pay attention. Don't explain too much; just listen. That doesn't mean all your solutions will be self-explanatory, but if most of the users get hung up at the same point, and it happens time after time, think again. Be humble. You might want to take a look at some user interface sites on the web like the Interface Hall of Shame at http://homepage.mac.com/bradster/iarchitect/shame.htm, which provides examples of both the good and the bad.

Know What You Like

Look at more than one of the template files. Even though they use the same theme, each of the template files offers a little different approach, especially the integrated files in the Registration file under the Business - General heading. When you look at the Manage Database, Tables tab, you'll see there are three tables in this file. For a real eye-opener, click the Relationships tab and look at the graph. Since the table occurrences have been named according to function, hover your mouse pointer over the arrow in the upper-left corner of each TO to find out which table they're associated with. Notice that by not using the anchor-buoy system, it's difficult to tell what the base table is for the three TOs in the upper right.

The companion files for this book, which you can download from the publisher's web site (www.wordware.com/files/fmpro10), include the Asset Management template FileMaker provided with earlier versions of the software. Look in the Book files\Chapter 17 folder. When you open the file:

1. Ask yourself what you might do differently.
2. Duplicate one of the data entry layouts.
3. Start moving the layout parts around to see how the background is constructed. Some parts, like the black rectangle that provides the background in the header, may be locked. Click to select them and choose Arrange, Unlock so you can move them around, too. Some layout objects are text blocks, while others are colored rectangles with transparent or "None" borders. A few items are actually buttons formatted with the Do Nothing script step. You can figure them out because when you double-click them, the cursor goes immediately to the center and flashes, waiting for you to enter the button text.

Let's say that you like this layout, and you'd like to use it in your own solution. The only improvement you'd like to make is to change the colors to reflect your corporate logo colors. Let's do that now.

1. Go back to the original data entry layout in the template, and make another copy.
2. Delete all the fields and their labels, and change the colors to suit you.
3. Now choose **Edit, Select All**, then **Arrange, Group**, and copy the elements to the clipboard.
4. Open your Business file to the Invoice layout, and go to Layout mode.
5. Duplicate the layout, paste the background elements onto your layout, and read the next step.
6. Before you do anything else, choose **Arrange, Send to Back**, and move them into place. (If you click off the parts before you send them to the back, it would be better to delete them and start over. Otherwise they won't be stacked the same way.) You may have to work with the layout parts to get it to look right. Don't forget that the entire background is now grouped. You can select it and choose **Arrange, Ungroup** so you can work with individual elements again.
7. Remember that all your buttons will need to be reattached to the proper scripts (some not created as yet) and other Button Setup options. That means the tab buttons would need to be attached to the proper layouts. An alternative would be to use the Tab Control tool, which I'll show you later in this chapter. When I do a transfer like this, I use the procedure described in the following Tip to remind myself to fix them.

⌘ **TIP** After transferring a set of buttons from another file or layout, you should assume they'll be attached to the wrong scripts and identify them as still needing work. Use the Text tool and type an X somewhere on the layout. Format the X as red, bold, and at least 18 points. Then make as many copies as you need to put one on each questionable button. As you fix the buttons, you can remove the Xs one at a time until the job is done. This allows you to work on other things and come back to finish this job at a later time. Regardless of how you make this look now, when you're doing work for other people, be sure you always think of your users.

Keep It Consistent

In most layouts in the templates, you'll notice similar buttons are in exactly the same location. As much as possible, buttons that provide the same function should be in the same place on all the layouts. Don't try to provide all buttons for everything on every page. Too many buttons can be overwhelming. You may need to provide separate areas, usually for specific reports, where similar groups of functions will have matching buttons within that area only. Maybe some of those areas will apply to different groups of users.

One thing you should always do is provide a Main Menu or Home button on every layout. The upper-left corner is the position most often used by designers. That's not what FileMaker has done in these templates, but you'll want that in your more complex solutions.

Notice that sometimes when you arrive in an area, the button or tab that got you there changes color, but it's still on the page. You should also strive to let users know when they've changed layouts, but make it consistent enough that they understand how to go back to where they were.

Make the field labels conform to the same style and terminology from layout to layout. If you use Invoice No. on one layout, don't switch to Inv. # on another and InvNum on yet another. Using that same approach in the selection of short, descriptive file, table, layout, and script names will also help you to understand your own files when you have to come back to work on them later.

Group Formatting

Too many different fonts can add confusion to a layout. Use the same one or two fonts and font sizes as much as possible throughout your layouts. If you find you have too many font styles and sizes on one layout, you can reformat all of them at once. First, you need to select the group of items you want to change. You could be changing the fields themselves, their labels, or some other text on the layout. This technique will also work for other object types.

1. Select one of the items you want to change.
2. Press **Option+Command+A** (Macintosh) or **Ctrl+Shift+A** (Windows) to select all of that type of object.
3. To deselect any items you don't want to change, hold down the **Shift** key and click on the object.

4. To reformat all selected items on the Macintosh, hold down the **Control** key and click on one of the selected objects in the group. On Windows machines, right-click on one of the selected objects.
5. Make the formatting changes.

Another way to select all of one type of object is to:

1. Click on the first object.
2. Click on the **Select Objects by Type** icon on the right side of the Arrange palette as seen in Figure 17-1.

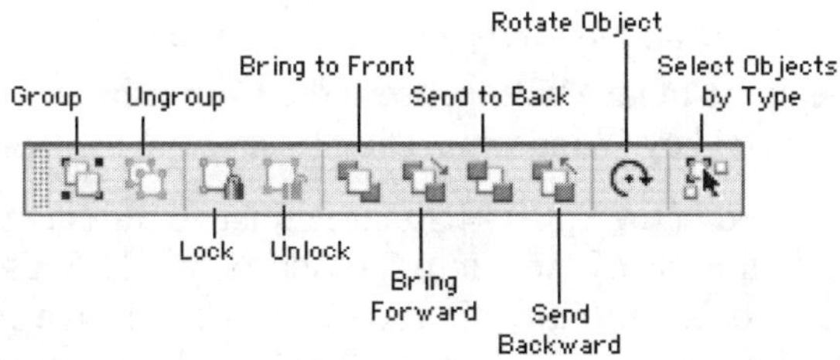

Figure 17-1
By clicking on a layout item and using the Select Objects by Type icon from the Arrange palette, you can select all layout elements of the same type.

3. If you think you might want to change them again later, choose **Arrange, Group.** Now you can get to all of them at one time. You can always ungroup them later should you need to move or otherwise work with them separately.

You can also reformat items by selecting just a couple of objects or text items. You don't have to select all items of one type on the layout.

Remember that you can use the Format Painter when changing the attributes of layout objects. For a complete discussion of the Format Painter, see Chapter 3, "Creating Your First Database."

CAUTION Be careful when choosing the Field Format window options on multiple fields. Any fields that have been formatted with value lists will either lose all their value lists or acquire the same value list as one of the other items — a major pain that you might not even discover for some time! That doesn't happen with the Format Painter tool.

TIP Sometimes the default settings for fonts and graphics change mysteriously. If there is an object on the layout that has the formatting you want to make into the default, press Command (Macintosh) or Ctrl (Windows) while you click on the object. If you don't have a default you like, click in a blank space on the layout so that nothing is selected. Then make choices from the appropriate menus. Those will become the default settings. And finally, add graphics or text to the layout using any of the layout tools. (Pasting something onto the layout from the clipboard won't work.) Now make changes to it before you deselect it. You guessed it — those are the new defaults.

Selecting Groups of Layout Objects

Here are some techniques you might find helpful when selecting a group of objects.

The first is by surrounding the objects. In Chapter 3, I described a method for selecting a group of objects by clicking and dragging with the Selection tool until you surrounded the objects. This method allows you to select a group of objects that are within or touching the selection rectangle.

The second is by touching the objects.

1. In Layout mode, click outside of the group and drag until the selection rectangle is touching all the items you want to include.
2. Before releasing the mouse button, press the **Command** key (Macintosh) or **Ctrl** key (Windows). Then release the mouse button.

In Figure 17-2, I started in the upper-right corner above the NameFirst field label and dragged until I was partway into the AddrCity field. This selects all four fields and their labels. With the other method, I would have also had to surround the NameLast, State, and Zip fields and their labels as well, only to have to deselect them before proceeding. You can see the advantage! (On Macintosh computers you'll know you have it right because the whole area of the rectangle turns gray.)

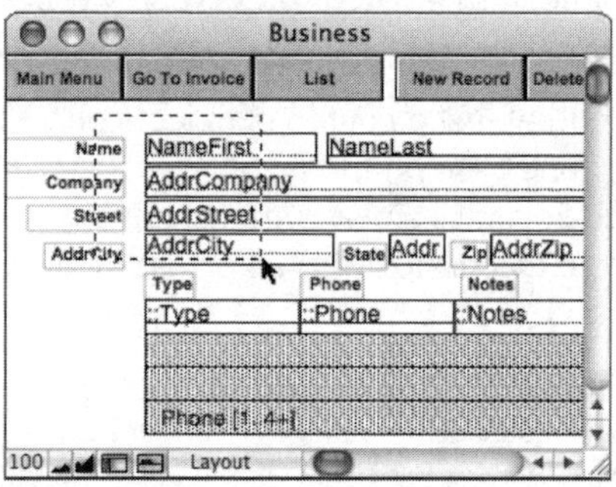

Figure 17-2
Selecting a group of objects without completely surrounding them.

Remember, you can always deselect any objects after they've been selected as part of a group.

Here's another helpful trick. To deselect an object underneath another:

1. Select both objects, then deselect the upper object by Shift+clicking somewhere on it. The bottom object is now the only item selected.
2. Choose **Arrange**, **Lock**. Now you can work with the upper object separately since the locked, lower object won't move even if it's included in the selection.

This is especially helpful when you then want to select and move a group of objects but include just that upper element.

How to Make It Pretty

Aside from using soft colors, the overriding rule to making layouts look nice is to keep it simple. It's not too early to discuss the final step in cleaning up your layouts. Stated simply: If you don't need it, take it out. Clutter is confusion. Your layout is not done when everything is there. It's done when you can't possibly take anything else out. Also note that something about the way our brains are organized seems to respond better if buttons, fields, and labels are aligned and uncluttered. If you're afraid you might need a layout object later, create a layout using the same base table and name it with a three-letter base table code and the word Developer. Remove it from the layout list in Browse mode and put your deleted items there.

Arrange and View Menus

Use the tools in the Arrange and View menus to organize your layouts. Take a look at the tools in the View menu in in Figure 17-3. When you choose Show from this menu, there are some options we haven't seen before. Try them out on your own to see what they do. If there aren't any sliding or non-printing objects on your layout, select any object and format it with one of the two options. Then turn on the menu choice by choosing View, Show, Non-Printing Objects so you can see how it changes in appearance. (Once an item is selected, a check mark appears in front of it in the list. Of course, you can't see the check mark because the menu disappears. Selecting the menu item again turns if off.) I find Show, Text Boundaries especially helpful for aligning text items on the layout.

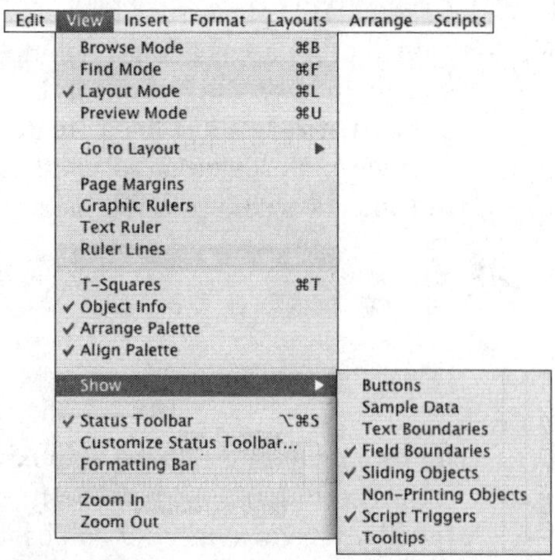

Figure 17-3
The list of tools and options under the View menu.

Rotate Layout Objects

You can also rotate any layout object (except a layout part or a portal) by selecting it and choosing Arrange, Rotate. Objects rotate in 90-degree clockwise increments. The keyboard shortcut is Command+Option+R (Macintosh) or Ctrl+Alt+R (Windows). In reports, if the field is short and the field label is long, rotate it. You may still have to abbreviate it or break it into two lines to make it fit in a narrow header part.

Part 4

Icons

There has been a proliferation of icons in software in recent years. FileMaker Pro itself includes toolbars that are full of icons. The reason is that our brain can grasp an image more quickly than it can read words. After all, a picture is worth a thousand words. But you'll also notice that you can choose not to display the toolbars. Don't get carried away with too many icons in your files. If the same button is the same color and in the same place on the layout, users will know where to go automatically. Again, notice how simple the templates are.

⌘ **TIP** If you decide to provide icons on your buttons, don't fall in love with them. If your users don't understand one or more of them, it doesn't matter how much time you spent on them — the ones that don't work have to be taken out or redesigned.

The arrow icons (in the Asset Management template in the downloadable companion files) that indicate next, previous, first, and last record are simple and fairly universal in meaning. You see similar icons on cassette recorders, CD and DVD players, as well as VCRs. In some files these buttons are created in other applications and imported. In the Asset Management file, when you zoom in on the buttons in Layout mode, you'll find out they're made up of a series of very short lines created with FileMaker's Line tool. Graphics created with FileMaker's tools will usually draw faster on the screen, as long as the objects are not too complex.

⌘ **TIP** When you do create icons, try to construct them with FileMaker's own graphics tools. Also, large graphics brought in from other sources can slow down screen redraws. In rare cases, they may contain a bit of information that causes a layout not to print properly.

If you simply must create graphics in other applications, use a 256-color (8-bit) setting rather than 32-bit. Storing a batch of 32-bit graphics will make the file large in a hurry. If you have the choice, it would be even better to use the web-safe 212-color palette, which is easy to share between Macintosh and Windows computers, not to mention the web. If you do decide to use external graphics, it is more efficient to use the same image over again whenever possible, rather than creating separate images. Once the graphic has loaded, FileMaker will redraw it from memory each time instead of returning to the disk or the server. If you have a layout that won't print, be suspicious of any imported graphics on the layout.

⌘ **TIP** To locate a layout object that may be causing print problems, make a copy of the layout and try deleting half of the objects. If it still won't print, make another copy and delete the other half. Now if it prints, start working your way down to one quarter of the part that won't print until you finally determine the culprit.

Locking Objects on a Layout

There are times when you may want to lock objects on your layouts. For instance, you may have a set of background objects right where you want them, but you want to move a few items in the foreground. If you try to click and drag to surround them, the background object(s) will move instead. In that case, lock the background elements by selecting them and choosing Arrange, Lock. Then you can easily work with the items in the foreground.

If other people will have access to Layout mode in the files, you may have to lock objects to prevent them from being moved. That can be especially problematic with portals and the fields in them. If a field extends even one pixel out of the portal, you may not be able to see or create anything beyond the first portal row. (You could also group the portal and the fields in it so that if they get moved, they'll at least move together.) Most users don't want to deal with Layout mode, but in situations where there are problems, you have the tool to handle it, at least until they discover the Unlock command!

I've also had to protect fields from myself. Occasionally, I've created scripts that performed a copy, paste, replace, or insert step. All of those commands require that the chosen field be on the current layout. And there is no warning if FileMaker can't find the field it needs on the layout. I spent 32 hours one weekend tracking down a bug in a long string of scripts. In the end, I found I had deleted the field referred to in the script. Seems I thought I didn't need that field on that layout. Now I lock fields referred to by scripts that might not otherwise seem essential to a layout.

NOTE Find/Replace script steps also require that any field they operate on be on the layout. So any script that uses the Find/Replace step should include a step to choose the correct layout.

TIP Here's a way to hide a script-essential field that might not otherwise need to be on a layout.

1. Move the field to one of the corners of the visible screen (upper left is a good choice) and turn off all four borders.
2. Choose a font and field background color that matches the layout background.
3. Remove the field from the tab order, and uncheck the box next to "Allow entry into field" in the Field Format window.
4. Now choose **View**, **Object Info**.
5. If "cm" or "in" appears to the right of the boxes, click until you see **px** (for pixels).
6. Type **1** in both of the bottom boxes (width and height), pressing the Tab key between entries.
7. Before deselecting it, use the up and down arrows to move it farther into the corner, send it to the back, and lock the field.

The point here is to keep the field accessible to the script but not to a human. A script doesn't care what size or color the text in the field is; it can find the field as long as it's somewhere on the layout. But remember, a user must have access to the field for a script to run properly. You can check the box next to "Run script with full access privileges." More about that in Chapter 22, "Keeping Your Data Secure."

Adding Graphics and Movies to a Layout

You can place graphics directly in the layout in Layout mode or into a container field in Browse mode using one of a number of methods. When you're in Layout mode, use drag-and-drop, copy and paste, or Insert, Picture. When in Browse mode, you have the same choices with one exception. In order to choose Insert, Picture, you first have to click in the container field or use a script to get you into the field. Then your choices are Insert, Picture, QuickTime, Sound, and File. On the Windows platform, your choices also include Object. (See Chapter 21 for information about importing a folder of files.) When the graphic or movie goes into a field, you'll then want to format the field as described in the next section.

Formatting Graphics on a Layout

Remember back in Chapter 13 where I showed you how to use GetRepetition in a calculation to highlight a negative invoice amount with a red rectangle? There was a little problem in that the color didn't completely fill up the calculated field. This is where I show you how to fill the rectangle to the edges.

1. Go back to the Invoice table. Since the Color field we want to work with is underneath Invoice Total, let me show you a technique to work with it.

⌘ **TIP** When layout objects are stacked or very near each other, you may need to move some objects so you can work on others. Select the objects that are in the way, and move them by pressing the appropriate arrow key 10 times. When you're done working on the other field or layout element, you'll always know the other items have to go back into place exactly 10 clicks.

2. Select the **InvoiceTotal** field and move it 10 clicks downward.
3. Now highlight the **Color** field, and choose **Format**, **Graphic**. This will bring up the window shown in Figure 17-4.

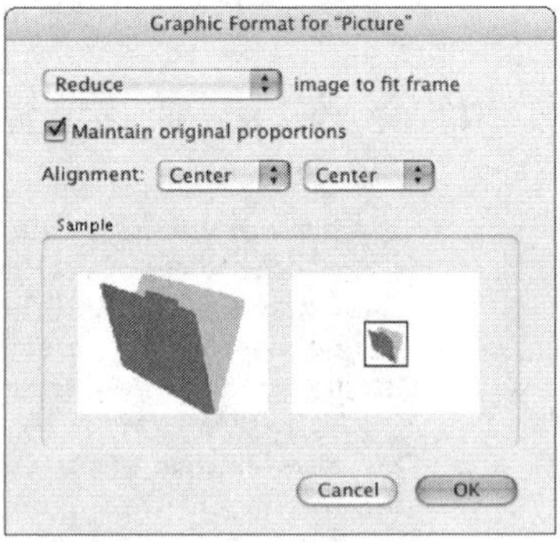

Figure 17-4
The Graphic Format window.

Take a look at the choices in this window. As you make selections from the three drop-down lists, the Sample area gives you some idea of how they will affect your final image. With photographs and movies, you'll almost certainly want to choose the check box next to "Maintain original proportions." Otherwise, the images may appear unnaturally squashed or stretched. Since our goal is a simple patch of color, it may not be clear that these choices also apply to photos, movies, and objects placed in container fields.

4. Choose **Enlarge** from the "image to fit frame" drop-down.

5. Deselect the "Maintain original proportions" check box, and click **OK**.
6. Now select and move **InvoiceTotal** back up the layout — exactly 10 clicks.
7. Go to the record with the negative amount in it to see if it aligns the way you expect.

CAUTION Be aware that images with lots of detail will cause the screen to redraw more slowly. If you have a fast machine, that may not be a problem. If the files are shared over a network, however, it could cause traffic to slow to a crawl. Most computer screens cannot display images with more than 72 dots per inch of detail anyway. If the images are absolutely necessary, it's better to use image-editing software to downsample the image before importing. You can also place the container field that holds the image on a layout that will be referred to only when needed rather than one that comes into view constantly.

Customizing the Appearance of Objects on a Layout

As you develop your own style, you will want to make choices about how specific layout objects will look. Just remember, it takes time to do this work. If you're working on a project for yourself or a set of files that will be a commercial product, it's okay to labor over it. If someone else hired you, be sure they're willing to pay for some of the finer details. If you've quoted someone a price, you may end up absorbing the polish work yourself. This is one reason the Layout Assistant is so valuable.

Adding Borders, Baselines, and Fills to Fields

Once your cursor is in any of the fields in a form, you can see all the other fields outlined. But I find it disconcerting to be in Browse mode with the cursor out of the record and not be able to tell where the borderless fields are. Since field labels can logically be either to the side, above, or (less often) below the fields they identify, I prefer to make the borders visible.

You can use the method outlined in the section called "Group Formatting" earlier in this chapter to format one, a few, or all of the fields on your layout. Choose Format, Field/Control, Borders to open the Field Borders dialog. You can choose border and fill patterns in this window as well as add a text baseline. In the Sample area on the right, you can watch the effect of your choices. Afterward, you may also want to add Embossed, Engraved, and Drop Shadow effects from the Object Effects palette in the Layout bar. The Format Painter will work with all these attributes, including the object effects.

Adding Object Effects

Using the Object Effects palette (see Figure 17-5) can really help give a finished look to your files. Of course, building your layouts with the Layout Assistant using themes will go a long way toward giving you a finished look with little effort.

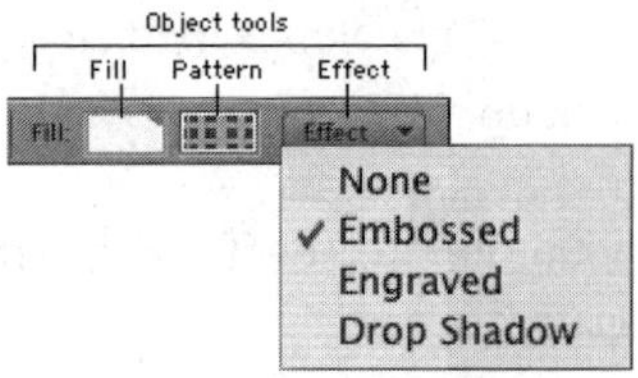

Figure 17-5
FileMaker's Object Effects palette available in Layout mode.

As I mentioned before, some of the background objects in the older template files are really buttons. However, they could just as easily be rectangles. In earlier versions of FileMaker Pro, you had to jump through hoops to get rectangles to have a 3D appearance, so buttons were often used instead. Now, providing depth to rectangles, ellipses, and fields is just a click away.

Embossed

To try out this effect:

1. Draw a button about 1 inch by 1 inch.
2. Now draw a rectangle with the same color and border width as the button, and use the Embossed effect. They should look identical.
3. While the rectangle is still selected, choose a wider border, say 3 point, just to see what it looks like.

Engraved

Using the Engraved effect gives the appearance that the layout object is etched into the surface. It's most effective against a background color other than white.

Select your rectangle, give it the Engraved effect, and then try some different point sizes for the border. Now try some different color combinations of border and fill.

Drop Shadow

Now choose Drop Shadow with a transparent border, but make the border 8 point. This gives you a nice floating rectangle effect. You don't get separate control over the color of the shadow. If you really need that much control, you can offset a stack of two rectangles like us old-timers used to do before FileMaker Pro 5.0! Then you can format each rectangle separately.

Changing Colors

We haven't talked much about the details of changing colors of layout objects. When you're in Layout mode and have an object selected, you've been selecting colors by using the Fill Color palette in the Layout bar. Click the color patch to the right of the word "Fill" and scroll down to Other Color. On Windows, you can create your own custom color by clicking anywhere on the graduated color rectangle. You can also enter numbers directly in the Hue, Saturation, and Luminescence or Red, Green, and Blue fields. On Macintosh, you have five different tools for choosing colors. Three of the five tools have a number of additional options available from the drop-down list in each tool. If you're not happy with the standard color sets, this is where you make your own personal choices. Just remember, not everybody's computer will be able to display your favorite colors.

Tab Control[8]

In earlier versions of FileMaker, we often had certain fields that repeated at the top of different layouts. We developers would create elaborate tab systems for switching to the various layouts. Not to mention that the layout list would often get quite long. With this multi-layout method you had to be careful not to make a change in the look of the repeated information. If you did, you would have to change it on every single layout. And aligning layout items across multiple layouts was a nightmare. No more!

The Tab Control (TC) feature, introduced in version 8, lets you place items in different "layers" of a tabbed panel on a single layout. It helps you organize your layouts and makes updating much easier. Hooray!

To get an idea of how this works, let's add a tab control to our Business file so we can display both a Notes area and an invoice list.

1. Go to the **CON_Contact** layout.
2. Click the **Tab Control** tool, which looks like a file folder and lies just above the Field tool. (You can also choose Insert, Tab Control, or use the button in the Tool panel.)
3. Click and drag to make a rectangle about 8 inches wide and 2 inches tall. In my file I'm placing it directly on top of the Notes field so it covers it up. This will bring up the Tab Control Setup window shown in Figure 17-6 — except it won't be filled in yet.

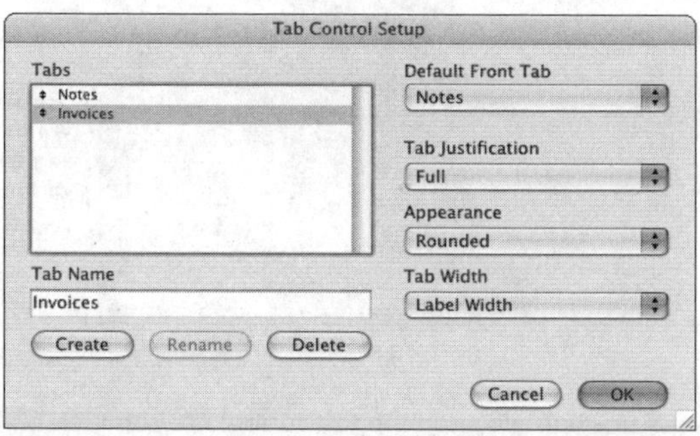

Figure 17-6
The Tab Control Setup window showing two tabs with Full justification.

4. In the Tab Name box, type **Notes** and click the **Create** button.
5. Now type **Invoices** and click the **Create** button again.
6. In the Tab Justification drop-down, select **Full**. This will make the two tabs the same size and fill the whole top area of the control.

With the Tab Justification drop-down set to Full, any selections in the Tab Width[9] drop-down really don't have any effect. However, if you choose one of the other justification settings, you can tell FileMaker exactly how to handle the width of the tabs. This was a new feature for FMP9 and it makes it a lot easier to have your tabs look the way you like. Previously (unless you selected Full justification) the tabs were the size of the text on them. I personally like my tabs to look like the tabs on file folders, exactly the same width. This Tab Width feature lets me do that and a lot more!

Notice that the Notes tab is chosen in the Default Front Tab[9] drop-down. That means whenever you return to Browse mode, the Notes tab will be the front tab. In previous versions, whichever tab you were on when you left Layout mode became the front tab. After making layout changes to one of the "lesser" tabs, it was easy to forget to select the one you wanted to be in front when you went back to Browse mode. People complained and FileMaker listened. Obviously, you can choose whichever tab you want to always be the front tab.

7. Look around this dialog at the other choices in the drop-down lists. When you're done, click **OK**.
8. Under the Arrange menu, choose **Send to Back**. If your Notes field had been hidden by the tab control, it should now be on top of it.

   You may need to resize either the tab control or the Notes field at this point. Ideally, you would want the Notes field to fit just under the tabs themselves without having the bottom of the field extend below the bottom edge of the tab control. Placing the items on the tab control can be a little bit fussy. You want to make sure the Notes tab is the front tab as you place the Notes field. If the Invoices tab was in front, you'll need to move the Notes field down until the bottom of the field is below the tab control. Then click the Notes tab to bring it forward, and move the Notes field back up into place as I have done in Figure 17-7.

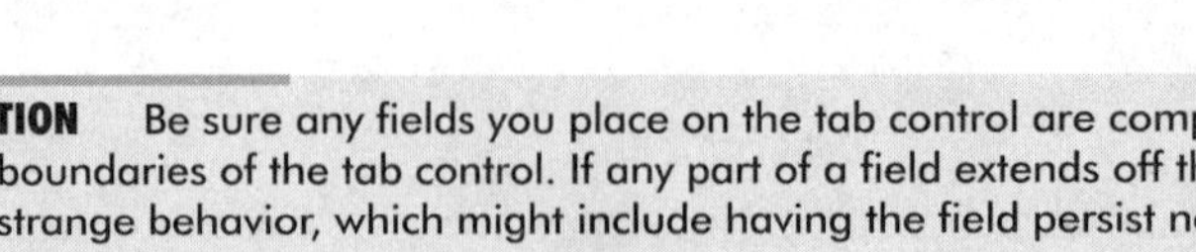

Figure 17-7
A tab control showing the placement of the Notes field.

CAUTION Be sure any fields you place on the tab control are completely within the boundaries of the tab control. If any part of a field extends off the TC, you will get strange behavior, which might include having the field persist no matter which tab you click.

9. Click the two tabs to make sure the Notes field alternately shows and disappears. If not, go back to the previous paragraph and study the instructions about positioning items there.

10. Once you have that set, click to select the Invoices tab.
11. Using the Portal tool, draw a portal in the Invoices area roughly the size of the Notes field.
12. When the Portal Setup window appears, choose **con_INV__ConSerNum** from the drop-down.
13. Check the box next to **Sort portal records**. Double-click **Date**, change it to **Descending order**, and click **OK**.
14. Check the box next to **Show vertical scroll bar**, and click **OK**.
15. In the Add Fields to Portal window, choose **Date**, **InvoiceNum_pk**, and **Invoice Total**, and click **OK**.
16. Resize the fields and format them in a way that makes sense. I removed a portal row so I had room to give the fields some labels.
17. Add a Go button. You don't need a script. In the Button Setup dialog, just click the **Specify** button and choose **con_INV__ConSerNum** from the "Get related record from" drop-down and **INV_Invoice** from the "Show record using layout" drop-down. Check the box next to **Show only related records** and select the radio button next to **Match current record only**. Click **OK**.

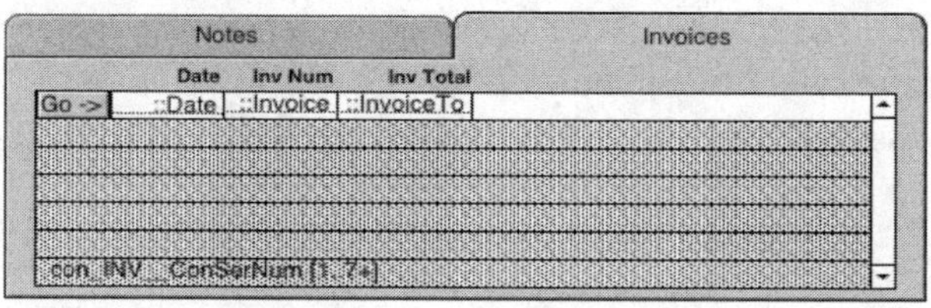

Figure 17-8
A tab control showing placement of a portal and the portal fields.

Does your layout look like Figure 17-8? Seems as if we have a lot of extra space in the portal. We could probably resize the Notes field and the portal and make the whole tab control area smaller. Now that I look at it, doesn't it seem as if the Phone portal might belong in the tab control area?

1. Double-click the tab control to bring up the Tab Control Setup window again.
2. Add a new tab called **Phones**.
3. When it appears in the Tabs box, move it to the top of the list, choose it from the Default Front Tab drop-down, and click **OK**. (The tabs will appear in order from left to right the way they appear from top to bottom in the Tab Control Setup window.)
4. Make sure the **Phones** tab is selected.
5. Highlight the entire Phone portal, the fields in it, the labels above it, and the Delete button, and move them onto the new Phones tab control. If you added the CountPhone field we talked about back in Chapter 13, make sure that goes into the Phones tab too.
6. Finally, position the whole tab control into the space that was occupied by the Phone portal so it looks something like Figure 17-9.

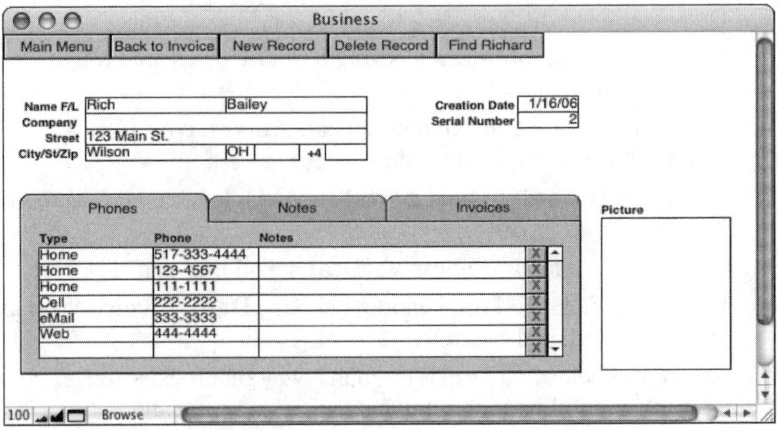

Figure 17-9
A tab control in Browse mode with three tabs.

This uses the screen space so efficiently, I opened up the Phone portal and made the Phone portal's Notes field wider. I also added extra portal rows. If you do that, it will mean the CountPhone field calculation will need to change to accommodate the number of rows you choose to display. I did a little more work to rearrange my other fields, bringing them closer together and changing some of the labels. See Figure 17-9.

This looks great! Now that everything is so much more organized, I wonder if maybe we could have used slightly larger fonts for everything. It's all to your taste. Personally, I prefer to have my screens organized so I don't need to scroll up and down.

You can change the background color of the tab control, as well as use all the font formatting tools. In fact, by double-clicking any individual tab to highlight it (it will display with a heavy rectangle inside the tab), you can change the background color and pattern of each tab independent of the other tabs.

A nice feature of a tab control is that once items are properly placed on it, if you move it, everything moves together. In other words, you don't need to make a selection rectangle to surround the entire tab control area. Just click one of the corners to select it. Everything will move as if it were grouped. If you want to get something off it, you have to click on the tab where the item is and explicitly move it off.

If you include a tab control in the tab order of the layout (see Chapter 5), it behaves as one object. That means that pressing the Tab key won't take you to each of the tabs. To switch between tabs, you need to press one of the arrow keys until you get to the tab you want. Then you press the Return or Enter key to view its contents. When you use the Set Tab Order dialog, you switch between the tabs on the tab control to assign the fields your preferred tab order.

Once you are viewing a particular tab in the tab control area, it stays active and you can use the arrow keys followed by Return or Enter to view the contents of the other tabs. It stays active until you tab out of that area, select or tab into a field, click onto the background, or press the Return or Enter key.

You can have a tab control within a tab control in case you need another layer of information.

If you select View, View as Table, all the fields will show as if they were on a normal layout without a tab control.

Each tab has its own layout object stacking order. Stacking items on a specific tab will act as if the tab itself were the layout background. In other words, by selecting Arrange, Send to Back, a layout object on one of the tabs will only go as far back as the tab it's on, not behind it.

Something you may be disappointed to learn is that neither the tab control nor its tabs can be made into buttons. Developers often want specific processes to occur before users leave one area for another. That isn't currently possible using any simple tools. You may be able to perform some of these processes using script triggers, but it's still somewhat of a work-around. There are also some methods of placing invisible buttons on the layout slightly above the tabs, but they can be difficult to maintain when moving layout objects around — you know, because they're invisible. I cross my fingers with each revision.

One thing to watch out for: If you cover any layout object with a tab control and set it down by releasing the mouse button, the layout object becomes part of the tab control. The object is placed on the frontmost tab at the time. But if you didn't notice it and changed tabs, you might think things were disappearing from your layout.

The tab control is also supported in FileMaker's Instant Web Publishing feature. See Chapter 20, "Sharing Your Data on the Web."

Now that I look at it, maybe the Notes tab should have a Notes portal instead of one large field. I mean, won't I want to identify each interaction I have with the person with a date and time? Hmmm….

Object Names[8.5]

Using the Object Info palette, you can name any item on a layout. Since we've just been talking about the tab control, I want to start by saying that you can name each tab on a tab control. First, of course, you need to make the Object Info palette visible by choosing View, Object Info. Simply clicking one of the tabs won't be enough. You need to click a tab once or twice so that the thick rectangle appears, showing that it's active. (Too many clicks and you'll bring up the Tab Control Setup dialog.) Then type the name in the Object Name field in the Object Info palette. The name you choose must be unique from any other objects on this layout. Note that the calculation engine is not available when it comes to the object name. (Wouldn't it be nice if the default Object Info name for a tab was the same as the text that's already on the tab? Stay tuned for future versions.)

Okay, now that you've named a tab, what can you do with it? Well, you can refer to it in various scripts. When the tab control (TC) was introduced in

FMP8, developers were asking for more control over it. One request was the ability to get to a layout via a script (which could be attached to a button or a script trigger) and have a specific tab selected instead of the default tab. Now you can do that by adding the Go to Object script step under the Navigation heading. You can simply type the object name directly, or you can use the calculation engine to name it more dynamically based on what's happening in the script.

Just because we're talking about using the object name with the TC here, don't forget that you can name other objects on the layout — such as fields. You can use layout object names in calculations in scripts to make the scripts more modular. You can use logic such as, "If this layout object is active, run this routine." One developer said he was able to take a script with 400 lines and distill it into just a couple of lines using the object name. Additionally, you can use the GetLayoutObjectAttribute step (a logical function) to get the object name. It sounds kind of powerful, doesn't it?

Here are some additional rules, advantages, and limitations of named objects:

- You can use up to 100 characters in an object name. Since you can only see about 16, brevity would seem to make development somewhat easier. On the other hand, you can also use tooltips to display the full object names. That would probably be most useful during development, and likely an irritation for everyday users.
- If you group objects, you can give the group a name. Objects within the group can also be named, but they need to be named before they're part of the group. To see the name of an object within a group, you need to ungroup it.
- You can now place multiple copies of the same field on a layout and navigate to the specific copy (using the Go to Object script step) by giving it a unique object name.
- If an object is locked, you need to unlock it to edit its name.
- Each object name must be unique. Don't worry — FileMaker will warn you if you try to use a name twice.
- Remember that during scripting, if you do anything that causes the script to lose focus on the object (such as Commit Records/Requests), you need to include another Go to Object step to bring the focus back to the object. You can store the name of the object in a variable or a global field if you need to.

If you have FileMaker Pro Advanced, you can also build custom menus. If you then assign keyboard commands to the menu items, users can switch between tabs with a quick keystroke.

Autoresize Layout Objects[9]

When you display the Object Info palette in Layout mode (View, Object Info), one of its features is Autoresize. It's indicated at the bottom of the palette with check boxes in the middle of four anchors.

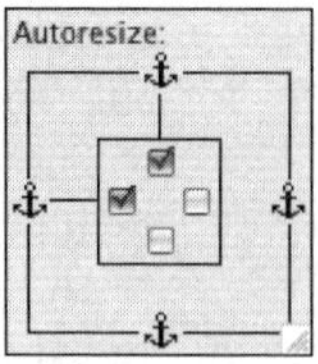

Figure 17-10 The Autoresize feature found at the bottom of the Object Info palette.

The easiest way to understand what Autoresize does is to look at a web page. If you want to resize the window, you grab the lower-right corner and make it bigger or smaller. When you do that with most web pages, some or all of the objects on the page will change their size or position. A PDF may slide back and forth to stay centered (but not change size), or a column of text may expand or contract to accommodate your moves. Well, Autoresize is FileMaker's way of letting you do that to objects on your layouts. I think they added it so the Web Viewer can act more like a web page, but it has a lot of other uses.

Now as fun as that might sound, getting it to work so it's truly usable can be a bit of a trick. Depending on the settings of various objects on your layout, one item may go sliding over or under another layout object. And objects on a tab control might not appear to respond at all to the Autoresize settings.

Getting Autoresize to Work

The default setting for all layout objects is with the left and top anchor boxes checked as they are in Figure 17-10. If you change the size of a FileMaker window in Browse mode by dragging the lower-right corner, none of the objects move or change size at all. Since the right and bottom anchor boxes are not checked, the objects are not anchored or attached to the right and bottom of the window. Once you start choosing the other check boxes, depending on which combinations of boxes you use, objects can slide up and down, side to side, or even stretch wider, taller, or both.

Let's try this out. Back in our Business file, go to Layout mode on the CON_Contact layout and click the Picture field to select it. Make sure the Object Info palette is showing and check the bottom and right anchors in addition to the top and left anchors. Now go to Browse mode and resize the window. (If you don't have an image in the field, you want to be sure that you have the field borders turned on.) Notice that at some point (when the scroll bars disappear either vertically or horizontally), the lower-right corner of the Picture field sort of chases your mouse pointer as you pull the window corner. If there's an image in the field, it may or may not stretch depending on the settings in the Graphic Format window. (Unchecking "Maintain original proportions" can provide you with a couple minutes of funhouse mirror silliness. Guess how I know.)

Now try anchoring just the top and bottom, go back to Browse mode, and resize the window. Then test for left and right anchors. Next, select the ContactSerNum_pk field, set it to top and bottom anchors only, and test that out. With the possibility that objects may overlap each other, you can probably see how making the right combination of settings is critical to getting the results you want.

As you experiment, think in terms of anchoring the edges of the object a specific distance from the edges of the window. Notice that objects will only stretch bigger than they appear in Layout mode, but they never get smaller. You'll also see that an object doesn't resize at all until the window scroll bar reaches its limit and disappears. The scroll bars tell you where the last layout object ends and thus the boundary of the layout.

> **NOTE** If you're on a Windows machine and you can't grab the resize square in the lower-right corner, you may need to go to the upper-right corner and click the middle button called Restore Down. Then you should be able to resize the window.

Return the Picture and ContactSerNum_pk fields to the default setting (top and left anchors only). Click on the Phones tab of the tab control and add the bottom anchor. Do the same for the portal itself (not the fields), go to Browse mode, and make the window taller. Even though the portal is set to display a specific number of rows, you're no longer limited to that number. It can be up to the size of the user's screen. Pretty cool! (But now the CountPhone field won't be very informative, will it? But maybe with a nice tall portal that won't be an issue anymore.) Switch to the Notes tab. That field is pretty small. Try using Autoresize on it.

Autoresize Rules

Let me give you a set of rules you can use when working with Autoresize:

- An object with one anchor selected will lock to the anchored side and will not resize. But it will move vertically or horizontally (depending on the anchor) when the window exceeds the layout boundaries.
- Objects with a single anchor on the right or bottom will move in the direction of the anchor when the window exceeds the layout boundaries.
- Objects with top and bottom anchors will get taller, stretching downward when the bottom of the window exceeds the bottom layout boundary.
- Objects with left and right anchors will get wider, stretching to the right when the right of the window exceeds the right layout boundary.
- With all anchors turned off, the object maintains its distance from the center of the layout.
- Form view can take advantage of all the Autoresize features. List view can take advantage of horizontal (wide) stretching but not vertical stretching. Nothing happens at all to any Autoresize objects in Table view.

- A tab control or portal needs to be set to Autoresize in order for objects inside it to respond to their own settings. But the tab control and the objects within its borders don't have to use the same Autoresize settings.
- Objects inside a tab control or portal (let's call the TC or portal a "container," not to be confused with container fields) will resize with respect to their container. So in most circumstances it will be best to use the same settings for both the container and object within — that is, if you intend for them to resize.
- You can apply settings to more than one object at a time without affecting the position settings or Object Name in the upper part of the Object Info palette.
- Autoresize objects in the header and footer are affected, too. If there are Autoresize objects in the header and/or footer with top and bottom anchors activated, it causes the parts themselves to stretch taller — something they don't normally do. If there are also Autoresize objects in the body, it appears there is an algorithm that distributes the stretching between the parts, giving the largest amount of stretch to the body. Knowing this can give you a lot of flexibility when building layouts for different size monitors.

Depending on your Autoresize settings, you may be able to use the same layout to print on paper of various heights and widths. It's also an excellent tool if you have users on different size monitors.

Tooltips[8]

Tooltips can only be set up using FileMaker Pro Advanced — a little more feature-rich version preferred by developers. Using the Tooltips feature can help to make your solutions look more professional. A tooltip gives users extra information about an object when they hover the mouse over it. Now FileMaker lets you add that extra little touch to your layouts. They work in both Browse and Find modes, and in Form, List and Table views, and they show up on the web in Instant Web Publishing. (Buttons disappear from the body part in Table view.) Again, you can only create tooltips if you have a copy of FMPA.

1. Go to Layout mode on the CON_Contact layout. Be sure you're on the Phones tab.
2. Click the **X** button — that's the one we're using to delete — and choose **Format, Set Tooltip.** (You can also get to the Set Tooltip dialog by calling up the context menu.)
3. When the Set Tooltip dialog appears, type **Use this to delete a phone and the notes associated with it.**
4. Click **OK** and go back to Browse mode.

5. Hover your mouse pointer over the X button, but don't click it. You should see the yellow tooltip appear. (To be a little more clear, you need the tip of the mouse pointer to be somewhere within the bounds of the object that owns the tooltip.)

NOTE FileMaker's tooltip text wraps when the text reaches 40 percent of the screen width.

6. You might prefer to have the tooltip appear with shorter lines. In order to change that, you have to go back to the Set Tooltip dialog and click the **Specify** button. Now you have full access to FileMaker's calculation engine.

   That means you can provide dynamic text on the little strip that appears. For instance, you could refer to the specific phone listing type. The way I set mine up not only included the type, but also the Return character so it fits on two lines (see Figure 17-11) like this:

```
"Use this button to delete the <" & con_PH__SerNum::Type & "> ¶listing
and the notes associated with it."
```

   Back in Browse mode, the tooltip changes as I roll the mouse down the list of X buttons. See if you like where I placed the Return character in the code. Obviously that only scratches the surface of what you can do with this feature. Using 8.5's Object Name feature, you could display the name of the object in the tooltip if you thought that might be of some value. It would probably be more helpful for the developer than for a group of users.

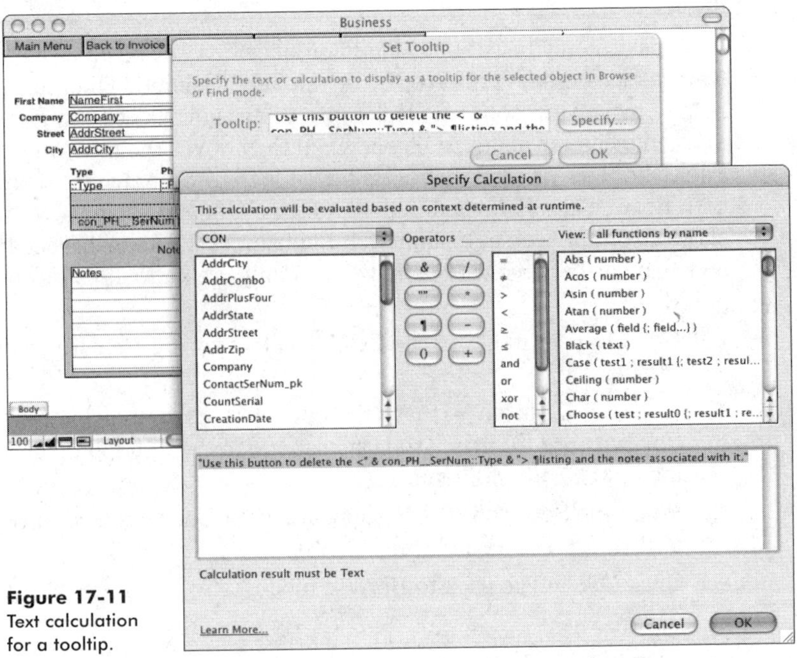

Figure 17-11
Text calculation for a tooltip.

When you're in Layout mode, you can choose to display layout objects that have tooltips in Browse mode. Choose View, Show, Tooltips. A small yellow icon will show in the lower-right corner of each tooltip object.

Conditional Formatting[9]

At last! Developers have been asking for this feature for years. It completely does away with the need for a trick I showed you in Chapter 13 in the section titled "GetRepetition Example." And it does it brilliantly. Same with the text color exercise we did in Chapter 13 under "Text Formatting Functions."

1. Go to the INV_Invoice layout and switch to Layout mode.
2. Click on the **LineTotal** field in the portal and choose **Format, Conditional** to bring up the Conditional Formatting window.
3. Click the **Add** button and the window should look like Figure 17-12. Before we actually make our choices, let's look around a little more.

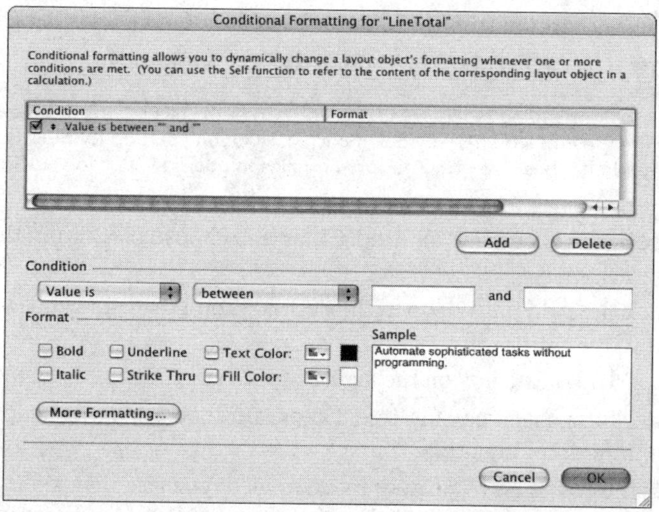

Figure 17-12 The Conditional Formatting window after clicking the Add button.

4. If you look in the Condition area in the middle and click the second drop-down from the left, you'll see all the preset choices shown in Figure 17-13. As you make various selections from that drop-down, the number of boxes to the right can change from two to one and even none. This is a heck of a start toward making this tool easy for you to work with. But you can also use FileMaker's calculation engine to do just about anything you can think of.

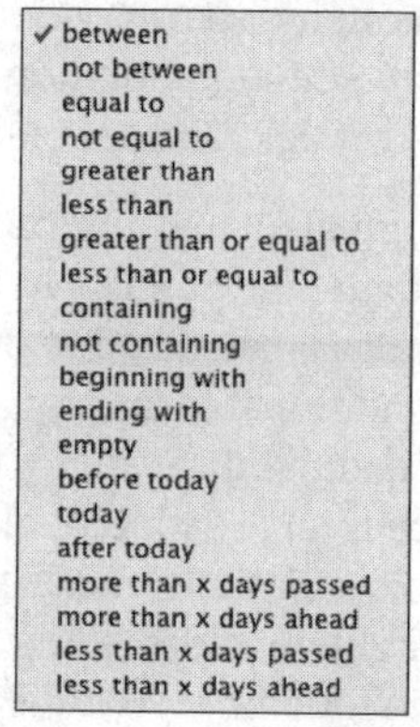

Figure 17-13 Conditional formatting preset list for the second drop-down.

5. Click on the "Value is" drop-down in the Condition area and choose **Formula is.** FileMaker will start a formula for you. But if you click the **Specify** button all the way over on the right (which will only appear when you choose **Formula is**), you get the Specify Calculation window. You probably already have a pretty good idea of how you might use that. Any calculation you choose does not need to refer to this specific field. It would be anything from the user name to whatever you can dream up. We don't really need that for our exercise, so click **Cancel** to leave the Calculation window and return to the Conditional Formatting window.
6. Use the left drop-down to select **Value is** again and choose **less than** from the second drop-down.
7. Enter **0** (zero) in the box next to the drop-down, check the check box for **Text Color**, and choose one of the shades of red from the color square. Notice that you can also choose a background color and other text styles. If you click the More Formatting button in the lower-left corner, you have full access to more styles and all the fonts and font sizes.
8. Click the **Add** button, go to the second drop-down, and choose **between.**
9. Type **0** in the first box and **100** in the box on the right.

> **NOTE** You don't need to worry that the "0" is in both calculations. FileMaker will start at the top and work its way down each calculation you add to this area, stopping when it has a match. The same applies to adding "100" in step 12.

10. Check the check box for **Text Color** and choose black from the color square.
11. Click the **Add** button, go to the second drop-down, and choose **greater than.**
12. Type **100** in the box on the right.
13. Check the check box for **Text Color** and choose a dark shade of green from the color square.
14. Click **OK** and go to Browse mode to view your handiwork.

    You may have to flip through a few of the invoices in order to get enough different values to be able to see all the variations. If you don't have enough line items to show all colors, add a few until you can see red, black, and green text.

Conditional formatting can be applied to any field, button, block of text (including field labels), or Web Viewer object. That means that if the customer has a balance due in the Invoice Total and it's over 90 days old, you can use conditional formatting on the customer Go button to turn it red. Now that's cool! You can see why I said the methods I described to format the InvoiceTotal are kind of old-fashioned. And you don't need those extra fields and colors in the repeating field. This is a lot easier, don't you think? In fact, you might consider going back into the Invoice table and changing the InvoiceTotal field so it displays normally. Then use conditional formatting on the layout to control the color. Oh, go ahead and do it. It will only take a few minutes.

By the way, the Self function can be used very effectively with conditional formatting.

Summary

In this chapter, we talked about the overall appearance of files and the importance of simplicity and clarity of appearance and navigation. Then I showed you methods for working on individual objects and groups of layout objects so they can be formatted with a consistent appearance. Finally, we looked at the Autoresize feature, tab controls, tooltips, and conditional formatting features.

Q & A

Q What if I don't want to go beyond the layouts provided by the Layout Assistant?

A That shouldn't be a problem. Most of them look just fine, and anyone you work for will be happy that it takes you less time to do a job. However, some of the tools and shortcuts provided in this chapter can help you make requested changes very quickly once you've learned to use them.

Q What if I really want to go beyond the Layout Assistant? Where can I see more of what other people are doing?

A Look at other software programs first. See how they make navigation clear and understandable (or more confusing in many cases). Look at web pages that win awards for design and easy navigation. Go to the FileMaker web site and other sites listed in Appendix B, and download files created by other FileMaker professionals to see what work inspires you. If you develop a good eye, maybe you'll be the one to inspire other FileMaker users.

Workshop

Take the files we've been working on and try to find ways to tie them together with a similar appearance. Use the same fonts for field labels and in the fields themselves. Make the backgrounds the same color. If the layouts will print, make any backgrounds and buttons non-printing. Some developers strive to make a group of files feel as if they're one file. See if you can do that.

Just a few paragraphs ago I suggested you go back to the Invoice table and change the InvoiceTotal field so it displays normally. Then use conditional formatting on the layout to control the color. Well, go do it. How many times do I have to tell you it's really a great tool?!

Chapter 18

Designing Your Printed Report Layouts

Introduction

In earlier chapters, we created some basic reports. Now we'll do some real reporting. In this chapter, we'll look at:

- What a report is
- Two questions you need to answer before you start a report
- Two real-life reports we'll add to our file
- How to get to and from the reports with ease

What Is a Report?

Even though a single record can technically be a report, a report is usually thought of as a group of records and some summarized information about them. Whether the report is simply displayed on the screen, exported, or printed depends on how the data is to be used.

My concept of a report goes a bit further than how the data looks on the layout. It includes getting to and from the report in a way that makes it effortless to the user. If that process isn't well designed, the report will end up unused, and an unused report is not a report at all.

Creating a Useful and Attractive Report

You need to think about how the report will be organized so that users can find what they need without reading every single line. Summaries should be set apart visually, with lines, shading, or different type size or style, or all three. Section heads are just as important. When the reader finishes one area with a sub-summary, he or she should instantly know what the next section is about.

You can save time for your users by helping them get to the information they need more quickly. How many times have you looked for a piece of information in an advertisement or on a web page only to find it buried in some illogical place? Ask yourself: "What are the most important pieces of data?" and "How can I set them apart so they can be found quickly?"

Figures 18-1 and 18-2 show two versions of the same report. The first example is the rough draft. It's hard to read because you can't easily tell where charge card transactions leave off and deposits begin. By adding a leading sub-summary part with shaded, merged text as a divider, there's no longer any question where a new type of entry begins. In the second version, there is also a little shading around the totals, and there are borders around the section grand totals.

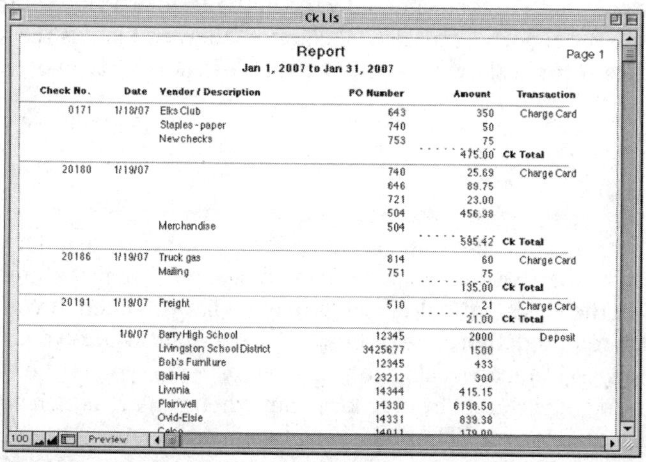

Figure 18-1
Rough draft of a checking account report. It's hard to tell where charge card entries end and deposits begin.

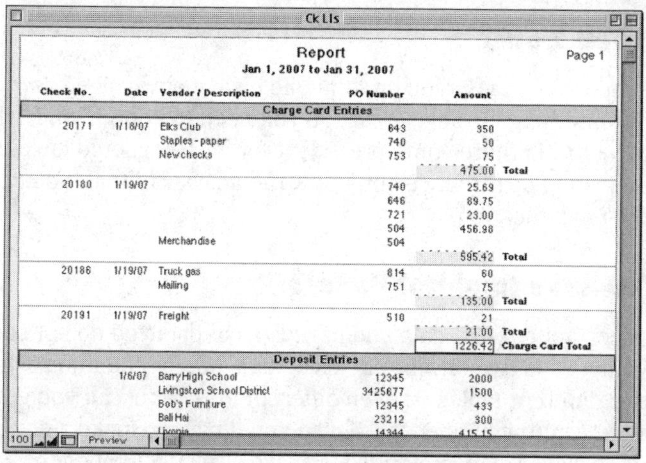

Figure 18-2
Finished checking account report with sections set apart for easier reading.

Report Types

A list of invoices or phone numbers can be a report. A printout of a customer's information layout can be a report. For that reason, even the standard form or List view can be considered a report. At a school, someone may ask for a list of students whose grade point average has dropped to a D so they can meet for counseling. Putting together one of these reports is pretty straightforward. But even if that's all you'll be doing, in this chapter there are some techniques for getting to and from these reports that you will find very helpful.

Generally, reports include detail information along with some type of summary information. That's why we use the Columnar and Extended Columnar reports. The only difference between the two is that the Extended Columnar report can extend up to 111 inches in width. The Columnar report is confined to the width of the paper selected in the Page or Print Setup window at the time the report is created. Of course, "View as List" is the key to making multiple records show on a report regardless of what type of report it is.

Creating a Report

With FileMaker's Layout Assistant, creating reports is quite easy, but you still need to answer some questions. In many cases, you can just stumble through and let the Assistant help you figure out what you need. If you find another field is required, there are places in the Assistant where you can access the Manage Database dialog so you can create it. If you're the type who just likes to go for it, feel free to do so, but when you hit a brick wall, I'll make recovery easy for you. There are only two main questions to ask.

What Results Do You Want?

Whether the report is for yourself or someone else, it always begins with a need to know something. So ask, "What do you need to know?" and "How do you want it to look?" Is there some precedent for what it should look like, such as a pre-existing form? Once you know the answer to that, you can move on to the next question.

What Data Do You Have (and Not Have)?

Yes, just as important as what data you have is what data you do not have. Often what you need is two or more fields of data. Maybe the information is available in two different tables or even different files. How can you get the data into one file where you need it? Maybe you'll have to make a new field and import some data. Maybe you need to make a calculation field or a relationship to one or more tables or files.

Example Reports

The rest of this chapter will be spent creating two fairly typical reports. Many other reports can be made using the same concepts. The first one is necessarily lengthy, because it introduces all of the basic elements. The second report is less than half as long because we'll simply copy sections from the first. Understanding the copy and modify process is as important as creating the first report.

Customer Sales Report

Let's say we want to create a report to tell us how much each of our customers spends with us each year. That answers the question about what we want to know. We could pretty easily search our Invoice table using a date range, sort by ContactSerNum, and display a sub-summary, but let me save you the trouble. Since we're not using a true double-entry bookkeeping system, most of the invoices would show a balance of zero, because they'll be paid off.

So it appears that, once again, the report should be done in the "many" table of our one-to-many relationship; that means on a layout that uses the InvoiceLineItems table. The reason for this is that when we do our find, we can omit any payment, discount, and interest item records. All that will be left is what the customer spent. That partly answers the question about what data we have, even though, as you'll see, we'll still need another field.

Setup — Making the Data Available

What's missing from the InvoiceLineItems table is the customer data. At the end of Chapter 7, I said you needed the ContactSerNum in the InvoiceLineItems table so you could use the contact information on the Invoice layout. Then I suggested you try it out in the Workshop. If you did that exercise and it worked, you should have a field called ContactSerNum that looks up from the Invoice. In that case, you may be interested in an alternative way of getting the information. If not, skip ahead to the next section. If you didn't do that Workshop, here's another way.

In the InvoiceLineItems table, create a new calculation field named ContactSerNum_l (that's a lowercase "L," which is the keyboard shortcut for calculation type field), with a numeric result:

```
ContactSerNum_l(Calculation) = ili_INV__InvNum::ContactSerNum_fk
```

That's it! Now that we have the contact data available, let's make the report.

Building the Report

1. Go to Layout mode, and choose **Layouts**, **New Layout/Report**.
2. Choose **ILI** from the drop-down menu and name it **ILI_CustomerSalesReport**.
3. Choose **List/Report** and click **Next**.
4. Click the radio button next to **Report with grouped data**.
5. Check both of the check boxes for **Include subtotals** and **Include grand totals**, and click **Next**.
6. Oddly enough, you really only need to choose one field at this point, the Customer field. So in the Specify Fields window, click on **Current Table** and come down to — uh, oh! There's only one table occurrence related to the ILI TO, and it doesn't have the Customer field in it.

It will happen to you sometimes that the information you need to use won't be set up yet. So we'll have to do that now.

Go to the bottom of the table occurrence list and choose **Manage Database** and go to the Relationships tab. Add a new TO called **ili_CON__ConSerNum** and connect it to ContactSerNum_1 in ILI with ContactSerNum_pk in CON. Interesting that we just added ContactSerNum_1 to that table! Click **OK** and continue on.

Now that we have the new ili_CON__ConSerNum TO, use it to get the **Customer** field, then click **Next.**

7. In the Organize Records by Category screen, double-click the **ili_CON__ConSerNum::Customer** field to move it to the Report categories list. Here's another dialog that doesn't open wide enough to read both the relationship and the field name. Good thing there's only one field to choose from. Click **Next.**
8. Just click the **Next** button in the Sort Records window.
9. Click the **Specify** button under "Summary field" and choose **InvoiceTotal** from the Specify Field window. That's where we get the other piece of information we need. Click **OK.**
10. Then, from the "Subtotal placement" pop-up, choose **Above record group** and click the **Add Subtotal** button. When you've done all that, your screen should look like Figure 18-3. Click **Next.**

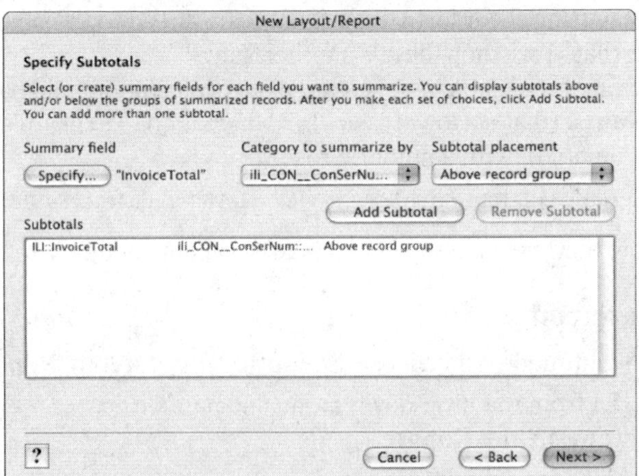

Figure 18-3
The Specify Subtotals screen showing the settings in the pop-ups and InvoiceTotal in the Subtotals area.

11. At the Specify Grand Totals screen, you could choose a Grand Total using the InvoiceTotal. It would tell you the total sales for all customers for the time period, but you don't need it. If you don't want it, just click the **Next** button.
12. Choose a theme you like, and click **Next.**
13. You are at the Header and Footer Information screen. From the "Top center" pop-up, choose **Large Custom Text**, type **Customer Sales Report**, and click **OK** and **Next.**

14. We'll be creating our own scripts, so just click **Next**.
15. At the You are finished! screen, select **View the report in Layout mode.**
16. Now click **Finish**.
17. Go into Layout mode, click on the Body label, and press **Delete**. FileMaker will ask you if you really want to delete it. Click **OK**.
18. Now, go to Preview mode to see how your report would look if you printed it.

Depending on the records that are in the current found set when you started building the report, the report may not look like the one in Figure 18-4. When I built mine, it only had one record showing. To get it to look like a report, I had to choose Records, Show All Records and sort the records again. Then I could see the summarized information. Starting in FMP10 you can see the sub-summaries in Browse mode, but the records still have to be sorted.

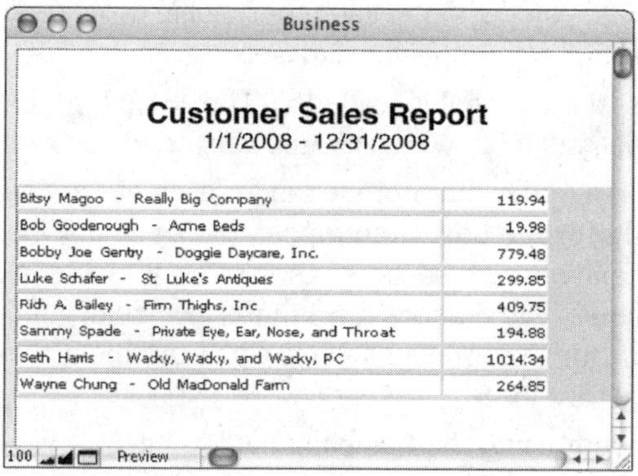

Figure 18-4
Final version of Customer Sales Report listing just the customer and what they spent in the year.

Touch-up Work

Whenever I create a report this way I often get too much information. Don't let that worry you, though. It's considerably easier to remove information than it is to figure out what's missing. You'll find it's not too hard to make your reports look the way you want them to. You may want to change the fonts, field sizes, or some other part of the layout, but the information is usually all there. Figure 18-4 shows my final report. Don't worry about the dates shown in the header part. I'll show you how to change that shortly.

How to Set Up a Find Layout

Now the report looks simple and clear, but how will we limit it to a specific date range? There's also a problem in that the amount shown reflects *all* transactions by each customer. That includes payments and various other such data with negative values. We only want to see their purchases, so we'll have to do a little more work here to omit the unwanted data.

1. Go to Browse mode and choose **Records, Show All Records.**

2. Sort the records by **ili_CON__ConSerNum::Customer**. (That sort may still be in memory from the previous exercises). To view the report, return to Preview mode, but it should also show in Browse.

You may have some customers showing zero or negative balances.

What I want to show you is a Find Setup layout I use for many of the reports for my clients. I use a pair of global fields for start and end dates. That way, no matter what mode the users are in, they won't be touching any active data. They'll be on a layout in the Null table, so they can't accidentally delete any important data. Another advantage is that the script can take them to the layout in Browse mode and end without leaving the script paused. Paused scripts are too easy to unintentionally bypass while the user is still in Find mode, and there are a number of problems with that. Finally, if the search fails, you can bring the users back to the Find Setup layout. Their data request will still be in place so they can see what they asked for and make a minor edit if they need to. That's not so critical with a date range, but this system will also work should you decide to add other global fields to filter the find for names, companies, and other specific data sets.

1. Create two text fields (not date fields) called **zi_DateStart_gt** and **zi_DateEnd_gt** in the Null table we created in Chapter 14.
2. Go into the Options area under the Storage tab for each of the fields and check the **Use global storage** box. (Remember, the z will put these non-data fields at the end of the field list so they're easy to find when fields are sorted by name. The i means it's an interface field, g indicates global, and the t stands for text. You could also add a comment to remind yourself what the fields are for.)
3. Create a new blank layout using the Assistant, and call it **NUL_FindDateRange**.
4. Choose **NUL** from the "Show records from" drop-down (although that's not strictly necessary). If you've been using a certain theme you may want to create a new standard form layout with the two global fields on it. I usually delete the header and footer parts of the layout.

   The reason we're using the Null table is because a user could accidentally delete a record in one of the other tables. The Null table is meant to hold no data and will help avoid such problems. Also, we can protect addition or deletion of data by users by using security settings. But that's a topic we'll deal with in Chapter 22.
5. Add the text from Figure 18-5. (Don't worry about the buttons just yet.)

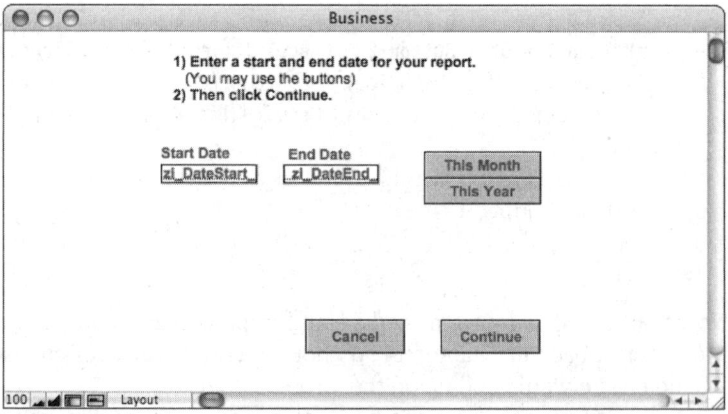

Figure 18-5
The FindDateRange layout showing the suggested position of text, buttons, and fields.

6. Drag the two new fields onto the layout.
7. Now create the following scripts:

```
Script Name: 20 - Setup for Report
Enter Browse Mode [] (Navigation)
Go to Layout ["NUL_FindDateRange" (InvLI)] (Navigation)
Set Field [NUL::zi_DateStart_gt; ""] (Fields)
Set Field [NUL::zi_DateEnd_gt; ""]
Go to Field [NUL::zi_DateStart_gt] (Navigation)
```

> **Note** At the Set Field step, you'll first select the Specify target field button and then the calculated result Specify button. At the calculated result, type "" (two quotes right up against each other), which indicates that we will be emptying out the field. When you use quotation marks, you are indicating literal text or a text constant. In this case, we are indicating that there is no text.

Remember, when we give you script steps, we've identified the category in which you can find script steps in parentheses after the script step.

```
Script Name: 21 - Check for Complete Dates
If [IsEmpty (NUL::zi_DateStart_gt) or IsEmpty (NUL::zi_DateEnd_gt)]
(Control)
   Beep (Miscellaneous)
   Show Custom Dialog ["You must choose a Start AND End date."]
(Control)
   #Button 1 = OK (Comment - Miscellaneous)
   Halt Script (Control)
End If

Script Name: 22 - If None Found
If [Get (FoundCount) = 0] (Control)
   Beep (Miscellaneous)
```

```
    Show Custom Dialog ["None Found. Want to try again?"] (Miscellaneous)
    #Button 1 = OK / Button 2 = Cancel (Comment - Miscellaneous)
    If [Get (LastMessageChoice) = 2] (Control)
       Perform Script ["1 - Main Menu (Halt)"] (Control)
    Else
       Go to Layout ["NUL_FindDateRange" (NUL)]
       Halt Script
    End If
 End If
```

Now you can see why we placed a Halt Script step at the end of the Main Menu script back in Chapter 14. Without it, should the user choose button #2, he or she would end up on the wrong layout.

This next script uses a number of things we learned elsewhere in the book. It looks complex, and it is — if you look at it as a whole. But again, it can be broken down into simpler parts by asking these questions — "Where am I now?" and "Where do I want to be when I finish?" — and then writing it out in plain English. Some of the work is handled by subscripts.

The most complicated part is the Set Field step. It's only complicated because we're using dates from the two global fields and an ellipsis (three dots) between them. Make sure your step looks exactly like mine when you're in the Edit Script window — except your script text won't spill down onto the next line.

The second part that could be confusing is that after we complete the find for the items with the dates we want, we turn around and constrain the found set by omitting items we don't want. Looking at the script, you can't tell what those items are or even that they're items to be omitted without double-clicking the Constrain step. But you will know what they are after you finish with these instructions.

And third, we have to use the If None Found subscript twice in this script because we essentially perform two different finds, each of which could result in records not being found. So let's give it a go.

```
Script Name: 23 - Continue Report
Perform Script ["21 - Check for Complete Dates"] (Control)
Set Error Capture [On] (Control)
Go to Layout ["ILI_CustomerSalesReport" (ILI)] (Navigation)
Enter Find Mode [] (Navigation)
Set Field [ini_INV__InvNum::Date; NUL::zi_DateStart_gt & "..." &
   NUL::zi_DateEnd_gt] (Fields)
Perform Find [] (Found Sets)
Perform Script ["22 - If None Found"] (Control)
#Omit: ==Payment / ==Discount / ==Refund / ==Interest
Constrain Found Set [] (Found Sets)
Perform Script ["22 - If None Found"] (Control)
#Sorted by ili_CON__ConSerNum::Customer (Comment - Miscellaneous)
Sort Records [Restore, No dialog] (Found Sets)
```

```
Enter Preview Mode [Pause] (Navigation)
Enter Browse Mode (Navigation)
```

The reason Set Error Capture is set to On is because FileMaker's default error messages can be confusing. We'll provide more meaningful error messages.

Now we need to touch it up a little.

8. Go back to the Constrain Found Set step and click the **Specify** button. If there are any actions already in this window, click on them and delete them until the window is empty.
9. Click the **New** button.
10. In the Action drop-down, choose **Omit Records.**
11. In the "Omit records when" drop-down, be sure you are looking at fields from the InvLI table and choose the **Description** field.
12. In the Criteria area, type **==Payment** (see Figure 18-6).

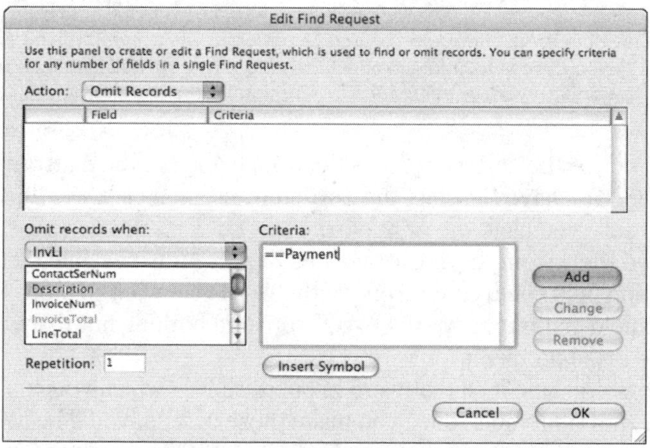

Figure 18-6
The Edit Find Request window.

13. Click the **Add** button and **OK.** Don't leave the Specify Find Requests window just yet.
14. Click the **Duplicate** button and the **Edit** button.
15. Highlight the Action listed there. That will allow you to change Payment to **Discount.**
16. Click the **Change** button and then **OK.**
17. Repeat steps 14 through 16 two more times, substituting the words **Refund** and **Interest** where Payment or Discount is.
18. When you're done, the window should look like Figure 18-7. Click **OK.**

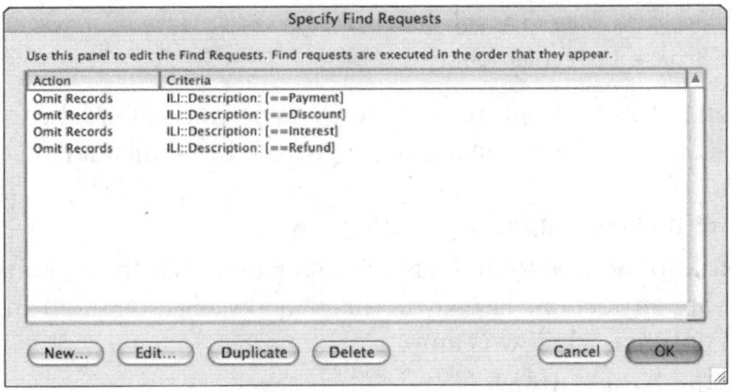

Figure 18-7 The details of the Specify Find Requests window showing the items to be omitted.

19. Now the Constrain Found Set should have "Restore" in brackets after it.

CAUTION During data entry you'll have to make sure that the exact words for Payment, Discount, Refund, and Interest are used. A misspelling will cause the item to be included in the report. You may want to take care of that in the Invoice table by using a pop-up that includes those specific items. It will only be used when someone clicks in the Description field. It won't be disruptive to data entry since all product descriptions are entered by a lookup when the ProdID is chosen. You might even choose to create product codes for Payment, Discount, Refund, and Interest and prevent entry into the Description field altogether.

Did you notice the comment steps that told you what the constrain and sort should be? You have to select the Sort step and then click the Specify button to make sure you have the right sort.

I used the == in the Constrain step because it is possible that a product description field could contain one of the words we want to omit. By insisting that the field contents have the exact word and nothing but that word in each case, we avoid problems.

Whew! Imagine if all that were in one script — which you could do if you wanted. And remember, once you make these scripts, you'll be able to import them into other files in the future. This is a report I use for nearly all my clients, in one form or another, although not necessarily with the Constrain step.

TIP If a report that contains sub-summaries doesn't look right, be suspicious of the sort. Check the sub-summary layout part information against the actual sort that occurs after performing the script. If they don't match, you've found the culprit. To fix it, go into the script, double-click the Sort Records step, and click the Specify button. Set up the proper sort criteria, click OK to save the sort order, then OK to save the script.

A second possible problem could be the position of the sub-summary field(s) in the layout part. If the top of the field is parallel to the part line, try moving it one click lower.

Notice the Set Error Capture step. That prevents FileMaker from displaying its own error message. Instead, the user will see the message we made in the If None Found script.

> **NOTE** Once you choose Set Error Capture [On], there are other possible errors that could occur during the execution of the script. I have had good luck with the script as it is, but if the possibility of other errors concerns you, add the following script steps:
>
> ```
> If [Get (LastError)0 and Get (LastError)401]
>    Beep
>    Show Message ["An unknown error occurred [Script 23]"]
>    Halt Script
> End If
> ```

Until FMP10 the Get (Last Error) step had to appear immediately after the step that would generate the error. Even though that's no longer necessary, if you're trying to check for a specific error, you wouldn't want to wait until a new error might be generated. I always place Get (Last Error) right after the step that might cause an error. In the case of script 23 - Continue Report, we already have a step that would do this for us. Notice that it comes right after the Perform Find step. I also like to put the number of the script in brackets in messages so users can report what script they saw if they have a problem.

20. Now, to make data entry easier, add this date range script:

```
Script Name: 24 - Date Range Buttons
If [Get (ScriptParameter) = "This Month"]
   Set Field [NUL::zi_DateStart_gt; Date (Month (Get (CurrentDate)), 1,
   Year (Get (CurrentDate)))] (Fields)
   Set Field [NUL::zi_DateEnd_gt; Date (Month (Get (CurrentDate)) + 1;
   1;
   Year (Get (CurrentDate))) - 1]
Else If [Get (ScriptParameter) = "This Year"]
   Set Field [NUL::zi_DateStart_gt; Date (1; 1; Year (Get
(CurrentDate)))]
   Set Field [NUL::zi_DateEnd_gt; Date (12; 31; Year (Get
(CurrentDate)))]
End If
```

21. Add the four buttons shown in Figure 18-5 to the layout, and attach them to the appropriate scripts. The Cancel button should be connected to the Main Menu script. Be sure you add the parameters to the This Month and This Year buttons. You could also add buttons for Last Month, Last Year, etc. Each would have its own parameters and fit within an Else If step followed by the date ranges you'll need. If you need help, take a look at the Workshop at the end of the chapter.
22. In Layout mode, select both the **DateStart** and **DateEnd** fields and choose **Format**, **Field/Control**, **Setup**. From the "Display as" drop-down, choose **Drop-down Calendar**, and click **OK**. Take a look in Browse mode. Now your users can use either the quick preset date range buttons or the drop-down calendars. Couldn't be easier!

⌘ **TIP** Interestingly, scripts can enter data into fields that are otherwise locked up tight from manual entry. They can even work on areas where certain groups of users otherwise don't have access — as long as you check the box next to "Run script with full access privileges" in the Edit Script window.

23. You may want to add a button to the Customer Sales Report layout to take you to the Main Menu since there's no navigation on that layout once you return to Browse mode. If you'll be printing this report, make a script for that with the settings you need and add a Print button. I often provide a button to start the report over right there on the report layout itself so users don't have to make the extra click to go to the Main Menu in case they asked for the wrong date range.
24. Now go to the Main Menu layout and add a button. Attach it to script 20 - Setup for Report, type **Customer** in the parameter box, and click **OK**. Label the button **Customer Report**. See how this works?
25. One other thing I like to do is add the date range to the report just under the title like I did in Figure 18-4. I use merge fields that pull the data from NUL::zi_DateStart_gt and NUL::zi_DateEnd_gt.

In reality, you may prefer to sort by Contact Last Name, but be cautious. The sort will place all people with the same last name in the same sub-summary! You'll be better off making a concatenated field. I'll leave it up to you to figure it out. Just remember you'll have to change your sub-summary part(s) and the script to match.

Percent of Sales by Product Report

Let's look at another report where you want to know what percent of the total sales each item in the product line is earning. Using the information in this report, you can make decisions such as whether a product is overpriced, falling out of favor with your buyers, or just not being promoted properly.

Start by looking at what data we have and don't have. In the InvoiceLineItems table, we have a ProdID, a Description, and a dollar amount as our LineTotal. What we don't have is the percentage of total sales. We can get sub-summaries of the LineTotal when sorting by ProdID, but we can't do a calculation from that. However, if we use the GetSummary function, we can use that in a calculation. To accomplish that, we'll need two new fields:

Field Name	*Type*	*Options*
GetSumProdAmount	Calculation	GetSummary(SumLineTotal; ProdID_fk)
PercentSalesAmount	Calculation	Round(GetSumProdAmount/SumLineTotal; 2)

Building the Report

1. Start a new layout called **ILI_PercentSalesByProdID**, use **ILI** from the "Show records from" drop-down, choose **List/Report**, and click **Next**.

2. Click the **Report with grouped data** radio button, check both the **Include subtotals** and **Include grand totals** boxes, and click **Next**.
3. Move the following fields to the Layout fields column on the right:

   ProdID_fk
   Description
   PercentSalesAmount

   You don't need the SumLineTotal because we'll pick that up in the sub-summary. Click **Next**.
4. Double-click the **ProdID_fk** field to move it to the Report categories list, and click **Next**.
5. In the Sort Records window, just click the **Next** button.
6. Click the **Specify** button under Summary field and choose **SumLineTotal**, then click **OK**.
7. Then from the "Subtotal placement" pop-up, choose **Below record group**.
8. Click the **Add Subtotal** button, and click **Next**.
9. You could choose a grand total using the SumLineTotal. It would tell you the total sales for the time period, but you don't need it. If you don't want it, just click the **Next** button.
10. Choose a theme that fits your overall plan, and click **Next**.
11. Choose **Large Custom Text** from the "Top center" pop-up, type **Percent Sales by Product ID**, and click **OK** and **Next**.
12. No need to create a script here. We'll be making our own. Click **Next**.
13. Select **View in Layout Mode**.
14. Finally, click **Finish**.

Touch-up Work

15. Move both Description and PercentSalesAmount into the lower sub-summary part.
16. Now delete the body and upper sub-summary parts.
17. When you go back to either Browse or Preview mode, you should only see one line per ProdID. If you don't see those results, choose **Records**, **Show All Records**, **Sort by ProdID**. Your report won't look like mine. I did a lot of reformatting of my layout, and you won't have the date range that appears under the title in Figure 18-8. We'll add that shortly.
18. Take a look at Figure 18-8 and see how your report compares to mine. Another year like 2008 and we might consider dropping Small Widgets from our product line. Being able to make decisions like that is what good reporting is all about.

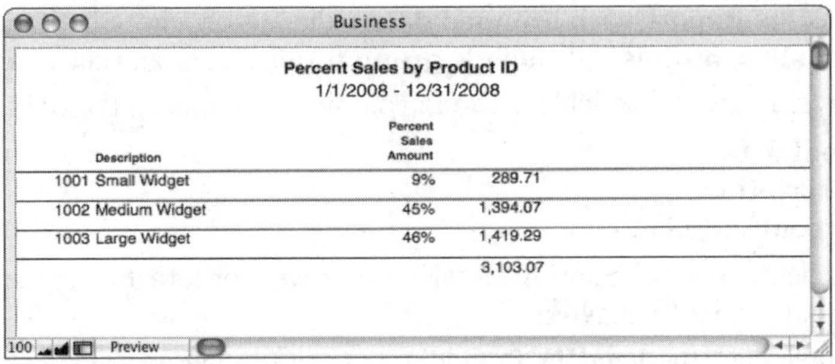

Figure 18-8 Percent Sales by ProdID report in Browse mode.

How to Set Up This Find Layout

The way I had to do this in old versions of FileMaker was to add a separate set of layouts and scripts. But using some of the features introduced in FileMaker 7 and later, we can use the same NUL_FindDateRange layout and only make a few changes to a couple of the scripts. Very efficient! Let's go!

1. Go to the NUL_MainMenu layout and duplicate the Customer Report button. Change the text on it to read **Products Report**.
2. Double-click your new button, and click the **Specify** button. Change the parameter to **Products**, click **OK**, and **OK** again.
3. Go into Manage Scripts and edit script 20 - Setup for Report.
4. Right after the first step (Enter Browse Mode), add the following step:

   ```
   Set Variable [$$Report; Value: Get (ScriptParameter)]
   ```

   Set Variable was new in FileMaker 8. Earlier we used Set Variable with a single dollar sign ($). That means it's only good for that script. The double dollar sign ($$) means you're setting it for your session in the file. You can use it again and again until you close the file. It's very much like putting data in a global field.

   In this case, we've already added parameters (Customer and Products) to the buttons on the Main Menu. This script step says, "Please, Mr. Script, memorize whatever word was attached to the button the user just clicked. We'll be using it later." And indeed we will!
5. Click **OK** and double-click the 23 - Continue Report script.
6. Single-click on the 10th script step, Perform Script ["22 - If None Found"].
7. In the left column, double-click the If step. It will pop over under the Perform Script step and also add an End If step. (To get an idea of where we want to end up, look ahead to the upcoming code to see what the second half of the script will look like when we're done.)
8. Pull the End If step down below the Sort Records step.
9. Click to highlight the Comment step, then Shift+click the Sort step so they're both highlighted. Click the **Duplicate** button in the lower middle of the window. Yes, you can duplicate multiple script steps at one time! In

fact, you can duplicate multiple items that are separated by other script steps.

10. Insert an Else If step after the first Sort.
11. Under that, insert a Go to Layout step.
12. Double-click the If step, enter **$$Report = "Customer"** in the Calculation box, and click **OK.**
13. Double-click the Else If step, enter **$$Report = "Products"** in the Calculation box, and click **OK.**
14. When you're done, the second half of the Continue Report script should look like this:

```
Perform Script ["22 - If None Found"] (Control)
If [$$Report = "Customer"]
   #Sorted by ili_CON__ConSerNum::Customer (Comment - Miscellaneous)
   Sort Records [Restore, No dialog] (Found Sets)
Else If [$$Report = "Products"]
   Go to Layout ["ILI_PercentSalesByProdID" (ILI)] (Navigation)
   #Sorted by ILI::ProdID_fk (Comment - Miscellaneous)
   Sort Records [Restore, No dialog] (Found Sets)
End If

Enter Preview Mode [Pause] (Navigation)
Enter Browse Mode (Navigation)
```

Do you see what's happening? By passing the parameter from the button into the file variable, we use it to decide which report to run. If the parameter is "Customer," we stay on the same layout and sort by Customer. If the parameter is "Products," go to the PercentSales layout and sort by Product ID. One script, multiple uses.

Of course, you will probably want to put a Main Menu and a Print button on the Percent Sales report layout, too. Starting with FMP10, you can skip the Enter Preview Mode and Enter Browse Mode steps since you can see the sub-summaries in Browse mode. However, the report will only show exactly as it will print when you're in Preview mode. Since this report is a simple, one-page list based on just a few invoices, it's probably not so important. But a real year-end report would have multiple pages to it, maybe adding page numbers and the date the report was printed. If you want the users to see it exactly as it will print, you need those last two steps. In that case you would have to instruct users that the Print button will actually print the report properly even though it will look a little different when they're back in Browse mode after previewing the report. I would say that most users find the difference between Browse and Preview modes a bit confusing. It's somewhat more helpful that FMP10 started showing sub-summaries in Browse mode. It's just that unless you go to Preview mode in more complicated reports you won't be able to see page breaks or special printing data, and fields that use sliding/printing won't squeeze down when they're not filled with data.

15. Create a generic Print script and button and add it to your layout.
16. Now run both reports for various date ranges. You can run one report multiple times without going back to the Main Menu — if you added the "Start Report Over" button I suggested when we created the previous report. It works because the variable remembers which report you're running. Use the Main Menu to switch reports.

Yes, it was a lot of work, but somebody's gonna be very happy these reports are so fast and easy to run.

Other Common Reports

Other reports you might be interested in would be Sales by Salesperson and Overdue Invoices. Of course, we don't have salespeople in our file, but they could certainly be added fairly easily — probably in the Invoice table. And maybe all these reports could be run using script parameters and the file variable using the one script.

Avoiding the Today and Get (CurrentDate) Functions in Calculation Fields

An Overdue Invoices report tells which invoices still have a balance due after 30, 60, and 90 days. A lot of people working with FileMaker Pro in the past have used the Today function in a calculation field to build this report. Their files have a field that calculates Today and subtracts 30 (or 60 or 90) from it. In FileMaker 7, the Today function was replaced with Get (CurrentDate), although files converted from previous versions will calculate correctly using the old Today function. You can still type the word Today anyplace a function would appear and it will work, even though it is no longer in the list of functions in the upper-right corner of the Specify Calculation window.

I'll do almost anything to keep from using the Today and Get (CurrentDate) functions in a calculation field because every record must be recalculated whenever the file opens if the field indexing is stored. You can't trick these functions by leaving the file open, either. After midnight, any calculation using them won't update until the file is closed and reopened. In tables with lots of records, this can be agonizing, especially after a computer crash where the file has to go through a checking process first. Let me add that I have used both these functions in scripts quite often, since their placement in a script has nothing to do with what happens when the file opens.

Using the Today or Get (CurrentDate) function in a calculation field is especially problematic with FileMaker Server, since the files are sometimes open continuously (on the server). That means the files have to be closed and opened at least once a day or either of these functions won't get recalculated. If you only closed and backed up the files on your server once a week (on

Sunday morning, for example), then your calculation would only be updated once a week, and then only if the files were closed, not just paused.

There are a number of strategies used by FileMaker professionals to avoid these functions in a calculation. The one I prefer for this report is to base the calculation on a global date field. The disadvantage of using a field stored globally is that it cannot be indexed. That means that finds performed on the field will be slower, and the field can only be used on the "master" side in relationships. But it's still worth doing if the report will not be run on a daily basis.

NOTE The only way to identify "related" records is if they're indexed. The "master" record/table/field is the current record/table/field of context (i.e., where you are). The "related" field must be indexed in order to ensure expected behavior through the relationship. The field used on the master side does not have to be indexed. That's why you can use a global field on the master side to find related records.

1. Create a date field in the Invoice table and call it **zi_Date_gd**. Click the **Storage** tab and check the box next to **Use global storage**.
2. Make a calculation field called **Overdue** with a text result:

   ```
   Table: Invoice
   Field Name: Overdue
   Case (Date < zi_Date_gd - 90; "Over 90";
   Date < zi_Date_gd - 60; "Over 60";
   Date < zi_Date_gd - 30; "Over 30"; "")
   ```

   You can make a script that finds all invoices with a balance due and fills in the zi_Date_gd field with today's date (Get (CurrentDate)).
3. Finally, sort the records by the Overdue field. Now you have a current report, and your file will open quickly.

There are two other common ways to avoid the problems associated with using the Today or Get (CurrentDate) functions in a calculation:

- Use Get (CurrentDate) wherever you would use Today and leave the field unstored (Storage Options in the Field Definition area). This has the same problems as a global date field, but the advantage is that you don't have to make sure the global date field is populated with the right date value. FileMaker will take care of it.
- Here is the method I prefer. Use a date field (*not* specifying global storage) on the layout, and run a Replace script step on it just before the field is needed so that it has the most recent date in it. This method is probably the worst in terms of making sure that the field has today's date in it, and you get a performance hit when running a script that needs it. However, it can be invaluable when you are dealing with a small found set or in a case where you absolutely must be able to index the field for finds or building relationships. (Remember, you will have a small found set if you first find all invoices with a balance due.)

Organizational Details

Since our file is starting to get a little more complicated, it's probably time to do a little cleanup work. First of all, I like to see layouts based on the same base table grouped together.

1. Choose **File, Manage, Layouts.**
2. Move NUL_MainMenu to the top of the list. It could be considered the starting place of your solution, so it seems it should have the top position. Then move any other NUL tables after it.
3. Follow that with any layouts that begin with CON — except if you have one called CON_Developer. I suggest leaving developer layouts for the end of the list.
4. Next are layouts based on INV, followed by ILI.

There's probably only one each of the remaining layouts. Any order is fine.

Now let's organize the relationships graph a little better using one version of the anchor-buoy standard.

1. Go to the Relationships tab of Manage Database.
2. Select all TOs and move them down the work area a few inches.
3. Use the Table Note tool to draw a rectangle about 2 inches tall and 6 inches wide in the area at the top of the graph. Type **LEGEND** in the Note field and click **OK**.
4. Next we'll add one table occurrence for each base table to the graph. Starting with Contact, I'm calling this one **z CON__Contact**. Using this name as an example, follow the pattern of beginning each name with "z " (z and space), the base table code, two underscores, and the table name.
5. Use the Table Display toggle in the upper-right corner of each of these "dummy" TOs to close them so they only show their names. But make them wide enough so the entire name shows.
6. Place these dummy TOs in columns and rows on the LEGEND note block. These will provide us with the base table name and the code for each table. Because they begin with z, they'll sort to the bottom of any dialog that displays TOs. If you ever need to remember what a code means, you'll be able to spot it, both in the dialog and in the graph. You may choose to alphabetize these dummy TOs.
7. Now click on any TO that starts with CON.
8. Use the Select Tables tool (to the right of the Zoom Percentage indicator — usually set to 100%) to select tables with the same source table.
9. Use the Set Color tool and select a dark shade of yellow. I like to think of my contacts as "good as gold."
10. Click in one of the INV TOs.
11. Use the Select Tables tool to select all the same source tables and make them a reasonably dark shade of green. After all, this is where your money comes from!

12. Do the same with ILI, but use a lighter shade of green.

    Now you can quickly spot all TOs with the same base table. The base table code does the same thing, but this adds a quick visual cue. If you have some level of color blindness, you can use various shades of gray that suit the same purpose.

    You can provide color keys to the other TOs if you like. But to my thinking, they're not yet in sufficient use to warrant the time.

13. Finally, if you haven't done so already, align the TOs as if they were in columns. All TOs directly connected to the anchor TO should be lined up vertically as if in a second column. All TOs with the table code in caps in the third position of their name will make up a third column, and so on. See Figure 18-9, but you may need a magnifying glass.

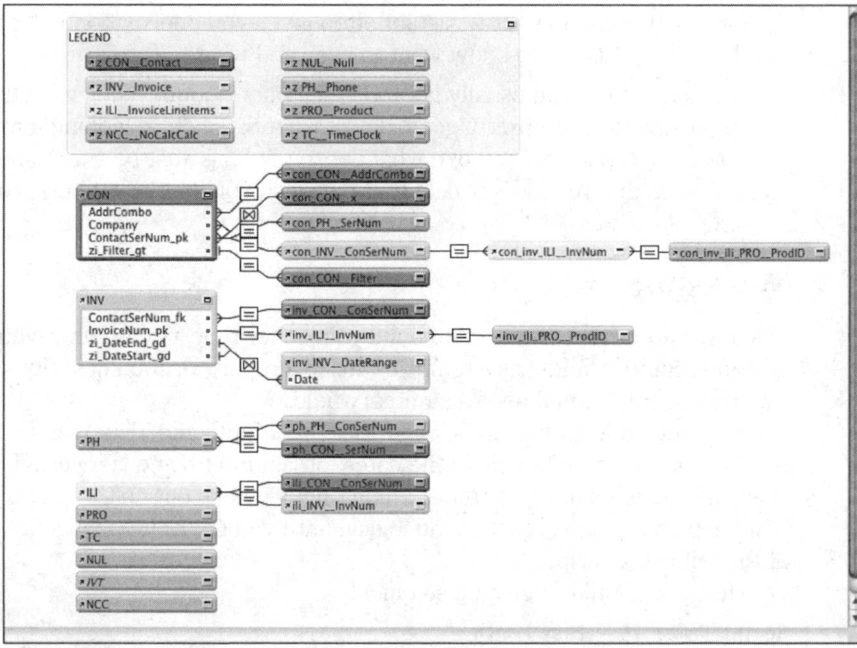

Figure 18-9
The relationships graph organized in columns and showing a legend and TO color coding.

Part 4

Summary

Am I wrong, or is your file starting to look and act like something almost professional? In this chapter we looked at reports in detail, and created two reports in our file that can be used as is or as templates for other types of reports. We also went quite a bit further by adding buttons that create the reports automatically right from the Main Menu.

Q & A

Q When we made the scripts for the Find Date Range layout, why couldn't we have just gone to a layout based on the Invoice table, put the file in Find mode, and let the users type in a date range — or maybe use the buttons?

> **A** You could. But what if the user accidentally leaves Find mode and ends up entering a date range in a real date field in Browse mode? What if they don't know how to use the ellipsis? What if they decide to delete their date range attempt instead of just starting over? Right, they might delete a real invoice! And isn't it nice and clear to see Start Date and End Date fields? Remember, one of the things we need to ask is, "What can go wrong?" The answer is, "Lots of things."

Q You say that the Layout Assistant often gives you information you don't need. How am I going to know what to keep and what to throw away?

> **A** Remember, you usually get too much information. When you start a report, you have a pretty good idea of what data you're looking for. Preview the report and remove what doesn't belong. Just be sure to perform a find on different sets of data to preview so you'll be able to test your expectations.

Workshop

Using the steps that you used to build your other reports (scripts, layouts, and any required fields) as a template, make a report for total quantity sales by ProdID. Hint: You'll need a summary field.

Test your calculation skills. Copy the This Month and This Year scripts, and change them so they fill in the dates for last month and last year. This is really a troubleshooting exercise. I didn't figure these out on the first try. You just keep trying things that sound logical until you get it. If you give up, look at the following scripts.

Hey, you shouldn't give up so quickly!

```
Script Name: 25 - Last Month
Set Field [InvLI::zi_DateStart_gt; Date (Month (Get (CurrentDate)) -1; 1;
Year (Get (CurrentDate)))]
Set Field [InvLI::zi_DateEnd_gt; Date (Month (Get (CurrentDate)); 1; Year
(Get (CurrentDate))) -1]
```

```
Script Name: 26 - Last Year
Set Field [InvLI::zi_DateStart_gt; Date (1; 1; Year (Get (CurrentDate)) -1)]
Set Field [InvLI::zi_DateEnd_gt; Date (12; 31; Year (Get (CurrentDate)) -1)]
```

Now add the buttons to the layout.

Part 5

Sharing Your Database

Chapter 19

Personal Data Sharing

Introduction

Databases become more valuable when you can share them over a network, especially in an office environment. Different users have access to the same information, and many people can be involved in data entry. FileMaker Pro allows both Macintosh and Windows users to share the same database files transparently on the same network at the same time. As more people are working away from the office, the fact that FileMaker can share files remotely by way of a modem and the Internet makes it all the more valuable.

The information in this chapter may not apply to everyone. It's mostly instructional and we won't be adding any functionality to our files. If your files will not be used on a network, this will only serve as a reference for when that day arrives.

In this chapter, we'll look at:

- How to share FileMaker files using built-in sharing capabilities
- The network requirements for sharing
- How to optimize sharing performance
- The capabilities and limitations of personal file sharing

What Is Personal Data Sharing?

There are a number of techniques for sharing data in FileMaker files:

- You can use a special product called FileMaker Server.
- You can share data from your files by way of an intranet or the Internet using a browser and FileMaker's Instant Web Publishing capabilities.
- You can just share the files on a network by turning on FileMaker's Sharing option.
- You can export exact copies of layouts as PDFs that you can send to clients.
- You can export your data as an Excel spreadsheet and share it with any user who has Excel.
- You can export the contents of any one field with FileMaker's Fast Send feature. Or use a script that builds a Fast Send as part of an export of any number of fields in any number of records.

- E-mail a link to a published database[9]

We'll look at sharing data using a browser in Chapter 20, "Sharing Your Data on the Web." To share a large number of files with many users, you'll need FileMaker Server. For sharing files with Instant Web Publishing or Custom Web Publishing through a browser with more than 10 users, you'll need FileMaker Server Advanced. We've already seen the PDF maker in Chapter 14 in the section titled "Printing to PDF." So the discussion in this chapter will deal mostly with the standard FileMaker Pro program, and the spreadsheet maker (Save/Send Records as Excel) and Fast Send features introduced in FMP8.

Capabilities

FileMaker's sharing is independent of other types of file sharing. Of course, if the network is down, you won't be able to share FileMaker files. You do not need to see the icon of the network hard drive of the computer that contains the files you want to share on your desktop in order to use remote FileMaker files. Nor do you need to have file-level access to the files. No one has to set up any file sharing of any kind other than FileMaker's own Network Sharing. If you are accessing the Internet through a modem, you can share files that are open on another machine connected to the Internet (as long as you can figure out how to get through any firewalls, which we'll discuss later in this chapter). You can even open shared files remotely through an older dial-up modem by dialing directly to another computer. In order to make that work, you'll need to use a product like PCAnywhere, Timbuktu, or Apple Remote Desktop (all of which can be used much more efficiently via a fast Internet connection). FileMaker does not actually dial up the other computer. But once you've established the connection by other means, you can share your files. Otherwise, FileMaker is pretty flexible about communicating over whatever networks are available.

As long as you are on a network and your account privileges allow, as a host or guest you can:

- View, edit, create, delete, sort, and print records
- Change modes, layouts, and views
- Import and export records
- Perform and create scripts
- Edit and create value lists
- Define user privilege sets and passwords
- Create fields and tables

Network Requirements

Early versions of FileMaker allowed file sharing using up to three different network protocols. Starting with FileMaker 7, all sharing is done via TCP/IP, the language of the Internet as well as many other networks. That simplifies sharing, because if two computers were set to different protocols, they couldn't see each other across the network.

> **NOTE** The network protocols are simply the languages used by the computers to talk with each other.

You'll want to set up the machines so that the various copies of the FileMaker program on the network will be able to speak with each other. You do this by choosing File, Sharing, FileMaker Network. Then click the radio button next to On, select each open file, and decide if and with whom you want to share the file or files. You have to do this on all machines that will be hosting files across the network. Just to be clear, it won't be necessary to do this with copies of FileMaker on machines where users want to have access to the files being hosted on other machines — only on machines where users want to say, "Hello, I have files to share with everyone."

In Figure 19-1 you can see a screen shot of the FileMaker Network Settings window.

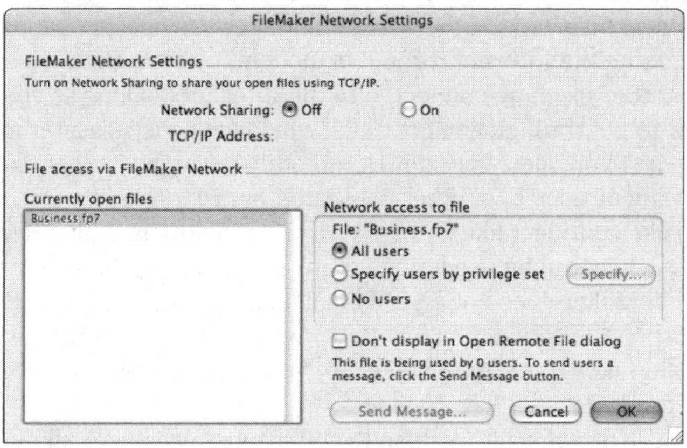

Figure 19-1
The FileMaker Network Settings window showing Network Sharing via TCP/IP currently turned off.

Using Personal File Sharing

Making your files available to other FileMaker users on your network is almost as easy as clicking a button. Of course, the network must be set up properly, FileMaker's own networking support software must be installed, and the files you want to share must be open. But all you need to do is choose File, then Sharing, FileMaker Network, select the files from the list of currently open files, and click the "All users" button. You can choose more details by selecting one file at a time and selecting "Specify users by privilege set." Figure 19-1 shows Business.fp7 to be the only currently open file.

Here are a few more items to be attentive to:

- Files must be compatible with the FMP7 format. (FileMaker Pro 8, 8.5, 9, and 10 files still have the .fp7 extension and are compatible, but features in each newer version won't be available to users of any of the previous versions of the client program.) Files created in versions previous to 7 must be converted first.

- If you have a client outside your LAN firewall, the network administrator must remove blocking from TCP port 5003.
- Windows users must be sure only one network adapter is installed for the protocol being used. If more than one network card is installed, FMP broadcasts only from the card with ID 0 (zero).
- On a Mac, the FMP app must remain in the FMP folder and the TCP/IP OT Network file must be properly installed.

The check box next to "Don't display in Open Remote File dialog" is used for files that you do not want other users to see as hosted files. You can select multiple open files and check this box to affect them all at once.

Why would you want to have any files effectively invisible on the network?

If you create a solution that consists of a group of files, you may want one file to open and control when and how the other files open. Set up the control file without checking that box and set the other files as "Don't display." All the hidden files will be called as needed by relationships, value lists, and scripts.

In a network environment with shared FileMaker files, you can be either a host of a file or a guest. The host is the first person to open a file. (Technically, that could include the FileMaker Server application as well.) Anyone else who wants to use the file will be a guest. The details for how to do that are in the following section. Of course, you can still have files open on your computer that are not shared.

There is another situation in which a user can become a remote host. To become a remote host, you must have access to the files on the hard drive of another machine. Double-clicking on the icon of one of these files will bring up a warning that you are about to become the host of a file on another machine. Opening files this way works, but it can really slow down the network. (See the section on optimizing performance later in this chapter.) Remote hosting can also make recovery more precarious in the case of a crash. For all of these reasons, you should think of remote hosting as useful in temporary or emergency circumstances, but as a general practice, I would strongly discourage it.

Using Files as a Guest

Once files are open on a host machine, guests can access the files. Guests must be hooked up to the same network and be running FileMaker. (Again, a guest does not have to turn FileMaker Network Sharing on.) Then, to become a guest:

1. Choose **File**, **Open.** (If you choose File, Open Remote you can skip to step 3.)

2. When the File window appears, click the **Remote** button.
3. After a few seconds, you'll be able to see a list of all hosts on the network. Click on a host and you'll see a list of the open (non-hidden), shared FileMaker files. Of course, you'll need to know the name of the file you're supposed to open.

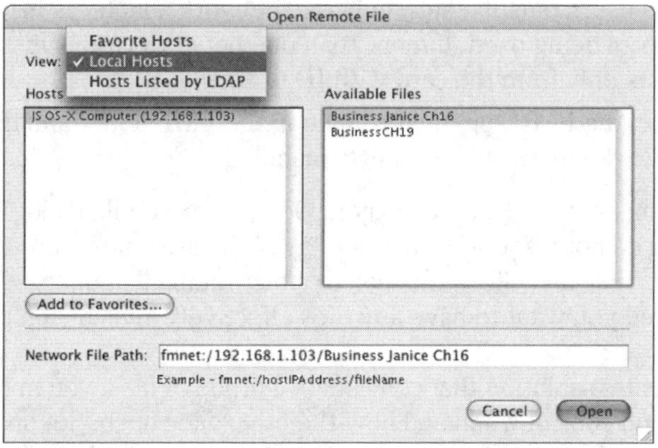

Figure 19-2
The Open Remote File window showing the available host(s) and files.

4. Just open it as you would any other file.

With the exception of the limitations of shared files, working in the files is the same as working with a file on your own machine.

NOTE You can open a file using the Open File script step. Notice in Figure 19-3 that the Specify pop-up list includes choices to add and manage data sources. Figure 19-4 shows the Edit Data Source window. This window allows you to define multiple paths to a file in case one copy of the file is unavailable. Before FileMaker Pro 7, FileMaker would search the entire network for a file. This was time consuming, slowed down the network, and sometimes opened files with the same name that were not intended to be opened. Generally, you'll be looking for a specific file along one path in this window. You have access to this window from the Import Records, Open, Close, or Recover script steps as well as when you choose a relationship or a value list from another file.

You can still run into trouble if you have multiple files on the same volume with the same name. (See the Caution about renaming older versions of your files in the section titled "InvLI and Product" in Chapter 7.) Be aware that you can lose track of a file if it gets moved to a different server. The biggest advantage of the Manage External Data Sources feature is that when FileMaker has finished searching for the specific files, it stops, thereby speeding up the search and preventing accidental use of unintended files.

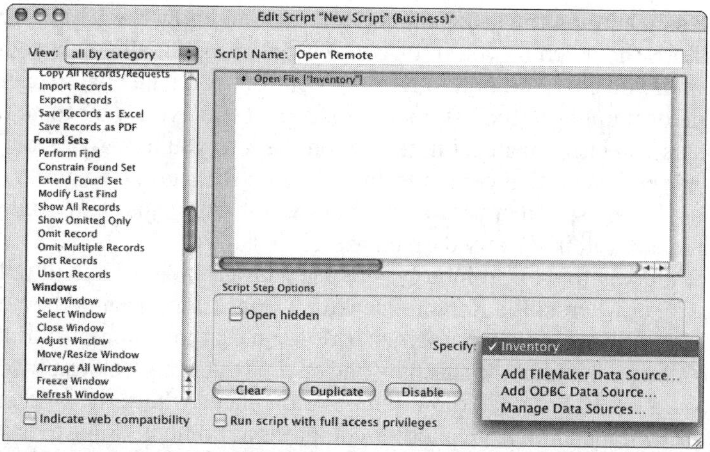

Figure 19-3 The Open File script step and the Specify pop-up list.

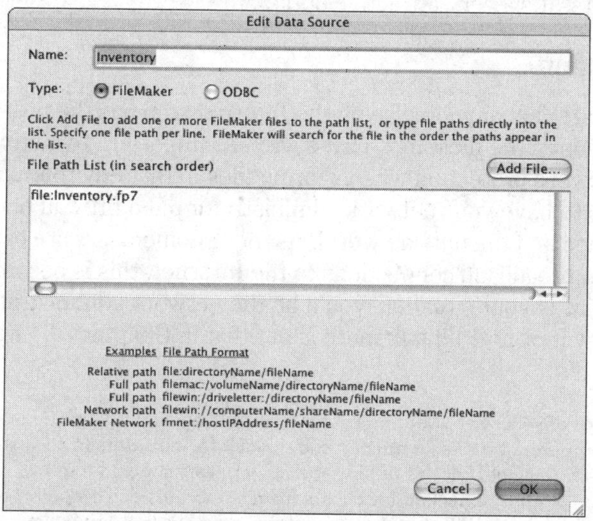

Figure 19-4 The Edit Data Source window showing a single path to the Inventory file.

Sharing Remotely by Way of Modem

You can also share files across the Internet. There are two ways to access files: by way of a phone modem (a pretty antiquated method these days) or with another TCP Internet connection. If you have permission to open other files on the remote hard drive, and you know how to log on with a modem, you can mount the drive using TCP. Then, as long as no one else has the file open, you can simply double-click the icons that appear on your desktop.

The other way of sharing files is to use FileMaker's own sharing capabilities. For that to work, the host file has to be open with FileMaker Network Sharing set to on, on a computer connected to the Internet. Once you establish a connection to the Internet with your modem or other network, bring FileMaker to the front and choose Open Remote from the File menu, just as in the last section. You should see the window shown in Figure 19-2.

Unless you're on the same subnet, you have to know the IP address or the URL for the machine you're trying to connect to, but all you have to do is type it in. If you click the Add to Favorites button, you'll be able to click on the name or number in the list under Hosts next time you want to go there. As soon as you click on a host in the list on the left, you'll see a list of all the open, shared files on that computer in the list on the right. Of course, you'll be limited by the speed of your connection, but it works just fine. And when you think about it, it's pretty darn amazing!

Another way to work remotely is to use a program like Timbuktu, PC Anywhere, or Microsoft's Remote Desktop Connection to bring the remote computer's desktop onto your screen. (More on that in a moment.) But you end up taking control of the machine and anybody at that desk can't work while you do it. However, I know a number of offices where the workers log into their own machine from another computer at home in order to have more flexible work hours. It's a very attractive option.

File Sharing Caution

You should be aware that anyone else on the Internet who has the host name or IP address can open the files, too. That's why it's important to institute some sort of password protection when sharing files in that environment. Another choice is to have your network administrator put a firewall between your local machines and the outside world. As more home users are establishing permanent broadband connections to the Internet, this is becoming a critical issue. If that is your situation, you'll be the network administrator whether you know it or not! I'll talk more about that in Chapter 20, "Keeping Your Data Secure."

> **NOTE** For the sake of security I bought a router that sits between my cable modem and my computer. It makes it much more difficult for outsiders to get in and play around with my files. Prior to getting the router, tests showed that my machine was being "pinged" (checked for access from some outside computer) at least once every two minutes. With the router in place, whether the pinging is from a hacker or for some legitimate purpose, I haven't had any problems for the past six years.

It might not seem like there'd be much of a chance of someone guessing one particular IP address. But I had only begun experimenting with this technique when I transposed the numbers of a friend's IP address. I found a database of student grades on a server at a school in New Hampshire. The file was not password protected, and I discovered I could actually change the grades! If someone a little more warped or mischievous than me (not to mention a disgruntled student) were to have gotten to those files...well, just make sure you protect any files that you share on the Internet.

This warning doesn't only apply to machines with a permanent connection to the Internet. If you don't have a static IP address, your provider assigns you a temporary (dynamic) address every time you turn your machine on and connect to the Internet. That's so that when you make a request to view a web page, the other machine knows how to find you with the results of your request. Any FileMaker files you have open and shared on your computer are vulnerable during the time you're online (if you're not behind a router). It's a little creepy when you think about it. You can always quit or exit FileMaker before going online. But you can also password protect your files or just leave them set to "No users."

Now that I've sufficiently scared you, let me show you a script you can run before going online:

```
Script Name: 24.5 - Multi-User Off
Set Multi-User [Off] (Files category)
```

That script's not too hard, eh? It effectively turns FileMaker Network Sharing off. You can put that script in the files you use most often, and then create a single script in one of your favorite files that runs all the external scripts. Then you'll want to make another script for turning multi-user back on. Nevertheless, I really think that password protection is your best defense. It's just too easy to forget to activate the script. Besides, more often these days, we're online all the time.

Another major caution has to do with working in files over the Internet. I know some developers who log into their client's databases using the Open Remote dialog and then work in the Manage Database area. If you lose your connection to the Internet, you can destroy the file. And you increase your chances of being disconnected if you work wirelessly. It's much better to use a program like Timbuktu, PC Anywhere, or Remote Desktop Connection to bring the remote computer's desktop onto your screen. If you lose the connection, someone on the remote machine can finish up your work. I do have one client that has me log on with Open Remote, but I have him back up just before I do.

Limitations

Although personal file sharing is a valuable tool, there are some limitations. Two people cannot edit the same record, but one person can edit a record while another person views it. If a record is included in a report and someone edits it, the report won't reflect the change until the report is called up again. In versions of FileMaker prior to 7, while the files were being shared, neither the host nor the guest could define fields, change the order of layouts, or open the Access Privileges window. All that has changed starting with FMP7, increasing the power to developers a great deal. Guests of a file still cannot use the Save a Copy As command, but the host of the file can. And starting with FMP9, multiple users can work on different scripts inside the Manage Scripts area.

File and Guest Limits

There are some limits to FileMaker's standard, built-in file sharing. You may host up to eight guests at the same time not including yourself. If your needs are greater than that, it's time to get a copy of FileMaker Server, which is optimized for sharing large numbers of files with a group of workers, or FileMaker Server Advanced, which can share files with the FileMaker client software as well as through a web browser using Instant Web Publishing. (Beginning with the standard version of FileMaker Server 9, users are allowed to connect using Custom Web Publishing. Previously CWP for more than five users was limited to the Advanced version of the server product.)

Global Fields and Shared Files

Here's a seemingly unrelated item that actually turns out to be pretty important. The values in fields formatted as global are local. The values users see when they first open a file are those stored in fields formatted as global on the server (keeping in mind that some opening scripts may alter those values). When I say that the values are local, it means that when a guest opens a file hosted on another machine, any changes that occur to values in global fields do not travel back to the host file. I had quite a few surprises in my first major design using global fields on a network, because I thought data was being saved in the host file when it was actually being dumped.

Even changes to global fields in the host file do not travel out to the guests until they sign off and back on. As long as you understand that, there are some marvelous things you can do with global fields that take advantage of this "limitation." You'll just have to work out some other arrangement for moving values to other machines on the network.

Optimizing Performance

There are a number of things you can do to get the best performance out of a network with shared FileMaker files. First, use the fastest machine possible to host the files (see the next section, "Hardware Considerations"). Next, make sure any other network software issues are resolved. If there are intermittent problems, check that all connectors are tightly seated between wires, computers, and hubs. Sometimes worn or poor quality wiring can be the cause of the trouble. I have a client who tried to save money by having a "friend" install some wiring for him. After his files crashed numerous times, he realized the $100 he saved on wiring had cost him nearly $1,000 in data recovery.

As I mentioned before, if you have access to the files on the hard drives of other computers, you can open and host FileMaker files remotely. The problem with this arrangement is that when anyone else signs on as a guest, all the requests have to travel down the network through the remote host machine, back to the computer where the files are actually stored, back through the remote host machine, and back to the guest. This effectively doubles the network traffic, not to mention that it slows down the machine that is doing the remote hosting. Figure 19-5 illustrates the inefficiency of this arrangement. (More arrows mean more traffic. More traffic means slower speeds.) Avoid remote hosting whenever possible. It's better to go to the computer with the stored files and open them so they can be hosted there. Even then, if somebody is working on the host machine in a processor-intensive program, FileMaker's hosting sits politely in the background. I've been to a few offices where everybody thought FileMaker was a terribly slow program until I showed them how to set it up properly.

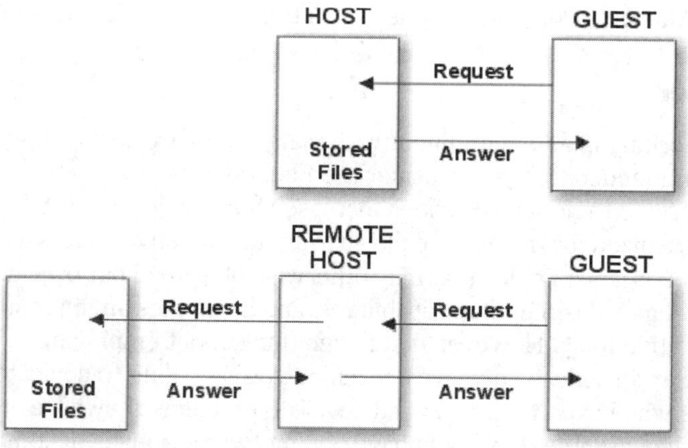

Figure 19-5 Diagram showing how remote hosting of files doubles the network traffic.

Processing large reports can also slow down a network, especially if print jobs with complex graphics are traveling down the same lines. Try to work out such activities so they take place when there is low network traffic.

Hardware Considerations

The best way to share files, short of using FileMaker Server (see the next section), is to devote a machine to the FileMaker files. The computer should only be running FileMaker Pro, and no one should be running other programs on it. Additionally, the faster the machine, the better the response for all users. It can often be hard to convince the staff that the fastest computer should be devoted to FileMaker. Everyone wants the newest, fastest machine on his or her own desk. Almost every office I've been to that shares FileMaker files has relegated their oldest machine to be the server. Then they complain about how pokey FileMaker is, but it's not FileMaker's fault. A trip to the grocery store in a Model-T is pretty slow, too, even if the driver is an Indy 500 champion.

As a database, FileMaker Pro's functions are hard-drive intensive. Data is moved back and forth to the computer from the hard drive. That means that a faster hard drive will get better results, as long as the computer can use the information quickly enough. Simply installing a screamingly fast hard drive in an old clunker of a computer will not necessarily improve the operation of your databases.

CAUTION Years ago I had dreams of speeding up FileMaker by putting files on a RAM disk. A RAM disk is a software trick that allows computer memory to act as if it were an extremely fast hard drive. Good idea! The only problem is, if you have a crash, all changes to the files are lost. It's much better to get the fastest hard drive you can afford.

The speed of the network can also influence the apparent speed of FileMaker. In its day, 10baseT Ethernet was pretty quick, and many offices still operate fairly efficiently using that system. Most new machines, however, ship with built-in Ethernet chips or 100baseT cards installed. Whatever system is put to use, FileMaker can operate only as fast as the weakest link in the chain.

FileMaker Server

If you are working in an environment with many users accessing files, it is highly recommended that you consider the FileMaker Server product. You should experience a noticeable speed increase when using the files, because Server is optimized for this type of file sharing over a network. It is also a better way of organizing files that may otherwise be spread out over multiple machines, it has built-in backup capabilities, and it contains an impressive set of administrative tools. However, don't even think about employing FileMaker Server unless you have a machine you're willing to dedicate to it. I have clients who haven't taken that advice. The problems they have are their own fault. I'll guarantee they could have bought two reasonably fast machines for the amount they've spent on having me and another network professional come in to fix problems this "inexpensive" arrangement has caused. Running an e-mail server on the machine with FileMaker Server causes the most problems.

Some Final Words

If you move a set of shared files to a single-user environment, depending on the settings on that machine, FileMaker may turn sharing off. If you then return the files to a multi-user environment, be sure to turn FileMaker Network Sharing back on for each file in the solution.

Closing Hosted Files

If you are the host, when you attempt to close a file, you will be presented with a dialog box listing any guests of the file. Clicking the Ask button will alert any users that you need to close the file. Users can delay the closing of the file by clicking Cancel on their end, but the dialog box will continue to present itself at irritatingly short intervals. If guests don't click either button (e.g., they're away from their desk), the file will close in 30 seconds. If all users click the Close Now button, the file closes immediately.

Slow Network Traffic

Because file sharing makes use of the network, there are times that other network traffic may affect the performance of your files. When network traffic causes a slowdown, your cursor will change to a double-pointed, zigzagged arrow or a coffee cup. It's best just to be patient at times like these, but I have seen these icons stay on the screen when the network is completely locked up. My advice is to wait about five minutes. If the cursor hasn't returned to normal, quit or exit FileMaker. Worst case, you may find your machine locked up, and you'll have to reboot.

Save/Send Records as Excel[8]

A discussion about sharing wouldn't be complete without some features introduced in FMP8 — Sending as Excel, Printing to PDF, and Fast Send. We already discussed the PDF maker in Chapter 14, so we'll skip that here.

Prior to 8, you could get an Excel spreadsheet by exporting data as a tab-separated file and importing that into Excel. But there were a lot of steps involved. Starting with 8, you can get a spreadsheet by making a few simple choices in a dialog. Not only that, but the same choices are available inside Manage Scripts. That means you can create it once and users can run it at the click of a button!

To look at how it works:

1. Choose **File, Save/Send Records As, Excel**.
2. Take a look at Figure 19-6. The Save as type drop-down at the bottom of the window lets you choose the type of Excel Workbook you want. The .xlsx extension applies to Excel 2007 for Windows and 2008 for Macintosh. The Save drop-down at the bottom of the window is where you choose whether you save all records being browsed or just the current record. As you can see, there are check boxes so you can automatically create an e-mail and/or open the file as soon as you create it. Click the **Options** button to see the Excel Options window. Notice the check box at the top that lets you choose if you want the spreadsheet to use the field names in the first row.
3. Once you make your selections, click **Save.** That's it! Since one of the choices is to "Create email with file as attachment," all you need to do is finish out the e-mail message.

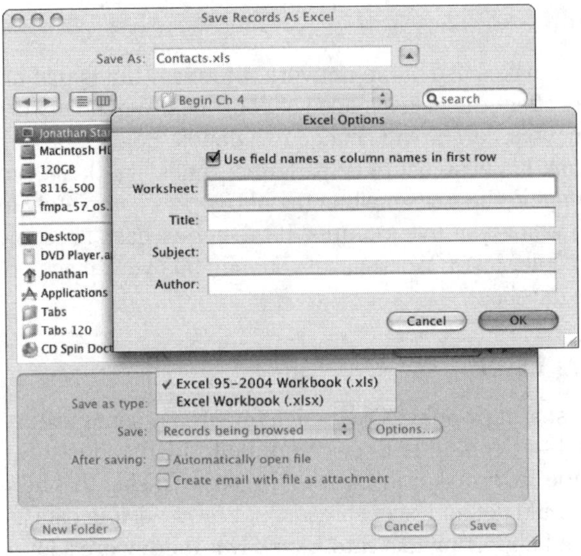

Figure 19-6
The Save Records As Excel and Excel Options windows.

If you want to script this feature, the script step is called Save Records as Excel. It has many of the options Save a PDF has. Remember that we used a variable to give the PDF a unique name and path using Get (TemporaryPath). I tried to do this using a date as part of the file name. It turns out that FileMaker is very fussy about that. It didn't want me to use slashes (/) in the file name because the slash character indicates a different level of the directory. I set it up to use underscore characters instead.

One difference about saving or sending as Excel from a "normal" export is that all fields on the current layout are exported. You won't find the Specify Field Order window that you see when you choose File, Export Records. You can control what is exported by carefully choosing which layout you're on when the export takes place. Alternatively, you could export the old-fashioned way where you have complete control over what fields go out, and then import the text file into Excel.

Both the window and the script are limited to a user's ability to access the field. You can still script the export for them as long as you check the box next to "Run script with full access privileges." But there should be some consideration as to why they might be allowed to export with the script but not otherwise have access to the field. You wouldn't want just anybody exporting credit card numbers, would you?

Export Field Contents/Fast Send[8]

The Export Field Contents choice at the bottom of the context menu hides a lot of power. FileMaker 8 and later allow you to export the contents of any single field and send it automatically as an attachment to an e-mail. Since field contents can include anything in a container field, such as images, PDFs,

Word documents — virtually any type of file — there's quite a lot of power here. Here's how:

1. Control+click (Macintosh) or right-click (Windows) on the field you want to send as an e-mail, and choose **Export Field Contents** from the context menu.
2. At the top of the Export Field to File window, FileMaker already knows what type of file it should be. In the case of a container field, there could be quite a few options. So it's nice to have that taken care of. Of course, you can choose to name it something else.
3. Use the check boxes to decide whether to automatically open the file and/or create an e-mail with the file attached.
4. Click **Save**. Fast and easy.

If you want to script this command, use the Export Field Contents step under the Fields heading. The choices are virtually the same, except you can decide what field gets exported, name the file beforehand, and make the decisions for the users as to whether everything happens automatically.

I tried to go one step further with a container field and get the script to name the file with an extension based on the contents of the field. No such luck. It seems you would only want to script the file name if you know what the extension is expected to be. For example, if you knew you always intended to export a specific text field, you would know that the extension has to be .txt. Otherwise, you can leave the "Specify output file" box unchecked and leave it up to the user to click the Save button to verify the file name and type.

Of course, the ability to use this function is limited to the user's ability to access the field. If users are not allowed to export from the field, they obviously won't be able to use the context menu. But you could still script the export as long as you checked the box next to "Run script with full access privileges."

Email Link to Published Database[9]

And finally, FileMaker, Inc. really wants to keep their program the easiest to use database in the world. So they added a feature that lets you tell other users on your local network where to find your file. Instead of expecting you to figure out the network address of your machine, FileMaker grabs it for you and starts an e-mail. Beginning with FileMaker 10, we now have support for IPv6 Internet addresses. You don't need to know what that is. You can just take it for granted that when it comes to sending an e-mail link, FileMaker will take care of it for you.

Before you even get started, FileMaker Network Sharing must be turned on (File, Sharing, FileMaker Network) and the specific file must be open and set to be shared. Oh, and make sure you keep the file open during the time you expect other users to connect.

1. Choose **File**, **Send Link**.

2. FileMaker opens your e-mail program and starts a message that includes the IP address of your machine. Choose the recipient, add your own message, and send it off.

   That's it. Only two steps. Wow!

Okay, there is a little more to it than that:

- The user must have the FileMaker program installed on his or her machine.
- You can use the FileMaker Network Settings window to set up the file so that any user can get in, or you can limit it to specific users. Keep in mind the security of your files.
- Of course, you should provide your friend with a user name and password if you'll be limiting access to specific users.
- If you have a firewall between the server (which may be your computer) and theirs, you have to open port 5003 in the firewall to allow FileMaker sharing. (Port 5003 is registered exclusively to FileMaker, Inc. for FileMaker sharing. It is possible to assign that port to other software, but that doesn't change the fact that FileMaker has the right to it.)
- Also, if you have a router between your machine and your friend's, the link will only show the local network number of your machine — probably something like 192.168.1.101. (The link itself will look like fmp7://192.168.1.101/Business.fp7.) Unfortunately, that won't help him or her find your file. This only works on a local network, not across the Internet.
- If your files are being shared by the FileMaker Server program, the Send Link is smart enough to use the machine number of the server rather than your personal machine.
- If you don't have an e-mail program on your computer, you'll see a dialog from which you can copy the machine link. But how are you going to e-mail it? I guess you can call and tell the other user how to link up. At least it's a quick way to know your machine number.

When my Entourage program opens, for some reason it sticks the messages in the Drafts folder instead of in the Outbox. (I've spent an hour looking in the Preferences and the Help file. Any program that can't make it clear to me in an hour doesn't deserve my business. I use a plug-in and let FileMaker be my e-mail program because I can make it do what I want.)

Summary

In this chapter, we looked at how to use FileMaker Pro's built-in sharing, how to set it up to work on a network, and the capabilities and limitations of the arrangement. We also saw how to optimize FileMaker's sharing and how to access files remotely with a modem. Finally, we were introduced to two ways to share data using Save/Send As Excel and Export Field Contents, otherwise known as Fast Send, and how to e-mail a link to share your database.

Q & A

Q What if I need to change a field definition and I'm hosting a shared file?

A As long as no one else is in the Manage Database area, you can do any of the things you can do if you were the only user. But remember, there are dangers to working in the Manage Database area when you're working remotely on a file. If you lose the connection, your file could be permanently damaged. Back up the file first.

Workshop

If you're on a network with multiple copies of FileMaker on different machines, open one of the files and set network access to the file for all users. Go to one of the other computers, open a copy of FileMaker, make sure Network Sharing is on, and see if you can access the file remotely.

Chapter 20

Sharing Your Data on the Web

Introduction

FileMaker Pro 5.0 added an amazing built-in feature: If your computer is connected to the Internet or an intranet, you can make the data in your files available to other people through a browser — without any third-party software. To protect your privacy, you can control who can access the information with the use of passwords or by limiting what machine IP addresses are allowed to connect to your files. For many people, this opens up a whole new world of possibilities.

In this chapter, you'll learn:

- How to set up your computer to take advantage of FileMaker's Instant Web Publishing
- How to set up FileMaker and your files to serve the data
- How to keep your data secure

Why Publish on the Web?

There are quite a few reasons why you might want to make some of your files available through a browser on an intranet or the Internet. Maybe you have a business or a hobby you would like to share with other people. Maybe you occasionally need to get to some of your data from a machine that doesn't have a copy of FileMaker Pro on it but does have an Internet browser. Perhaps other people in your office need to occasionally update information in your files. Maybe you want to start an Internet business where people will make purchases from your web site.

When I first heard about being able to publish on the web, I couldn't figure out what I'd do with it. About six months later, I had a lot of ideas. On my web site, potential clients can see screen shots of some of my databases. Before I built my web site, I used to print brochures and mail or hand them out. Now I can give someone my business card, and they can get a lot more information about what I do by checking out my web site than they could ever get from my printed materials. I've posted articles I've written about FileMaker, links to other FileMaker sites, and even some short stories I've written. Plus, I can update my site quickly and easily. Maybe once you realize web publishing with FileMaker Pro is something you can do, you'll start to think of some uses of your own.

FileMaker and Instant Web Publishing (IWP)

Other databases can be set up to be available on the web, as long as they have all the right accessory software and all those programs are talking nicely to each other. FileMaker makes this easy, and you can do it without having to buy any extra software. With the click of a few buttons and some check boxes, you can literally make your databases instantly available on an intranet or the web. There are some considerations for protecting your data that require a little more than a couple of clicks, but you'll find you can handle that using the information in this and the next chapter. You'll also want to look at a file called fm10_instant_web_publish_en.pdf, which you'll find inside the FileMaker Pro 10\English Extras\Electronic Documentation folder on your hard drive. What FileMaker's software is actually doing here is turning your machine into a web server. If you have any other software that is doing web serving on the machine, we'll be turning it off as part of our setup.

Setting Up Your Computer

To make your files available to other users on a regular basis, you'll need a static IP address and a machine that's connected to the network all the time. (However, you won't need that just to try it out. You can test on a single machine without a network. But your machine must still have an IP address. Read the next section called "If You Don't Have an Internet Account.") If you're on an intranet, you already have an IP number assigned to your computer — even if you don't know it. However, I've seen some companies that routinely reassign IP numbers to their users. You need to find out how that is handled on your network and make sure the address stays the same. Then, of course, you'll need to tell other people how to find you. (See the section titled "Email Link to Published Database" near the end of Chapter 19.) As you go through the steps for your machine, you may find it's already set up as described. If not, these instructions should get you there.

If You Have an Internet Account

CAUTION A little disclaimer before you get very far with this: There seem to be a ton of system software versions. While the instructions that follow are correct for the versions of software I used to write this section (Mac OS X 10.4.11 and Windows XP SP2), it's completely possible that you might have an older version of Mac OS X. (FileMaker Pro 7 and later will not operate under Mac OS 9 or even on versions of OS X previous to 10.3.9.) Remember to check for software updates for your system, browser, and even FileMaker Pro. The reason the software is updated is that people report problems that need to be fixed.

The settings I talk about here are something that you should get from your Internet service provider. Otherwise, tread lightly with the awareness that things may go awry when making changes to your TCP/IP settings on the Windows platform. In other words, don't start this five minutes before an important deadline.

NOTE You can make Instant Web Publishing work through a router. The instructions that follow do not include the details of how to do that. The router will assign your machine a generic IP address. In order to serve through a router, you'll need the IP address assigned to the router by your Internet service provider. You probably have software on your computer that can look at the router and tell you what the IP address is. I prefer to bring up a browser and use http://www.findmyip.com/ to get the router address. Then you may need to open up a port on the router so it can communicate with your FileMaker server. To avoid all this, you may just want to disconnect your router and temporarily connect directly to the cable (or other service type) modem. Then you'll probably have to restart your machine. Don't get freaked out about all this right now. If you're just looking at IWP and testing this out on your own machine, you don't need to concern yourself with such things.

To share regularly on the World Wide Web, you'll need a permanent connection to the Internet if you want people to be able to get to your data 24 hours a day. That can be accomplished with an ISDN, ADSL, cable modem, second phone line, or perhaps some arrangement with a satellite dish. However, when this becomes something you want to do all the time, you could also consider hiring the services of a provider who will keep your files on a web server for a monthly fee. On the other hand, assuming you don't have one of these services, you could specify certain times that your files will be available and only leave your phone line open during those hours, but that really defeats the convenience of Instant Web Publishing.

This may seem like a silly example, and most of it won't make sense until after you've read the rest of the chapter, but here goes. I wanted to show my mother some pictures I had taken, and I needed her opinion quickly. I stuck the images in a container field in a FileMaker file and turned on IWP. I was using a dial-up connection and only had one phone line. (This was a few years ago. I have a fast Internet connection now.) I called her and told her to check her e-mail in about five minutes. Then I hung up and dialed into my Internet provider. I went to TCP/IP on the Control Panel and copied down the IP address temporarily assigned to my machine. I sent Mom an e-mail giving her the URL including that machine number (something that looks like http://192.168.0.2/) and telling her how to click on the file on the FileMaker IWP homepage. I left my connection open for 15 minutes. She went online with her browser and 20 minutes later we talked about the pictures she had seen. (This won't work quite as easily if you're using a router between your computer and the Internet if it assigns generic machine addresses. You'll need to open port 5003 on the router.)

Mac OS X 10.4.11 or Greater To prepare a Macintosh computer so that you can use FileMaker for Instant Web Publishing, do the following:

1. In the System Preferences area, click the **Sharing** control panel and select the **Services** tab.

2. Make sure Personal Web Sharing is turned off because it will conflict with FileMaker's web sharing.
3. Go to the Network control panel. You'll need to be able to connect to some kind of network using either the built-in Ethernet or the internal modem. Select the one you want to work with from the drop-down.
4. Once it's open, click the **Assist me** button at the bottom of the window to make your settings.
   - When you're finished, if you're using the Built-in Ethernet option, you should see an IP address in the TCP/IP tab. Write that down so you can work with it later. If you don't see the numbers, restart your machine and return to the Network control panel; the new location should appear. You may have to reselect Built-in Ethernet in the Show pop-up to see the IP address. We tested on several machines and found it irritating that this process worked better on some machines than others.
   - If you're working with the internal modem, you won't be able to get the machine number until you dial in. That may be exactly what you want. But for testing Instant Web Publishing on the same machine as the browser, you can just go to the TCP/IP tab and choose Manually from the Configure pop-up. Then you can type in something like 192.168.0.2. Just make sure that the IP address on the other machine(s) you're connecting to is different. I set my system up so my second machine's IP number is 192.168.0.3, and so on sequentially.
5. Close the Network window. Now you can skip ahead to the section called "Setting Up FileMaker Pro for IWP."

Windows 2000 SP4 The bad news here is that FileMaker 9 and 10 will not work with Windows 2000. But I'm including this little section just in case you're actually using this book with an older version of FileMaker.

Have your Windows 2000 installation CD handy before you start this process. You probably won't need it, but you don't want to get stuck.

1. Click the **Start** button in the lower-left corner of the window.
2. Choose **Settings**, **Control Panel**, then **Network and Dial-up connections.**
3. Double-click the **Local Area Connection** icon. The Local Area Connection Properties window appears, displaying the network adapter in use and the network components used in this connection.
4. Click **Internet Protocol (TCP/IP)** and verify that the check box to the left of the entry is selected. (If you don't see the TCP/IP protocol, install it using the directions in the Windows Help files.)
5. Click the **Properties** button. The Internet Protocol (TCP/IP) Properties window appears.

6. Click the **Use the following IP address** radio button, and enter the number for your machine that has been provided by either your network administrator or your Internet service provider. You'll also want the subnet mask information.
7. Click **OK**, and **OK** again. Now you can skip down to the section called "Setting Up FileMaker Pro for IWP."

Windows XP SP2 Have your Windows XP installation CD available before you start this process. You probably won't need it, but it's better to have it handy.

1. Click the **Start** button in the lower-left corner of the window.
2. Choose **Control Panel**, then double-click **Network Connections**.
3. Double-click the **Local Area Connection** icon. You may be taken directly to the Local Area Connection Properties window. If not, when the Local Area Connection Status window appears, click the Properties button.
4. Click to highlight **Internet Protocol (TCP/IP)** and verify that the check box to the left of the entry is selected. (If you don't see the TCP/IP protocol, install it using the directions in the Windows Help files.)
5. Click the **Properties** button. The Internet Protocol (TCP/IP) Properties window appears.
6. (If you want to save this setting, click the Alternate Configuration tab — if it's available — before entering the IP address. If it's not available, write down the settings so you can re-enter it if needed.) Click the **Use the following IP address** radio button, and enter the number for your machine that has been provided by either your network administrator or your Internet service provider. You don't need to concern yourself with the subnet mask unless your network administrator has given it to you.
7. Click **OK**, and **OK** again, then **Close** (it may take up to one minute for the first window to close), and **Close** again. Now you can skip down to the section called "Setting Up FileMaker Pro for IWP."

If You Don't Have an Internet Account

You may not have an Internet account or even be on a network, but you still might want to try this out. I worked with this technique quite a bit when I was developing my web site before I put it up on a server. You can experiment by tricking your computer into looking at itself as if it were a machine on the Internet. Just follow all the other directions for setting up TCP/IP, Instant Web Publishing, and FileMaker Pro in this chapter. When it comes time to put in the URL address, simply type http://localhost in the URL Address box. You could also use the number of the machine you used in the machine settings area — something like 192.168.0.3. Look at the Tip in the upcoming "Advanced Options" section for information on a special situation that may arise during this process. Of course, you must have the FileMaker files open and each file's web sharing option turned on in order to see them in the browser. That's what we'll be describing next.

Sometimes setting up Instant Web Publishing to serve files to yourself using a browser can act squirrelly. Recently I had FileMaker open before I set up TCP/IP. When it wouldn't work, I found I had to quit and restart FileMaker before I could activate IWP.

Setting Up FileMaker Pro for IWP

FileMaker Pro 7 greatly simplified the setup needed to activate Instant Web Publishing (IWP). But to say it is simplified doesn't mean that there isn't an amazing depth to what is possible here. In fact, all of the accounts and privilege sets of FileMaker 7 and later can be brought to bear in IWP.

There is now one main setup area in FileMaker Pro to activate Instant Web Publishing. Here are the three functions we'll be setting up:

- FileMaker needs to use the TCP/IP network protocol and you must be connected to a network.
- You'll have to allow Instant Web Publishing access to any files you want to share.
- You'll select each individual file you want to share in the Instant Web Publishing window.

NOTE First I told you that you don't need to be connected to a network in order to get a web page to show the IWP shared files. But then I tell you that you need to be connected to a network to activate IWP. So which way is it?! You may be able to trick your machine into thinking it's connected to a network by plugging it into an Ethernet hub. Before I had network access, I had a very inexpensive hub that I plugged my computer into and I could turn IWP on. You may be able to borrow an older hub and try it out this way. I know for a fact that there are a lot of old 10baseT hubs sitting around on shelves because they're outdated and not even worth $5.

You can also connect one computer directly to another, but you really need a special crossover cable. Don't try it without the right cable because you can damage your network card.

Instant Web Publishing Settings

Within each specific file, there are quite a few choices you can make, but you can keep it very simple if you prefer. You must be connected to a network for this to work; otherwise, you'll get a message that FileMaker cannot share any files.

1. With FileMaker as the frontmost application, open the files you want to share.
2. On Windows, choose **Edit, Sharing, Instant Web Publishing**. On Macintosh, choose **File, Sharing, Instant Web Publishing**. You should see the window in Figure 20-1.

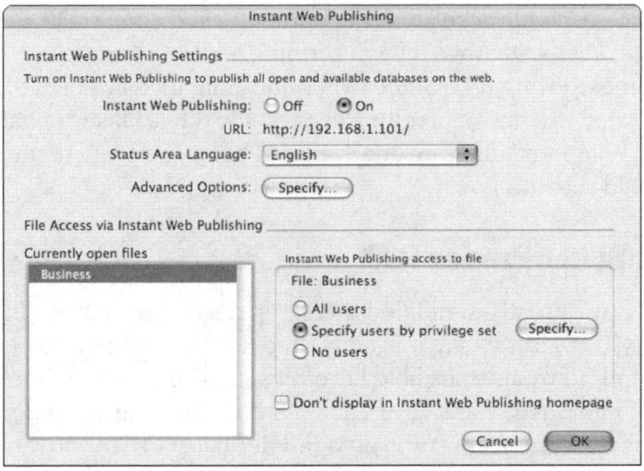

Figure 20-1
FileMaker's Instant Web Publishing window showing the feature turned on and the Business file as currently open.

3. Click the radio button next to **On**. On Windows, you may see the hourglass for a few seconds. (On Macintosh, it would be the spinning rainbow beach ball.) When you enable IWP on Mac OS X, you may see the Mac dialog asking for your user name and password. This is not a FileMaker dialog and actually requires the account information for the computer. After you provide your password and click OK, wait until your cursor turns back into the pointer.
4. Click on one of the files in the list in the **Currently open files** area.
5. Look over on the right and notice that you can choose to share with No users. Click the **Specify** button and take a look at how you can determine access by privilege sets. (Privilege sets are discussed in detail in Chapter 22.)
6. Click **Cancel.**
7. For now, click the **All users** radio button.

Advanced Options

1. Before you leave here, look at the middle of the window and click the **Specify** button next to Advanced Options. You should see the window shown in Figure 20-2.
2. Take a look around the Advanced Web Publishing Options window to get an idea of what other controls you can have over web access to your files. One important option is near the bottom where you choose how many minutes before you disconnect inactive accounts. You might feel generous and bump up the default time, but I'd advise against it. Some users will certainly quit their browsers without clicking the Log Out button. When that happens, they could tie up the file until the disconnect time runs out. For more on that, see the section called "IWP Browser Interface" later in this chapter.

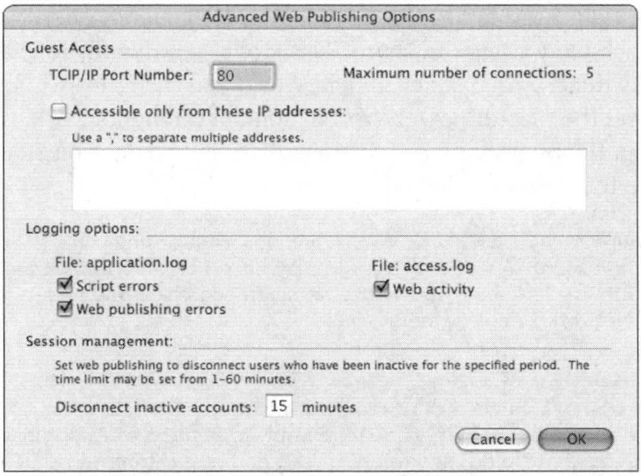

Figure 20-2 Advanced Web Publishing Options window showing the default settings.

3. Click **OK** twice to leave here.

   Even though we'll go into it detail in Chapter 22, since you can control user access to IWP with FileMaker's Accounts & Privileges system, we need to preview it now.

4. Go to **File**, **Manage**, **Accounts & Privileges**, choose the **Privilege Sets** tab, and double-click any one of the items in the list.
5. In the Edit Privilege Set window, look at the Extended Privileges area in the lower left. You can switch IWP access on and off for each account. This has the same effect as the check box in the IWP Sharing window.
6. Click **Cancel**.
7. Go to the **Extended Privileges** tab, and double-click **[fmiwp]**. Here again you can turn IWP on and off for any privilege set. The same check boxes are available in the Sharing, Instant Web Publishing, Specify users by privilege set area.

   One setting that was particularly troubling to me a couple of years ago was the TCP/IP port number. Apparently, I had some other application that took over port 80. Port 80 is the default web server port. If you have two versions of FileMaker running (say, FMP9 and FMP10), they will both try to monopolize port 80, which will result in the error. Also, programs such as Lasso, Webstar, and Personal Web Sharing (Mac OS X) will try to use port 80. I never did figure out what program was causing the problem for me. If that happens to you, try using the information in the next Tip.

   I wouldn't suggest making any changes in the Accounts & Privileges area until you get more familiar with everything else. The default settings should work for you. You can find out more about the other settings in the electronic documentation or the Help files.

8. Click **Cancel** and close the Instant Web Publishing window by clicking **OK**.

What we've done here is turn on Instant Web Publishing. Then we turned on access to each file we want to share. Think of it like this: In your home, you have light switches. To make each light work, you turn the switch on and off. If you turn off the master power switch, none of the lights work. Instant Web Publishing in the Sharing area is the master switch. The choices you make for each file are the individual light switches.

NOTE If you're in the FileMaker Network Settings window and you find you cannot turn on Instant Web Publishing, you may have TCP/IP turned off for the computer. After you turn it on, you'll have to restart FileMaker and reset FileMaker's Network Settings window.

TIP If you cannot connect with your machine from a remote browser, try changing the port setting to 591. (This is probably more than you want to know, but port 591 is a User Datagram Protocol (UDP) port, not a Transmission Control Protocol (TCP) port. Too much? Okay, let's move on.) However, when you do, you'll have to change the address where users will find you by adding ":591" on the end. For example, if your machine number is 192.168.0.5, people will now have to use 192.168.0.5:591 instead. Likewise, if you're using a domain name, it will have to read something like http://JonathanStars.com:591 or http://localhost:591. (By the way, I don't have a web site called JonathanStars.com. You can find me at DataDesignPros.com.) You can actually use any port number you want that's not in use. This can be a nice tool to keep your info one step more secure. It's called "security by obscurity." Hackers can't simply find your FileMaker homepage by guessing the machine's IP number or domain name. Adding a port number is not foolproof, however. Hackers can still run a port scan — and believe me, they do!

By assigning FileMaker a port address, you can actually have two web servers on the same machine. But that's getting a bit beyond the scope here.

Setting Up Your Database

There are a number of little things you might miss when getting everything ready to go. Here are some finer points of setting up the files:

- Web sharing is completely separate from FileMaker Network Sharing, so you do not need to set the network access to your files to All (or specific) users for web sharing to work. On the other hand, if you intend to share your files with other users who will be using their copy of the FileMaker application on an intranet or remotely through the web at the same time, you will need to have network access to those files turned on. In either case, you'll need to be attentive to password protecting your files. For more on that, see the "Web Security" section later in this chapter and Chapter 22, "Keeping Your Data Secure." Pay special attention to the section called "A Word about Passwords" in Chapter 22.
- If you're familiar with Instant Web Publishing in versions of FileMaker prior to 7, note that you can no longer control access to the web version of files in the File Options window. You used to be able to check the box next to "Log in using" and select a password. Starting in version 7, that check box only controls how users enter the files using their version of

the FileMaker Pro program. Instead, you activate the Guest account and have IWP turned on for the Guest account. Now all users have access to the file(s) without needing to see the Account Name and Password dialog.

- If the Guest account is enabled and has the IWP privilege set enabled, web users open the database without being prompted for an account name and password when they access the file. But keep in mind, if the Guest account has IWP turned off, each user will still be presented with the Account Name and Password dialog.
- To force users to log in when using a browser, the Guest account must be inactive or the Guest account must be turned off for fmiwp in the Extended Privilege area. For a user to be able to log in, his or her account must be active, and extended privileges must be turned on for Access via Instant Web Publishing. Any users set for auto login in the File Options area will not have any effect on IWP.
- In versions of FileMaker prior to 7, you needed to make sure users had Export Records turned on. That is no longer necessary in order to make IWP work.

Browsers

Users who are looking at your database in a browser will see pages that look nearly identical to your layouts. Unfortunately, IWP is only certified to be used with a limited set of browsers.

FileMaker's IWP is only certified to host the specific browsers listed below for the specific operating systems. Other browsers might work, but you can't guarantee the results — either in appearance or what might happen when users click the various buttons and/or try to enter data. When I tested IWP with different browsers for the FMP6 book, we actually locked up the server when we tried to use Netscape. IWP for FileMaker Pro 7 and later is much more robust, however. I have not tried any browsers other than those listed. Just be aware that you might be wise to post a list of the certified browsers somewhere on your pages. Keep in mind that many users of AOL don't even know they're using a browser. (They just think of it as AOL.) Here are the certified browser/OS combos:

- Windows Vista, XP SP4 or later, Server 2003, Server 2008 — Internet Explorer 7 or Firefox 3.0
- Mac OS X 10.4.11 or 10.5.4 — Safari 3.1.2.x or Firefox 3.0

Note that JavaScript must be enabled in the web browser.

As a developer, it might help to know that even though people may be able to log into your files if they're on Mac OS X 10.2 and 10.3, you yourself can't run FMP8 or 8.5 on any version of OS X below 10.3.9. FMP9 requires 10.4.8 or later, and FMP10 needs 10.4.11 or later.

Some earlier versions of Internet Explorer and Safari are blocked from IWP. If you try to access the files using some other browser, you may not get anything at all. Or you may get the following message displayed on the database homepage just above the list of open files: "This site has been optimized for use with Internet Explorer 6.0 or later. Using another browser to access this site is not recommended." You will want to have your users stick with the browsers recommended by FileMaker. It may seem like a lot to ask of your users. But, hey, browsers are cheap.

Layouts

You can do some fancy design work to your FileMaker layouts so they look more like web pages. For the most consistent results, you should choose colors from the Web palette in FileMaker's Preferences. You won't get as much control as you would by having a custom-built web site, but this is for basic data viewing and/or entry, and it's free!

You'll probably want to make some special web layouts. There should be as few fields and graphics as possible on these layouts so they'll load more quickly in the browsers. Look at the simplified web layout I created in Figure 20-3 to get some idea of how a few fields can be arranged on the layout. The picture I used is a 72 dpi JPG image resized to fit the field so it's web compatible and loads quickly. If none of your layouts seem appropriate, create a new layout, change access in Accounts & Privileges, and come back to choose it from the pop-up on the web page.

Figure 20-3
A layout optimized for web viewing.

There are a few things you should be aware of when designing your layouts:

- Buttons you create on layouts will work in a browser, with some very specific limitations. The details are rather complex, but the results can give you a lot of control over what you can accomplish without having to build custom web pages.

- Any buttons that appear on your layouts need to be attached to scripts that contain only web-compatible script steps.

There are now almost 80 script steps that can be run using a button on a web page. Since there are 137 script steps, that means not all steps can be run via buttons on the web. You need to check each script attached to each button on the layouts you'll be sharing on the web. When you're in the script editing window, if you click the Show Compatibility drop-down and select Web Publishing, any steps that won't run turn gray.

Here are a few other important considerations:

- Some steps will depend on having the actual data sent back to the database from the web. You'll need to include a Commit Records/Requests step where necessary.
- When scripts run via the web interface, all scripts are run with Error Capture on. If you have any scripts that depend on Error Capture being off, you'll want to redesign.
- The user account must be able to run the script.
- Buttons may display only one line of text. If you're in the habit of creating buttons with two lines of text (as I am), you'll need to check what it looks like and consider making changes. Some of the text on my buttons seemed crowded in the browser, while others were spread out.
- Round (circular or round-cornered) layout objects do not translate to IWP. They get converted to square or rectangular objects. This applies to buttons too.
- Tab controls work in IWP. Rounded corner tabs will be squared just like buttons.
- Web Viewers work in IWP. This gives you the option to have a web page within a web page. You can also display other types of documents in the Web Viewer. (For more on the Web Viewer, see Chapter 25, "FileMaker and the Internet.")

So yes, you can put your files up on the Internet. And you can do it instantly. But it's not advisable to make it an everyday tool without consideration for your users and the security of your data.

Now we come to the issue of various users' privilege sets. Before you put the files out on the web, you should log in under each user account and test each button to see that they operate as you expect. All I can do for you here is scratch the surface. There is a more comprehensive, 44-page document titled fm10_instant_web_publish_en.pdf that discusses the finer points. You can find it by going to the FileMaker Pro 10\English Extras\Electronic Documentation folder. The details include information about which script steps work and how they operate differently on the web. There is also information about extra steps that might be needed to ensure the results of the script.

Working with FileMaker Pro using a browser is not the same as working with your files using FileMaker. I say this because when IWP was first introduced a few years ago, some companies got the idea they could buy one copy of FileMaker and have everyone in the company work with the data using a browser. They were trying to avoid buying a site license for other copies of the FileMaker application. You simply do not get all of FileMaker's rich feature set via the web. I know of one company that spent over $50,000 having one of their people design a solution this way before they realized they couldn't get everything they wanted. Their site license would have cost far, far less. The IWP interface should be thought of as a convenience for rudimentary work with data. You can go further with custom web publishing in combination with products like Lasso. And working that way makes FileMaker a serious contender indeed. Just don't get the web interface confused with FileMaker's own capabilities.

Also, portals can appear on your page, and you can even edit data in the portals. So be sure you actually want the information in the portals to show. Even if the table from which the portal originates is protected from data entry, the data will show. If you don't want that information displayed, remove it from the layout or create a special web-only layout.

⌘ **TIP** Web sharing is where your layout names become critical. Name your layouts so you'll know what they are, but remove any spaces or non-web-compatible characters such as # @ % & *. Actually, spaces will work, but the URL inserts "%20" wherever spaces appear. If you really need a space, use the underscore character instead.

When you make decisions about which layouts to display on the web, choose layouts with as few fields and elements on the page as you can, so they'll draw faster. Even fast Internet connections can be frustratingly slow when your users have to wait between screen redraws.

IWP Browser Interface

Early versions of Instant Web Publishing were very limited with regard to what users could see and do to FileMaker files using a browser. Much of the work developers (that's you) needed to do to ready files for the web has been transferred to the new web interface. Although you can override many of the following functions based on accounts and privileges (see Chapter 22), your users can otherwise basically:

- Change modes
- Change layouts
- Change views (Form, List, or Table)
- Create, edit, duplicate, and delete records
- Perform finds
- Omit records

- Sort records
- Print records

That's a lot of responsibility for the user. It means you may need to train anyone coming to your IWP pages so they'll be able to get around. Of course you can remove access to the Status toolbar and have them use buttons you've created instead, but that's more work for you.

NOTE Visitors of your web site who use the Find Mode icon (magnifying glass) have access to the find symbols, which will appear beneath the Requests area under the Book.

Look at Figures 20-4 and 20-5 for information about what the icons on the interface are for. There is a lot to this interface. You can click the "?" button under the magnifying glass to bring up a complete set of instructions for your users. When you see what's there, you'll realize why I can't cover it all here.

The way the IWP Status toolbar is laid out is very similar to the way FileMaker's status area looked in the desktop software in versions previous to FMP10. Since these icons are different from those in the desktop software, it's all the more reason to understand the icons in these figures.

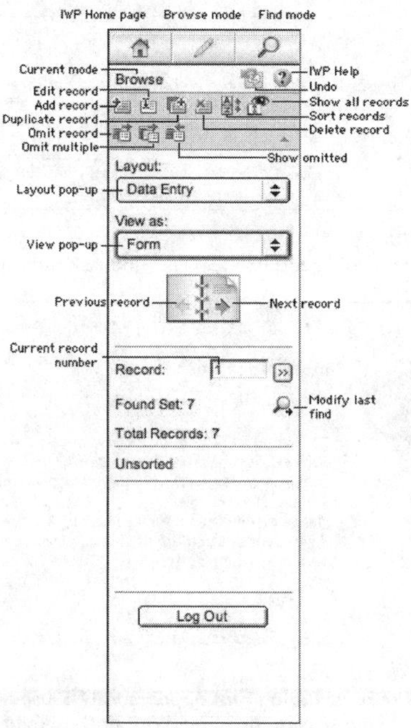

Figure 20-4
The Instant Web Publishing Browse mode tools as seen in a browser.

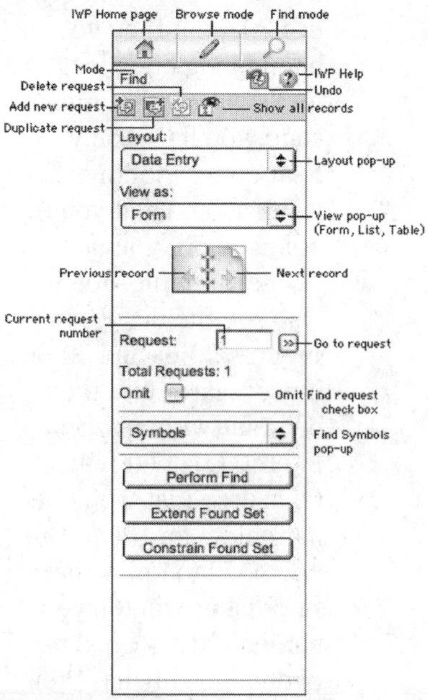

Figure 20-5
The Instant Web Publishing Find mode tools as seen in a browser.

Most important are the instructions regarding the log out. On each web page, there is a Log Out button near the bottom left. Users should log out when they're done. If they simply quit their browser, their connection to the FileMaker file stays active until it reaches the timeout limit. (To set the disconnect time, see the section called "Advanced Options" earlier in this chapter.) Other people could potentially access the files via the web. It also could prevent other users from accessing the files.

Here are some of the finer points to consider:

- You might wonder what will happen to IWP users if you close a web-shared file. Well, first you'll see the message shown in Figure 20-6a. The trick here is to click the Ask button, which will take you to the dialog seen in Figure 20-6b. Interestingly, it tells you that if you click OK, the IWP users who still have their browser open or hidden won't really be asked anything. They'll just be kicked out without warning. The next time they try to do anything to the FMP file in their browser, they'll see the message in Figure 20-6c. If they've been filling out a long form and get that message, you'll probably hear some shouting. So think about what you're doing before you quit an IWP-shared file. You'll also see the dialogs in Figures 20-6a and 20-6b if users have quit their browser without clicking the Log Out button. Of course that won't be a problem for them. But you need to know that FileMaker will tell you somebody is logged in even if nobody has their browser open.

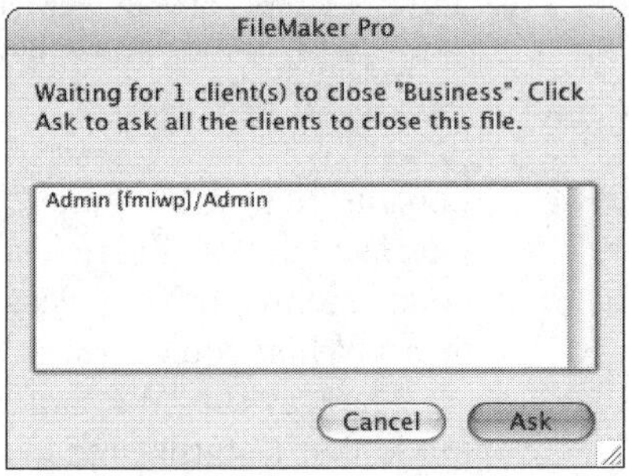

Figure 20-6a
The first dialog you'll see when trying to close a file that is being shared via IWP.

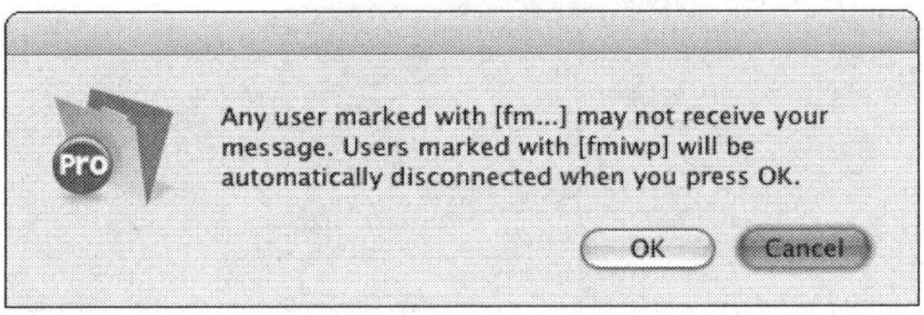

Figure 20-6b
The dialog you'll see after you click the Ask button.

Figure 20-6c
The Bad Request dialog that appears to IWP users after a FileMaker web session has timed out or the file has been closed.

- If the user clicks the IWP Log Out button after their connection time has expired, they'll see a dialog that looks like Figure 20-6c.

TIP On my Windows XP laptop machine, the screen is so small that the Log Out button is not visible even when using the scroll bar on the right. I have to force the top of the browser window up beyond the edge of the display. If you have any users on laptops with this problem, see if you can get them to change the resolution of their screen to something higher than 800 x 600.

- If you want a layout to appear on the web in a particular view (Form, List, or Table), you need to make that decision at the layout level in your file (View, Layout mode, Layouts menu, Layout Setup, Views tab, and use the check boxes). In some cases, you may find it easier to use a specific layout for the web.
- The List view of the web interface may be confusing over on the left by the word "Record" because it is not the familiar FileMaker interface. Once you enter a specific record number in the box next to Record and click the > button next to the box, the records previous to that record are no longer visible. Instead, your users will see that record and the next 24 of the current found set (for a total of 25), if there are that many records available.
- Sometimes the web page gets hopelessly scrambled — even after you click the Refresh button on the browser. To clear the browser's memory, I will often log out, quit the browser, and start it up again. That's probably the kind of thing you'll want to communicate to your users, but you might also want to provide that information somewhere on the various pages they'll be accessing. And again, they should always click the Log Out button first.
- My test showed that the browser allowed the user to click the "Edit current record" button, even when there was no place to edit the record — no active fields. It even displayed Submit and Cancel buttons on the right side of the browser. I would have expected the browser to display an error telling the users that they are not allowed to edit any records (on this layout — or in this table) or better yet, the Edit Current Record button should be inactive.
- Also, I logged in and logged out to test switching various accounts on and off. FileMaker seemed to remember that the Guest privilege account was still active. If I quit and restarted the browser, I would be presented with the window shown in Figure 20-7. Once I filled in the User ID and Password fields, the browser remembered the privileges until I quit and restarted the browser again.

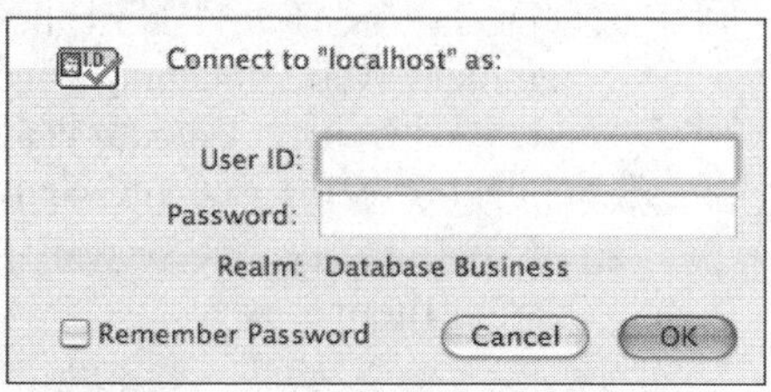

Figure 20-7
The Connect to localhost window users will see when they are required to log in to the database via their browser.

- You can create a button attached to a script using the Relogin script step. That way all users can come in easily on the Guest account and then users who need a higher level of access can get it as needed.
- On one layout I had the header part overlapping the first field in the browser. I changed it on the layout, then changed it back and it was okay. It just means you may see some inconsistencies.
- Mostly, check your work, see what your users will see, and test what will happen when they use the web interface. And try it on any of the approved browsers they may use on both Mac and Windows.

Web Security

Whether or not you've had to protect your FileMaker files with passwords in the past, you'll surely want to protect them before they go up on the web. When you're in a browser, that string of letters and numbers in the URL box (called Location or Address in various browsers) provides the information that tells the remote computer what to do. Starting with FileMaker 7, the whole request doesn't show in the Address area, but it does show in the lower-left corner of the browser momentarily. With FileMaker, that string can mean something like "Find and sort certain records from that faraway computer and display them on my screen in a specific way." If you haven't taken security measures, hackers may be able to take that string and substitute another command for Find, which could adversely affect your data. That means it's a good idea to secure your master files somewhere and only put copies on the web.

Don't serve files that include sensitive data, even if you don't intend to display it. Why? Because it is possible for technically savvy users to remotely access that data. It's better to make a smaller file with just the essential information you want to share and leave out the sensitive fields. This means someone will have to go through the extra effort to keep the office and web files synchronized with each other. But the safety of your data is at stake here, and that could have legal ramifications.

The first line of defense is to require users to log in with an account and password. Here's how:

1. Deactivate (FileMaker calls it Inactivate) the Guest account either in the Instant Web Publishing window or in the extended privileges area. (Anytime the Guest account is active, the file(s) will be available without displaying the Account Name and Password dialog.)
2. Create an account for web users, deciding which layouts and data you want them to see.

A second protective measure is to restrict which IP addresses can get to your files. That certainly shrinks down the "World Wide" part of the web, though, doesn't it? Nevertheless, allowing a limited number of machines to connect may be all that you need. Groups on an intranet will find their machines are on a very specific range of IP addresses. Those are the numbers you would work with to limit access to only your local users.

1. To do that, go to **File**, **Sharing**, **Instant Web Publishing**, and click the **Specify** button next to Advanced Options.
2. Now you simply enter the list of IP addresses you want to have access to your web-shared data. Just remember, some networks (including Internet service providers) routinely reassign IP addresses to machines. You need to consider how often you'll need to re-enter those addresses. If your company or a company you want to serve data to has a range of IP addresses, you can serve to all of them. In the last position of the web address, you simply substitute an asterisk (*) so the address looks something like 192.168.123.*. The only trouble with this shorthand is that you may want to serve only to addresses .10 to .30. Your data would be available to any other companies who have the rest of the IP range from .31 to .99. Of course they would need to know your data was there in the first place. And they would need to know your account names and passwords. You did protect your data with account names and passwords, didn't you?

You can also restrict which users can see which records by setting up record-level security in the Accounts & Privileges area of your files. See the section called "Record-Level Security" in Chapter 22. There you'll learn how to protect your files with passwords using FileMaker's Accounts & Privileges system. You'll be able to individually control what your remote users can do with your files. You may decide that some users can only view certain data, while others will be able to add and delete records.

IPv6 Support[10]

The explosive popularity of the Internet has caused an interesting problem. We're running out of IP addresses! IPv6 is a protocol allowing for ten billion billion billion times more addresses than the current IPv4 standard. That ought to cover us for a while. FileMaker is getting ready now for the changeover, which is coming surprisingly soon.

It's not my intent to provide an IPv6 primer here, but I thought I should at least mention it. One of FileMaker's functions is Get (HostIPAddress). That function can now grab the IPv6 address if the host machine is running the protocol. An example address might look like this:

https://[2001:0db8:85a3:08d3:1319:8a2e:0370:7344]:443/

where the final number appearing outside the brackets represents the port number. The adoption of this new standard will also help users developing solutions for governmental agencies that are already requiring it.

Try It Out

CAUTION Before you jump too far into this, make sure you're not working with files that have important data in them. Make some backup copies and experiment with those instead. The same applies to any files that might be called by these files.

To check out your work, you'll have to be connected to an intranet or the web. (On my Mac, I found all I needed to do was connect to a hub — even if there were no other computers connected to it. Machines that have wireless networking built in don't even need a hub. That would include computers equipped with infrared or AirPort networking. However, you must turn the wireless protocol on.)

Open a browser and type one of the following in the URL field:

- http://192.168.0.2/ (if you set up your machine the way we discussed earlier)
- http://localhost
- 127.0.0.1 (which is the absolute, cross-platform guaranteed "loopback" machine number)

If everything works correctly, you should be able to click to perform the various View, Search, Edit, Delete, and New Record functions. Then go to another machine that has access to the same network.

1. Establish a connection to the network. Some browsers do this for you.
2. Open the browser if it's not already open.
3. Type in the IP address or URL. (If 80 doesn't work, try the :591 discussed earlier.)
4. You should see the Instant Web Publishing portal page similar to Figure 20-8. Click on the database name.
5. Enter a password if required.

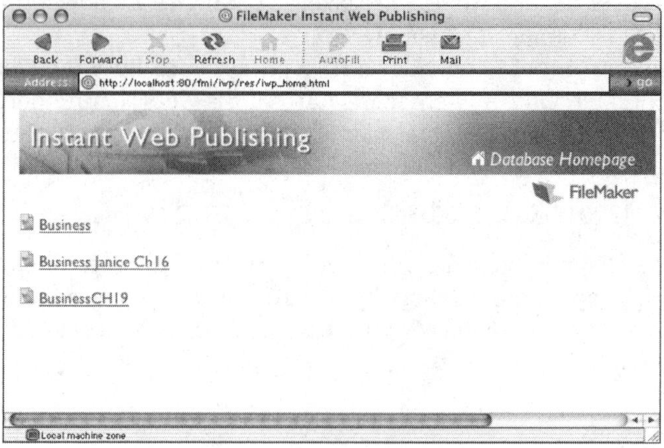

Figure 20-8 The Instant Web Publishing homepage.

See if you can perform the View, Search, Edit, Delete, and New Record functions. What functions you can perform will depend on what account you came in under. And remember, not all buttons may act as you expect since not all script steps are supported. If you see the layout with nothing in it, it might be that no records are selected. Click on the eye icon under Browse. This eye stands for Show All. Click on that now.

If the files are vulnerable and you haven't been able to work out password protection yet, go back to the host machine and turn off Instant Web Publishing or disconnect the machine from the network. If you had TCP/IP turned off for that machine before you started and you turned it on for this exercise, you'll probably want to turn it back off. If you previously turned off other web sharing services on your machine, you might want to turn them back on now.

Other Notes and Options

You can also create customized web sites that incorporate FileMaker data. Some of the other web page building programs now include the FileMaker tags. ("Tags" refer to the HTML code that represents the fields in FileMaker.) You should check out the details before buying any of those products since features change — sometimes on a daily basis. If you were heavily into Instant Web Publishing in the past, take note that CDML (Claris Dynamic Markup Language) is no longer supported. You will be able to convert your web pages created in CDML by replacing it with XSLT. FileMaker Server 10 Advanced ships with a tool for converting CDML called FileMaker CDML Converter. Instructions for using Converter are in a document called FMS 10 Custom Web Guide.pdf. I found it in the FileMaker Server 10\Web Publishing Tools\Electronic Documentation folder. Once the file or files are converted, you'll likely still have some work ahead of you to make them usable. When I tried converting one of my pages, it ended up complete gibberish, so don't expect too much there. FileMaker Server 10 comes with a tool to create a web site using PHP, a popular web language. The tool goes a long way in getting developers started building their own pages using Custom Web Publishing.

A different approach would be to use FMWebschool's Blackbelt tool. It's supposed to let you use your old CDML code with your FMP7 and later files. I haven't tried it, so I can't vouch for it. But you can find out more at http://www.fmwebschool.com/blackbelt.php.

Another big improvement in IWP since FMP9 is that files can be served regardless of what the files are doing at the time. In previous versions, if any one of the FileMaker files you were trying to connect with was in anything except Browse mode or displayed the window for Define Fields (currently Manage Database, Fields), Define Relationships (currently Manage Database, Relationships), or Manage Scripts, among others, it would prevent the browser from connecting with any of the files. Now even an error dialog on the host machine won't stop the browser from connecting.

Files can be anywhere on your machine, but FileMaker has to be running with the specific files open. One thing that wasn't clear to me when I started working with files on the web was that you do not need to put your FileMaker files into the Web folder inside the FileMaker folder. In fact, it's better if they're not in the Web folder. Because of the way Instant Web Publishing works, it actually makes the Web folder shared and vulnerable. Sneaky hackers can mess with data that's in the Web folder. That's another good reason to keep backups.

- The regular version of FileMaker Pro will only allow web sharing using Instant Web Publishing with up to 10 files and up to five users at the same time. If you need better network speeds and the ability to serve to more simultaneous users than you can with regular FileMaker, you should get FileMaker Server Advanced, which allows much greater Instant Web Publishing sharing capacity, not to mention many other file sharing options. For users of older versions of FileMaker's IWP, the FileMaker Pro Unlimited product has been eliminated in favor of the more powerful and flexible FileMaker Server Advanced version.
- You can prevent users from seeing the area on the browser that looks like FileMaker's Status toolbar. You do that by creating a script that runs whenever the file opens. Then you include Toggle Status Toolbar [Hide; Lock] (the script category is Windows) early in the script. To make the script run at startup, choose File, File Options, and go to the Open/Close tab. In the "When opening this file" area, check the box next to Perform Script, and choose the script that should run on opening. But be sure this is your intent. Users will only be able to navigate your files with the button you provide for them. That could mean a lot of testing depending on how complex your solution is. If you choose not to display the Instant Web Publishing homepage (check box in the Instant Web Publishing Settings window), you'll need to provide buttons to take your users through your web pages and consider what you want to use as the "home" page. You'll also need to provide your own Log Out method.
- If you suspect trouble with hackers, you can check the access log file. You'll find it inside the FileMaker Pro 10 folder in a folder called Web logs. As long as you had the "Web activity" box checked in the Advanced Web Publishing Options window, you'll be able to see what machine numbers have made requests for information from your files. Don't expect to instantly know who the attack is from, though. Hackers often use other machines as aliases to keep their identities hidden. But if it's important enough, you can hire someone to trace it back and find out who's been messin' wit'cha.
- Instant Web Publishing has a lot of power, but there are many finer points you need to be attentive to. If you go to the Help files, choose Index, and type "Instant Web Publishing," you'll be presented with a long list of topics. Also look inside FileMaker Pro\English Extras\Electronic Documentation for a file called fm10_instant_web_publish_en.pdf. Once you get an

idea of the scope of IWP, you'll see why I can't cover it all in just one chapter. It could easily take a whole book.

Making files available on the web can be costly unless you already have a full-time connection. The more important the application, the more you may want to consider having your FileMaker connected site hosted by companies that specialize in this service. For a partial list of such services, go to the FileMaker web site. Depending on your budget, you might consider purchasing a machine to provide FileMaker IWP right in your building where you can be in charge of the files. Or you could talk to your web provider about having them take your machine into their facility where they will likely have a number of safety features for automatically backing up your data, uninterruptible power supplies, and perhaps even generators.

Cool Web Sites Powered by FileMaker

More and more web sites are powered by FileMaker all the time. Go to http://www.filemaker.com for a listing of sites powered by FileMaker. You may have to search for the specific page since the FileMaker site gets redesigned occasionally. Sites tend to jump around, but I will try to keep a list up on my site as well (www.DataDesignPros.com). Some of these sites are very interesting, and some have FileMaker files that you can download.

If you talk to someone about hosting your site and they don't want to bother with it, go to FileMaker, Inc.'s web site for a list of companies that provide FileMaker web hosting. Just don't let any web hosting company talk you out of using FileMaker. It's perfectly suited to those types of services. There are even some special high-end methods of serving busy web sites that consist of networking a series of inexpensive computers to handle the load.

Summary

In this chapter, we looked at how you can make the data in your FileMaker Pro files available to other people on an intranet or the Internet through a browser using Instant Web Publishing. You learned how to set up your computer, how to set up FileMaker Pro, and some basic considerations for keeping your shared data secure.

Q & A

Q I'd like to try this out, but it's not easy for me to get to another machine. Is there some other way I can see what the pages look like in my browser?

A If your machine is wired for Ethernet and you can get your hands on an inexpensive Ethernet hub, connect to it as if you were connecting to a network. Then follow the directions for the other settings. When it comes time to find your FileMaker files with the browser, use the same

IP address you entered for the machine you're on. The browser will go out to the hub and come back to your own machine. I've also made this work on a laptop with an infrared network option instead of Ethernet. It didn't even require a hub.

Q This sounds pretty good, but some of my friends don't have Internet Explorer, Firefox, or Safari. I'm sure a lot of other people don't either. I want the pages to look the way I plan them.

A The IWP-certified browsers are free downloads. To control the look of the page, you'll need to purchase specialized software for designing web pages. But be aware that it will take some time to develop your skills with any of these other programs. And don't forget, even with all your planning, users have the ability to change the way things look in their browsers.

Workshop

Choose one of your files and set it up the way you want it to appear on the web. Set up the Guest account to display only a couple of the layouts. Then go to the browser and take a look at how the choices you made in the files affect what you see. Come back to the file and make a few more changes to the layouts and what is available to the Guest account. Then see what that looks like in the browser.

Click the Log Out button, inactivate the Guest account, and try signing in under various other accounts. Don't forget to log out of each one before trying to log in under another. (I had to quit and restart the browser each time I wanted to log in under a different account.)

Chapter 21

Sharing Your Data with Other Applications

Introduction

At some point, you may find a need to share FileMaker information with other programs, or maybe you'll need to get data from other applications for use in FileMaker Pro. Depending on the application and your needs, FileMaker provides the answer with the Import Records and Export Records commands, the ODBC control panel, the ODBC/JDBC Sharing Settings window, and the Manage External Data Sources window.

In this chapter, I'll explain:

- The use of imports and exports to share data between FileMaker and other applications
- How to use the ODBC control panel
- How to use the ODBC/JDBC Sharing Settings window

We'll cover the details of how to work with external database systems in Chapter 26, "Working with External Data Sources." It's for a feature added in FMP9 and there's so much to it, it deserves its own chapter.

Using FileMaker's Import and Export Commands

FileMaker has a nice array of file types it can import and export.

1. Open any FileMaker file, choose **File**, **Import Records**, and select **File**.
2. Now click the **Show** pop-up (Macintosh) or **Files of type** pop-up (Windows). Click **Cancel**.
3. To see the list of exportable file types, make sure you have at least one record in the current found set. Then choose **File**, **Export Records** and click on the **Type** pop-up (Macintosh) or **Save as type** pop-up (Windows) to view that list.

By exporting and importing records in a common format, FileMaker is capable of communicating with applications such as Microsoft Office, Corel Office, WordPerfect, Quattro Pro, Lotus Smart Suite, and Word Pro, among others. You aren't going to see these applications listed in the Type pop-up list. The options that are given are common file formats. You need to check the manual of the application you're working with to find out what file formats it can read. For more on the basics of importing and exporting records, take a look at the sections called "FileMaker Techniques" and "Importing Data" in Chapter 23. Although not exhaustive, you should get a pretty good idea of the steps required. Later in this chapter I'll show you how to import a folder of files, a feature introduced back in FileMaker Pro 6.

As important and valuable as importing and exporting are to FileMaker, these methods don't actually transmit and receive directly with the other programs in real time. For that, we need ODBC.

NOTE At one point, XML (which was introduced with FileMaker 6) was predicted to be *the* new standard for sharing live data. Although still used, it has failed to be more than another tool with which to work. For now, ODBC is a more established method. Always on the forefront, FileMaker 9 introduced an impressive method of bringing table occurrences from a number of other database systems right into the relationships graph using ODBC. See Chapter 26, "Working with External Data Sources."

ODBC Sharing

Open Database Connectivity (ODBC) is an interface used to communicate between various computer programs in real time. The ODBC drivers provided on the FileMaker CD allow other applications to use FileMaker data via ODBC, and the ODBC Administrator application (Mac OS X) and Data Sources control panel (Windows) tell FileMaker where to find data from the other applications.

You might think of the drivers and the control panel as translators. As long as the other programs you want to use support ODBC, and the plug-ins, drivers, or control panels for both applications are configured properly, you can get FileMaker to send and receive data. That includes being able to send Structured Query Language (SQL — pronounced *sequel*) requests back and forth.

Let's take the translators analogy a bit further. Imagine that you have a friend in another country. You want to call him or her for some information, but neither of you speaks the same language. Each of you has an acquaintance who speaks a second language, but it's not your friend's language. Fortunately, your interpreters speak each other's language, SQL. You speak FileMaker Pro, and your interpreter speaks FileMaker and SQL. Your friend speaks Excel, and his interpreter speaks Excel and SQL. Using these interpreters, you can ask a question, and your friend can answer. That's exactly how SQL works over ODBC. Think of SQL as the language and ODBC as the translator.

This capability allows you to share data with programs like Oracle, Microsoft Access, Excel, Microsoft SQL Server, and more than 50 others. The ODBC components for most applications are not normally installed unless you perform a custom install. Any of the ODBC drivers not available with your other programs are available for purchase from third-party companies. Since ODBC is a Microsoft Windows standard (based on COM), drivers and ODBC-savvy applications are much more common on the Windows platform than on the Mac.

One terrific advantage of using ODBC is that it lets users work with the easy-to-learn FileMaker front end to access data in systems that are much harder to use. Even if you understand and can use such systems, your end users may not be able to. You can build solutions for them that they will find easy to use and modify. And it only takes about one-fourth of the time it would take to build something similar with other ODBC tools.

Maybe you work for a company where the IT people don't want to mess with FileMaker because they don't consider it a "serious" database. With ODBC sharing, FileMaker absolutely needs to be taken seriously!

Making FileMaker Data Available to Other Applications

To make your data available to other applications, you first have to set up your file correctly.

1. Choose **File**, **Manage**, **Accounts & Privileges.**
2. Choose any of the existing accounts and click the **Edit** button. You need to choose the Guest account if you want everyone to have access to your data. If you want more control over who has access to the data, follow this procedure for each account that will have access.
3. Click the **Edit** button to the right of the Privilege Set pop-up. That will take you to the Edit Privilege Set window shown in Figure 21-1.

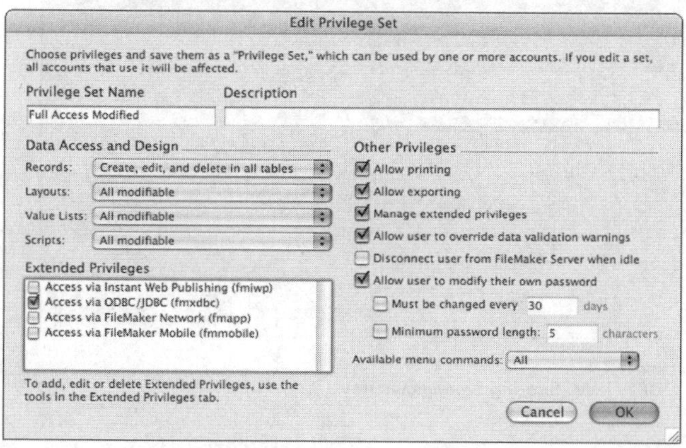

Figure 21-1 The Edit Privilege Set window with the Access via ODBC/JDBC box checked.

4. Check the box in the lower left next to **Access via ODBC/JDBC (fmxdbc)**. When you click **OK** to leave here, you'll see the Account Name and Password dialog, which will require the information for an account with All Access. When you convert or create a file, an Administration account is created automatically. You can read more about this in Chapter 22, "Keeping Your Data Secure." If you haven't already assigned

a password, type **Admin** for the Account Name and leave the password blank.

You can double-click the Admin account to look at it. If there are a number of bullets in the password area, a password has already been assigned. If you are having trouble with the passwords, read Chapter 22 first. You need to have Administration-level access (full access) to change the password. If someone else sets up the account and leaves the company without making a record of that password and letting you know where it's recorded, you'll be up the creek without a paddle. The password is not stored with the file. So be careful to keep records of all the passwords.

In our current set of files, the Admin account does not have a password.

5. You know enough to click **OK** as many times as needed to finish up from here, don't you?
6. If you see a blinking cursor at the Edit Account window, ignore it, and click **OK**.
7. If you see the Confirm Full Access Login dialog, type **Admin** for Full Access Account and no password.

Now you need to allow users to get to the data. Here's how:

1. On a Mac, choose **File**, **Sharing**, **FileMaker Network**, **ODBC/JDBC**. On Windows, choose **File**, **Sharing**, **ODBC/JDBC**. That will bring up the ODBC/JDBC Sharing Settings window shown in Figure 21-2.

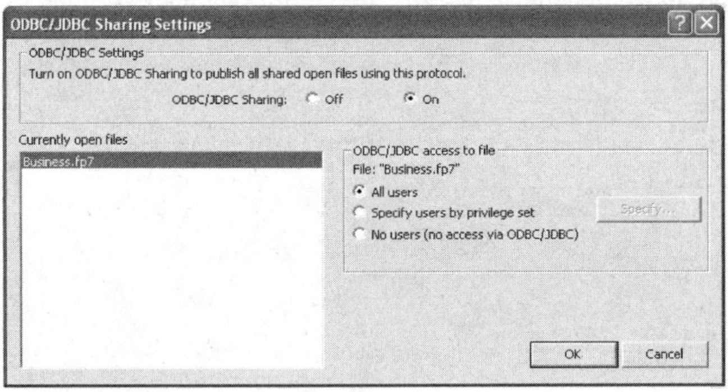

Figure 21-2
The ODBC/JDBC Sharing Settings window.

2. Click the **On** button to the right of ODBC/JDBC Sharing.
3. Select the file or files you want to share and click the radio buttons on the right to select the privilege sets. Notice that if you select more than one file, you can only choose to share with All users or No users. The only way to choose "Specify users by privilege set" is by selecting one file at a time. Clearly you need to have the files you intend to share open at the time you work with this window.

4. Finish by clicking **OK**, etc.

This process is like the light switches I told you about when explaining web sharing: First you turn on the master switch, then you turn on the individual lights. The master switch here is the On button. The individual light switches are the specific files and the users allowed to connect.

Once you've made these settings, any other program that talks ODBC can get information from the switched-on FileMaker files. The specifics of how to accomplish that in the other application is something you'll have to find out by looking in the manual for that program.

NOTE Keep in mind that sharing FileMaker data with other applications via ODBC is subject to any password restrictions placed on the individual files.

NOTE The database you want to share needs to be open to share its data.

Getting Data from Another Application

Even if you never do anything else with ODBC, you'll need to perform the setup described in the following sections in order to bring table occurrences into FileMaker from other database systems. One important detail to pay attention to is that if you are preparing to bring External SQL Sources (ESS) into your FileMaker files, you must set up a System DSN. User DSNs are not supported by FileMaker's ESS.

In my previous books, I took readers through an exercise that used ODBC to import data into a FileMaker file from a text file. But FileMaker, Inc. no longer provides the text driver the exercise depended upon. Then I realized that no matter what demo I show you, if you ever wanted to set up any other driver, you'd be no further ahead. Drivers are provided by a variety of vendors and there are no standard interfaces. So instead, I'll show you the basics of the dialogs that are common. Then it will be up to you, and the (hopefully well-written) documentation provided by the vendor, to finish the setup.

The ODBC components are provided in the FileMaker package, but you must perform a separate install to get them in place. For instructions, look under the Help menu. And there should be a file called fm10_odbc_jdbc_guide_en.pdf inside English Extras\Electronic Documentation.

When you're running on a network, there are quite a few other settings to be considered. In most cases, someone else will be administering the other data sources. Hopefully, they'll know the settings from their side. Just be sure that you have a line open to the machine with the data you want to access. Of course, you'll get a message if something is set up improperly.

NOTE You do not need to activate the ODBC/JDBC sharing settings in order to import data from external data sources. They are only necessary when you want to make FileMaker data available to other applications.

At this point, Macintosh and Windows users will say "bye-bye" to each other. The screens and steps are similar but just different enough to be confusing if I jumble them all together. We'll meet up again at the section called "Importing the Data (Windows)." If you're a Windows user, skip ahead to the section titled "Setting Up the Data Source (Windows)." Mac users, keep reading here.

Setting Up the Data Source (Macintosh OS X)

1. Go into the Applications, Utilities folder and double-click **ODBC Administrator.** Mine opens to the User DSN tab, but I clicked to the Drivers tab as shown in Figure 21-3. (DSN stands for Data Source Name.) Your window may or may not have some items in the list, so don't worry about trying to match my screen.

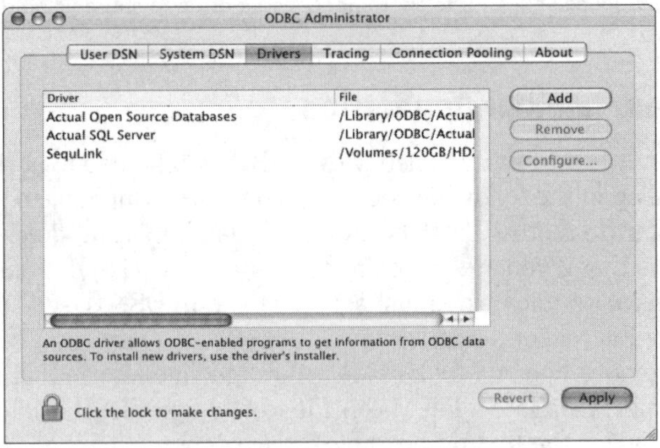

Figure 21-3
The ODBC Administrator window with the Drivers tab selected.

2. To have complete control over what you do from here, you'll need to click the lock in the lower-left corner of the dialog. You'll be asked for your System Administrator User Name and Password. Enter the correct information and click **OK** to return to the ODBC Administrator window.
3. Click the **Add** button to add a new driver. A little window slides down in front of the list area (Figure 21-4) and you enter information there. You can provide any description you want. Then you select the driver. I don't want to go any further here because locating the correct driver can be somewhat complicated and specific to the company that makes the driver.

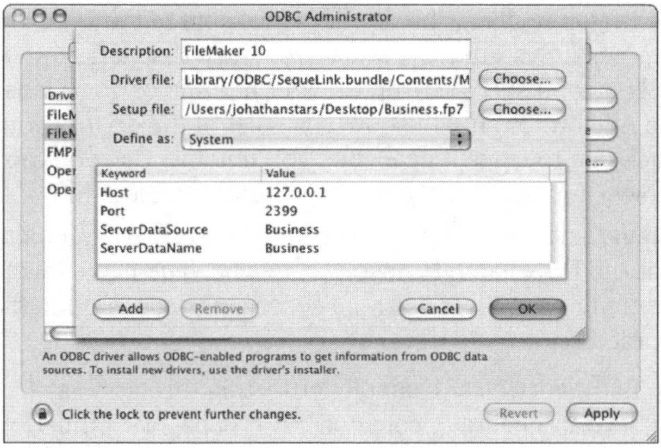

Figure 21-4 The window that allows you to configure the new driver.

As I worked my way through an example, I came to the conclusion that it would require a book to explain everything properly. When writing the 8.5 book, I worked with an ODBC support person at FileMaker, Inc., and we finally had to stop after an hour and a half. Unfortunately, this ODBC Administrator window does not have Apple's characteristic easy-to-use interface. Nevertheless, part of the process will involve selecting the specific file or files, tables, fields, and maybe the types of values found in the fields (date, time, text, number, etc.). Here are some of the other details of the Administrator windows:

- Once you have the upper boxes filled in, you'll want to add keywords and values to the lower area. It's not completely intuitive so here are the steps:
  a. Click the **Add** button in the lower-left corner. The words "Key" and "Value" will appear below the column heads.
  b. Click on the word **Key** and you can enter your own word. Examples might be "Host" and "Port."
  c. Click on the word **Value**, and enter the appropriate value. Examples might be "127.0.0.1" for Host and "2399" for Port.

> **NOTE** When it comes to External SQL Sources (ESS), the port will likely be something other than 2399. The one I worked with that appears to be a SQL standard is port 1433. If both you and the person serving the data have separate firewalls, each firewall must have the matching port open.

  d. When you have everything set up, click **OK**.

- I also found that sometimes when I tried to reconfigure a driver, the window went gray and I couldn't get any further. When that happens, you need to reactivate the lock in the lower-left corner. Other times the only way to activate the lock was to quit the ODBC Administrator and restart from scratch. Very frustrating!

- When you're done, the driver is available to the User DSN or System DSN. System DSN lets anyone use that data source. User DSN is for a specific user. Click either one of those tabs and click the Add button. It will show you a list of the drivers you've set up. Click one to make it available. You'll notice that you can make choices for keywords and values in this window, too.
- When I tried to click OK after selecting a DSN, I got a message that the DSN name I chose was invalid. The name must consist of letters and numbers, with no spaces, periods, or underscore characters.

You can find a very clear example for testing this process at http://www.fmpromigrator.com/doc/fmp7_odbc_mac.html. (I've included a PDF of the demo in the Chapter 21 folder of the downloadable files just in case they remove that page from their web site.) Their Macintosh demo is as long as an entire chapter in this book and only gives one example of one setup. Even at that, some of their windows look a little different from what you'll see when you work on your machine. After you look at what is provided there, you can see why I think it would take a book to go into much detail. FileMaker's own documentation suffers from the problem I have with giving you enough examples. But I'm not sure it's their job. They're giving us a tool to connect to another application. At some point you have to take responsibility for learning that other application yourself. That doesn't mean this isn't a marvelous tool. But you would do well to look to the people who provided the clear example above for documentation.

Importing the Data (Macintosh)

Once you've set up your data source outside of FileMaker, you can perform an import. Choose File, Import Records, ODBC Data Source. You select the DSN from the list and click the Continue button. Since the rest of the process is essentially the same for Windows users, I'll have you jump ahead now to the section called "Importing the Data (Windows)." The example I'm giving is based on the text driver that is no longer available. But the dialogs for creating a SQL query are exactly the same regardless of the other application you're reaching out to. I want you to see that by using ODBC, you can perform a SQL query to draw data into FileMaker.

Remember, this process can be reversed to make FileMaker the data source and pull data from it into other applications.

Setting Up the Data Source (Windows)

The first thing you have to do is tell FileMaker where to find the data you want.

1. Click the **Start** menu, and choose **Settings**, **Control Panel, Administrative Tools**, and double-click **Data Sources (ODBC)**. If you can't find

it, perhaps you didn't do the full install from the FileMaker CD-ROM or the web download.

When the ODBC Data Source Administrator window opens, it will look similar to Figure 21-5, but yours probably won't show any data sources listed. DSN on the tabs stands for Data Source Name. User DSN is for a specific user, while System DSN is for all users. Click the tab for which DSN you want to set up.

2. Click the **Add** button to bring up the window shown in Figure 21-6 where you'll pick a driver you want to work with. Since every driver is different, it would take an entire book to demonstrate every option. Look to the vendor's documentation for the specifics. Nevertheless, part of the process will involve selecting the specific file or files, tables, fields, and maybe the types of values found in the fields (date, time, text, number, etc.).

   After you've set up the driver, it will be available in the list.

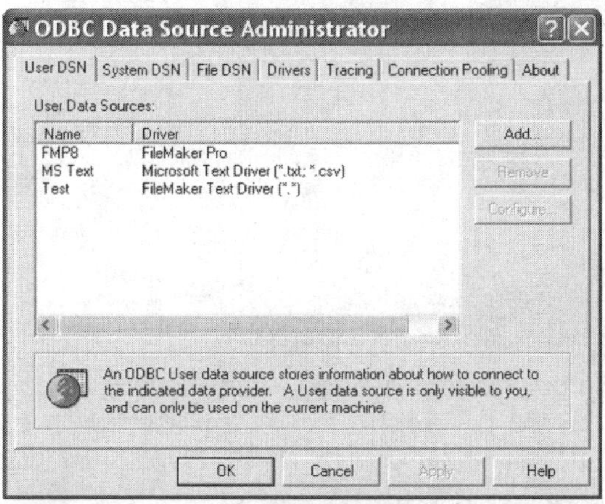

Figure 21-5
The ODBC Data Source Administrator window.

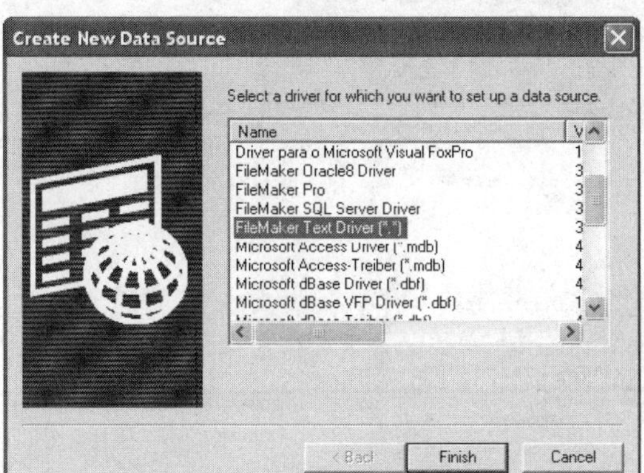

Figure 21-6
The Create New Data Source window with the FileMaker Text Driver selected.

Importing the Data (Windows)

The following steps are from the exercise that used the text driver in my previous books. Once you've selected your driver, you can apply the steps to your specific data source. Be sure to name it **Test**, as that's the name we'll be using in this example. I'll be talking about a sales report and how to construct a SQL query using a relationship between two tables and sorting the results.

You may already have the Sales Reports file open. If you don't, open it now.

1. Choose **File**, **Import Records**, **ODBC Source**. This will bring up the Select ODBC Data Source window.
2. Choose the **Test** data source described above. Click the **OK** button.

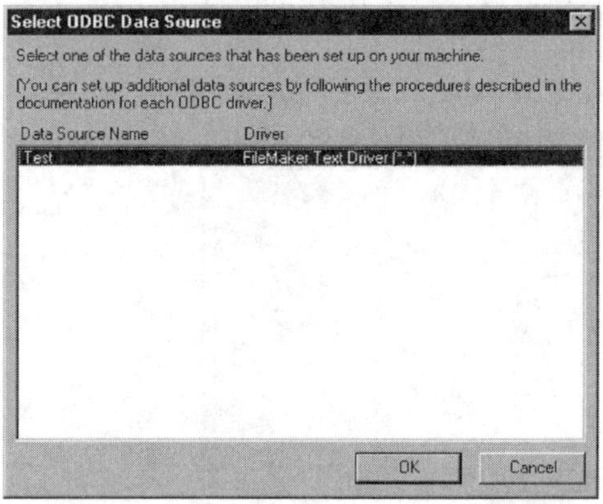

Figure 21-7
The Select ODBC Data Source window with the Test data source selected.

3. You'll likely be prompted for a user name and password. If you haven't set up any for this file, use **Admin**, leave the password blank, and click **OK**. That should bring up the Specify ODBC SQL Query window.

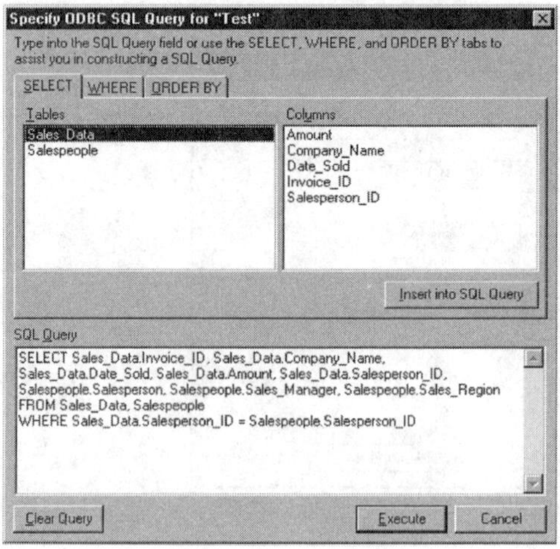

Figure 21-8
The Specify ODBC SQL Query window where you construct the request for the specific data you want to find.

4. If there is any text in the SQL Query box in the lower part of this window, click the **Clear Query** button to empty it out. When you're asked if you're sure, click the **Clear** button.

   If you know SQL, you can type right in the SQL Query box. However, FileMaker makes it easy to construct your own query without all that typing and without knowing the SQL syntax.

> **NOTE** This is where some of the field-, table-, and file-naming guidelines we talked about earlier come into play again. SQL (as well as HTML — the language of the Internet) cannot deal with periods, spaces, or special characters in the names of files or fields. Actually, you can work with spaces by using single quotes around the field names. When FileMaker builds the query, it takes care of that for you.

5. Select **Sales_Data** from the Tables list and **Amount** from the Columns list, and click the **Insert into SQL Query** button. Notice that the proper SELECT and FROM headings are added, and the fields and tables are placed in the query box.
6. You don't have to click the Insert into SQL Query button. Once a table is selected, you can double-click on the column names. Continue by double-clicking on the other column names.
7. Select **Salespeople** from the Tables list, and double-click each of the column names from the Columns list except Salesperson_ID. When you're done, the data in your window should match the first five lines of the SQL Query box in Figure 21-9.

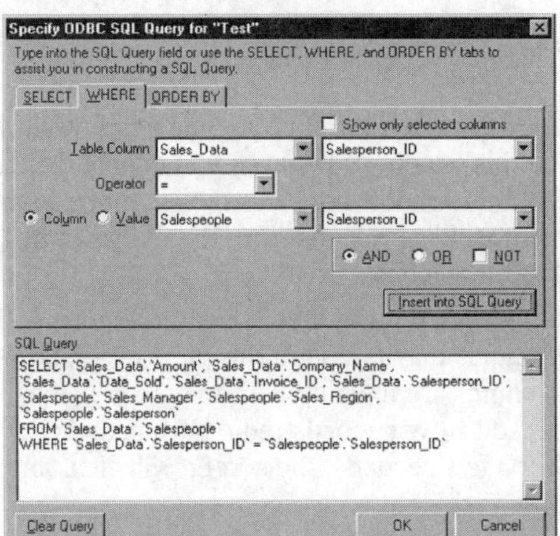

Figure 21-9
The WHERE tab of the Specify ODBC SQL Query window with the Test selections inserted into the query.

8. Click the **WHERE** tab. This is where you create a relationship between the two text files, or a "join between tables" to use a SQL term. Select **Sales_Data** from the Table.Column pop-up and **Salesperson_ID** from the pop-up to the right of that. Choose = as the Operator. Then select **Salespeople** from the lower-left pop-up and **Salesperson_ID** from the

Part 5

lower-right pop-up, and make sure the **Column** radio button is selected. Look at Figure 21-9 to see what your screen should look like. To move this part of the query into the SQL Query box, click the **Insert into SQL Query** button.

9. Click the **ORDER BY** tab. This window is similar to FileMaker's Sort window. Double-click **Sales_Data.Amount** in the Columns list to move it to the Order By area. Be sure Sales_Data.Amount is selected in the box on the right, click the **Descending** radio button, and click the **Insert into SQL Query** button. When you're done, your screen should look like the one in Figure 21-10. Click **Execute** or **OK**, whichever appears on your button.

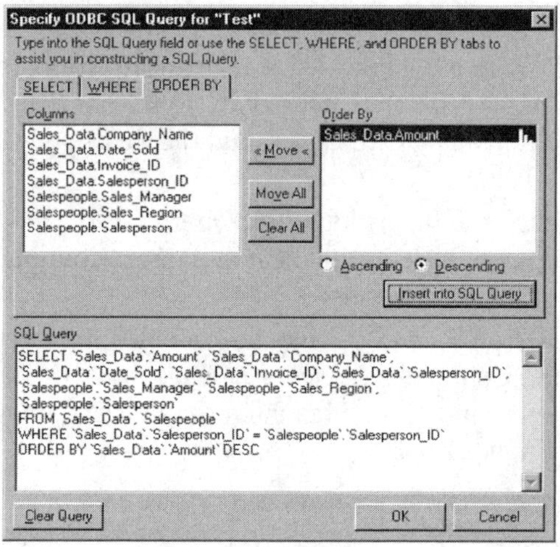

Figure 21-10
The ORDER BY tab of the Specify ODBC SQL Query window with Sales_Data.Amount inserted into the query.

10. FileMaker will display the Import Field Mapping window shown in Figure 21-11. You'll see this window whenever you import data from other files. The specifics of this window are discussed in more detail in Chapter 23. For now, choose **matching names** from the "Arrange by" drop-down in the middle right of the window.
11. Make sure the fields are lined up as they appear in Figure 21-11, including the arrows. Your fields may not be in the same order, but you should make sure the field names are lined up with matching names in the two columns. Select the **Add new records** radio button, and click the **Import** button. After a few seconds, the screen will clear and you should have 250 new records in the file.

NOTE You don't necessarily need to import the data into an existing table. Using the Import Field Mapping window, you can add a new table on the fly. For the details, see the section called "Import Table" in Chapter 7. And you can create fields on the fly in an existing table in case you don't have a field that matches some data that you're importing. In the Import Field Mapping window, click the Manage Database button.

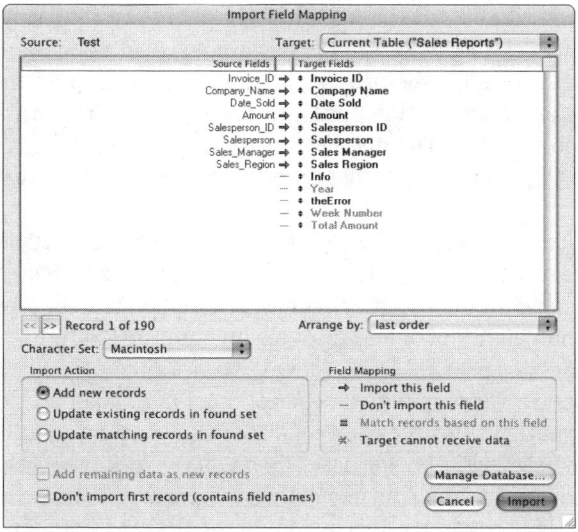

Figure 21-11
FileMaker's Import Field Mapping window.

Saving the Import as a Script

After you've created your ODBC import, if you expect to run it again, it would be very wise to create a script that will handle all the work automatically, especially while the details are still fresh in your mind. The process is slightly different from other imports described in this book. Here's how:

1. Choose **Scripts**, **Manage Scripts**, start a new script, and call it **Test ODBC Import**.
2. Find the **Import Records** step from the Records heading, and double-click it.
3. Click the **File** pop-up and choose **ODBC Data.** Then choose **Test** from the Select ODBC Data Source window, and click **OK** (on Macintosh) or **Continue** (on Windows).
4. The Enter Password window will show up next. Fill in the User name and Password boxes and click **OK.** (If your Guest account has been activated and it doesn't require a password, you can leave both boxes empty.)
5. In the Specify ODBC SQL Query window, make sure the query is the one you want, and click **OK.** This will return you to the Script Definition window. (In Windows XP, you may need to rebuild the query. I found a shortcut to that tedious process. I left the script and started the import process over with the query still in the box. I just copied it, backed out of the import, and went back to the script where I pasted it into the box.)
6. You'll also probably want to check the box next to **Perform without Dialog.** If you don't, users will be presented with the Data Source, Password, and Specify ODBC SQL Query windows before they actually import. That would only be an invitation to future errors.
7. When you're done, click the **Close** button, and then click **Save.**

Now try it out by running the script. This works fine with the sample text file, but if you're working with other applications, you'll need to turn on any plug-ins for that application before the data will actually import properly. Those plug-ins are what provide our "interpreter." If you're getting data from a remote computer, you'll also need to make sure the network is open and set to TCP/IP, and that you include the number of the machine you're trying to get data from.

Although some of this terminology may be new to you, stepping through these windows makes the complexities of ODBC queries considerably easier than learning standard ODBC query construction. If you are interested in SQL, you can find plenty of online tutorials by entering "SQL tutorial" in a search engine.

This has been a very simplified description of FileMaker's ODBC capabilities. Don't forget that this process works the other way around. In other words, you can access FileMaker data when you're working in other ODBC-compliant programs. You can get more information from the manual and the Help files. Look in the indexes under ODBC and SQL. Depending on the ODBC driver you work with, the windows may give you different options.

Execute SQL Script Step

Starting with version 5.5, FileMaker has been able to execute SQL statements with the Execute SQL script step. That means that not only can you get data into FileMaker from other SQL-savvy applications, but you can also manipulate and export data to them. This feature (along with the XML features introduced in FMP6) expands FileMaker's value as a serious application in an enterprise setting.

In the previous section, "Saving the Import as a Script," that import is actually a static activity. With the Execute SQL step, you can run SQL statements based on data stored in fields (including calculation and global fields). The statements can operate dynamically for each record in the file if you want.

Working hand in hand with the Execute SQL step is the Get (LastODBCError) function. You'll want to have FileMaker check for any errors by placing this step immediately after any Execute SQL script step so you can plan a course of action in case it doesn't run properly (i.e., display an error message onscreen and/or halt the script). I would use it like this:

```
SetField [Invoice::zi_ODBCError_gt; ""]
Execute SQL []
SetField [Invoice::zi_ODBCError_gt; Get (LastODBCError)]
If [not IsEmpty (Invoice::zi_ODBCError_gt)]
   Beep
   Show Message [There was an ODBC Error]
   Go to Layout [ODBC Error] (display the error in a field on this
      layout)
```

```
    Halt Script
End If
```

Getting the correctly matched set of drivers is critical and can cause a lot of frustration. Getting the right syntax for your query can be equally trying. Since a problem with either drivers or syntax will produce the same result — nothing — it's hard to know where to look. You may need to check out FileMaker, Inc.'s web site to find resources and get on a discussion list. But prepare yourself before asking your question. Find out the version numbers of each database (FMP and the other database — e.g., Oracle) and the ODBC drivers you're trying to use. Using FMP's window to help you construct the query (assuming you may not know the syntax) will go a long way in ruling out syntax as the problem. You may want to run a simplified query as a test before working on a more complex one.

I won't go into any more detail here. Maybe it's just the clients I work with, but in all my years as a FileMaker developer, none of them have asked me to implement any ODBC or SQL functions. That doesn't mean the functions aren't important, just that it's beyond the scope of this tutorial. There's a little more information in the Help files, but even they suggest you get a book on SQL if you want to go further. Good luck!

Converting and Importing Data from Microsoft Excel

You can send and receive data from Excel spreadsheets using ODBC. You can also convert an Excel spreadsheet into a FileMaker file. Then you can import the data when you need it, or build an ODBC connection to transfer data back and forth in real time.

FileMaker Pro 5.5 added functionality for importing named ranges from Excel. That becomes useful when there's more than one row of description in the Excel file, when there is more than one set of tabular data on the spreadsheet, or when data is labeled in the row above the data you want to import.

Assuming you have the Excel application and an Excel spreadsheet on your computer or accessible on a network:

1. Choose **File, Open** from within FileMaker.
2. Choose **Excel 95-2004 Workbook (.xls) or Excel Workbook (.xlsx)** from the pop-up list next to Show (Macintosh) or Files of type (Windows), select the file you want to convert, and click the **Open** button.
3. As shown in Figure 21-12, select a worksheet or named range and click **OK**.

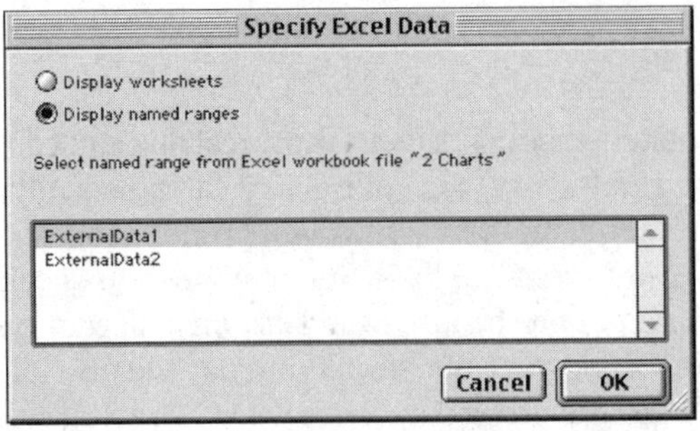

Figure 21-12 The Specify Excel Data window where you can select worksheets or named ranges to be converted.

4. The window in Figure 21-13 should appear. Choose the radio button for whether the first row or named range should be used as field names or data and click **OK**. This window will not appear if there are no named ranges.

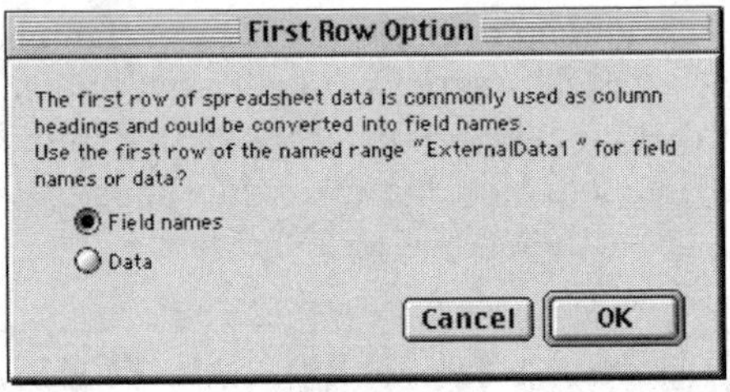

Figure 21-13 The First Row Option window.

5. Choose a name and location for your file, and click the **Save** button.

Depending on the size of the spreadsheet, this could take some time. With most files people have sent to me, it only takes a couple of seconds.

Once your new file has been created, you can build an ODBC connection to it. If you only need to import information occasionally, you might choose to create a script to import from the spreadsheet. To do that, start a script and choose the Import Records step from the Records heading. Click the Specify File button, select the file, and run through the same windows as in steps 3 and 4.

To read more about this and other conversions and imports, see the FileMaker Help files. For more on field mapping when importing data, see the section called "Importing Data" in Chapter 23.

Importing a Folder of Files in a Single Operation

I've been very happy with this feature, which was introduced in FileMaker Pro 6. It allows you to import a whole folder of files at one fell swoop. That includes importing graphics (GIF, JPG, EPS, TIFF, PICT, BMP, and a bunch of other file types), PDFs, and QuickTime movies into container fields, as well as text files into text, number, date, and time fields. Along with the data, you can choose to import the file name and path and thumbnails of the images. This is a terrific time-saving organizational tool. Let me show you how I used it on a folder of pictures from my digital camera.

I first started taking film photographs about 20 years ago. It wasn't long before I had trouble keeping track of where the pictures were, and I wasted a lot of time trying to find them and keep them organized. So I started to number the envelopes that came back from the developer and listing the shots in a FileMaker database. Before long I started scanning some of my favorites and keeping thumbnails in the file along with the text. A picture may be worth a thousand words, but it was sure a lot easier to find those photos using text than to look through that box of envelopes.

Scanning all those pictures was a very time-consuming process, and I soon found I wasn't keeping up with it. I was thrilled when I got my first digital camera and found I could simply hook it up to my computer and save the images to CD. But it was still pretty tricky trying to find them when I wanted them.

Enter FMP6 and its feature for importing a file of folders! Just follow along with my first experience and see if this might be useful to you as well.

First I dragged the folder of new images from my digital camera onto the desktop of my computer. Then I went to Program Files, FileMaker Pro 10\English Extras\Templates\Home - Collections and opened the Photo Catalog.fp7 file. I chose File, Import Records, Folder. That brought me to the window in Figure 21-14.

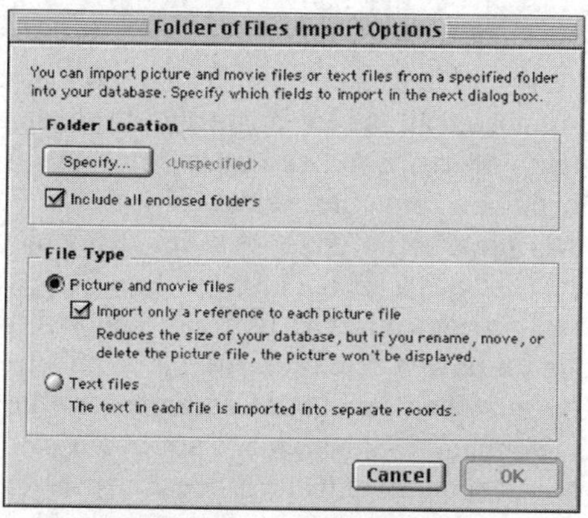

Figure 21-14
FileMaker's Folder of Files Import Options window.

Clicking the Specify button took me to the usual window for finding any folder or file. I hunted around on the desktop until I found the folder. It confused me when I double-clicked the folder to open it and found nothing inside. Backing out one level, I discovered you're just supposed to highlight the folder and click the Choose button. That took me back to the Options window and the folder name appeared next to the Specify button. Since there were no enclosed folders, I simply unchecked that box.

Then I moved on to the File Type area and clicked the "Picture and movie files" radio button. I made sure to check the box next to "Import only a reference to each picture file." If you store the pictures right in the file, the file can get large pretty quickly. Think about it: My pictures come in at about 320 K each. I had 167 pictures in this folder. The whole folder weighed in at 52.4 MB. Even though FileMaker files can now hold up to 8 terabytes of data, the size of your hard drive will more likely be the limiting factor. Storing a reference to the images keeps the file size down.

Next, I clicked the OK button, which brought up FileMaker's Import Field Mapping window, similar to the one in Figure 21-11. Of course, the fields are different from that figure. Since you may actually want to try this, I mapped the fields as follows (although your fields may be somewhat different):

Image	Image Data
File Name	Image File Name
File Path	Location
Image Thumbnail	Thumbnail Image Data

After clicking the radio button next to "Add new records" in the Import Action area, I clicked the Import button. In the Import Options window I checked the box next to "Perform auto-enter options" and clicked the OK or Import button.

It took a couple of minutes for all the pictures to come in. Sure enough, there were my pictures of the chili cook-off, my niece's graduation, my trip to Chicago for the FileMaker tech update, and my buddy Gene Burd's band at a jam session. I entered a little text about each of the important images.

The template I used has a List layout that shows the thumbnails, as shown in Figure 21-15. Clicking the thumbnail takes you to a larger version of the image. If I had taken advantage of FileMaker's ability to import directly from the camera, I could have imported all the metadata about the shots as well. I do a lot of goofy things with aperture and exposure times, and it would be interesting to have that information come in automatically.

In the old days, I would never have bothered to scan this many pictures. It would have taken way too long. This was a snap. I also like that I can choose to store the file path. I'll store the images on a CD-ROM as well; even if I delete them from the hard drive (or have a drive failure), I'll be able to find that folder on the CD. That's because I index all my CDs and store the index in — what else — FileMaker. The main trick is to make sure your camera is set up so the images are numbered sequentially and it doesn't reset to image number DSC00001 when you insert a new memory card. When each image has a unique name, it's a lot easier to find a particular one. With all the batches of photos I've taken, I'd have a hard time finding the particular DSC00001 I'm looking for when I have 80 with the same name.

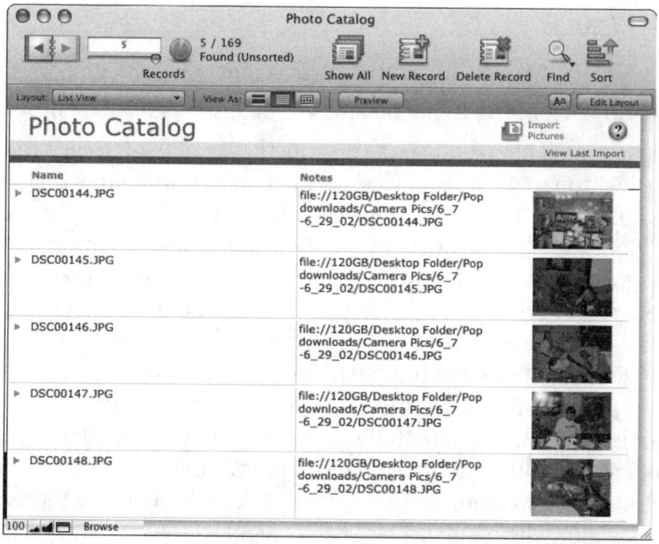

Figure 21-15
FileMaker's Photo Catalog template shows List view and fields for metadata from a digital camera.

Just because I used this feature with my digital camera doesn't mean you have to stop there. You can also import a folder of text files. That means you can get all your text for many documents into one, easy-to-search place — FileMaker. The files must be straight .txt files. That means if the files are in Word or WordPerfect, you'll have to save them as text first, which means you'll likely lose some of the formatting. (FileMaker can now hold up to one billion characters in a text field.) Even though importing a folder of files only works with folders of pictures and movies, or text files, keep in mind that you can import any type of file into a container field. You're just limited to importing them one at a time.

Summary

In this chapter, we looked at using the Import and Export commands, as well as how to use the ODBC control panel and the ODBC/JDBC Sharing Settings window to share data between FileMaker and other applications. Then we looked at the Folder of Files Import Options window, which allows us to import an entire folder at a time. In particular, the ODBC features place FileMaker in a very respectable league regarding its place in large organizations.

Q & A

Q When we did the ODBC import, I noticed the "Update matching records in found set" radio button. Does this mean FileMaker does file synchronization?

A Well, sort of. The main use of this function is to update files from a laptop to a desktop machine and vice versa. The assumption is that you know which of the files is the "master" file. You pick a field that has a unique identifier (usually a serial number) in both files, perform a find in each file for the specific records you want to update (or choose Show All Records), and choose which fields you want updated (or choose matching names). When you import, it will overwrite the selected data in the current file with the data from the file being imported from.

Some people mistakenly think this feature will provide file synchronization between multiple users and a master database in the home office. It would take some truly sophisticated scripting to avoid duplicating serial numbers for new entries. That's also true for making decisions about which entries will be considered the "master" when the same records in the "twin" files on two different machines have changed since the last update. For more on this specific feature, see the FileMaker manual PDF file or the Help files.

There are some subtleties to the "Update matching" option that we haven't covered anywhere else. Only the current found set of records will be updated, and they'll only be updated from the data in the current found set in the other file. For that reason, if you intend to update all the records in the current file with the records in the other file on a regular basis, you would want to create a script that finds all records in both files before performing the update.

At the end of the update process, the number of records updated in the current file will become the found set. That caused me some grief recently when I was refining an import. I didn't realize my found set had continued to diminish each time I performed the update. Each attempt reduced the found set until finally no records at all were being updated. After my initial "Huh?" I figured out what was happening. Now you'll know better. You are memorizing this entire book, aren't you?

Workshop

If you're serious about the ODBC functions, I doubt I'll need to encourage you in any way. I would just suggest that you make a backup before you do anything that might be permanent to your files.

Part 6

Protecting Your Information

Chapter 22

Keeping Your Data Secure

Introduction

After all the work you've done to build your files, you'll want to protect the information you've collected either for yourself or for your employer.

In this chapter, we'll look at:

- How to set up FileMaker Pro's security
- How to protect data through scripts
- How to protect data through calculations

Why Protect Your Data?

There are three main reasons you'll need to protect FileMaker files: confidentiality, accidents, and vandalism. If you're storing information about customers, employees, finances, or medical records, it should be obvious that only certain people should be able to get to that data. Since the data is valuable (otherwise, why collect it?), you don't want it accidentally erased. Likewise, after all the time you've spent on the layouts, you'd hate to have someone go in and unintentionally rearrange or even delete your layouts. And let's not forget the Internet hacker or disgruntled employee. All of these situations point to reasons to put a little extra time into making sure everything stays secure.

FileMaker Security

FileMaker Pro's security system changed dramatically with version 7. Developers who have been working with the new model are very pleased with it. The newer approach is more logical than the old one and offers better protection. And after all, isn't that what security is all about?

Setting up FileMaker Pro's security consists of creating accounts, choosing passwords, and assigning privilege sets to the various records, layouts, and fields. That's right, you can even control whether specific users can enter or even see data in individual fields.

The two primary domains you control with FileMaker security are what users can do and what users can access. When you create a privilege set, you make decisions about what users can do, ranging from printing and going to

Layout mode to viewing and deleting records. You decide what layouts they can go to and what fields they're allowed to see and enter data into.

Every account is assigned a privilege set and a password. Because a privilege set can easily be added and removed from an account, one or more accounts (and the individuals who go with them) can be temporarily assigned a privilege set for a particular project and removed when the job is done. The same applies to what records, layouts, and fields are available to a privilege set. Access to specific areas can be changed for an entire privilege set fairly quickly and easily.

Although FileMaker's built-in security scheme does not cover every combination of control functions you might be able to dream up, it's quite powerful and should take care of the majority of the user's needs. Let's take a look.

Accounts Tab[7]

Go to your Business file, and choose File, Manage, Accounts & Privileges. You should be presented with a window similar to the one in Figure 22-1 except there will probably be fewer accounts in yours. Take a look at the View by pop-up in the lower right of this window. Just another way to help you organize. Since you see columns here, you might think that clicking the column headings might change the sort order. No such luck. Oh, well. You can, however, resize the columns by clicking and dragging the line between the column names. And if you're on a Macintosh, once you've selected an item in the View by pop-up, you can reverse the sort by clicking the triangle to the right of the Description column. Windows users don't get that choice. For both Mac and Windows users, if you click the Account column heading after selecting one of the other choices in the pop-up, the View by will switch back to "account name."

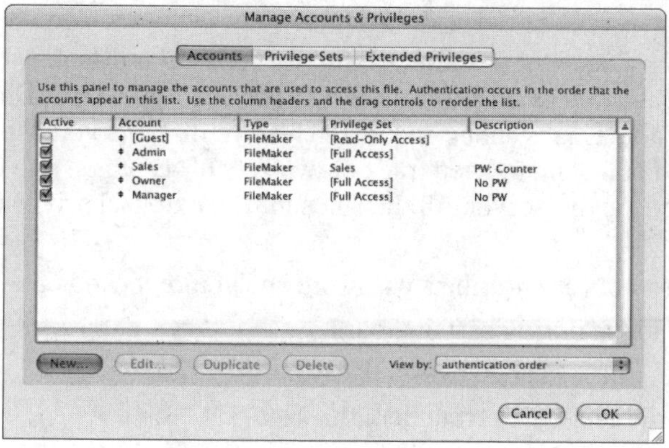

Figure 22-1
The Accounts tab of the Manage Accounts & Privileges window for the Business file showing five example accounts.

Edit Account[7]

Guest Account[7]

Click the [Guest] account to highlight it. Notice the Duplicate and Delete buttons remain gray. There can only be one Guest account in a file. That's why you can't duplicate it. And at the same time there absolutely must be a Guest account in each file. That's why you can't delete it. Also notice that when a file is first created, the box in the Active column next to the Guest account is unchecked. FileMaker wants to make sure you decide for yourself whether that account should be active.

Click the Edit button to bring up the Edit Account window in Figure 22-2. (You can also double-click an account to open this window.) At this point you'll notice that you cannot rename the Guest account, and you cannot assign it a password. By definition the Guest account does not require a password. That would seem to be a security risk, wouldn't it? But notice the Account Status radio buttons in the middle of the window. At any time you can choose to deactivate the Guest account.

Figure 22-2
The Edit Account window.

Notice also that the "Account is authenticated via" pop-up is disabled. Other accounts can be validated by an external server such as Apple OpenDirectory or Windows Domain. This is a long-requested feature that lets you use the server list instead of having to keep track of two sets of accounts, one for FileMaker and one for the server. All the rules for the external privilege set apply, such as:

- Too many attempts at entering a password and you're locked out.
- You can only log in during certain hours.
- Your password must change every 30 days.
- Your password must be a certain length.

The default privilege set for the Guest account is Read Only. But you can use the pop-up list to choose any privilege set you like, including the Full Access and Data Entry Only sets. You can type a description at the bottom of this window. Currently, I'm using this to remind myself what the account is for and to store the password. I'm not sure that's the best place for passwords, but that's what I'm doing until I figure out something better. If other people using your files have access to Accounts & Privileges, you certainly won't want to do that. Besides, even low-level users can be set up with the right to change their passwords, so what you put here may mean nothing. The text in this Description field shows up in the Description column of the Accounts tab seen in Figure 22-1.

Click the Edit button to bring up the Edit Privilege Set window in Figure 22-3. We'll go into the details of this window later. But the reason I wanted you to see it now is that this is actually the very same window we've seen before. You're just accessing it from a different direction. You need to be aware that any changes you make here to a privilege set will affect all accounts with that privilege set. Don't assume that because you got here by way of a specific account that you're having an effect on that account alone.

Make sure your Guest account is still set to Data Entry Only, and you'll notice the only changes you can make here are the Extended Privileges in the lower-left corner. (There's more to this Extended Privileges thing than meets the eye. For more on that, read the section called "Extended Privileges Tab" later in this chapter.) Click Cancel and Cancel again to take you back to the Accounts tab.

Admin Account[7]

Click the Admin account. Notice the Duplicate and Delete buttons are active. If you delete the account, you'll just have to create it again before leaving the Manage Accounts & Privileges window (unless you click the Cancel button).

> ⌘ **TIP** At least one of the accounts must have the Full Access privilege set selected. This is a FileMaker requirement, so if you try to make some other arrangement, FileMaker will prevent you from making the change when you try to leave Manage Accounts & Privileges.

By the way, you can experiment all you want in this window. If you click the Cancel button when you decide to leave Manage Accounts & Privileges (regardless of which tab you're in), all your changes will be discarded.

Double-click the Admin account. You can make nearly any choices you want in the Edit Account window, including leaving Password empty. However, you are not allowed to have an account without a name. Also, every file must have one account with the Full Access privilege set. At this point in the file, since the Guest account has limited access, you may as well leave the Admin privilege set alone. Oh, you can choose some other set of privileges all right. But when you finally click the OK button to exit Manage Accounts & Privileges, you'll get a dialog that tells you that at least one account must have Full Access. If you didn't intend to make any changes, click Cancel to restore your previous settings.

CAUTION You can click the Cancel button to discard all changes since you entered the Manage Accounts & Privileges window. Just be sure that's what you want to do. It's possible to work here for hours, only to discard everything at the click of a button!

You should still be looking at the Edit Account window for the Admin account. You can click the Edit button next to the Privilege Set pop-up to bring up the Edit Privilege Set window similar to Figure 22-3. The Full Access set is similar to the Data Entry Only set in that you can only make changes to the Extended Privileges area. Click Cancel and Cancel again.

New Account[7]

Click the **New** button to bring up an empty Edit Account window. Every account name must be unique. Of course, if you try to use the same name twice, you'll get a warning dialog. Even though account names must be unique, more than one account can have the same password. Name this account **Sales** and use **Counter** for the password. (See the following Caution.) Pay attention to the capitalization of the password. You'll need to retype it exactly. Account names aren't that fussy. Type **PW: Counter** in the Description field as a reminder. Notice the "User must change password on next login" check box in the middle of this window. If you want the user to create his or her own password, you can create one here or leave it blank and let him change it next time he logs in.

What problems might that cause? First of all, you have to give the user the first password you created before he can enter his own password. Of course that first password could be the same as the account name (or blank) to make your job easier. If the user creates a new password, the password you just typed into the Description area won't work anymore. That could be a good thing. Since there is no way to know the user's password, passwords are truly personal. However, if the user forgets his password, you have to come back in here as the Administrator and create a new one. (At least he's not locked out forever — as long as you remember the master password!) Regardless of the administrative problems this feature may cause, this version of FileMaker's security is tremendously more powerful than past versions.

By the way, you can create accounts without ever assigning any passwords. Of course that cuts your security level quite a bit. But if you're not too worried about people getting into the files, maybe one level of security is okay.

CAUTION Never use the password "Master" in your files. A study was done recently that found that "Master" was used as a high-level password in an unbelievable number of corporate systems. If you want people to come in and mess with your work, I suppose that's a different thing. But otherwise, avoid the obvious.

A Word about Passwords

Choosing good passwords is a completely separate issue from keeping track of users' passwords. Even if you don't get too fancy, do keep in mind that passwords shouldn't be so easy that anyone can guess them or pick them up too easily by watching over someone's shoulder. Of course, if users are allowed to create their own passwords, a tutorial for them is in order. Maybe you'll decide that the security of your system is more important than your user's choices.

Be careful what you do with the passwords because there is no way to see them once you've created them. After you leave the window and return, whatever password you entered will be replaced with 22 dots, regardless of the length of the password you actually entered. So you won't even be able to guess based on counting the dot characters. You can assign a new password if you come in under an account with the Full Access privilege set.

Whatever you do, you should never use a password that consists of a word found in the dictionary. Hackers use software that tirelessly tries every word in the dictionary to break into files while they go to lunch. Use a combination of letters and numbers, and make it at least seven characters long — unlike what we've done here.

Privilege Set[7]

Click the pop-up next to Privilege Set and choose **New Privilege Set** to open the Edit Privilege Set window shown in Figure 22-3. In the Privilege Set Name box, type **Sales**. Notice that you can access all the check boxes and pop-ups now that you're no longer working with the Guest or Admin privilege sets. But also notice that the default settings have nearly everything turned off. That's so you don't accidentally give a new account any power without intending to. In a minute we'll be coming back here via the Privilege Sets tab. What I'm saying is you can get to this window from more than one direction. Since you can access a privilege set when you're in an account, don't forget that any set you are editing may be attached to other accounts. Since we've been talking about passwords, notice in the lower right that you can decide a minimum password length for users who change their passwords. Click **OK** and **OK** again to take you back to the Manage Accounts & Privileges window.

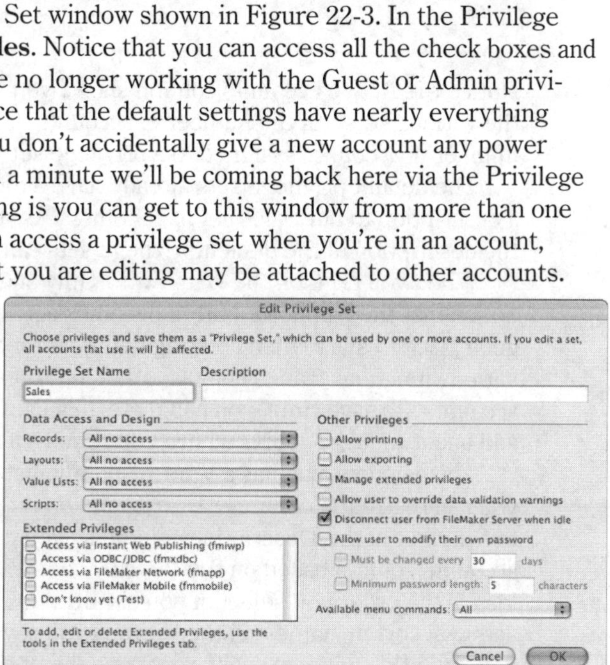

Figure 22-3
The Edit Privilege Set window.

Privilege Sets Tab[7]

Click the Privilege Sets tab to open the window shown in Figure 22-4. There are three default privilege sets (shown in brackets) created with every file: Full Access, Data Entry Only, and Read-Only Access. They're in brackets to tell you they can't be changed or deleted. If you click on the Full Access set, you'll notice that the Duplicate button is gray. The Full Access set is the only privilege set that has absolute power over the file. You can assign it to as many accounts as you like. And get this — you can create a privilege set where you manually make all the same choices that appear in the Full Access account, but it will not have the same power over the file.

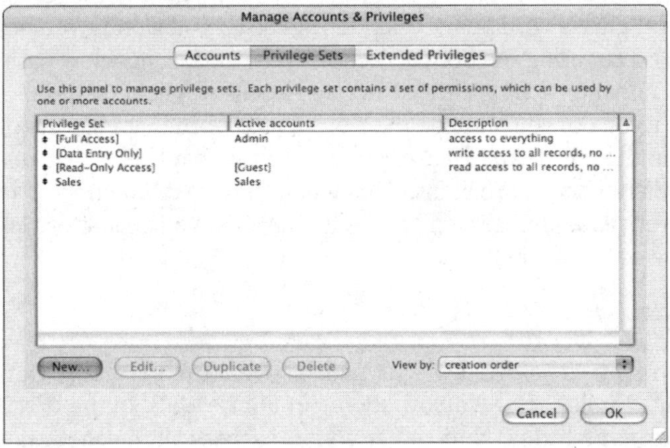

Figure 22-4
The Privilege Sets tab of the Manage Accounts & Privileges window.

Notice the Active accounts column shows you what accounts are assigned to the various sets. As the number of accounts in your file grows, it's likely the number of accounts assigned to a privilege set will grow as well.

The default privilege sets already have a description. We'll be able to add a description to our Sales set in a moment. By the way, neither the name nor the description of the default privilege sets can be changed.

When you click on the Data Entry Only and Read-Only Access accounts, notice that the Duplicate button becomes active. Both of these accounts are a good place to start when creating new sets for a file. You can add and delete various functions from a copy of either set. It can be tedious adding access to accounts. To save time, you could create an account with access to everything and use it to make copies where you remove a few privileges as needed.

This window also has a View by pop-up list in the lower-right corner, and you can resize the columns. Here again, on the Macintosh there's a triangle to the right of the Description column so you can reverse sort the Active accounts column based on the View by choice. Sorry, Windows users. Regardless of the order you select, if you click the Privilege Set column header, the sets will sort by name and the View by will revert to "name." The View by pop-up in this window is different from the one in the Accounts window in that you can rearrange the sets manually. Click the two-headed arrow to the left of the set name and drag the set where you want it in the list. The View by will change to "custom order."

One more detail: If you try to delete a privilege set that is being used by one or more accounts, you'll get a message saying you can't do it. After you reassign different sets to the accounts, you can come back and delete the set.

(For info on how groups in earlier versions of FileMaker become privilege sets during conversion, see the section called "Conversion Issues" at the end of the chapter.)

Edit Privilege Set[7]

Double-click the Full Access set to open the same window we saw in Figure 22-3. As I already mentioned, you can also get to this window from the Accounts tab. Click the Cancel button. Now double-click the **Sales** set. In the Description field, type **Cash register workers**. In the Other Privileges area, check the box next to **Allow printing**. Let's not check the box next to "Allow exporting" for now. I've had some of my clients express concern that departing employees might walk off with their customer list. When you think about it, that could be more of a concern for people in a managerial capacity. On the other hand, you may need to have various people export data to create text reports outside of FileMaker. Lots to think about, eh?

Data Access and Design

Look in the Data Access and Design area. There are four drop-downs here; each influences the user's ability to work with and view data in different ways.

Records Click the drop-down to the right of Records in the Edit Privilege Set window. Figure 22-5 shows the default choices, which are pretty much self-explanatory. And then there is the Custom privileges option, which leads to an area that is deep indeed! Ready? Choose "Custom privileges" and let's go!

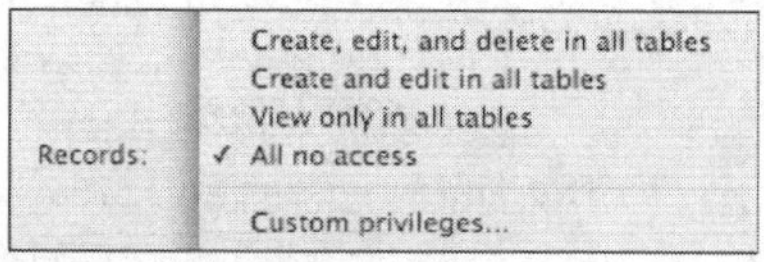

Figure 22-5
The Records pop-up under Data Access and Design.

You should now see a window similar to the Custom Record Privileges window shown in Figure 22-6. Click the Contact table, and the Set Privileges area will probably more closely match the figure. You can start making choices from the pop-up lists, but notice you can't touch the Edit pop-up. Instead, click the Cancel button. Click the Records pop-up and choose "Create and edit in all tables." Click the pop-up again and select "Custom privileges." Look at the difference when you click the Contact table. Now not only can you use the Edit pop-up, but all except the Delete pop-up have a higher level of privileges preset. You only need to disable the ones you want to protect. Interestingly, if you click OK at this point, Sales now shows "

"Custom privileges" although the privileges are the same as "Create and edit in all tables" privileges.

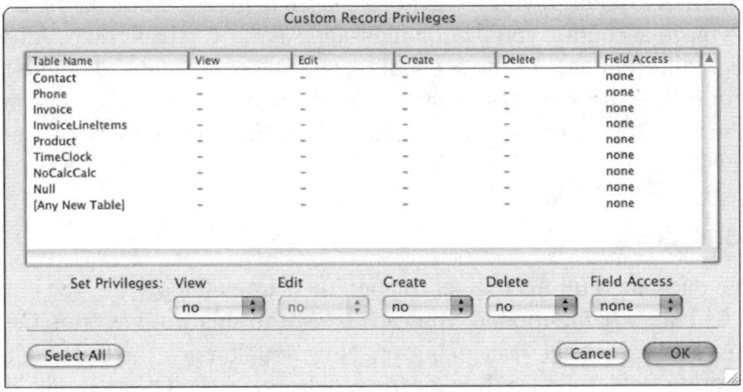

Figure 22-6 The Custom Record Privileges window.

You can edit multiple tables at one time by Shift-clicking them, or all tables with the Select All button (or the keyboard equivalent). That way you can make changes to, let's say, the Edit privileges, for all tables at once and still work on the Delete privileges separately for each table. That's smooth! In the old FileMaker, since every table was actually a different file, you had to do this separately for each file. You can see why I might be enthusiastic about this change.

The tables from External SQL Sources (ESS)[9] will be included in this list of tables just as if they were tables right in the current file. (ESS is discussed in Chapter 26, "Working with External Data Sources.") There is nothing to indicate that these tables are anything other than FMP tables, so you do need some awareness about how your database is structured. What's very powerful here is that you can apply the same limitations to ESS tables as you do to the FMP tables.

Let's dig a little deeper here before we move on to the other choices in the Data Access and Design area.

Now select a specific table and choose "limited" from the Field Access pop-up. That should bring up the Custom Field Privileges window seen in Figure 22-7. Here you can choose one or more fields and determine whether the user can modify, view, or have no access. When someone with the view only privilege is working in a field, he or she can actually click into the field and copy the data if necessary, but cannot make changes. If the user is assigned the no access privilege, the data is not viewable. The fields will still be on the layout, but the words <No Access> will appear where the data would be, as shown in Figure 22-8. Click Cancel to return to the Custom Record Privileges window.

TIP You could change any <No Access> fields so that the text disappears into the background by using conditional formatting on any of the affected fields. For example, you could use a calculation like Get (PrivilegeSetName) = "Low Level" to produce white text on a white background. The user still won't be able to click into the field, but the layout will look somewhat less in-your-face to those "less privileged."

Notice the last entry in the Table Name column, [Any New Table]. You can determine in advance what will happen in the file for this privilege set in any new tables as they are created. This is a particularly handy feature. I created a set of files for a client in a previous version of FileMaker that caused me some problems because this feature was not available. As I added new functions to the files, the new fields inherited the most restrictive characteristics of the other fields in that privilege. (They were called "groups" at the time.) Scripts were failing left and right, and it took me some time to figure out what had happened.

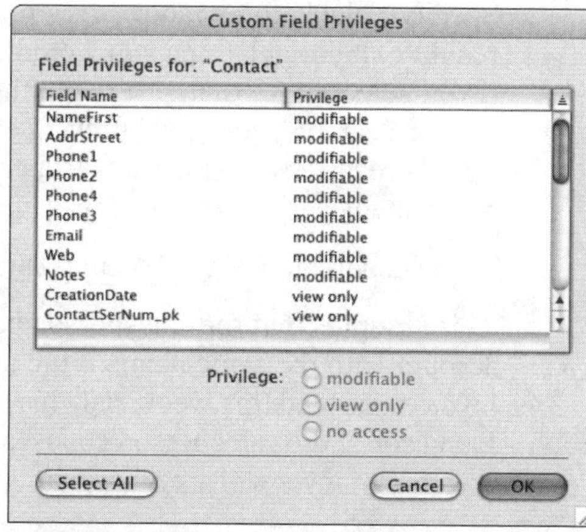

Figure 22-7
The Custom Field Privileges window.

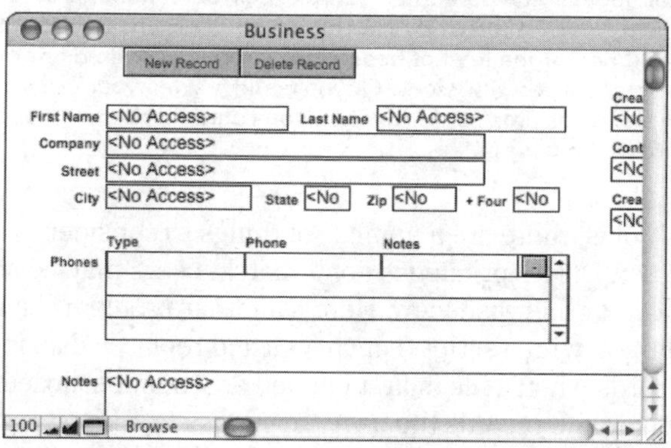

Figure 22-8
A FileMaker layout showing what fields look like when Custom Field Privileges are set to "no access."

Look at the other drop-down lists in the Set Privileges area. You'll notice they're not all alike. Not only that, but the window you see when you select "limited" is different in some of the lists. We already saw the window that appears when you choose Field Access. But in order to show you what happens when you choose "limited" from some of the other Set Privileges drop-downs, we need to take a little side trip. This next part is where the records part of privilege sets can really get deep. I don't want to scare you with this; I've rarely needed to use this for my clients. But it is powerful, and you should know it's here. And honestly, it is pretty cool.

Record-Level Security FileMaker allows you to set up security on a record-by-record level based on calculations. If you've been following along, you should already be at the Custom Record Privileges window shown in Figure 22-6. Look at the Set Privileges area in the lower part of the window. Notice the pop-up lists under View, Edit, and Delete. Select a table and choose "limited" from one of the pop-up lists. You will be presented with a Specify Calculation window. This requires a calculation with a Boolean result. (The calculations you would use here need to be done table by table. If you select more than one table, the "limited" option will appear in gray.)

For example, you could prevent salespeople from viewing or editing each other's records. If you had a Salesperson field where a name is entered when a new invoice is created, your calculation might look like this:

Salesperson = Get (AccountName)

This assumes that the salesperson list and each worker has their own account with the same name. If the salesperson were to perform a find for all invoices created this week, only his or her own records will turn up in the found set. If the salesperson chooses Records, Show All Records, invoices created by anyone else will appear with <No Access> in all the fields.

CAUTION Get (UserName) is determined in FileMaker Pro, Preferences (Macintosh) or Edit, Preferences (Windows) under the General tab. If a user changes the user name on his or her copy of the program, it can mess up your carefully crafted solution. That's why we're using Get (AccountName) instead in the example table. In my solutions, I have users enter a login name and password in a special layout. Their login is compared to an Employees table. It then stores the name in a global field, which is referred to in various script and password validations. It's complex and not for the faint of heart since it requires quite a few safeguards and some potential security issues. Or you could just tell your users not to mess with the Preferences area. Unfortunately, you cannot lock users out of the Preferences area without a plug-in.

As powerful as this tool is, there are a number of things to consider when using it. If the View and Delete privileges don't match, users may be able to delete records they can't otherwise view. Here's another problem scenario: You could build a solution with a script that checks and replaces data in a field across a group of records when a file is first opened or when it's closed. That script would only update the records the user has access to, skipping the others. And it would do that without displaying a warning. Similar problems can occur when using lookups, relookups, Find and Replace, and spell check. And value lists that are drawn from data in fields where the records are not accessible to the user will simply not show the entire list.

I'm not saying you shouldn't use record-level security. On the contrary — developers have requested this feature for years. With it you can control access based on time, IP address, values in a number field, and just about anything you can dream up. You should just thoroughly consider the effects and carefully test your solution before putting it to use.

Later in this chapter in the "Limiting Access through Field Calculations" section, I provide an example that could just as easily be handled with record-level security. The Help files also provide some examples and address the limitations and potential problems in more detail than I can here. In the Help files, search on "limiting access." Click and read the topic titled "Editing record access privileges." Record-level security is also available for databases published on the web.

A couple of notes before we leave Custom Record Privileges:

- You can sort columns by clicking the column headers. For Windows users, clicking the column header a second time will reverse sort them. On the Macintosh, you have to click the triangle in the upper right next to Field Access.
- If you click the Cancel button, any changes you make to the Custom Record Privileges window will disappear without warning. So be careful which button you click.
- If you have the View option set to "no," it won't matter if you have Field Access set to "all." Users won't be able to get to the data.
- If you have an account with records set to any of the privileges above "All no access" but have the Layouts pop-up set to "All no access," the user won't see any data.
- In the Custom Record Privileges window, you can make many of the settings apply to multiple tables by Shift-clicking the tables in the list. However, to make changes in the Custom Field Privileges window, which appears when you select "limited" from the Field Access pop-up, you must select a single table at a time.

Don't make any changes here just yet. If you already did, click the Cancel button and come back in by choosing "Custom privileges" from the Records pop-up. (If you really got messed up, make sure you are customizing the "Create and edit in all tables" privilege set.) Let's make a couple of changes that we'll keep for the sales crew.

1. Click the **Product** table and choose **no** under Create. We'll let the managers add new products.
2. Click the **Contact** table and select **limited** under Field Access.
3. Make sure all fields are modifiable. Then select **CreationDate**, **ContactSerNum_pk**, and **CreationTime**, and change them to **view only**.

Well, locking down ContactSerNum_pk for the sales team isn't much of a challenge. We locked it down for everybody when we created the field. Isn't it interesting that there are so many places you can lock things down? Yeah, and it can be pretty confusing if you find something locked and need to figure out how to unlock it. Lots of places to look.

4. Click **OK**.
5. From the Layouts drop-down, choose **All view only**. Next to Value Lists, choose **All view only**. Next to Scripts, choose **All executable only**,

then click **OK** again so these changes are memorized for the Sales privilege set.

6. Click **OK** one final time. If you have a full access account that has no password, you'll see a dialog now. It's okay to allow that. But you ought to make sure you know what accounts and passwords you've set up before leaving here. At the Confirm Full Access Login window, you will be required to enter a name and password (even if it will be blank) for a full access account. In this case, type **Admin** in the Full Access Account box, leave the Password box empty, and click **OK**.
7. Under the **File** menu, choose **File Options**. There should be a check next to "Log in using." Uncheck it now. That will force you (and other users) to log in when the file opens. Otherwise, it opens with all privileges. Click the **OK** button.
8. Close the file and reopen it using the **Sales** account and **Counter** password, remembering to be attentive to case. Go to the Contact layout and try to change CreationDate or CreationTime. You don't need to test ContactSerNum. You wouldn't be able to change it anyway.
9. Close and reopen the file with all privileges. That will probably mean the Admin account and no password.

Layouts

1. Go back into the Business file, and choose **File**, **Manage**, **Accounts & Privileges.**
2. Click the **Privilege Sets** tab and double-click the **Sales** privilege set.
3. Click the pop-up next to Layouts (see Figure 22-9) and choose **All view only** if it's not already selected.
4. Click on the pop-up again and choose **Custom privileges** to open the Custom Layout Privileges window shown in Figure 22-10.

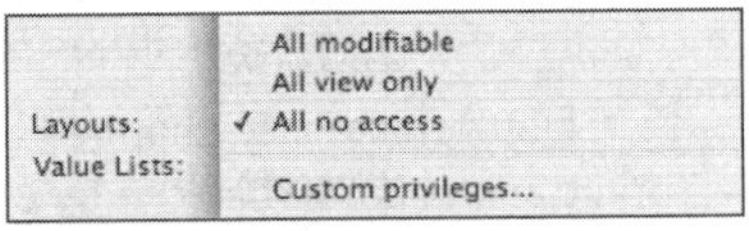

Figure 22-9
The Layouts (and Value Lists) pop-up under Data Access and Design.

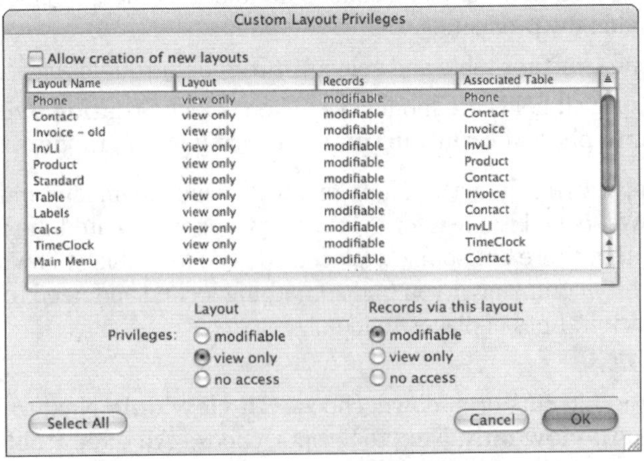

Figure 22-10
The Custom Layout Privileges window.

Here's where you decide what changes a privilege set can make to layouts. Clicking the column headers will sort them by that header. For Windows users, clicking the column header a second time will reverse sort them. On the Macintosh, you have to click the triangle in the upper right next to Associated Table.

Regardless of how you sort the list, at the bottom is [Any New Layout]. This is just like the [Any New Table] option discussed previously. You get to decide in advance what will happen in the file for this privilege set in any new layouts as they are created.

Click on one or more of the tables to activate the radio buttons in the lower part of the window. If you choose the "no access" radio button under Layout, the buttons under "Records via this layout" turn gray. That makes sense. If you choose "view only" under Layout, you can also choose "no access" under "Records via this layout." That provides you with a layout with no visible data. I don't know why you might want to do that, but it's there.

Here are some specifics to consider:

- You can make a privilege set so all layouts are "no access," and [Any New Layout] is set to "modifiable." Then by selecting the radio button next to "view only," you can prevent the user from altering data in the very layout he or she created.
- There's something rather interesting about the "Records via this layout" option. Even if you set up the file so users have full access to one of the tables in the file (say the Phone table), if you put a portal using data from that table on a different layout with "view only" or "no access," the user access will be limited accordingly. They won't have full access from that specific layout.
- If you go to the Custom Layout Privileges window and select the "no access" radio button under "Records via this layout," even if you have the Custom Record Privileges window set up with Field Access set to All, the users will only see <No Access> in every field.
- When you turn off access to layouts, the layout names will not even show up when those users click the Layout list drop-down below the Book. In fact, they won't show up in List Layout mode even if the user is allowed access to other layouts in Layout mode. This brings control over specific layouts to specific users in both Browse and Layout modes. It's similar and yet subtly different from using the Layout Setup window in Layout mode and selecting whether layouts appear in the list for all users in Browse mode.
- If the file opens automatically to a specific layout and the user doesn't have access to that layout, he'll see a screen that looks like Figure 22-11. That's something to be concerned about since the user won't be able to see or click on any buttons that might be on that layout. For the same reason, you should be cautious that any buttons on layouts users can access don't take them to layouts they can't get out of. That applies to the web interface as well.

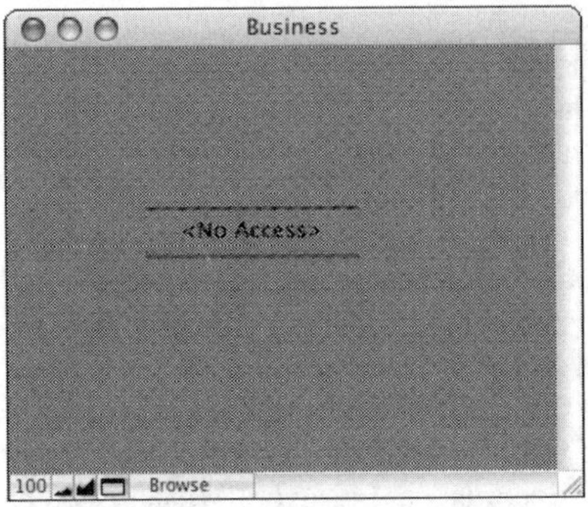

Figure 22-11
What a FileMaker layout looks like to an account where the custom layout privileges are set to "no access."

- There is a check box in the upper-left corner of the window that allows the account to create new layouts. That means you can prevent users from working in Layout mode throughout the file and still let them create their own letters and reports. Try that with earlier versions of FileMaker!
- The layouts from External SQL Sources (ESS)[9] will be included in the list, and you can apply the same limitations to the ESS layouts as you do to the FMP layouts.

Don't make any changes here just yet. If you already did, click the Cancel button and come back in by choosing "Custom privileges" from the Layouts pop-up. (If you really got messed up, make sure you are customizing the "All modifiable" privilege set.) Let's make a couple of changes that we'll keep for the Sales group.

1. Click the **Select All** button and set it to **view only** under Layout and **modifiable** under "Records via this layout."
2. Now select the **PH_Phone** and **PRO (Products)** layouts and set them to **no access.**
3. Select the **CON_Contact** layout in the list and click the **modifiable** radio button.

   Remember, your users will be able to see the phone information in the portal on the Contact layout, and they'll be able to see the products in the drop-down list on the Invoice layout. They just won't be able to see those layouts in the Layout drop-down below the Book.
4. Click **OK** and **OK** again so these changes are memorized for the Sales privilege set.
5. Click **OK** one final time. Deal with any windows that appear.
6. Close the file and reopen it using the **Sales** account and **Counter** password.
7. Go to the **CON_Contact** layout and click the Layout drop-down below the Book. You should no longer be able to see either the PH_Phone or PRO layouts.

8. Go to Layout mode and move something. No problemo. Use Undo to move it back. Now switch to the ILI_InvoicePrint layout and try to move something. Aha! Foiled again!
9. Close and reopen the file with all privileges. That will probably mean the Admin account and no password.

Value Lists

1. Go back into the Business file, and choose **File, Manage, Accounts & Privileges.**
2. Click the **Privilege Sets** tab and double-click the **Sales** privilege set.
3. Click the pop-up next to Value Lists (see Figure 22-9) and choose **All view only**, if it's not already set that way from our earlier exercise.
4. Click on the pop-up again and choose **Custom privileges** to bring up the Custom Value List Privileges window shown in Figure 22-12.

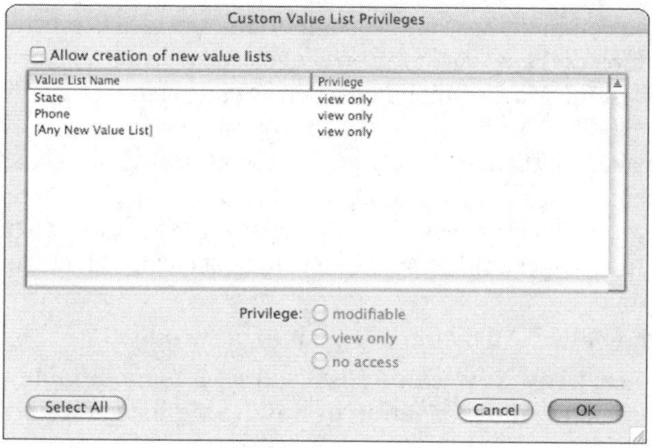

Figure 22-12
The Custom Value List Privileges window.

Here's where you decide what changes a privilege set can make to various value lists. Clicking the column headers will sort them by that header. For Windows users, clicking the column header a second time will reverse sort them. On the Macintosh, you have to click the triangle in the upper right next to Privilege.

Regardless of how you sort the list, at the bottom is [Any New Value List]. This is just like the [Any New Table] and [Any New Layout] options. You get to decide in advance what will happen in the file for this privilege set in any new value lists as they are created.

Here are some things to be aware of:

- If you create a list to which a privilege set has no access, users won't even see the list. That means if you make a list using radio buttons, they won't even show on the layout!
- If you create a drop-down list that uses values from a field and the privilege set can type in the field, users will be able to add the new value to the list. Doesn't sound much like it's "view only," does it?

- If you're in Layout mode and you format the field by checking the box next to Include Edit, the privilege set can change the value list even though the privilege would indicate that the user is allowed to view only.
- In the upper-left corner of the window is a check box for "Allow creation of new value lists." That means you can prevent specific users from messing up your carefully created lists while letting them create lists they need for themselves. But you'll also have to select [Any New Value List] and click the "modifiable" radio button to make it work.
- If you allow a privilege set the right to create new value lists but prevent users from having access to all layouts, they won't be able to attach their value lists to any fields.
- When a privilege set says "view only" and users go to the File menu, Manage will be grayed out. So they can't even view the lists, let alone modify them.

My own little comment here is, although I think the idea is pretty good, the implementation of these particular privileges seems contradictory and not particularly useful. Maybe you'll find a better use for them than I've been able to.

Don't make any changes here just yet. If you already did, click the Cancel button and come back in by choosing "Custom privileges" from the Layouts pop-up. (If you really got messed up, make sure you are customizing the "All modifiable" privilege set.) Let's make a couple of changes that we'll test on the Sales group.

5. Click the **Select All** button and set it to **view only.**
6. Now select **[Any New Value List]** and set it to **modifiable**, and check the box next to **Allow creation of new value lists**, if it's not checked already.
7. Select the **State** value list and click the radio button next to **no access.**

   Remember, your users will be able to see the phone information in the portal on the Contact layout, and they'll be able to see the products in the drop-down list on the Invoice layout. They just won't be able to see those layouts in the Layout drop-down below the Book.
8. Click **OK** and **OK** again so these changes are memorized for the Sales privilege set.
9. Click **OK** one final time. Deal with any dialogs that appear.
10. Close the file and reopen it using the **Sales** account and **Counter** password.
11. Go to the Contact layout and click the **State** field. You should no longer be able to see the drop-down list of states.
12. Go to **File**, **Manage**, **Value Lists.** Double-click any of the lists; you should get a dialog saying your access privileges prevent editing.
13. Click the **New** button. You don't really need to create a new value list, do you? Click the **Cancel** button.

14. Close and reopen the file with all privileges. That will probably mean the Admin account and no password.
15. You'd better go back and give the sales folks access to the State drop-down list. They might need it. You might also want to limit their ability to create new lists.

Scripts

1. Go back into the Business file, and choose **File**, **Manage**, **Accounts & Privileges**.
2. Click the **Privilege Sets** tab and double-click the **Sales** privilege set.
3. Click the pop-up next to Scripts (Figure 22-13) and choose **All executable only**, if it's not set that way already.
4. Click on the pop-up again and choose **Custom privileges** to open the window shown in Figure 22-14.

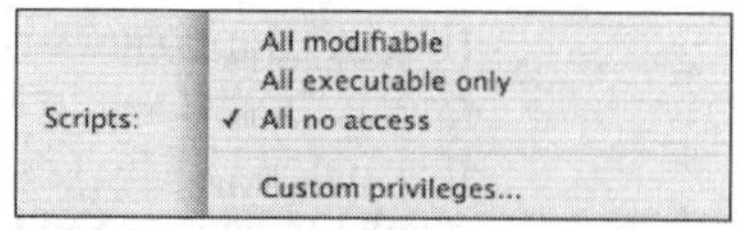

Figure 22-13
The Scripts pop-up under Data Access and Design.

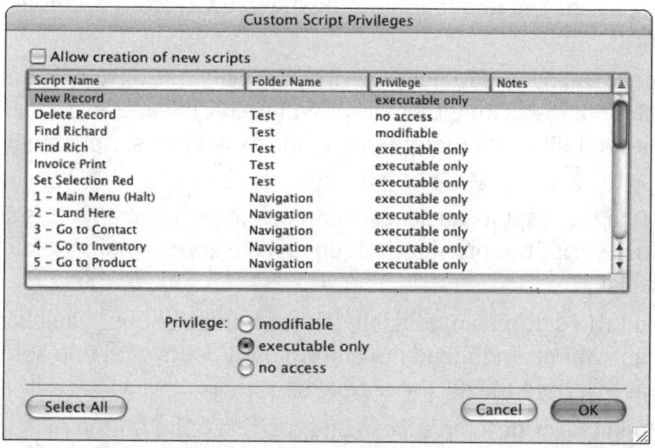

Figure 22-14
The Custom Script Privileges window.

Here's where you decide what changes a privilege set can make to various scripts — or if the script can be executed at all! Clicking the column headers will sort the scripts by that header. That means you can sort the script by name. That's something you can't even do in the Manage Scripts dialog! For Windows users, clicking the column header a second time will reverse sort them. On the Macintosh, you have to click the triangle in the upper right next to Notes. There is also a Folder Name column header, which was introduced as Group Name in FileMaker 9.

Regardless of how you sort the list, at the bottom is [Any New Script]. You get to decide in advance what an account can do with each script.

This Custom Privileges window is the only one that includes a Notes column. You can't actually add any notes here, though. The only note that might currently show here is if a script has the box checked next to "Run script with full access privileges."

Here are some things to be aware of:

- In the upper-left corner of the window is an "Allow creation of new scripts" check box. With this option you can prevent specific users from messing up your carefully created scripts and still let them create scripts they need for themselves. But you'll also have to select [Any New Script] and click the "modifiable" radio button to make it work.
- If the privilege set is allowed entry into Manage Scripts, any scripts that are tagged as no access to those users will not even be visible in the list.
- That also means any numbering scheme you may be planning for the first 10 scripts could go out the window. If you're passing out a list of scripts that are supposed to be run with those key combinations, make sure you check the list while logging in under each account first. What will happen if you don't? The key combinations will shift down the list to the next available script, and you could be in for some unhappy surprises! Think what might happen if one user with one set of 10 F key scripts is helping out another user who has a different set of 10 F key scripts without relogging in. You know, something like New Record becomes Delete All Records.
- If a user can access Manage Scripts but only has executable access to a script, double-clicking that script will result in a message that his privileges don't allow modifying the script. However, scripts tagged as modifiable for that privilege set open right up.
- If you tag a script as no access for a privilege set and it runs as part of another script the privilege set does have access to, it could mess up your plans.
- If you tag a script as modifiable for a privilege set but you change the available menu commands to editing only, users won't be able to open Manage Scripts to edit the script.
- If you set a script to no access but you leave the button on a layout accessible to the privilege set users, you would probably expect them to be somewhat frustrated and lose faith in the effect of any buttons.

Don't make any changes here just yet. If you already did, click the Cancel button and come back in by choosing "Custom privileges" from the Scripts pop-up. (If you really got messed up, make sure you are customizing the "All executable only" privilege set.) Let's make a couple of changes that we'll keep for the Sales group.

5. Click the **Select All** button and set it to **executable only**. That probably won't change a thing since that's the privilege set we began with.
6. Select the **Find Richard** script and set it to **modifiable**.
7. Select the **Delete Record** script and click the radio button to make it **no access**. Those salespeople shouldn't be deleting sales records anyway, right?

8. Click **OK** and **OK** again so these changes are memorized for the Sales privilege set.
9. Click **OK** one final time. Deal with any dialogs that appear.
10. Close the file and reopen it using the **Sales** account and **Counter** password.
11. Go to the **Contact** layout and click the **Delete Record** button. You should no longer be able to delete any records. But remember the confusion that might cause.
12. Go to **Scripts, Manage Scripts**. First notice that the Delete Record script is nowhere to be found!
13. Double-click the **New Record** script. Can't go there, eh?
14. Double-click **Find Richard**. We're in! Don't make any changes though. Click the **Close** buttons to leave Manage Scripts.
15. Close and reopen the file with all privileges. That will probably mean the Admin account and no password.

Other Privileges[7]

Look under the Other Privileges heading on the right side of the Edit Privilege Set window. "Allow printing" and "Allow exporting" are pretty clear. "Manage extended privileges" generally refers to allowing access to items found on the Macintosh under FileMaker Pro, Sharing and on Windows under Edit, Sharing. These include the preset sharing items Instant Web Publishing, ODBC/JDBC, and FileMaker Network, as well as any additional extended privileges FileMaker and third-party companies may make available in the future. We'll look at that in a minute in the section called "Extended Privileges Tab."

Next is the check box for "Allow user to override data validation warnings." I'm used to seeing that option at the field definition level under the Validation tab from previous versions of FileMaker. It's still there, although it's been moved near the top of that window. Using this check box with the privilege set gives you more flexibility. And in a way it does make sense that some users should have the ability to override those warnings. Leave the box unchecked in the Validation tab of the Options for Fields window and turn it on here to force specific users to stay within the data entry requirements. When users are allowed to override the value, they'll see a dialog like this: "Price is defined to contain only specific values. You must enter a valid value." They'll see three buttons: Revert Record, No, and Yes. With the restriction placed by this check box, users will see this dialog: "Price is defined to contain only specific values. Allow this value?" They'll only see two buttons: Revert Record and OK.

"Disconnect user from FileMaker Server when idle" can be set for each privilege set. The idle time length is set to the same variable number of minutes for all users in FileMaker Server.

The next three items were introduced in FileMaker Pro 7 and add a great deal to the security of a solution while reducing administration.

Take a look at the pop-up next to "Available menu commands." The choices here provide some manner of control over menu access. The Editing Only choice shuts out access to Manage Scripts (users can still run scripts depending on their privileges), all of the Records menus, the ability to change modes or views, and most of the choices under the File menu. That means that you'd have to create buttons to provide any of those functions that you still wanted users to be able to access. The Minimum choice also removes all the choices under the Edit menu.

It would be nice to have more control over specific commands, but that's the way it is. However, there are some plug-ins created for just that purpose. FileMaker 8 Advanced and later let you create custom menus for your files. We won't cover that here since it's for the product used by developers, but you should know it's available and can be quite effective.

Extended Privileges[7]

And finally, in the lower-left corner as we work our way clockwise around the window, is the Extended Privileges area. As you can see, these include Instant Web Publishing, ODBC/JDBC, and FileMaker Network. Again, you can control which privilege sets have access to these various functions simply by using the check boxes here. Some of the check boxes are repeated in other windows. For instance, in the Sharing, Instant Web Publishing window, when you click the Specify button you can choose which privilege sets have access to the file. Under the Sharing menu, you work with all privilege sets at once. In the Edit Privilege Set window, you work with one privilege set at a time, but all the extended privileges at once. That brings us to the details of the Extended Privileges tab.

Extended Privileges Tab[7]

The final tab of the Manage Accounts & Privileges window is Extended Privileges, as seen in Figure 22-15. FileMaker, Inc. has provided add-on software products that work along with FileMaker. These add-on products are similar to plug-ins but often have wider capabilities. In fact, some of the current sets of extended privileges were former plug-ins. The Extended Privileges area is where you assign various accounts access to these accessories. As time goes on, we may see other such products from FileMaker and third-party software developers. With the release of FileMaker 7, the only extended privileges available were Instant Web Publishing, ODBC/JDBC, FileMaker Network, and FileMaker Mobile (which is still included even though FileMaker, Inc. is discontinuing the product). FileMaker 8 added two more: XML Web Publishing and XSLT Web Publishing. These last two allow the files to be available to the privilege set when users log in using some other application using XML or XSLT Web Publishing as opposed to Instant Web Publishing. It's limited to files being served with FileMaker Server Advanced. You can't test it out using the standard client version of FileMaker even though you can serve up to five users with IWP. And FileMaker 9 introduced PHP Web Publishing, which is only active when files are available through FileMaker Server.

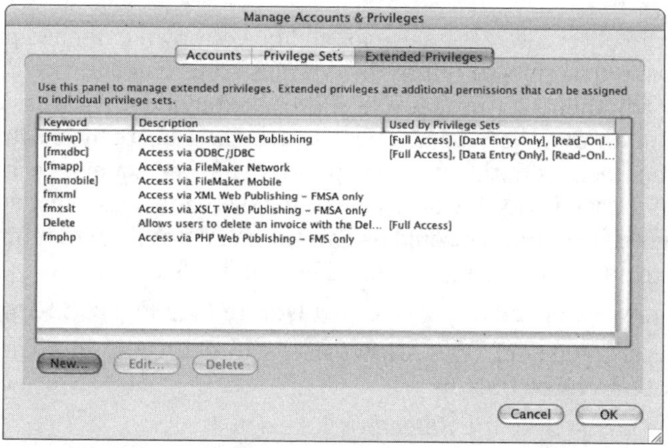

Figure 22-15 The Extended Privileges tab of the Manage Accounts & Privileges window.

Click the Extended Privileges tab to examine the area. Clicking on the column headers does nothing. The four preset items we see here (the ones with brackets in the Keyword column) cannot be deleted. (The Delete extended privilege is a special one we'll be creating in a minute.) The other privileges can be edited by double-clicking them — although I wouldn't advise that.

Double-clicking Access via Instant Web Publishing brings up the Edit Extended Privilege window seen in Figure 22-16. Hey, we've seen this window before. Yep, there's one very similar in the Sharing, Instant Web Publishing area. There's also one each for Sharing, ODBC/JDBC and Sharing, FileMaker Network. By clicking the check box in the On column over on the left, you can toggle access to this extended privilege for each privilege set. When you're in this window, you cannot change the keyword or the description for these presets. About all you can do is check the check boxes and sort by privilege set. The advice from the people at FileMaker is to avoid enabling extended privileges unless you need to. Uncheck all the boxes for each extended privilege set and only add them when users need the functions.

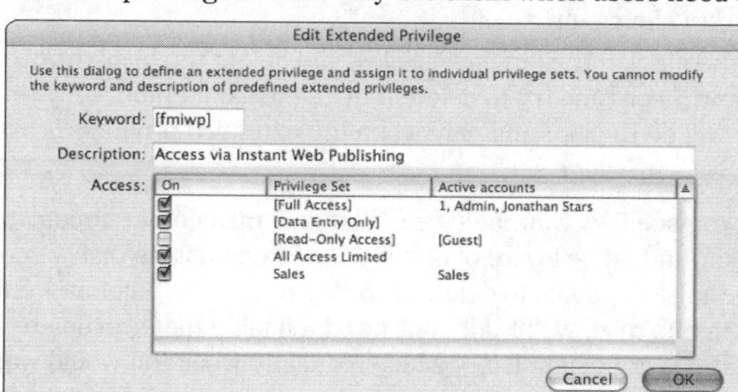

Figure 22-16 The Edit Extended Privilege window for Instant Web Publishing.

Click the Cancel button to take you back to the Extended Privileges tab. Notice the **New** button in the lower-left corner. You might use it if you're installing a new extended privilege provided by FileMaker or a third-party vendor. In that case, you'd follow their directions for installing and naming the keyword.

There is one other interesting use for adding your own extended privilege. You can set up scripts to run so that various steps will only occur depending on whether the user has one of these extended privileges. You could then grant or deny various functions to groups of users by checking or unchecking their access to the extended privilege. As an example, earlier we had turned off the ability for the salespeople to delete invoices. That seems like a pretty good idea. But we could use an extended privilege to temporarily let them delete an invoice using a scripted button. Let's try it.

1. Create a new extended privilege called **Delete** (see Figure 22-15).
2. In the Description field, type **Allows users to delete an invoice with the Delete Invoice button**.
3. Check the box next to the **Sales** privilege set.
4. Click **OK**, **OK**, and deal with any dialogs.
5. Create a script called **27 - Delete Invoice [EP Delete]**. EP stands for extended privilege. It's just a way to remind ourselves what's going on. Use these steps:

```
Script Name: 27- Delete Invoice [EP Delete]
If [PatternCount (Get (ExtendedPrivileges) ; "Delete") ≥ 1]
   Delete Record/Request [No dialog]
End If
```

6. Check the box near the bottom of this dialog next to **Run script with full access privileges**.
7. Click the **Close** button and continue to exit Manage Scripts.
8. Now add a **Delete Invoice** button to the INV_Invoice layout and attach that script.
9. Go to Browse mode, create a new record, and click the button. Hey! Even as the Admin level user, you can't delete the record using that button. Pretty clever, eh?
10. Close the file, log back in under Sales, and delete the blank record. Create a new record and try to delete it by the usual method. Only the button will do the job. And only when the extended privilege is assigned to the Sales privilege set.

I think you can see how this could be effective in many other circumstances. One thing you should be aware of in this specific example is that we currently don't allow the salespeople to delete records from the InvoiceLineItems table either. But in this case, we're not limiting which table they can delete from. So the line items are deleted, too, which is exactly what you would want to have happen.

Expand and/or Reduce Privileges

There is no dialog to expand or reduce privileges, but FileMaker's Manage Accounts & Privileges makes this capability a snap — and very powerful. One of the features introduced with FMP7 is that it allows you to instantly add to or subtract privileges from any account on the fly. Now here comes the good part: That also means you can duplicate a complex privilege set, change only as many of the specific privileges as you need to, then assign it to the account for as long as needed.

To show you how powerful this can be, let's take a privilege set we've already created and duplicate it. Then we'll change it to temporarily expand the privileges to allow changes to all the layouts.

1. Click the **Privilege Sets** tab.
2. Highlight and duplicate the **Sales** account. Then double-click it to edit it. Under Privilege Set Name, change Sales Copy to **Sales + Layout Access.** In the Description area, type **Access to all layouts.**
3. In the Data Access and Design area, next to Layouts, select **All modifiable.** Click the **OK** button.
4. Click the **Accounts** tab and double-click the **Sales** account.
5. Click on the pop-up list next to Privilege Set and select **Sales + Layout Access.**
6. Click **OK**, **OK** again, and deal with any dialog that may be required as you leave Manage Accounts & Privileges.
7. Close the file and open it using the **Sales** account and **Counter** password.
8. See if you can get to Layout mode and see all the layouts.

Once you've created the modified privilege set, changing privileges this way is something you can do by simply accessing an account and making a different selection from the pop-up list. It couldn't be easier. With this feature you can expand or reduce anyone's privileges any way you want. The only challenge will be remembering to remove the extra privileges after the task is done. Speaking of that, you should probably go back and reset the Sales account to the Sales Access privilege set. You might consider removing the Delete extended privilege, too. When you do, you'll notice that the Sales + Layout Access privilege set got use of the Delete EP. Uncheck that box.

NOTE For simplicity, we've set this file up with only two additional accounts. Normally, you would set up a file so that each user would have his or her own account and password. Each member of the sales team would be assigned to the Sales privilege set. That way a single person can be assigned the new privileges rather than a whole group of people.

NOTE Changing a password in one file of a multi-file solution can affect how groups of files open. When users first open a file in a multi-file solution, if subsequent files use the same account, FileMaker opens them without displaying the account and password window. If the account has been changed in the first file, FileMaker will display the login window for every subsequent file that opens — a major pain. This used to be a big issue before FileMaker implemented multiple tables per file. But you may inherit a solution that uses the old format. And, as we've said before, there are reasons to build multi-file solutions even with the availability of the multi-table structure.

That brings up another issue. Changing accounts in a group of files on a regular basis can be a big job. The DialogMagic plug-in from New Millennium Communications allows you to change accounts across a multi-file solution by entering information in one window. For more on plug-ins, see the files available at www.wordware.com/files/fmpro10 and the FileMaker, Inc. web site.

TIP FileMaker's password system is now case sensitive. That means variations of the same password can be assigned to different people. Counter, counter, CoUnTeR, COUNTer, and coUNTer are all considered different passwords starting with FMP7. That much variety is not required because different accounts are allowed to use the same password. However, account names must be unique, and are not case sensitive.

Editing and Deleting Accounts[7]

Making a change to an account's privileges couldn't be easier. Go to the Edit Account window, click on the Privilege Set pop-up, choose a different set of privileges, and click OK.

Editing

Any time you need to, you can come back to Manage Accounts & Privileges and make changes by making selections that move you through the other windows. You can make any number of changes to a selected item without committing yourself. At any time you can click the Cancel button. However, if you click the OK button in any of the windows, *all* those changes become final once you click the final OK button to leave Accounts & Privileges.

Cautions

You should test your solution very carefully before foisting it upon your end users. Try every combination of layouts and fields with each of the various accounts to be sure they perform the way you expect them to. As I mentioned before, I recently built a solution that was locked down pretty tightly with various accounts. Then the client asked for some new features. I added new fields and didn't realize field access privileges were being assigned by FileMaker based on current restrictions. (Remember those items in brackets? Any New Table, Layout, Value List, and Script.) That meant accounts with lower-level privileges were not able to perform scripts that used fields to which they didn't have access. I had assumed all accounts would have access to the new fields unless I changed it — and I didn't test it. I found out pretty quickly that it doesn't work that way!

NOTE If you want to test the results of changes to an account, you could set up a script to relogin. But if you're networked, you can also choose File, Open Remote to open a second copy of the file on the same machine you're working on. When the Open Remote File window appears, you will see a list of hosts. Just choose your machine and you'll see a list of files appear on the right. Select the file you want, click the Open button, and enter the account and password information. (If the Account window does not appear, you'll need to hold down the Shift key on Windows or the Option key on Macintosh when you click the Open button.) With both a high privilege set window and a restricted privilege set window open, you can click back and forth between them to run various tests without having to login over and over. You are limited to having two sessions open, and you must be networked. Of course, Network Sharing must be on and the network access to the file(s) must allow access to the account you want to test.

Keep careful records of your administrative passwords, and keep them somewhere they won't be easily found, but make sure someone else knows where they are. For goodness sake, don't put them in a file on your computer that isn't being backed up! And don't put them on a Post-it note and stick it to your monitor. Files that can't be updated can cause a lot of problems for an organization. A company with proper proof of ownership used to be able to get passwords from FileMaker, Inc., but this was a time-consuming process and a last resort for poor planning. Starting with version 7, the passwords are no longer accessible to anyone — even at FileMaker, Inc. You've been warned!

If a button takes users to a layout that says Access Denied, they won't be able to see any buttons on the page to get them out of there. If you choose to have the Status toolbar hidden, you should add appropriate script steps to prevent those groups from being able to go to those layouts. Your only other alternative is to provide a script to the Main Menu that will appear under the Scripts menu. Then you'll have to teach everyone in that group how to find it.

Many times you will be building a set of files that work together. If you use the same set of accounts and passwords for each of the files, the users will only have to enter their password once, and the other files will open without calling up the dialog. This is a great feature, but it can also cause problems. For example, if you want to change the access for a particular account, you may have to make the change in multiple files. Depending on the complexity of the files involved, you may want to make use of one of the other ways of limiting access discussed in the rest of this chapter.

If you intend to modify a solution offsite and then install it by importing the onsite data into your file(s), consider this: What if users have changed their passwords? What if administrators have changed privilege sets or created new accounts? None of those changes will be in the file or files you're installing.

One suggestion would be to use some of the Get functions to collect account names, extended privileges, and privilege set names. You would then write a looping script to create a new record for each account in a special table. The script would have to be set up ahead of time in the onsite file. Then you'd need a second looping script that would create the new accounts in the updated solution. And you still wouldn't have the passwords. It would require a lot of setup and it's beyond the scope of this book to show you the details.

A second suggestion would involve using the Data Design Report in FileMaker Advanced to gather the information using XML. Once again, pretty complicated, and no passwords — but it may be necessary.

To handle the passwords, you would need to set them back to blank or some other more generic word and have the users enter a password at next login. That could also cause some confusion if the update required setting passwords in multiple files — some of which might only open once a week.

The main point is you need to think about what could happen. It might just be easier to have everyone lock in their settings and passwords. Depending on the scope of the application, that may be just as difficult as creating the updating scripts.

Limiting Access through Scripting

One way of controlling where users go is with scripts. The best way is to have a script check what privilege set the user has to determine where he or she can go. The following script is an example.

Go to the Invoice table, and create a new script called "28 - Open" with the following steps:

```
Table: Invoice
Script Name: 28 - Open
If [Get (PrivilegeSetName) = "Sales"]
   Go to Layout ["INV_Invoice" (INV)]
Else
   Go to Layout ["NUL_MainMenu" (NUL)]
End If
```

(You can do the same thing with account names using the Get (AccountName) function.) Click the Close button, uncheck the box in front of the script so it won't appear in the Scripts menu, and click the Close button to exit Manage Scripts. Now let's make this script run automatically when opening the file.

Startup Script

Choose File, File Options, Open/Close, and click the box next to "Perform script." Then click on the word <unknown>, and pull down to the 28 - Open script. Figure 22-17 shows what the window should look like when you're done. Click OK. What this will do is run the Open script when anyone opens the file. Of course, users will have to put in their account name and password when opening the file. The account name determines what privilege set they're in, and the Open script puts them on the appropriate layout.

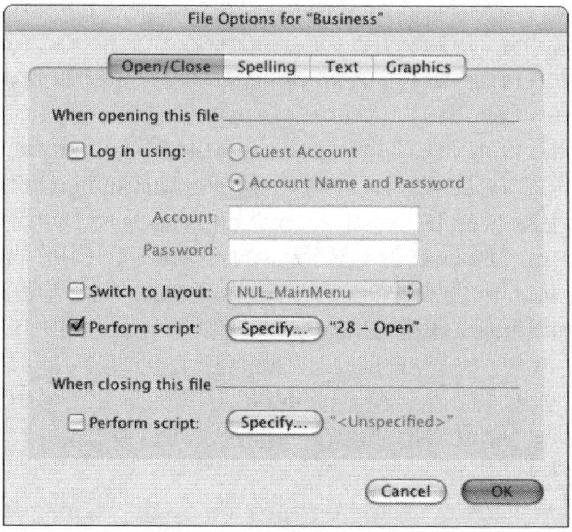

Figure 22-17 File Options window showing that the 28 - Open script will perform automatically when the file is opened.

To test it out, close the file, and reopen it using the Sales account and the Counter password. Notice which layout you're on. Close the file, and open it with one of the other passwords. It's magic!

This is only one example of such a script. I've seen some amazing solutions that control every move through the files, yet they appear completely transparent to the user. I used some of those ideas to create a solution for a bakery with areas for owners, managers, order takers, bakers, and decorators. Each worker only went to the areas they used, and often didn't even know that other areas of the files existed. New employees could learn how to take orders in half a day using a point-and-click FileMaker system. Previously, the full training process using a paper system had taken six weeks.

Controlling Layout Access

Sending users to specific layouts isn't much help if they can just choose a different layout from the Layout drop-down list below the Book. But the Layout drop-down can be set so users only see the current layout. Starting with FMP7, you can change the order of layouts even while other users are in the files. Go to the File menu and choose Manage, Layouts. (If the Manage icon is available in the Status toolbar, you can click the icon and choose Layouts.) By clicking the check box to the left of each layout name, you can hide or show specific layouts from the Layout drop-down.

Of course, anyone who has access privileges that allow them to view or modify all layouts will be able to see and select from the list when they're in Layout mode. Then you need to use privilege sets to prevent various users from having access to Layout mode or specific layouts. You'll have to follow that up by making sure users can get to the layouts they need with the buttons you provide for them. It requires a lot more work to set up files this way, but some situations will require that level of control.

Limiting Access through Field Calculations

Another method that is less often used (but is no less effective) is to limit access using field calculations. This method is used less often because it is more difficult to set up. One thing that can be done with this method that cannot be done with FileMaker's security in versions prior to 5.5 is that you can adjust who can see data based on the data in the records. For example, a group of marriage counselors needs to be able to access the same fields and layouts, but they shouldn't be able to see the troubles, sins, and confidential foibles of the patients of other counselors. Prior to version 5.5, FileMaker's password system was useless in this "record-level" security. The field calculation method (though much more difficult to establish) is more capable. I've seen about three different ways to limit access through calculations, but I'd like to offer my own version that uses validation by calculation. It won't make data invisible to other users, but it will prevent changes to specific records. Let me show you.

Let's assume that all invoices need to be approved by the manager or owner. Once they're approved, you don't want anyone except a manager or owner changing the invoice to prevent, for example, anyone from giving one of their buddies a price break so they can get a kickback. (This widget business is just full of corruption.)

1. Go to the Invoice table, and create a new text field called **Approved**. Then click **OK**.

The Script

Now we need a script that only the owner or manager can use to approve an invoice. What the script will do is check to see what privilege set the user is from. If they're from the Owner or Manager group, clicking on the Approved field puts an X there. Since they may have to unapprove an invoice, it allows for that in the Else section of the script.

You could just as easily control this with field validation, but I think making a field into a button is a great technique.

2. Go to Manage Scripts and make a script called **29 - Approved** with the following steps:

```
Table: Invoice
Script Name: 29 - Approved
If [Get (AccountName) = "Owner" or Get (AccountName) = "Manager"]
   If [IsEmpty (INV::Approved)]
      Set Field [INV::Approved ; "X"]
   Else
      Set Field [INV::Approved ; ""]
   End If
End If
```

3. Click the **Close** button and **Save**, uncheck the box in front of **Script Name**, and click the **Close** button to exit Manage Scripts. This, of course, assumes that you've created accounts for the Owner and Manager. If you haven't done that, make sure you do it now.
4. Now make the field into a button. Go to Layout mode, and put a copy of the Approved field in a logical place on the layout if one didn't appear automatically. Be sure the field is selected, and choose **Format**, **Button**. Choose **Perform Script** from the list on the left, select the new **29 - Approved** script from the pop-up on the right, and click **OK.**
5. You will also need to remove the Approved field from the tab order.
6. To test it out, click the field. Since these are new accounts, unless you've logged back in you shouldn't be able to change the field.
7. Close and reopen the file using one of the new accounts. Make sure this script only works if you have the right password. You don't want order takers approving invoices.

The Calculation

8. Now choose **Manage Database**, go to the **InvoiceLineItems** table, and double-click the **ProdID_fk** field. Click on the **Validation** tab, click the box next to **Validated by calculation**, and use the following:

```
ili_INV__InvNum::Approved <> "X"
```

   Notice that we can't just choose INV::Approved. We need to look at the calculation from the point of view of the InvoiceLineItems table. INV is not a related TO.

9. Check the box next to **Display custom message if validation fails** and type **You cannot make changes to an invoice once it has been approved.** Once your dialog looks like Figure 22-18, click **OK** and **OK**.

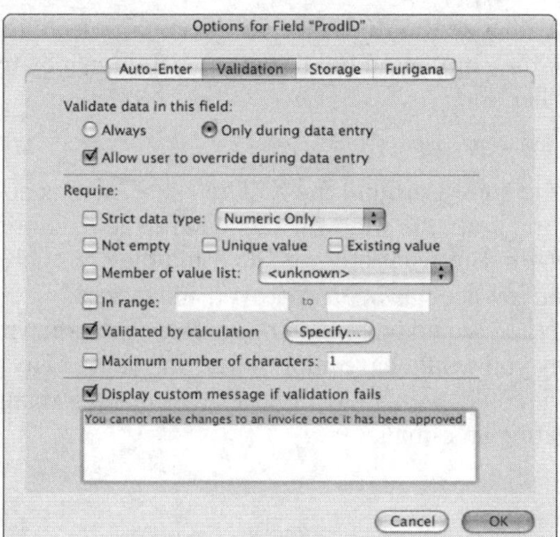

Figure 22-18
The Validation tab in the field definition for ProdID showing the text that will display when the validation fails.

10. Go to **File**, **Manage Accounts & Privileges**, and select the **Accounts** tab. Double-click the **Sales** account and click the **Edit** button on the middle right. In the Other Privileges area on the right, make sure there is *not* a check mark in the box next to **Allow user to override data validation warnings**. (For users of previous versions of FileMaker, this check box used to be in the field definition Validation tab.)
11. Repeat step 10 for any other accounts you want to force to respond to the strict message.
12. Before you log back in, make sure there's an X in the Approved field on at least one invoice.
13. Log in as one of the sales team. Go back to Invoice, and try to change the ProdID. As part of the Sales group, you should get the validation message, and you'll be forced to revert the field.
14. Log in as the boss and uncheck the Approved box. Now log in under Sales and try to change ProdID. Pretty cool, huh? To really make this complete, you'll need to use the same validation for the Quantity, Description, and Price fields.

Here's a slightly different approach. It would be much faster in tables where you need to prevent changes to all the fields at once. In this case, you can prevent specific privilege sets from making changes to any fields in records in the InvoiceLineItems table once the Approved field has been checked by management in the related invoice.

1. Go to **Manage Accounts & Privileges**, click the **Privilege Sets** tab, and double-click the **Sales** privilege set. In the Data Access and Design area, choose the pop-up next to Records and choose **Custom Privileges**.
2. Click the **InvoiceLineItems** table in the list. In the Set Privileges area at the bottom of the page, choose **limited** under the Edit column. That brings up the Specify Calculation window.
3. In the upper left, choose the **ili_INV__InvNum** table from the pop-up and double-click the **Approved** field from the list. Finish by making the calculation look like this:

   ```
   ili_INV__InvNum::Approved <> "X"
   ```

   Be sure to use the quotes around the X. The "< >" means not equal to. Remember, setting it up this way will affect all the fields in that table for the restricted users. But what other fields could they possibly need access to once an invoice has been approved and locked?

   One final method would be to use the same calculation with a script trigger. That way you would have a lot more control over any dialogs you want to display. It could even allow the user to request a change from the manager by creating an e-mail.

Internet Considerations

If you'll be sharing a file on the web, you can turn off various privileges with the expected consequences.

FileMaker's Instant Web Publishing feature can now encrypt data using a Secure Sockets Layer (SSL) when you use the FileMaker Server Advanced product.

Beyond that, you may need to purchase other software such as Blue World Communications' Lasso, which also provides SSL between FileMaker Pro and the outside world. Solutions like this are not for beginners, but if you need it, you'll have to start somewhere. For more information, see FileMaker's web site.

Conversion Issues

If you convert a solution created in a version of FileMaker previous to 7, groups will be converted to privilege sets. In earlier versions of FileMaker, passwords could be associated with multiple groups. Since an account in FMP7 or later can belong to only one privilege set, an account will inherit a privilege set named after all groups it was associated with. The privilege set will inherit the access privileges of the least restrictive group to which it belonged. If you'd rather not redesign very complex privilege sets after conversion, make sure that each password (that doesn't have full access to the file) is assigned to only one group in the old solution before converting.

Summary

In this chapter, we looked at protecting your data and layouts using FileMaker's built-in password security system. We also looked at controlling file use with scripts and calculations.

Q & A

Q I want the owner to be able to have access to everything except the master password. How can I do that without taking away one of the other privileges?

A Simply uncheck the box next to "Access the entire file."

Q Most users just fit under one account and password. Isn't there some way to have the files open without having to type in the password?

> **A** Yes. Choose File, File Options, check the box next to "Log in using," and enter the default account and password in the boxes. When you want to access the file with some other password, holding down the Option key (Macintosh) or Shift key (Windows) as you open the file will bring up the password window. Or create a relogin script that you can access from a button somewhere.

Workshop

If you didn't finish "locking down" the Description and Price fields in InvLI using validation by calculation, do it now and try it out. Make sure you try it with other passwords.

Create a special layout in Invoice to perform finds. Make the Find button run scripts that take the user to a special layout where all fields are locked if the invoice has been approved and their privileges don't allow changing the data. If the user is the owner or manager, the script should take them to a layout where data can be edited.

Try controlling access to invoice fields using a script trigger. You can go back to Chapter 16 for more information if you need to.

Chapter 23

Backup and Recovery

Introduction

Perhaps more important than protecting your files with passwords is keeping good backups. Any number of things can happen to your files. Let's face it, without your data, your business is — well, out of business! This chapter is mostly a discussion, but I will have you save a clone and experiment with exporting and importing some records.

In this chapter, we'll look at:

- Why you need to do backups
- Commercial backup products
- Making a clone of a file
- Backups you can do with software you already have
- Good backup routines (schedule)
- Techniques from within FileMaker
- How to recover your data when the time comes

Why Back Up?

Power fluctuations or outages, hard drive mechanisms that go bad, and computer system conflicts can all spell trouble for your data, and let's not even mention fire, flood, and tornado. Stuff happens, and it can happen to your data.

In the old pre-computer days, people kept their records on paper. Remember those days? Business people had to worry about fire and flood, and most companies didn't make a copy of every sheet of paper they generated. The loss of a company's records was devastating. Well, it still is today; it's just that all those records can now be concentrated on a hard drive. Because of the nature of digital information, making backups of a company's entire set of records is a simple procedure. Now you can make backups onto media the size of a pack of chewing gum so they can easily be stored in multiple locations for added security. So what's the problem?

Sometimes people just forget. I try to back up every day, but when I started this chapter, I realized I'd forgotten to back up a couple of important files for about four days. Backing up is usually everybody's last thought when leaving the office after a long day.

Hardware cost is another issue. Many people strain their budget to get their computer. Then they go over budget to get some software. Now someone tells them they have to buy another machine to make backups. Forget it!

I know of a state agency that decided not to buy a backup system because it cost $2,000. (This was a few years ago.) Their computer tech kept warning them they were skating on thin ice. His favorite saying was, "There are two kinds of hard drives: those that *have* lost data and those that *will* lose data." The day finally came when their only hard drive bit the dust and the data on it was unrecoverable. They lost the equivalent of eight people entering data 40 hours a week for one year, or about $250,000 of employee pay and benefits. The little $2,000 backup device looked pretty cheap by comparison. That's why you need to make backups. Any questions?

FileMaker Server Backup Features

We haven't spent much time discussing FileMaker Server in this book because it is a separate product. However, it's worth mentioning Server's backup features, because they have much to offer the users of shared files that just aren't available when using standard FileMaker Pro sharing.

In a nutshell, FileMaker Server has the capability to automatically save copies of files while multiple users are sharing those files. You can save to different backup devices on any schedule you choose. This is an extremely convenient feature when you consider that using peer-to-peer sharing in the standard version of FileMaker Pro requires you to have all users disconnect before you can make backups.

Using Commercial Backup Applications

There are some good products on the market for both Macintosh and Windows machines that will take care of scheduled backups for you. Retrospect for the Macintosh and PC Backup for Windows come to mind. You can also program AppleScript to perform backups on the Macintosh. In Windows NT, you can use NT Scheduler. I'm currently using SuperDuper! for the Mac because I find its interface much more clear than Retrospect. They also have great customer support.

You can (but shouldn't) perform any of these backups while your FileMaker files are up and running, and even while they're being shared by other users (see the following Caution). That's something you can't do from within FileMaker itself unless you're using the Server version.

CAUTION Although it looks as if you can back up while FileMaker is running, it is not the recommended procedure. Even FileMaker Server pauses the database before performing its own backup. That gives it a chance to empty the cache for all users to the hard drive. Files that are backed up while they are active run the risk of corruption. The best solution is to close all files before running the backup (unless you're using FileMaker Server). It's a pain, but you'll feel a much greater pain if you can't use your files any more. Keep in mind that file corruption may not show up for quite some time after you begin using a backup. Your backup software may tell you the procedure was successful, but if the file was open at the time, don't you believe it!

When FileMaker Server performs a backup, it pauses the files and only updates the areas that have been changed since the last backup. That takes a lot less time than writing the entire set of files to disk. Then you can use a different backup utility to make a normal, complete duplicate of the backup files. It seems like one step extra, but it's a well-established method.

I highly recommend that you back up to removable media or a portable hard drive. You can back up to the so-called thumb drives, but they're slower than hard drives — for today, that is. Don't forget to remove it from the mechanism after backing up. Non-removable backup hard drives are not a good choice because they are also subject to damage from power surges and lightning. And you should have multiple backups anyway.

Problems with Tape

Over the years, I've had 10 different clients tell me they couldn't restore their data from tape backups. I suspect it's because they didn't replace the tapes in the required time. You should retire tapes after six to eight weeks of daily use or about 45 backups. Contrast that with CD-RW disks that can be rewritten 10,000 times. The problem with tape is that when it touches the heads, tiny amounts of the oxide material wear off. After many uses of an audiotape, you may begin to notice some high-frequency loss. This is not a big deal with music, but with digital data, if you lose a single zero or a one, the backup software may not be able to reconstruct your files.

You shouldn't use the same tape 45 days in a row, anyway. The suggested backup routine discussed shortly recommends that you use any given media only once every two weeks. Besides, there are plenty of removable alternatives to tape, including CD-R, CD-RW, DVD, Syquest, plug-in hard drives, and removable media like USB drives. I currently have a stack of inexpensive hard drives I swap in and out. Over the years I've wasted so much time getting everything back to normal after crashes, I've come to the conclusion that my time is worth too much to mess with slower media or compressed backups. Part of that decision has been influenced by the steady increase in hard drive space along with the steady decline of hard drive prices. I've been able to buy Seagate drives with a five-year warranty for about 16 cents per gigabyte.

CAUTION Don't count on any backup media forever. Even the durable CD only has an expected shelf life of 25 years. That is a good long time, but it's not forever, and that's as good as it gets. This means that every other media falls somewhere short of that. I've also read that the 25-year lifespan is for commercial CDs only. Some of the homemade disks are reported to be good for as little as five years! That's quite a letdown. But if you make backups regularly, there won't be much of a need to go back five years — except for that CD you made of Fleetwood Mac.

NOTE (to Windows 98 and 2000 users) (FileMaker 10 won't run on Windows 98 or 2000, but if you're upgrading and bringing files over from another machine, you might run into the glitch this note addresses.) When a FileMaker file is written to a CD-ROM and you bring it back onto a Windows 2000 machine, the file may have become "read only." That means you'll be prevented from entering data in the files. You can make the files work, but you'll have to jump through a few hoops:

1. Copy the normal FileMaker Pro file from the CD onto your hard drive.
2. Using Windows Explorer, locate the file or files you want to return to read/write status.
3. Right-click on the file(s) and choose Properties from the list.
4. In the window, uncheck the box next to Read-only.
5. Click the Apply button and then OK.

Now you can use the files in the normal way. (However, sometimes file names may have been truncated. You may need to find related files to rebuild relationships using the newly shortened file names.)

Whatever media you choose, date each backup and move it off the premises. You might try to get into the habit of taking the most recent backup home with you when you leave for the day. Don't do anything with it. Just take it home and bring it back the next day. It's also a good idea to keep a copy onsite. When there's a failure and you're not in the office, you don't want your co-workers stuck without a backup.

Another offsite backup method would be to use one of the Internet disks that are now available, such as the iDisk portion of Apple's iTools or a Dot Mac account. (To take a look at discussions about how this works, go to www.apple.com and click the Support tab. Type in iDisk or Dot Mac and click the Search button.) This method of storage provides users with a low-cost, offsite, easily accessible, backed-up hard drive. Of course, using such a system would depend on how secure you feel about the possibility of your files being intercepted while traveling across the Internet or sitting on someone else's servers. You'll also want a fast Internet connection to take advantage of this option. I found it a bit slow for my taste. But you can schedule an automatic backup in the middle of the night, so the length of time it takes won't matter to you.

Database Corruption

Quite apart from the data, the database structure itself can be damaged beyond repair. That includes the field descriptions, relationships, scripts, and layouts. After all the time you've spent creating that structure, just getting back a list of customers and invoices probably wouldn't be very comforting. Even more worrisome is that this type of corruption can creep into a file over time and not be noticed for weeks or even months. To protect yourself against that event, you should work out a system of making clones of your files.

In versions of FileMaker previous to 7, your data was often spread across multiple files. Since FMP7 and later let you create all your tables in a single file, this data corruption has the potential for even greater harmful consequences. I've heard developers tell stories about having to recreate single-table files from scratch after they had been damaged beyond repair. Imagine having to recreate a very complex multiple-table database from scratch.

Starting with FileMaker 7, files are much more resistant to crashing and corruption. But resistant is not the same as immune. The biggest problem seems to arise when people are working remotely in Manage Database and they lose their Internet connection even for a second. Hosed! (That's not the case if you're logged in through a utility like Timbuktu, Remote Desktop Connection, or PC Anywhere. Someone on the far end can close the dialog — assuming their power didn't go off. Save a copy before you start work, though.) Aside from that, just because FileMaker is stable under most circumstances doesn't mean hard drives can't go bad. And even a small hard drive failure will corrupt your files. All it takes is one little area of the magnetic media to go bad and your database will have a lurking corruption that may not show up for months. Making a clone is so easy and the consequences for failing to perform this type of backup so dire, it just doesn't make sense to avoid learning the process. It could cost you weeks or months of your life trying to rebuild what you lost by not taking one minute out of every day of the development process.

What Is a Clone?

A *clone* of a FileMaker database is an empty copy of a file that includes all structure elements of the file: the tables, fields, relationships, scripts, and layouts.

Files usually get corrupted when they're closed improperly. That happens when FileMaker crashes or you have a power outage. Oh, I know, some of you have uninterruptible power supplies. But if the computer's power cord gets knocked out of the UPS, believe me, your work *will* be interrupted. The idea is to make a clone of each file, and then make copies of those clones in which to enter data, never again opening the original clone. When you want to make changes to the structure of a file, make a copy of the clone and work in that. If it turns out later that the data file has been corrupted, you can always go back to the untouched (or "golden") clone, make another copy, and pull the data into it. Figure 23-1 shows how the process works over a series of updates to a file.

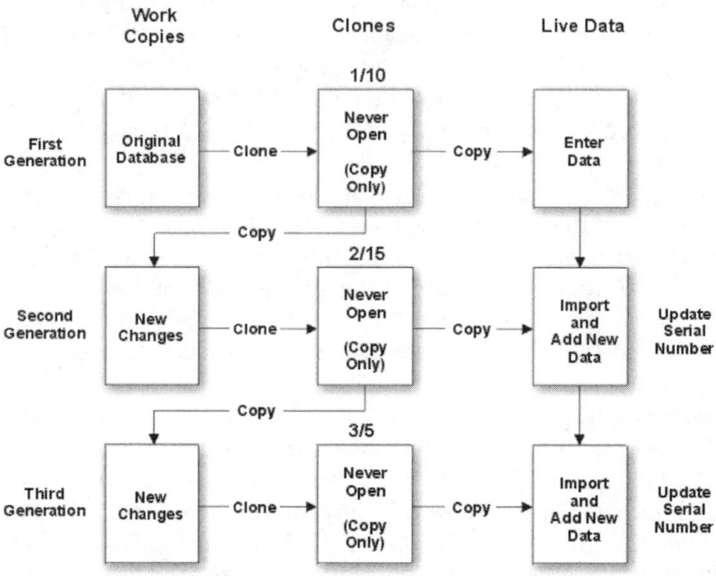

Figure 23-1
This diagram shows the recommended procedure for making clones of a file to reduce the likelihood of corruption over generations of changes to the file.

Date, label, and make backup copies of the clones of your files. This may seem like overkill, but there are more than a few horror stories of businesses nearly brought to their knees by data corruption. I won't even tell you about the terror experienced by the creators of those files. Needless to say, you don't want to be a member of that fraternity. And don't get the idea that this is just a FileMaker Pro problem. Every database on this planet experiences its share of corruption woes. When it comes to data recovery, FileMaker is among the best, but you need to help out, too.

Saving a Clone

Open your Business file. Choose File, Save a Copy As, which will bring up the window in Figure 23-2. The first time you open this window, the Type pop-up box will default to "copy of current file," and the word "Copy" appears after the name of the file you're currently in. Click and pull down to "clone (no records)." As soon as you release the mouse button, the word "Clone" will replace "Copy" at the end of the file name. Click the Save button but pay attention to where the file is being saved.

Figure 23-2
FileMaker's Create a copy window showing the pop-up list of types.

Before you open the file, make a copy of it from the Finder (Macintosh) or with Windows Explorer. Remember, you never want to open the clone itself, only a copy of it. Now open the copy of the Business clone. You'll see a big empty file. Go into Manage Database. Look familiar? If you look in Manage Scripts, you'll see the scripts you made. Keep this file handy. We'll pull some data into it later in this chapter.

An even better method is to script the process. It's similar to what we did with the 6.5 - Print One PDF script and when we looked at Save/Send Records as Excel in Chapter 19. Here's the two-step script I use:

```
Script Name: 30 - Clone This File
Set Variable [$clone; Value: Get (FileName) & " clone " & GetAsNumber
    (Get (CurrentTimeStamp))]
Save a Copy as ["$clone"; clone]
```

Every clone is guaranteed to have a unique name because of the timestamp. You can go further by naming a specific folder you want the file to land in rather than cluttering up your desktop.

Backup Routine

Aside from making clones of files whenever you add new features, you need to back up the files with the data in them. There are a number of approaches I've seen recommended over the years. The one I use seems to be a good compromise between the different methods I've seen described. I run a backup of all my files at least once a day for two weeks, using new removable media each day (which can include external hard drives). Assuming a five-day workweek, I archive the copies at the end of days five and 10. At the beginning of the third week, I reuse the media I used on the first day. I do the same until day 15 at the end of that week. Since I don't want to touch the archived copy, I bring in new blank media. I follow the same procedure of reusing media and archiving the last weekday copy. Look at Figure 23-3 for a quick overview of this technique.

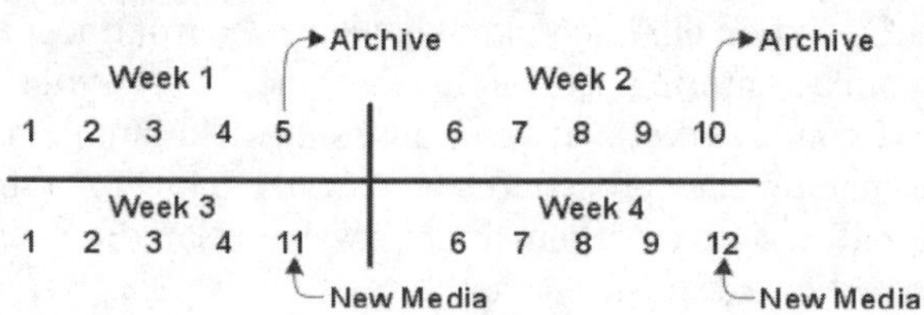

Figure 23-3
In this diagram, each number represents a backup. At the beginning of Week 3, begin to reuse the media.

After another month goes by, you can begin reusing your archived copies, but always keep at least one archive for each month. Archive more often if you're in a period of heavy development. If you insist on using tape against my advice, put a mark on the label each time you use it. After 45 uses, discard it. With any other media, put a date on it for the day it went into service. I'd start to question the reliability of media that gets to be three years old.

Maybe I'm obsessive, but when I was looking for something recently my old computer couldn't read a lot of those floppies I relied on as little as 10 years ago. The stuff just doesn't last. When I take this approach, my blood pressure stays just fine. I've had Zip disks that went bad in less than a year, and hard drives that went bad in as little time.

Whatever your method, the worst thing in the world is to set up a backup schedule and not test out the backups until the day they're needed. It could be tragic to discover that you weren't backing up "properly" after a disaster had hit. Every so often you should try to reconstruct the files from the backups to see if they work. Be warned: Some backup software has settings that overwrite the original file. Make sure you change that setting before you attempt the recovery test. And don't trust the software when it tells you the recovery is complete. Open the files and muck around a bit to see if they're really OK. Just don't get them mixed up with your current set of files.

While You Work

Depending on how much data you can live without, you may want to run a backup more than once a day. I have some customers who back up their main data files every couple of hours. When I work on files, if I've put in three or four hours, I'll make a backup. I'm not anxious to do all that work over. And let me tell you, when you're developing a set of files, it's not too hard to cause a crash while you're trying out scripts and calculations on files containing a few thousand records. Backing up only takes a few seconds. Trying to recreate your work takes much, much longer.

Other Related Measures

Another way to reduce problems is to devote one machine to serving FileMaker files. Again, use the fastest machine you can spare. On this machine, run as few other programs as possible to prevent conflicts where the other programs may compete with FileMaker Pro for memory. That includes little accessories such as screen savers. If you're afraid of screen "burn in," just turn the screen off. FileMaker should be the frontmost application, and no one should be entering data on this machine. In my experience, sharing FileMaker with mail server software causes the most problems.

Below are other maintenance procedures you should follow to protect your data. Although only a couple of them are FileMaker related, a problem in any of these areas could threaten your data.

Daily

- Restart your computer. This takes care of any RAM fragmentation problems.

Weekly

- Run virus detecting software. Be sure to get the latest updates from the web. (This is a Windows procedure. There still don't seem to be any viruses for the Mac. But stay aware of news reports, as this could change. Hackers love a challenge.)

- Run software to check the hard drive and system for errors.
- You should have an uninterruptible power supply (UPS) and test it weekly. Keeping the power line steady will go a long way in preventing crashes and data corruption.

Monthly

- Once a month, save a "compacted copy (smaller)" version of the files you use every day. The process is similar to saving a clone. You can see this option in the Type pop-up in Figure 23-2. This can take some time for larger files, since FileMaker copies the file one block at a time. In that case, you may want to perform this task overnight.
- Keep track of and install the most recent updates to FileMaker Pro. These updates include valuable bug fixes.
- Run disk optimization software.
- Defragment the hard drive once a month — but only after backing up.
- On the Macintosh, repair disk permissions.

Annually

- Completely back up and reformat the hard drive.
- Have the computer and keyboard cleaned out.

Put these events on a calendar and don't forget to copy each activity to the next year's calendar. I have a FileMaker reminder file (what else?) that I use for everything from my daily phone calls and birthdays to file and computer maintenance.

FileMaker Techniques

If you're the only user of a FileMaker file and you have the right account privileges, you can export records from within FileMaker Pro as a backup technique. Be sure to go to each table and choose Show All Records so that the current found set includes everything in all tables. Figure 23-4 shows the window that appears when you choose File, Export Records. By looking at this list, you can probably tell there are many other uses for an export besides backing up your data.

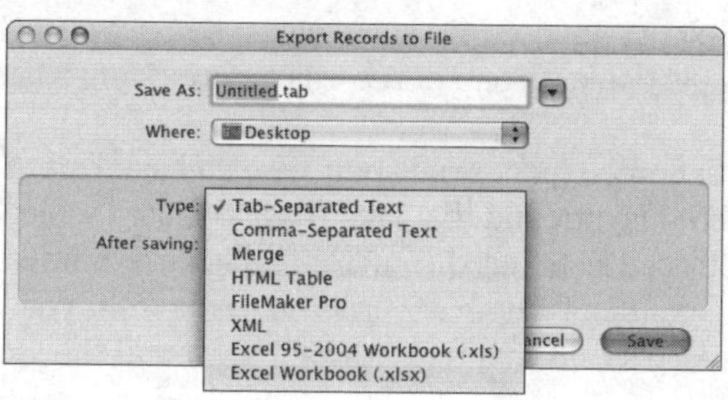

Figure 23-4
FileMaker's Export Records to File window showing the pop-up list of the various file export options.

When you click the Save button, you'll be presented with the Specify Field Order for Export window in Figure 23-5. First you select the table or the current layout from the drop-down in the upper left. Then you can select fields from the list on the left and move them to the list of fields that will be exported on the right, or just click the Move All button. Finally, you can reorder the fields to determine how they'll appear in the new file.

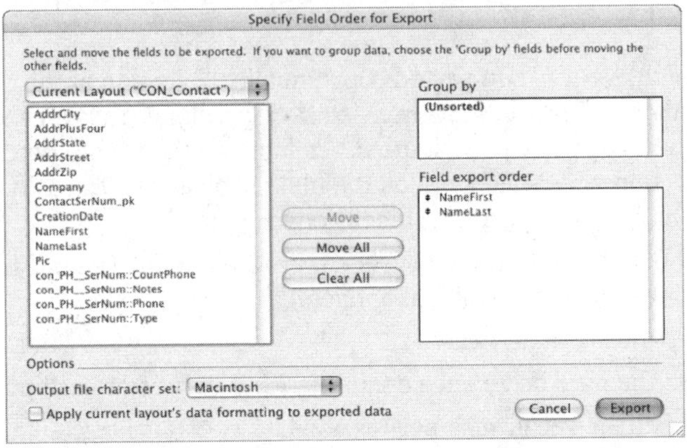

Figure 23-5
The Specify Field Order for Export window where you choose what fields will be exported in what order.

The ability to choose the current layout as your source of fields was introduced in FileMaker 8. I didn't fully appreciate this feature until I needed to export from a client's database that had over 300 fields in a single table. When you're performing an export, you're often on the layout from which you intend to export. This feature can really shorten the list of fields you need to choose from and lightens your work. After you pick from the short list, you can still return to the drop-down and select the base table (or any other table for that matter) to get access to the remaining fields if you need to. If you're used to the drop-down in earlier versions, you may be confused by the shortened list of fields because the default list is for current layout rather than current table. If you can't figure out where the rest of your fields went, go back to the drop-down and make another selection. These types of exports will not output any stored files or images. (That's not the same as files that have been imported using a reference only.) You need to export as a FileMaker file in order to maintain stored files and image data.

Once you've performed a particular export manually, you can create a script that will repeat the export for you in the future. One thing you need to be aware of is that all exports only export the current found set of records for the table selected in the Export window. Be sure to choose Show All Records or create a script to find a particular group of records before doing a backup export.

Another "gotcha" is that any export sends out the data based on the context of the currently selected layout and that layout's associated table. If you think you're exporting your contacts but the current table at the time of the export is Invoice, only the contacts who have ordered items from you will be exported! Since FMP7, every script that exports data must add the Go to

Layout [] (with the layout name filled in, of course) script step to make sure the correct data is exported.

To protect against that I would recommend a script similar to this:

```
Script Name: 31 - Export Contacts
Go to Layout ["Contact" (Contact)]
Show All Records
Export Records [No dialog; "Contact.mer"; Unicode]
```

You would repeat that, making appropriate changes that refer to every table in your file.

The following is a list of steps to use in performing an export:

1. Go to the layout with the table you want to export.
2. Find the records you want to export.
3. Choose **File, Export.**
4. Choose the file format you want to export and the final location of the file.
5. Choose the fields and the field order.
6. Click the **Save** button.
7. Create a script to do the next export automatically.

If you export all the data in all fields as tab-separated or comma-separated text with the intention of pulling the data back into FileMaker, consider this: When you import a text file, you'll have to tell FileMaker which data you want to go into which fields. Depending on how many fields you have, this can be a tedious job. It's easier to go into Manage Fields and reorder the fields by creation order before exporting the data. I've had very good luck exporting as a merge file. Merge files maintain the field names, so it's easy to match the fields back up by choosing "matching names" in the View by pop-up.

If you want to save the font style or color formatting of your text, you'll need to export as a FileMaker Pro file. All other exports drop any such formatting, although they will maintain number and time formats based on the current layout *if* you click the radio button next to "Apply current layout's data formatting to exported data" on the Specify Field Order for Export window.

When you export as a FileMaker file, FileMaker creates a new file without any of the layouts or scripts. Any calculation fields do not retain their formulas. Instead, they become the "Calculation result is" type chosen when you created the formula. If you have to pull the records back into the original file, matching field names is a lot easier. Any calculation fields in the original file will show in gray since you can't import into them.

Another interesting technique for running backups is to have a script run when your files either close or open. After you create the script, you tell it when to run in the File Options area as demonstrated in Chapter 22. To make sure it only runs on the file server, use an If statement that uses Get

One-Record Table

There is a trick used in the past by FileMaker developers in which they would create a one-record file that would hold special settings used in all the files in a solution via relationships. Included in such a file might be colors, logos, the corporate address, and advancing serial numbers (when not using FileMaker's auto-enter serial number feature).

Now that we have multiple tables in a file, storing those settings in a one-record table would seem a perfect opportunity to eliminate that external file and all those relationships. You could also create the layout, add the data you need, and delete the layout, thereby preventing anyone from accidentally changing that data. But what about exporting that data for backups and updating files?

Because you can only reliably export records from a table at the time you are on a layout associated with that table, if the layout is gone, how would you export the data? Here's how:

1. Go to the Manage Database, Relationships tab and create a relationship between any field in the Settings table (my name for the one-record table) and ContactSerNum in the Contact table. Instead of using the equal sign between the tables, use the "x" from the pop-up.

Field Name	Type	Options
Constant	Calculation	=1

2. When it comes time to export the data from the Settings table, use the following script:

```
Go to Layout ["Contact" (Contact)]
Show All Records
Omit Record
Show Omitted Only
Export Records [No dialog; "Settings.mer"; ASCII]
```

Since a script can import to a table that has no layout associated with it, you don't have to make any special arrangements there. However, you must have a layout available associated with that table if you intend to import manually.

Nice trick! But it might just be easier to use FileMaker's Accounts & Privileges settings to remove the special Settings layout from the layout list of all users except those with the highest privilege sets. The only thing to keep in mind is that any account that has the Full Access privileges can create new records. So what? Well, if you're on the Settings layout with full access and create a new record, you no longer have a one-record table. I have a calendar file I created in FMP4. It automatically opens with a password that prevents me from adding records to it and messing it up. I had to do that because more than once I added new records to the file when I pressed Command+N (Mac) accidentally when trying to hit Command+B or Command+J. With this multi-table arrangement, you'd have to come in with access to everything except the ability to create new records in that table, or make getting to that layout darn difficult. You could use a script trigger to warn yourself about multiple records in the table. Another choice would be a calculation field that only shows up in bright red text when there is more than one record in the table. I'll leave that up to you to figure out.

How far do you want to go with backups? One of my clients prints out a list of new orders and new customers at the end of every day as well as backing up to a removable hard drive. He does this because one time some data corruption got into his Invoices file, and he lost two weeks of orders. He did have backups, but each of them had been damaged and couldn't be recovered. Since his Customers file was okay, he looked at all customers at the end of the file that weren't attached to an invoice. His staff called the people and recreated their orders. He just had to wait for his repeat customers to come in to pick up their order, and do the best he could to satisfy them. It was a very uncomfortable time for the company, and he doesn't intend to go through that again.

More about Exporting

When you perform an export in FileMaker, you need to be aware of the context. The data you export depends on the table you're in and the found set in the active window — and that could lead to some surprises.

For instance, let's say you go to the Phone table and find all records with the intent of exporting all of them for backup. Now you go to the Invoice table and you see that only 10 of your 200 contact records are in the current found set. "No problem," you think. "It's the phone number I'm going to export anyway." You choose File, Export Records or run a script with the Export Records step in it and choose the Phone table. When you look at the data that you exported, you're surprised to find only the phone numbers associated with the 10 contacts. In order to get the data you really want in this case, you need to switch to a layout that is connected to the table where your data lives.

Don't get me wrong. Sometimes you may want only the phone numbers associated with a specific group of contacts. If that's what you want, stay right on the Contact layout and export the Phone table data.

In previous versions of FileMaker you were allowed only one Export script step per script. You could call any number of subscripts, each of which could have its own Export script step. Starting with FMP7 you can include unlimited exports in one script. It's just that you would probably want to make sure each Export step was preceded by a Go to Layout step and perhaps a Find All Records step. Your script might look like this:

```
Go to Layout ["CON_Contact" (Contact)]
Show All Records
Export Records [No dialog; "Contact.tab"; Macintosh]
Go to Layout ["PH_Phone" (Phone)]
Show All Records
Export Records [No dialog; "Phone.tab"; Macintosh]
```

Oh, and you can export the same data (i.e., Contact) to multiple locations and in different formats in the same script step using the Specify Output File window. For instance you could export the contacts as both a tab-separated text file (.tab) and a merge file (.mer) at the same time, sending one copy to the local hard drive and another copy to a computer on the other side of the world over the Internet! Now that's flexibility!

Apple's Time Machine

If you use a Mac running OS X v10.5 (Leopard) or later and you use Time Machine for backup, you may feel pretty comfortable about skipping the method I've been talking about. You would be wrong to do so.

The process of backups established over a number of years is described as Automatic, Redundant and Restorable, or ARR. It's a slight misnomer because, although the software can provide automatic backups, there is nothing automatic about taking that hard drive with you. Anyway, Apple's system does not provide the Redundant part of ARR. If you have a flood, fire, or theft and you lose not only your main drive but your Time Capsule backup hard drive, you're outta luck, Chuck! The software will let you target different drives on different schedules. You can probably guess that's what I would suggest.

Using Your Backups

When things go wrong, and they eventually will, you'll need to know how to use the backups you've created to get up and running again. You'll know you're in trouble if you see the dialog in Figure 23-6.

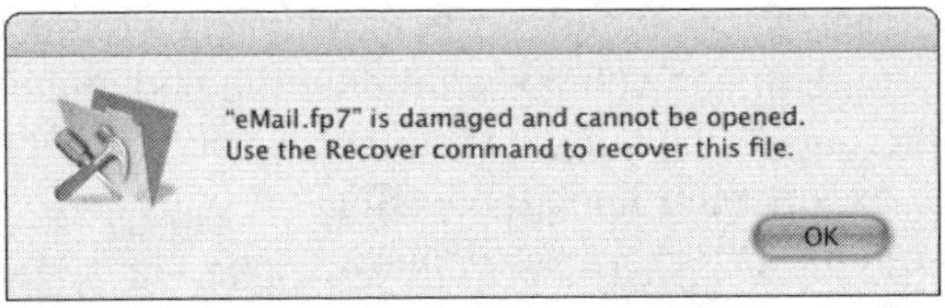

Figure 23-6
This scary dialog will appear when you try to open a file that is damaged.

Figure 23-7 shows one other message you'll see when a file is not closed properly. The message will stay onscreen while FileMaker goes through the file and corrects any errors it can find. I found it disconcerting the first few times I saw the warning, but the file usually turns out okay. It's only irritating and painful when it appears while opening large files. Keep in mind there could be unseen problems with the file after that. Fortunately, FileMaker Pro 7 and later have a different way of handling these kinds of problems. I started working with early alpha versions of FMP7 and have rarely seen any of these dialogs — even after what seemed like bad crashes. And this process has been improved with each version since then. Hurray!

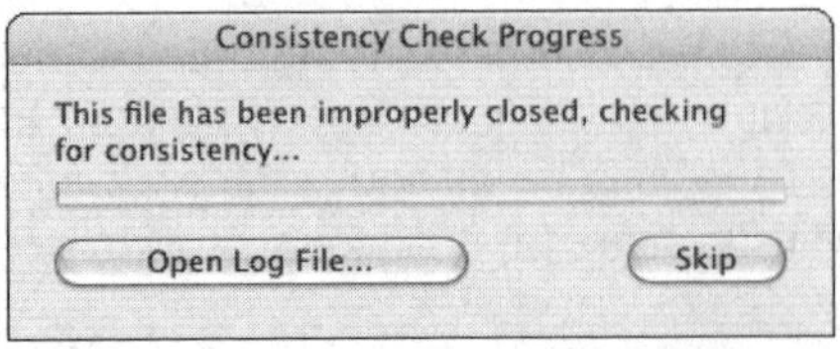

Figure 23-7
The message FileMaker displays the first time a file is opened after it has been closed improperly.

Restoring

When you get a message that the file has been damaged, what you do next depends on a couple of issues. If you haven't entered much data since the last backup, it may be more economical to go to the last backup and recreate the new data.

The other choice is to open FileMaker Pro, choose File, Recover, find the damaged file wherever it lives on your hard drive, and open it. You will be prompted to name the file (see the following Tip) as shown in Figure 23-8. By checking the box next to Use Advanced Options, you will bring up the Advanced Recover Options[10] dialog seen in Figure 23-9, where you can get very specific about what you intend to recover.

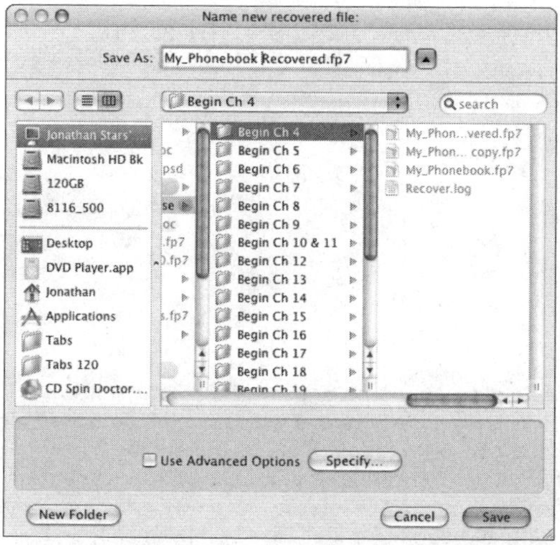

Figure 23-8
The Name new recovered file dialog.

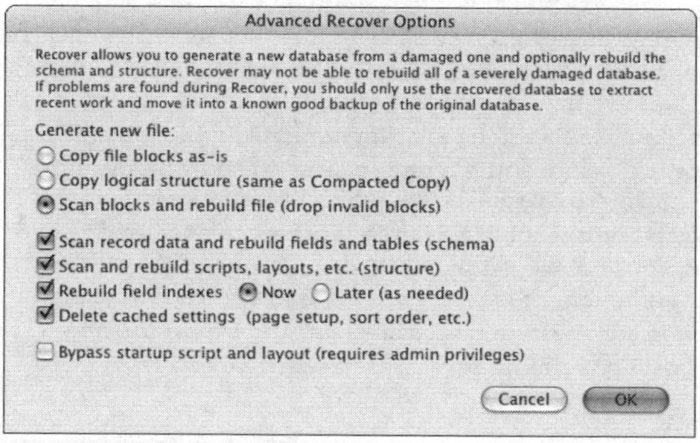

Figure 23-9
The Advanced Recover Options dialog.

These choices are a welcome change starting with FileMaker 10. Previously, if the entire file could not be recovered, you lost both data and structure since your last backup. Now you can recover each part separately. For instance, maybe the only changes you've made have to do with layouts, table occurrences, and scripts. If the file has a lot of data you can get from a backup, it may be more efficient to recover the file by selecting the second check box to Scan and rebuild scripts, layouts, etc. and import the "good" data from your recent backup. Regardless of whether you use the Save button (which uses the default recover settings) or the advanced options, FileMaker will run a process that attempts to recover your data and/or the file structure. This can take anywhere from less than a minute to several hours depending on the size of the file, the options you choose, and the speed of your computer. Don't do this on a hard drive that's not attached to your computer. If the file is on a server somewhere, go to that machine or move the file to your machine first. Don't work on the file through the network. Make sure you have enough room on your hard drive to create the new copy. It will take at least as much space as the original, and in some cases more. Again, you may just want to go to your last backup of the file. At the end of the process, you will see the dialog box shown in Figure 23-10.

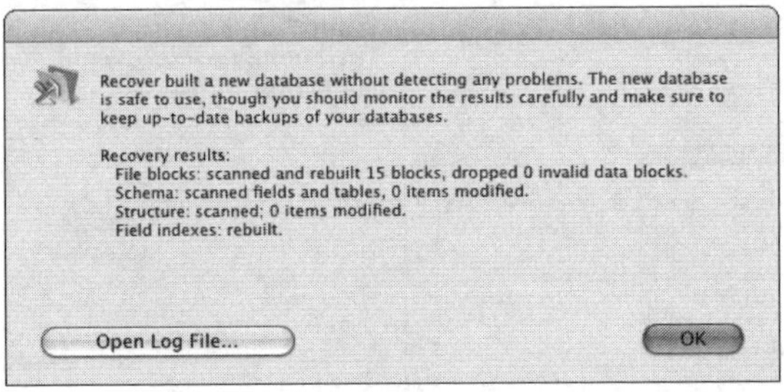

Figure 23-10 The dialog displayed at the end of file recovery.

⌘ **TIP** FileMaker's method of helping you name a recovered file has caused many problems for my clients. The program suggests you leave the damaged file with the file's original name and name the repaired file by appending the word "Recovered" to the original file name. But here's what happens: When you next open your solution, any other files that need to refer to the new file through relationships will try to connect to the old damaged file (based on its unchanged file name), and FileMaker will tell you that "this file is damaged and needs to be recovered." Kind of confusing since you're positive you just recovered the file. I've gone to clients' offices where their solution folder was littered with half a dozen files named Invoice_Recovered1.fp7, Invoice_Recovered2.fp7, etc.

Instead, I recommend that when you have a damaged file, you name it something like Business_broke.fp7 before you attempt recovery. Then when you use the Recover command and you're asked what to name the recovered file, give it the name the file has always had. That way all relationships, scripts, and field calculations will work immediately after you reopen the solution. Better yet, see if you have a fairly recent, undamaged backup you can use and skip the whole recovery process. You could still perform a recovery and just import the new records into your clean backup copy.

If any of the items in this dialog show a number greater than zero (other than the scanned and rebuilt blocks), you may have lost some of your data. In that case, you'll need to be vigilant to errors in any of your records. Sometimes the file is so severely damaged that the recovery process is unsuccessful. In that case, you have no alternative but to revert to your last saved copy.

My experience has been that more than 95 percent of the time the recovery is complete, and you can use the file as is. The problem is the other 5 percent of the time where there may still be some lurking damage to the file that could cause trouble days or even weeks later, leading to another crash. And there's no way to know after a recovery if you're in the 95 or 5 percent group. Rather than take any chances, I recommend exporting the data as a FileMaker Pro or merge file and importing it into a copy of your most recent clone. Of course you'll lose any changes you've made to the structure of the files (new tables, fields, layouts, and scripts) since saving your last clone.

One thing we've run into is when you try to compact a corrupted file, FileMaker can get stuck in an endless loop trying to fix the bad block(s) and you'll have to force quit. This is potentially destructive to other files that may be open at the time. My recommendation is to exit all files before attempting a recover or compact process.

If you get into some real problems with recovered files, you may want to look into a program called FMDiff created by Winfried Huslik. Go to www.fmdiff.com/ to find out more. The application can tell you if a file is still corrupted after it's been recovered. It can also tell you what has changed from one version to another. Many developers who work with a number of customers swear by it and consider it an indispensable tool.

One other potential problem you should be attentive to at this point: Sometimes any custom formatting of the text itself in various fields can contribute to the corruption of the file. When you export as a FileMaker Pro file, text formatting is exported whether or not you chose "Don't format output" in the Specify Field Order window. A merge file strips off any such formatting but retains the field names. That way, when you re-import the data, field mapping is a cinch. On the other hand, it might cause me some pain, since I like to format text in text fields to call attention to important details. But it's better to have unformatted data than no data at all.

Importing Data

Although our intent here is to get the data into an undamaged clone, most of what follows also applies to updating a file by bringing in a clone with new changes.

1. Open the copy of the clone.
2. Go to the layout associated with the table where you want the data to go.
3. Choose **File**, **Import**, and find the file you want to import from.
4. If it's a FileMaker file, choose the matching table from the data source file.
5. If the file is a FileMaker or merge file, choose **matching names** from the Arrange by drop-down. Otherwise, you'll have to match the data manually by moving the field names in the list on the right.

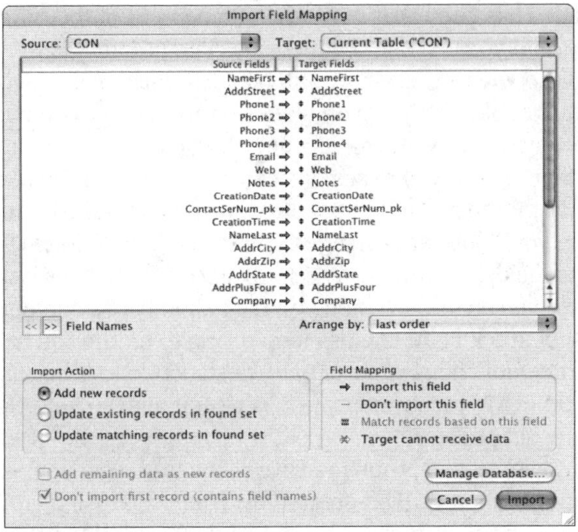

Figure 23-11
The Import Field Mapping window where you choose how the data will come into the current database.

6. Select the **Add new records** radio button and click on **Import.**
7. Make selections from the Import Options window. Most of the time you will use the settings in Figure 23-12.

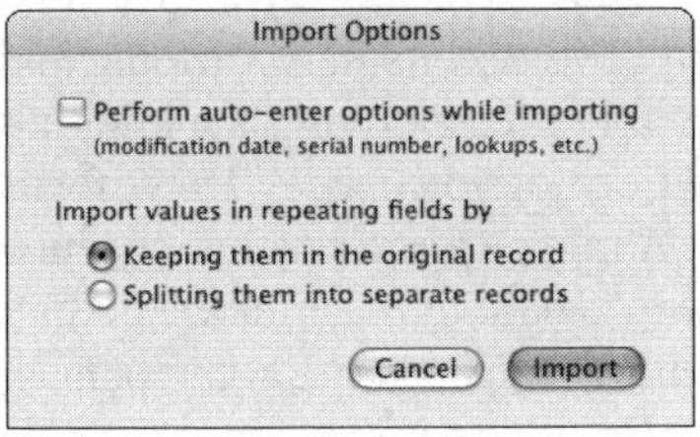

Figure 23-12
The Import Options window.

8. Update any serial numbers (see the section titled "Tying Up the Loose Ends").

To try this out on the files we've been using, open the Business file, go to each table and choose Show All Records, and close it again. This will be the data source, so imagine that it's the damaged file that's just been recovered. Now open the copy of the clone you created earlier in this chapter, and import the records from each of the tables in the Business file using the directions just listed. Before importing from a table, make sure you change to a layout that matches the table you'll be importing.

NOTE You can only import data manually into a table if you are currently on a layout associated with the table into which you want the data to go. The window only shows the name of the current table in the upper-right corner. However, the window you use when importing records using a script is slightly different in that it allows you to choose the target table from a pop-up that appears in the upper-right corner.

That means whenever you want to update a file by importing data into a clone manually, you'll need to make sure you switch layouts before each import. If you create a script that runs a routine for you, you won't need to worry about which layout you're using as long as you select the target table from the pop-up.

TIP If you perform the same import regularly, you might want to create a script that uses the Import Records script step. You can even have FileMaker match field names dynamically every time the script is run. To do that, begin your import. When the Import Field Mapping window appears, select "matching names" from the Arrange by pop-up. Finish the import and then define your script. Just make sure you never change any field names!

If you're trying to change an existing script, go back into the script and click the Import Records script step. Be sure you have the right data source. Then click the Specify button and make sure the import is what you want. A second option would be to create a new script with the Import Records step and just click the Specify button. The import will already be memorized.

If you want to make sure the field mapping remains static, choose "custom import order" as part of your import (Arrange by: custom import order), then save the script.

TIP The Import Field Mapping window has a couple of other interesting features. Just above the Import Action area there are double arrow buttons (>>) that let you preview the data before bringing it into your file. You can also click the Manage Database button (if your access privileges permit) to create fields on the fly if there is incoming data you want to place into fields other than the ones previously created.

CAUTION If you are importing from a file that is open, there's something you need to check for. Remember that you can have multiple windows of the same file open with various found sets of the same table. Your import will include the found set of the frontmost window. If this will be a regular process, you'll probably want to create a simple script in the other file with the single step Show All Records as the first step in your routine. If a file is closed, FileMaker automatically assumes you want to import all records. But a file can be opened in the background by another file and end up in the Window, Show Window menu without you knowing it. The Show All Records script step avoids any questions.

More about Importing

By using the Import script step you can import from multiple source files in multiple locations in the same script. For instance, you could import potential customers into the Client table from a tab-separated text file (.tab) on your desktop and a merge file (.mer) on a remote server in the same script. Simply select the Import Records script step in your script on the right, then click the check box next to "Specify data source" in the Script Step Options area.

When you get to the Specify File window, click the Add File button and locate the file you'll be using. You'll notice the Add File button is still active and you can indeed select other files, but it won't do any good since additional files can't be imported in a single script step. Instead, finish your work of field mapping with the file you've selected. Then create another Import script step and target your other file for import.

In previous versions of FileMaker you were allowed only one Import step per script. You could call any number of subscripts, each of which could have its own Import script step, but it was a pain. Starting with FMP7, you can include unlimited imports in one script.

Tying Up the Loose Ends

To finish off this process, you'll need to perform a few other tasks. First, close all the files and make sure they have the right names. Remember what I told you a couple of Tips ago about the naming of recovered files.

Next, you should update any serial numbers in each table of the new clone. I can't tell you how important this is. If you have related records that use the serial number as the key and forget to update, here's what happens: Let's say you're working with the Invoice table, and just before a crash you were at InvoiceNum 1025. The last time you backed up or made a clone, that file was at InvoiceNum 1000. So you recover the file and import the data into the clone. When you create your next invoice record in the clone, the serial number will be 1001, but when you look at the portal, there will already be some data in it. Now you have two invoices with the number 1001 and each of them has a different customer. This is not good!

One way to handle this is to go into Manage Fields in the Invoice table of the recovered file, and double-click the InvoiceNum field. Make sure you're on the Auto-Enter tab, and write down the number to the right of "next value." Exit Manage Fields, and close the file. Now go back into the new clone file and put the number you just wrote down into the same field definition. You need to do that for every table that has an auto-enter serial number.

An even better way to handle the serial number issue is to use the Set Next Serial Value script step. With it, you can reach into a file (for example, a recovered file) for the number in the Next Value box (Manage Database Fields tab, Auto-Enter tab) without having to enter the Manage Fields area. First you would have to create a relationship to the file. Such a script has only one step:

```
File: Business Clone
Script Name: 32 - Update Next Serial Number
Go to Layout ["INV_Invoice" (INV)]
Set Next Serial Value [INV::InvoiceNum_pk; GetNextSerialValue
   ("Business.FP7"; INV::InvoiceNum_pk)] (Fields)
```

Set Next Serial Value is one of the design functions. Make sure you include the quotes around the database name — "Business.FP7" in this case.

FileMaker will let you close the window without warning you there is a problem, and you'll get no other warning that it didn't work the way you expected.

Using Set Next Serial Value and GetNextSerialValue in a single step like this will even grab serial number values that include text. Setting the next serial number using some other function would require a more complex calculation in order to incorporate text.

With versions of FileMaker Pro prior to 5.5 (and unless you use Set Next Serial Value), you won't be able to update the serial number while the files are being shared. However, if you've just recovered the files, you should perform this operation one way or another before making the files available to the other users anyway.

My most recent favorite method of updating serial numbers bypasses the potential problems associated with file names. After the records are imported, it works like this:

```
Go to Layout ["INV_Invoice" (INV)]
Sort Records [Restore] (InvoiceNum_pk; ascending)
Go to Record/Request/Page [Last]
Set Next Serial Value [INV::InvoiceNum_pk; INV::InvoiceNum_pk) + 1]
      (Fields)
```

Prior to version 5.5, some developers had to create complex schemes whereby the serial number is created somewhere besides Manage Fields, so that changes can be made while the files are being shared. It's beyond the scope of this book to explain them, but you should know there are some other options available for handling serial numbers.

Finally, file away the damaged and recovered files just in case there are still problems and you need to get to the data in them.

Summary

In this chapter, we looked at reasons to back up your files, how to make a clone of a file, a backup routine, some methods you can use to avoid database corruption, and how to recover from a problem using your backups and clones. You also learned about some commercial backup programs and some ways to back up from within FileMaker Pro.

Q & A

Q Why not just make a clone of the most recent backup when a file turns out to be damaged instead of adding a cloning routine?

A You don't know when the corruption may have occurred to the file. You also don't know whether it was the data or the file structure that was damaged. Golden clones are much more reliable because damage happens most often when files are closed improperly.

Workshop

Go to your other files and make clones of them. Make extra copies on some removable media and take a copy offsite. Export some data using the various formats. Then import it back into the original file, and notice the problems and advantages of each format. Remember to delete the extra data afterward or you'll have duplicate records.

Part 7

Beyond FileMaker

Chapter 24

FileMaker and XML

Introduction

Starting with FileMaker Pro 6.0, FileMaker, Inc. chose to embrace Extensible Markup Language (XML) technology. FileMaker can export, import, and open files using XML. XML is also the backbone of Instant Web Publishing. But what is this XML stuff all about? What can we who use FileMaker do with it? That's exactly what I wanted to know. So I started asking around.

In this chapter I want to tell you a little about what XML is and some ways I've seen it used. Then I'll take you through an exercise to create a document using an XML export from the files we've already created.

Unfortunately, I cannot provide you with a primer on XML in this book. All I can do is tell you a bit about what it is and why it is important based on the little research I've done. Whether or not it will be important to you with regard to your use of FileMaker is up to you and the requirements of your work. If you get excited about XML, go to FileMaker.com, click the Support link, and choose Knowledge Base. Then do a search for XML. You'll find a list of items where you can learn the basics. Don't forget Google. You'll find more links than you can possibly imagine. I mean, I found over a billion! Seriously!

What Is XML?

XML is a language standard for exchanging data in agreed-upon formats. Its primary purpose is similar to HTML: "mark up" some data in a way that enables it to be parsed and displayed in a specified fashion by the end user or an agent thereof (a browser, some other parser, style sheet, or whatever). That's the textbook way of saying that when you and I send data back and forth, we're going to put it in a form we both can understand. And the form will not necessarily be FileMaker files. Groups can create their own languages for their own purposes. They just have to work within the XML standard.

XML is different from ODBC in that ODBC is sort of a pipeline for sending data between applications. XML actually translates the data into different forms. Using ODBC, you can pull data from a FileMaker file into an Excel spreadsheet. Using XML, you can export FileMaker data so that it ends up as an Excel spreadsheet. It will actually hit your desktop as a fully formatted spreadsheet complete with the little Excel icon ready for double-clickin'. In fact, FileMaker uses XML to accomplish the Save/Send Records as Excel that we looked at in Chapter 19. (Note: You must be using Microsoft Excel 2002 (XP) for Windows or later to take advantage of XML format for spreadsheets.)

Just because I use the Excel example doesn't mean it stops there. What form do you need the data in? Word? You can do that. PageMaker? You can do that, too. And much, much more. You can transform data from *any* application format that supports XML. Wow! Currently onboard are applications such as QuickBooks, Microsoft Office, Lotus Notes, MySQL, Keynote, QuarkXPress, Adobe Acrobat, FedEx package tracking, SAP, Siebel, and PeopleSoft, to name a few. And there are over 450 vocabularies for various business and government applications rapidly replacing EDI as the primary means to exchange data.

Additionally, FileMaker can connect to SQL servers using XML without the need for ODBC drivers. (Well, that's not such a big deal now that FMP can connect directly to many SQL sources. For more on that, see Chapter 26, "Working with External Data Sources.") Regardless, using XML instead of ODBC can be a great advantage since ODBC tends to be a bit slow. It can also be good news for system administrators who may find it difficult to keep up with the latest ODBC drivers for their systems. And let's not forget the licensing fees. XML may eventually do away with the licensing issue entirely.

Add in XSL

Extensible Stylesheet Language (XSL) is what tells your data how to look and act. Put XML with XSL and you get a document for a specific use. Using different style sheets, you can have the same data appear in a number of different forms. For example, you could have the data show as a list, and by simply clicking a link that calls a different style sheet, you could display the same data as a graph. There is actually a lot more to it than I'm telling you. But that pretty much covers the basics.

What Can I Use It For?

Starting with FileMaker 5.0, the people from FileMaker, Inc. have been using XML behind the scenes to provide us with the themes we choose when we create layouts. On Windows, look in FileMaker Pro 10\English Extras\Extensions\Themes. On Macintosh, look in the FileMaker Pro 10 folder, Control+click on the FileMaker Pro application icon, and choose Show Package Contents. Choose Contents\Resources\English.lproj\Themes. In Chapter 9 I talked about how you can create your own themes by opening a copy and editing an existing theme in a word processing program. XML looks a lot like HTML, but don't get too scared. Since the folks at FileMaker want us to use this tool, you can find a list of XML style sheets for all types of uses on their web site.

XML is used to make the Web Companion work some of its magic in browsers that support cascading style sheets. Before XML, if you were using a dial-up modem, you would call for some data from a web site, watch the stuff start to load into your browser, and go get a cup of coffee. If you wanted to sort the data, you went for another cup because the browser would go get the data all over again along with all the information about what the page should look like. With XML, the browser says in effect, "Hey, I've already got the data. Why don't I just use XSL and display it in a different order?" There's no need to go back across the web and get the data all over again with a description of what the page should look like. This change in method speeds up the process a great deal, and it helps to keep from clogging up the network, too. Of course, these days we want the Net to deliver movies on demand and play networked games, but let's not go into that.

Ever have a client who doesn't use FileMaker and wants you to give them data in a Word file? Ever spent a lot of time formatting data for the accounting department? I have a client who puts out a booklet with all the company's vendors listed. They retype the booklet every year in PageMaker. We began discussing how the vendor list could come out of FileMaker with the PageMaker tags already attached so the headings were 16-point bold followed by a gray underline and double spaces between vendors. The process would take a couple of minutes rather than a week. I was going to create FileMaker fields to calculate all the tags. But I can use XSL to do that for me.

I saw a demonstration where the presenter clicked various clauses of a contract to build a custom document. When he exported it, it arrived on the desktop as a fully formatted Word document ready to be attached to e-mail for client approval. Using something like that could help more than one office I know do away with folders and folders of contract templates. Using XML they'd be able to build custom contracts on the fly.

You can export records from FileMaker and build a fully formatted web page. FileMaker has been able to export data as HTML since version 5.0. But the pages were quite generic — and boring. Using XSL, you can make it look as pretty as you please. And guess what. That's exactly what we'll be doing in this chapter — in a rather rudimentary form.

How about using XML to encrypt data before sending it out and then unscramble it on the other end? You can take your data and build complex graphs to make it easier to understand. How about getting access to headlines on the web and pulling them into FileMaker, then turning them out as a custom newsletter? You can track packages from FedEx on the web. Or maybe you'd rather track your stock prices. Is this giving you any ideas?

When Chris Trytten was director of product management for FileMaker, Inc., he said that XML would allow for more focused results in search engines. How many times have you requested data in a search engine only to have 50 to 100 results? Most of them are not related at all to what you want to know. XML can do more than display the data — it can tell you what it means.

If you go to http://www.filemaker.com/products/technologies/xslt_library.html, you'll find the FileMaker XSLT library describing a whole rack of uses and the files you can use for translating data back and forth from FileMaker.

Examples: Exporting XML as HTML

The following examples are something I dreamed up and Dave Dowling built. He's an FSA member and a very clever FileMaker developer who lives in Okemos, Michigan. He'd been experimenting with XML for some time, so I asked him to help out by providing the example for the downloadable files. He has some other examples on his web site, which you'll find at www.davedowling.com. Look in the Downloads area.

What I/we will be showing you is how to take some data in the file we've been building in the chapters of this book and export it using XML and an XSL style sheet to create an HTML page you can open with a browser. Using the same export method, I'll also show you how to use the same data to build an HTML page using a style sheet that actually sits on my web site. Of course, you'll need to be online to access the second XSL document. I'm using this example because most people have a web browser on their machine, and I can't know what other applications you might have. If you haven't built the file, you can open the folder for Chapter 24 from the book's downloadable files and copy the folder onto your hard drive.

Using a Local XSL Style Sheet

If you are using your own files, there is a file you'll need from the book's downloadable files. Look for Book files\Chapter 24\contact.xsl. Drag it into the same folder as your Business file.

1. Open your Business file, go to the **CON_Contact** layout, and choose **File, Export Records.**
2. Choose **XML** from the Type pop-up, and name the file **Contacts.htm.** You decide what directory you want it to go into. In this case, I prefer the folder where you keep the Business file because it will be easier to connect the XSL style sheet. Click the **Save** button. You will see a window like Figure 24-1, but it won't be filled out yet.

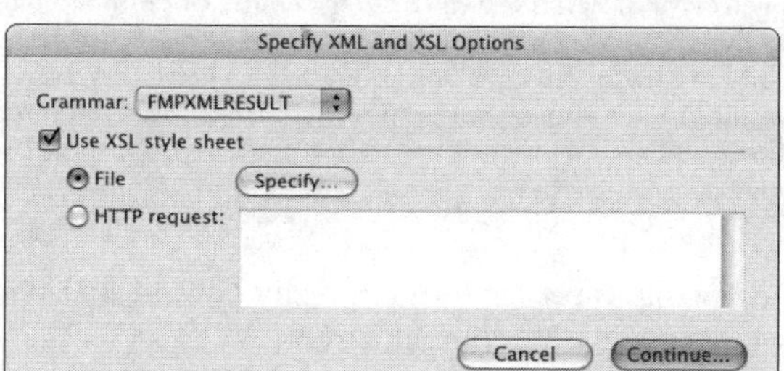

Figure 24-1
The Specify XML and XSL Options window.

3. Be sure the Grammar drop-down says FMPXMLRESULT, click the box next to "Use XSL style sheet" so a check mark appears there, then click the **File** radio button. (Notice that you could also type a web address in the HTTP request field.) You'll need to work your way through your directories until you find the contact.xsl file you got from the downloadable. When you find the file, select it and click the **Open** button. That will bring you back to the Specify XML and XSL Options window. Click **Continue**.
4. Make your field choices. I simply used NameFirst and NameLast. Then click the **Export** button.
5. You can hide or minimize FileMaker and open the Contacts.htm file with a browser to take a look at it. It's nothing fancy, but there it is! It's even got a little background color.

NOTE Once again, the field- and file-naming guidelines we discussed earlier come into play. XML cannot deal with periods, spaces, or special characters in the names of files or fields. You'll also want to avoid using numbers at the beginning of any field name.

Creating the Export XML Script

Follow the next set of directions carefully. The Specify Output File and Specify (XSL) File windows look almost identical, and it's easy to get confused when working your way through them.

1. Start a new script and call it **33 - XML test**. (This is assuming you have followed the steps in the previous section so the export is still in FileMaker's memory.)
2. Under the Records heading, double-click the **Export Records** step.
3. While the step is highlighted, click the **Specify** button next to "Specify output file." In the Specify Output File window, click the **Add File** button, choose **XML** from the Type pop-up, and name the file **Contacts2.htm**. (Be very careful not to give it a name that overwrites one of the XSL files in this folder.) You decide what directory you want it to go into. In this case, I prefer the folder where you keep the Business file because it will be easier to connect the XSL style sheet.

CAUTION Starting with FMP6, when I tried to overwrite my original file from the export window using the same file name, all buttons in the window turned gray and I had to force quit FileMaker. This problem persists into FMP10. When I used the Contacts2.htm name, I didn't have that problem. So if you use a different name you'll avoid that headache. However, the script itself will run, replacing the file each time without any problems.

4. Click the **Save** button to return to the Specify Output File window. You should now see the file path in the white box.

5. Choose **XML** from the File Type pop-up. Notice that you can choose to automatically open the file after saving. Go ahead and do that. Then click **OK** and you will see a window like Figure 24-2. (Clicking that OK button when choosing XML is the only time you'll see this window. There is no other way to get here.) Notice that in the script you not only have the option to use a web address (http request), but you can also use a calculation.

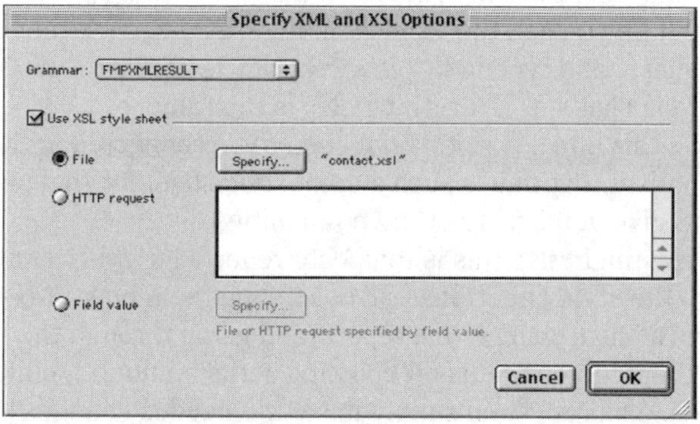

Figure 24-2
The Specify XML and XSL Options window found in the Export Records script step in Manage Scripts.

6. If there's a check in the box next to "Use XSL style sheet," click the **Specify** button. If the box is not checked, click it so a check mark appears there, then click the **File** radio button. The contact.xsl file may already appear in the File Path window, but if not, you'll need to work your way through your directories until you find the contact.xsl file you got from the downloadable file. When you find the file, select it and click the **Open** button. That will bring you back to the Specify XML and XSL Options window. Click **OK** and **OK** again.
7. Now click the **Specify** button next to "Specify export order." NameFirst and NameLast should already be in the "Field export order" box in the lower right, but if they're not, add them now. If there's anything in the "Group by" box, clear it out, then click **OK**.
8. At this point, you can choose to click the "Perform without dialog" check box. It's up to you. If you're doing this for an organization, you may want to check the box next to "Run script with full access privileges." Then click **OK**.

    Now run the script to try it out. You do need to be on a layout that uses the CON base table. It would probably be smart to change the script to make sure you're on one of those layouts before exporting the records.

One other small detail: Export Records is not a web-compatible script step.

You can place a button on one of the layouts to perform the script automatically if you like. Each time you run the script, it will overwrite the previous file. That means you can choose a different set of records manually, click the button, and look at the file.

You should be able to look at the style sheet by opening it with a text editor, although I found that opening and saving it in Word caused the file to break. A plain text editor would be a better choice, but be sure to test the file afterward.

Using a Remote XSL Style Sheet

About the only thing you'll need to do differently for this exercise is make sure you have an open line to the web and change the XSL request in the Specify XML and XSL Options window. You'll be attaching a style sheet from my web site. When you see the window in Figure 24-2, click the button next to "HTTP request" and type in http://www.DataDesignPros.com/XSL/contact8Web.xsl. That's it. Everything else is the same.

If you make this into a script, you'll need to be connected to the web each time you run it. Not that this is such a great style sheet for that purpose. I only did this to give you a taste of the possibilities.

One way you might use this is to update reports for your clients by making changes to the style sheet. Instead of sending them new FMP files each time they need a small change to a report (and going through the process of importing all their current data and updating serial numbers), build the reports as XML exports. Then simply make the needed changes to the XSL style sheet that lives on the web somewhere. Big time-saver!

My final script reads like this:

```
Script Name: 34 - XML Test Web
Beep
#1 = Yep! / 2 = No / 3 = Cancel
Show Custom Dialog ["WARNING"; "You should not perform this script
unless you are connected to the web. Are you connected?"]
If [Get (LastMessageChoice) = 2 or Get (LastMessageChoice) = 3]
   Halt Script
End If
Go to Layout [CON_Contact]
Export Records [No dialog; "Contacts.htm"; Automatically open;
"FMPXMLRESULT"; http://www.DataDesignPros.com/XSL/contact8Web.xsl;
Unicode (UTF-8)]
```

Of course the paths to your files will be different from mine — all except the path to the XSL style sheet on my web site.

Before you run the script to open the page, make sure you're still connected to the web. There are a couple of things about this page that are different from the earlier example that gathered information from the Net. You are opening an HTML page that lives on your machine, using a style sheet that lives on my web site, and displaying elements (my picture) that come from elsewhere on the web. Starting to get the idea? Cool, eh?

And Beyond...

The HTML file we just built (Contacts.htm) uses a static export. If you open the file in a text editor, you'll see the data embedded in the XML text. But XML can operate on files that are shared on a network — whether that network is an intranet or the Internet. That means you can have a file on a server, and, using XML and an XSL style sheet, you can build reports that draw from the data as it is called for. You can also have different style sheets for various ways you might want to display the same data. For a simple set of demo files and different style sheets that demonstrate this capability, go to http://www.filemaker.com/products/technologies/xslt_library.html.

Profile of a FileMaker XML Web Request

Just so you know a little bit more about what happens with FMP and XML on the web, here is how FileMaker uses XML and XSL to provide the final web page with a browser that uses cascading style sheets (Microsoft Internet Explorer, Firefox, or Apple's Safari):

1. The user fills out a form and/or clicks a button or link to make a request.
2. The browser sends the request to the server where the FMP files live.
3. The copy of FileMaker on the server sends the XML data back to the browser, but the data waits until...
4. The browser finds the required style sheet wherever it might live.
5. The browser takes the style sheet and formats the FileMaker XML data from step 3 into what will appear on the final page.

The value of this system over the old way of building a web request is that the FileMaker server is only required to send the data. Previously, the server was also required to format the data into the final web page and send the whole thing over the web channel. Using XML, the web browser on the user's machine builds the final page. That means less information needs to be sent down the pipeline to and from the server. The server can process more requests. And it means a big improvement in speed. It's even more efficient if the user then clicks a Sort button in their browser. The data and the style sheet are already on the user's machine. Only the order of the data needs to change — and very quickly at that.

Import XML

I'm not going to go into any detail regarding importing XML. If you choose File, Import Records, XML Source, you'll see the window in Figure 24-3. You can see the method is virtually the same as exporting from FMP using XML. The only difference is you'll have to map the incoming data to the proper fields in the FileMaker file.

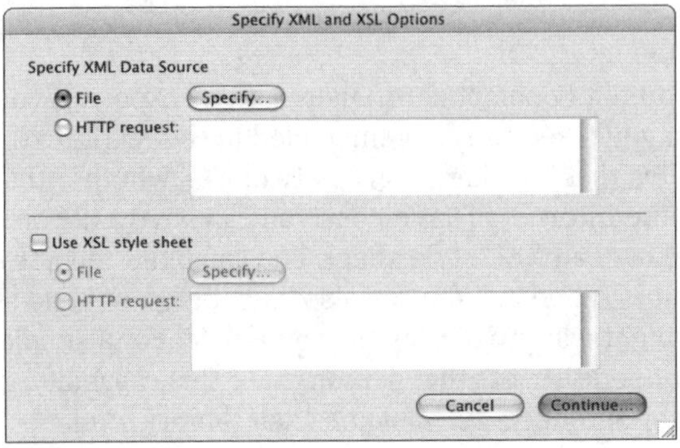

Figure 24-3
The Specify XML and XSL Options window that displays when importing and opening XML.

Open XML

Not to disappoint you, but I'm not going to go into any detail regarding opening XML either. If you choose File, Open, and select XML Source from the Show pop-up, you'll see the same window as in Figure 24-3. Again, you can see the method is virtually the same as exporting and importing from FMP using XML. You can handle it.

Summary

In this chapter I introduced you to FileMaker's Import, Export, and Open XML features. I gave you some reasons you might find XML a valuable tool and some links to pages on the FileMaker web site to get more information. Then we created a simple export example and made a script so we could run it again.

Q & A

Q How can I find out what other people are doing with XML and FileMaker?

A You can go to FileMaker XML Talk (http://filemaker2.webcrossing.com/) to join a discussion group dedicated to the exchange of XML ideas among FileMaker users.

Q Can I use XML without having to use XSL too?

A Yes. XSL just gives you more options, like sorting, different formats, etc. XML allows you to separate your data from formatting. Theoretically, XSL allows you to provide any other formatting to that data.

Workshop

Download one of the examples that interests you from http://www.filemaker.com/products/technologies/xslt_library.html and work with it. See if you can start to come up with more ways you might use XML for your company, clients, or yourself.

If you have a little XML knowledge, make some changes to a copy of the contact.xsl style sheet we used in the example in this chapter. Then run an export using that style sheet to see the results of your work.

Chapter 25

FileMaker and the Internet

Introduction

With each release, FileMaker continues to add new features to expand its power as a data source. FMP8.5 gave us the Web Viewer, which allows us to reach out to the World Wide Web and bring web pages right back into FileMaker.

Web Viewer[8.5]

The advance documentation for 8.5 touted the Web Viewer as a "major technical achievement opening a myriad of information management possibilities." I read that and with doubt in my voice said, "Oh, sure." But I have to admit, as soon as I saw it, I said, "Wow!"

NOTE Other programs like Apple Mail, Access, and Outlook (among others) use similar technologies to display such things as HTML formatted text, spreadsheets, and charts.

Quite simply, the Web Viewer (WV) layout object allows you to display anything you can open in a browser right inside your database. That might not sound too impressive until you find out that you can use fields in your database to populate fields in web sites and bring back results. Results like a MapQuest map, FedEx tracking number, Google search, dictionary definition, or Wikipedia entry — right there in FileMaker — without having to retype the data that's already in your file. Now that's a database to the *n*th power! After all, as a database, FileMaker is a repository of information. And what could be a more logical addition to a database than the entire Internet?

The Web Viewer makes FileMaker a virtual one-stop information station. The people at FileMaker, Inc. are saying that the FileMaker application is not just about storing data, it's about assembling data. By extending its reach to the web, FMP allows the user to compare and contrast data. Keep in mind that just a few years ago, the concept of downloading music and movies from the Internet was an impossible dream. Where this is going is anybody's guess. Maybe one day we'll be reading each other's minds remotely via FileMaker.

Just because the tool is called Web Viewer doesn't mean it's only for displaying web pages. You may not realize that a browser can display other types of files, too. That includes certain types of documents that reside on your own computer, a local network, and the Internet. So the Web Viewer supports all web formats from HTML to Flash, Java, SVG, and more. Getting the syntax just right to make something display can take some fussing around, but it certainly can be done — as long as the file can be displayed in a browser. And the WV has the capability to combine data from within the FMP file with little applications stored on servers on the web to build graphs.

If you leave the viewer set so users can interact with the display, they can even click links in the WV and cruise the Internet almost as if they were using a browser. I say "almost" because among other things, a browser allows you to save favorite web pages. Even though WV doesn't offer that, you can accomplish something similar using script steps. Using one of the logical functions, if you had a layout object named Picker, you might try something like GetLayoutObjectAttribute ("Picker"; "source") to get the URL. (See "Working with the Web Viewer" later in this chapter.) Save that URL in a portal with a place for notes about what the site provides and you have your own bookmark. The portal could list items tied to each specific record or show the list of all records from the portal.

Oh, and in case you hadn't guessed, you have to be connected to the Internet in order to have the Web Viewer display web pages. And remember from the discussion in Chapter 13 that for GetLayoutObjectAttribute you can choose a repetition number, a portal row number, or both.

Creating a Web Viewer

1. Open your Business file and go to the **CON_Contact** layout.
2. Because we'll be making some radical changes to all the careful work we've done, let's duplicate the layout by choosing **Layouts**, **Duplicate Layout**.
3. Immediately go to the **Layouts** menu, choose **Layout Setup**, and rename it **CON_WebViewer**. Click **OK**.
4. The Web Viewer loves screen real estate, so grab the Body tab and pull it downward so the layout is about 12 inches tall.
5. There are a number of ways to place a Web Viewer object onto your layout. In the Status toolbar, just to the left of the Field tool, is an icon that looks like a globe. The same globe icon is available in the Tool panel. You can also go to the Insert menu and choose Web Viewer. Whichever method you use, when you move your cursor onto the layout, your pointer will turn into a crosshair.
6. Somewhere in the blank space under the tab control, click and drag to create a Web Viewer roughly 6 by 6 inches.

   As soon as you let go of the mouse button you'll be presented with the Web Viewer Setup window as shown in Figure 25-1. Google Maps (US) is the default web site. Notice there's already a calculation in the Web Address box in the lower part of the window. That calculation will change as we select fields from our database to fill in the boxes along the right side. But before we do anything else, click on some of the other web sites in the list. Notice that the calculation in the Web Address box changes, as does the set of fields on the right side of the window. Clearly a lot of thought has gone into this tool. At the top of the list is Custom Web Address. When you click it, the Web Address box at the bottom still holds what was in it previously. You can put your own site in there if you like.

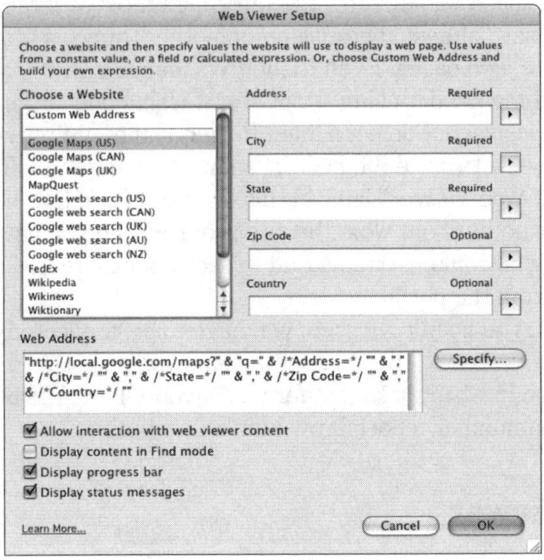

Figure 25-1
The Web Viewer Setup window.

7. For now, click back on **Google Maps (US)**.
8. Click on the arrow to the right of the Address field. Notice that you can specify a field or a calculation. Lots of power here.
9. For now, choose **Specify Field**. Make sure you're viewing fields from the **CON** table, select **AddrStreet**, and click **OK**.

   Look in the Web Address box and notice that the calculation now includes CON::AddrStreet.
10. Do the same for the **City** and **State** fields (CON::AddrCity and CON:AddrState).

    Notice that there is a Specify button to the right of the Web Address box. You could certainly use that and add the elements manually. But selecting fields from the drop-down list sure seems a lot easier. Before we leave here, notice the four check boxes in the lower-left corner. You can set the viewer so that users can't click links in it once a web page displays. They can still get results in the viewer by making selections from fields on the layout. In our current example, that would be the address fields. If you were to build a viewer based on Wikipedia or Wiktionary and prevent users from interacting with WV, they would only be able to view the entry that came up based on the word they typed into a field you provide for them on the layout. It keeps people from wasting away the workday cruising the Internet. (Can you say parental control?) The next option is to display content in Find mode. You may want to activate this so the WV will display data you would like to see while performing a find in the file. The other two check boxes give you features a little more like a web browser. When you're in Browse mode and a page is loading, you can see how the download is progressing and you can see the URL and any other messages in the lower quarter inch of the Web Viewer. The text in the status message area is subject to conditional formatting, which was discussed in Chapter 17. I'm not sure how that would be particularly helpful since it's only onscreen while the page is loading and then disappears.

11. Go ahead and click **OK** to finish out this WV, then go to Browse mode to take a look.

In my case, I'm looking at a fictitious address, so it asks if I meant an address that's something like the fake one I have in the file. Click through a few records and notice how the viewer changes the map. Did you say "Wow!" yet?

Why not create a new record with your own address? In Figure 25-2 you can see what my layout looks like in Browse mode. If you're from another

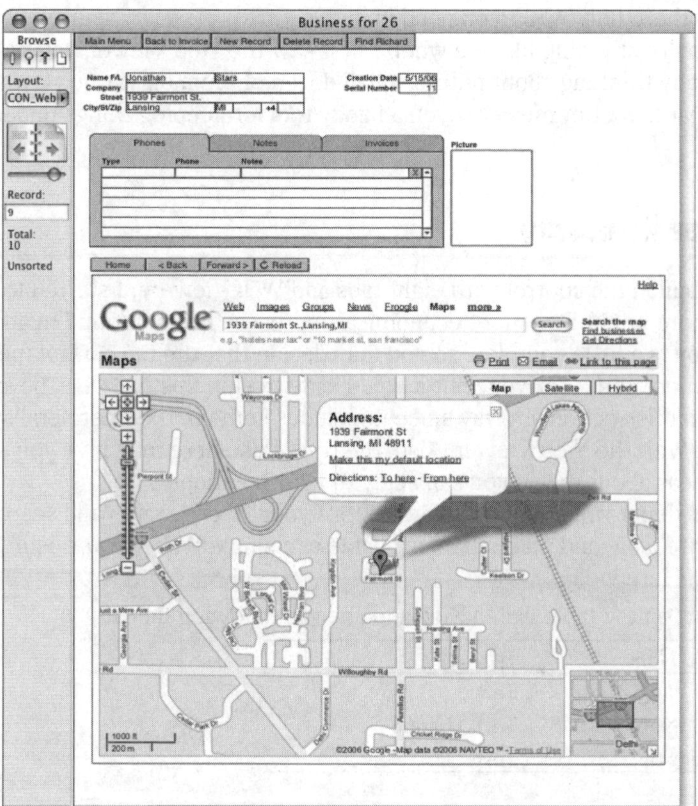

Figure 25-2
The Web Viewer added to the layout displaying the current address in Google Maps.

country, use the address of FileMaker, Inc.: 5201 Patrick Henry Drive, Santa Clara, CA. My WV displays a map that's a little cramped, so you can see why I say it loves screen real estate, you know, like a browser. If you want, you can go back to Layout mode and make the WV bigger. By the way, have you ever noticed the Satellite button on the Google Maps page? If not, try it out. Amazing! You also may not know that you can click on the map and drag it around so you can see areas adjacent to the address you selected. There are quite a few other interesting tools in Google Maps. It's worth a look.

The web links at the top of the WV are also active. Click the News link. All the links are active on the News page as well. Now go back to the map. Uh, oh… Umm, there doesn't seem to be a way to do that. You can click to another record in your file and click back to the current record, but that seems a little awkward. That's why there are also some script steps you can attach to buttons to bring you back to where you started. We'll add some Back and Ahead buttons in a little bit. As I said before, it's not quite a browser, but we've only scratched the surface.

You will probably want to consider the fact that the WV will update the map every time you click through your records. That could slow down your other work, especially if you only need to refer to the WV occasionally. It might make sense to put your WV in a tab control and keep it from being the primary tab. You could also put it on a separate layout and provide a button to get you there only when you need it.

If you're anything like me when I first saw the Web Viewer, you're probably already thinking about putting a half dozen of them on various layouts. Whoa, pardner! Let me show you a handy tool for keeping things under control.

Web Viewer Economy

After I built a tab control with eight tabs and Web Viewers, I started to wonder if there might be a more economical approach. The solution I'm about to show you is a little complex, so you may decide that the tab control method makes more sense for you. But if you decide to skip this exercise, be sure you read this section anyway since it includes some of the finer details of how to work with the Web Viewer. Also, the trick I use here may give you some other ideas about magic you can apply to your solutions.

This demo will show you how to store your favorite sites and searches in a separate table and make them available in a single Web Viewer using radio buttons. Here we go!

1. Start a new table called **Site** and add the following fields:

Field Name	*Type*
Site	Text
ShortName	Text, Unique
Extension	Text

2. Before leaving the Fields tab, switch to the **Contact** table, add a text field, and call it **zi_WebAddress_gt**.
3. Click the **Options** button, choose the **Storage** tab, and check the box to make it a global field. Click **OK**.
4. Add one more text field called **zi_SearchTerm_gt** and make it global as well.
5. Go to the relationships graph. Using the anchor-buoy method, move the new TO over to the left column and rename it **SIT**. You can add a copy to the Legend area.
6. Add yet another copy of the Site TO and call it **con_SIT__ShortName**. Connect it to the CON table occurrence using **zi_WebAddress_gt** and **ShortName**.
7. Tidy up the relationships graph and click back to the **Fields** tab.
8. Make sure you're in the **Contact** table and add a field called **SiteCalc**. Make it a calculation field and click **Create**. At the top of the dialog, make sure **CON** shows in the drop-down next to "Evaluate this calculation from the context of." Use this calculation:

```
con_SIT__ShortName::Site & Evaluate(con_SIT__ShortName::Extension)
```

9. Be sure to select **Text** from the "Calculation result is" drop-down in the lower-left corner. Click **OK** and **OK** again to finish.

Layout Work

Now let's set up the layout.

1. Go to Layout mode and double-click the Web Viewer object to open the Web Viewer Setup dialog. Click on **Custom Web Address** at the top of the list and click the **Specify** button in the lower right. Be sure that **CON** is selected in the drop-down in the upper left, then double-click **SiteCalc** from the field list. It should replace the original Google calculation in the box. Click **OK** and **OK** again.
2. Go to the **File** menu and choose **Define**, **Value Lists**. Start a new value list and name it **Sites**.
3. Click the radio button next to **Use values from field**. Click the drop-down underneath "Use values from first field" and choose **SIT**. Click on **ShortName** in the field list and click **OK** three times to bring you back to either Browse or Layout mode.
4. Go to Layout mode and add the new **zi_WebAddress_gt** and **zi_SearchTerm_gt** fields to a convenient place on the layout near (but not overlapping) the Web Viewer.
5. Resize the WebAddress field so it's about 2 inches by 2 inches.
6. While it's still selected, go to the **Format** menu and choose **Field/Control**, **Setup**. Click the drop-down next to "Display as" and choose **Radio Button Set**.

7. Click the drop-down next to "Display values from," choose **Sites**, and click **OK**.

Now we need to add a site or two in order to populate our value list.

1. Go to the **SIT** layout in Layout mode. Go to the **Layouts** menu, choose **Layout Setup**, and choose the **Views** tab.
2. Uncheck the Form View and List View boxes and click **OK**.

If you've downloaded the companion files from the publisher's web site (www.wordware.com/files/fmpro10), you'll find a file in the Chapter 25 folder called JSLinks.mer, which we'll import. That file has a mix of examples of what you can do with this method, some of them fairly complex. So if you haven't downloaded it, I recommend that you do. Directions for importing the data are in the next section. Otherwise, you can just enter one or two of your favorite sites in the Site field.

You'll also need to enter a short name for the site. For example, the site http://www.amazon.com/ might have the short name Amazon.

Importing Some Data

1. To import the file, switch to the **SIT** layout and choose **File**, **Import Records**, **File**.
2. Set the Open File window to show **All Available files**, find the **JSLinks.mer** file wherever you downloaded it, and click the **Open** button.
3. In the Import Field Mapping window, go to the "Arrange by" drop-down and choose **matching names**. (When you created your fields, you used exactly the same names I suggested, didn't you?)
4. Click the **Import** button. When the Import Summary dialog appears, click **OK** to dismiss it.
5. You may want to adjust your column widths so you can see the details better.

Working with the Radio Buttons

Now that you have some data, switch back to the CON_WebViewer layout and try out the radio buttons. If you're working with Google Maps, you'll want an address in the record you're viewing. If you're using either of the Wiki items, you'll need to put a word in the Search Term field.

Of course the weather link likely won't be right for where you live. The basic link is pretty much set up for the United States. You can enter your own city and state right on the page that comes up for Lansing, Michigan. Then examine the link that it creates to figure out how to phrase the data in the Extension field back on the SIT layout to return your area. Be especially attentive to the fact that there are quotes in that field.

I couldn't make the Web PDF item work with FMP8.5. The Help file says you may need some additional software. What that means is that you'll need the PDF viewer plug-in for your default browser. Many web sites that offer PDF files also provide you with a link to install the plug-in for your browser. You could go to www.adobe.com to see if you can find what you need there. I found out that on my OS X machine using 8.5, the WV wouldn't display PDF files if Acrobat 7 is installed. That appears to have been solved because the PDF file now displays in the viewer in FMP10 even though I still have Acrobat on my machine.

Look at how the extension for the link to Google Maps is constructed. In order to include both fields and the commas that need to appear between them, you have to jump through some hoops. Kinda makes you appreciate how nicely the Google preset in the WV is set up. But if you want this to be a more flexible WV that can do it all, you need to set it up manually this way.

Take a look at the JS Web Pic example. All it does is display a picture from my site. It's interesting that you can display a file that is really meant to appear embedded in a web page. Maybe this will be useful to you if you want something to display quickly without the rest of the web page it's meant for. Possible uses would be for PDFs and QuickTime movies. You'll need the appropriate plug-ins installed in your default browser in order to see them in the WV. Once you see the file in the WV, you can Control+click (Mac) or right-click (Windows) to open it in a browser, download it, or copy it to the clipboard — the same as if it were displayed within a web page.

Working with the Web Viewer

Getting the URL

Once you start constructing your own searches, you'll want to display the URLs of the pages you go to. That way you can copy and paste them and tweak them until you get the details just right. In order to make the default WV choices easier to work with, there are some fancy calculations that take place behind the scenes. Since the WV sometimes adds to the string you provide for it, getting the syntax just right to work the same as the defaults when using the radio button version can be a bit fussy. For example, the WV automatically takes care of spaces in searches by entering the "%20" characters you may have noticed in many URLs. If you examine the URL generated for Google maps, you'll see these characters are added into the street item. In order to get easy access to the URL, we need to add a field. But before we do, we'll need to name our Web Viewer.

1. Go to Layout mode and click on the Web Viewer object.
2. If the Object Info palette doesn't show, bring it up by choosing **View, Object Info**.

3. In the Object Name box, type **Picker** as shown in Figure 25-3.
4. Go to **Define Database**, open the **Fields** tab, and choose the **Contact** table from the drop-down.
5. Add a calculation field called **URL** with the following definition. It uses a logical function. (Be sure to type the quotes.)

```
GetLayoutObjectAttribute ("Picker"; "source")
```

6. Make the calculation result **Text** and click the **Storage Options** button.
7. Check the box next to **Do not store calculation results**.
8. Click **OK** three times to bring you back to Layout mode.
9. Add the field to the layout and open it up enough to view a few lines.
10. As you click the radio buttons, you should see the URL change. Go to the Lansing Weather item. You'll see a box at the top right where you can enter a city and two-character state abbreviation. (You may need to scroll to see it.) Type in **Santa Clara, CA** and click the **Go** button. When I did that, I could see the weather, but the URL didn't update until I clicked into the field.
11. Copy the URL and switch to the **SIT** layout.
12. Duplicate the Lansing Weather item and change the short name to **Santa Clara**.
13. Now paste the URL from your clipboard into the URL field and clear the Extension field.

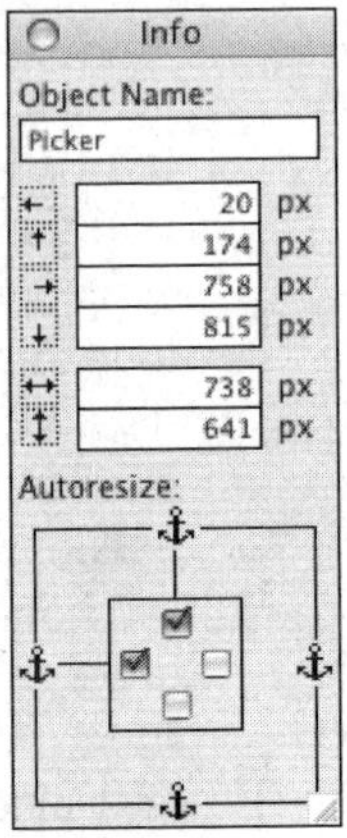

Figure 25-3
The Object Info palette showing the name, size, position, and Autoresize settings of the Picker Web Viewer object.

You could actually split the URL between the URL and the Extension fields at the question mark. (If you do that, don't forget to put quotes around the text in the Extension field.) But it's unnecessary to split the URL. Apparently there are other parts of the initial Lansing and Santa Clara URLs that are different enough from each other that you can't just add a city and state.

So you can see why I say figuring out exactly how to phrase your custom pages can be a bit fussy — and why having the URL right there on the page can be a great help. You might also get some use out of having the SiteCalc field on the layout. As you click links within the WV, the basic SiteCalc will remain constant, but the URL field will reflect the current location as long as you click in it.

There is also a text function called GetAsURLEncoded. You could use it to create a calculation either in a field or a script to automatically add the extra characters needed to turn a text string into the string the URL box in a browser expects to see. For example, when you send an address to Google Maps, the WV takes the address 5201 Patrick Henry Drive and converts it to

5201%20Patrick%20Henry%20Drive. You could put that address in a field and use the GetAsURLEncoded function to add the string for you. It's probably not a big deal in our case because our URL field provides that for us. You can see how the text gets converted by comparing what's in the SiteCalc field against what's in the URL field. But if you want to use GetAsURLEncoded for some other purpose, you now know what it's for.

Mini Web Viewer

As I said before, the WV loves screen real estate. But using cell phone web page technology, you can bring up web sites displayed the way they would on a cell phone and use less space on the monitor. To get Google to display in a smaller window, use http://www.google.com/xhtml. Many people are using their cell phones this way; all you have to do is go to the more popular sites and look around to find information about how to view their pages on a cell phone. Use that link in your WV and you're ready to harvest data even on the most economical screen. I would have to say that finding the specific link can be frustrating. Some sites tell you that you can use your mobile phone but don't explain what link to log in with. I guess I'll leave that up to you.

Automatically Filling Out Forms — Not

When you look at how the Google Maps preset works, you might get the idea that you can use it to fill in all kinds of forms on the web using information from your database fields. Sorry to burst your bubble — and mine. When the WV makes a request to a web site, all it does is build a URL string. Even if a web site is set up to receive data in that string, it most likely won't do more than a simple query. But I can safely say if a site is set to fill a form completely with the URL, you will be able to use it for that purpose.

That being said, developers are creating sophisticated solutions that use fairly complex URL strings to build charts in the Web Viewer using data from a file. You can find out more on the FileMaker web site. In one of the example files I saw during testing before 8.5 was released, there was a charting example that didn't make it into the final file. Even without the charts, the Web Viewer Example.fp7 is worth taking a look at. You can find it in the Chapter 25 folder of the downloadable files. Now look at the bar chart example in Figure 25-4. There should be a working example at http://www.filemaker.com/products/fmp/wvg/details_dynamic_charts.html. The people at FileMaker also have a Web Viewer gallery with many useful examples at http://www.filemaker.com/products/fmp/wvg/.

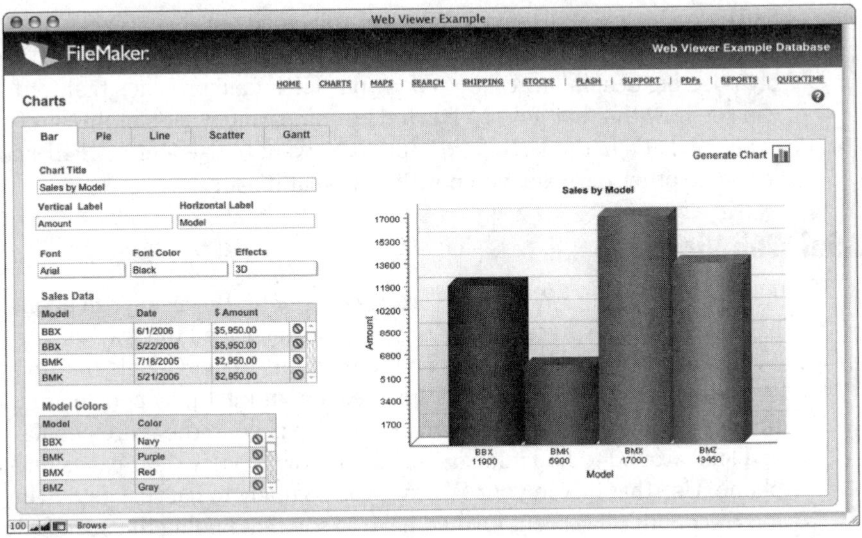

Figure 25-4
The Web Viewer showing a bar chart.

As an example, the WV can use data in your database and a tool on a web site to draw a graph. If you read Chapter 24, "FileMaker and XML," and did the exercise in the "Using a Remote XSL Style Sheet" section where you used your own data and grabbed the format from my web site, the idea is similar. This can be a great tool to serve multiple clients. You can make up a tool that's easy to update in one place — your web site. That way, instead of sending updates to every client, you simply put the update on your site and it's automatically available to all users without the need to notify them or require them to download anything.

Which Way Did He Go?

In order to get directions in the Google Maps item, I needed to make the WV wider and type the second address. But there is a better way. You can make the WV use two different addresses and display the directions without all the typing. Take a look at the Web Viewer example file. Click the MAPS link/button and go to the Directions tab. Wouldn't this be a handy tool for companies that send out drivers on a different route every day?

Back and Ahead Buttons

Since the Web Viewer isn't exactly a browser, we could sure use some tools to make it act more like a browser. Fortunately, FileMaker provides us with a script step that can give us some of that functionality. Since the Set Web Viewer script step has multiple options, and since you only need one step to perform most of the functions you would want, you don't even need to create a script.

1. Instead, go to Layout mode.
2. Use the Button tool and add a button about a quarter inch tall and an inch wide.
3. When the Button Setup window appears, scroll to the bottom and click the **Set Web Viewer** step from the Miscellaneous steps.
4. Now click the **Specify** button and enter **Picker** in the Object Name field.
5. Choose **Go Back** from the Action drop-down and click **OK** twice.
6. The cursor should be blinking in the button, so type **< Back** and click somewhere on the background to deselect the button and set the text.
7. Now duplicate the button and double-click it to open the Button Setup window.
8. Click the **Specify** button, change the Action drop-down to **Go Forward**, and click **OK** twice.
9. Change the text on the button to **Forward >** and click off the button to set it.

By now you've probably noticed the other choices from the drop-down, so create two more buttons for Reload and Reset. The Go to URL option will only work if you want to choose a particular alternative web address. Even if you clear the Specify Calculation window, it won't present you with a window that allows you or your other users to enter a URL directly. But can you think of another way you would be able to enter a web address manually? (Hint: You need another SIT record. Then you could use the Search Term field somehow. Make sure whatever you place there begins with "http://www." if it's a web page. The WV isn't quite as forgiving as a regular browser when it comes to filling in the beginning of the URL for you.)

Try out the buttons. I found that the Back button didn't always take me on a step-by-step trip back through the pages where I'd been. Reset is sort of like the Home button. In fact, I relabeled the Reset button so it reads Home. It goes back to the place your WV considers the starting place. In our case, that would be the currently selected Web Address radio button. You may have already noticed that the Back button won't go back beyond your last selection on the radio button panel. With our radio buttons, we basically provide a method that resets the Home. That's quite a bit more flexible than a regular browser.

Screen Scraping

When I started investigating the WV, I came across a term I'd never heard before — "screen scraping." I'll bet that you've occasionally highlighted and copied text from web pages. But there are some pretty fancy tricks programmers are using to grab specific data from sites, sometimes without even viewing the whole page. They get the data they want from the HTML code that's used to determine what the page will look like in the browser. Have you ever been looking at a web page and gone to the View menu and selected

View Source? You get a lot of text that may look like junk to you. Most of it is just a bunch of code that describes how the page should look, and much of the time the data is embedded in that jumble. It's possible to use calculations to parse out the specific data you want. I'm not going to teach that to you since it's a fairly large topic. But it could be helpful for you to know the possibility is there. And beyond that, there are developers who are using XML style sheets parked on servers to only grab specific parts of the data rather then return the entire HTML so the parsing job is a lot easier. So much to learn! When is there time for TiVo?

Even though I don't show you the parsing process, I can still show you how to do screen scraping.

1. Create a field in the Contact table called **HTML.**
2. Add it to the CON_WebViewer layout and open it up so it's about 2 inches wide by 4 inches tall.
3. Add a button with one script step:

   ```
   Set Field [CON::HTML; GetLayoutObjectAttribute ("Picker"; "content")]
   ```

4. Now go to one of the web pages from your radio button choices, click the button, and look at the text that appears in the HTML field. Switch to another page and click the button again.

If grabbing the HTML content of every web page is important to you, you could make the HTML field a calculation field so it filled in automatically rather than requiring you to click a button. But remember it takes time to display both the web page in the WV and the HTML in the field. Consider your connection speed and your users — and what might happen if every user on your network were pulling that data down every time they switched records in their files. You could have a traffic jam! Or you could park your WV in a tab control.

Along the same line, there's a little something you need to take into account if you want to try script screen scraping. The web page needs to be loaded in the viewer before the data from the page will be available. It can take anywhere from a couple of seconds to a minute for a page to get loaded — if the server is available at all. There is no script step to test that the viewer is loaded. So it may be more logical to provide users with a button to grab the data after the page is obviously loaded.

One other note about screen scraping: If you choose the JS Web Pic, there is no HTML web content. Of course not. It's a picture, not a web page. The same would be true with a PDF file and some of the other uses you might make of the WV. And some pages use cascading style sheets that pull data by pointing at it rather than including it in the source code. No big deal. It's just that if there is HTML to get, you'll have access to it.

Saving the URL

Now, how about a method for saving your favorites? Try a script like this:

```
Script Name: Save URL as Favorite
Set Variable [$URL; Value:CON::URL]
Go to Layout ["SIT" (SIT)]
New Record/Request
Set Field [SIT::Site; $URL]
Go to Field [SIT::ShortName]
```

That last step puts the cursor in the ShortName field ready for you to give the URL a meaningful name. If you plan to do this a lot, you might want to consider how large the radio button field will need to be to accommodate all the sites. Instead of radio buttons, you could use a drop-down list and save a considerable amount of screen space. You also might want to add a Category field to the Site table to keep your list better organized.

The Example File

Be sure you take a look at the Web Viewer Example.fp7 downloadable file I mentioned earlier. It's chock full of examples of how to build reports, get directions, display a Flash or QuickTime video (and maybe some charts) — just about every option that developers had come up with by the time this book went to print. Certainly some examples are more complicated than others.

Take a look at the Reports tab. It's done with a script. Go into Manage Scripts and scroll to the bottom. The first script under the Reports heading is Generate Matrix Report. Take a look at it. Whoa! That's not too difficult, is it? What it does is build an HTML file based on the data in the Sales Data tab and drops it onto your hard drive. Then it displays the file in the WV. Back in Browse mode, over on the right you have to click the Generate Report button to see the report. If you click the Report Builder tab, you can make choices from the drop-down lists to determine what this report will look like. It uses the data in the portal on the Report Data tab. Again, you have to click the Generate Report button. The script behind this one is Generate Custom Report. In some cases, you might want to put a copy of the field that fuels the example WV somewhere on the layout so you can see how the calculations are built. However it's being done, it's all pretty amazing if you ask me.

The Web Viewer and Other Applications

The WV can also be used to work with other applications — both commercial and custom. Some applications listed in the literature are QuarkXPress, QuickBooks Online (for Windows only), Power School, Microsoft SharePoint Services, and Microsoft Office, to name a few. Some of them will operate on

Windows only. The basic rule is, if you can drive the application with a web browser, you can make it work in the Web Viewer.

An example is Power School. You can use student IDs in a FileMaker file to display the student data stored in Power School online. You would build a URL the same way you do with Google to get a map.

The ability of any other application to work with the WV is dependent on how that app can be driven by a URL.

Cleaning Up

When you're done, if you're happy with your new layout, you might consider copying the layout elements to your main Contact layout. After all, you were experimenting on a copy of the layout, weren't you?

Rules

Even though we've looked at quite a few examples and created our own URL links, here's a list of rules that might save you some time when working with the WV:

- Don't stack any layout objects within the confines of a WV. They'll just disappear in Browse mode.
- You can put a WV into a tab control. (In fact, if you think it's valuable enough, you might consider combining the three main functions of the Business tab control (Phones, Notes, and Invoices) into one tab, eliminating one tab, and putting the WV on the remaining tab.)
- WVs won't fill in until they're visible on the computer screen.
- The Web Viewer cannot be formatted like a graphic, but you can make it any size you choose. You can also format it with the Autoresize feature discussed in Chapter 17.
- The Web Viewer uses Internet Explorer on Windows and a program called the WebKit for Safari on the Mac. If you (or your users) don't have one of those browsers installed, your WV won't work.
- Because the WV actually operates off the approved browser, when you click a link that requires the passing of cookies, the cookies will be sent to the browser, even if it's closed. If you go to the browser and clear cookies, you'll be logged out of the site in the WV.
- Certain versions of Flash and Adobe plug-ins may be required to be installed in the browser in order to make some WV functions work.
- Once you are displaying a page in the WV, if you click on a link that includes instructions to open in a new browser window, the new window will be displayed in a browser, not a new window in FileMaker. The URL may not provide any clue to the new window instruction, so you can't

necessarily look there. For instance, http://www.cnn.com will pop open a browser when called from FileMaker.

- The settings in your browser have everything to do with how the WV works. If you set the browser to open a new window every time you click a link, you'll keep jumping out of FileMaker and into your browser. Keep in mind that your users can have their own browser settings, which may override your intent for the WV. Be prepared to provide them with instructions or to answer questions about how to get the best results.
- Since a WV is not the same as a container field, you can watch a movie or play music from it at the same time you enter data. (A container field needs to be selected in order to view a movie or play music from it.)
- Web Viewers don't work in portals.
- The WV is available to people who access your solution via Instant Web Publishing. You can even view other IWP solutions inside the WV and display them in your files online.
- The Back (Go Back) and Ahead (Go Forward) script steps are not supported in IWP.

Suggested Uses

Because this is a fairly new technology, I expect to see amazing uses continue to emerge as developers get their teeth into this great tool. FileMaker provides a link on their web site at http://www.filemaker.com/products/fmp/wvg/, where wvg stands for webviewer gallery.

Here are a few other ideas to get your imagination going:

- Fixed links — Store a URL in a WV that applies to that specific record. For example, a purchasing agent wants access to a page for the specific product showing price and specs.
- Get a list of phone numbers based on names and addresses.
- How about checking webcams for building security?
- Create a pointer to your own web site with updates to your solutions or a webchat.
- Combine information from multiple web sites onto one page of your database. For example, you might want your favorite news site, weather page, and Apple's iTunes all inside your database.
- Provide training videos in your solution.
- Process credit card payments by bringing the payment web site inside of FileMaker.
- Make the opening page of a solution display news events from the company web site.
- Display different web sites based on selections users make for reservations or to compare prices.

- Display files on your network. This is similar to the JS Web Pic example, but the syntax is file:///Volumes/ followed by the complete path and file name. I was able to make this work with images and a QuickTime movie but not with a Word document. For more about the limits of this use, see the Q & A below.

Data URLs[9]

FMP9 introduced the ability to create data URLs in the Web Viewer. This feature lets you put the text from a page of HTML, a Cascading Style Sheet (CSS), or JavaScript into a field and then tell a WV to display the results. I judge this to be a rather advanced feature, so I won't spend a lot of time on it. If you want to see how it works, go to the downloadable companion files for Chapter 26 (*not* Chapter 25), open the Business file, and go to the last layout, called NUL_DataURL. You'll see three examples — two that display buttons and one that displays a digital clock. I've seen some wonderful examples including one that tells you the value of a resistor by selecting the colors of the bands painted on the resistor from drop-down menus. The most impressive part was that you could see the colors shown on an example resistor.

If you have experience writing these specialized codes, you may find this feature very interesting. In order to take advantage of data URLs, you must structure the URL statement like this:

```
"data:text/html," & TableName::FieldName
```

You can put the code directly into the WV calculation box itself rather than referring to a field. (See the third example in the Chapter 26 Business file.) However, you need to escape any quotes by preceding the quote with the backslash character. Even then, many sets of code won't render properly. By putting the code into a field, you can use the coded text as it is. And you can make changes in the text field and see the results immediately. Don't forget that the code itself can refer to other fields in your database. That means you can render graphs and reports based on your data as it changes in real time right in the WV.

I expect developers to come up with some amazing uses for this functionality. With data URLs, FileMaker could turn into a highly flexible tool with features that stretch way beyond those of a database.

Summary

I hope I've given you enough of an idea of what the Web Viewer can do that you'll find it a tool you (and your customers) can use. Maybe you even said "Wow!" It's a big time-saver when you find you don't have to retype addresses and other data in order to access maps and work with other online applications. I use it all the time. It really *is* more than a browser once you consider that you can use the screen scraping capability to harvest data for use right in FileMaker. What will they think of next!

Q & A

Q I can't seem to make an Excel document show up in the Web Viewer.

A Sounds like you may be working on a Macintosh. The test is easy. Open a browser, go to the File menu, and choose Open File. Navigate your hard drive to the file you're trying to see in the Web Viewer. If it's grayed out, that means you can't open it in the browser or the Web Viewer.

Q I was able to open a PDF in Safari on my Mac, but it won't open in the Web Viewer.

A As I said earlier, the WV won't work with FMP8.5 on a Mac if Acrobat 7 is installed, but it should work in FMP10. If you can live without it, uninstall Acrobat 7 (by throwing it in the trash). Then as long as you have the plug-in installed in Safari (which it must be because you could open the PDF in Safari), it will work in the WV.

Workshop

Hopefully you imported the example URLs into your file. Now it's time to see if you can add some of your own in the Links table and make them work. Don't be afraid to experiment. Getting the syntax right can be frustrating, but once you have it, it's yours.

You might also go back to Chapter 17 and look at the section titled "Autoresize Layout Objects." Autoresize gives you the same effect as changing the size of a web page. Try applying Autoresize to the Web Viewer. Don't forget that the tab control that contains the WV needs to include Autoresize settings in order to see any changes.

Chapter 26

Working with External Data Sources

Introduction

For some time FileMaker has provided tools to help users work with data from other sources. FileMaker 9 opened up many ODBC data sources in a revolutionary new way — from within our own databases! And now that Bento is part of the Macintosh culture there have been requests to get that data into FileMaker.

My thanks to Beverly Voth from Tier3 Data & Web in London, Kentucky, who put some test files on a remote server for developers to use so I didn't have to learn some other database system in order to tell you how this great feature works.

And thanks also to Jonathan Monroe from Actual Technologies in Libertyville, Illinois, makers of ODBC drivers for Mac OS X, who provided test drivers for developers and authors so we could try before we buy, and spread the word about their easy-to-use interface.

External SQL Sources (ESS)[9]

FileMaker users have had access to ODBC data sources for years. But working with them has been a bit cumbersome, especially when it came to learning how to construct SQL queries. After all, one of the most intuitive features of FileMaker is using Find mode. You don't have to know the name of a field in order to perform a find. Just go into Find mode in a form you're familiar with. Then click in a field where you know you've seen the data before, type your request, and finish the find. No complicated interface to deal with. With previous versions of FileMaker, in order to work with ODBC, you needed to leave the standard FileMaker interface behind and learn that SQL stuff.

With the Manage External Data Sources window, you can target a supported External SQL Source (ESS) and bring table occurrences right into the relationships graph. (External SQL Source (ESS) is also sometimes referred to as External SQL Data Source.) You can then build layouts around the TOs and work with the data almost as if it were FileMaker data. You get the advantages of fast development and FileMaker's familiar toolset, and you get access to legacy systems that may have been tied up in knots with the IT department. This certainly adds a whole new level of Wow! to FileMaker.

FileMaker 10 supports the following eight SQL data sources — as of the second foray into this territory:

- SQL Server 2000
- SQL Server 2005
- Microsoft SQL Server 2008 (10.0.1049)
- Oracle 9g
- Oracle 10g
- Oracle 11g (11.1.0.6)
- MySQL Mini Edition 5.0
- MySQL Community Server 5.1

Before you can use this feature, you'll have to struggle through the setup described briefly in Chapter 21, "Sharing Your Data with Other Applications." I say it was described briefly because there are just too many variations of the drivers and even the ODBC Administrative tools on both Mac and Windows platforms to do any more than point you in the right direction. Unfortunately, the dialogs aren't under FileMaker's control. But once you've done that, the setup inside FileMaker couldn't be much easier. On the other hand, if you're familiar with these other database programs or have someone who will work with you on the setup, the ODBC configuration should not be all that hard. FileMaker will be the easiest link in the whole process.

NOTE When it comes to External SQL Sources (ESS), any firewalls will likely need the ports set to something other than 2399 as mentioned in Chapter 21. The one I worked with that appears to be a SQL standard is port 1433. If both you and the person serving the data have separate firewalls, each firewall must have the matching port open.

NOTE Another important detail is that you must set up a system DSN. User DSNs are not supported by ESS in FileMaker.

I can't provide you with an exact description of the changes to our Business file because there is no permanent test database I can have you connect to. Besides, you'd need the drivers and I can't see you purchasing the specific driver you would need just to run these tests. With those excuses out of the way, I can still show you the steps and the windows you can expect to see.

Selecting the Data Source

Once you've conquered the DSN hurdle and are back inside the comfort of FileMaker, nothing could be easier. The following assumes you have an external data source set up. If not, you can still follow along until you hit a brick wall in your windows.

1. Choose **File, Manage, External Data Sources.** We've already looked at this window, but we'll be heading in a little different direction this time.

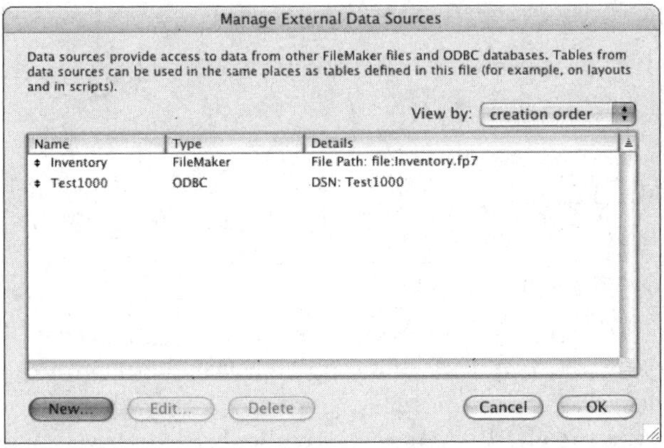

Figure 26-1
The Manage External Data Sources window.

2. Click the **New** button in the lower-left corner. When the Edit Data Source window appears, type any meaningful name for your data source in the Name box at the top.
3. Click the **ODBC** radio button, and the window will change to show the ODBC appropriate fields as shown in Figure 26-2.

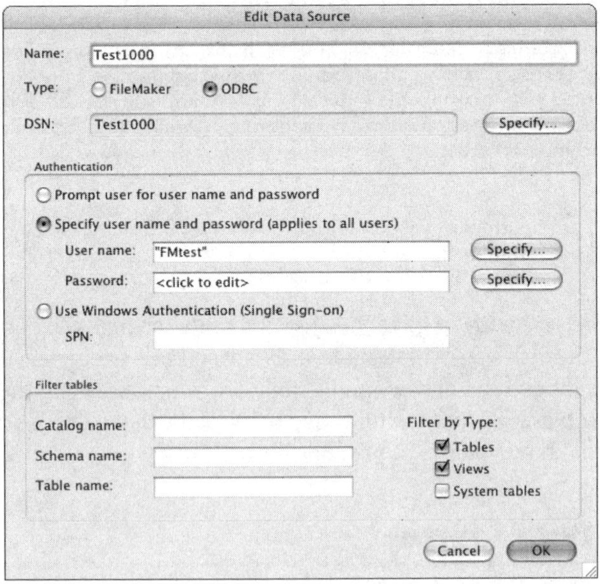

Figure 26-2
The Edit Data Source window showing the ODBC settings.

NOTE If there are a large number of tables available on your network, it would probably be wise to filter the data source using some combination of the check boxes in the Edit Data Source window. Otherwise, it might take a very long time whenever you attempt to add an ESS table to FileMaker.

4. To enter your DSN, click the **Specify** button in the upper right, which will bring up the Select ODBC Data Source window in Figure 26-3. Any system DSN ODBC data sources you have set up will appear in the list here. (Again, FileMaker only supports system DSNs.) Simply make your selection and click **OK**.

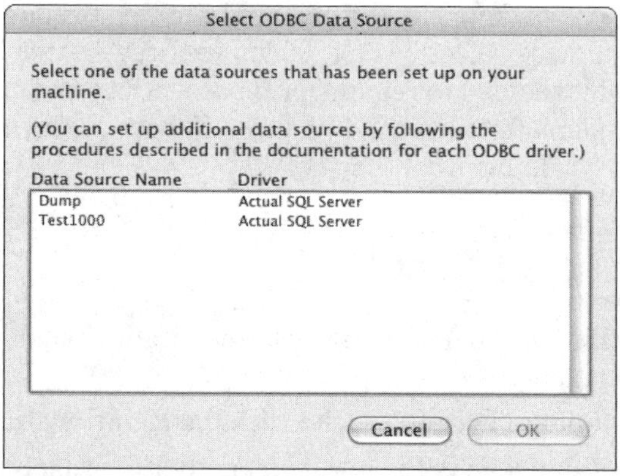

Figure 26-3
The Select ODBC Data Source window.

5. Back at the Edit Data Source window, I filled in the User name and Password fields. If you don't, you will be prompted every time you open the file. If you have multiple data sources, you would have to enter those bits of information for every source every time you open your file. That can get more than a bit tedious, so I suggest filling these in if at all possible. On the other hand, you may have security reasons for not allowing that. If your files are set for external authentication and single sign-on, as long as the SQL data sources use the same authentication, you would use the "Prompt user for user name and password" radio button and it will bypass the request. This seems counterintuitive, but that's what you need to do to force FMP to check for external authentication first. If it doesn't find any, the user will be presented with the authentication dialog. Using the radio button next to "Specify user name and password (applies to all users)," you can fill in the boxes to preset a user name and password. Alternatively, you can leave both boxes empty. If everything is set up in the DSN and SQL Server to use Windows authentication, the user should be connected. If not, the system will fall back to prompt for the user name and password. Starting with FMP10, when working with SQL Server and for Windows users only, you can select the Use Windows Authentication radio button and add the Service Principal Name (SPN). That allows the host of the FMP files to pass the user's security settings along to the SQL Server.

   When you enter the password in the Edit Data Source window, it shows "in the clear" rather than as a series of dots as it does in many other password boxes. You might want to check to see if anyone is watching you when you work with this window. After you have exited the Password field, it changes to "<click to edit>" as shown in Figure 26-2.

Also notice the Specify buttons to the right of User name and Password. Yep, you get the full use of FileMaker's calculation engine to provide something more specific — like different names and passwords depending on who is logged into the file.

6. Still referring to Figure 26-2, you'll see the Filter tables section in the lower third of that window. These items relate to the world of database administration. I made selections for Tables and Views when I set up my data source, and it seemed to remember those settings and checked the boxes for me. I just left it alone and clicked OK, but you can make changes here if you know what they do.

Using ODBC Tables in the Graph

Now let's see how this data source works with the existing table occurrences in the relationships graph.

1. Choose **File**, **Manage**, **Database**, and click the **Relationships** tab.
2. Click the **New Table** icon in the lower-left corner to bring up the Specify Table window, which you can see in Figure 26-4.

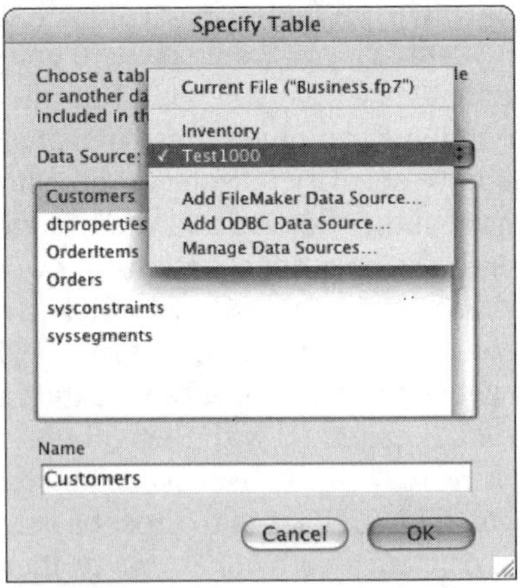

Figure 26-4
The Specify Table window showing the Data Source drop-down with the ODBC test data source selected.

3. It automatically appears with the current file as the Data Source. Click on the drop-down and you should see the ODBC data source. Notice that you can add an ODBC data source right from here, or you can even go to Manage External Data Sources. That's right; you can do it all without exiting the Manage Database window if you prefer.

At this point, the tables I choose will certainly not match up with whatever you have available to you. But you can still follow along with the windows and bits of advice.

4. I selected the **Customers** table and renamed it **CUS**. As soon as I clicked **OK**, I got a TO that looks just like any of the FileMaker TOs. If you hover your mouse pointer over the Table Info Control icon in the

upper left of the TO, it will show you information about the data source as shown in Figure 26-6. If you go to the Tables tab, you'll also find that a new table has been added to the list, unless there's already one based on the same table.

As part of this arrangement, FileMaker must identify a unique key in the ESS table. But sometimes none of the fields have been defined as unique. In that case, you will see the window shown in the background in Figure 26-5. You can make a guess by checking one of the Column boxes and click OK again. FileMaker will then examine that field in every record in the table and if it determines uniqueness, the TO will appear on the graph.

If that field does not prove to provide a unique key, you will then see the dialog shown in the foreground in Figure 26-5. In that case, click OK and try to add another field to build a concatenated unique key. You may have to select a number of fields before FileMaker recognizes the combination as unique. In some cases I had to put a check mark next to each field before FMP accepted it. It is possible that no combination will yield a unique key. Once you get to that point, it would really help if you had some kind of idea about the structure of the database with which you're trying to connect. Any "temporarily unique keys" could change and cause difficulties for users after you thought you had it worked out. Better to work with the administrator of the back-end database and have him create a unique key and add data to it in order to avoid the issue altogether.

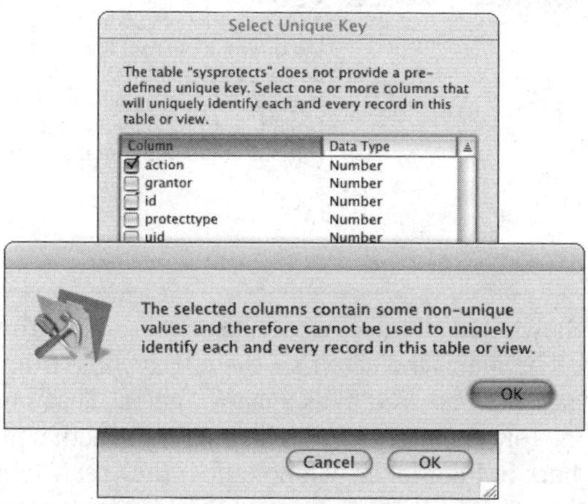

Figure 26-5
The window and dialog you may see requiring a unique key when inserting an ESS table into the graph.

Once you've established one incidence of that table, FMP remembers the key and you can add other TOs of the base table without seeing the window. In order to reset the key selection process, you would need to delete all instances of the TOs that belong to that base table, then switch to the Tables tab and remove the table from that list as well. Depending on how much work you had done with the ESS tables, that could be a painful choice!

5. I continued by adding Orders and Order Line Items tables to the graph. Then I built relationships between them just as I had with the other tables in the Business file. You can also create relationships between the

ESS and FMP tables. And you aren't limited to making them equal relationships. But you must remember that many relationships require that one side be indexed, so in some cases you may not get the results you expect.

You can set the relationships between ESS table occurrences (or ESS and FMP TOs) to allow auto-creation of related records via the relationship. For instance, an ESS Order table can have a portal displaying records from an ESS OrderLineItem table with an empty last row for adding new items. But if your permissions do not allow you to create (or delete) records in that table, you will generate errors. That's another reason to have some idea of how the ESS database has been set up — and why you should have some agreement with the administrator of that database. You wouldn't want the administrator changing the settings on a table without keeping you up to date.

One thing you might find a little confusing is that the lines between the ESS table occurrences don't look quite like the usual links between FileMaker resident TOs. If you look at Figure 26-6, you'll see the lines terminate without quite touching the TO — the same way that the lines look when you try to connect using a global field. It just means that these TOs are unindexed as far as FileMaker's way of working is concerned. Even if you have a one-to-many relationship, you won't be able to tell by looking at the graph.

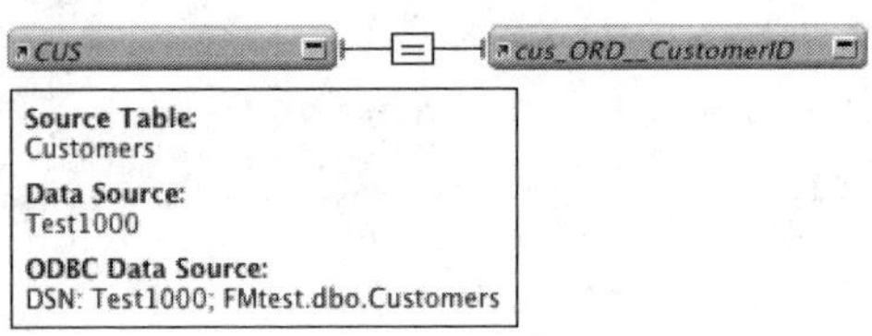

Figure 26-6
A pair of related ESS table occurrences from the graph. Note that the line between them does not touch the TO borders; this indicates that the TOs are unindexed. Hovering over the Table Info Control icon will display a tooltip with information about the table source.

Shadow Tables

Clicking the Tables tab shows that all table occurrences you added from any ESS tables are italicized. The italics indicate that the tables come from External SQL Sources, which are also referred to as shadow tables. That's because they are simply shadowing (or you might say "following") the actual SQL tables. Making changes here in FileMaker will not affect the "real" tables.

When you click the Fields tab and choose one of the ESS tables from the drop-down, you'll see that the field names are also italicized. That's another indication that the fields belong to a shadow table. Any fields that you add to the table will not be italicized. That's right; you are allowed to add "supplemental fields" to the ESS tables, although you are limited to unstored calculation and summary fields. In fact, as you attempt to add a field here, the Type drop-down switches to Calculation and all other choices except Summary are grayed out. Even with that limitation, being able to build on the ESS data is really valuable stuff!

Notice that in the Options/Comments column you can see details about the ESS fields. Some details include whether the field data will be validated, if it requires numeric entry, if it can't be modified, if it's a lookup, and if there are a maximum number of characters (although you can't tell how many).

You cannot rename the italicized fields in the field list. But you can apply such FileMaker features as lookups and field validation. However, you must stay within any restrictions enforced by the SQL database. For instance, if your SQL file limits the State field to two alpha characters and the 50 U.S. states, you can make the FMP field limited to something like five states if you like. But you cannot expand to values beyond the 50 states without generating an error message. In other words, you can always provide more restrictions than the "back-end" database allows, but never fewer.

You can also remove fields from the Fields tab if you don't need them or if you want to prevent users from finding them for some reason. (Don't worry: they won't be deleted from the SQL database.) And you can bring them back again by clicking the Sync button, which you'll find just below the Fields tab. Another advantage of removing fields from an ESS table is you reduce the overhead involved with getting and displaying the data. But you'll need to remove them again if you click Sync.

> **NOTE** When you click the Sync button, if the primary key you selected for the table is no longer unique, you will see the dialog in Figure 26-5 again. You'll need to reselect a unique key. If one cannot be established, <primary key missing> will appear in the Manage Database area and on the layouts. If FileMaker later finds that an ESS data source field has been redefined as a unique key, that key will be used instead of the key previously selected in FMP.

ODBC Tables in Browse Mode

When you return to Browse mode, you'll find that a new layout has been created for each base table added to the graph with all the fields in the Standard Form format. You can add, delete, and duplicate records as long as the back-end database allows you to. And remember that those back-end settings may be different for different users.

The fields can also be added to your layouts based on FMP tables as long as you've built a relationship to the ESS tables. You'll be able to perform finds in the fields just as if they were FileMaker fields. However, since SQL data sources are often known for large record counts, the finds could be somewhat slower than those on FileMaker resident data.

ESS-based Value Lists[10]

Starting with FileMaker 10, you can create value lists using data that lives in the SQL database. That value list is available to any table in the file whether the field is a FileMaker field or a SQL field that shows up on a FileMaker layout. You create the value list the same way you do any value list that uses values from a field in FileMaker. You choose the "Use values from field" radio button and select the ESS table occurrence. When you see the list of fields, you'll know they're ESS fields because they'll be italicized as in Figure 26-7.

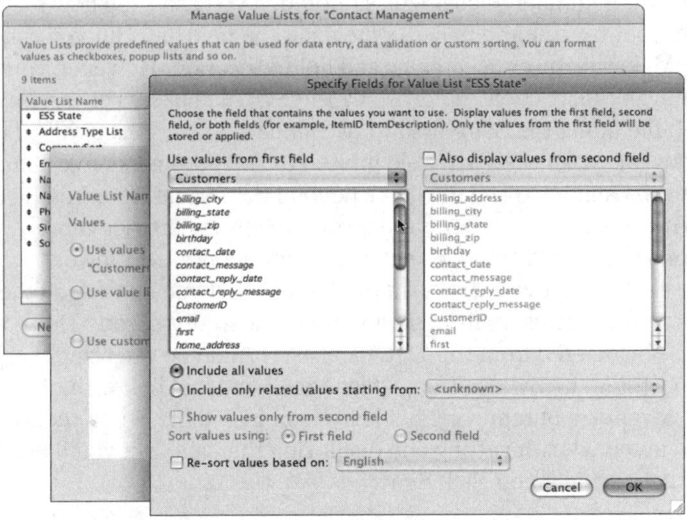

Figure 26-7
The windows you will see when defining ESS-based value lists.

Other Stuff You Need to Know

Here are a few odds and ends regarding working with ESS tables:

- Some date fields in SQL databases are actually timestamps. So you need to be aware that if you're writing any scripts to handle a date, you'll have to format it the way the back-end database system expects or you will get an error. In a SQL 2000 file I tested, I entered a date and it was converted to a timestamp in the back-end database without displaying an error. Regardless of how you force data entry, you can still format the field on your layout so the date (or timestamp) looks any way you like.
- SQL Server databases use full timestamp data in their fields, which is not always what we want in our FMP databases. FileMaker 10 lets you choose the date, time, or full timestamp for the appropriate fields in your shadow table.
- The engineers at FileMaker set this system up using a trick so that you can display a group of about 50,000 records very quickly. However, if you move the Book slider to view more records, it takes longer to pull down the data. For that reason, views may be a better way to filter the data coming from ESS files. (See the following Note.) Or you may simply plan to wait the extra time needed. But you would probably want to avoid working directly with tables that hold millions of records. The same caution applies to sorting large sets of data. Be prepared to wait! Or filter the records using a view first.

NOTE SQL views can help you avoid long waits by filtering the amount of data that comes to you. But views need to be set up in the external database. They're sort of like finds in FMP. For example, if you only need to look at the past year's invoices, you wouldn't want to have FMP pull down perhaps millions of records worth of data from the ESS file in order to look at just a few thousand.

- How fast all of this operates will depend on the speed of your computer, the speed of the connection between your computer and the server (including network traffic), the speed of the server itself, and the size of the data sets you'll be accessing.
- It is possible for ESS records to be locked in their back-end database during data entry, just as if another user were entering data into a record in an FMP file. If that happens and you are trying to make a change to that record, you will see an error message. When you think about it, it does seem logical. But I mention it because if you were the only user of a FileMaker file, you might be surprised to see an error message that another user has control of the record — which for all appearances is actually a FileMaker record.
- One thing you may find a little confusing is that ESS table occurrences look like any other external FMP table occurrence in the graph. Nothing except the italicized TO name in the graph indicates that it's anything other than an external table — until you hover your pointer over the Table Info Control icon in the upper left of the TO.
- When working with FileMaker Server, as long as the ESS is set up on the server, the clients do not need to individually set up ODBC on their computers. Users would more than likely be completely unaware that the data lives anywhere other than in FileMaker — except for the speed issues already discussed when dealing with large data sets.
- You can use the Open File and Close File script steps and name your ESS data source as if it were any other file. Open File allows users to reconnect if a connection fails or is cancelled. Close File allows users to re-login, perhaps with a different set of privileges. Without these scripts, you would have to close and reopen the FileMaker file to re-establish the ESS connection. Alternatively, if you've lost contact with an ESS database, you can go into Manage Database in the Fields tab and click the Sync button for the ESS table.
- You can export from and import into the ESS tables as if they were FMP tables. I experimented by exporting 24 records and re-importing them. Since OrderItemID was the key field, I held my breath at the possibility of ending up with duplicate keys. Not to worry! When the import was complete, the SQL 2000 file had ignored the imported duplicates in that field and provided the new sequential IDs. In this case, the OrderItemID field was defined in the SQL file to create a unique ID during record creation. If that were not the case, I would have likely gotten an error.

- You will need to purchase ODBC drivers. They don't appear to be too expensive — somewhere in the neighborhood of $30 or so per user.
- Working with ESS is similar to working with the separation model that I discussed in Chapter 14. One of the drawbacks of working this way is that development is spread across multiple interfaces, which makes it more difficult to control. If you are not the one in charge of the SQL database, everything depends on your relationship with that administrator.
- If you or someone else redefines the ODBC data source to point to a different database or even a different table in the same database, you are almost guaranteed to mess up everything in your file relating to the ESS table. That includes the table, table occurrences, the layouts the fields appear on, and any scripts that point to anything related to that source. The only way to avoid complete failure is if you intentionally point to a different data source with exactly the same name and structure. But you could still run into trouble since the fields aren't likely to match up, and that would certainly cause problems with any supplemental fields you may have added. My advice is just don't do it.
- When fields are added or renamed in the ESS database, FileMaker tries to make repairs based on where the fields are in the ESS table. FMP can make mistakes in this regard. Any scripts that run using these incorrectly targeted fields could have disastrous results. It's just one more reason to have an agreement with the ESS database administrator.
- In Chapter 22 I talked about FileMaker's accounts and privileges. When you edit a privilege set and choose the Records drop-down, the ESS tables appear in the Tables list as if they were tables right in this database. That is particularly interesting since even FMP tables from other files don't appear there. You can exercise full FMP control over the privileges given to users of the records in these ESS data sources. The same applies to control over the ESS layouts. Don't overlook this detail when you're setting up access to the ESS data sources. You get to decide exactly which users can perform specific activities.

Whatever you might say about the speed of this amazing feature (or the ponderous setup in the ODBC administration windows), it lets you work with SQL data without learning one bit of SQL language. The engineers at FileMaker have done a great job. This is power not to be scoffed at!

Getting Your Data from Bento[10] (Macintosh Only)

Now that Bento has been around for a little while, there have been requests to bring that data into FileMaker. Maybe you've been using Bento for Mac OS X and decided it doesn't do all you need it to, so you're stepping up to FileMaker Pro. Of course, you don't want to leave all your data behind. Well, the friendly folks at FileMaker, Inc. have provided you with a tool to get your data into a FileMaker file. You can either import into an existing FMP file or convert your Bento data into a new file. This really only works if you are using Bento 2. However, you can get at your Bento 1 data by saving it as a .csv file and then importing that into FMP. It's only one extra step and no big deal.

The only thing that might be a disappointment to you is that FileMaker won't automatically stay connected to your Address Book and iCal the way Bento does. You're basically saying goodbye to Bento and hello to FileMaker. I personally don't use those apps because I've recreated their functions in FileMaker, although not as elegantly. I wouldn't expect you to go that far with FileMaker, so you might want to prepare yourself for tracking some people in both locations or maybe using a FileMaker plug-in to integrate with the Apple apps.

There are three methods you might use to get your Bento 2 data into FileMaker: create a new file, import the data into an existing table, or create a new table in an existing file. You can create a new file using the Quick Start dialog. Bring that up by choosing File, New Database. Click the radio button next to "Create a database from an existing" and choose Bento Source from the drop-down. There will be a pause as FileMaker gathers the data sources, and then you'll see the dialog in Figure 26-8.

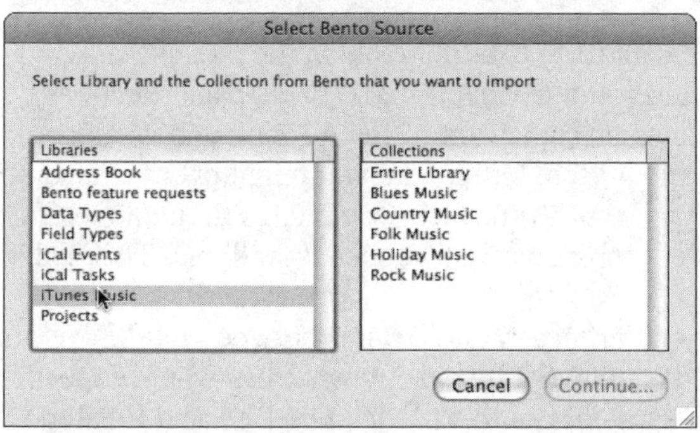

Figure 26-8
The Select Bento Source dialog.

When you click on the items in the Libraries list, most of them will only say Entire Library in the Collections list. Once you make a selection in the Collections list, click the Continue button. When the process is complete, you'll be looking at a FileMaker window with a table of your Bento data in front of you. It won't look like your Bento database, so it will be up to you to make it look and act the way you want. But if you've made it this far in the book, you're probably up for the challenge.

If you just want to get your data into an existing file, go to the File menu and choose Import Records, Bento Data Source. Once you make a selection from the window in Figure 26-8, you'll see FileMaker's Import Field Mapping dialog as shown in Figure 26-9.

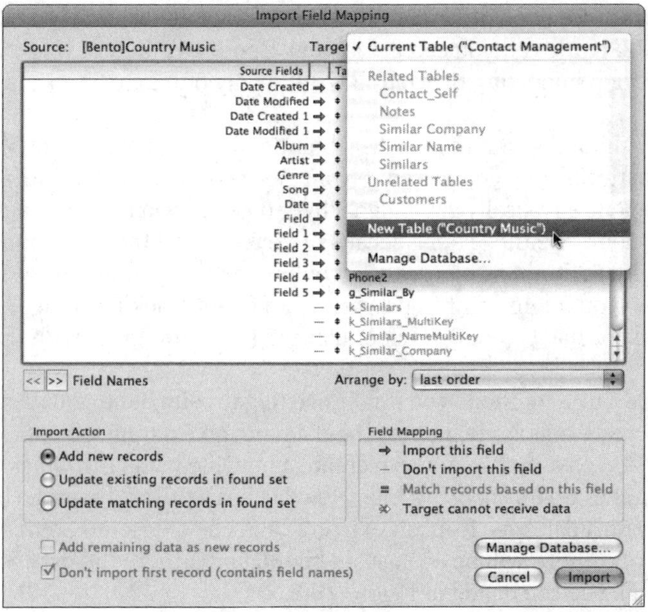

Figure 26-9
The Import Field Mapping dialog from Bento 2.

If you want to add the data to an existing table in the file, use the Import Field Mapping window as described in Chapter 23, "Backup and Recovery," to get the data into the fields where you want it. Just be sure you've selected the "Add new records" radio button. Otherwise you might overwrite some of your current data. If you want to start a new table, go to the upper-right corner, click the Target drop-down, and choose New Table. That's all there is to it.

Because there are differences in field types between FileMaker and Bento, some of your data may not be exactly what you would expect once it's been converted. For example, Bento's Media, File List, and Related Records List are not supported in FMP. Hopefully you haven't started using those field types too heavily. Also, any calculation fields you might have built in Bento will be converted to straight data fields. They'll end up as either Text, Number, Time, or Timestamp depending on what they were in Bento. As long as you imported the fields that were used to create the Bento calculation field, you can recreate your calculations in FileMaker.

Summary

In this chapter we looked at how FileMaker lets you bring tables from SQL data sources right into the relationships graph and into your layouts. We looked at how you can work with the data almost as if it were FileMaker data, and, rather than constructing complex SQL queries, how you can perform FileMaker-type finds on that data. Then we looked at getting data from Bento 2 into FileMaker.

Q & A

Q When I was looking at a layout that was supposed to have some ESS data on it, all I saw was a bunch of fields that said "<Data Source Missing>." What's up?

> **A** You've lost connection with the remote database. You can first try to sync with the data source by using the Sync button in the Fields tab of Manage Database. If that fails, check to see if other connections on your network are working okay — maybe by seeing if you have access to the Internet or other machines on the network. Then check with the database administrator to be sure the remote file is still available.

Q What else can I do with this ESS data?

> **A** Aha! I forgot to mention that you can make PDFs of your reports and you can also export as Excel. And of course you can then use the instant e-mail features to send any of those files to people who need the info.

Workshop

If you've just been reading about this, you really need to try it. As I said, setting up the data source is likely to be the most frustrating part of the process. Once it's working, try creating some supplemental fields even if you don't need them. Also, remove some of the ESS fields that you won't be using, and then click the Sync button to see how they come back to haunt you.

Chapter 27

File Conversion Issues and Answers

Introduction

Because FileMaker Pro 7 and later files are structurally quite different from previous versions, converting files from the FMP5 format (usable with FMP6) cannot be done without some attention to detail. This chapter will address the process of converting, some problems you might run up against, and what to do to make the transition as smooth as possible. There were rarely issues when upgrading between earlier versions. The fact that you have to pay any attention to the conversion process might make you wonder if the upgrade would be worth the trouble. But after working for a few years with the great new tools available, I definitely think it's worth it.

Documentation

This chapter will only be an overview. What you really need to do is look at a document that comes with this book's companion files. You can download the files from the publisher's web site at www.wordware.com/files/fmpro10. Then look in the folder called "Begin Chapter 27" for the file titled fm8_converting.pdf. Why would I tell you to read that document instead of this chapter? Because it's a very comprehensive 84 pages. The longest chapter I have in this book is only 30-some pages.

Don't get too scared by the length of the primer. There's a three-page table of contents, a three-page index, and a bunch of blank pages between sections, and quite a few items are repeated for clarity. You don't even get to the meat and potatoes until page 7. Much of what is covered has to do with complex solutions heavily laden with lots of scripting between files. That might have nothing to do with what you'll be converting. I converted a number of single-file solutions without incident. Be sure to look at the checklist on page 10 of that document.

What I'll do here is take you on a tour of a conversion I did while following the directions in that document back with the release of FMP7. I actually wrote this chapter while performing my first multi-file solution conversion. You won't find any significant difference in your process. Since I'm usually confused when dealing with installation, new software, and such, I think I can give you a pretty good idea of the worst of what you'll be up against. Let's just see what trouble I can get into.

> **NOTE** FileMaker 10 now uses Manage Database, Manage Scripts, and Manage External Data Sources. Previously, these had been called Define Database, ScriptMaker, and Define File References. In the following sections I will use the current terminology while I talk about converting FMP7 files. Just trying to keep it simple.

Step By Step

Before you even get started, it might be wise to look at how you have your preferences set up in the previous version of FileMaker. Write them down or take a screen shot (or a digital photo) of the Preferences screens so you can use the same settings in FMP10. When you upgrade, FileMaker doesn't move those settings for you.

You should also consider any plug-ins that you might be using. You'll need to check with the makers of the plug-ins to be sure they'll work with 10 or get a license in case you need to upgrade them — assuming the company is still in business. I can't tell you the number of times I've had clients upgrade only to find they no longer had the functions provided by the plug-ins. And don't forget, if all you do is buy a new machine and move your FileMaker license to that machine, you need to get into the folder that holds the plug-ins and move them (and any of their license files), too.

There are different sets of instructions depending on whether your database consists of just a few files or if it's a more complex, multi-file solution. The conversion document has a great checklist where you can determine which items you need to pay attention to.

The solution I'll be converting is the one that went with the version of this book for FileMaker Pro 6. By the time we hit Chapter 15 in the FileMaker 6 book, we had created eight files (which have since become a single file with eight tables). It's not a terribly complex set of files, but it should work as a nice start.

A big part of what needs to be considered has to do with how the database is being used. Here are some pertinent questions:

1. Are the files being hosted with FileMaker Server or are they your own personal files?
2. Are the files being published on the web with Instant Web Publishing or Custom Web Publishing?

Both these questions have a lot to do with FileMaker's new Accounts & Privileges model. If you're not using passwords in your files, many conversion issues will fall by the wayside, even though all new files will now have default accounts associated with them.

3. Are you using any plug-ins that need to be updated? (At least check with the vendor.)
4. Does anything in your files work with ActiveX, Apple events, or ODBC/JDBC? (May need updates there.)

5. Would it just be better to rebuild in FMP10 and import your data from the old files?
6. Are there any functions in your files that depend on undocumented behavior? (That functionality may disappear.)

It might be a really good idea to print the scripts, field definitions, and layouts in your current file before starting. If you use FMP Advanced, it might be better to create a database design report rather than a printed copy. I set two computers side by side so I could see the differences file by file.

The first thing to be aware of is that multi-file solutions will not be instantly converted to a single-file, multi-table solution. That might be a big disappointment. But the differences in file structure make that kind of conversion impossible.

As the file(s) convert, FileMaker creates a Conversion.log file in the same folder as the files. Look at the report to see what problems need to be solved. This will be one of your best tools. More on how to do that in a bit.

After reading the conversion document it seems clear to me that if I mess up the first conversion, converting a second time wouldn't be that hard. So rather than checking everything out, I'm just going to convert and then take a look at the log file. I'll open both the old and new versions on computers next to each other and see how they look. (Converting hundreds of thousands of records or records that have many hundreds of fields could be time consuming, so that might not be the best solution for everybody. But that's what I'll be doing here. I can do a larger file later and clock it out — with consideration for the fact that I currently have the fastest personal computer on the planet!)

First I created a new folder on my hard drive called "Chapter 27 convert from 6." I copied the files I'm converting from another folder and put them in this new folder. I added a folder at the same level called "Chapter 27 converted to 7" so both folders showed up next to each other.

I started the FileMaker Pro 7 program. Then I dragged the folder with the files in it (Chapter 27 convert from 6) onto the FMP7 icon in my (Mac OS X) Dock and I got the window shown in Figure 27-1. Since I already created a folder where I want the files to go, I clicked the Specify button and found the folder. But you can see you're allowed to create a folder anywhere you want while you're in the middle of the process. Then I clicked the Open button.

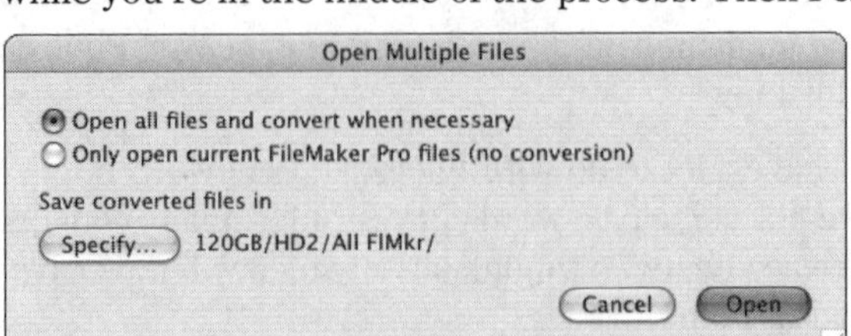

Figure 27-1
The Open Multiple Files window.

I got Mac OS X's "spinning beach ball of death" for about four seconds. This is a very fast computer and the files really are quite small with very little data. Then I got a message that "FileMaker cannot share a file because FileMaker network sharing is turned off." Sounds logical, because another version of FileMaker has control over the FileMaker sharing "channel." When I clicked OK to dismiss that dialog, all the files popped open.

I was then presented with the Account Name and Password window for the Invoice file. My name was already in the Account Name field. I figured I could use the Admin account, so I typed Admin where my name was and left Password empty. No dice! Uh, oh. I tried Admin, Admin. That didn't work. Finally I typed Master and Master. It worked! (Hum... Didn't I tell you never to use Master as a password?) FileMaker 7 converts passwords to both account names and passwords and requires you to use the same name in both fields. Since FMP7 passwords are case sensitive, users who have not needed to pay attention to that in previous versions may be baffled when they can't get into the file using a password they've been using for years. So anyway, I'm in now. If you can't get into a file, you can always go back to your previous file and see what passwords you used — if you can remember them. I found the biggest problem with passwords turned out to be capitalization errors. The old FileMaker was less fussy about that. But in the new FileMaker, you'll need to know exactly what the old passwords were in all their upper- and lowercase glory.

As I moved files around so I could find the Contact file (remember, this is the old system where I have multiple files) I saw the Phones file displaying <Field Missing> where FirstName should go. I looked at the Manage Database window's Relationships tab and saw that the Phones ContactSerNum field seemed to be connected to the Contacts Notes field. What's that about? I went back into the original FMP6 files and sure enough, that's what it looks like there. Not FMP7's fault.

Just for fun I chose File, Manage, External Data Sources. I double-clicked the Contact file and got the following:

file:/Macintosh HD/Buttons/Part 3/All FlMkr/JSSA business files/FMP 5 book/Contact
file:/Contact

Apparently, FileMaker remembers some version of the files a couple of hard drives ago. The first one listed is a drive that committed suicide by self-immolation about five years ago. Kinda upset me to remember that sad time. I believe the dead drive was followed by an incident involving an object flying through a window, the police, handcuffs...

We'll look at data sources in more detail in a little bit.

Conversion Log

It's time to look at the conversion log. Wow! There are over four pages in the log with close to 200 items listed. It begins with the Contact file. One note says "Poor field name." Well! I think I should be the judge of that. The field was called Field::Name experiment. Right! I was experimenting with the problems a field would have with relationships, Instant Web Publishing, and ODBC if you used the double colon. Poor field name indeed! A field name should never have a double colon in it. I also wouldn't recommend using a single colon in a field name.

Some relationships converted. The Today function was replaced with a Today field and a startup script to update it. Interesting, since I dislike the Today function. Looked around but didn't see any field named Today. There is a text field called DateTest. In the field validation area of the Options for Field window, I had used the Today function, which has been converted to Get (CurrentDate). It was a field I was experimenting with in one of the earlier books but never used. Hey, maybe this will help me clean up the files!

Mostly it just says that fields, layouts, scripts, value lists, indexes, and records were converted just fine. In fact, as I scan down the list it appears that everything was converted correctly. No errors appear anywhere that I can see. Looking for errors at this point is actually very helpful, but since the list is so long, they can be hard to spot. Open the log with a word processing program and search for the word "error." Better yet, open the log in FileMaker!

Comparing Fields

Now I'm setting the two databases next to each other on two machines to see what differences appear in various places. I'll start with field definitions. The first difference I notice is that Phone1 shows the number 10 after the word Text in the Type column. I like knowing at a glance how many repetitions there are to a repeating field.

Fields that were indexed before are indexed now, and fields that weren't indexed before are not indexed now. Makes sense. When I look behind the Storage tab, where indexing used to be On or Off, now the index is shown to be Minimal. When I look behind the Validation tab on State (AddrState), I see the window looks different with regard to the placement of "Allow user to override during data entry." In the FMP6 version, this check box reads "Strict: Do not allow user to override data validation." Where that box used to be empty unless checked, the new one is checked until you uncheck it. No big deal, just different.

Oh, I also see that calculations are identified with specific tables. For example in FMP6, the AddrCombo field reads "NameFirst & " " & NameLast &…" In FMP7, it reads "from Contact, = NameFirst & " " & NameLast & …" I suppose if I were to combine elements from other tables, I'd see those tables identified as well. A little test shows that the calculation is still associated with the specific table. The related field was tacked onto the end of the calculation. But when I switched back, removing the related field, the storage showed to be Unstored and I had to change it manually. Okay.

Global fields appear different according to the newer model. Instead of the word Global in the Type column, it's now in the Options column as expected.

Everything else is simply a repetition of the things I already mentioned. I looked at a couple of the other files in the solution. More of the same. It's interesting that I now see how much I would gain by having this old, multi-file solution in a single file like we've built over the course of this book. Now let's see what happens with layouts.

Comparing Layouts

The first thing I noticed was that the buttons were colored slightly differently. Probably a difference in the displays I'm using and between Mac OS 9 and OS X. Next, I found the converted file didn't remember the found set in my Contact file. That's not surprising.

The Status area that was on the left has been replaced with the Status toolbar along the top of the window, and there are other differences from the previous version. The Book now works from left to right (more like a book) where it used to work top to bottom (like a Rolodex). The new mode buttons appear above the layout names, but that's about it. None of these are conversion issues.

Finally, the text aligns differently horizontally in the fields on my OS X machine than on my OS 9 Macintosh. The fonts also look ragged. That's because I turned off Font Smoothing, which makes my eyes feel as if I've got something smeared on my glasses. I don't like what I see either way, but it's a Mac problem, not FileMaker's.

Accounts & Privileges

In the Invoice file of my FMP6 files I had two passwords: Master and Sales. Master was defined with full privileges, so it took the place of the Admin account that it normally created when a file gets started. That explains my confusion when I couldn't get into the file with the Admin password.

Along with the Master account, I got an inactive Guest account with the Read-Only Access privilege set, and an active Sales account. When I click the Privilege Sets tab, I see the Data Entry Only privilege set and the Read-Only Access, neither of which is assigned to any accounts. Then there's a new Sales account faithfully based on the privileges assigned to the password in my old FMP6 file.

I clicked over to the Contact file, which was not protected with any passwords. There were only two accounts there: Admin and Guest. The Privilege Sets tab revealed the standard three sets: Full Access, Data Entry Only, and Read-Only Access. I looked at the File Options window. To prevent locking you out of a converted file that has no passwords, I see FileMaker sets the Admin account to log in automatically when opening the file. It's clear I'll want to change that if I intend to take advantage of all the new security tools available in FMP7. Looking back at the Invoice file, I see that check box is empty, forcing the user to log in when opening. Beyond that, there's nothing I can see here in Accounts & Privileges. It's all new.

Comparing Scripts

When I clicked the Main Menu button in my Contact file, it should have taken me to the Main Menu layout in the Invoice file. Instead, it hid the Contact file and left me with a blank screen. Looking at the scripts I see that a final step has been added, Select Window [Name: "Invoice"]. Well, that didn't seem to help much. Windows now have three states: Active, Minimized, and Hidden. Many of my scripts on the Mac use the Toggle Window [Hidden] script step. Since Select Window can't find the Invoice window when it's hidden, it can't select it. I had to add an Adjust Window [Restore] step in the Main Menu script in the Invoice file to make it come to the front. Nothing tragic, but you will probably need to make adjustments to your files after conversion.

I have a script called Find All Records. It simply shows all records and sorts them. There's an extra step in the FMP7 version, Go to Record/Request/Page [First]. That's because after sorting, FileMaker now stays on the record that was selected when you started your sort. In order to act like the old FileMaker (which put you on the first record of the found set), you need this extra step. Some developers' solutions depend on this behavior. That's why the conversion adds the step.

Oh, here's an interesting one. I have a script called Function Test that looks at numbers in a Zip Code field. Since FMP7 recognized that the Zip field was a number field (I don't recommend that, but…), it changed every reference to the Zip field to GetAsNumber (Contact::Zip). No problem.

Many of the places that used to show field names now have table names added to the front of them. The only other alteration I noticed was that one of the export files I used for XML had "Unicode (UTF-8)" tacked onto the end of it.

Other scripts just seem to show changes to some script step and function names. But it sure is nice to double-click a find, sort, import, export, or print step and see the details stored and editable. These are the good new days!

Comparing Relationships

Relationships have changed quite a bit. The old version showed three columns: Relationship Name, Relationship (the related fields), and Related File. FMP6 showed two relationships in the list in my main file, Contact. Looking at the Relationships tab of Define Database in FMP7 (now Manage Database), I see the three table occurrences all strung together. One of the relationships is between a set of constant fields (calculation = 1). We used to need those constant fields to connect files to pass information back and forth between them. That's pretty much a thing of the past now. In the old version I needed to create calculations in the in-between file to pipeline data to the far ends of the relationships. Now you can pass it with no special calculations at all. That should reduce file and indexing overhead, not to mention a lot of extra work needed to figure out how to get information where you need it. You may see table occurrences here that don't seem to make sense to your solution. I recommend you don't delete anything here. You may end up with layouts and scripts unattached from the rest of your solution.

External Data Sources

After converting an FMP5 solution, you may see a large number of data sources (referred to as file references post FMP7), many of which don't seem to make any sense at all and may have been valid years ago on different computers — both yours and those of your clients. In general, if things worked before, they'll continue to work. That's because, even with extra data sources, there is usually a current valid one. Sometimes there are multiple pointers to the same file with different reference names.

You should be cautious about deleting these references. I left every data source in the list, but I edited them by removing references to long-gone machines. When I'd finished, all that was left was the relative reference. For example, in the Contact file I edited the Invoice data source so it now reads file:Invoice. That means these connected files will look inside the immediate solution folder for the file it needs. If you see data sources named Invoice and Invoice 2, don't delete the second one just because it refers to the same file. That's where you'll get into trouble. You don't really need to clean them up at all as long as you have one valid item in the File Path List. For the set of files I had converted, only one reference had no valid item in the Path List. I simply added file:Contact so there would be no problems in case it were ever called from the solution.

FileMaker has always had an area where it kept track of data sources; it was just hidden from the user. There's no harm in leaving this area alone except when you need to add new references. You can consolidate data sources if it makes you crazy. But you shouldn't do it without checking every relationship, value list, and script to find out what file reference they expect, or you may be in for a few unpleasant surprises. There are also some script steps that store their own data sources apart from the Manage External Data Sources window. Only three script steps refer to the files listed in the Manage External Data Sources window. Any others keep track of their own sources. If you have persistent calls for a file you know you're no longer using, you can delete it. Otherwise, my advice is to leave well enough alone.

New Millennium Communications makes a special tool called MetadataMagic. It can be a bit pricey depending on the number of files involved, but if you value your time and want to clean up the data sources before you convert them to the FMP7 format, it's a great tool and has a lot of other uses. Find them at www.newmillennium.com.

More on Accounts and Passwords

When files are converted from earlier versions of FileMaker, both the account name and the password are identical. If an eavesdropper who knew this little bit of information were to observe an administrator signing into an account shortly after a file conversion, all he or she would have to do is watch the account name the administrator typed. For that reason, FileMaker allows you to log in using just the password (which appears as bullets) when both the account name and the password are identical. Since the user name (set in FileMaker's Preferences area) fills the Account name field on login, all you have to do is empty it out, tab to the Password field, and type the secret word. The real advice is this: After file conversion, get to a private machine and change the passwords so they're not the same as the account names. Or, if you allow users to make up their own passwords, check the box next to "User must change password on next login" in the Edit Account dialog for each account.

Finishing Up

That's about all there is to it. I had it easy because the solution I converted was fairly uncomplicated and had so little data in each of the files. If you really want to talk about conversion that will take advantage of all the great tools starting in FileMaker Pro 7, you'll need to recreate your database by building your tables into a single file. That's where you'll really begin to unleash the power of the tools the software engineers at FileMaker, Inc. have been working on for years.

Fortunately, FileMaker 8 added the ability to import a table complete with field definitions. You'll still have to recreate the layouts, but you'll be able to copy elements of your layouts from your converted multi-file solution. (For a primer on the details of file consolidation, see Appendix A.) The big work will be scripting. Even then, you can import or copy and paste scripts and use what you need. FMP7 began a new age for FileMaker. These are very good times!

Summary

In this chapter I showed you what it was like to convert a FileMaker 6 solution to FileMaker 7. The process is virtually the same in FMP8 and later. I showed you some of the things I ran into as I examined the differences between how layouts, scripts, relationships, fields, accounts, and privileges looked in the two sets of files.

Q & A

Q We have a complicated solution that we want to convert over the weekend. What's the best way to approach a mission-critical conversion?

A Whoa, cowboy! Not so fast. Print and read the conversion document with a highlighter in hand. After you've carefully noted items that are important to your particular conversion, do a test run and put the solution on a machine that's disconnected from the network where you can test it out in detail. Make notes about what doesn't work and how you corrected it so you'll be prepared when you make your final conversion.

One company I know about started their conversion late Friday afternoon, but their files were so large that the computer was still working the following Wednesday! If you have both Mac and Windows users, be sure you test it on both platforms through a network. Then do the conversion at a time when the company isn't too rushed. You don't want your business to come to a screeching halt because you were in such a hurry.

Q Our company has a five-file solution. We just want to put everything into one file. How should we go about that?

A First convert to an FMP10 multi-file solution and see if everything works using the advice I gave in the answer to the previous question. Then decide which will be your main file and import a table to it, using the method explained in Chapter 7 when we imported the Product table. Remember, you don't have to go live with it just yet. Duplicate your main layouts and see if you can make them work with the new table similar to the way everything worked with the other file. It may take some getting used to the new way of working from previous versions of FileMaker. Once you really have it working the way you want, make a backup of your files in their current state. Delete all the records from the new table and re-import the current set of live data from the other file. Replace the layouts with the work layouts. After that's been in use for a while, try another table. Also see the method outlined in Appendix A.

Workshop

If you have some pre-FMP7 files, convert one of your solutions and take a careful look at the Conversion.log file. Don't forget to watch for the word "error."

Appendix A

Leftover, but Important Stuff

There are just a few things that didn't seem to fit anywhere else in the book but I feel are important enough that I don't want to leave you without mentioning them.

Cleaning Up After Yourself

You may want to go back through your files and delete the unused fields. For example, in our Contact table, you still have fields Phone1 through Phone4, Web, and FunctionTest. In the Invoice table you still have the Design field. It's not absolutely necessary to delete these fields. In all likelihood, if you tested the speed of two copies of the file, one with the fields and one without them, even with sophisticated equipment you wouldn't be able to measure any difference. It just depends on how obsessive you are.

With more complex systems of files, it can be a problem to delete fields that haven't been carefully documented as being for experimentation only. Get in the habit of documenting things you do to solve a problem, if you can train yourself. It'll make this cleanup work a whole lot easier.

You may also want to uncheck the scripts in Manage Scripts so none of them are available from the Scripts dialog. Some of those scripts can be destructive out of context.

Selecting Multiple Fields, Scripts, and Relationships

Deleting some of these fields gives me a chance to show you another feature you might need. You can choose multiple fields by selecting the first field, then holding down the Command key (Macintosh) or Ctrl key (Windows), and clicking on the other fields you want to select. Then you can delete or duplicate the fields all at once. This can be a big time-saver depending on what work you're doing. Holding down the Shift key will select all fields between your first and second selection.

You can do the same thing in the Manage Scripts window and in the Relationships tab of the Manage Database window.

Circular File Opening

If you try to close a file (let's call it the "first file") but a second file is open that has the first file listed among its data sources, the first file will open back up hidden. If you try to close the second file, and then bring the first file to the foreground to close it but the first file lists the second file among its data sources, the second file will reopen. This circular opening can be very frustrating! There is currently no way around it. If you're concerned that users might open files that are in the Window, Show Window menu, you may want to get a copy of FileMaker Pro Advanced. By using that developer-level product, you can better control the menus of your solution.

Network Errors

In versions of FileMaker prior to 7, if you had FileMaker Network Sharing turned on and you lost your network connection, you would get a message that TCP/IP networking could not be started. That could certainly be a helpful bit of information, but alas, it's now gone. You may not know that, for example, your Ethernet cable has been kicked out until someone calls you saying they can't find your files, or until you can't connect to your e-mail.

There are a few things you can do before calling a professional. First, check both ends of the Ethernet cable to make sure they're secure. (You might also check the cable itself to make sure nothing has crushed the cable.) Then check the hub or router and the modem. You may need to restart your machine after making any changes in those areas. See if you can go online with a browser. If you can, check to see that FileMaker sharing is still turned on for the specific files. Those steps will often solve 95 percent of your problems.

Preferences Including Dial Phone

I did not cover some of the other application and file Preference tabs. Most of them are not too difficult, although I don't think the Modem and Dialing Preferences (Windows only) are particularly intuitive. That's not FileMaker's fault. That's just the way it has to be because of the way modems operate.

Other than that, being able to make FileMaker dial phone numbers stored in your database at the click of a button is a terrific tool, especially if you do a lot of calling at your computer. I mean, once you've typed those numbers into the database, why should you have to retype them into the phone? I think I may be a touch dyslexic, so it sure makes dialing easier for me.

After you work out the Modem and Dialing settings, make a script that uses the Dial Phone step near the bottom of the list. Remember, you can tell the script to use a number in a related field if you're using the Contact file. Then place a button in the portal row. Once you get used to it, you'll never want to go back. You can read more about these preferences in the manual and the Help files.

Unfortunately, this will not work on Mac OS X. There is a workaround that uses AppleScript, but I find it somewhat slow in that it takes a full 10 to 15 seconds before the modem starts dialing the phone. It's somewhat complicated, but if you write to me, I'll pass the information on to you. If I hear from enough of you, I'll post it on my web site.

Script and Key Field Weirdness

Occasionally I make a script that will create a new record and enter some data in the first portal row. Sometimes it works and sometimes it doesn't. I seem to be able to make it work consistently by putting a Commit Records/Requests script step before entering the portal. I'm guessing that by doing so, the data in the key field gets sent to the hard drive so the portal has the key it needs to create the new portal record. If that's really the case, I don't know why the script without the step would work some of the time. But if you run into this, add the Commit Records/Requests script step and see if it doesn't solve your problem.

If you're entering data in row after row of a portal, be sure to exit the portal occasionally. Until you do, the portal rows aren't actually committed. If you are a single user and the power goes out or if you are a guest of a hosted file and you lose connection with the host, all those portal rows will be lost.

Sending E-mail from FileMaker

Since version 5 I've been enthusiastic about using FileMaker as my e-mail program. I use a plug-in called MailIT to both send and receive e-mail. (You can find a complete list of registered plug-ins on the FileMaker web site at www.filemaker.com.)

Apart from plug-ins, FileMaker has a Send Mail script step and a Send Mail dialog under the File menu. With it, you can build an e-mail message you can send to one of a few e-mail programs. Version 5.5 expanded the usable e-mail programs on the Macintosh platform. You can find out more about how to send messages in the Help files.

FileMaker 10 lets you send e-mail right from your file without first sending the message to your e-mail client. The Send Mail option has been in FileMaker since version 8. You can get to it by going to the File menu and choosing Send Mail. It's also one of the script steps, which means you can automate it. You can type directly in the fields, but you also have full access to FMP's Calculation engine by clicking the triangles or Specify buttons on the right. The big change here is the little SMTP Server option from the "Send via" drop-down in Figure A-1. Once you select that, you'll be taken to the SMTP Options dialog in Figure A-2. I can tell you from my own experience that getting all these settings just right can be quite tricky. Many e-mail programs provide you with a setup wizard, but even then knowing what you need to put in each of the boxes can be daunting. Here you're on your own. Probably the easiest way to fill out these dialogs would be to just go into your e-mail client and copy the settings from there. If SMTP Send Mail isn't working, try using Authentication and using your account name and password. You might also try removing spaces from the Name field.

This can be a great tool when combined with the ability to create PDFs or Excel files and attach them to the e-mail messages. I included an example in Chapter 14 in the section titled "Get (TemporaryPath) and Send Mail." This capability will be supported on FileMaker Pro Server.

Unfortunately, working this way only provides you with half an e-mail solution. You are sending messages with no way to track what you've sent (unless you script something) and no way to receive messages. That means your sent and received messages aren't in the same place and you would need to bounce back and forth between FileMaker and your e-mail program to follow your conversations. If you think of it as a tool for specific uses rather than a replacement for your e-mail program, you'll do just fine.

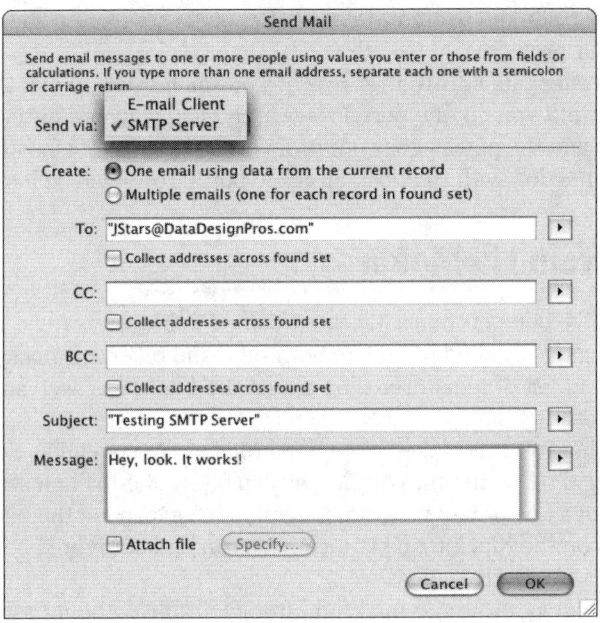

Figure A-1
The Send Mail dialog showing SMTP Server selected from the drop-down.

Figure A-2
The SMTP Options dialog.

Personally, I like using the plug-in better because I have control over both the sent and received messages. One thing that always frustrated me about e-mail programs was that I couldn't edit the messages I received. I always wanted to highlight part of the message someone sent to me or add my own text between the lines. When my messages are sent and received in FileMaker, I can edit the text to my heart's content since the text is right there in an editable text field.

Another advantage is that I can search the text of my saved e-mails way faster than any of the e-mail programs I've used. I export all of my messages to an archive file that is attached to my Contact database. That way I can trace my exchanges with anyone through a portal. The e-mail programs I've used in the past kept my sent messages apart from the received ones in ways I found confusing. I can organize the messages any way I want in FileMaker. If you're interested, look at the e-mail plug-ins on FileMaker's web site.

I do want to add that some of the documentation with MailIT (as well as many other plug-ins) is pretty technical. Fortunately, most plug-ins come with example files that make it reasonably easy to copy and paste the functions you need.

E-mail Merge[8]

This is an extremely powerful feature introduced in FileMaker 8. As I said, I prefer to both send and receive my e-mail with FileMaker as the e-mail client. This feature gets you part of the way there by allowing you to use the data in your fields to create e-mail messages that go out to your e-mail program. And it's scriptable. With it you can go from record to record and send personalized messages with the data in your file. Or you can send one message to all of the people in a found set of contact records — assuming they have an e-mail address in your files, that is. If you're interested, take a look at the Send Mail script step. You can find it in the Miscellaneous category. Many of the options are similar to Save/Send as PDF and Save/Send as Excel. Since we covered those elsewhere in the book, you should find it easy to work with this tool. Keep in mind that depending on how your e-mail service is set up, you may be blocked from sending "too many" e-mail messages at one time without upgrading your Internet service package. I got around this with one of my clients by having them send messages to themselves with 75 blind carbon copies that consisted of sections of their member e-mail list.

Prevent Users from Creating Databases

You can choose to prevent users from creating databases when you install a copy of FileMaker Pro on a machine. Now why would you want to do that? This is really a tool for network administrators, and following are a couple of reasons why you might want to implement it.

FileMaker connects to related files based on file names. If workers are creating their own shared files with names that might accidentally match those in a solution somewhere else on the network, there is a danger that data could end up in the wrong files. This danger has been significantly reduced since users now have control over external data sources. But it's possible to mess that up if a user doesn't know what he's doing.

Secondly, creation of new files could potentially duplicate functions in files that might already be in use in other departments. This isn't dangerous, just a waste of time. Administrators can better control the data using this option.

Automatic Record-Saving[8]

In previous versions of FileMaker, when you clicked out of all fields, the record was automatically saved. FileMaker 8 now lets you choose to have users verify that they really want to save the record. You can set this up on a layout-by-layout basis. The default is to save automatically. Here's how to make users confirm their changes:

1. Go to the layout where you want to display the confirmation dialog and switch to Layout mode.
2. Choose **Layouts**, **Layout Setup**.
3. Uncheck the box next to "Save record changes automatically," and click **OK**.

To test this, go back to Browse mode, change something, and click out of all fields. You'll see a dialog asking if you want to "Save changes to this record?" The user gets to choose between Save, Don't Save, and Cancel. In case you're wondering, Don't Save and Cancel are not the same. Cancel gives the user the opportunity to change the record in some other way. Don't Save returns the record to its former state.

I'm not sure I'd really use this feature. It might be helpful for some special-purpose layouts. But in that case I'd probably prefer to script something.

Getting Around Your Database

Now that we have the ability to include multiple tables in one file, the number of layouts and scripts in the file usually increases as well. (Although the total number of scripts is usually less compared to the old multiple-file system.) So how do you get around? In Manage Scripts and Layout mode, you can get around by typing the first few letters or digits of the name of the item. If you were to use the naming conventions I suggest in the upcoming section titled "Notes to Developers about Naming Conventions," typing a number would make this a snap.

Say your scripts are organized by number. You were just in Layout mode and double-clicked a button to find out it triggers script 223 - Find Invoices. Go into Manage Scripts and type "223." You're instantly transported to the script! If instead you organize your scripts by categories (BUTTONS, REPORTS, etc.) and type "BU", you'll be looking at the first script that begins with those letters. You can do the same by tying in the Filter Edit Control box by the magnifying glass in the upper right of the Manage Scripts window. Of course, putting your scripts into folders can go a long way in keeping organized.

The same works with layouts (except for the folders bit). I have to admit, I have found it more difficult to keep layouts organized by number. Especially now that it's recommended that a layout name should include a table occurrence code as well as the layout function. The darn layout names get pretty long. And eventually I need to reorganize the layouts — reordering them, deleting some, adding others — until a layout number preceding the layout name may not be accurate. But remember, with all these tables in one file, layout lists can get pretty unwieldy. I've found it particularly frustrating on the Windows platform because the layout list scrolls so slowly. There's gotta be a better way.

If each layout is preceded by a unique number, you can get to the layout in a snap. Click the Layout drop-down below the Book to reveal the layout list. Then type the unique layout number and you're there. No muss, no fuss. If you're dead set against layout numbers, you can organize the layouts by keeping them together based on the TO to which they refer. As long as all CONTACT and INVOICE layouts are grouped together, you can at least get to the first layout that begins with "CO" or "IN" by simply typing those letters.

Consolidating Multiple Files into a Single File

If you have converted a multi-file, pre-7 solution and want to take full advantage of the FMP7 multiple-table format, you'll need to know how to consolidate files. First of all, remember that you can import tables from other files. Once that's out of the way, follow these steps to save yourself a lot of time. It will help if you start by adding anchor-buoy style prefixes to all layouts, scripts, and value lists in each of your files. I use a program called QuicKeys to automate the task for files that have lots of each.

1. First, create the TOs using the *exact* same names as the old file. Some of this can be accomplished by importing tables from the other files involved. You may want to rename TOs with the anchor-buoy standard in the old file before bringing them into your consolidated file.
2. Create the necessary table occurrence groups and connect them using the same fields as in your old files. When possible, you should point the TOs that refer to "outside" tables to the new internal tables. That way most scripting and calculations will resolve with the least effort. Be sure to check the various check box options in the Edit Relationship window.
3. Check that all calculation fields are resolved properly. (Some imported calculation fields may be commented out if all the referenced fields can't be found.) This may include fields that use lookups and auto-enter calculation values.
4. Add the layouts in the new file using the *exact* same layout names. Add all the layout parts using the Object Info palette to make sure the height of each section is exactly the same as the parts on the old layout. Leave the layouts empty for now. You need to check the Layout Setup window. Consider the views that are available for the layout. If the old one was set to list, be sure you set it up that way for the new layout. You may also need to check the Printing tab in the Layout Setup window so that your print margins are the same.
5. Add the value lists using the *exact* same names and relations as the old file. Then change any existing value lists that point to the old file.
6. Import all the scripts.
7. Copy layout elements from the old file to the matching layouts in the new one.
8. You'll need to check that scripts and various buttons work correctly. My experience is that there are little surprises in items like Go to Layout, Go to Related Record, and Select Window.
9. Remove the data sources to the tables you've internalized. If you don't, your "main file" will keep calling for them every time you open it. I usually avoid deleting the unused file for a few months. I rename it something like Link_RETIRED.fp7 so I can call it back if I need to.
10. You may have scripts that refer to the old file. Scripts hold their own data sources. If a script is set to run a subscript in the old file, create a new

Perform Script step and point to the newly imported script. Then delete the old Perform Script step. Editing the old Perform Script step doesn't seem to work properly.

11. You should also consider any other files that might be trying to find the file you just retired. There could be data source references to the file in the Manage External Data Sources area, in a value list or in a script somewhere. Maybe there's an import that's looking for your old file. Be sure to point it to the correct table in the new file. Another good reason to keep the old files around for a while before putting them into the trash.

One other trick I use to position layout objects precisely goes like this:

1. Draw a small red rectangle and put it tightly into the upper-left corner of the layout in the old file.
2. Choose **Edit**, **Select All**, followed by **Edit**, **Copy**.
3. Go to the new layout, click in the upper-left corner, and choose **Edit**, **Paste**.
4. Deselect all objects, select the red rectangle, and delete it.

Notes to Developers about Naming Conventions

The naming of fields and relationships is particularly important to developers who create new and related files on a daily basis. Being able to quickly and easily come back and spot problem areas is critical to doing a good job — and keeping yourself sane. There are some naming conventions I became aware of since the first version of this book that I think are especially valuable.

Key fields — that is, fields that will be used to build relationships with other tables or files — should end with "_pk" (lowercase letters pk preceded by an underscore). The pk stands for primary key. So a field called ContactSerNum would be ContactSerNum_pk. If you are creating a field for use on the remote (child) side of the relationship, you should use "_fk" after the main part of the field name to represent foreign key. The main reason for these tags is that you'll be reminded not to delete these fields since it might really mess up the structure of the files.

Relationship names are dealt with shortly in the "Anchor-Buoy Method" section.

For a wonderfully comprehensive set of standards, see the downloadable files for a file named Standards.pdf (in the Developer files folder) prepared by CoreSolutions Development, Inc., or go to www.coresolutions.ca.

FileMaker, Inc. also provides a set of standards they've collected at http://www.filemaker.com/downloads/pdf/FMDev_ConvNov05.pdf. They are only suggestions, and various developers may have reasons for going in different directions. These were collected in 2005 before anchor-buoy had gotten as well established as it has since become. But the document addresses far more than table occurrence names.

Script Numbering

Here's a method I developed that has speeded up my debugging and development by about 50 percent. I number my scripts beginning with the first script in a file. It's the same method we've been using throughout the book. Then I follow the number with a space, hyphen, space, and the name I choose for the script. A script might read "1 - Main Menu" or "12 - Check Current User Name."

This speeds up debugging work tremendously. When you want to find out what a scripted button does, simply double-click it in Layout mode. When you see the name of the script, just memorize the number and head to Manage Scripts. The old standard required that you memorize the script name, which may or may not give you a clue as to where it lives in the list of possibly hundreds of scripts. If the name in the Button Setup window wasn't particularly helpful, sometimes you would have to click on the script name pop-up and locate the script position in the scripts list. Often, I'd find more than one script with a similar name and have to exit Manage Scripts and go back to the layout to the Button Setup window again. It can get pretty tedious.

Once the scripts are numbered this new way, I rarely move one to a different position in the list unless it just absolutely needs to be near another, related script. Then I renumber it.

Oh, and speaking of renumbering, watch out when duplicating scripts. You need to renumber the script immediately once it's copied in the list. Then move it to the new location in the list. This is also helpful when you want to find scripts in other files. The name and number appear in the current file for quick memorization.

Debugging scripts that call other scripts is a cinch. You don't have to memorize or write down the names of the subscripts. Just write down their numbers and whisk yourself off to check 'em out.

This numbering system may cause some difficulties when trying to comply with the grouping standards set forth by CoreSolutions. There are probably a few ways to work with both standards, especially now that we have script Group folders. You can easily leave spaces between script numbers to make room for future scripts under specific headings. And you can use some version of the Dewey Decimal System to insert a script between two other scripts with consecutive integers. Simply add a decimal point and one or more places to the right of the decimal. But most of the time I try to keep it to whole numbers.

If you do choose to group scripts by categories, a list might look like this:

100 - BUTTONS
101 - Close Window
102 - Spellcheck
103 - Add Attachment
-
200 - REPORTS
201 - Monthly Report

202 - Annual Report
203 - Daily Report
-
300 - NAVIGATION
301 - Main Menu
302 - Invoices
303 - Customers
-
400 - SORTING
401 - Sort by Customer ID
402 - Sort by Invoice ID
403 - Sort by Customer and Invoice ID
-
500 - PRINTING
501 - Print Setup
502 - Print Windows - Landscape
503 - Print Windows - Portrait
504 - Print Mac - Landscape
505 - Print Mac - Portrait

Notice the spacer before each heading. It makes it easy to spot the heading itself.

Windows users have one possible inconvenience to be aware of. Any script you check to appear in the Scripts menu will be assigned a number that will appear before the number you give the script in the script name box. A possible solution would be to leave off the number in your script name if you'll use it in that menu. Depending on where they are in the list, that can be okay or more complicated. Another solution would be to put a few spaces before the number in the script name so the two numbers don't sit so close to each other.

All I can tell you is, I move like the wind under my new system. And I challenge anyone using any other system with the standard version of FMP to beat me in a session that requires tracing your way back through a set of scripts that call subscripts.

Try it. You'll like it. Trust me.

Here's one other little trick you can use in debugging if you're using FileMaker Pro Advanced (a tool well worth the money if you do a lot of development). I often want to find out what script a button is attached to so I can go work on it. As I already explained, I used to go to Layout mode, double-click the button to find out the script number, then choose Scripts, Manage Scripts as described above. For a faster way to get to the script, go to the Tools menu, and choose Debug Scripts. Now just click the button in Browse mode and you're taken to the Script Debugger dialog. Press Command+F10 (Windows users should press Ctrl+F10). You're instantly taken to the scripts list with the script highlighted. Press the Enter key and you're in. Much quicker than my old method. Maybe faster than the numbering method. But the two in tandem beat anything! And if you go onsite where a client doesn't have a copy of FMPA or maybe you're working on another machine on your company network, you'll still be glad you numbered the scripts.

Anchor-Buoy Method

I finished my FileMaker 7 book with these words, "As I write this, developers are furiously discussing how to best use the new tools we've been given. FileMaker 7 is so radically different from previous versions, best practices and optimum procedures will continue to emerge over the next few years." The anchor-buoy method of organizing relationships is exactly the type of best practice I had in mind when I wrote that. I wish I'd had it when I began developing my first big project in FMP7.

Anchor-buoy is a method of organizing the graph and naming table occurrences (TOs) so you can more easily work your way around your solution. It is especially valuable as a solution becomes more complicated.

Take a look at Figure A-3. This is the graph of an early version of a solution I built for insurance agents to track their clients. As the solution became more complicated, I began to dread returning to the graph when it came time to add new features or debug the earlier ones. It was even worse when I would need to select TOs from various drop-down menus (Figure A-4). Names for TOs that had meant something to me at the time I created them turned to useless gibberish in as little as a few minutes — even when they included the name of the base table. Then I began to hear murmurs about a thing called anchor-buoy in the daily stack of FileMaker e-mails I got.

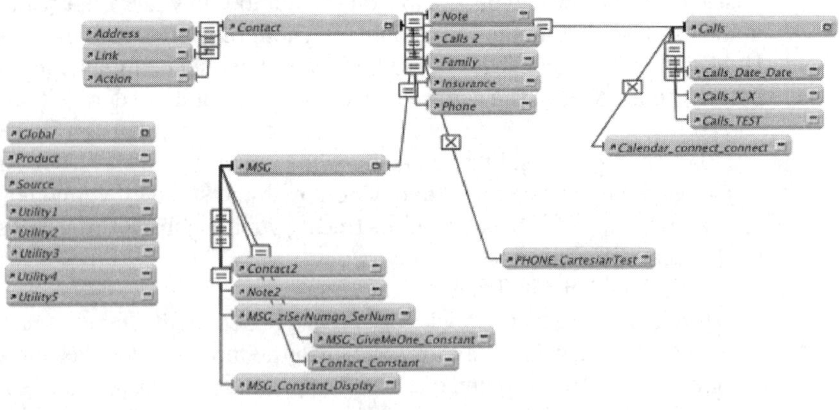

Figure A-3
The relationships graph of a moderately complex solution before the anchor-buoy method.

I didn't understand what it was until I downloaded a PowerPoint presentation by Kevin Frank, a FileMaker developer from Arcata, California. The presentation was both humorous and crystal clear to me. Even though we've used it in some of the book exercises, and the basics appear here, I encourage you to download the long presentation at www.kevinfrank.com/anchor-buoy.html. He has asked to be referred to as an unofficial chief evangelist for the technique and not its originator. Kevin explained that database and web development company Soliant Consulting evolved the technique in order to better control their processes when working with FileMaker. *FileMaker Advisor* magazine ran an article in the August/September 2005 issue titled "Managing the FileMaker Pro 7 Relationship Graph," written by Soliant project leader Roger Jacques.

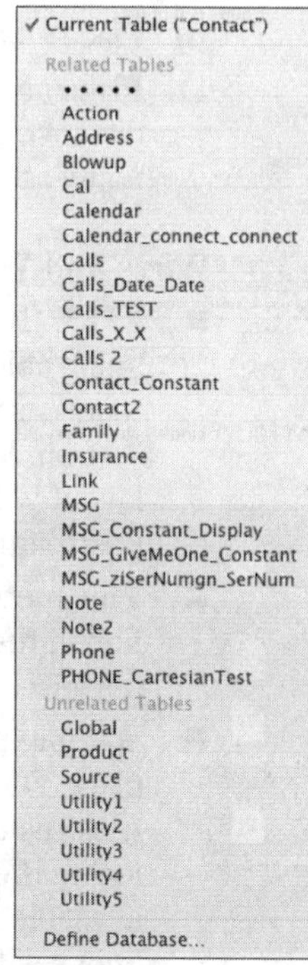

Figure A-4
A table occurrence list before the anchor-buoy method.

Basic "Rules" for the Anchor-Buoy Method:

1. Only one anchor TO per base table.
2. Layouts are attached to nothing except anchors. You can have many layouts attached to the same anchor, but you never attach a layout to a buoy.
3. The graph will only be as wide as one page. You may make it as tall as you like. This facilitates printing as well as searching.
4. Anchors will have a capitalized code name. (I try to use three letters, but occasionally have to make it two or four.) For example, CON = Contacts. Among the other advantages to this is that anchors will always appear at the top of related TOs in lists. (For both anchors and buoys, use ODBC-compliant characters (upper- and lowercase alpha, numerals, and underscores — no special characters) and never any spaces.)
5. Buoys will be named with the anchor name first (in lowercase), followed by an underscore, (followed by any intervening buoys and underscores), and ending with the final buoy's base table code in caps. You can also choose to extend the name by adding an underscore and the link field. (I usually add the field name, but I precede it with two underscores. Often I'll skip the pk and fk extensions.) For example, "con_inv_ILI__InvNum," where "con" stands for the Contact table, "inv" is Invoice, "ILI" is InvoiceLineItems, and "InvNum" is the key field.
6. Never connect two table occurrence groups (TOGs).
7. Create a legend area at the top of the graph. Name the legend TOs beginning with "z_" followed by the code in caps, and end with the base table name. With the z at the start, all these TOs will be at the bottom of any lists. The rest of the legend TO names relate the code to the base table name so you can remind yourself of what the code stands for either while you're in the graph or when you're viewing one of the lists.
8. Use color-coding to identify all TOs that belong to the same base table.
9. Put any unused or single anchor TOs at the bottom of the graph. You do not need to create a layout for anchor TOs that don't need them.

10. Place all anchors down the left side of the graph.
11. Place all buoys in columns to the right of the anchors depending on their distance in the relationship chain from the anchor. You'll rarely go as many as five columns deep.

Whys and Wherefores:

- FMP7-10 relationships can be bidirectional. But you can't count on data being able to travel in both directions because keys can be unstored. For that reason, if you build all relationships as if they only go in one direction — from left (anchor) to right (buoy) — you'll never be surprised. Any layout will only display data that is downstream. There is never an upstream when it comes to the layout.
- This method may increase the total number of TOs. But each is easier to find in the graph and in lists. And it's often easier to understand a TO's purpose.
- You might consider alphabetizing TOGs based on the anchor name. If you place TOs in columns, the graph will be like a grid. When you need to add features to a layout, you'll instantly know where to look in the graph to locate the base table. Then you'll be able to see what data is already available from any attached buoy TOs. You might also consider taking buoys with the same base table in each TOG and grouping them together.
- Since every layout is connected to a base table, there will never be any question about the context when it comes to the Calculation window. In other words, when you're looking at the Calculation window, you will always be looking at the right TO.
- You'll never wonder what to name a TO, and its name will tell you where to find it in the graph and often give you a strong clue as to its purpose. I can tell you that learning the TO naming pattern takes a relatively short time. I can also tell you that working without it provides hours of frustration.
- Reworking a solution that has not been set up with A-B can be difficult since TO relationships affect field calculations, scripts, layouts, and value lists. It can be done, but you need to pay attention to every detail.
- Sometimes you'll be on a layout and need to perform a Go to Related Record action that puts you on a layout with a different base table. Since anchors are never connected on the graph, here's what you do: In the Go to Related Record dialog, from the "Get related record from" pop-up, choose the buoy TO that *is* related to the anchor. (If there isn't one, create it.) Then, from the "Show record using layout" drop-down, select the layout you need.

This may sound more complicated than it is. We've already done it in exercises in the book. For example, when we ran the monthly invoicing in Chapter 14, we started by finding all invoices with a balance due. Script 6 -

Print One Invoice says "Get related record from" inv_ILI__InvNum. But of course there is no layout for that TO. So instead we "jump" TOGs by choosing to "Show record using layout" ILI_InvoicePrint where the layout is more conducive to printing than the data entry layout.

With all that in mind, take a look at Figures A-5 and A-6. Go back and compare them to A-3 and A-4. The pictures may be too small to really tell what's going on, even with a magnifying glass, but believe me, using the anchor-buoy method has made a great difference in how I'm able to work. It's important enough that I decided to redesign one client's project on my own time because working in it the old way was too frustrating. I hope you get the same value out of it — without the cost I had to pay.

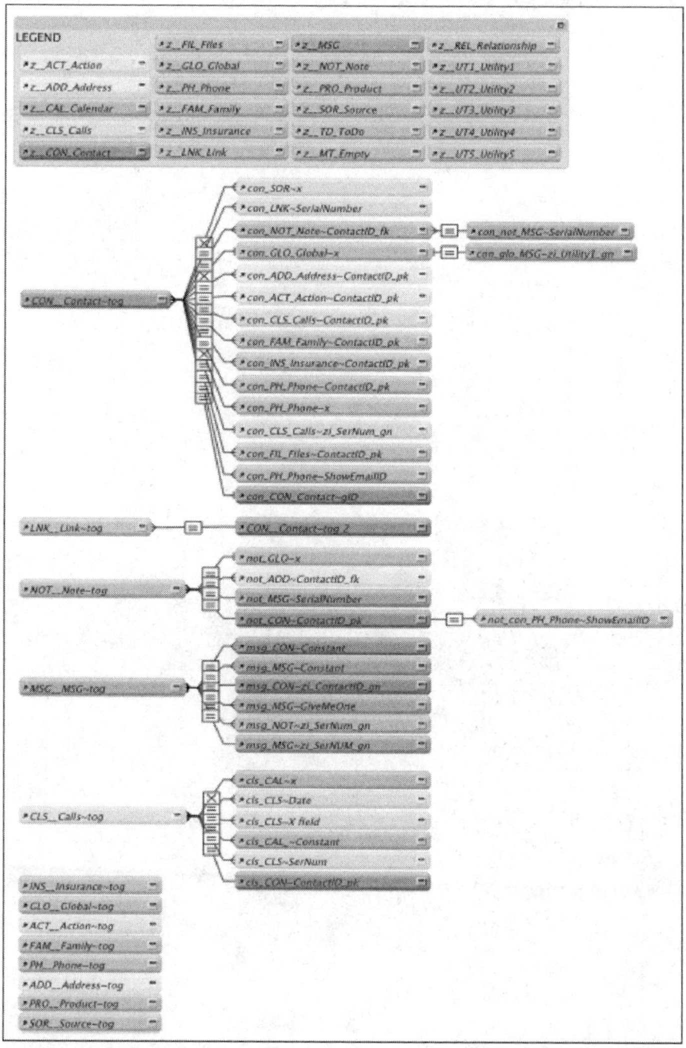

Figure A-5
The relationships graph of the same solution as in Figure A-3 after using the anchor-buoy method.

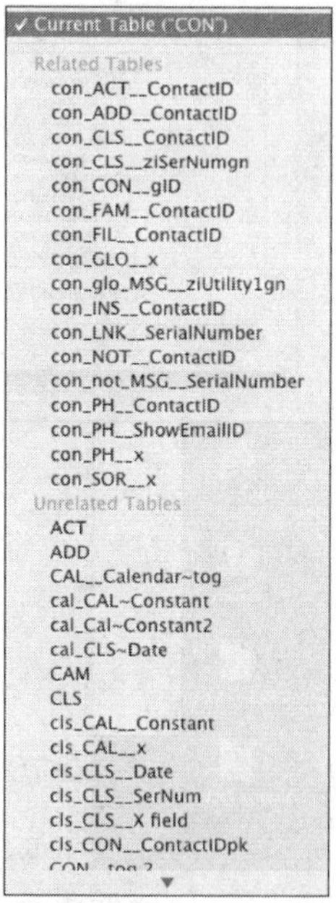

Figure A-6
The same table occurrence list as Figure A-4 after anchor-buoy.

One final note. When you're retrofitting an existing solution to take advantage of anchor-buoy, be very careful that all the fields on your layouts refer to the proper table occurrences. This is especially true of fields in portals. And make sure the portals point to the right table occurrences. Since portal fields all have the four dots in front of the field name, it's easy to be lulled into thinking you have the right relationship. Just double-check everything.

Appendix B

Getting More Help

Okay, you've read the book, you've done the exercises, but you're still having trouble. What do you do now? Read the pertinent parts and do the exercises again. Really! If it were me, it would take more than one repetition for all the concepts to sink in — and there are a lot of concepts to absorb. Oh, you've already done that?

Tech Support

You may have a complimentary call to tech support coming to you. When you buy FileMaker Pro, a card for that call comes in the box, or there's a PDF if you downloaded the product. If you're part of a company with a site license, you may have a support agreement with FileMaker, Inc. Ask your IT people about that.

To get the best out of any tech support services, prepare yourself. Make notes about what happened just before the problem started. Has it done this before? Under what conditions? What equipment are you using? What computer (model, OS, RAM, etc.), printer, scanner, etc.? Yes, you're frustrated, but if you don't get your information together before making the call, you'll be even more frustrated once you get on the phone and can't describe the problem.

Keep in mind that the tech support people don't know your level of knowledge. They'll have to ask you some questions that may sound like they think you're an idiot, but let me tell you a short story to clarify their plight:

I was trying to help a new, non-computer-literate worker for one of my clients over the phone late one night after everyone else had gone home. She was trying to use a time clock I had built for them to punch in. I told her to take the mouse so that the cord was pointing away from her and move it toward the screen. I asked if the arrow on the screen moved. She said it hadn't moved at all. We tried moving the mouse left and right. After checking that the mouse was actually plugged in and the screen was on, I asked her where the mouse was. She said, "In front of the screen, about eight inches above the table in my hand."

Tech support is great, but you need to work with them and give them as much information about your situation as you can. They don't know if you're on the level of my client's employee or not.

Hire a Consultant

After you use tech support, as a second choice you could hire me. Yes, this is a shameless plug, but I do this for a living, and there's nothing wrong with a little advertising. I've built complete systems and trained employees for a number of clients. On other occasions, companies brought me in to provide answers for a specific problem. Their people already worked with FileMaker Pro and took over from there to implement the changes.

A third situation is where I've been brought in to be the architect of a system so that a solution would be designed correctly before anybody started creating files. Then in-house people built the system. Sometimes another developer created a set of files but had since moved from the area. I work remotely a lot these days. On some occasions I'll instruct an in-house person on the changes that need to be made as they make them at their computer. I've also worked using software that temporarily takes control of their computer through the Internet.

Sometimes it's simply more cost effective to bring in a professional who can put the thing on course again. If you're a small company, your time might be better spent on other things. If you're part of a larger company, ask yourself: How many people's time is being wasted waiting for the answer I need?

That being said, let me point out that no consultant knows everything — not even me. There are times that clients request work that is beyond my areas of expertise. In cases like that, I'll consult with other developers I know who do have that expertise. I usually know who to call because I've been doing this for 24 years and I go to the conventions.

Don't want me? I'm crushed. To find some other consultant, go to the FileMaker, Inc. web site at http://www. filemaker.com/. On the main FileMaker tab, hover your mouse pointer over "Support" and click Consultants from the drop-down. You can search by company, state, zip code, country, and keywords to find a list of developers in your area. If you put Data Design Pros in the Company field, you'll find me!

Just keep in mind that you don't have to hire the first person you talk to. Not everyone has the same amount of experience. You'll also want to choose someone whose personality will work with yours. If your project is so large that it requires a full-time FileMaker person, you may need to look for an employee to do the work. A full-time consultant could get expensive.

If you think you might get even more involved in FileMaker yourself, you could consider joining the FileMaker Business Alliance (FBA), an organization sponsored by FileMaker, Inc. with many useful resources and discussion lists. See http://filemaker.com/fba/. An alternative is the FileMaker Technical Network (FTN). Go to http://filemaker.com/technet/.

FileMaker's Web Site

FileMaker's web site is a fantastic source for FileMaker resources. Aside from consultants, the site has everything from trainers to plug-ins, books, magazines, templates, commercial solutions, and other sites powered by FileMaker. Once you head out to any of the other sites, you'll find each of them leads to other sites — each with resources of their own. The FileMaker community is large, active, and growing along with the great product they represent. Of course, the hard part is finding exactly what you need.

Companion Files

There is quite a variety of files available to be downloaded from www.wordware.com/files/fmpro10. These are divided into the following folders:

- Book files — These files go along with the book, chapter by chapter, for readers to learn to work with FileMaker Pro. The index is also included here as a PDF file.
- Developer files — Most of these solutions were provided by other FileMaker developers; some of these may require a fee to use beyond a trial period.
- Author files — These include an explanation of what they're for. Simply click the question mark button on the main page of each file.

I had originally intended to provide all the links to the plug-ins for you in a clickable database. But the links keep changing and companies come and go. So instead, here is the URL for the page on FileMaker, Inc.'s web site where they are updated more frequently than I would be able to on my own site:

http://developer.filemaker.com/solutions/results/?sol_category=5&sol_region_amr=1

Third-party developers created most or all of the plug-ins at the link above. FileMaker, Inc. only offers information about them as an aid to users, but does not vouch for the plug-ins themselves or the makers of them.

I myself had recommended a plug-in to one of my clients. Once it was installed and we had a problem, the developer seemed to disappear from the face of the earth. Many of the plug-ins you'll find at the link have had a long history. But since they are small companies, things can change — as they can with large companies. (Ever hear of Enron?)

See the included Read Me file for more information.

FileMaker Pro CD-ROM

The PDF files that came with your FileMaker Pro 10 installation CD-ROM or in the download are chock full of information. They list solutions, partners, consultants, publications, and trainers, along with ads from many of the companies and some special price offers. If you are part of a large organization with a site license, ask your IT representative about materials that came with the company purchase.

Training Resources

There are companies that specialize in FileMaker Pro training. Some of them have sessions that move around the country and the world. You could even hire them to come to your site and train a group of workers.

It just so happens that I am an instructor for FMPTraining. It is "The world's best hands-on FileMaker Pro training." And it must be, because I'm doing it, right? Go to FMPtraining.com for the lowdown. Or contact me directly.

There are also sets of audio and video training tapes, workbooks, and CDs you can purchase, as well as online training. A fairly comprehensive list of these resources can be found on FileMaker's web site.

FileMaker Hosting

If there comes a time that you need to put information from your files up on the Internet, you may want to contact a company that specializes in FileMaker web hosting. The value of working with one of these companies is that they can help you avoid some of the pitfalls you're likely to run into by doing it yourself. The more important the project is, the more you'll need an expert. FileMaker used to provide a list of hosting companies on their web site, but that seems to have disappeared. However, if you do a Google search for FileMaker Pro Hosting, you'll get over a half million hits. You'll have to figure out for yourself who you want to work with.

FileMaker Advisor Magazine

The reason I wanted to write for *FileMaker Advisor* magazine in the first place is that I thought it was such a great product. The editors include articles that appeal to every level of user. I find it most exciting when other developers demonstrate techniques they've created to solve their own problems, only to find that it solves my own. Additionally, the advertisements often put you in touch with other products and services you may need. The magazine is completely independent from FileMaker, Inc.

My Web Site

Of course, I have a web site. The URL is: http://www.DataDesignPros.com.

Among other things on my site, I have a list of sites that deal with FileMaker issues and some that have downloadable files. Many of those sites are listed in the Web_Sites.fp7 file in the Author files folder of the companion files.

I mentioned this earlier in the book, but it bears repeating. FileMaker 7 was so radically different from previous versions that best practices and optimum procedures will continue to emerge. I've done my best to test and explain everything I've learned about it over the past six years and I've included a number of these procedures in this edition. We'll continue to understand what we're dealing with as we build more projects for our customers. That's why I'm adding an area to my web site where I'll post new information and clarifications to items in the book. Go to my homepage at www.DataDesignPros.com and click the link near the bottom titled "FileMaker 10 book updates." Hopefully this book will be perfect, and I won't have to post any updates. I'm only half joking when I say that. It's interesting that I posted very few updates to the FMP9 book compared to the FMP7 book, because I've been working with the new structure for a few years now. Also, if you make discoveries on your own that you think others might benefit from, e-mail me at JStars@DataDesignPros.com and I'll try to include them.

Index

B

U